GLEIM® Aviation

2018 EDITION

FLIGHT/GROUND INSTRUCTOR
FAA Knowledge Test Prep

for the FAA Computer-Based Pilot Knowledge Test

Flight Instructor - Airplane
Advanced Ground Instructor
Basic Ground Instructor

Pilot Examiner - Airplane
Flight Instructor - Airplane - Added Rating
Flight Instructor - Sport - Airplane

by
Irvin N. Gleim, Ph.D., CFII and Garrett W. Gleim, CFII

Gleim Publications, Inc.
P.O. Box 12848 · University Station
Gainesville, Florida 32604
(352) 375-0772
(800) 87-GLEIM or (800) 874-5346
Website: www.GleimAviation.com
Email: admin@gleim.com

For updates to the first printing of the 2018 edition of
Flight/Ground Instructor FAA Knowledge Test Prep

Go To: www.GleimAviation.com/updates

Or: Email update@gleim.com with **FIGI 2018-1** in the subject line. You will receive our current update as a reply.

Updates are available until the next edition is published.

ISSN 1553-6912
ISBN 978-1-61854-126-0

This edition is copyright © 2017 by Gleim Publications, Inc. Portions of this manuscript are taken from previous editions copyright © 1986-2016 by Gleim Publications, Inc.

First Printing: July 2017

ALL RIGHTS RESERVED. No part of this material may be reproduced in any form whatsoever without express written permission from Gleim Publications, Inc. Reward is offered for information exposing violators. Contact copyright@gleim.com.

YOU CAN HELP

This 2018 edition is designed specifically for pilots who aspire to obtain the Flight Instructor Certificate and/or Ground Instructor Certificate. Please send any corrections and suggestions for subsequent editions to us via the feedback links within the online components or using the form at www.GleimAviation.com/AviationQuestions.

A companion volume, *Fundamentals of Instructing FAA Knowledge Test Prep*, is available, as is *Flight Instructor Flight Maneuvers and Practical Test Prep*, which focuses on the FAA practical test, just as this book focuses on the FAA knowledge test. Save time, money, and frustration--order online at www.GleimAviation.com today! Please bring these books to the attention of flight instructors, fixed-base operators, and others with a potential interest in acquiring their flight instructor certificates. Wide distribution of these books and increased interest in flying depend on your assistance and good word. Thank you.

Environmental Statement -- This book is printed on recyclable, environmentally friendly groundwood paper, sourced from certified sustainable forests and produced either TCF (totally chlorine-free) or ECF (elementally chlorine-free).

Our answers have been carefully researched and reviewed. Inevitably, there will be differences with competitors' books and even the FAA. If necessary, we will develop an UPDATE for *Flight/Ground Instructor FAA Knowledge Test Prep*. Visit our website or email update@gleim.com for the latest updates. Updates for this 2018 edition will be available until the next edition is published. To continue providing our customers with first-rate service, we request that technical questions about our materials be sent to us via the feedback links within the online components. We will give each question thorough consideration and a prompt response. Questions concerning orders, prices, shipments, or payments will be handled via telephone by our competent and courteous customer service staff.

ABOUT THE AUTHORS

Irvin N. Gleim earned his private pilot certificate in 1965 from the Institute of Aviation at the University of Illinois, where he subsequently received his Ph.D. He is a commercial pilot and flight instructor (instrument) with multi-engine and seaplane ratings and is a member of the Aircraft Owners and Pilots Association, American Bonanza Society, Civil Air Patrol, Experimental Aircraft Association, National Association of Flight Instructors, and Seaplane Pilots Association. He is the author of flight maneuvers and practical test prep books for the sport, private, instrument, commercial, and flight instructor certificates/ratings and the author of study guides for the remote, sport, private/recreational, instrument, commercial, flight/ground instructor, fundamentals of instructing, airline transport pilot, and flight engineer FAA knowledge tests. Three additional pilot training books are *Pilot Handbook*, *Aviation Weather and Weather Services*, and *FAR/AIM*.

Dr. Gleim has also written articles for professional accounting and business law journals and is the author of widely used review manuals for the CIA (Certified Internal Auditor) exam, the CMA (Certified Management Accountant) exam, the CPA (Certified Public Accountant) exam, and the EA (IRS Enrolled Agent) exam. He is Professor Emeritus, Fisher School of Accounting, University of Florida, and is a CFM, CIA, CMA, and CPA.

Garrett W. Gleim earned his private pilot certificate in 1997 in a Piper Super Cub. He is a commercial pilot (single- and multi-engine), ground instructor (advanced and instrument), and flight instructor (instrument and multi-engine), and he is a member of the Aircraft Owners and Pilots Association and the National Association of Flight Instructors. He is the author of study guides for the sport, private/recreational, instrument, commercial, flight/ground instructor, fundamentals of instructing, and airline transport pilot FAA knowledge tests. He received a Bachelor of Science in Economics from The Wharton School, University of Pennsylvania. Mr. Gleim is also a CPA (not in public practice).

REVIEWERS AND CONTRIBUTORS

Paul Duty, CFII, MEI, AGI, Remote Pilot, is a graduate of Embry-Riddle Aeronautical University with a Master of Business Administration-Aviation degree. He is our aviation marketing specialist and an aviation editor. Mr. Duty is an active flight instructor and remote pilot. He researched questions, wrote and edited answer explanations, and incorporated revisions into the text.

Char Marissa Gregg, CFII, ATP, Glider, ASES, LTA, Remote Pilot, is the Gleim Part 141 Chief Ground Instructor and an aviation editor. Ms. Gregg has over 16 years of aviation experience with a background in flight instruction and as a corporate pilot. She researched questions, wrote and edited answer explanations, and incorporated revisions into the text.

The CFIs who have worked with us throughout the years to develop and improve our pilot training materials.

The many FAA employees who helped, in person or by telephone, primarily in Gainesville; Orlando; Oklahoma City; and Washington, DC.

The many pilots who have provided comments and suggestions about *Flight/Ground Instructor FAA Knowledge Test Prep* during the past several decades.

A PERSONAL THANKS

This manual would not have been possible without the extraordinary effort and dedication of Julie Cutlip, Blaine Hatton, Belea Keeney, Kelsey Olson, Bree Rodriguez, Teresa Soard, Justin Stephenson, Joanne Strong, Elmer Tucker, and Candace Van Doren, who typed the entire manuscript and all revisions and drafted and laid out the diagrams, illustrations, and cover for this book.

The authors also appreciate the production and editorial assistance of Jacob Bennett, Steven Critelli, Melody Dalton, Jim Harvin, Jessica Hatker, Kristen Hennen, Katie Larson, Diana León, Jake Pettifor, Shane Rapp, Drew Sheppard, and Alyssa Thomas.

Finally, we appreciate the encouragement, support, and tolerance of our families throughout this project.

Returns of books purchased from bookstores and other resellers should be made to the respective bookstore or reseller. For more information regarding the Gleim Return Policy, please contact our offices at (800) 874-5346 or visit www.GleimAviation.com/returnpolicy.

TABLE OF CONTENTS

	Page
Preface	vi
Introduction: The FAA Pilot Knowledge Test	1
Study Unit 1. Airplanes and Aerodynamics	19
Study Unit 2. Airplane Performance	53
Study Unit 3. Airplane Instruments, Engines, and Systems	89
Study Unit 4. Airports, Airspace, and ATC	117
Study Unit 5. Weight and Balance	145
Study Unit 6. Aviation Weather	169
Study Unit 7. Federal Aviation Regulations	225
Study Unit 8. Navigation	283
Study Unit 9. Flight Maneuvers	327
Study Unit 10. Aeromedical Factors and Aeronautical Decision Making (ADM)	359
Appendix A: Additional Ground Instructor Questions	373
Appendix B: Sport Pilot Instructor – Airplane	377
Appendix C: Practice Test	381
Appendix D: Interpolation	391
FAA Listing of Learning Statement Codes	393
Cross-References to the FAA Learning Statement Codes	399
Abbreviations and Acronyms	407
Index of Figures	408
Index	409

NOTE: The FAA does not release its complete database of test questions to the public. Instead, sample questions are released on the Airman Testing page of the FAA website on a quarterly basis. These questions are similar to the actual test questions, but they are not exact matches.

Gleim utilizes customer feedback and FAA publications to create additional sample questions that closely represent the topical coverage of each FAA knowledge test. In order to do well on the knowledge test, you must study the Gleim outlines in this book, answer all the questions under exam conditions (i.e., without looking at the answers first), and develop an understanding of the topics addressed. You should not simply memorize questions and answers. This will not prepare you for your FAA knowledge test, and it will not help you develop the knowledge you need to safely operate an aircraft.

Always refer to the Gleim update service (www.GleimAviation.com/updates) to ensure you have the latest information that is available. If you see topics covered on your FAA knowledge test that are not contained in this book, please contact us at www.GleimAviation.com/AviationQuestions to report your experience and help us fine-tune our test preparation materials.

Thank you!

PREFACE

The primary purpose of this book is to provide you with the easiest, fastest, and least expensive means of passing the FAA knowledge test for the flight instructor (CFI) and/or the ground instructor certificate. The publicly released FAA knowledge test bank does **not** have questions grouped together by topic. We have organized them for you. We have

1. Reproduced all previously released knowledge test questions published by the FAA. We have also included additional similar test questions, which we believe may appear in some form on your knowledge test.
2. Reordered the questions into 122 logical topics.
3. Organized these topics into 10 study units.
4. Explained the answer immediately to the right of each question.
5. Provided an easy-to-study outline of exactly what you need to know (and no more) at the beginning of each study unit.

Accordingly, you can thoroughly prepare for the FAA pilot knowledge test by

1. Studying the brief outlines at the beginning of each study unit.
2. Answering the question on the left side of each page while covering up the answer explanations on the right side of each page.
3. Reading the answer explanation for each question that you answer incorrectly or have difficulty answering.
4. Facilitating this Gleim process with our **FAA Test Prep Online**. Our software allows you to emulate the FAA test (CATS or PSI). By practicing answering questions on a computer, you will become at ease with the computer testing process and have the confidence to PASS. Refer to pages 17 and 18.
5. Using our **Online Ground School**, which provides you with our outlines, practice problems, and sample tests. This course is easily accessible through the Internet. Also, we give you a money-back guarantee with our **Online Ground School**. If you are unsuccessful, you get your money back!

Also included in the FAA test bank of flight and ground instructor test questions are the fundamentals of instructing test questions that we have as a separate book entitled *Fundamentals of Instructing FAA Knowledge Test Prep* (which you must also pass for your initial flight or ground instructor certificate). Go to www.GleimAviation.com for additional information and to order.

Authors' Recommendation: Since both the flight and ground instructor tests are taken from the same set of questions (those appearing in this book), all CFI aspirants should take the ground instructor test as they take the CFI test. It is an additional credential that may be helpful.

Additionally, this book will introduce our entire series of pilot training texts, which use the same presentation method: outlines, illustrations, questions, and answer explanations.

Many books create additional work for the user. In contrast, this book and its companion, *Flight Instructor Flight Maneuvers and Practical Test Prep*, facilitate your effort. The outline/illustration format, type styles, and spacing are designed to improve readability. Concepts are often presented as phrases rather than as complete sentences – similar to notes that you would take in a class lecture.

Also, recognize that this study manual is concerned with **airplane** flight training, not balloon, glider, or helicopter training. We are confident this book, **FAA Test Prep Online**, and/or **Online Ground School** will facilitate speedy completion of your knowledge test. We also wish you the very best as you complete your flight and/or ground instructor certification in related flying and obtain additional ratings and certificates.

Enjoy Flying Safely!

Irvin N. Gleim
Garrett W. Gleim
July 2017

INTRODUCTION: THE FAA PILOT KNOWLEDGE TEST

What Is a Flight Instructor Certificate?	2
Requirements to Obtain a Flight Instructor Certificate without a Sport Pilot Rating	2
Requirements to Obtain a Flight Instructor Certificate with a Sport Pilot Rating	4
Requirements to Obtain a Ground Instructor Certificate	5
FAA Pilot Knowledge Test and Testing Supplement	6
FAA's Knowledge Tests: Cheating or Unauthorized Conduct Policy	7
FAA Pilot Knowledge Test Question Bank	7
FAA Questions with Typographical Errors	7
Reorganization of FAA Questions	8
How to Prepare for the FAA Pilot Knowledge Test	8
Multiple-Choice Question-Answering Technique	11
Educated Guessing	12
Simulated FAA Practice Test	12
Authorization to Take the FAA Pilot Knowledge Test	13
When to Take the FAA Pilot Knowledge Test	13
What to Take to the FAA Pilot Knowledge Test	13
Computer Testing Centers	14
Computer Testing Procedures	14
Your FAA Pilot Knowledge Test Report	14
Applying for Your Ground Instructor Certificate	15
Failure on the FAA Pilot Knowledge Test	16
Gleim Online Ground School	16
Gleim FAA Test Prep Online	17

The beginning of this introduction explains how to obtain a flight instructor and/or ground instructor certificate, and it explains the content and procedures of the Federal Aviation Administration (FAA) knowledge test, including how to take the test at a computer testing center. The remainder of this introduction discusses and illustrates the Gleim **Online Ground School** and **FAA Test Prep Online**. Achieving an instructor certificate is fun. Begin today!

Flight/Ground Instructor FAA Knowledge Test Prep is one of six related books for obtaining your flight and/or ground instructor certificate. The other five books are

1. *Fundamentals of Instructing FAA Knowledge Test Prep*
2. *Flight Instructor Flight Maneuvers and Practical Test Prep*
3. *Pilot Handbook*
4. *FAR/AIM*
5. *Aviation Weather and Weather Services*

Fundamentals of Instructing FAA Knowledge Test Prep prepares you to pass the FAA's fundamentals of instructing (FOI) knowledge test. This test is required for instructors. If you are planning to obtain both the flight and ground instructor certificates, you only need to pass the FOI test once.

Flight Instructor Flight Maneuvers and Practical Test Prep is a comprehensive, carefully organized presentation of everything you need to know to prepare for your flight training and for your flight instructor practical (flight) test. It integrates material from FAA publications and other sources.

Pilot Handbook is a complete pilot reference book that combines over 100 FAA books and documents, including *AIM*, Federal Aviation Regulations, ACs, and much more. Aerodynamics, airplane systems, airspace, and navigation are among the topics explained in *Pilot Handbook*.

FAR/AIM is an essential part of every instructor's library. The Gleim *FAR/AIM* is an easy-to-read reference book containing all of the Federal Aviation Regulations applicable to general aviation flying, plus the full text of the FAA's *Aeronautical Information Manual (AIM)*.

The Gleim *Aviation Weather and Weather Services* book combines all of the information from the FAA's *Aviation Weather* (AC 00-6), *Aviation Weather Services* (AC 00-45), and numerous FAA publications into one easy-to-understand reference book.

WHAT IS A FLIGHT INSTRUCTOR CERTIFICATE?

A flight instructor certificate is similar in appearance to your commercial pilot certificate and will allow you to give flight and ground instruction. The certificate is sent to you by the FAA upon satisfactory completion of your training program, two knowledge tests, and a practical test. It expires at the end of the 24th month after issue. A new certificate is sent to you by the FAA upon renewal. A sample flight instructor certificate is reproduced below.

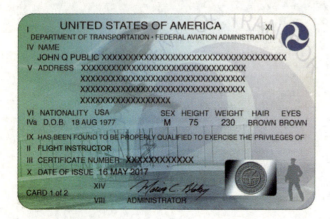
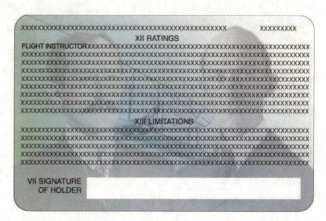

REQUIREMENTS TO OBTAIN A FLIGHT INSTRUCTOR CERTIFICATE WITHOUT A SPORT PILOT RATING

1. Be at least 18 years of age.
2. Be able to read, write, and understand English (certificates with operating limitations may be available for medically related deficiencies).
3. Hold a commercial or airline transport pilot (ATP) certificate with an aircraft rating appropriate to the flight instructor rating sought (e.g., airplane, glider).
   a. You must also hold an instrument rating to be a flight instructor in an airplane.
4. Study this book, **Fundamentals of Instructing FAA Knowledge Test Prep**, **Flight Instructor Flight Maneuvers and Practical Test Prep**, **FAR/AIM**, **Aviation Weather and Weather Services**, and **Pilot Handbook** or use the Gleim **Online Ground School** to learn
   a. Fundamentals of instructing
   b. All other subject areas in which ground training is required for recreational, private, and commercial pilot certificates
5. Pass both the FOI and the flight instructor knowledge tests with scores of 70% or better.
   a. All FAA knowledge tests are administered at FAA-designated computer testing centers.
      1) Page 14 contains additional details.
   b. The FOI and flight instructor tests consist of 50 and 100 multiple-choice questions, respectively, selected from the airplane-related questions in the FAA's flight and ground instructor knowledge test bank.
   c. The FAA's published airplane-related questions, along with our own similar questions, are reproduced in this book with complete explanations.
   d. You are not required to take the FOI knowledge test if you
      1) Hold an FAA ground instructor certificate,
      2) Hold a current teacher's certificate authorizing you to teach at an educational level of the 7th grade or higher, or
      3) Are employed as a teacher at an accredited college or university.

6. Demonstrate flight proficiency (14 CFR 61.187).
    a. You must receive and log flight and ground training and obtain a logbook endorsement from an authorized instructor on the following areas of operations for an airplane category rating with a single-engine or multi-engine class rating.
        1) Fundamentals of instructing
        2) Technical subject areas
        3) Preflight preparation
        4) Preflight lesson on a maneuver to be performed in flight
        5) Preflight procedures
        6) Airport and seaplane base operations
        7) Takeoffs, landings, and go-arounds
        8) Fundamentals of flight
        9) Performance maneuvers
        10) Ground reference maneuvers
        11) Slow flight, stalls, and spins (single-engine only)
            a) Slow flight and stalls (multi-engine only)
        12) Basic instrument maneuvers
        13) Emergency operations
        14) Multi-engine operations (multi-engine only)
        15) Postflight procedures
    b. A CFI who provides training to an initial applicant for a flight instructor certificate must have held a flight instructor certificate for at least 24 months and have given at least 200 hr. of flight training as a CFI.
    c. You must also obtain a logbook endorsement by an appropriately certificated and rated flight instructor who has provided you with spin entry, spin, and spin recovery training in an airplane that is certificated for spins and has found you instructionally competent and proficient in those training areas, i.e., so you can teach spin recovery.
7. Alternatively, enroll in an FAA-certificated pilot school that has an approved flight instructor certification course (airplane).
    a. These are known as Part 141 schools or Part 142 training centers because they are authorized by Part 141 or Part 142 of the Federal Aviation Regulations.
        1) All other regulations concerning the certification of pilots are found in Part 61 of the Federal Aviation Regulations.
    b. The Part 141 course must consist of at least 40 hr. of ground instruction and 25 hr. of flight instructor training.
8. Successfully complete a practical (flight) test that will be given as a final exam by an FAA inspector or designated pilot examiner. The practical test will be conducted as specified in the FAA's Flight Instructor Practical Test Standards (FAA-S-8081-6).
    a. FAA inspectors are FAA employees and do not charge for their services.
    b. FAA-designated pilot examiners are proficient, experienced flight instructors and pilots who are authorized by the FAA to conduct flight tests. They do charge a fee.

The FAA's Flight Instructor Practical Test Standards are outlined and reprinted in the Gleim **Flight/Ground Instructor Flight Maneuvers and Practical Test Prep** book.

REQUIREMENTS TO OBTAIN A FLIGHT INSTRUCTOR CERTIFICATE WITH A SPORT PILOT RATING

1. Be at least 18 years of age.
2. Be able to read, speak, write, and understand English. If you cannot read, speak, write, and understand English because of medical reasons, the FAA may place limits on your certificate as are necessary for the safe operation of light-sport aircraft.
3. Hold at least a current and valid sport pilot certificate with category and class ratings or privileges, as applicable, that are appropriate to the flight instructor privileges sought.
    a. Have at least 150 hours of flight time as a pilot. That must include (for airplane certification)
        1) 100 hours of flight time as pilot in command, of which 50 hours are in a single-engine airplane.
        2) 25 hours of cross-country flight time, of which 10 hours are in a single-engine airplane.
        3) 15 hours of flight time as pilot in command in a single-engine airplane that is a light-sport aircraft.
    b. Refer to 14 CFR 61.411 for time requirements of other categories of aircraft.
4. Study **Flight/Ground Instructor FAA Knowledge Test Prep**, **Fundamentals of Instructing FAA Knowledge Test Prep**, **Flight Instructor Flight Maneuvers and Practical Test Prep**, **FAR/AIM**, **Aviation Weather and Weather Services**, and **Pilot Handbook** or use the Gleim **Online Ground School** to learn
    a. Fundamentals of instructing
    b. All other subject areas in which ground training is required for sport pilot certificates
5. Receive a logbook endorsement certifying that you are prepared for the knowledge tests from an authorized instructor who trained you or evaluated your home-study course on the aeronautical knowledge areas listed in 14 CFR 61.407.
6. Pass knowledge tests on
    a. The fundamentals of instructing.
        1) Item 5.d. on page 2 contains information on when the FOI knowledge test is not required.
    b. The aeronautical knowledge areas for a sport pilot certificate applicable to the aircraft category and class for which flight instructor privileges are sought.
7. Demonstrate flight proficiency in the areas below that are appropriate to the category and class of aircraft privileges you seek (14 CFR 61.409).
    a. *Technical subject areas*
    b. *Preflight preparation*
    c. *Preflight lesson on a maneuver to be performed in flight*
    d. *Preflight procedures*
    e. *Airport, seaplane base, and gliderport operations, as applicable*
    f. *Takeoffs (or launches), landings, and go-arounds*
    g. *Fundamentals of flight*
    h. *Performance maneuvers and, for gliders, performance speeds*
    i. *Ground reference maneuvers*
    j. *Soaring techniques (for gliders)*
    k. *Slow flight (not applicable to lighter-than-air, powered parachutes, and gyroplanes)*
    l. *Spins (applicable to airplanes and gliders)*
    m. *Emergency operations*
    n. *Tumble entry and avoidance techniques (for weight-shift-control aircraft)*
    o. *Postflight procedures*

8. Receive a logbook endorsement from an authorized instructor who provided you with flight training on the areas of operation specified in 14 CFR 61.409 that apply to the category and class of aircraft privileges you seek. This endorsement certifies that you meet the applicable aeronautical knowledge and experience requirements and are prepared for the practical test.
   a. If you are seeking privileges to provide instruction in an airplane or glider, you must receive
      1) Flight training in those training areas in an airplane or glider, as appropriate, that is certified for spins, and
      2) A logbook endorsement from an authorized instructor indicating that you are competent and possess instructional proficiency in stall awareness, spin entry, spins, and spin recovery procedures.
9. Pass a practical test on the areas of operation specified in 14 CFR 61.409 that are appropriate to the category and class of aircraft privileges you seek, using an aircraft representative of that category and class of aircraft.

REQUIREMENTS TO OBTAIN A GROUND INSTRUCTOR CERTIFICATE

1. To be eligible for a ground instructor certificate, you must
   a. Be at least 18 years of age.
   b. Be able to read, write, and understand English (certificates with operating limitations may be available for medically related deficiencies).
   c. Exhibit practical and theoretical knowledge by passing the FOI and the appropriate ground instructor knowledge tests.
      1) Item 5.d. on page 2 discusses when the FOI knowledge test is not required.
2. Ground instructor certificates cover three levels of certification:
   a. Basic ground instructor (BGI) may provide
      1) Ground training in the aeronautical knowledge areas required for a sport, recreational, or private pilot certificate
      2) Ground training required for a sport, recreational, or private pilot flight review
      3) A recommendation for the sport, recreational, or private pilot knowledge test
   b. Advanced ground instructor (AGI) may provide
      1) Ground training in the aeronautical knowledge areas required for any certificate or rating (except for an instrument rating) issued under Part 61
      2) Ground training required for any flight review, but not for an instrument proficiency check (IPC)
      3) A recommendation for a knowledge test required for any certificate issued under Part 61 except for the instrument rating knowledge test
   c. Instrument ground instructor (IGI) may provide
      1) Ground training in the aeronautical knowledge areas required for an instrument rating to a pilot or instructor certificate
      2) Ground training required for an instrument proficiency check
      3) A recommendation for the instrument rating knowledge test for a pilot or instructor certificate

      NOTE: The Gleim *Instrument Pilot FAA Knowledge Test Prep* covers the IGI knowledge test, which consists of 50 questions with a 2.5 hr. time limit.
3. If you are not a CFI, the Federal Aviation Regulations require you to have a ground instructor certificate to teach ground school or to sign off applicants for the appropriate pilot knowledge test.

> Your BGI or AGI knowledge test may have a few non-airplane questions. We have excluded all non-airplane questions from this book. Take your best guess at these questions without worry. It is not worth the few points to study all of the extra questions unless you are going to teach subjects related to rotorcraft, gliders, or lighter-than-air aircraft. Recall that this book has its primary focus on flight instructor -- airplane, and that is why non-airplane questions are excluded.

FAA PILOT KNOWLEDGE TEST AND TESTING SUPPLEMENT

1. This book is designed to help you prepare for and pass
   a. Flight Instructor -- Airplane (FIA), which consists of 100 questions and has a time limit of 2.5 hours.
   b. Advanced Ground Instructor (AGI), which consists of 100 questions and has a time limit of 2.5 hours. Refer to pages 374 through 376 for 10 additional questions.
      1) Authors' note: We suggest you take the AGI rather than the BGI, as the AGI gives you more privileges. The BGI is not a prerequisite to the AGI.
      2) If you are not a commercial pilot or flight instructor, you should be aware that your BGI or AGI test may include some questions about how to perform the commercial pilot flight maneuvers (chandelles, lazy eights, and eights-on-pylons). Having experience with flying these maneuvers is helpful in, but not necessary for, understanding these questions. Refer to *Flight Instructor Flight Maneuvers and Practical Test Prep* for a discussion of these maneuvers.
   c. Basic Ground Instructor (BGI), which consists of 80 questions and has a time limit of 2.5 hours. Refer to page 374 for two additional questions.
   d. Flight Instructor -- Airplane -- Added Rating (AFA), which consists of 25 questions and has a time limit of 1 hour.
      1) This test is for a person who currently holds a helicopter or gyroplane instructor certificate and wants to add an airplane rating to his or her instructor certificate.
      2) This test consists of questions relating to airplane aerodynamics and airplane flight maneuvers and emphasizing airplane differences. Topics such as aeromedical factors and aviation weather are not covered.
   e. Flight Instructor -- Sport Airplane (SIA), which consists of 70 questions and has a time limit of 2.5 hours.

2. The FAA figures are contained in a book titled *Airman Knowledge Testing Supplement for Flight Instructor, Ground Instructor, and Sport Pilot Instructor*, which you will be given to use at the time of your test.
   a. For the purpose of test preparation, all of the FAA airplane-related figures (except those related to topics the FAA has removed from the test) are reproduced in color in this book.

3. In an effort to develop better questions, the FAA frequently **pretests** questions on knowledge tests by adding up to five "pretest" questions. The pretest questions will not be graded.
   a. You will NOT know which questions are real and which are pretest, so you must attempt to answer all questions correctly.
   b. When you notice a question NOT covered by Gleim, it might be a pretest question.
      1) We want to know about each pretest question you see.
      2) Please contact us at www.GleimAviation.com/AviationQuestions or call 800-874-5346 with your recollection of any possible pretest questions so we may improve our efforts to prepare future instructors.

FAA'S KNOWLEDGE TESTS: CHEATING OR UNAUTHORIZED CONDUCT POLICY

The following is taken verbatim from an FAA knowledge test. It is reproduced here to remind all test takers about the FAA's policy against cheating and unauthorized conduct, a policy that Gleim consistently supports and upholds. Test takers must click "Yes" to proceed from this page into the actual knowledge test.

14 CFR part 61, section 61.37 Knowledge tests: Cheating or other unauthorized conduct

(a) An applicant for a knowledge test may not:
(1) Copy or intentionally remove any knowledge test;
(2) Give to another applicant or receive from another applicant any part or copy of a knowledge test;
(3) Give assistance on, or receive assistance on, a knowledge test during the period that test is being given;
(4) Take any part of a knowledge test on behalf of another person;
(5) Be represented by, or represent, another person for a knowledge test;
(6) Use any material or aid during the period that the test is being given, unless specifically authorized to do so by the Administrator; and
(7) Intentionally cause, assist, or participate in any act prohibited by this paragraph.

(b) An applicant who the Administrator finds has committed an act prohibited by paragraph (a) of this section is prohibited, for 1 year after the date of committing that act, from:
(1) Applying for any certificate, rating, or authorization issued under this chapter; and
(2) Applying for and taking any test under this chapter.

(c) Any certificate or rating held by an applicant may be suspended or revoked if the Administrator finds that person has committed an act prohibited by paragraph (a) of this section.

FAA PILOT KNOWLEDGE TEST QUESTION BANK

In an effort to keep applicants from simply memorizing test questions, the FAA does not currently disclose all the questions you might see on your FAA knowledge test. We encourage you to take the time to fully learn and understand the concepts explained in the knowledge transfer outlines contained in this book. **Using this book or other Gleim test preparation material to merely memorize the questions and answers is unwise and unproductive, and it will not ensure your success on your FAA knowledge test.** Memorization also greatly reduces the amount of information you will actually learn during your study.

The questions and answers provided in this book include all previously released FAA questions in addition to questions developed from current FAA reference materials that closely approximate the types of questions you should see on your knowledge test. We are confident that by studying our knowledge transfer outlines, answering our questions under exam conditions, and not relying on rote memorization, you will be able to successfully pass your FAA knowledge test and begin learning to become a safe and competent instructor.

FAA QUESTIONS WITH TYPOGRAPHICAL ERRORS

Occasionally, FAA test questions contain typographical errors such that there is no correct answer. The FAA test development process involves many steps and people and, as you would expect, glitches occur in the system that are beyond the control of any one person. We indicate "best" rather than correct answers for some questions. Use these best answers for the indicated questions.

Note that the FAA corrects (rewrites) defective questions as they are discovered; these changes are explained in our updates (discussed on page ii). However, problems due to faulty or out-of-date figures printed in the FAA Computer Testing Supplements are expensive to correct. Thus, it is important to carefully study questions that are noted to have a best answer in this book. Even though the best answer may not be completely correct, you should select it when taking your test.

REORGANIZATION OF FAA QUESTIONS

1. In the public FAA knowledge test question bank releases, the questions are **not** grouped together by topic; i.e., they appear to be presented randomly.

    a. We have reorganized and renumbered the questions into study units and subunits.

2. Pages 399 through 406 contain a list of all the questions in FAA learning statement code order, with cross-references to the study units and question numbers in this book.

    a. For example, question 2-31 is assigned the code PLT004, which means it is found in Study Unit 2 as question 31 in this book and is covered under the FAA learning statement, "Calculate aircraft performance - climb / descent / maneuvering."
    b. Questions relating to helicopters, gliders, balloons, etc., are excluded.

HOW TO PREPARE FOR THE FAA PILOT KNOWLEDGE TEST

1. Begin by carefully reading the rest of this introduction. You need to have a complete understanding of the examination process prior to initiating your study. This knowledge will make your studying more efficient.

2. After you have spent an hour analyzing this introduction, set up a study schedule, including a target date for taking your knowledge test.

    a. Do not let the study process drag on and become discouraging; i.e., the quicker, the better.
    b. Consider enrolling in an organized ground school course, like the Gleim **Online Ground School**, or one held at your local FBO, community college, etc.
    c. Determine where and when you are going to take your knowledge test.

3. Work through Study Units 1 through 10, unless you are taking the Flight Instructor -- Sport Airplane (SIA) test.

    a. SIA applicants should study the specified study units or parts of the 10 items listed below and on the next page.

       1) Study Unit 1, all subunits
       2) Study Unit 2, all subunits except

          5. Multi-Engine Performance

       3) Study Unit 3, all subunits except

          7. Manifold Pressure Gauge
          11. Turbocharged Engines
          18. Oxygen Systems

       4) Study Unit 4, all subunits
       5) Study Unit 5, all subunits except

          4. Weight Change Calculations

       6) Study Unit 6, all subunits
       7) Study Unit 7, all subtopics except

          61.23 Medical Certificates: Requirement and Duration
          61.31 Type Rating Requirements, Additional Training, and Auth. Requirements
          61.69 Glider Towing: Experience and Training Requirements
          61.101 Recreational Pilot Privileges and Limitations
          61.109 Aeronautical Experience
          61.123 Eligibility Requirements: General
          61.129 Aeronautical Experience
          61.133 Commercial Pilot Privileges and Limitations
          91.109 Flight Instruction; Simulated Instrument Flight and Certain Flight Tests

Introduction: The FAA Pilot Knowledge Test

91.117 Aircraft Speed
91.135 Operations in Class A Airspace
91.157 Special VFR Weather Minimums
91.211 Supplemental Oxygen

8) Study Unit 8, all subunits except

6. Distance Measuring Equipment (DME)
7. VHF Omnidirectional Range (VOR)

9) Study Unit 9, all subunits except

9. Eights-on-Pylons
12. Chandelles
13. Lazy Eights
14. Flight by Reference to Instruments

10) Study Unit 10, all subunits

b. All previously released questions in the FAA's flight and ground instructor knowledge test question bank that are applicable to airplanes have been grouped into the following 10 categories, which are the titles of Study Units 1 through 10:

Study Unit 1 -- Airplanes and Aerodynamics
Study Unit 2 -- Airplane Performance
Study Unit 3 -- Airplane Instruments, Engines, and Systems
Study Unit 4 -- Airports, Airspace, and ATC
Study Unit 5 -- Weight and Balance
Study Unit 6 -- Aviation Weather
Study Unit 7 -- Federal Aviation Regulations
Study Unit 8 -- Navigation
Study Unit 9 -- Flight Maneuvers
Study Unit 10 -- Aeromedical Factors and Aeronautical Decision Making (ADM)

c. Within each of the study units listed, questions relating to the same subtopic (e.g., thunderstorms, airplane stability, sectional charts, etc.) are grouped together to facilitate your study program. Each subtopic is called a subunit.

d. To the right of each question, we present

1) The correct answer.
2) The appropriate source document for the answer explanation. These publications can be obtained from the FAA (www.faa.gov) and aviation bookstores.

AC	Advisory Circular	14 CFR	Federal Aviation Regulations
ACL	Aeronautical Chart Legend	Fl Comp	Flight Computer
AFH	*Airplane Flying Handbook*	FTP	*Flight Theory for Pilots* – Jeppesen Sanderson, Inc.
AIH	*Aviation Instructor Handbook*		
AIM	*Aeronautical Information Manual*	IFH	*Instrument Flying Handbook*
AvW	*Aviation Weather*	NTSB	National Transportation Safety Board regulations
AWBH	*Aircraft Weight and Balance Handbook*		
AWC	Aviation Weather Center	PHAK	*Pilot's Handbook of Aeronautical Knowledge*
AWS	*Aviation Weather Services*		
Chart Supplement		RFH	*Rotorcraft Flying Handbook*
		RMH	*Risk Management Handbook*

a) The codes may refer to an entire document, such as an advisory circular, or they may refer to a particular chapter or subsection of a larger document.

i) Page 407 contains a complete list of abbreviations and acronyms used in this book.

3) A comprehensive answer explanation, including

a) A discussion of the correct answer or concept
b) An explanation of why the other two answer choices are incorrect

4. Each study unit begins with a list of its subunit titles. The number after each title is the number of questions that cover the information in that subunit. The two numbers following the number of questions are the page numbers on which the outline and the questions for that particular subunit begin, respectively.

5. Begin by studying the outlines slowly and carefully. The outlines in this part of the book are very brief and have only one purpose: to help you pass the FAA knowledge test.
    a. **CAUTION:** The **sole purpose** of this book is to expedite your passing the FAA knowledge test for the flight and/or ground instructor certificate. Accordingly, all extraneous material (i.e., topics or regulations not directly tested on the FAA knowledge test) is omitted, even though much more knowledge is necessary to be an instructor. This additional material is presented in five related Gleim books: ***Fundamentals of Instructing FAA Knowledge Test Prep***, ***Flight Instructor Flight Maneuvers and Practical Test Prep***, ***FAR/AIM***, ***Aviation Weather and Weather Services***, and ***Pilot Handbook***.
6. Next, answer the questions under exam conditions. Cover the answer explanations on the right side of each page with a piece of paper while you answer the questions.

 Remember, it is very important to the learning (and understanding) process that you honestly commit yourself to an answer. If you are wrong, your memory will be reinforced by having discovered your error. Therefore, it is crucial to cover up the answer and make an honest attempt to answer the question before reading the answer.

   a. Study the answer explanation for each question that you answer incorrectly, do not understand, or have difficulty with.
   b. Use our **Online Ground School** or **FAA Test Prep Online** to ensure that you do not refer to answers before committing to one AND to simulate actual computer testing center exam conditions.
7. Note that this test book contains questions grouped by topic. Thus, some questions may appear repetitive, while others may be duplicates or near-duplicates. Accordingly, do not work question after question (i.e., waste time and effort) if you are already conversant with a topic and the type of questions asked.
8. As you move through study units, you may need further explanation or clarification of certain topics. You may wish to obtain and use the following Gleim books described on page 1:
   a. ***Flight Instructor Flight Maneuvers and Practical Test Prep***
   b. ***Pilot Handbook***
   c. ***Aviation Weather and Weather Services***
9. Keep track of your work. As you complete a subunit, grade yourself with an A, B, C, or ? (use a ? if you need help on the subject) next to the subunit title at the front of the respective study unit.
   a. The A, B, C, or ? is your self-evaluation of your comprehension of the material in that subunit and your ability to answer the questions.
      A   means a good understanding.
      B   means a fair understanding.
      C   means a shaky understanding.
      ?   means to ask your CFI or others about the material and/or questions, and read the pertinent sections in ***Flight Instructor Flight Maneuvers and Practical Test Prep*** and/or ***Pilot Handbook***.
   b. This procedure will provide you with the ability to quickly see (by looking at the first page of each study unit) how much studying you have done (and how much remains) and how well you have done.
   c. This procedure will also facilitate review. You can spend more time on the subunits that were more difficult for you.
   d. **FAA Test Prep Online** provides you with your historical performance data.

Follow the suggestions given throughout this introduction and you will have no trouble passing the FAA knowledge test the first time you take it.

With this overview of exam requirements, you are ready to begin the easy-to-study outlines and rearranged questions with answers to build your knowledge and confidence and PASS THE FAA's FLIGHT AND GROUND INSTRUCTOR KNOWLEDGE TEST.

The feedback we receive from users indicates that our materials reduce anxiety, improve FAA test scores, and build knowledge. Studying for each test becomes a useful step toward advanced certificates and ratings.

MULTIPLE-CHOICE QUESTION-ANSWERING TECHNIQUE

Because the flight instructor knowledge test has a set number of questions (100) and a set time limit (2.5 hours), you can plan your test-taking session to ensure that you leave yourself enough time to answer each question with relative certainty. The following steps will help you move through the knowledge test efficiently and produce better test results.

1. **Budget your time.** We make this point with emphasis. Just as you would fill up your gas tank prior to reaching empty, so too should you finish your exam before time expires.
   a. If you utilize the entire time limit for the test, you will have about 1.5 minutes per question.
   b. If you are adequately prepared for the test, you should finish it well within the time limit.
      1) Use any extra time you have to review questions that you are not sure about, cross-country planning questions with multiple steps and calculations, and similar questions in your exam that may help you answer other questions.
   c. Time yourself when completing study sessions in this book and/or review your time investment reports from the Gleim **FAA Test Prep Online** to track your progress and adherence to the time limit and your own personal time allocation budget.

2. **Answer the questions in consecutive order.**
   a. Do **not** agonize over any one item. Stay within your time budget.
      1) We suggest that you skip cross-country planning questions and other similarly involved computational questions on your first pass through the exam. Come back to them after you have been through the entire test once.
   b. Mark any questions you are unsure of and return to them later as time allows.
      1) Once you initiate test grading, you will no longer be able to review/change any answers.
   c. Never leave a multiple-choice question unanswered. Make your best educated guess in the time allowed. Remember, your score is based on the number of correct responses. You will not be penalized for guessing incorrectly.

3. **For each multiple-choice question,**
   a. **Try to ignore the answer choices.** Do not allow the answer choices to affect your reading of the question.
      1) If three answer choices are presented, two of them are incorrect. These choices are called **distractors** for good reason. Often, distractors are written to appear correct at first glance until further analysis.
      2) In computational items, the distractors are carefully calculated such that they are the result of making common mistakes. Be careful, and double-check your computations if time permits.

b. **Read the question carefully** to determine the precise requirement.
   1) Focusing on what is required enables you to ignore extraneous information, to focus on the relevant facts, and to proceed directly to determining the correct answer.
      a) Be especially careful to note when the requirement is an **exception**; e.g., "Which of the following is **not** a type of hypoxia?"
c. **Determine the correct answer** before looking at the answer choices.
d. **Read the answer choices carefully.**
   1) Even if the first answer appears to be the correct choice, do **not** skip the remaining answer choices. Questions often require the "best" answer of the choices provided. Thus, each choice requires your consideration.
   2) Treat each answer choice as a true/false question as you analyze it.
e. **Click on the best answer.**
   1) You have a 33% chance of answering the question correctly by blindly guessing; improve your odds with educated guessing.
   2) For many multiple-choice questions, at least one answer choice can be eliminated with minimal effort, thereby increasing your educated guess to a 50-50 proposition.

4. After you have been through all the questions in the test, consult the question status list to determine which questions are unanswered and which are marked for review.
   a. Go back to the marked questions and finalize your answer choices.
   b. Verify that all questions have been answered.

EDUCATED GUESSING

 The FAA knowledge test sometimes includes questions that are poorly worded or confusing. Expect the unexpected and move forward. Do not let confusing questions affect your concentration or take up too much time; make your best guess and move on.

1. If you don't know the answer, make an educated guess as follows:
   a. Rule out answers that you think are incorrect.
   b. Speculate on what the FAA is looking for and/or the rationale behind the question.
   c. Select the best answer or guess between equally appealing answers. Your first guess is usually the most intuitive. If you cannot make an educated guess, re-read the stem and each answer choice and pick the most intuitive answer. It's just a guess!
2. Avoid lingering on any question for too long. Remember your time budget and the overall test time limit.

SIMULATED FAA PRACTICE TEST

Appendix C, "Practice Test," beginning on page 381, allows you to practice taking the FAA knowledge test without the answers next to the questions. This test has 100 questions randomly selected from the questions in our flight and ground instructor knowledge test bank. Topical coverage in the practice test is similar to that of the FAA knowledge test.

It is very important that you answer all 100 questions in one sitting. You should not consult the answers, especially when being referred to figures (charts, tables, etc.) throughout this book where the questions are answered and explained. Analyze your performance based on the answer key that follows the practice test.

It is even better to practice with Test Sessions in the Gleim **FAA Test Prep Online**. These simulate actual computer testing conditions, including the screen layouts, instructions, etc., for CATS and PSI.

More information on the Gleim **FAA Test Prep Online** is available on pages 17 and 18.

AUTHORIZATION TO TAKE THE FAA PILOT KNOWLEDGE TEST

The FAA does not require an instructor endorsement for your initial attempt of any ground instructor knowledge test or conventional flight instructor knowledge test. Applicants seeking a flight instructor certificate with a sport pilot rating need a knowledge test endorsement to take both the FOI and SIA tests. If you fail the knowledge test, you will need an instructor endorsement before you can retake the exam.

WHEN TO TAKE THE FAA PILOT KNOWLEDGE TEST

1. You must be at least 16 years of age to take the flight or ground instructor knowledge test.
    a. You must be 18 years of age to obtain your certificate.
2. Take the FAA knowledge test within 30 days of beginning your study.
    a. Get the knowledge test behind you.
3. Your practical test must follow within 24 months.
    a. Otherwise, you will have to retake your knowledge test.

WHAT TO TAKE TO THE FAA PILOT KNOWLEDGE TEST

1. An approved flight computer (ideally the one that you use to solve the test questions in this book, i.e., one you are familiar with and have used before)
2. Navigational plotter
3. A pocket calculator you are familiar with and have used before (no instructional material for the calculator is allowed)
4. Proper identification that contains your
    a. Photograph
    b. Signature
    c. Date of birth
    d. Actual residential address, if different from your mailing address

NOTE: Paper and pencils are supplied at the examination site.

It is essential for each student to own an approved E6B flight computer (manual or electronic) and a navigation plotter. These tools are necessary to answer some questions on the knowledge test and to use during your check ride. Go to www.GleimAviation.com/E6B to access complete instructions on the use of the Gleim E6B flight computer.

COMPUTER TESTING CENTERS

The FAA has contracted with two computer testing services to administer FAA knowledge tests. Both of these computer testing services have testing centers throughout the country. To register for the knowledge test, call one of the computer testing services listed below. More information can be found at www.GleimAviation.com/testingcenters.

        CATS   (800) 947-4228   PSI   (800) 211-2754

COMPUTER TESTING PROCEDURES

When you arrive at the testing center, you will be required to provide positive proof of identification and documentary evidence of your age. The identification must include your photograph, signature, and actual residential address if different from the mailing address. This information may be presented in more than one form of identification. Next, you will sign in on the testing center's daily log. Your signature on the logsheet certifies that, if this is a retest, you meet the applicable requirements (discussed in "Failure on the FAA Pilot Knowledge Test" on page 16) and that you have not passed this test in the past 2 years.

Next, you will be taken into the testing room and seated at a computer terminal. A person from the testing center will assist you in logging onto the system, and you will be asked to confirm your personal data (e.g., name, Social Security number, etc.). Then you will be given an online introduction to the computer testing system, and you will take a sample test. If you have used our **FAA Test Prep Online**, you will be conversant with the computer testing methodology and environment and will breeze through the sample test. When you have completed your test, an Airman Computer Test Report will be printed out, validated (usually with an embossed seal), and given to you by a person from the testing center. Before you leave, you will be required to sign out on the testing center's daily log.

Each testing service has certain idiosyncrasies in its paperwork, scheduling, and telephone procedures as well as in its software. It is for this reason that our **FAA Test Prep Online** emulates both of the FAA-approved computer testing companies.

YOUR FAA PILOT KNOWLEDGE TEST REPORT

1. You will receive your FAA Pilot Knowledge Test Report upon completion of the test. An example test report is reproduced on the next page.
   a. Note that you will receive only one grade as illustrated.
   b. The expiration date is the date by which you must take your FAA practical test.
   c. The report lists the FAA learning statement codes of the questions you missed so you can review the topics you missed prior to your practical test.
2. Use the FAA Listing of Learning Statement Codes on pages 393 through 398 to determine which topics you had difficulty with.
   a. Look them over and review them with your CFI so (s)he can certify that (s)he reviewed the deficient areas and found you competent in them when you take your practical test. Have your CFI sign off your deficiencies on the FAA Pilot Knowledge Test Report.
3. Keep your FAA Pilot Knowledge Test Report in a safe place because you must submit it to the FAA inspector/examiner when you take your practical test.

Introduction: The FAA Pilot Knowledge Test

Computer Test Report

U.S. DEPARTMENT OF TRANSPORTATION
Federal Aviation Administration

Airman Knowledge Test Report

NAME:

APPLICANT ID: EXAM ID:

EXAM: Flight Instructor - Airplane

EXAM DATE: 10/08/2017   EXAM SITE:

SCORE: 96   GRADE: PASS   TAKE: 1

Learning statement codes listed below represent incorrectly answered questions. Learning statement codes and their associated statements can be found at **www.faa.gov/training_testing/testing/airmen**.

Reference material associated with the learning statement codes can be found in the appropriate knowledge test guide at **www.faa.gov/training_testing/testing/airmen/test_guides**.

A single code may represent more than one incorrect response.

PLT229 PLT306

EXPIRATION DATE: 10/31/2019   CTD's Embossed Seal

DO NOT LOSE THIS REPORT

AUTHORIZED INSTRUCTOR'S STATEMENT: (If applicable)

On _____ (date) I gave the above named applicant ____ hours of additional instruction, covering each subject area shown to be deficient, and consider the applicant competent to pass the test.

Name _____ Initial ____ Cert. No. _____ Type _____
(Print clearly)

Signature _____

FRAUDULENT ALTERATION OF THIS FORM BY ANY PERSON IS A BASIS FOR SUSPENSION OR REVOCATION OF ANY CERTIFICATES OR RATINGS HELD BY THAT PERSON. THIS INFORMATION IS PROTECTED BY THE PRIVACY ACT. FOR OFFICIAL USE ONLY.

APPLYING FOR YOUR GROUND INSTRUCTOR CERTIFICATE

Flight instructor applicants will take their FAA Pilot Knowledge Test Reports to their FAA practical tests. A ground instructor applicant (BGI, AGI, or IGI) does not, however, have to take an FAA practical test.

You must take your FAA Pilot Knowledge Test Report and a completed Airman Certificate and/or Rating Application (FAA Form 8710-1) to your local FSDO where you will be issued an appropriate temporary ground instructor certificate. An FAA-designated examiner cannot issue a ground instructor certificate. Also, on FAA Form 8710-1, the Instructor's Recommendation block does not require an instructor's signature.

Your permanent ground instructor certificate will be mailed to you from the FAA in Oklahoma City.

FAILURE ON THE FAA PILOT KNOWLEDGE TEST

1. If you fail (score less than 70%) the knowledge test (which is virtually impossible if you follow the Gleim system), you may retake it after your instructor endorses the bottom of your FAA Pilot Knowledge Test Report certifying that you have received the necessary ground training to retake the test.
2. Upon retaking the test, you will find that the procedure is the same except that you must also submit your FAA Pilot Knowledge Test Report indicating the previous failure to the computer testing center.
3. Note that the pass rates on the flight and ground instructor knowledge tests average out to about 90%; i.e., about 10% fail the test initially. Reasons for failure include
   a. Failure to study the material tested and mere memorization of correct answers. (Relevant study material is contained in the outlines at the beginning of Study Units 1 through 10 of this book.)
   b. Failure to practice working through the questions under test conditions. (All of the previously released FAA questions appear in Study Units 1 through 10 of this book.)
   c. Poor examination technique, such as misreading questions and not understanding the requirements.

This Gleim Knowledge Test book will prepare you to pass the FAA knowledge test on your first attempt! In addition, the Gleim *Flight/Ground Instructor Flight Maneuvers and Practical Test Prep* book will save you time and frustration as you prepare for the FAA practical test.

Just as this book organizes and explains the knowledge needed to pass your FAA knowledge test, *Flight/Ground Instructor Flight Maneuvers and Practical Test Prep* will assist you in developing the competence and confidence to pass your FAA practical test.

Also, flight maneuvers are quickly perfected when you understand exactly what to expect before you get into an airplane to practice the flight maneuvers. You must be ahead of (not behind) your CFI and your airplane. Our flight maneuvers books explain and illustrate all flight maneuvers so the maneuvers and their execution are intuitively appealing to you. Visit www.GleimAviation.com or call (800) 874-5346 and order today!

GLEIM ONLINE GROUND SCHOOL

1. Gleim **Online Ground School (OGS)** course content is based on the Gleim Knowledge Test Prep books, **FAA Test Prep Online**, FAA publications, and Gleim reference books. The delivery system is modeled on the Gleim FAA-approved online **Flight Instructor Refresher Course**.
   a. Online Ground School courses are available for
      1) Private Pilot
      2) Sport Pilot
      3) CFI/CGI
      4) FOI
      5) Instrument Pilot
      6) Commercial Pilot
      7) ATP
      8) Flight Engineer
      9) Canadian Certificate Conversion
   b. OGS courses are airplane-only and have lessons that correspond to the study units in the Gleim FAA Knowledge Test Prep books.
   c. Each course contains study outlines that automatically reference current FAA publications, the appropriate knowledge test questions, FAA figures, and Gleim answer explanations.
   d. OGS is always up to date.
   e. Users achieve very high knowledge test scores and a near-100% pass rate.

f. **Gleim Online Ground School is the most flexible course available!** Access your OGS personal classroom from any computer with Internet access 24 hours a day, 7 days a week. Your virtual classroom is never closed!
g. **Save time and study only the material you need to know!** Gleim **Online Ground School** Certificate Selection will provide you with a customized study plan. You save time because unnecessary questions will be automatically eliminated.
h. **We are truly interactive. We help you focus on any weaker areas.** Answer explanations for wrong choices help you learn from your mistakes.

Register for Gleim Online Ground School today:
www.GleimAviation.com/OGS
or
Demo Study Unit 1 for FREE at
www.GleimAviation.com/Demos

GLEIM FAA TEST PREP ONLINE

Computer testing is consistent with aviation's use of computers (e.g., DUATS, flight simulators, computerized cockpits, etc.). All FAA knowledge tests are administered by computer.

Computer testing is natural after computer study and computer-assisted instruction is a very efficient and effective method of study. The Gleim **FAA Test Prep Online** is designed to prepare you for computer testing because our software can simulate both CATS and PSI. We make you comfortable with computer testing!

FAA Test Prep Online contains all of the questions in this book, context-sensitive outline material, and on-screen charts and figures. It allows you to choose either Study Mode or Test Mode.

In Study Mode, the software provides you with an explanation of each answer you choose (correct or incorrect). You design each Study Session:

Topic(s) and/or FAA learning statement codes you wish to cover
Number of questions
Order of questions -- FAA, Gleim, or random
Order of answers to each question -- Gleim or random

Questions marked and/or missed from last session -- test, study, or both
Questions marked and/or missed from all sessions -- test, study, or both
Questions never seen, answered, or answered correctly

In Test Mode, you decide the format: CATS or PSI. When you finish your test, you can and should study the questions missed and access answer explanations. The software emulates the operation of FAA-approved computer testing companies. Thus, you have a complete understanding of how to take an FAA knowledge test and know exactly what to expect before you go to a computer testing center.

The Gleim **FAA Test Prep Online** is an all-in-one program designed to help anyone with a computer, Internet access, and an interest in flying pass the FAA knowledge tests.

Study Sessions and Test Sessions

Study Sessions give you immediate feedback on why your answer selection for a particular question is correct or incorrect and allow you to access the context-sensitive outline material that helps to explain concepts related to the question. Choose from several different question sources: all questions available for that library; questions from a certain topic (Gleim study units and subunits); questions that you missed or marked in the last sessions you created; questions that you have never seen, answered, or answered correctly; questions from certain FAA learning statement codes; etc. You can mix up the questions by selecting to randomize the question and/or answer order so that you do not memorize answer letters.

You may then grade your study sessions and track your study progress using the performance analysis charts and graphs. The Performance Analysis information helps you to focus on areas where you need the most improvement, saving you time in the overall study process. You may then want to go back and study questions that you missed in a previous session, or you may want to create a Study Session of questions that you marked in the previous session. All of these options are made easy with **FAA Test Prep Online**'s Study Sessions.

After studying the outlines and questions in a Study Session, you can further test your skills with a Test Session. These sessions allow you to answer questions under actual testing conditions using one of the simulations of the major testing services. In a Test Session, you will not know which questions you have answered correctly until the session is graded.

Recommended Study Program

1. Start with Study Unit 1 and proceed through study units in chronological order. Follow the three-step process below.
    a. First, carefully study the Gleim Outline.
    b. Second, create a Study Session of all questions in the study unit. Answer and study all questions in the Study Session.
    c. Third, create a Test Session of all questions in the study unit. Answer all questions in the Test Session.
2. After each Study Session and Test Session, create a new Study Session from questions answered incorrectly. This is of critical importance to allow you to learn from your mistakes.

Practice Test

Take an exam in the actual testing environment of either of the major testing centers: CATS or PSI. **FAA Test Prep Online** simulates the testing formats of these testing centers, making it easy for you to study questions under actual exam conditions. After studying with **FAA Test Prep Online**, you will know exactly what to expect when you go in to take your pilot knowledge test.

On-Screen Charts and Figures

One of the most convenient features of **FAA Test Prep Online** is the easily accessible on-screen charts and figures. Several of the questions refer to drawings, maps, charts, and other pictures that provide information to help answer the question. In **FAA Test Prep Online**, you can pull up any of these figures with the click of a button. You can increase or decrease the size of the images, and you may also use our drawing feature to calculate the true course between two given points (required only on the private pilot knowledge test).

Order FAA Test Prep Online today
(800) 874-5346 or www.GleimAviation.com

or

Demo Study Unit 1 for FREE at
www.GleimAviation.com/Demos

Free Updates and Technical Support

Gleim offers FREE technical support to all users of the current versions. Call (800) 874-5346, send an email to support@gleim.com, or fill out the technical support request form online (www.GleimAviation.com/contact). Additionally, Gleim **FAA Test Prep Online** is always up to date. The program is automatically updated when any changes are made, so you can be confident that Gleim will prepare you for your knowledge test. More information on our email update service for books is on page ii.

STUDY UNIT ONE
AIRPLANES AND AERODYNAMICS

(10 pages of outline)

1.1	Flaps	(10 questions)	19, 29
1.2	Lift and Drag	(28 questions)	21, 32
1.3	Load Factor	(15 questions)	24, 38
1.4	Wings	(17 questions)	25, 42
1.5	The Axes of Airplanes	(4 questions)	26, 45
1.6	Angle of Attack	(3 questions)	26, 45
1.7	Turns	(8 questions)	26, 46
1.8	Airplane Stability	(11 questions)	27, 48
1.9	Spiraling Slipstream and Gyroscopic Precession	(3 questions)	28, 50
1.10	Stalls and Spins	(5 questions)	28, 50
1.11	Ground Effect	(4 questions)	28, 51
1.12	Turbulence	(2 questions)	28, 52

This study unit contains outlines of major concepts tested, sample test questions and answers regarding aerodynamics, and an explanation of each answer. The table of contents above lists each subunit within this study unit, the number of questions pertaining to that particular subunit, and the pages on which the outlines and questions begin, respectively.

 Recall that the **sole purpose** of this book is to expedite your passing of the FAA pilot knowledge test for the CFI, BGI, or AGI certificate. Accordingly, all extraneous material (i.e., topics or regulations not directly tested on the FAA pilot knowledge test) is omitted, even though much more knowledge is necessary to become a proficient flight or ground instructor. This additional material is presented in *Pilot Handbook* and *Flight Instructor Flight Maneuvers and Practical Test Prep*, available from Gleim Publications, Inc. Order online at www.GleimAviation.com.

1.1 FLAPS

1. Flaps are the most common high-lift devices used on aircraft. These surfaces, which are attached to the trailing edge of the wing, increase both lift and induced drag for any given angle of attack. Flaps allow a compromise between high cruising speed and low landing speed because they may be extended when needed and retracted into the wing's structure when not needed. There are five kinds of trailing edge flaps:

    a. A **plain flap** is a portion of the trailing edge of the wing on a hinged pivot that allows the flap to be moved downward, thereby changing the chord line, angle of attack, and camber of the wing.

    b. A **slotted flap** is similar to a plain flap but provides a gap between the trailing edge of the wing and the leading edge of the flap.

    c. The **split flap** is a hinged portion of only the bottom surface of the wing.

    1) Extending a split flap creates the least change in pitching moment.

    d. A **fowler flap** not only tilts downward but also slides rearward on tracks.

    1) The fowler flap creates the greatest change in pitching moment.
    2) The fowler flap also provides the greatest increase in lift coefficient with the least change in drag.

    e. A **slotted fowler flap** is a combination of the slotted and fowler flaps.

2. High-lift devices can also be applied to the leading edge of an airfoil (i.e., a wing). There are four common types:
   a. A **fixed slot** directs airflow to the upper wing surface and delays airflow separation at higher angles of attack.
   b. A **movable slot** is a leading edge segment that moves on tracks.
      1) At low angles of attack, each slot is held flush against the wing's leading edge by the high pressure that forms there. As the angle of attack increases, the high-pressure area moves aft below the lower surface of the wing, allowing the slots to move forward.
      2) By moving to high angles of attack, the slot allows the air below the wing to flow over the wing's upper surface, delaying airflow separation.
   c. **Leading edge flaps** are used to maximize lift and the camber of the wings.
      1) This type of device is frequently used in conjunction with trailing edge flaps and can reduce the nose-down pitching movement produced by the latter.
   d. **Leading edge cuffs**, like leading edge flaps, are used to maximize lift and the camber of the wings.
      1) Unlike leading edge flaps and trailing edge flaps, leading edge cuffs are fixed aerodynamic devices.
      2) In most cases, leading edge cuffs extend the leading edge down and forward. This causes the airflow to attach better to the upper surface of the wing at higher angles of attack, thus lowering an aircraft's stall speed.
3. The following image shows each of the types of flaps and leading edges:

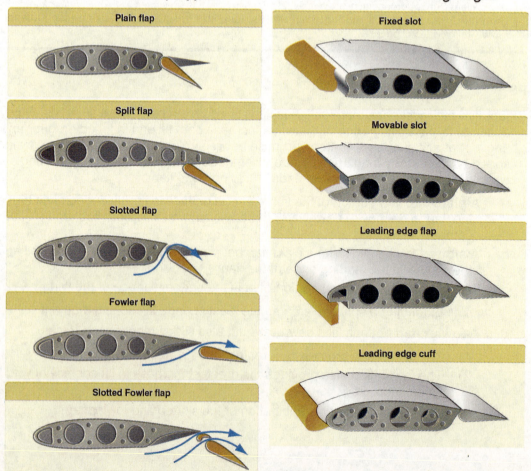

1.2 LIFT AND DRAG

1. The **lift** provided by a wing is based in part upon Bernoulli's principle that the internal pressure of a fluid (liquid or gas) decreases at points where the speed of the fluid increases, and in part upon Newton's Third Law of Motion that for every action, there is an equal and opposite reaction.

    a. During flight, air must travel farther in the same amount of time to flow over the curved upper surface of the wing than across the lower surface. Thus, according to Bernoulli's principle, the pressure above the wing is less than the pressure below the wing.

    1) In other words, there is a positive air pressure below the wing's surface and a negative air pressure above the wing's surface, even at zero angle of attack.

    NOTE: Negative pressure is any pressure less than atmospheric, and positive pressure is pressure greater than atmospheric.

    b. An increase in the speed at which an airfoil passes through the air increases lift because the increased impact of the relative wind on the airfoil's lower surface creates a greater amount of air being deflected downward (Newton's Third Law of Motion).

2. Lift is considered to be the net force developed perpendicular to the relative wind.

3. The center of pressure is the point on the airfoil through which the lift acts.

    a. The change in the center of pressure of a wing affects the airplane's aerodynamic balance and controllability.

    b. When the center of pressure is forward of the center of gravity, an airplane has a tendency to nose up and has an inherent tendency to enter a stalled condition.

    c. When the angle of attack of a symmetrical airfoil is increased, the center of pressure will remain unaffected.

4. **Thrust** is the force that imparts a change in the velocity of a mass.

5. **Induced drag** is the portion of drag created by the production of lift.

    a. Induced drag varies inversely as the square of the airspeed.

    b. It increases total drag as airspeed is reduced below the maximum lift/drag (L/D) speed.

6. **Profile drag** is the resistance, or skin friction, due to the viscosity of the air as it passes along the surface of the wing.

7. **Parasite drag** increases with airspeed and increases total drag above the maximum L/D speed.

8. **Interference drag** comes from the intersection of airstreams between adjacent parts of the airplane that creates eddy currents, turbulence, or restricts smooth airflow.

    a. For example, the intersection of the wing and the fuselage at the wing root has significant interference drag.

    1) Air flowing around the fuselage collides with air flowing over the wing. These airstreams merge into a current of air different from the two original currents.

    b. Placing two objects adjacent to one another may produce turbulence 50–200 percent greater than the parts tested separately.

    c. The most interference drag is observed when two surfaces meet at perpendicular angles.

    d. Fairings and distance between lifting surfaces and external components (such as radar antennas hung from wings) reduce interference drag.

9. An angle-of-attack chart (illustrated in Figure 19 below) has curves that represent the coefficient of drag (C_D), coefficient of lift (C_L), and the L/D ratio for various angles of attack.

   a. The maximum lift-drag (L/D_{MAX}) ratio occurs at only one angle of attack, at which the total drag is at a minimum.

      1) Any other angle of attack increases the total drag for a given airplane.
      2) L/D_{MAX} is the angle of attack at which the airplane will travel the maximum horizontal distance per foot of altitude lost.

   b. Of interest is that the L/D ratio can be the same for two different angles of attack.

      1) EXAMPLE: At a 2° angle of attack and at 16.5° angle of attack, the L/D ratio is approximately 7.4.

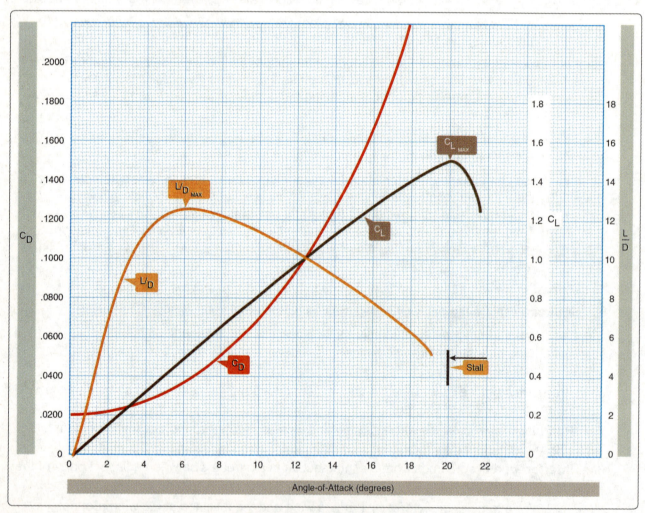

Figure 19. – Angle-of-Attack vs. Lift.

10. The drag chart below has curves that represent parasite drag, induced drag, and total drag.

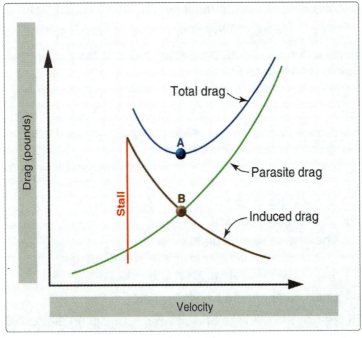

Figure 20. – Drag Chart.

   a. The L/D$_{MAX}$ airspeed occurs at the minimum (lowest) point on the total drag curve and at the intersection of the parasite and induced drag curves, i.e., when induced drag and parasite drag are equal.

      1) This airspeed represents the airplane's maximum glide range in still air.

11. When the line of thrust is below the center of gravity, an increase in power will make the nose of the aircraft rise.

12. In steady-state flight, the sum of the opposing forces (thrust and drag; weight and lift) is equal to zero.

   a. In a constant-power, constant-airspeed descent, thrust is equal to drag and lift is equal to weight.
   b. In a steady-state climb, the sum of all upward forces is equal to the downward forces.

13. For a given weight of the airplane, the **rate of climb** depends on the difference between the power available and the power required, i.e., the excess power.

14. For a given weight of the airplane, the **angle of climb** depends on the difference between thrust and drag, i.e., the excess thrust.

15. Weight always acts vertically toward the center of the Earth.

1.3 LOAD FACTOR

1. To determine the load acting on an airplane, multiply the load factor by the airplane's weight.

    a. A level 60° bank imposes a load factor of approximately 2.0.

2. When an airplane is forced into an accelerated stall at twice its normal stalling speed, the load factor is approximately 4 Gs.

3. Velocity/load factor charts have the indicated airspeed on the horizontal axis and the load factor on the vertical axis.

    a. For various operations, one can plot the load factor and the possible impact on the airplane, as illustrated in the chart below.
    b. One can also plot gusts of various strengths against airspeed to find the resultant load factor.
    c. Point A is the stalling speed (V_S).
    d. Point B is the accelerated stall.
    e. Point C is the maneuvering speed (V_A).
    f. Point D is the maximum structural cruise speed (V_{NO}).
    g. Point E is the never exceed speed (V_{NE}).
    h. Points C and I represent the limit load factor.
        1) Exceeding the load factor limit would subject an airplane to structural damage.

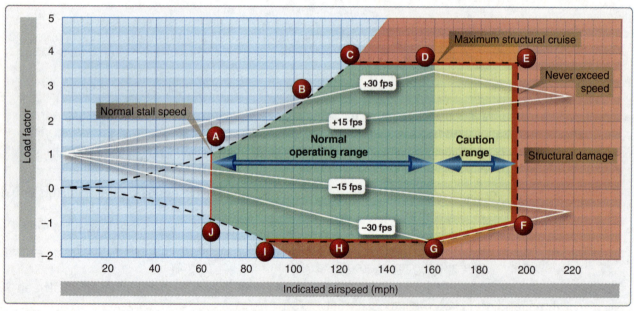

Figure 17. – Velocity/Load Factor Chart.

4. A load factor/stall speed chart relates these variables to the degree of bank angle for a particular airplane, as illustrated in the chart below.

   a. Determine the load factor (or G units) for any bank angle by finding the bank angle on the horizontal axis and moving vertically up to the intersection with the load factor curve. Then proceed horizontally to the right of the graph to determine the load factor.

   b. To determine the increase in stall speed for any load factor, begin with the load factor on the vertical axis and move horizontally to the left to intersect the load factor curve. From that point of intersection, move up vertically to the intersection with the stall speed curve. From that point, move horizontally to the left to the vertical axis to determine the percentage increase in stall speed.

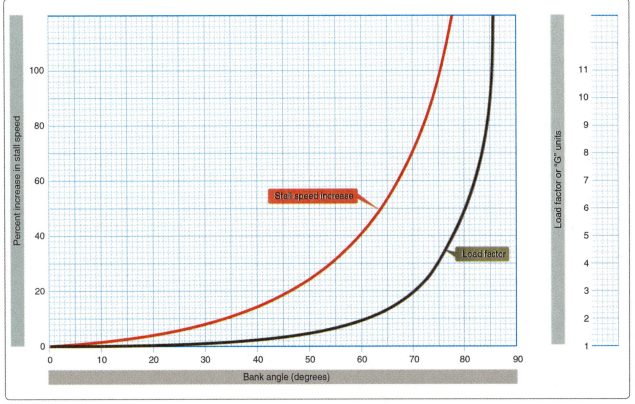

Figure 18. – Stall Speed vs. Load Factor.

1.4 WINGS

1. A **rectangular wing**, when compared to other wing planforms, has a tendency to stall first at the wing root, with the stall progression toward the wingtip. This provides adequate stall warning.

2. The **angle of incidence** is the acute angle formed by the chord line of the wing and the longitudinal axis of the airplane.

3. A reference line drawn from the leading edge to the trailing edge, which is equidistant at all points from the upper and lower contours, is the **mean camber line**.

4. The subsonic wing planform that provides the best lift coefficient basis is the **elliptical wing**.

5. A sweptwing airplane with weak static directional stability and increased dihedral causes an increase in Dutch roll tendency.

   a. A sweptback wing has a tendency to stall at the wingtip first and progress inward to the wing root.

   b. Sweepback is the rearward slant of a wing, horizontal tail, or other airfoil surface.

6. Wing dihedral angle increases lateral stability.
7. The **aspect ratio of a wing** is the ratio of the wingspan to the mean (average) chord.
    a. A wing with a very high aspect ratio will have a lower stall speed than a low aspect ratio wing.
    b. At a constant velocity in airflow, a high aspect ratio wing will have decreased drag, especially at a high angle of attack.
    c. Airplanes with higher aspect ratios generate the greatest lift and the least drag, all other factors held constant.
8. The use of a slot in the leading edge of the wing enables an airplane to land at a slower speed because it delays the stall to a higher angle of attack.

1.5 THE AXES OF AIRPLANES

1. The three axes of an airplane (lateral, longitudinal, and vertical) intersect at the center of gravity.
2. The elevators move the airplane on its lateral axis.
3. The ailerons move the airplane on its longitudinal axis.
4. The rudder moves the airplane on its vertical axis.
    a. If the pilot applies right rudder pressure to a stable airplane, the tail deflects to the left, causing the nose to yaw to the right.
    b. The opposite is true when left rudder pressure is applied.

1.6 ANGLE OF ATTACK

1. The **angle of attack** is the angle between the chord line of an airfoil and the relative wind.
    a. The angle of attack directly controls the distribution of positive and negative pressure acting on the wing.
2. The critical angle of attack is determined by the design of the wing.

1.7 TURNS

1. A turn is said to be coordinated when the horizontal component of lift (HCL) (which acts toward the inside of the turn) equals centrifugal force (CF) (which acts toward the outside of the turn), i.e., the ball in the inclinometer is centered.
    a. CF is greater than HCL in skidding turns (the ball is on the outside of the turn).
    b. CF is less than HCL in slipping turns (the ball is on the inside of the turn).
2. To coordinate a turn, you should center the ball on the turn-and-slip indicator or the turn coordinator.
    a. Center the ball by applying rudder pressure on the side where the ball is (e.g., if the ball is on the left, use left rudder) to "kick" the ball back to center.
3. As the angle of bank is increased, the vertical component of lift decreases and the sink rate increases.
4. To increase the rate of turn and decrease the radius at the same time, steepen the bank and decrease airspeed.
5. To make an airplane turn, it is necessary to change the direction of lift by banking the wings.

6. Adverse yaw during a turn entry is caused by decreased induced drag on the lowered wing and increased induced drag on the raised wing.
7. When rolling out of a steep-banked turn, the lowered aileron (on the inside wing) creates more drag than when rolling into the turn because the wing's angle of attack is greater as the rollout is started.

1.8 AIRPLANE STABILITY

1. The quality of an aircraft that permits it to be operated easily and to withstand the stresses imposed on it is the **maneuverability** of the aircraft.
2. The capability of an aircraft to respond to the pilot's inputs, especially with regard to flight path and altitude, is its **controllability**.
3. The tendency of an aircraft to develop forces that restore it to its original condition when disturbed from a condition of steady flight is known as **stability**.
4. Static stability is the initial tendency that the airplane displays after its equilibrium is disturbed.
    a. Positive static stability can be illustrated by a ball inside a round bowl. If the ball is displaced from its normal resting place, it will eventually return to its original position at the bottom of the bowl.
    b. Neutral static stability can be illustrated by a ball on a flat plane. If the ball is displaced, it will come to rest at some new, neutral position and show no tendency to return to its original position.
    c. Negative static stability is actually instability. It can be illustrated by a ball on the top of an inverted round bowl. Even the slightest displacement of the ball will activate greater forces, which will cause the ball to continue to move in the direction of the applied force (e.g., gravity).
5. Dynamic stability is the overall tendency that the airplane displays after its equilibrium is disturbed.
    a. Positive dynamic stability is a property that dampens the oscillations set up by a statically stable airplane, enabling the oscillations to become smaller and smaller in magnitude until the airplane eventually settles down to its original condition of flight.
    b. Neutral dynamic stability means the oscillations remain unchanged.
    c. Negative dynamic stability is actually dynamic instability. It means the oscillations tend to increase.
6. The most desirable type of stability for an aircraft to possess is positive dynamic stability, because this means it will also possess positive static stability.
    a. If an aircraft has negative dynamic and positive static stability, this will result in divergent (increasing) oscillations.
7. Spiral instability occurs when an airplane has strong static directional stability (stability about the vertical axis) and weak dihedral effect (weak lateral stability).
8. If airspeed increases and decreases during longitudinal phugoid oscillations, the airplane is maintaining a nearly constant angle of attack.
    a. "Phugoid" means long period (10 to 100 sec.).

1.9 SPIRALING SLIPSTREAM AND GYROSCOPIC PRECESSION

1. A propeller rotating clockwise, as seen from the rear, creates a spiraling slipstream that tends to rotate the aircraft to the left around the vertical axis and to the right around the longitudinal axis.
2. With regard to gyroscopic precession, when a force is applied at a point on the rim of a spinning disc, the resultant force acts in the same direction as the applied force, 90° ahead in the plane of rotation.
   a. As a result of gyroscopic precession, any yawing around the vertical axis will result in a pitching movement.

1.10 STALLS AND SPINS

1. An airplane stalls when the critical angle of attack is exceeded.
2. The critical angle of attack remains constant regardless of gross weight.
3. The critical angle of attack is independent of the speed of airflow over the wings.
4. A spin occurs when, after a full stall, the wing that drops continues in a stalled condition while the rising wing regains and continues to produce some lift, causing the rotation.
   a. The difference between a spin and a steep spiral is that in a spin, the wings are stalled.

1.11 GROUND EFFECT

1. It is possible to fly an aircraft just clear of the ground at a slightly slower airspeed than that required to sustain level flight at higher altitudes.
   a. This is the result of interference of the ground surface with the airflow patterns about the airplane in flight.
   b. If the same angle of attack is maintained in ground effect as when out of ground effect, lift will increase and induced drag will decrease.
2. Ground effect is usually experienced at altitudes of less than half of the airplane's wingspan.
3. An airplane leaving ground effect will experience a decrease in stability and a nose-up change in moments.

1.12 TURBULENCE

1. If severe turbulence is encountered, the aircraft's airspeed should be reduced to design maneuvering speed (V_A).
2. The best technique for minimizing the wing-load factor when flying in severe turbulence is to set power and trim to obtain an airspeed at or below V_A, maintain wings level, and accept variations of airspeed and altitude.

QUESTIONS AND ANSWER EXPLANATIONS: All of the AGI/CFI knowledge test questions chosen by the FAA for release as well as additional questions selected by Gleim relating to the material in the previous outlines are reproduced on the following pages. These questions have been organized into the same subunits as the outlines. To the immediate right of each question are the correct answer and answer explanation. You should cover these answers and answer explanations while responding to the questions. Refer to the general discussion in the Introduction on how to take the FAA knowledge test.

Remember that the questions from the FAA knowledge test bank have been reordered by topic and organized into a meaningful sequence. Also, the first line of the answer explanation gives the citation of the authoritative source for the answer.

QUESTIONS

1.1 Flaps

1. (Refer to Figure 23 below.) Which is a fowler flap?

   A. 2.
   B. 3.
   C. 4.

Answer (C) is correct. *(PHAK Chap 6)*
   DISCUSSION: The fowler flap, when extended, not only tilts downward but also slides rearward on tracks. This increases the angle of attack, wing camber, and wing area, thereby providing added lift without significantly increasing drag.
   Answer (A) is incorrect. Image 2 in Fig. 23 is a split flap. Answer (B) is incorrect. Image 3 in Fig. 23 is a slotted flap.

2. (Refer to Figure 23 below.) Which is a slotted flap?

   A. 1.
   B. 3.
   C. 4.

Answer (B) is correct. *(PHAK Chap 6)*
   DISCUSSION: A slotted flap is similar to a plain flap but provides a gap between the trailing edge of the wing and the leading edge of the flap. This permits air to pass through and delays airflow separation.
   Answer (A) is incorrect. Image 1 in Fig. 23 is a plain flap. Answer (C) is incorrect. Image 4 in Fig. 23 is a fowler flap.

3. (Refer to Figure 23 below.) Which is a split flap?

   A. 2.
   B. 3.
   C. 4.

Answer (A) is correct. *(PHAK Chap 6)*
   DISCUSSION: The split flap is a hinged portion of only the bottom surface of the wing. When extended, it increases the angle of attack by changing the chord line.
   Answer (B) is incorrect. Image 3 in Fig. 23 is a slotted flap. Answer (C) is incorrect. Image 4 in Fig. 23 is a fowler flap.

4. (Refer to Figure 23 below.) Which type of flap creates the greatest change in pitching moment?

   A. Plain.
   B. Split.
   C. Fowler.

Answer (C) is correct. *(PHAK Chap 6)*
   DISCUSSION: The fowler flap provides the greatest amount of lift with the least amount of drag. When extended, it not only tilts downward but slides rearward on tracks. This increases the angle of attack, wing camber, and wing area, therefore providing added lift without significantly increasing drag. This creates the greatest change in pitching moment.
   Answer (A) is incorrect. The fowler flap, not the plain flap, creates the greatest change in pitching moment. Answer (B) is incorrect. The split flap creates the least, not greatest, change in pitching moment.

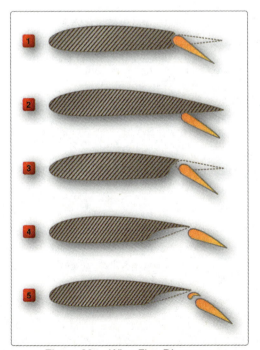

Figure 23. – Wing Flap Diagrams.

5. Which type of flap creates the least change in pitching moment?

A. Split.
B. Fowler.
C. Slotted.

Answer (A) is correct. *(PHAK Chap 6)*
DISCUSSION: The split flap creates the least change in pitching moment because, although it provides lift, it also results in considerably more drag than other types of flaps. Accordingly, it requires more power during approaches.
Answer (B) is incorrect. The fowler flap does not produce as much drag as the split flap. Answer (C) is incorrect. The slotted flap does not produce as much drag as the split flap.

6. Which type of flap is characterized by large increases in lift coefficient with minimum changes in drag?

A. Split.
B. Fowler.
C. Slotted.

Answer (B) is correct. *(PHAK Chap 6)*
DISCUSSION: When extended, the fowler flap increases the angle of attack, wing camber, and wing area, which provides added lift without significantly increasing drag. Thus, the fowler flap produces large increases in lift coefficient with minimum changes in drag.
Answer (A) is incorrect. The split flap does not increase the lift coefficient as much as the fowler flap. Answer (C) is incorrect. The slotted flap does not increase the lift coefficient as much as the fowler flap.

7. (Refer to Figure 56 on page 31.) Which of the following illustrations is a fixed slot?

A. 1
B. 2
C. 4

Answer (A) is correct. *(PHAK Chap 6)*
DISCUSSION: Fixed slots direct airflow to the upper wing surface and delay airflow separation at higher angles of attack.
Answer (B) is incorrect. Illustration 2 is a movable slot. Movable slots consist of leading edge segments, which move on tracks. At low angles of attack, each slot is held flush against the wing's leading edge by the high pressure that forms there. As the angle of attack increases, the high-pressure area moves aft below the lower surface of the wing, allowing the slots to move forward. Answer (C) is incorrect. Illustration 4 is a leading edge cuff. In most cases, leading edge cuffs extend the leading edge down and forward. This causes the airflow to attach better to the upper surface of the wing at higher angles of attack, thus lowering an aircraft's stall speed. The fixed nature of leading edge cuffs extracts a penalty in maximum cruise airspeed, but recent advances in design and technology have reduced this penalty.

8. (Refer to Figure 56 on page 31.) Which of the following illustrations is a movable slot?

A. 1
B. 2
C. 3

Answer (B) is correct. *(PHAK Chap 6)*
DISCUSSION: Movable slots consist of leading edge segments, which move on tracks. At low angles of attack, each slot is held flush against the wing's leading edge by the high pressure that forms there. As the angle of attack increases, the high-pressure area moves aft below the lower surface of the wing, allowing the slots to move forward.
Answer (A) is incorrect. Illustration 1 is a fixed slot. Fixed slots direct airflow to the upper wing surface and delay airflow separation at higher angles of attack. Answer (C) is incorrect. Illustration 3 is a leading edge flap. Leading edge flaps, like trailing edge flaps, are used to maximize lift and the camber of the wings. This type of leading edge device is frequently used in conjunction with trailing edge flaps and can reduce the nose-down pitching movement produced by the latter.

SU 1: Airplanes and Aerodynamics

9. (Refer to Figure 56 below.) Which of the following illustrations is a leading edge cuff?

- A. 2
- B. 3
- C. 4

Answer (C) is correct. *(PHAK Chap 6)*
DISCUSSION: Illustration 4 is a leading edge cuff. In most cases, leading edge cuffs extend the leading edge down and forward. This causes the airflow to attach better to the upper surface of the wing at higher angles of attack, thus lowering an aircraft's stall speed. The fixed nature of leading edge cuffs extracts a penalty in maximum cruise airspeed, but recent advances in design and technology have reduced this penalty.
Answer (A) is incorrect. Illustration 2 is a movable slot. Movable slots consist of leading edge segments, which move on tracks. At low angles of attack, each slot is held flush against the wing's leading edge by the high pressure that forms there. As the angle of attack increases, the high-pressure area moves aft below the lower surface of the wing, allowing the slots to move forward. Answer (B) is incorrect. Illustration 3 is a leading edge flap. Leading edge flaps, like trailing edge flaps, are used to maximize lift and the camber of the wings. This type of leading edge device is frequently used in conjunction with trailing edge flaps and can reduce the nose-down pitching movement produced by the latter.

10. (Refer to Figure 56 below.) Which of the following illustrations is a leading edge flap?

- A. 1
- B. 2
- C. 3

Answer (C) is correct. *(PHAK Chap 6)*
DISCUSSION: Leading edge flaps, like trailing edge flaps, are used to maximize lift and the camber of the wings. This type of leading edge device is frequently used in conjunction with trailing edge flaps and can reduce the nose-down pitching movement produced by the latter.
Answer (A) is incorrect. Illustration 1 is a fixed slot. Fixed slots direct airflow to the upper wing surface and delay airflow separation at higher angles of attack. Answer (B) is incorrect. Illustration 2 is a movable slot. Movable slots consist of leading edge segments, which move on tracks. At low angles of attack, each slot is held flush against the wing's leading edge by the high pressure that forms there. As the angle of attack increases, the high-pressure area moves aft below the lower surface of the wing, allowing the slots to move forward.

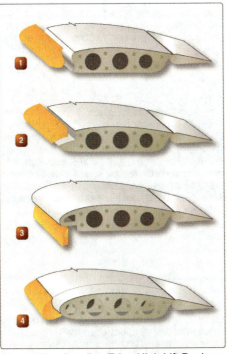

Figure 56. – Leading Edge High Lift Devices.

1.2 Lift and Drag

11. Which statement relates to Bernoulli's principle?

A. For every action there is an equal and opposite reaction.

B. An additional upward force is generated as the lower surface of the wing deflects air downward.

C. Air traveling faster over the curved upper surface of an airfoil causes lower pressure on the top surface.

Answer (C) is correct. *(PHAK Chap 4)*
DISCUSSION: Bernoulli's principle states in part that the internal pressure of a fluid (liquid or gas) decreases at points where the speed of the fluid increases. This same principle applies to air flowing over the curved upper surface of a wing.
Answer (A) is incorrect. Newton's Third Law of Motion states that for every action there is an equal and opposite reaction. Answer (B) is incorrect. The additional upward force that is generated as the lower surface of the wing deflects air downward is related to Newton's Third Law of Motion.

12. An aircraft wing is designed to produce lift resulting from

A. Negative air pressure below the wing's surface and positive air pressure above the wing's surface.

B. Positive air pressure below the wing's surface and negative air pressure above the wing's surface.

C. A larger center of pressure above the wing's surface and a lower center of pressure below the wing's surface.

Answer (B) is correct. *(PHAK Chap 4)*
DISCUSSION: In the same period of time, the air flowing over the curved top of the wing must travel farther than the air flowing along the flat bottom for most wings. This means the air on the top must go faster. According to Bernoulli's principle, the pressure on the wing top decreases, resulting in a lower pressure on top of the wing and a higher pressure below. This generates a lifting force over the upper curved surface of the wing in the direction of the low pressure.
Answer (A) is incorrect. The pressure is positive, not negative, below the wing and negative, not positive, above the wing. Answer (C) is incorrect. The larger center of pressure is beneath, not above, the wing and the lower center of pressure is above, not below, the wing.

13. During flight with zero angle of attack, the pressure along the upper surface of a wing would be

A. Equal to atmospheric pressure.

B. Less than atmospheric pressure.

C. Greater than atmospheric pressure.

Answer (B) is correct. *(PHAK Chap 4)*
DISCUSSION: Zero angle of attack means that the chord line of the wing coincides with the relative wind. Because air flows a greater distance over the upper wing surface than the lower wing surface of an asymmetrical airfoil, the upper surface has a lower pressure (less than atmospheric pressure) than the lower surface.
Answer (A) is incorrect. If the pressure on the upper surface of the wing were equal to atmospheric pressure, there would be no lift. Answer (C) is incorrect. The pressure along the lower, not upper, surface of the wing would be greater than atmospheric pressure.

14. Why does increasing speed also increase lift?

A. The increased velocity of the relative wind overcomes the increased drag.

B. The increased impact of the relative wind on an airfoil's lower surface creates a greater amount of air being deflected downward.

C. The increased speed of the air passing over an airfoil's upper surface increases the pressure, thus creating a greater pressure differential between the upper and lower surface.

Answer (B) is correct. *(PHAK Chap 4)*
DISCUSSION: Increasing speed increases the air flowing over and under an airfoil. The increased impact of the relative wind on an airfoil's lower surface creates a greater amount of air being deflected downward, producing greater lift.
Answer (A) is incorrect. The thrust, not the velocity of the relative wind, overcomes increased drag as speed increases. Answer (C) is incorrect. The increased speed of air passing over an airfoil's upper surface decreases, not increases, the pressure.

15. Lift produced by an airfoil is the net force developed perpendicular to the

A. chord.

B. relative wind.

C. longitudinal axis of the aircraft.

Answer (B) is correct. *(PHAK Chap 4)*
DISCUSSION: Lift produced by an airfoil is the net force developed perpendicular to the relative wind.
Answer (A) is incorrect. The chord is an imaginary straight line through a cross-section of the wing between the leading edge and the trailing edge. Answer (C) is incorrect. The longitudinal axis of the aircraft and the chord line of the wing determine the angle of incidence.

16. The point on an airfoil through which lift acts is the

A. center of gravity.
B. center of pressure.
C. midpoint of the chord.

Answer (B) is correct. *(PHAK Chap 4)*
DISCUSSION: Although lift is generated over the entire wing, an imaginary point is established that represents the resultant of all lift forces. This single point is the center of lift, also known as the center of pressure.
Answer (A) is incorrect. The center of gravity is the point along the longitudinal axis at which all weight is considered to be concentrated. It is the point of balance. Answer (C) is incorrect. The midpoint of the chord is the midpoint of an imaginary line between the leading edge and the trailing edge of the wing.

17. Changes in the center of pressure of a wing affect the aircraft's

A. lift/drag ratio.
B. lifting capacity.
C. aerodynamic balance and controllability.

Answer (C) is correct. *(PHAK Chap 4)*
DISCUSSION: Center of pressure (CP) is the imaginary but determinable point at which all of the upward lift forces on the wing are concentrated. In general, at high angles of attack the CP moves forward, while at low angles of attack the CP moves aft. The relationship of the CP to center of gravity (CG) affects both aerodynamic balance and controllability.
Answer (A) is incorrect. The lift/drag ratio is determined by angle of attack. Answer (B) is incorrect. Lifting capacity is affected by angle of attack and airspeed.

18. When the angle of attack of a symmetrical airfoil is increased, the center of pressure will

A. remain unaffected.
B. have very little movement.
C. move aft along the airfoil surface.

Answer (A) is correct. *(RFH Chap 2)*
DISCUSSION: Unlike that of an asymmetrical airfoil (generally used in conventional wing design), the center of pressure of a symmetrical airfoil remains unaffected, regardless of angle of attack.
Answer (B) is incorrect. The center of pressure of a symmetrical airfoil has no movement, not little movement, as angle of attack changes. Answer (C) is incorrect. The center of pressure of an asymmetrical, not symmetrical, airfoil would move forward, not aft, if the angle of attack were increased.

19. An airplane would have a tendency to nose up and have an inherent tendency to enter a stalled condition when the center of pressure is

A. below the center of gravity.
B. aft of the center of gravity.
C. forward of the center of gravity.

Answer (C) is correct. *(PHAK Chap 4)*
DISCUSSION: As the angle of attack increases, the center of pressure moves forward. If it moves forward of the center of gravity, it will tend to raise the nose of the airplane, thus increasing the angle of attack even more. This will lead to a stalled condition.
Answer (A) is incorrect. Pitching moments are caused by the center of pressure being forward or aft of the center of gravity, not below or above. Answer (B) is incorrect. When the center of pressure is aft of the CG, the nose tends to drop, decreasing the angle of attack.

20. The force which imparts a change in the velocity of a mass is called

A. work.
B. power.
C. thrust.

Answer (C) is correct. *(PHAK Chap 5)*
DISCUSSION: Thrust is the force that imparts a change in the velocity of the mass. It may be measured in pounds but has no element of time or rate.
Answer (A) is incorrect. Work is the product of a force moving an object over a distance. Answer (B) is incorrect. Power is the rate of doing work, or units of work per unit of time.

21. That portion of the aircraft's total drag created by the production of lift is called

A. induced drag, and is not affected by changes in airspeed.
B. induced drag, and is greatly affected by changes in airspeed.
C. parasite drag, and is greatly affected by changes in airspeed.

Answer (B) is correct. *(PHAK Chap 5)*
DISCUSSION: Induced drag is the undesirable but unavoidable by-product of lift and is greatly affected by changes in airspeed. The slower the airplane flies, the greater the coefficient of lift and thus the greater the induced drag.
Answer (A) is incorrect. Induced drag is greatly affected by changes in airspeed. Answer (C) is incorrect. Parasite drag is resistance to the air produced by any part of the airplane that does not produce lift.

22. Airflow from two adjacent surfaces that merge and create eddy currents, turbulence, or restrict airflow is called

A. form drag.
B. interference drag.
C. skin friction drag.

Answer (B) is correct. *(PHAK Chap 5)*
DISCUSSION: Interference drag comes from air flowing from two adjacent surfaces colliding and creating a current of turbulent air different from the original currents. Fairings and distance between lifting surfaces reduce interference drag.
Answer (A) is incorrect. Interference drag comes from air flowing from two adjacent surfaces colliding and creating a current of turbulent air different from the original currents, not form drag. Form drag is the portion of parasite drag generated by the aircraft due to its shape and airflow around it. Answer (C) is incorrect. Interference drag comes from air flowing from two adjacent surfaces colliding and creating a current of turbulent air different from the original currents, not skin friction drag. Skin friction drag is the aerodynamic resistance due to the contact of moving air with the surface of an aircraft.

23. As airspeed increases in level flight, total drag of an aircraft becomes greater than the total drag produced at the maximum lift/drag speed because of the

A. increase in induced drag.
B. decrease in induced drag.
C. increase in parasite drag.

Answer (C) is correct. *(PHAK Chap 4)*
DISCUSSION: As airspeed increases, the total drag of an aircraft becomes greater than the total drag produced at L/D_{MAX} because of the increase in parasite drag.
Answer (A) is incorrect. As airspeed increases above L/D_{MAX}, induced drag decreases, not increases. Answer (B) is incorrect. As airspeed increases above L/D_{MAX}, the decrease in induced drag is less than the increase in parasite drag.

24. As airspeed decreases in level flight, total drag of an aircraft becomes greater than the total drag produced at the maximum lift/drag speed because of the

A. decrease in induced drag.
B. increase in induced drag.
C. increase in parasite drag.

Answer (B) is correct. *(PHAK Chap 5)*
DISCUSSION: As airspeed decreases, the total drag of an aircraft becomes greater than the total drag produced at L/D_{MAX} because of the increase in induced drag. The lower the airspeed, the greater the angle of attack required to produce lift to equal the sum of the downward forces and, consequently, the induced drag will be greater.
Answer (A) is incorrect. As airspeed decreases below L/D_{MAX}, induced drag increases, not decreases. Answer (C) is incorrect. As airspeed decreases below L/D_{MAX}, parasite drag decreases.

25. Which relationship is correct when comparing drag and airspeed?

A. Induced drag increases as the square of the airspeed.
B. Induced drag varies inversely as the square of the airspeed.
C. Profile drag varies inversely as the square of the airspeed.

Answer (B) is correct. *(PHAK Chap 5)*
DISCUSSION: Parasite drag increases as the square of the airspeed, and induced drag varies inversely as the square of the airspeed.
Answer (A) is incorrect. Induced drag varies inversely, not directly, with airspeed. Answer (C) is incorrect. Profile drag is an element of parasite drag, which varies directly, not inversely, as the square of the airspeed.

26. (Refer to Figure 19 on page 35.) Which statement is true regarding airplane flight at L/D_{max}?

A. Any angle of attack other than that for L/D_{max} increases parasite drag.
B. Any angle of attack other than that for L/D_{max} increases the lift/drag ratio.
C. Any angle of attack other than that for L/D_{max} increases total drag for a given airplane's lift.

Answer (C) is correct. *(PHAK Chap 5)*
DISCUSSION: The maximum lift/drag ratio (L/D_{MAX}) occurs at one angle of attack. If the airplane is operated in steady flight at L/D_{MAX}, the total drag is at a minimum. Any angle of attack lower or higher than that for L/D_{MAX} reduces the lift-drag ratio and consequently increases the total drag for a given airplane's lift.
Answer (A) is incorrect. Parasite drag is a function of speed, not angle of attack. Answer (B) is incorrect. L/D_{MAX} is the angle of attack that provides the highest L/D ratio; i.e., any change from that decreases the L/D ratio.

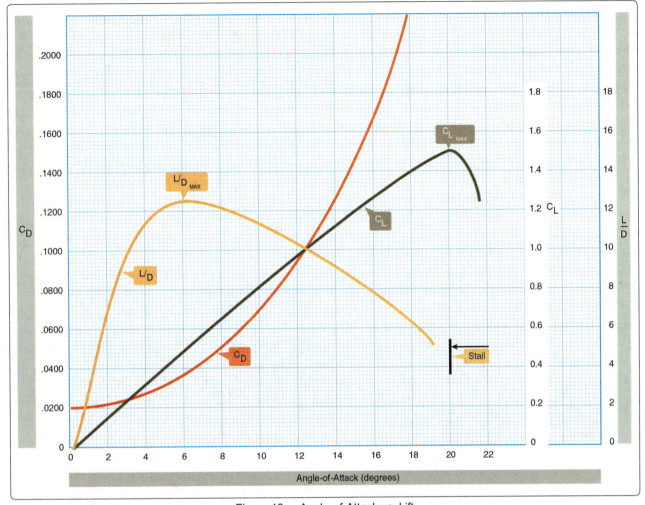

Figure 19. – Angle-of-Attack vs. Lift.

27. (Refer to Figure 19 above.) The lift/drag at 2° angle of attack is approximately the same as the lift/drag for

A. 9.75° angle of attack.
B. 10.5° angle of attack.
C. 16.5° angle of attack.

Answer (C) is correct. *(PHAK Chap 5)*
DISCUSSION: Enter the bottom of the chart in Fig. 19 at 2° angle of attack and move vertically up to the L/D curve. From this point move right horizontally until you again reach the L/D curve. Then move vertically down to the bottom of the chart to determine a 16.5° angle of attack. Thus, the L/D ratio is approximately the same at both 2° and 16.5° angle of attack.
Answer (A) is incorrect. An angle of attack of 9.75° would have approximately the same L/D ratio as a 3.75°, not 2°, angle of attack. Answer (B) is incorrect. An angle of attack of 10.5° would have approximately the same L/D ratio as a 3.5°, not 2°, angle of attack.

28. (Refer to Figure 19 above.) At which angle of attack does the airplane travel the maximum horizontal distance per foot of altitude lost?

A. 6°.
B. 12.3°.
C. 20°.

Answer (A) is correct. *(PHAK Chap 5)*
DISCUSSION: When gliding at L/D$_{MAX}$, the least drag is experienced and the airplane will travel the maximum horizontal distance per foot of altitude lost. On the chart in Fig. 19, locate L/D$_{MAX}$ and drop down vertically to the bottom of the chart to determine a 6° angle of attack.
Answer (B) is incorrect. An angle of attack of 12.3° is the point where the coefficient of drag (C_D) and the coefficient of lift (C_L) are equal, not L/D$_{MAX}$. Answer (C) is incorrect. An angle of attack of 20° is the maximum lift or $C_{L(MAX)}$, not L/D$_{MAX}$.

29. Maximum gliding distance of an aircraft is obtained when

A. parasite drag is the least.
B. induced drag and parasite drag are equal.
C. induced drag equals the coefficient of lift.

Answer (B) is correct. *(PHAK Chap 5)*
DISCUSSION: The maximum gliding distance of an aircraft is obtained when the total drag is at the minimum, and L/D ratio is at the maximum. Minimum drag occurs when induced drag and parasite drag are equal.
Answer (A) is incorrect. When parasite drag is least, the total drag is very great. Answer (C) is incorrect. It is a nonsense concept.

30. If an increase in power tends to make the nose of an airplane rise, this is the result of the

A. line of thrust being below the center of gravity.
B. center of lift being ahead of the center of gravity.
C. center of lift and center of gravity being collocated.

Answer (A) is correct. *(PHAK Chap 5)*
DISCUSSION: If an increase in power tends to make the nose of an airplane rise, it is an indication that the line of thrust is below the center of gravity. This combines with the changing load on the tail surfaces to create a pitch-up attitude.
Answer (B) is incorrect. An increase in angle of attack, not thrust, tends to make the nose of the airplane rise due to the center of lift being ahead of the center of gravity. Answer (C) is incorrect. This is the ideal balanced point. It is not maintained, however, because the changing angle of attack moves the center of pressure or lift.

31. When considering the forces acting upon an airplane in straight-and-level flight at constant airspeed, which statement is correct?

A. Weight always acts vertically toward the center of the Earth.
B. Thrust always acts forward parallel to the relative wind and is greater than drag.
C. Lift always acts perpendicular to the longitudinal axis of the wing and is greater than weight.

Answer (A) is correct. *(PHAK Chap 5)*
DISCUSSION: Weight is the force that is caused by gravity accelerating the mass of the airplane and always acts vertically toward the center of the Earth.
Answer (B) is incorrect. During straight-and-level flight at constant airspeed, thrust and drag are equal in magnitude. Answer (C) is incorrect. During straight-and-level flight at a constant airspeed, lift and weight are equal in magnitude.

32. Which statement is true regarding the forces acting on an airplane in a steady-state climb?

A. The sum of all forward forces is greater than the sum of all rearward forces.
B. The sum of all upward forces is greater than the sum of all downward forces.
C. The sum of all upward forces is equal to the sum of all downward forces.

Answer (C) is correct. *(PHAK Chap 5)*
DISCUSSION: In a steady flight condition, the opposing forces are equal. Thus, in a steady climb, descent, or straight-and-level flight, total upward forces equal total downward forces.
Answer (A) is incorrect. The forward forces are equal to, not greater than, the rearward forces in steady-state flight. Answer (B) is incorrect. The upward forces are equal to, not greater than, the downward forces in steady-state flight.

33. During a steady climb, the rate of climb depends on

A. excess power.
B. excess thrust.
C. thrust available.

Answer (A) is correct. *(PHAK Chap 5)*
DISCUSSION: For a given weight of the airplane, the rate of climb depends on the difference between the power available and the power required, or the excess power. The maximum rate would occur where there exists the greatest difference between power required and power available.
Answer (B) is incorrect. Excess thrust is the determining factor in the angle, not rate, of climb. Answer (C) is incorrect. The thrust available is not the total equation. You must first determine how much thrust or power is needed and then determine how much is available beyond that.

SU 1: Airplanes and Aerodynamics

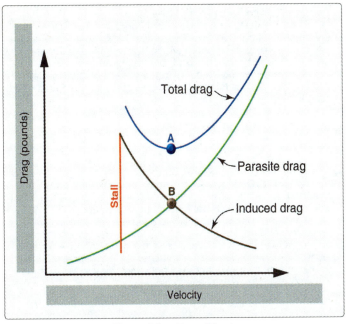

Figure 20. – Drag Chart.

34. (Refer to Figure 20 above.) At the airspeed represented by point A, in steady flight, the aircraft will

A. have its maximum lift/drag ratio.
B. have its minimum lift/drag ratio.
C. be developing its maximum coefficient of lift.

Answer (A) is correct. *(PHAK Chap 5)*
    DISCUSSION: In Fig. 20, points A and B both represent the airspeed at which minimum drag occurs and the maximum lift/drag ratio occurs. That is the point at which the least power is required for both maximum lift and minimum total drag.
    Answer (B) is incorrect. Point A is the airspeed where lift/drag is at its maximum, not minimum. Answer (C) is incorrect. The aircraft develops its maximum coefficient of lift just prior to the critical angle of attack or at the greatest angle of attack prior to stall, where induced drag is substantial.

35. (Refer to Figure 20 above.) At an airspeed represented by point B, in steady flight, the pilot can expect to obtain the aircraft's

A. maximum coefficient of lift.
B. minimum coefficient of lift.
C. maximum glide range in still air.

Answer (C) is correct. *(PHAK Chap 5)*
    DISCUSSION: In Fig. 20, points B and A both represent the airspeed at which minimum drag occurs. At this speed, the pilot can expect to obtain the aircraft's maximum glide range in still air.
    Answer (A) is incorrect. An airfoil develops its maximum coefficient of lift just prior to the critical angle of attack or at the greatest angle of attack prior to stall, where induced drag is substantial. Answer (B) is incorrect. A cambered airfoil minimum coefficient of lift is zero at a negative angle of attack, which occurs in a vertical climb or vertical dive, both of which do not occur in normal flight.

36. During a steady climb, the angle of climb depends on

A. excess thrust.
B. power available.
C. thrust required.

Answer (A) is correct. *(PHAK Chap 5)*
    DISCUSSION: For a given weight of the airplane, the angle of climb depends on the difference between thrust and drag, or the excess thrust. The maximum angle of climb would occur where there exists the greatest difference between thrust available and thrust required.
    Answer (B) is incorrect. The power available is only a portion of the equation. The amount of thrust or power needed must be determined to get the net left over beyond that needed. Answer (C) is incorrect. The thrust required is only a function of the minimum needed to maintain a specific configuration.

37. Which statement describes the relationship of the forces acting on an aircraft in a constant-power and constant-airspeed descent?

A. Thrust is equal to drag; lift is equal to weight.
B. Thrust is equal to drag; weight is greater than lift.
C. Thrust is greater than drag; weight is greater than lift.

Answer (A) is correct. *(PHAK Chap 5)*
DISCUSSION: In a steady flight condition, no change in speed or flight path occurs. The forces that oppose each other are also equal to each other. Lift equals weight, and thrust equals drag in a steady climb, descent, or straight-and-level flight.
Answer (B) is incorrect. Weight equals lift in steady-state flight. Answer (C) is incorrect. Weight equals lift and thrust equals drag in steady-state flight.

38. During flight, advancing thrust will

A. increase airspeed.
B. cause the aircraft to climb.
C. cause the aircraft to increase airspeed and climb.

Answer (C) is correct. *(PHAK Chap 5)*
DISCUSSION: Increasing engine thrust will increase airspeed. As a side effect of the increased airspeed, additional lift will be produced, which will in turn cause a climb.
Answer (A) is incorrect. While airspeed will increase with an increase in engine thrust, this answer is not correct because an increase in thrust will also result in a climb. Answer (B) is incorrect. While a climb will result after an increase in engine thrust, this answer is not correct because an increase in thrust will also result in an increase in airspeed.

1.3 Load Factor

39. If an airplane's gross weight is 3,250 pounds, what is the load acting on this airplane during a level 60° banked turn?

A. 3,250 pounds.
B. 5,200 pounds.
C. 6,500 pounds.

Answer (C) is correct. *(PHAK Chap 5)*
DISCUSSION: Load factor is the ratio of the total load supported by the airplane's wing to the actual weight of the airplane and its contents. A level 60° bank imposes a load factor of approximately 2.0. Thus, imposing a load factor of 2.0 on an airplane that weighs an actual 3,250 lb. would impose a wingload of 6,500 lb. (3,250 × 2.0).
Answer (A) is incorrect. The figure of 3,250 lb. implies a load factor of 1.0 (3,250 ÷ 3,250). Answer (B) is incorrect. The figure of 5,200 lb. implies a load factor of 1.6 (5,200 ÷ 3,250).

40. (Refer to Figure 17 on page 39.) A positive load factor of 4 at 140 MPH would cause the airplane to

A. stall.
B. break apart.
C. be subjected to structural damage.

Answer (C) is correct. *(PHAK Chap 5)*
DISCUSSION: The velocity/load factor chart (Fig. 17) has indicated airspeed on the horizontal axis and load factor on the vertical axis. Plotting a positive load factor of 4 at 140 MPH by going up the vertical axis to 4 and over to 140 shows that you would be in the shaded area, which would cause the airplane to be subjected to structural damage.
Answer (A) is incorrect. The velocity/load factor chart indicates the impact of combined airspeed and load factor on the structural strength of the airplane, not on stalls. Answer (B) is incorrect. The airspeed causing the airplane to break apart is not measured or documented.

41. (Refer to Figure 17 on page 39.) What load factor would be created if positive 30 feet per second gusts were encountered at 130 MPH?

A. 3.8.
B. 3.0.
C. 2.0.

Answer (B) is correct. *(PHAK Chap 5)*
DISCUSSION: Begin at the bottom of Fig. 17 by locating 130 MPH and then move up vertically to the positive 30-feet-per-second (+30 fps) diagonal line. Then move left horizontally to determine a load factor of 3.0.
Answer (A) is incorrect. A load factor of 3.8 would be created if gusts above 30 fps were encountered at 130 MPH. Answer (C) is incorrect. A load factor of 2.0 would be created if +15 fps, not +30 fps, gusts were encountered at 130 MPH.

42. (Refer to Figure 17 on page 39.) The horizontal dashed line from point C to point E represents the

A. positive limit load factor.
B. airspeed range for normal operations.
C. maximum structural cruise airspeed range.

Answer (A) is correct. *(FTP Chap 14)*
DISCUSSION: The horizontal dashed line between points C and E on Fig. 17 is the positive limit load factor of 3.8. It indicates that structural damage may be possible when the airplane is operated beyond this limit.
Answer (B) is incorrect. The airspeed for normal operations is from point A to point D, not point C, to point E. Answer (C) is incorrect. The maximum structural cruise airspeed is the vertical line down from point D.

43. (Refer to Figure 17 below.) The airspeed indicated by point A is

A. maneuvering speed.
B. normal stall speed.
C. maximum structural cruising speed.

Answer (B) is correct. *(FTP Chap 14)*
DISCUSSION: Point A is the normal stall speed (V_S). At this speed in the clean configuration, the airplane will stall. The normal stall speed is shown on the airspeed indicator at the low-speed end of the green arc.
Answer (A) is incorrect. Maneuvering speed (V_A) is indicated by point C. Answer (C) is incorrect. Maximum structural cruising speed (V_{NO}) is indicated by point D.

44. (Refer to Figure 17 below.) The airspeed indicated by point C is

A. maneuvering speed.
B. never-exceed speed.
C. maximum structural cruising speed.

Answer (A) is correct. *(FTP Chap 14)*
DISCUSSION: Point C is the maneuvering speed, or V_A. It is not shown on the airspeed indicator. It is the speed below which you can move a single flight control, one time, to its full deflection, for one axis of airplane rotation only (pitch, roll, or yaw), in smooth air, without risk of damage to the airplane. A stall will occur before the aircraft is structurally damaged.
Answer (B) is incorrect. The never-exceed speed (V_{NE}) is indicated by point E. Answer (C) is incorrect. The maximum structural cruising speed (V_{NO}) is indicated by point D.

45. (Refer to Figure 17 below.) The airspeed indicated by point E is

A. maneuvering speed.
B. never-exceed speed.
C. maximum structural cruising speed.

Answer (B) is correct. *(FTP Chap 14)*
DISCUSSION: Point E is the never-exceed speed, or V_{NE}. This airspeed is indicated on the airspeed indicator by a red line. If flight is attempted beyond V_{NE}, structural damage or failure may result from a variety of phenomena.
Answer (A) is incorrect. Maneuvering speed (V_A) is indicated by point C. Answer (C) is incorrect. Maximum structural cruising speed (V_{NO}) is indicated by point D.

46. (Refer to Figure 17 below.) The airspeed indicated by point D is

A. maneuvering speed.
B. never-exceed speed.
C. maximum structural cruising speed.

Answer (C) is correct. *(FTP Chap 14)*
DISCUSSION: Point D is the maximum structural cruising speed, or V_{NO}. This airspeed is indicated on the airspeed indicator by the upper limit of the green arc (or lower limit of the yellow arc). This is the maximum speed for normal operation.
Answer (A) is incorrect. Maneuvering speed (V_A) is indicated by point C. Answer (B) is incorrect. Never-exceed speed (V_{NE}) is indicated by point E.

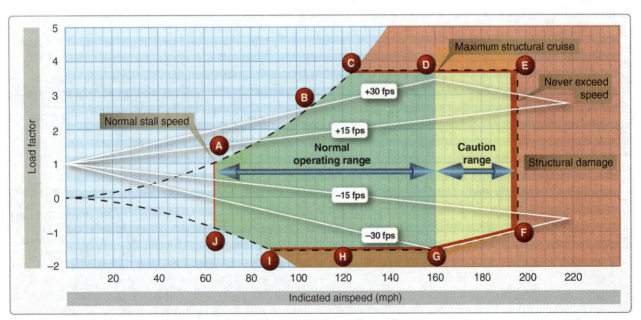

Figure 17. – Velocity/Load Factor Chart.

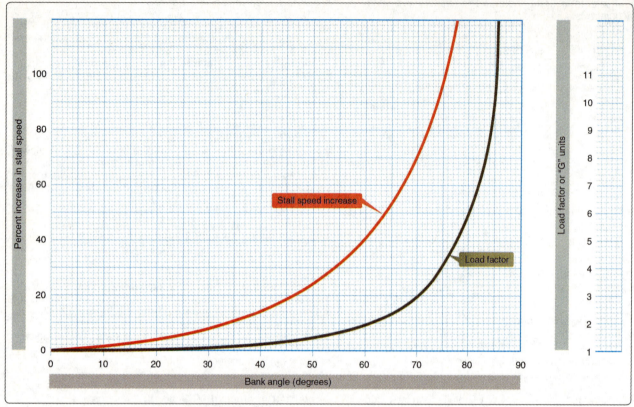

Figure 18. – Stall Speed vs. Load Factor.

47. (Refer to Figure 18 above.) If, during a steady turn with a 50° bank, a load factor of 1.5 were imposed on an airplane which has an unaccelerated stall speed of 60 knots, at what speed would the airplane first stall?

A. 68 knots.
B. 75 knots.
C. 82 knots.

Answer (B) is correct. *(PHAK Chap 5)*
DISCUSSION: Use Fig. 18 to determine the percentage of increase in stall speed in a steady 50° bank and a load factor of 1.5. First, find 50° angle of bank on the horizontal scale and move up vertically. Note 50° will intersect the load factor curve at 1.5. Continue moving up vertically on the 50° line to the stall speed increase curve. Next, move horizontally from that point to the left to the first scale to determine a 25% increase in stall speed. Thus, if the unaccelerated stall speed is 60 kt., the accelerated stall speed in a steady 50° bank turn is 75 kt. (60 × 125%).
Answer (A) is incorrect. In order to have a stall speed of 68 kt. under a load factor of 1.5 in a 50° bank, the unaccelerated stall speed would have to be 54 kt. (68/1.25). Answer (C) is incorrect. In order to have a stall speed of 82 kt. under a load factor of 1.5 in a 50° bank, the unaccelerated stall speed would have to be 66 kt. (82/1.25).

48. (Refer to Figure 18 above.) What is the stall speed of an airplane under a load factor of 4 if the unaccelerated stall speed is 70 knots?

A. 91 knots.
B. 132 knots.
C. 140 knots.

Answer (C) is correct. *(PHAK Chap 5)*
DISCUSSION: Use Fig. 18 to determine the percentage of increase in stall speed under a load factor of 4. First, find a load factor of 4 on the right vertical scale and move horizontally to the left to the load factor curve. Then move vertically up from that point to the intersection of the stall speed increase curve. Next, move left horizontally from that point to the percent increase in stall speed scale to determine a nearly 100% increase in stall speed. Thus, if the unaccelerated stall speed is 70 kt., the accelerated stall speed of an airplane under a load factor of 4 is 140 kt. [(70 × 100%) + 70 kt.].
Answer (A) is incorrect. The figure of 91 kt. is only approximately a 30% increase in the stall speed. Answer (B) is incorrect. The figure of 132 kt. is only approximately an 89% increase in the stall speed.

SU 1: Airplanes and Aerodynamics 41

49. (Refer to Figure 18 on page 40.) What increase in load factor would take place if the angle of bank were increased from 60° to 80°?

A. 2 G's.
B. 3 G's.
C. 4 G's.

Answer (C) is correct. *(PHAK Chap 5)*
DISCUSSION: Using Fig. 18, find 60° angle of bank on the horizontal axis, go up to the load factor curve, and then horizontally left to the far left scale to determine 2 Gs. At 80° there are 6 Gs. Thus, the increase in load factor is 4 Gs (6 – 2) when the angle of bank is increased from 60° to 80°.
Answer (A) is incorrect. For an increase of 2 Gs to occur, the bank would have to increase from 60° to 75°. Answer (B) is incorrect. For an increase of 3 Gs to occur, the bank would have to increase from 60° to 77°.

50. (Refer to Figure 18 on page 40.) What is the stall speed of an airplane under a load factor of 2 if the unaccelerated stall speed is 100 knots?

A. 115 knots.
B. 129 knots.
C. 140 knots.

Answer (C) is correct. *(PHAK Chap 5)*
DISCUSSION: Use Fig. 18 to determine the percentage of increase in stall speed under a load factor of 2. First, find load factor of 2 on the far left vertical scale and move horizontally to the right to the load factor curve. Then move vertically up from that point to the intersection of the stall speed increase curve. Next, move left horizontally from that point to the first scale to determine a 40% increase in stall speed. Thus, if the unaccelerated stall speed is 100 kt., the accelerated stall speed of an airplane under a load factor of 2 is 140 kt. (100 × 140%).
Answer (A) is incorrect. In order to have 115 kt. stall speed under a load factor of 2, the unaccelerated stall speed must be 82 kt. (115/1.4). Answer (B) is incorrect. In order to have 129 kt. stall speed under a load factor of 2, the unaccelerated stall speed must be 92 kt. (129/1.4).

51. (Refer to Figure 18 on page 40.) A 70 percent increase in stalling speed would imply a bank angle of

A. 67°.
B. 70°.
C. 83°.

Answer (B) is correct. *(PHAK Chap 5)*
DISCUSSION: Use Fig. 18 to determine the bank angle that would produce a 70% increase in the stalling speed. First, find 70% on the vertical scale labeled Percent Increase in Stall Speed. Then move horizontally to the right to the stall speed increase curve. Then move vertically down from that point to the bank angle scale to determine a 70° angle of bank.
Answer (A) is incorrect. A bank angle of 67° is determined if you incorrectly used 7 on the vertical scale labeled Load Factor or "G" units, not the percent increase in stall speed scale. Answer (C) is incorrect. A bank angle of 83° is determined if you incorrectly used the load factor curve, not stall speed increase curve.

52. (Refer to Figure 18 on page 40.) What is the stall speed of an airplane in a 30 degree bank turn if the level stall speed is 100 knots?

A. 100 knots.
B. 102 knots.
C. 108 knots.

Answer (C) is correct. *(PHAK Chap 5)*
DISCUSSION: Use Fig. 18 to determine the percentage of increase in stall speed in a steady 30° bank. Find 30° angle of bank on the horizontal scale and move up vertically. Next, move horizontally from that point to the left to the first scale to determine an 8% increase in stall speed. Thus, if the unaccelerated stall speed is 100 kt., the accelerated stall speed in a steady 30° bank turn is 108 kt. (100 × 108%).
Answer (A) is incorrect. In order to have a stall speed of 100 kt. under a 30° bank, the unaccelerated stall speed would have to be 93 kt. (100 ÷ 1.08). Answer (B) is incorrect. In order to have a stall speed of 102 kt. in a 30° bank, the unaccelerated stall speed would have to be 94 kt. (102 ÷ 1.08).

53. An airplane has a normal stalling speed of 60 MPH but is forced into an accelerated stall at twice that speed. What maximum load factor will result from this maneuver?

A. 4 G's.
B. 2 G's.
C. 1 G.

Answer (A) is correct. *(PHAK Chap 5)*
DISCUSSION: A rule for determining the speed at which an airplane will stall is that the stalling speed increases in proportion to the square root of the load factor. Thus, in order to force an accelerated stall at twice the normal stalling speed, the load factor would have to be 4 since the square root of 4 is 2.
Answer (B) is incorrect. An airplane forced into an unaccelerated stall that imposes a load factor of 2 would stall at 1.4 (square root of 2), not twice, the normal stall speed. Answer (C) is incorrect. The load factor of an unaccelerated, not an accelerated, stall is 1 G.

1.4 Wings

54. At a constant velocity in airflow, a high aspect ratio wing will have (in comparison with a low aspect ratio wing)

A. increased drag, especially at a low angle of attack.
B. decreased drag, especially at a high angle of attack.
C. increased drag, especially at a high angle of attack.

Answer (B) is correct. *(PHAK Chap 5)*
DISCUSSION: An increase in aspect ratio with constant velocity will decrease the drag, especially at high angles of attack, improving climb performance and decreasing stall speeds.
Answer (A) is incorrect. A high aspect wing will have decreased, not increased, drag, especially at high, not low, angles of attack. Answer (C) is incorrect. High aspect ratio wings will have decreased, not increased, drag, especially at high angles of attack.

55. The use of a slot in the leading edge of the wing enables an airplane to land at a slower speed because it

A. changes the camber of the wing.
B. delays the stall to a higher angle of attack.
C. decelerates the upper surface boundary layer air.

Answer (B) is correct. *(PHAK Chap 6)*
DISCUSSION: The use of a slot and/or slat in the leading edge of the wing provides for the passage of air, which accelerates the boundary layer on the upper surface. The stall is delayed to a higher angle of attack, thus enabling the airplane to land at a slower speed.
Answer (A) is incorrect. Wing flaps, not slots, change the wing camber. Answer (C) is incorrect. A slot accelerates, not decelerates, the upper surface boundary layer of air by allowing it to flow through the slot.

56. A rectangular wing, as compared to other wing planforms, has a tendency to stall first at the

A. wingtip providing adequate stall warning.
B. wing root providing adequate stall warning.
C. wingtip providing inadequate stall warning.

Answer (B) is correct. *(PHAK Chap 5)*
DISCUSSION: A rectangular wing, as compared to other wing planforms, has a tendency to stall first at the wing root, with the stall progression toward the wingtip, which provides adequate stall warning. Because the wingtips and the ailerons stall later, you are provided aileron control in avoiding and recovering from the stall.
Answer (A) is incorrect. With a rectangular wing, the wing root, not the wingtip, stalls first. Answer (C) is incorrect. With a rectangular wing, the wing root, not the wingtip, stalls first.

57. The angle between the chord line of the wing and the longitudinal axis of the aircraft is known as

A. dihedral.
B. the angle of attack.
C. the angle of incidence.

Answer (C) is correct. *(PHAK Chap 5)*
DISCUSSION: The angle of incidence is the acute angle formed by the chord line of the wing and the longitudinal axis of the aircraft.
Answer (A) is incorrect. The dihedral refers to the amount the wings are slanted upward from the root to the tip. Answer (B) is incorrect. The angle of attack is the acute angle between the chord line of the wing and the direction of the relative wind.

Aircraft	1	2	3	4	5	6	7	8	9	10	11	12	13	14	15	16
Wing span	40'	35'	48'	30'	33'	36'	36'	36'	52'	57'	51'	75'	59'	49'	117'	32'
Average wing chord	6'	5'	6'	6'	4'	4'	4'	4'	10.5'	4.5'	5'	3'	4'	2' 7"	13'	5'

Figure 21. – Aspect Ratio.

58. (Refer to Figure 21 above.) Which aircraft has the highest aspect ratio?

A. 2.
B. 3.
C. 4.

Answer (B) is correct. *(PHAK Chap 5)*
DISCUSSION: The aspect ratio is the wingspan divided by the average wing chord. Thus, aircraft 3 has the highest aspect ratio.

$$\text{Aircraft 2} = 35 \div 5 = 7.0$$
$$\text{Aircraft 3} = 48 \div 6 = 8.0$$
$$\text{Aircraft 4} = 30 \div 6 = 5.0$$

Answer (A) is incorrect. Aircraft 2 has an aspect ratio of 7.0. Answer (C) is incorrect. Aircraft 4 has an aspect ratio of 5.0.

59. (Refer to Figure 21 on page 42.) Which aircraft has the lowest aspect ratio?

A. 2.
B. 3.
C. 4.

Answer (C) is correct. *(PHAK Chap 5)*
DISCUSSION: The aspect ratio is the wingspan divided by the average wing chord. Thus, aircraft 4 has the lowest aspect ratio.

Aircraft 2 = 35 ÷ 5 = 7.0
Aircraft 3 = 48 ÷ 6 = 8.0
Aircraft 4 = 30 ÷ 6 = 5.0

Answer (A) is incorrect. Aircraft 2 has an aspect ratio of 7.0. Answer (B) is incorrect. Aircraft 3 has an aspect ratio of 8.0.

60. (Refer to Figure 21 on page 42.) Of aircraft 1, 2, or 3, which has the lowest aspect ratio?

A. 1.
B. 2.
C. 3.

Answer (A) is correct. *(PHAK Chap 5)*
DISCUSSION: The aspect ratio is the wingspan divided by the average wing chord. Thus, aircraft 1 has the lowest aspect ratio.

Aircraft 1 = 40 ÷ 6 = 6.6
Aircraft 2 = 35 ÷ 5 = 7.0
Aircraft 3 = 48 ÷ 6 = 8.0

Answer (B) is incorrect. Aircraft 2 has an aspect ratio of 7.0. Answer (C) is incorrect. Aircraft 3 has an aspect ratio of 8.0.

61. (Refer to Figure 21 on page 42.) Consider only aspect ratio (other factors remain constant). Which aircraft will generate greatest lift?

A. 1.
B. 2.
C. 3.

Answer (C) is correct. *(PHAK Chap 5)*
DISCUSSION: Airplanes with higher aspect ratios generate the greatest lift, all other factors held constant. Thus, aircraft 3 will generate the greatest lift.

Aircraft 1 = 40 ÷ 6 = 6.67
Aircraft 2 = 35 ÷ 5 = 7.0
Aircraft 3 = 48 ÷ 6 = 8.0

Answer (A) is incorrect. Aircraft 1 has an aspect ratio of 6.67. Answer (B) is incorrect. Aircraft 2 has an aspect ratio of 7.0.

62. (Refer to Figure 21 on page 42.) Consider only aspect ratio (other factors remain constant). Which aircraft will generate greatest drag?

A. 1.
B. 3.
C. 4.

Answer (C) is correct. *(PHAK Chap 5)*
DISCUSSION: Airplanes with the lowest aspect ratio generate the greatest drag, all other factors held constant. Thus, airplane 4 will have the greatest drag.

Aircraft 1 = 40 ÷ 6 = 6.67
Aircraft 3 = 48 ÷ 6 = 8.0
Aircraft 4 = 30 ÷ 6 = 5.0

Answer (A) is incorrect. Airplane 1 has an aspect ratio of 6.67. Answer (B) is incorrect. Airplane 3 has an aspect ratio of 8.0.

63. (Refer to Figure 21 on page 42.) Consider only aspect ratio (other factors remain constant). Which aircraft will generate the least drag?

A. 16.
B. 10.
C. 9.

Answer (B) is correct. *(PHAK Chap 5)*
DISCUSSION: Aircraft 10 has an aspect ratio of 12.6. Aircraft with the highest aspect ratio generate the least amount of drag, all other factors being constant. Thus, Aircraft 10 will have the least amount of drag.

Aircraft 16 = 32 ÷ 5 = 6.4
Aircraft 10 = 57 ÷ 4.5 = 12.66
Aircraft 9 = 52 ÷ 10.5 = 4.95

Answer (A) is incorrect. Aircraft 16 has an aspect ratio of 6.4. It would generate more drag than Aircraft 10 but less than Aircraft 9. Answer (C) is incorrect. Aircraft 9 has an aspect ratio of 4.9. It would have the greatest drag of the three listed.

64. Which subsonic planform provides the best lift coefficient?

A. Tapered wing.
B. Elliptical wing.
C. Rectangular wing.

Answer (B) is correct. *(PHAK Chap 5)*
DISCUSSION: The best subsonic wing planform from a lift coefficient standpoint is the elliptical wing.
Answer (A) is incorrect. The tapered wing is desirable from the standpoint of weight and stiffness, but not aerodynamic efficiency. Answer (C) is incorrect. Although the rectangular wing is most often used in low-speed aircraft due to its preferred low speed/stall characteristics, it does not provide as high a lift coefficient as the elliptical wing.

65. A line drawn from the leading edge to the trailing edge of an airfoil and equidistant at all points from the upper and lower contours is called the

    A. chord line.

    B. camber line.

    C. mean camber line.

Answer (C) is correct. *(PHAK Chap 5)*
    DISCUSSION: A reference line drawn from the leading edge to the trailing edge that is equidistant at all points from the upper and lower surfaces of the wing is the mean camber line.
    Answer (A) is incorrect. The chord line is a straight line drawn from the profiles connecting the extremities of the leading edge and the trailing edge. Answer (B) is incorrect. The camber line is the curvature of the upper and lower surfaces of the airfoil.

66. A sweptwing airplane with weak static directional stability and increased dihedral causes an increase in

    A. Mach tuck tendency.

    B. Dutch roll tendency.

    C. longitudinal stability.

Answer (B) is correct. *(PHAK Chap 5)*
    DISCUSSION: A sweptwing airplane has an increase in dihedral effect. When an airplane's dihedral effect is large in comparison with its static directional stability, its Dutch roll tendencies will increase.
    Answer (A) is incorrect. The Mach tuck tendency describes the control problems encountered when going through the sound barrier. Answer (C) is incorrect. Longitudinal stability is not affected by directional stability or dihedral.

67. On which wing planform does the stall begin at the wing root and progress outward toward the wingtip?

    A. Sweepback wing.

    B. Rectangular wing.

    C. Moderate taper wing.

Answer (B) is correct. *(PHAK Chap 5)*
    DISCUSSION: Rectangular wings have a tendency to stall first at the wing root, progressing toward the wingtip. This tendency gives adequate stall warning, adequate aileron effectiveness, and leads to a wing that is usually quite stable. Rectangular wings are therefore favored in the design of low-cost, low-speed airplanes.
    Answer (A) is incorrect. On sweptback wings, stalls begin at the wingtip and work inward toward the wing root. This tendency causes decreased aileron control and requires precise flying with professional techniques. Answer (C) is incorrect. The moderate taper wing stalls along the whole wing, thus not giving good prestall warnings.

68. The purpose of aircraft wing dihedral angle is to

    A. increase lateral stability.

    B. increase longitudinal stability.

    C. increase lift coefficient of the wing.

Answer (A) is correct. *(PHAK Chap 5)*
    DISCUSSION: Dihedral is the angle at which the wings are slanted upward from the root to the tip. When the airplane sideslips slightly, one wing is forced down. Then the greater angle of attack on the lower wing produces increased lift, with a tendency to return the airplane to wings-level flight; i.e., lateral stability is enhanced.
    Answer (B) is incorrect. Longitudinal stability is not affected by wing dihedral. Answer (C) is incorrect. The lift coefficient of the wing is not affected by dihedral angle.

69. Aspect ratio of a wing is defined as the ratio of the

    A. wingspan to the wing root.

    B. wingspan to the mean chord.

    C. square of the chord to the wingspan.

Answer (B) is correct. *(PHAK Chap 5)*
    DISCUSSION: The aspect ratio is the ratio of the wingspan to the mean chord.
    Answer (A) is incorrect. The aspect ratio is the ratio of the wingspan to the mean chord, not the wing root. Answer (C) is incorrect. The aspect ratio is the ratio of the wingspan to the mean chord, not the square of the chord to the wingspan.

70. A wing with a very high aspect ratio (in comparison with a low aspect ratio wing) will have

    A. a low stall speed.

    B. increased drag at high angles of attack.

    C. poor control qualities at low airspeeds.

Answer (A) is correct. *(PHAK Chap 5)*
    DISCUSSION: An increase in aspect ratio with constant velocity will decrease the drag, especially at high angles of attack, improving climb performance and decreasing stall speeds.
    Answer (B) is incorrect. A high aspect ratio wing decreases, not increases, drag at higher angles of attack. Answer (C) is incorrect. Control qualities at low airspeed are improved with a high aspect ratio wing.

1.5 The Axes of Airplanes

71. The three axes of an aircraft intersect at the

A. center of gravity.
B. center of pressure.
C. midpoint of the mean chord.

Answer (A) is correct. *(PHAK Chap 5)*
DISCUSSION: The three axes of an airplane intersect at the center of gravity.
Answer (B) is incorrect. The center of pressure is the imaginary point on the chord line through which the resultant lift vector crosses. Answer (C) is incorrect. The mean chord is the mean of the straight lines from the leading edge to the trailing edge of the wing.

72. Action of the elevators moves the plane on its

A. lateral axis.
B. longitudinal axis.
C. vertical axis.

Answer (A) is correct. *(PHAK Chap 5)*
DISCUSSION: An airplane is moved about its lateral axis (pitching motion) by action of the elevators.
Answer (B) is incorrect. An airplane is moved about its longitudinal axis (rolling motion) by action of the ailerons. Answer (C) is incorrect. An airplane is moved about its vertical axis (yawing motion) by action of the rudder.

73. Aileron deflection moves the airplane about its

A. lateral axis.
B. longitudinal axis.
C. vertical axis.

Answer (B) is correct. *(PHAK Chap 5)*
DISCUSSION: An airplane is moved about its longitudinal axis (rolling motion) by action of the ailerons.
Answer (A) is incorrect. An airplane is moved about its lateral axis (pitching motion) by action of the elevators. Answer (C) is incorrect. An airplane is moved about its vertical axis (yawing motion) by action of the rudder.

74. If the pilot applies right rudder to a stable airplane, the

A. tail deflects right and the nose moves right.
B. tail deflects left and the nose moves right.
C. tail deflects right and the nose moves left.

Answer (B) is correct. *(PHAK Chap 6)*
DISCUSSION: The rudder pedals and the rudder itself move in the same direction. By pressing the right rudder pedal in the cockpit, the pilot is causing the rudder to move to the right as well. This causes the tail to deflect to the left and the airplane to yaw to the right.
Answer (A) is incorrect. A rudder deflected to the right will cause the tail to deflect to the left. Answer (C) is incorrect. A rudder deflected to the right will cause the tail to move to the left and the nose to move to the right.

1.6 Angle of Attack

75. The angle between the chord line of an airfoil and the relative wind is known as the angle of

A. lift.
B. attack.
C. incidence.

Answer (B) is correct. *(PHAK Chap 4)*
DISCUSSION: The angle of attack is the acute angle between the chord line of the wing and the direction of the relative wind.
Answer (A) is incorrect. The angle of lift is a nonsense term. Answer (C) is incorrect. The angle of incidence is the acute angle formed by the chord line of the wing and the longitudinal axis of the airplane.

76. The critical angle of attack at which a given aircraft stalls is dependent on the

A. gross weight.
B. design of the wing.
C. attitude and airspeed.

Answer (B) is correct. *(PHAK Chap 5)*
DISCUSSION: The angle of attack at which an aircraft stalls is dependent upon the wing design. It is a fixed number, usually an angle of attack between 15° and 20°.
Answer (A) is incorrect. The gross weight will increase the stall speeds, but it does not change the critical angle of attack. Answer (C) is incorrect. It is the design of the wing, not attitude and airspeed, that determines the critical angle of attack.

77. The angle of attack of a wing directly controls the

A. angle of incidence of the wing.
B. amount of airflow above and below the wing.
C. distribution of positive and negative pressure acting on the wing.

Answer (C) is correct. *(PHAK Chap 4)*
DISCUSSION: The angle of attack of a wing directly controls the distribution of positive and negative pressure acting on the wing by altering the speed of the airflow over the wing surfaces.
Answer (A) is incorrect. The angle of incidence is the angle between the wing chord line and the airplane's longitudinal axis. It is a fixed angle determined by airplane design. Answer (B) is incorrect. The amount of airflow above and below the wing is controlled by airspeed, not the angle of attack.

1.7 Turns

78. As the angle of bank is increased, the vertical component of lift

A. increases and the sink rate increases.
B. decreases and the sink rate increases.
C. increases and the sink rate decreases.

Answer (B) is correct. *(PHAK Chap 5)*
DISCUSSION: In straight-and-level flight, the vertical component of lift acts directly opposite to the component of gravity or weight. Therefore, the vertical component of lift decreases. As a result, gravity is not offset by as much vertical lift, and the sink rate increases.
Answer (A) is incorrect. The vertical component of lift decreases, not increases, when the angle of bank is increased. Answer (C) is incorrect. The vertical component of lift decreases, not increases, and the sink rate increases, not decreases.

79. How can a pilot increase the rate of turn and decrease the radius at the same time?

A. Shallow the bank and increase airspeed.
B. Steepen the bank and decrease airspeed.
C. Steepen the bank and increase airspeed.

Answer (B) is correct. *(AFH Chap 4)*
DISCUSSION: The rate of turn is dependent upon the horizontal component of lift. As the horizontal component is increased (i.e., steepened bank), the rate of turn increases. The radius of a turn is dependent upon airspeed. As airspeed is decreased, the turn radius decreases.
Answer (A) is incorrect. The bank should be steepened, not made more shallow, and the airspeed should be decreased, not increased. Answer (C) is incorrect. The airspeed should be decreased, not increased.

80. What action is necessary to make an aircraft turn?

A. Yaw the aircraft.
B. Change the direction of lift.
C. Change the direction of thrust.

Answer (B) is correct. *(PHAK Chap 5)*
DISCUSSION: In straight-and-level flight, lift acts directly opposite to gravity or weight. As the aircraft is banked, the lift is divided into horizontal and vertical components. This horizontal component of lift pulls the aircraft around the turn.
Answer (A) is incorrect. Yawing the aircraft merely rotates it around its vertical axis. It does not produce force that is necessary to make an aircraft turn. Answer (C) is incorrect. The direction of thrust cannot be changed while in flight in propeller-driven aircraft.

81. (Refer to Figure 22 on page 47.) While rolling into a right turn, if the inclinometer appears as illustrated in A, the HCL and CF vectors would be acting on the aircraft as illustrated in

A. 2, and more left pedal pressure is needed to center the ball.
B. 2, and more right pedal pressure is needed to center the ball.
C. 4, and more right pedal pressure is needed to center the ball.

Answer (B) is correct. *(AFH Chap 4)*
DISCUSSION: If the ball is to the right in a right turn, right rudder (pedal) pressure is needed to center the ball; i.e., the horizontal component of lift (HCL) exceeds centrifugal force (CF).
Answer (A) is incorrect. Right, not left, rudder is needed to center the ball. Answer (C) is incorrect. HCL exceeds CF, not the opposite.

82. (Refer to Figure 22 on page 47.) While rolling into a right turn, if the inclinometer appears as illustrated in C, the HCL and CF vectors would be acting on the aircraft as illustrated in

A. 3, and less right pedal pressure is needed to center the ball.
B. 5, and less right pedal pressure is needed to center the ball.
C. 5, and more right pedal pressure is needed to center the ball.

Answer (B) is correct. *(AFH Chap 3)*
DISCUSSION: If the ball is to the left in a right turn, less right rudder (pedal) pressure is needed to center the ball; i.e., the CF exceeds the HCL.
Answer (A) is incorrect. In a right turn, the HCL is to the right, not to the left. Answer (C) is incorrect. More right rudder would only force the ball more to the left.

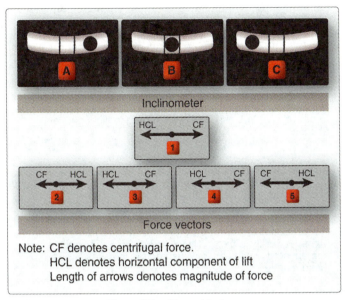

Figure 22. – Force Vectors.

83. (Refer to Figure 22 above.) While rolling out of a left turn, if the inclinometer appears as illustrated in A, the HCL and CF vectors would be acting on the aircraft as illustrated in

A. 4, and more right pedal pressure is needed to center the ball.

B. 4, and more left pedal pressure is needed to center the ball.

C. 2, and more right pedal pressure is needed to center the ball.

Answer (A) is correct. *(AFH Chap 3)*
DISCUSSION: If the ball is to the right while rolling out of a left turn, more right rudder (pedal) pressure is needed to center the ball; i.e., CF exceeds the HCL.
Answer (B) is incorrect. More left rudder pressure would only force the ball more to the right. Answer (C) is incorrect. The HCL is to the left, not right, in a left turn.

84. Adverse yaw during a turn entry is caused by

A. increased induced drag on the lowered wing and decreased induced drag on the raised wing.

B. decreased induced drag on the lowered wing and increased induced drag on the raised wing.

C. increased parasite drag on the raised wing and decreased parasite drag on the lowered wing.

Answer (B) is correct. *(AFH Chap 3)*
DISCUSSION: When the pilot applies pressure to the control stick or turns the control yoke to the left, the right aileron surface deflects downward and the left aileron surface deflects upward. The downward-deflected aileron produces more lift and more drag, which attempts to pull or veer the airplane's nose in the direction of the raised wing. This undesired veering is adverse yaw.
Answer (A) is incorrect. Induced drag is decreased, not increased, on the lowered wing and increased, not decreased, on the raised wing. Answer (C) is incorrect. Parasite drag is affected by airspeed, not aileron deflection.

85. When rolling out of a steep-banked turn, what causes the lowered aileron to create more drag than when rolling into the turn?

A. The wing's angle of attack is greater as the rollout is started.

B. The wing being raised is traveling faster through the air than the wing being lowered.

C. The wing being lowered is traveling faster through the air and producing more lift than the wing being raised.

Answer (A) is correct. *(AFH Chap 3)*
DISCUSSION: When rolling out of a turn, the adverse yaw effect caused by the lowered aileron is more apparent than rolling into a turn, due to the higher angle of attack, wing loading, and the slower airspeed of the lowered wing when rollout is started. This slower airspeed requires a greater deflection of the ailerons than is necessary when rolling into a turn. Thus, the lowered aileron produces more induced drag since the wing is at a greater angle of attack.
Answer (B) is incorrect. The low wing is traveling slower, not faster, than the high wing. Answer (C) is incorrect. The wing being raised, not lowered, is producing more lift than the wing being lowered.

1.8 Airplane Stability

86. The quality of an aircraft that permits it to be operated easily and to withstand the stresses imposed on it is

A. stability.
B. maneuverability.
C. controllability.

Answer (B) is correct. *(PHAK Chap 5)*
DISCUSSION: The quality of an aircraft that permits it to be operated easily and withstand the stresses imposed on it is the maneuverability of the aircraft.
Answer (A) is incorrect. Stability is the quality of an aircraft to correct for conditions that may disturb its equilibrium. Answer (C) is incorrect. Controllability is the ability of an airplane to respond to a pilot's control, especially with regard to flight path and attitude.

87. The capability of an aircraft to respond to a pilot's inputs, especially with regard to flightpath and attitude, is

A. response.
B. controllability.
C. maneuverability.

Answer (B) is correct. *(PHAK Chap 5)*
DISCUSSION: The capability of an aircraft to respond to the pilot's inputs, especially with regard to flight path and attitude, is its controllability.
Answer (A) is incorrect. Response is how the aircraft reacts to control inputs by the pilot. Answer (C) is incorrect. Maneuverability is the quality of an aircraft that permits it to be maneuvered easily and to withstand the stresses imposed by these maneuvers.

88. The tendency of an aircraft to develop forces which restore it to its original condition, when disturbed from a condition of steady flight, is known as

A. stability.
B. controllability.
C. maneuverability.

Answer (A) is correct. *(PHAK Chap 4)*
DISCUSSION: Stability is the inherent ability of a body after its equilibrium is disturbed to develop forces or moments that tend to return it to its original position. In other words, a stable airplane will tend to return to the original condition of flight if disturbed by a force such as turbulent air.
Answer (B) is incorrect. Controllability is the capability of an airplane to respond to the pilot's inputs especially with regard to flight path and attitude. Answer (C) is incorrect. Maneuverability is the quality of an airplane that permits it to be operated easily and to withstand the stresses imposed on it.

89. The most desirable type of stability for an aircraft to possess is

A. neutral static stability.
B. positive static stability.
C. positive dynamic stability.

Answer (C) is correct. *(PHAK Chap 5)*
DISCUSSION: An airplane should possess positive stability that is both static and dynamic in nature, but most desirable is the positive dynamic stability. Static stability (positive) means that if the airplane's equilibrium is disturbed, forces will be activated that will initially tend to return the airplane to the original position. Dynamic stability (positive) dampens the oscillations set up by a statically stable airplane, reducing the oscillations in magnitude until the airplane eventually settles to its original condition of flight. If an aircraft has positive dynamic stability, it will also have positive static stability, but an aircraft with only positive static stability does not necessarily possess positive dynamic stability. Thus, the most desirable type of stability to possess is positive dynamic stability.
Answer (A) is incorrect. Neutral static stability is not as desirable as positive static stability. Answer (B) is incorrect. An airplane with static stability does not necessarily possess positive dynamic stability.

90. Which aircraft characteristics contribute to spiral instability?

A. Weak static directional stability and weak dihedral effect.
B. Strong static directional stability and weak dihedral effect.
C. Weak static directional stability and strong dihedral effect.

Answer (B) is correct. *(FTP Chap 16)*
DISCUSSION: Spiral instability exists when the static directional stability of the airplane is very strong compared to the effect of its dihedral in maintaining lateral equilibrium. When one wing is lowered by gusts of air and the airplane moves into a sideslip, the strong directional stability tends to yaw the nose into the resultant relative wind; a comparatively weak dihedral lags in restoring the lateral balance.
Due to this yaw, the wing on the outside of the turning moment travels forward faster than the inside wing, and so its lift becomes greater. This produces an overbanking tendency that, if not corrected, will gradually increase into a steep spiral dive.
Answer (A) is incorrect. Spiral instability comes from strong, not weak, static directional stability. Answer (C) is incorrect. Spiral instability comes from weak, not strong, dihedral effect, coupled with strong, not weak, static directional stability.

SU 1: Airplanes and Aerodynamics

91. The tendency of an aircraft to develop forces that further remove the aircraft from its original position, when disturbed from a condition of steady flight, is known as

A. static instability.
B. dynamic instability.
C. positive static stability.

Answer (A) is correct. *(PHAK Chap 5)*
DISCUSSION: If an aircraft tends to continue in the direction of a disturbance, negative static stability or static instability exists.
Answer (B) is incorrect. Dynamic instability refers to the tendency for oscillations to increase, i.e., become greater. Answer (C) is incorrect. Positive static stability is the tendency of an airplane to develop forces that tend to return the airplane to, not move it farther from, its original position when disturbed.

92. If the aircraft's nose initially tends to return to its original position after the elevator control is pressed forward and released, the aircraft displays

A. positive static stability.
B. neutral dynamic stability.
C. negative dynamic stability.

Answer (A) is correct. *(PHAK Chap 5)*
DISCUSSION: Imagine that you trim the airplane for hands-off control in level flight and then momentarily give the controls a slight push to nose the airplane down. If within a brief period the nose rises to the original position and then stops, the airplane is statically stable. It is positively statically stable because it has returned to its original position after being displaced.
Answer (B) is incorrect. Neutral dynamic stability refers to oscillations continuing without a tendency to increase or decrease. Answer (C) is incorrect. Negative dynamic stability refers to oscillations that increase once they occur.

93. If the airspeed increases and decreases during longitudinal phugoid oscillations, the aircraft

A. will display poor trimming qualities.
B. is maintaining a nearly constant angle of attack.
C. is constantly changing angle of attack making it difficult for the pilot to reduce the magnitude of the oscillations.

Answer (B) is correct. *(FTP Chap 15)*
DISCUSSION: In a longitudinal phugoid oscillation, the angle of attack remains nearly constant when the airspeed and altitude increase and decrease. "Phugoid" means an oscillation with a long period (10 to 100 seconds). This kind of oscillation can easily be controlled by the pilot. The other type of oscillation is a neutral or short-period oscillation and is very dangerous because structural failure usually results if the oscillation is not damped immediately.
Answer (A) is incorrect. Normally, the phugoid oscillations can be trimmed out. Answer (C) is incorrect. The angle of attack remains constant as the airspeed increases and decreases.

94. If an aircraft has negative dynamic and positive static stability, this will result in

A. undamped oscillations.
B. divergent oscillations.
C. convergent oscillations.

Answer (B) is correct. *(PHAK Chap 5)*
DISCUSSION: If an airplane has positive static stability, the initial tendency of the airplane is to return to the original state after it is disturbed. With negative dynamic stability this movement creates divergent oscillations, which, instead of dampening, become progressively larger.
Answer (A) is incorrect. Undamped oscillations are a characteristic of neutral, not negative, dynamic stability. Answer (C) is incorrect. Convergent oscillations are characteristic of positive, not negative, dynamic stability.

95. If the aircraft's nose initially tends to move farther from its original position after the elevator control is pressed forward and released, the aircraft displays

A. negative static stability.
B. positive static stability.
C. positive dynamic stability.

Answer (A) is correct. *(PHAK Chap 5)*
DISCUSSION: When the airplane's nose moves farther from its original position, it has the undesirable characteristic of negative static stability.
Answer (B) is incorrect. If the aircraft had positive static stability, it would return to its original position. Answer (C) is incorrect. Positive dynamic stability refers to oscillations being dampened or decreasing, not the airplane's initial tendency after being disturbed.

96. If the aircraft's nose remains in the new position after the elevator control is pressed forward and released, the aircraft displays

A. neutral static stability.
B. negative static stability.
C. positive static stability.

Answer (A) is correct. *(PHAK Chap 5)*
DISCUSSION: If the airplane's nose remains in the new position after the elevator control is pressed forward and released, the aircraft displays neutral static stability.
Answer (B) is incorrect. A negative static stability means the airplane would tend to move even farther from the original position. Answer (C) is incorrect. With positive static stability, the airplane would return to its original position.

1.9 Spiraling Slipstream and Gyroscopic Precession

97. With regard to gyroscopic precession, when a force is applied at a point on the rim of a spinning disc, the resultant force acts in which direction and at what point?

A. In the same direction as the applied force, 90° ahead in the plane of rotation.
B. In the opposite direction of the applied force, 90° ahead in the plane of rotation.
C. In the opposite direction of the applied force, at the point of the applied force.

Answer (A) is correct. *(PHAK Chap 5)*
DISCUSSION: Gyroscopic precession applies to any object spinning in space, such as an airplane propeller. As the spinning propeller is moved to the left or right or raised or lowered, a deflective force is applied, which results in a reactive force called precession. Precession is the resultant action or deflection of a spinning wheel when a force is applied to its rim. The resultant force occurs 90° ahead in the direction of rotation and in the direction of the applied force.
Answer (B) is incorrect. Precession acts in the same, not opposite, direction as the applied force. Answer (C) is incorrect. The resultant force occurs in the same, not opposite, direction as the applied force and 90° ahead in the plane of rotation, not at the point of applied force.

98. As a result of gyroscopic precession, it can be said that any

A. pitching around the lateral axis results in a rolling moment.
B. yawing around the vertical axis results in a pitching moment.
C. pitching around the longitudinal axis results in a yawing moment.

Answer (B) is correct. *(PHAK Chap 5)*
DISCUSSION: The propeller acts as a gyroscope. Precession is the resultant action, or deflection, of a spinning rotor when a deflecting force is applied to the rotor's rim. Thus, as the airplane yaws around its vertical axis, it results in a pitching moment about its lateral axis.
Answer (A) is incorrect. Pitching about the lateral axis causes a yawing, not a rolling, moment. Answer (C) is incorrect. Pitch occurs about the lateral, not longitudinal, axis.

99. A propeller rotating clockwise, as seen from the rear, creates a spiraling slipstream that tends to rotate the aircraft to the

A. right around the vertical axis, and to the left around the longitudinal axis.
B. left around the vertical axis, and to the right around the longitudinal axis.
C. left around the vertical axis, and to the left around the longitudinal axis.

Answer (B) is correct. *(PHAK Chap 5)*
DISCUSSION: As the airplane propeller rotates through the air in a clockwise direction as viewed from the rear, the propeller blade forces the air rearward in a spiraling, clockwise direction of flow around the fuselage. This clockwise flow attempts to roll the airplane to the right about the longitudinal axis. A portion of this spiraling slipstream strikes the left side of the vertical stabilizer, forcing the airplane's tail to the right, causing the airplane to rotate to the left around the vertical axis.
Answer (A) is incorrect. The rotation is to the left, not right, around the vertical axis and to the right, not left, around the longitudinal axis. Answer (C) is incorrect. The rotation is to the right, not left, around the longitudinal axis.

1.10 Stalls and Spins

100. The angle of attack at which an airplane stalls

A. increases with an increase in engine power.
B. remains constant regardless of gross weight.
C. varies with gross weight and density altitude.

Answer (B) is correct. *(AFH Chap 4)*
DISCUSSION: While the stalling speed of a particular airplane varies, a particular airplane will always stall at the same angle of attack regardless of airspeed, engine power, weight, load factor, or density altitude.
Answer (A) is incorrect. While the airplane is stalled at a lower speed with increases in engine power, the airplane stalls at a constant angle of attack. Answer (C) is incorrect. While the airplane's stall speed may vary with gross weight, the angle of attack at which an airplane stalls is constant.

101. Which action will result in a stall?

A. Flying at too low an airspeed.
B. Raising the aircraft's nose too high.
C. Exceeding the critical angle of attack.

Answer (C) is correct. *(PHAK Chap 5)*
DISCUSSION: An airplane will always stall when the critical angle of attack is exceeded.
Answer (A) is incorrect. An airplane will stall at any, not only a low, airspeed. Answer (B) is incorrect. An airplane will stall at any, not only a nose-high, pitch attitude.

SU 1: Airplanes and Aerodynamics

102. Which statement is true relating to the factors which produce stalls?

A. The critical angle of attack is a function of the degree of bank.
B. The stalling angle of attack depends upon the speed of the airflow over the wings.
C. The stalling angle of attack is independent of the speed of airflow over the wings.

Answer (C) is correct. *(AFH Chap 4)*
DISCUSSION: Stalls are directly related to angle of attack (AOA), not airspeed. Above a wing's critical AOA, the flow of air separates from the upper surface and backfills, burbles and eddies, which reduces lift and increases drag. This condition is a stall, which can lead to loss of control if the AOA is not reduced. It is possible to stall the wing at any airspeed, at any flight attitude, and at any power setting.
Answer (A) is incorrect. A stall is the result of exceeding the critical AOA, which remains constant. Bank angle is directly related to load factor, which is a factor affecting the speed which the critical angle of attack is reached. It is possible to stall the wing at any airspeed, at any flight attitude, and at any power setting. Answer (B) is incorrect. A stall is the result of exceeding the critical AOA, which remains constant, not of insufficient airspeed. It is possible to stall the wing at any airspeed, at any flight attitude, and at any power setting.

103. Which characteristic of a spin is not a characteristic of a steep spiral?

A. Stalled wing.
B. High rate of rotation.
C. Rapid loss of altitude.

Answer (A) is correct. *(AFH Chap 4)*
DISCUSSION: During a spin, both wings are stalled although one wing is less stalled than the other. In a steep spiral (steep, descending turn), the wings are flying at a relatively low angle of attack and at a high airspeed.
Answer (B) is incorrect. A high rate of rotation is characteristic of both a spin and a steep spiral. Answer (C) is incorrect. A rapid loss of altitude is characteristic of both a spin and a steep spiral.

104. Which statement is true concerning the aerodynamic conditions which occur during a spin entry?

A. After a full stall, both wings remain in a stalled condition throughout the rotation.
B. After a partial stall, the wing that drops remains in a stalled condition while the rising wing regains and continues to produce lift, causing the rotation.
C. After a full stall, the wing that drops continues in a stalled condition while the rising wing regains and continues to produce some lift, causing the rotation.

Answer (C) is correct. *(AFH Chap 4)*
DISCUSSION: If, after a complete stall, one wing drops and the other rises, the higher wing will regain some lift and the airplane will begin to spin. To recover from a spin, the pilot should first apply full opposite rudder. Also, apply brisk positive straightforward movement of the elevator control, forward of the neutral position to break the stall.
Answer (A) is incorrect. The rising wing regains some lift. Answer (B) is incorrect. A spin is entered after a full stall, not after a partial stall.

1.11 Ground Effect

105. It is possible to fly an aircraft just clear of the ground at a slightly slower airspeed than that required to sustain level flight at higher altitudes. This is the result of

A. interference of the ground surface with the airflow patterns about the aircraft in flight.
B. a cushioning effect of the air as it is trapped between the ground and the descending aircraft.
C. ground interference with the static pressure system which produces false indications on the airspeed indicator.

Answer (A) is correct. *(AFH Chap 5)*
DISCUSSION: Ground effect is caused by the interference of the ground surface with the airflow patterns about the airplane in flight. As a result, it is possible to fly at a slower airspeed in ground effect than out of it.
Answer (B) is incorrect. It is the change in the wings' upwash, downwash, and vortices near the surface that causes ground effect, not a cushioning effect of air that is trapped between the ground and the airplane. Answer (C) is incorrect. While ground effect may cause an increase in the local pressure at the static source and produce a lower indication of airspeed and altitude, it is not the reason why an airplane will fly in ground effect at a slightly lower airspeed than normally required.

106. If the same angle of attack is maintained in ground effect as when out of ground effect, lift will

A. increase, and induced drag will decrease.
B. decrease, and parasite drag will increase.
C. decrease, and parasite drag will decrease.

Answer (A) is correct. *(AFH Chap 5)*
DISCUSSION: In ground effect, at the same angle of attack, lift is increased due to the decrease in wing downwash, and drag is decreased due to the reduction in wingtip vortices.
Answer (B) is incorrect. Lift increases, not decreases, and induced, not parasite, drag is affected. Parasite drag is not altered by ground effect. Answer (C) is incorrect. Lift increases, not decreases, and induced, not parasite, drag is affected.

107. An airplane is usually affected by ground effect at what height above the surface?

A. Three to four times the airplane's wingspan.
B. Twice the airplane's wingspan above the surface.
C. Less than half the airplane's wingspan above the surface.

Answer (C) is correct. *(AFH Chap 5)*
DISCUSSION: Ground effect is said to exist roughly between the surface and about one-half of the wingspan from the surface.
Answer (A) is incorrect. Ground effect does not extend to three or four times the airplane's wingspan above the surface. Answer (B) is incorrect. Ground effect does not extend to twice the airplane's wingspan above the surface.

108. An airplane leaving ground effect will

A. experience a decrease in thrust required.
B. experience a decrease in stability and a nose-up change in moments.
C. require a lower angle of attack to attain the same lift coefficient.

Answer (B) is correct. *(AFH Chap 5)*
DISCUSSION: An airplane leaving ground effect will:

1. Require an increase in angle of attack to maintain the same lift coefficient,
2. Experience an increase in induced drag and thrust required,
3. Experience a decrease in stability and a nose-up change in moment, and
4. Produce a reduction in static source pressure and increase in indicated airspeed.

Answer (A) is incorrect. Required thrust increases, not decreases. Answer (C) is incorrect. A higher, not lower, angle of attack is required.

1.12 Turbulence

109. If severe turbulence is encountered, the aircraft's airspeed should be reduced to

A. maneuvering speed.
B. normal structural cruising speed.
C. the minimum steady flight speed in the landing configuration.

Answer (A) is correct. *(PHAK Chap 5)*
DISCUSSION: In severe turbulence, the airplane should be slowed to its maneuvering speed (V_A), i.e., the speed below which you can move a single flight control, one time, to its full deflection, for one axis of airplane rotation only (pitch, roll, or yaw), in smooth air, without risk of damage to the airplane.
Answer (B) is incorrect. Normal structural cruising speed is greater than maneuvering speed and severe turbulence may result in structural damage to the airplane. Answer (C) is incorrect. The minimum steady flight speed in the landing configuration would be relatively close to stall speed. Thus, the airplane would be apt to stall in the changing wind gusts and directions associated with turbulence.

110. Which is the best technique for minimizing the wing-load factor when flying in severe turbulence?

A. Control airspeed with power, maintain wings level, and accept variations of altitude.
B. Control airspeed as closely as possible with elevator and power, and accept variations of bank and altitude.
C. Set power and trim to obtain an airspeed at or below maneuvering speed, maintain wings level, and accept variations of airspeed and altitude.

Answer (C) is correct. *(PHAK Chap 5)*
DISCUSSION: When in severe turbulence (i.e., turbulence in which it is very difficult to maintain control of the aircraft), your major concern should be to avoid structural damage to the airplane. Thus, you should be at or below maneuvering speed (V_A) so that the airplane will stall prior to incurring structural loads of a magnitude sufficient to cause structural damage. Also, you should attempt to keep the wings level and accept changes in airspeed and altitude.
Answer (A) is incorrect. You need only be at or below maneuvering speed. Further airspeed control will not be possible in severe turbulence. Answer (B) is incorrect. The first priority is to maintain level wings. In severe turbulence, it is impossible to maintain airspeed.

STUDY UNIT TWO
AIRPLANE PERFORMANCE

(12 pages of outline)

2.1	Density Altitude	(18 questions)	53, 65
2.2	Takeoff Distance	(12 questions)	55, 69
2.3	Maximum Climb	(3 questions)	59, 76
2.4	True Airspeed	(4 questions)	59, 77
2.5	Multi-Engine Performance	(10 questions)	59, 78
2.6	Glide Distance	(3 questions)	60, 80
2.7	Stall Speed	(3 questions)	61, 82
2.8	Landing Distance	(4 questions)	62, 83
2.9	Crosswind/Headwind Components	(7 questions)	64, 86

This study unit contains outlines of major concepts tested, sample test questions and answers regarding airplane performance, and an explanation of each answer. The table of contents above lists each subunit within this study unit, the number of questions pertaining to that particular subunit, and the pages on which the outlines and questions begin, respectively.

Recall that the **sole purpose** of this book is to expedite your passing of the FAA pilot knowledge test for the CFI, BGI, or AGI certificate. Accordingly, all extraneous material (i.e., topics or regulations not directly tested on the FAA pilot knowledge test) is omitted, even though much more knowledge is necessary to become a proficient flight or ground instructor. This additional material is presented in *Pilot Handbook* and *Flight Instructor Flight Maneuvers and Practical Test Prep*, available from Gleim Publications, Inc. Order online at www.GleimAviation.com.

2.1 DENSITY ALTITUDE

1. **Types of Altitude**

    a. **Absolute altitude** – the vertical distance of the aircraft above the terrain. It is expressed as a number of feet AGL (above ground level).

    b. **True altitude** – the vertical distance of the aircraft above sea level. It is expressed as a number of feet above MSL (mean sea level).

    1) Airport, terrain, and obstacle elevations found on aeronautical charts are given as true altitudes.

    c. **Indicated altitude** – the altitude read directly from the altimeter after it is set to the local altimeter setting.

    1) While indicated altitude is referred to as the height above MSL (i.e., true altitude), it is only an approximate true altitude.

        a) Indicated altitude and true altitude are the same only when the atmospheric conditions and the ISA values are the same.

    d. **Calibrated altitude** – indicated altitude corrected for mechanical errors.

    e. **Pressure altitude** – the altitude indicated on the altimeter when the altimeter setting window is adjusted to the ISA sea-level pressure of 29.92 in. of Hg.

    f. **Density altitude** – the pressure altitude corrected for nonstandard temperature variations.

2. Density altitude increases with

   a. Increases in temperature,
   b. Increases in moisture content (relative humidity) of the air, and
   c. Decreases in pressure.

3. As altitude increases, the indicated airspeed at which a given airplane stalls in a particular configuration will remain the same as at low altitude.

4. The standard lapse rate for pressure is approximately 1 in. mercury (Hg) per 1,000 ft. increase in altitude.

   a. To convert indicated altitude to pressure altitude, subtract the current altimeter setting from 29.92, multiply the result by 1,000, and add this to the indicated altitude.
   b. EXAMPLE: If indicated altitude is 1,850 ft. MSL and the altimeter setting is 30.18, what is the pressure altitude?

   $$29.92 - 30.18 = -.26$$
   $$-.26 \times 1,000 = -260$$
   $$-260 + 1,850 = 1,590 \text{ ft.}$$

5. The following describes the use of a density altitude chart (illustrated in Figure 24 on the next page):

   a. Adjust the airport elevation to pressure altitude based upon the actual altimeter setting in relation to the standard altimeter setting of 29.92.

      1) On the chart, the correction in feet (Pressure Altitude Conversion Factor) is provided for different altimeter settings.

   b. **To adjust the pressure altitude for nonstandard temperature**, plot the intersection of the actual air temperature (on the horizontal axis of the chart) with the pressure altitude lines that slope upward and to the right. The vertical coordinate (on the vertical axis of the chart) of the intersection is the density altitude.

   c. EXAMPLE:
   Outside air temperature (OAT)   30°C
   Altimeter setting   29.40 in. Hg
   Airport elevation   5,515 ft.

   Referring to Figure 24, determine the density altitude to be approximately 9,100 ft. This is found as follows:

      1) The altimeter setting of 29.40 requires a +485-ft. altitude correction factor.
      2) Add 485 to the field elevation of 5,515 ft. to obtain pressure altitude of 6,000 ft.
      3) Locate 30°C OAT on the bottom axis of the chart and move up to intersect the diagonal pressure altitude line of 6,000 ft.
      4) Move horizontally to the left axis of the chart to obtain the density altitude of about 9,100 ft.
      5) Note that, while true altitude is 5,515 ft., density altitude is about 9,100 ft.

SU 2: Airplane Performance

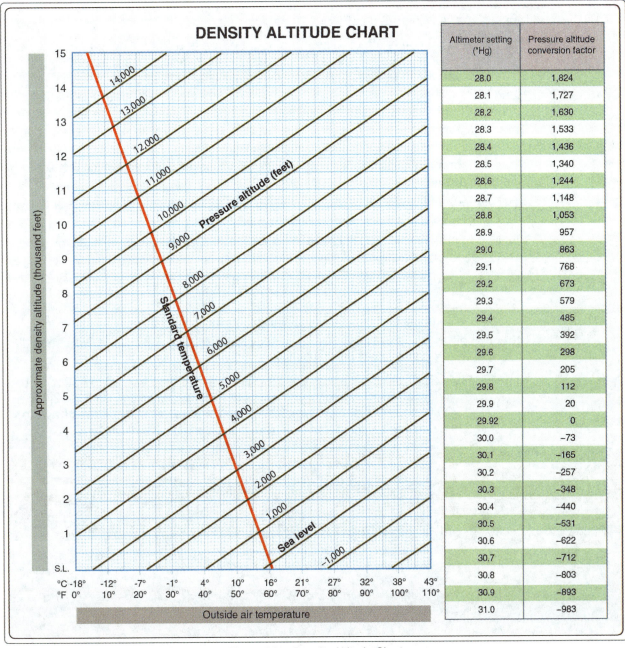

Figure 24. – Density Altitude Chart.

2.2 TAKEOFF DISTANCE

1. During takeoff with high density altitude conditions, the acceleration rate is slower because the engine and propeller efficiency is reduced.

    a. Thus, if pressure and temperature remain constant, an increase in humidity will result in longer takeoff distance because the air is less dense.

2. An uphill runway slope increases the takeoff distance.

3. Increased weight affects the takeoff distance of an airplane because the airplane accelerates more slowly with the same power output and a higher airspeed is required to generate necessary lift for takeoff.

4. Takeoff data charts incorporate several variables, including headwind, gross weight, altitude, and temperature, as illustrated in Figure 26 below.

   a. The length of takeoff is affected by the amount of gross weight. The chart gives the data for gross weight of 2,200, 2,600, and 3,000 lb. If gross weight for your airplane falls between these figures, you must interpolate (paragraph f.).

   b. Headwinds are given as 0, 15, and 30 kt. If the wind velocity lies between these figures, you must interpolate.

   c. Takeoff distances are also given for sea level, 2,500 ft., 5,000 ft., and 7,500 ft. You must interpolate for altitudes between these numbers.

   d. Note that separate distance columns are provided for ground roll and for the total distance required to clear 50-ft. obstacles.

      1) Be careful to determine whether you are being asked for the ground roll (i.e., on the runway) or the distance to clear a 50-ft. obstacle.

   e. Finally, the note at the bottom of the chart says to increase distances 10% for each 14°C above standard temperature at any altitude.

      1) The standard lapse rate is 2°C per 1,000 ft.

         a) EXAMPLE: Standard temperature at 2,500 ft. is 10°C, so the standard temperature at 3,500 ft. is approximately 8°C (10 – 2).

   f. When variables are presented that do not coincide exactly with a chart, you should interpolate (i.e., compute the difference).

      1) EXAMPLE: If your gross weight is 2,800 lb. with no headwind at 5,000 ft. and 5°C, your ground roll will be 848 ft. This is halfway between 705 ft. at 2,600 lb. and 990 ft. at 3,000 lb. However, if the temperature is 19°C, you will have to add 10%, or 85 ft. Thus, your total ground roll will be 933 ft. at 19°C.

Takeoff data

Takeoff distance with 10° flaps from hard-surfaced runway

Gross weight LB	KIAS at 50 feet	Head wind KTS	At sea level & 15 °C		At 2,500 feet & 10 °C		At 5,000 feet & 5 °C		At 7,500 feet & 0 °C	
			Ground roll	Total to clear 50' OBS	Ground roll	Total to clear 50' OBS	Ground roll	Total to clear 50' OBS	Ground roll	Total to clear 50' OBS
2200	55	0	345	680	405	770	480	885	580	1040
		15	205	460	245	525	295	615	365	725
		30	100	275	120	320	155	380	195	460
2600	60	0	500	915	585	1045	705	1230	855	1470
		15	310	635	370	735	455	870	560	1055
		30	165	395	200	465	255	565	325	695
3000	64	0	695	1210	820	1405	990	1675	1205	2045
		15	450	855	535	1005	660	1215	815	1505
		30	250	555	310	665	390	820	500	1030

Note: Increase distances 10% for each 14 °C above standard temperature for particular altitude.

Figure 26. – Takeoff Data Chart.

5. Another chart appearing on this written test is "Short-field takeoff distance chart," which appears as Figure 28 on the next page.

   a. Three temperatures appear across the top: 20°C, 30°C, and 40°C.

   b. Three weights appear along the left side: 5,500 lb., 5,100 lb., and 4,700 lb.

   c. For each of these weights, there are pressure altitudes of sea level to 10,000 ft. in 1,000 ft. intervals.

SU 2: Airplane Performance

d. As a result, for a given temperature, weight, and pressure altitude, you can determine "short-field takeoff distance," making additional adjustments for
  1) Use of a sod runway
  2) Any headwind
  3) Any tailwind
e. EXAMPLE: If the conditions are described as OAT of 20°C, weight of 5,500 lb., and a pressure altitude of 1,000 ft., use the second line for 5,500 lb. and 1,000 ft. The ground roll is 1,530 ft. and total distance over a 50-ft. obstacle is 1,950 ft.
f. Note that interpolation is required if the conditions do not coincide with the numbers prescribed in the chart.

Short-field takeoff distance

Conditions:
1. Power—FULL THROTTLE and 2700 rpm before releasing brakes.
2. Mixtures—LEAN for field elevation.
3. Cow flaps—OPEN.
4. Wing flaps—UP.
5. Level, dry, hard-surface runway.

Note:
1. Increase total distance 8% for operation on dry, sod runway.
2. Decrease total distance 7% for each 10 knots of headwind.
3. Increase total distance 5% for each 2 knots of tailwind.

Weight LB	Takeoff to 50 foot obstacle speed KIAS	Pressure altitude feet	20 °C		30 °C		40 °C	
			Ground roll feet	Total distance to clear 50' OBS	Ground roll feet	Total distance to clear 50' OBS	Ground roll feet	Total distance to clear 50' OBS
5500	82	Sea level	1390	1760	1490	1890	1590	2020
		1,000	1530	1950	1640	2080	1760	2230
		2,000	1680	2150	1810	2300	1940	2470
		3,000	1860	2380	2000	2550	2150	2750
		4,000	2060	2650	2220	2850	2380	3070
		5,000	2280	2950	2460	3190	2640	3450
		6,000	2530	3310	2730	3590	2950	3900
		7,000	2830	3750	3160	4190	3410	4570
		8,000	3280	4420	3540	4840	3830	5330
		9,000	3690	5170	4000	5730	4330	6420
		10,000	4150	6140	4500	6980	4880	8130
5100	78	Sea level	1160	1470	1240	1570	1330	1680
		1,000	1280	1620	1370	1730	1470	1850
		2,000	1400	1780	1500	1910	1610	2040
		3,000	1550	1960	1660	2100	1780	2260
		4,000	1710	2180	1840	2340	1970	2510
		5,000	1890	2410	2030	2590	2180	2790
		6,000	2090	2690	2250	2890	2420	3120
		7,000	2330	3010	2510	3250	2700	3520
		8,000	2600	3400	2800	3690	3030	4010
		9,000	2920	3890	3270	4360	3530	4760
		10,000	3390	4580	3660	5030	3960	5560
4700	75	Sea level	960	1220	1020	1300	1090	1380
		1,000	1050	1340	1120	1430	1200	1520
		2,000	1150	1460	1230	1560	1320	1670
		3,000	1270	1610	1360	1720	1460	1840
		4,000	1400	1770	1500	1900	1610	2030
		5,000	1540	1960	1650	2100	1780	2250
		6,000	1700	2170	1830	2330	1970	2500
		7,000	1890	2410	2030	2590	2190	2790
		8,000	2100	2700	2260	2910	2440	3140
		9,000	2350	3040	2540	3290	2730	3570
		10,000	2620	3430	2830	3730	3060	4060

Figure 28. – Short-Field Takeoff Distance Chart.

g. Aircraft performance charts have been tested by the aircraft manufacturer and have known values for their aircraft performance limitations. These values are what is seen on the manufacturer's published performance charts.

1) If values go beyond the charts, do not attempt a takeoff until conditions permit calculations that remain within the limitations of the published charts.
2) Some charts require interpolation to find the information for specific flight conditions. Interpolating information means that by taking the known information, a pilot can compute intermediate information. If the density altitude computed via interpolation is beyond capability as indicated on the performance chart, do not attempt takeoff until conditions permit calculations to provide the data to determine a safe takeoff and climb out.
3) It is not safe to extrapolate beyond the chart values, as that area has not been tested.

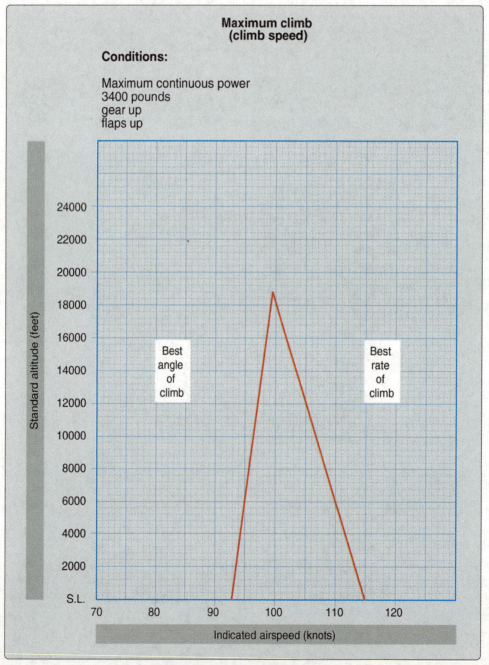

Figure 27. – Maximum Climb Chart.

SU 2: Airplane Performance

2.3 MAXIMUM CLIMB

1. The **best rate-of-climb speed** provides the greatest gain in altitude in a unit of time.
2. The **best angle-of-climb speed** provides the greatest gain in altitude for a given distance.
3. These climb speeds can be provided in a graph, such as Figure 27 on the previous page.
    a. Note the best rate-of-climb airspeed decreases approximately 0.8 kt. per 1,000-ft. increase of altitude.
    b. EXAMPLE: At 6,000 ft., the best angle-of-climb airspeed is 95 KIAS and the best rate-of-climb airspeed is 110 KIAS. At 12,000 ft., the best angle-of-climb airspeed is 97 KIAS and the best rate-of-climb airspeed is 105 KIAS.

2.4 TRUE AIRSPEED

1. When flying at a constant power setting and constant indicated altitude, a decrease in outside air temperature will
    a. Decrease the true airspeed and
    b. Decrease the true altitude.
2. When flying at a constant power setting and constant indicated altitude, an increase in outside air temperature will
    a. Increase the true airspeed and
    b. Increase the true altitude.
3. As density altitude increases with a constant indicated airspeed, true airspeed increases.
    a. In a no-wind situation, groundspeed also increases.
4. In a propeller-driven airplane, maximum range occurs at maximum lift/drag ratio.

2.5 MULTI-ENGINE PERFORMANCE

1. The critical engine on most light multi-engine airplanes with clockwise rotating propellers is the left engine because of the P-factor of the right propeller.
    a. The center of thrust of the right engine is farther away from the centerline of the fuselage than is the center of thrust of the left engine.
2. When one engine fails on a light twin-engine airplane, the resulting performance loss may reduce the rate of climb by 80% or more.
3. The blue radial line on the airspeed indicator of a light multi-engine airplane indicates the speed that will provide the maximum altitude gain in a given time when one engine is inoperative.
    a. It should be used for climb and final approach during engine-out operations.
4. When operating a light multi-engine airplane at V_{MC}, the pilot should expect performance to be sufficient to maintain heading only.
    a. V_{MC} means minimum controllable airspeed with the critical engine inoperative.
        1) V_{MC} is the calibrated airspeed at which, when the critical engine is suddenly made inoperative, it is possible to maintain control of the airplane.
        2) At V_{MC}, you will be able to maintain straight flight with an angle of bank of not more than 5°.
    b. V_{MC} decreases with altitude on reciprocating, nonturbocharged light twin-engine airplanes.
    c. Banking toward the inoperative engine increases V_{MC}.
    d. V_{MC} is the highest when the CG is at the most rearward allowable position.

5. In a twin-engine airplane, the single-engine service ceiling is the maximum density altitude at which V_{YSE} will produce a 50-fpm rate of climb.

   a. V_{YSE} is the best rate of climb speed with one engine inoperative.

2.6 GLIDE DISTANCE

1. For a given airplane configuration (e.g., flaps, gear, propeller, and at a specified glide speed), the glide distance in zero wind can be determined.

2. These data are frequently provided in airplane operating manuals as a graph, as in Figure 29 below.

3. Thus, given any altitude, you can determine the glide distance and make appropriate adjustments (as specified in the notes) for headwinds and tailwinds.

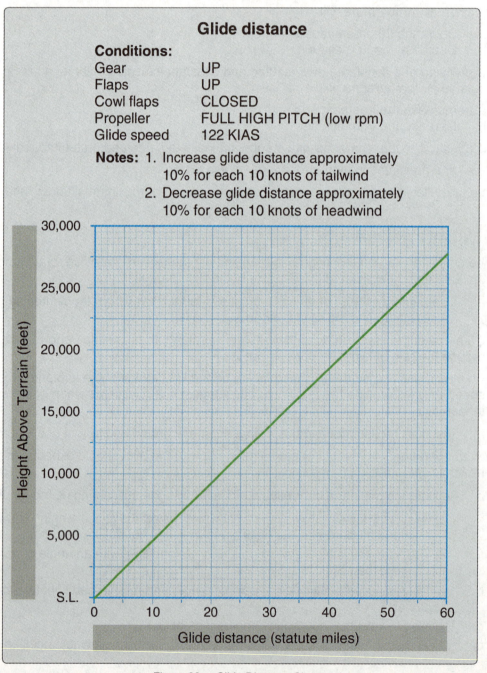

Figure 29. – Glide Distance Chart.

2.7 STALL SPEED

1. An airspeed calibration table is provided in airplane operating manuals so you can convert stall speed at calibrated airspeed (CAS) to indicated airspeed (IAS) in various airplane configurations with respect to flap angles and landing gear position, as illustrated in Figure 25 below.
2. EXAMPLE: If you are determining the stall speed in a 40° angle of bank with gear down and 15° flaps, the calibrated airspeed is 92 kt. Then, looking up at the airspeed calibration table, determine that 94 KCAS is 90 KIAS, or a correction of 4 kt. Apply that correction to 92 KCAS to determine an indicated stall speed of 88 kt.

Airspeed calibration—Normal system

Flaps 0°		Flaps 15°		Flaps 45°	
KIAS	KCAS	KIAS	KCAS	KIAS	KCAS
80	84	70	79	70	76
100	102	80	86	80	84
120	122	90	94	90	93
140	141	100	103	100	102
160	161	110	112	110	111
180	181	120	121	120	120
200	201	130	131	130	129
220	221	140	141	140	138
240	242	150	151		

KIAS—indicated airspeed in knots
KCAS—calibrated airspeed in knots

Stall speeds—KCAS   4,600 lb gross weight

Configuration	Angle of bank			
	0°	20°	40°	60°
Gear and flaps up	84	87	97	119
Gear down and flaps 15°	80	83	92	113
Gear down and flaps 45°	76	79	87	108

Figure 25. – Airspeed Calibration Stalls/Speeds Chart.

2.8 LANDING DISTANCE

1. Density altitude has an effect on landing performance.

   a. When landing at an airport located in the mountains, a pilot can expect higher true airspeed and a longer landing distance.

2. Landing distance information is given in airplane operating manuals in chart or graph form with sufficient data to adjust for headwind, temperature, and dry grass runways.

   a. It is imperative that you distinguish between total landing distance over a 50-ft. obstacle and ground roll distance.

3. Figure 31 on the next page illustrates a landing-distance graph.

   a. The graph shows total landing distance over a 50-ft. obstacle.

   b. The note on the graph states that ground roll is approximately 53% of total landing distance over a 50-ft. obstacle.

   c. EXAMPLE: Use the example data on the chart in Figure 31 to find the total landing distance over a 50-ft. obstacle.

       OAT: 27°C
       Pressure Altitude: 4,000 ft.
       Weight: 3,200 lb.
       Headwind: 10 kt.

   1) On the bottom left side of the chart, begin at 27°C and move up to the pressure altitude of 4,000 ft. Proceed horizontally to the first reference line, then up, parallel to the sloping line, to 3,200 lb. Next, proceed horizontally to the right to the second reference line. Since the headwind is 10 kt., move parallel to the headwind lines down to 10 kt. Finally, move horizontally to the right edge of the chart to determine the landing distance of approximately 1,475 ft. over a 50-ft. obstacle.

   2) If the question asks for ground roll, remember you must multiply by 53%. Here, the ground roll distance is 782 ft. (1,475 ft. × 53%).

SU 2: Airplane Performance

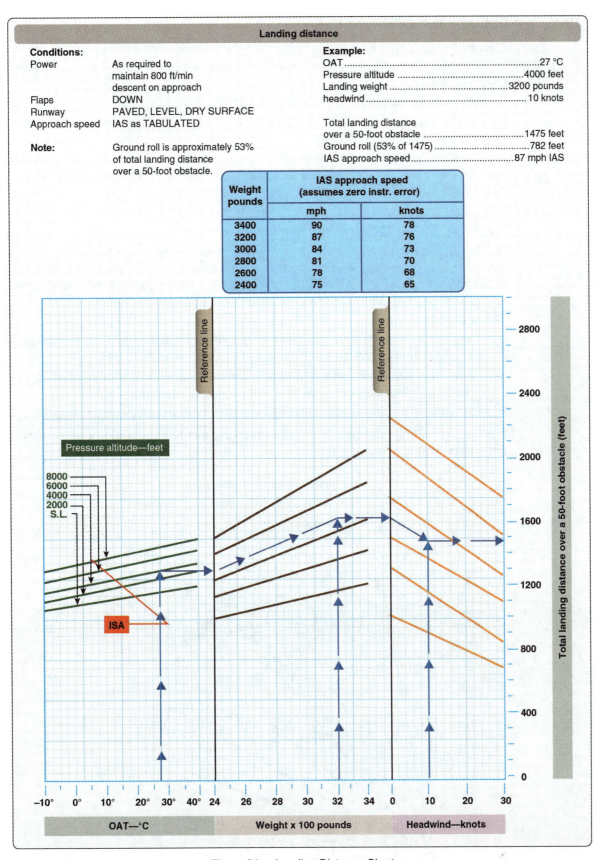

Figure 31. – Landing Distance Chart.

2.9 CROSSWIND/HEADWIND COMPONENTS

1. Each airplane has an upper limit to the amount of direct crosswind in which it can land. Crosswinds of less than 90° (i.e., less than direct) can be converted into a 90° component by the use of charts.

    a. Variables on the crosswind component charts are the
       1) Angle between wind direction and runway and
       2) Knots of total wind velocity.
    b. Both variables are plotted on the graph. The coordinates on the vertical and horizontal axes of the graph will indicate the headwind and crosswind components of a quartering wind.

2. Refer to the wind component chart, which is Figure 30 below.

    a. EXAMPLE: A 40-kt. wind at a 30° angle.
    b. Find the 30° wind-angle line. This is the angle between the wind direction and runway direction, e.g., between wind from 190° and runway 16 (RWY 16 means that, when landing, your course is 160° magnetic, measured clockwise from magnetic north).
    c. Find the 40-kt. wind velocity arc. Note the intersection of the wind arc and the 30° angle line.
       1) Drop straight down to determine the crosswind component of 20 kt.; landing in this situation would be like having a direct crosswind of 20 kt.
       2) Move horizontally to the left to determine the headwind component of 35 kt.; landing in this situation would be like having a headwind of 35 kt.

3. Many airplanes have a maximum demonstrated crosswind component equal to 0.2 V_{so}.

    a. Multiply V_{so} by .2 and compare the answer to the existing crosswind component to see if the maximum is exceeded.

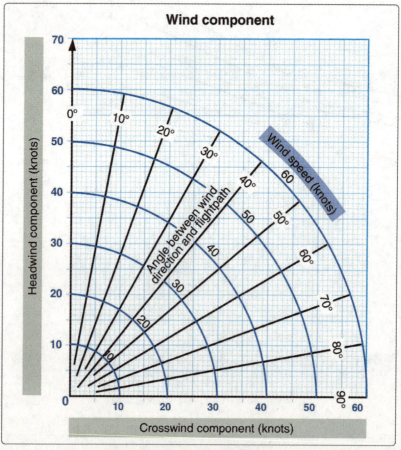

Figure 30. – Wind Component Chart.

SU 2: Airplane Performance

QUESTIONS AND ANSWER EXPLANATIONS: All of the AGI/CFI knowledge test questions chosen by the FAA for release as well as additional questions selected by Gleim relating to the material in the previous outlines are reproduced on the following pages. These questions have been organized into the same subunits as the outlines. To the immediate right of each question are the correct answer and answer explanation. You should cover these answers and answer explanations while responding to the questions. Refer to the general discussion in the Introduction on how to take the FAA knowledge test.

Remember that the questions from the FAA knowledge test bank have been reordered by topic and organized into a meaningful sequence. Also, the first line of the answer explanation gives the citation of the authoritative source for the answer.

QUESTIONS

2.1 Density Altitude

1. Density altitude increases with

    A. an increase in temperature only.
    B. increases in pressure, temperature, and moisture content of the air.
    C. increases in temperature and moisture content of the air, and a decrease in pressure.

Answer (C) is correct. *(PHAK Chap 4)*
   DISCUSSION: Density altitude varies inversely with pressure and directly with humidity and temperature. That is, an increase in the relative humidity and/or an increase in temperature would increase density altitude. It varies inversely with barometric pressure. An increase in pressure would decrease density altitude.
   Answer (A) is incorrect. An increase in humidity and a decrease in pressure also increases density altitude. Answer (B) is incorrect. An increase in pressure will decrease, not increase, density altitude.

2. What would increase the density altitude at a given airport?

    A. An increase in air temperature.
    B. A decrease in relative humidity.
    C. An increase in atmospheric pressure.

Answer (A) is correct. *(PHAK Chap 4)*
   DISCUSSION: When air temperature increases, density altitude increases because, at a higher temperature, the air is less dense.
   Answer (B) is incorrect. Density altitude decreases as relative humidity decreases. Answer (C) is incorrect. Density altitude would decrease with an increase in atmospheric pressure.

3. As altitude increases, the indicated airspeed at which a given airplane stalls in a particular configuration will

    A. remain the same as at low altitude.
    B. decrease as the true airspeed increases.
    C. increase because the air density decreases.

Answer (A) is correct. *(PHAK Chap 4)*
   DISCUSSION: The airspeed indicator is operated by impact air. At higher altitudes, air is less dense, so a less-than-true airspeed is indicated. The decreased air impact on the airspeed indicator at higher altitudes corresponds to the decreased lift produced by the wings in the thinner air. Thus, the airplane stalls at the same indicated airspeed.
   Answer (B) is incorrect. The indicated stall speed, determined by impact pressure, remains the same (does not increase). Answer (C) is incorrect. Indicated stall speed, determined by impact pressure, remains the same (does not decrease).

4. An altimeter indicates 1,850 feet MSL when set to 30.18. What is the approximate pressure altitude?

    A. 1,590 feet.
    B. 1,824 feet.
    C. 2,110 feet.

Answer (A) is correct. *(PHAK Chap 8)*
   DISCUSSION: First, to find the correct conversion factor, you must subtract the current altimeter setting of 30.18 from standard pressure of 29.92, resulting in –.26. Since the standard lapse rate for pressure is approximately 1 in. Hg/1,000 ft. increase in altitude, you must now multiply –.26 by 1,000 to find the altitude in feet. By doing this, the figure comes to –260 ft., which must now be subtracted (since it is a negative number) from the indicated MSL altitude of 1,850 ft. This results in a pressure altitude of 1,590 ft. (1,850 – 260).
   Answer (B) is incorrect. In the conversion, –.26 must be multiplied by 1,000, not 100 (remember, 1 in. Hg equals approximately 1,000 ft. in altitude). Answer (C) is incorrect. You must subtract, not add, the 260 ft. from 1,850.

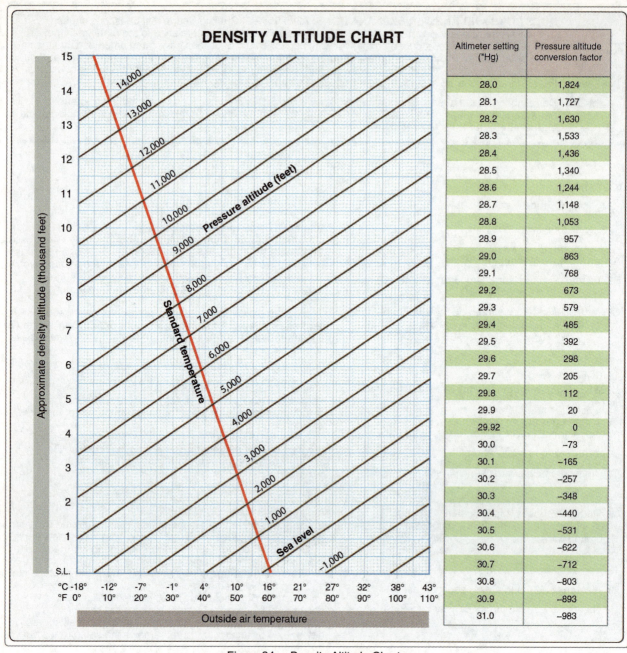

Figure 24. – Density Altitude Chart.

5. (Refer to Figure 24 above.) Determine the density altitude.

Airport elevation	5,515 ft
OAT	30°C
Altimeter setting	29.40" Hg

A. 6,000 feet.
B. 8,450 feet.
C. 9,100 feet.

Answer (C) is correct. *(PHAK Chap 4)*
DISCUSSION: With an altimeter setting of 29.40 in. Hg, 485 ft. must be added to the field elevation of 5,515 ft. to obtain a pressure altitude of 6,000 ft. On the chart, find the point at which the pressure altitude line for 6,000 ft. crosses the 30°C line. The density altitude at that point shows 9,100 ft. on the scale at the far left.
Answer (A) is incorrect. This is the pressure, not density, altitude. Answer (B) is incorrect. This is the density altitude without applying the pressure altitude conversion factor of +485 ft. to the airport elevation.

SU 2: Airplane Performance

6. (Refer to Figure 24 on page 66.) Determine the density altitude.

Airport elevation	3,795 ft
OAT	24°C
Altimeter setting	29.70" Hg

A. 5,700 feet.
B. 5,900 feet.
C. 4,000 feet.

Answer (B) is correct. *(PHAK Chap 4)*
DISCUSSION: With an altimeter setting of 29.70 in. Hg, 205 ft. must be added to the field elevation of 3,795 ft. to obtain a pressure altitude of 4,000 ft. On the chart, find the point at which the pressure altitude line for 4,000 ft. crosses the 24°C line. The density altitude at that point shows about 5,900 ft. on the scale at the far left. The approximate density altitude chart supplied by the FAA has known errors. We want you to be prepared to use this chart on your FAA exam. Gleim recommends using your E6B flight computer along with the pressure altitude conversion factor table to calculate density altitude accurately.
 Answer (A) is incorrect. This is the density altitude without applying the pressure altitude conversion factor of +205 to the airport elevation. Answer (C) is incorrect. This is the pressure, not density, altitude.

7. (Refer to Figure 24 on page 66.) Determine the density altitude.

Airport elevation	3,450 ft
OAT	35°C
Altimeter setting	30.40" Hg

A. 3,400 feet.
B. 6,650 feet.
C. 5,950 feet.

Answer (C) is correct. *(PHAK Chap 4)*
DISCUSSION: With an altimeter setting of 30.40 in. Hg, 440 ft. must be subtracted from the field elevation of 3,450 ft. to obtain a pressure altitude of 3,010 ft. On the chart, find the point at which the pressure altitude line for 3,010 ft. crosses the 35°C line. The density altitude at that point shows about 5,950 ft. on the scale at the far left.
 Answer (A) is incorrect. This is approximately the airport elevation, not the density altitude. Answer (B) is incorrect. This is the calculated altitude if the conversion factor of 440 ft. is incorrectly added instead of subtracted.

8. (Refer to Figure 24 on page 66.) What is the effect of a temperature increase from 30 to 50°F on the density altitude if the pressure altitude remains at 3,000 feet MSL?

A. 900-foot increase.
B. 1,100-foot decrease.
C. 1,300-foot increase.

Answer (C) is correct. *(PHAK Chap 4)*
DISCUSSION: On the chart, find the point where both 30°F and 50°F intersect the pressure altitude line for 3,000 ft. The two density altitude values for those conditions appear on the scale at the far left. The density altitude at 30°F is 1,700 feet, and the density altitude at 50°F is 3,000 ft. The difference between these values (when the temperature is increased from 30°F to 50°F) is an increase of 1,300 ft.
 Answer (A) is incorrect. A 900-ft. increase would occur if the temperature were only increased to 43°F (6°C), instead of 50°F (10°C). Answer (B) is incorrect. A 1,100-ft. decrease would occur if the temperature were reduced from 50°F (10°C) to 32°F (0°C), instead of 30°F (–1°C).

9. (Refer to Figure 24 on page 66.) Determine the pressure altitude at an airport that is 3,563 feet MSL with an altimeter setting of 29.96.

A. 3,527 feet MSL.
B. 3,556 feet MSL.
C. 3,639 feet MSL.

Answer (A) is correct. *(PHAK Chap 11)*
DISCUSSION: You must first find the pressure altitude conversion factor. On the right side of the chart, notice that 29.96 is not listed. You must interpolate between 30.0 and 29.92 to find the correct conversion factor. A setting of 29.96 is exactly in the middle of these two values. Therefore, the pressure altitude conversion factor will be halfway between –73 and 0, as shown in the rightmost column. Divide –73 in half to arrive at a pressure altitude conversion factor of –36.5 ft. Because it is a negative value, subtract 36.5 from the original altitude of 3,563 ft. to arrive at a pressure altitude of 3,527 ft.
 Answer (B) is incorrect. This would require a pressure altitude conversion factor of –7 ft. Answer (C) is incorrect. This would require a pressure altitude conversion factor of 76 ft.

10. What is pressure altitude?

A. The indicated altitude corrected for position and installation error.
B. The altitude indicated when the barometric pressure scale is set to 29.92.
C. The indicated altitude corrected for nonstandard temperature and pressure.

Answer (B) is correct. *(PHAK Chap 8)*
DISCUSSION: Pressure altitude is the airplane's height above the standard datum plane of 29.92" Hg. If the altimeter is set to 29.92" Hg, the indicated altitude is the pressure altitude.
 Answer (A) is incorrect. "Corrected for position and installation error" is used to define calibrated airspeed, not a type of altitude. Answer (C) is incorrect. It describes density altitude.

11. Under what condition is indicated altitude the same as true altitude?

A. If the altimeter has no mechanical error.
B. When at sea level under standard conditions.
C. When at 18,000 feet MSL with the altimeter set at 29.92.

Answer (B) is correct. *(PHAK Chap 8)*
DISCUSSION: Indicated altitude is the altitude read off of the altimeter when it is set to the local pressure setting. True altitude is the actual vertical distance of the airplane above mean sea level (MSL). These two values can only be the same when standard atmospheric conditions exist.
Answer (A) is incorrect. A lack of mechanical errors relates to calibrated altitude, which corrects indicated altitude. However, it does not correct the altitude to true altitude. Answer (C) is incorrect. Setting the altimeter to 29.92 when at 18,000 feet MSL indicates a pressure altitude, not true altitude above MSL.

12. What is true altitude?

A. The vertical distance of the aircraft above sea level.
B. The vertical distance of the aircraft above the surface.
C. The height above the standard datum plane.

Answer (A) is correct. *(PHAK Chap 8)*
DISCUSSION: True altitude is defined as the vertical distance of the aircraft above sea level.
Answer (B) is incorrect. The vertical distance of the aircraft above the surface is absolute, not true altitude. Answer (C) is incorrect. The height of the aircraft above the standard datum plane is pressure, not true altitude.

13. What is absolute altitude?

A. The altitude read directly from the altimeter.
B. The vertical distance of the aircraft above the surface.
C. The height above the standard datum plane.

Answer (B) is correct. *(PHAK Chap 8)*
DISCUSSION: Absolute altitude is defined as the vertical distance of the aircraft above the surface.
Answer (A) is incorrect. The altitude read directly from the altimeter is indicated, not absolute altitude. Answer (C) is incorrect. The height of the aircraft above the standard datum plane is pressure, not absolute altitude.

14. Density altitude may be determined by correcting

A. true altitude for nonstandard temperature.
B. pressure altitude for nonstandard temperature.
C. indicated altitude for temperature variations.

Answer (B) is correct. *(PHAK Chap 4)*
DISCUSSION: Density altitude is pressure altitude adjusted for nonstandard temperature. Pressure altitude is the height above the standard pressure plane. It is true altitude corrected for nonstandard pressure.
Answer (A) is incorrect. Density altitude is pressure, not true, altitude corrected for nonstandard temperature. Answer (C) is incorrect. Density altitude is pressure, not indicated, altitude corrected for nonstandard temperature.

15. What effect does high density altitude, as compared to low density altitude, have on propeller efficiency and why?

A. Efficiency is increased due to less friction on the propeller blades.
B. Efficiency is reduced because the propeller exerts less force at high density altitudes than at low density altitudes.
C. Efficiency is reduced due to the increased force of the propeller in the thinner air.

Answer (B) is correct. *(PHAK Chap 4)*
DISCUSSION: At density altitudes, the air density is decreased. There is, in effect, less air to move through the propeller, thus decreasing its efficiency.
Answer (A) is incorrect. Propeller efficiency decreases with an increase in altitude. Answer (C) is incorrect. The force (thrust) of the propeller is decreased in thinner air.

16. Which combination of atmospheric conditions will reduce aircraft takeoff and climb performance?

A. Low temperature, low relative humidity, and low density altitude.
B. High temperature, low relative humidity, and low density altitude.
C. High temperature, high relative humidity, and high density altitude.

Answer (C) is correct. *(PHAK Chap 11)*
DISCUSSION: Takeoff and climb performance are reduced by high density altitude. High density altitude is a result of high temperatures and high relative humidity.
Answer (A) is incorrect. Low temperature, low relative humidity, and low density altitude all improve airplane performance. Answer (B) is incorrect. Low relative humidity and low density altitude both improve airplane performance.

17. If the outside air temperature (OAT) at a given altitude is warmer than standard, the density altitude is

A. equal to pressure altitude.
B. lower than pressure altitude.
C. higher than pressure altitude.

Answer (C) is correct. *(PHAK Chap 11)*
   DISCUSSION: When temperature increases, the air expands and therefore becomes less dense. This decrease in density means a higher density altitude. Pressure altitude is based on standard temperature. Thus, density altitude exceeds pressure altitude when the temperature is warmer than standard.
   Answer (A) is incorrect. Density altitude equals pressure altitude only when temperature is standard. Answer (B) is incorrect. Density altitude is lower than pressure altitude when the temperature is below standard.

18. What effect does high density altitude have on aircraft performance?

A. It increases engine performance.
B. It reduces climb performance.
C. It increases takeoff performance.

Answer (B) is correct. *(PHAK Chap 11)*
   DISCUSSION: High density altitude reduces all aspects of an airplane's performance, including takeoff and climb performance.
   Answer (A) is incorrect. Engine performance is decreased (not increased). Answer (C) is incorrect. Takeoff runway length is increased, i.e., reduces takeoff performance.

2.2 Takeoff Distance

19. If the atmospheric pressure and temperature remain the same, how would an increase in humidity affect takeoff performance?

A. Longer takeoff distance; the air is more dense.
B. Longer takeoff distance; the air is less dense.
C. Shorter takeoff distance; the air is more dense.

Answer (B) is correct. *(PHAK Chap 11)*
   DISCUSSION: An increase in humidity decreases the density of air. Propeller, engine, and lift efficiency decrease, so a longer takeoff distance is required to obtain liftoff speed.
   Answer (A) is incorrect. A longer takeoff distance is the result of less, not more, dense air. Answer (C) is incorrect. Although a shorter takeoff distance is the result of denser air, an increase in humidity decreases air density, thereby increasing the takeoff distance.

20. Which statement is true regarding takeoff performance with high density altitude conditions?

A. The acceleration rate will increase since the lighter air creates less drag.
B. The acceleration rate is slower because the engine and propeller efficiency is reduced.
C. A higher-than-normal indicated airspeed is required to produce sufficient lift since the air is less dense.

Answer (B) is correct. *(PHAK Chap 11)*
   DISCUSSION: During takeoff in high-density altitude conditions, the acceleration rate is slower because both the engine and propeller efficiency are reduced by the less dense air.
   Answer (A) is incorrect. The decrease in drag does not offset the decrease in propeller and engine efficiency. Answer (C) is incorrect. At higher altitudes, the true airspeed must be greater, but the indicated airspeed for takeoff is the same at all density altitudes.

21. (Refer to Figure 26 on page 71.) Determine the ground roll required for takeoff.

Temperature	24°C
Pressure altitude	2,500 ft
Weight	2,400 lb
Headwind	25 kts

A. 256 feet.
B. 370 feet.
C. 230 feet.

Answer (C) is correct. *(PHAK Chap 11)*
DISCUSSION: To determine the ground roll required for takeoff, you must interpolate the distances for weight and headwind. Then adjust for the above standard temperature.

1. The schedule below interpolates the ground roll distances for a 15-kt. and 30-kt. headwind at a weight of 2,400 lb., which is 50% of the difference between 2,200 lb. and 2,600 lb.

	15 kt.	30 kt.
At 2,200 lb.	245 ft.	120 ft.
At 2,600 lb.	370 ft.	200 ft.
Difference	125 ft.	80 ft.
50% of difference	63 ft.	40 ft.
Add difference to 2,200-lb. value to obtain 2,400-lb. value	308 ft.	160 ft.

2. Now interpolate for a 25-kt. headwind, which is 2/3 (66%) of the difference between 15 kt. and 30 kt. The difference in the distances computed in the schedule is 148 ft. (308 − 160). Determine that 66% of 148 ft. is 98 ft. Subtract 98 ft. from 308 ft. to determine a ground roll distance of 210 ft.

3. Since the temperature is 24°C and the standard temperature at 2,500 ft. is 10°C, you must increase the ground roll distance by 10% per the note at the bottom of Fig. 26. Thus, the ground roll distance required is 231 ft. (210 × 1.1).

Answer (A) is incorrect. This is the approximate ground roll with a weight of 2,600 lb., not 2,400 lb., with a 25-kt. headwind at a pressure altitude of 2,500 ft. and a temperature of 10°C, not 24°C. Answer (B) is incorrect. This is the ground roll at a pressure altitude of 2,500 ft.; at 10°C, not 24°C; with a 15-kt., not a 25-kt., headwind; and at 2,600 lb., not 2,400 lb.

22. (Refer to Figure 26 on page 71.) Determine the ground roll required for takeoff.

Temperature	25°C
Pressure altitude	2,000 ft
Weight	2,200 lb
Headwind	15 kts

A. 205 feet.
B. 261 feet.
C. 237 feet.

Answer (B) is correct. *(PHAK Chap 11)*
DISCUSSION: To determine the ground roll required for takeoff, you must interpolate for the pressure altitude and then adjust for the above-standard temperature.

1. Interpolate for a pressure altitude of 2,000 ft., which is 4/5 (80%) of the difference between sea level and 2,500 ft., at a weight of 2,200 lb. and with a 15-kt. headwind.

	Distance
At sea level	205 ft.
At 2,500 ft.	245 ft.
Difference	40 ft.
80% of difference	32 ft.
Add difference to sea-level distance to obtain the 2,000-ft. distance	237 ft.

2. The standard temperature at 2,000 ft. can be determined by subtracting the standard lapse rate of 2°C per 1,000 ft. from the sea-level standard temperature of 15°C. Thus, at 2,000 ft. the standard lapse rate decreases 4°C (2° × 2°) to a temperature of 11°C (15° − 4°). Since 25°C is 14°C above standard temperature, you must increase the ground roll distance by 10% per the note at the bottom of Fig. 26. Thus, the ground roll distance required for takeoff is 261 ft. (237 × 1.1).

Answer (A) is incorrect. This is the ground roll required for takeoff at sea level and 15°C, not at a pressure altitude of 2,000 ft. and 25°C. Answer (C) is incorrect. This is the ground roll required with a weight of 2,200 lb., a 15-kt. headwind, pressure altitude of 2,000 ft., and a temperature of 11°C, not 25°C.

23. (Refer to Figure 26 below.) Determine the takeoff distance required to clear a 50-foot obstacle.

Temperature	23°C
Pressure altitude	3,000 ft
Weight	2,400 lb
Headwind	15 kts

A. 754 feet.
B. 718 feet.
C. 653 feet.

Answer (B) is correct. *(PHAK Chap 11)*
DISCUSSION: To determine the total takeoff distance to clear a 50-ft. obstacle, you must interpolate the distance for weight and pressure altitude. Then you must adjust for the above-standard temperature.

1. The schedule below interpolates the ground roll distances for pressure altitudes of 2,500 ft. and 5,000 ft. at a weight of 2,400 lb., which is 50% of the difference between 2,200 lb. and 2,600 lb.

	2,500 ft.	5,000 ft.
At 2,200 lb.	525 ft.	615 ft.
At 2,600 lb.	735 ft.	870 ft.
Difference	210 ft.	255 ft.
50% of difference	105 ft.	128 ft.
Add difference to 2,200-lb. value to obtain the 2,400-lb. value	630 ft.	743 ft.

2. Now interpolate for a pressure altitude of 3,000 ft., which is 1/5 (20%) of the difference between 2,500 ft. and 5,000 ft. The difference in the distances computed in the schedule is 113 ft. (743 − 630). Determine that 20% of 113 ft. is 23 ft. (113 × .2). Add 23 ft. to the 2,500-ft. value to obtain 653 ft.

3. The standard temperature at 3,000 ft. can be determined by subtracting the standard lapse rate of 2°C per 1,000 ft. from the sea-level standard temperature of 15°C. Thus, at 3,000 ft. the standard temperature is 6°C less (3 × 2) than sea level, or 9°C (15 − 6). Since 23°C is 14°C above standard temperature, you must increase the total takeoff distance by 10% per the note at the bottom of Fig. 26. Thus, the total takeoff distance required to clear a 50-ft. obstacle is 718 ft. (653 × 1.1).

Answer (A) is incorrect. This is the approximate total takeoff distance required to clear a 50-ft. obstacle at a pressure altitude of 3,750 ft. and at 14°C above standard temperature, not at a pressure altitude of 3,000 ft. Answer (C) is incorrect. The takeoff distance required at standard temperature is 653 ft. This figure must be adjusted for a temperature that is 14°C above standard temperature as specified in the note at the bottom of Fig. 26.

Takeoff data
Takeoff distance with 10° flaps from hard-surfaced runway

Gross weight LB	KIAS at 50 feet	Head wind KTS	At sea level & 15 °C		At 2,500 feet & 10 °C		At 5,000 feet & 5 °C		At 7,500 feet & 0 °C	
			Ground roll	Total to clear 50' OBS	Ground roll	Total to clear 50' OBS	Ground roll	Total to clear 50' OBS	Ground roll	Total to clear 50' OBS
2200	55	0	345	680	405	770	480	885	580	1040
		15	205	460	245	525	295	615	365	725
		30	100	275	120	320	155	380	195	460
2600	60	0	500	915	585	1045	705	1230	855	1470
		15	310	635	370	735	455	870	560	1055
		30	165	395	200	465	255	565	325	695
3000	64	0	695	1210	820	1405	990	1675	1205	2045
		15	450	855	535	1005	660	1215	815	1505
		30	250	555	310	665	390	820	500	1030

Note: Increase distances 10% for each 14 °C above standard temperature for particular altitude.

Figure 26. – Takeoff Data Chart.

24. (Refer to Figure 26 below.) Determine the takeoff distance required to clear a 50-foot obstacle.

Temperature	3°C
Pressure altitude	6,000 ft
Weight	3,000 lb
Headwind	15 kts

A. 1,464 feet.
B. 1,215 feet.
C. 1,331 feet.

Answer (C) is correct. *(PHAK Chap 11)*
DISCUSSION: To determine the takeoff distance to clear a 50-ft. obstacle, you must interpolate for the pressure altitude of 6,000 ft., which is 2/5 (40%) of the difference between 5,000 ft. and 7,500 ft.

At 3,000 lb. and with a headwind of 15 kt., the takeoff distance at 5,000 ft. pressure altitude is 1,215 ft., and at 7,500 ft. pressure altitude is 1,505 ft. The difference between the two values is 290 ft. (1,505 − 1,215). Determine that 40% of 290 ft. is 116 ft. (290 × .4). Add 116 ft. to the 5,000-ft. value to obtain a total takeoff distance to clear a 50-ft. obstacle of 1,331 ft.

No correction is required for temperature since the standard temperature at 6,000 ft. is 3°C. That is determined by subtracting the standard lapse rate of 2°C per 1,000 ft., or 12°C (2 × 6) from the sea-level temperature of 15°C.

Answer (A) is incorrect. This is the total takeoff distance required to clear a 50-ft. obstacle if the temperature is 17°C (14°C above standard), not 3°C (standard temperature at 6,000 ft.). Answer (B) is incorrect. This is the total takeoff distance required to clear a 50-ft. obstacle at a pressure altitude of 5,000 ft., not 6,000 ft.

Takeoff data
Takeoff distance with 10° flaps from hard-surfaced runway

Gross weight LB	KIAS at 50 feet	Head wind KTS	At sea level & 15 °C		At 2,500 feet & 10 °C		At 5,000 feet & 5 °C		At 7,500 feet & 0 °C	
			Ground roll	Total to clear 50' OBS	Ground roll	Total to clear 50' OBS	Ground roll	Total to clear 50' OBS	Ground roll	Total to clear 50' OBS
2200	55	0	345	680	405	770	480	885	580	1040
		15	205	460	245	525	295	615	365	725
		30	100	275	120	320	155	380	195	460
2600	60	0	500	915	585	1045	705	1230	855	1470
		15	310	635	370	735	455	870	560	1055
		30	165	395	200	465	255	565	325	695
3000	64	0	695	1210	820	1405	990	1675	1205	2045
		15	450	855	535	1005	660	1215	815	1505
		30	250	555	310	665	390	820	500	1030

Note: Increase distances 10% for each 14 °C above standard temperature for particular altitude.

Figure 26. – Takeoff Data Chart.

25. How does increased weight affect the takeoff distance of an airplane?

- A. The airplane will accelerate more slowly with the same power output, but the same airspeed is required to generate necessary lift for takeoff.
- B. The airplane will accelerate more slowly with the same power output, and a higher airspeed is required to generate necessary lift for takeoff.
- C. Every airplane has the same acceleration factor with the same power output, but a higher airspeed is needed to overcome the increased ground effect.

Answer (B) is correct. *(PHAK Chap 11)*
DISCUSSION: As weight is increased, the flight performance of an aircraft is degraded in nearly every respect. During takeoff, the airplane accelerates more slowly due to the increased mass, and a higher airspeed is required to generate the necessary lift for takeoff. Thus, takeoff distance is increased.
Answer (A) is incorrect. A higher, not the same, takeoff airspeed is required to generate additional lift to compensate for the additional weight. Answer (C) is incorrect. Weight as well as power determines acceleration.

26. What effect does an uphill runway slope have upon takeoff performance?

- A. Decreases takeoff speed.
- B. Increases takeoff distance.
- C. Decreases takeoff distance.

Answer (B) is correct. *(PHAK Chap 11)*
DISCUSSION: The upslope or downslope of a runway (runway gradient) is quite important when runway length and takeoff distance are critical. Upslope provides a retarding force, which impedes acceleration because the engine has to overcome gravity as well as surface friction and drag, resulting in a longer ground run or takeoff distance.
Answer (A) is incorrect. The indicated speed is the same on a level, downhill, or uphill runway at a given density altitude. Answer (C) is incorrect. A downhill, not uphill, slope will decrease the takeoff distance.

27. When density altitude is beyond capability as indicated on the performance chart,

- A. interpolate the data and attempt takeoff.
- B. extrapolate the data and attempt takeoff.
- C. do not attempt takeoff until conditions permit calculations to provide the data to determine a safe takeoff and climb out.

Answer (C) is correct. *(PHAK Chap 11)*
DISCUSSION: The performance charts have been tested by the aircraft manufacturers and have known values for their aircraft performance limitations. These values are what is seen on the manufacturer's published performance charts.
Answer (A) is incorrect. Some charts require interpolation to find the information for specific flight conditions. Interpolating information means that by taking the known information, a pilot can compute intermediate information. If the density altitude computed via interpolation is beyond capability as indicated on the performance chart, do not attempt takeoff until conditions permit calculations to provide the data to determine a safe takeoff and climb out. Answer (B) is incorrect. Extrapolation is the process of guessing an unknown beyond a known factor. If this unknown factor is beyond the chart, it has not been tested and may not be safe.

28. (Refer to Figure 28 on page 75.) Determine the approximate total distance required to clear a 50-foot obstacle.

Temperature	20°C
Pressure altitude	1,000 ft
Surface	sod
Weight	5,300 lb
Wind	15 kts headwind

A. 1,724 feet.
B. 1,816 feet.
C. 2,061 feet.

Answer (A) is correct. *(PHAK Chap 11)*
DISCUSSION: To determine the distance required to clear a 50-foot obstacle, you must interpolate for weight and then make the soft-field and headwind adjustments.
    At 5,100 lb., the charted distance is 1,620 ft.; at 5,500 lb., 1,950 ft. Interpolate for 5,300 lb., which is halfway between 5,100 and 5,500 lb. (1,950 − 1,620) × .50 = 165; 1,620 + 165 = 1,785 ft.
    Increase 1,785 ft. by 8% for a sod runway: 1,785 × 1.08 = 1,927.8 ft.
    Now decrease the distance by 10.5% (by multiplying the total distance by 89.5%) for the 15-kt. headwind: 1,927.8 × .895 = 1,725.4 ft.
    Answer (B) is incorrect. This is the approximate total distance required if the distance (after interpolation) is decreased, not increased, for the sod runway and then increased, not decreased, for the headwind. Answer (C) is incorrect. This is the approximate total distance required if the distance (after interpolating and correcting for the sod runway) is increased 7%, not decreased 10.5%, for the 15-kt. headwind.

29. (Refer to Figure 28 on page 75.) Determine the approximate total distance required to clear a 50-foot obstacle.

Temperature	35°C
Pressure altitude	3,000 ft
Surface	sod
Weight	5,100 lb
Wind	20 kts headwind

A. 1,969 feet.
B. 2,023 feet.
C. 2,289 feet.

Answer (B) is correct. *(PHAK Chap 11)*
DISCUSSION: To determine the distance required to clear a 50-ft. obstacle, you must interpolate for temperature and then make the soft-field and headwind adjustments.
    To find the charted distance under these conditions, interpolate for 35°C. At 40°C the charted distance is 2,260 ft.; at 30°C, 2,100 ft.: (2,260 − 2,100) × .50 = 80; 2,100 + 80 = 2,180 ft.
    To adjust for the sod surface, increase 2,180 ft. by 8%: 2,180 × 1.08 = 2,354.4 ft.
    Now decrease 2,354.4 ft. by 14% to adjust for the 20-kt. headwind: 2,354.4 × .14 = 329.6; 2,354.4 − 329.6 = 2,024.8.
    Answer (A) is incorrect. This is the approximate total distance required if the distance (after interpolation) is not corrected for a sod runway and is reduced 10%, not 14%, for the 20-kt. headwind. Answer (C) is incorrect. This is the approximate total distance required if the distance (after interpolation) is decreased, not increased, for the sod runway and then increased, not decreased, for the headwind.

30. (Refer to Figure 28 on page 75.) Determine the approximate total distance required to clear a 50-foot obstacle.

Temperature	25°C
Pressure altitude	2,500 ft
Surface	asphalt
Weight	5,500 lb
Wind	2 kts tailwind

A. 2,228 feet.
B. 2,294 feet.
C. 2,462 feet.

Answer (C) is correct. *(PHAK Chap 11)*
DISCUSSION: To determine the distance required to clear a 50-ft. obstacle, you must interpolate for pressure altitude and temperature and then make the tailwind adjustment.
    At 5,500 lb., first interpolate for a temperature of 25°C at 2,000-ft. and 3,000-ft. pressure altitudes.

	2,000 ft.	3,000 ft.
At 30°C	2,300	2,550
At 20°C	2,150	2,380
1/2 of difference	75	85
Interpolation	2,225	2,465

    Now interpolate for a 2,500-ft. pressure altitude: (2,465 − 2,225) × .50 = 120; 2,225 + 120 = 2,345 ft.
    Increase 2,345 ft. by 5% for the 2-kt. tailwind: 2,345 × 1.05 = 2,462.3 ft.
    Answer (A) is incorrect. This is the approximate total distance required to clear a 50-ft. obstacle at a pressure altitude of 2,000 ft., not 2,500 ft., and with a calm wind, not a tailwind of 2 kt. Answer (B) is incorrect. This is the approximate total distance required to clear a 50-ft. obstacle at a pressure altitude of 2,000 ft., not 2,500 ft.; at a temperature of 30°C, not 25°C; and with a calm wind, not a tailwind of 2 kt.

Short-field takeoff distance

Conditions:
1. Power—FULL THROTTLE and 2700 rpm before releasing brakes.
2. Mixtures—LEAN for field elevation.
3. Cow flaps—OPEN.
4. Wing flaps—UP.
5. Level, dry, hard-surface runway.

Note:
1. Increase total distance 8% for operation on dry, sod runway.
2. Decrease total distance 7% for each 10 knots of headwind.
3. Increase total distance 5% for each 2 knots of tailwind.

Weight LB	Takeoff to 50 foot obstacle speed KIAS	Pressure altitude feet	20 °C		30 °C		40 °C	
			Ground roll feet	Total distance to clear 50' OBS	Ground roll feet	Total distance to clear 50' OBS	Ground roll feet	Total distance to clear 50' OBS
5500	82	Sea level	1390	1760	1490	1890	1590	2020
		1,000	1530	1950	1640	2080	1760	2230
		2,000	1680	2150	1810	2300	1940	2470
		3,000	1860	2380	2000	2550	2150	2750
		4,000	2060	2650	2220	2850	2380	3070
		5,000	2280	2950	2460	3190	2640	3450
		6,000	2530	3310	2730	3590	2950	3900
		7,000	2830	3750	3160	4190	3410	4570
		8,000	3280	4420	3540	4840	3830	5330
		9,000	3690	5170	4000	5730	4330	6420
		10,000	4150	6140	4500	6980	4880	8130
5100	78	Sea level	1160	1470	1240	1570	1330	1680
		1,000	1280	1620	1370	1730	1470	1850
		2,000	1400	1780	1500	1910	1610	2040
		3,000	1550	1960	1660	2100	1780	2260
		4,000	1710	2180	1840	2340	1970	2510
		5,000	1890	2410	2030	2590	2180	2790
		6,000	2090	2690	2250	2890	2420	3120
		7,000	2330	3010	2510	3250	2700	3520
		8,000	2600	3400	2800	3690	3030	4010
		9,000	2920	3890	3270	4360	3530	4760
		10,000	3390	4580	3660	5030	3960	5560
4700	75	Sea level	960	1220	1020	1300	1090	1380
		1,000	1050	1340	1120	1430	1200	1520
		2,000	1150	1460	1230	1560	1320	1670
		3,000	1270	1610	1360	1720	1460	1840
		4,000	1400	1770	1500	1900	1610	2030
		5,000	1540	1960	1650	2100	1780	2250
		6,000	1700	2170	1830	2330	1970	2500
		7,000	1890	2410	2030	2590	2190	2790
		8,000	2100	2700	2260	2910	2440	3140
		9,000	2350	3040	2540	3290	2730	3570
		10,000	2620	3430	2830	3730	3060	4060

Figure 28. — Short-Field Takeoff Distance Chart.

2.3 Maximum Climb

31. (Refer to Figure 27 below.) The indicated airspeed that would give the greatest gain in altitude in a unit of time at 3,200 feet is determined to be

    A. 93 KIAS.
    B. 94 KIAS.
    C. 112 KIAS.

Answer (C) is correct. *(PHAK Chap 11)*
    DISCUSSION: By definition, the best rate-of-climb speed provides the greatest gain in altitude in a unit of time. Locate 3,200 ft. on the left margin of the chart and move horizontally to the right to the "Best Rate of Climb" diagonal line. Then move vertically down to determine an indicated airspeed of approximately 112 kt.
    Answer (A) is incorrect. The best angle-of-climb speed at sea level (S.L.), not 3,200 ft., is 93 KIAS. The best angle of climb provides the greatest gain in altitude for a given distance, not in a unit of time. Answer (B) is incorrect. The best angle-of-climb speed at 3,000 ft. is 94 KIAS. The best angle of climb provides the greatest gain in altitude for a given distance, not in a unit of time.

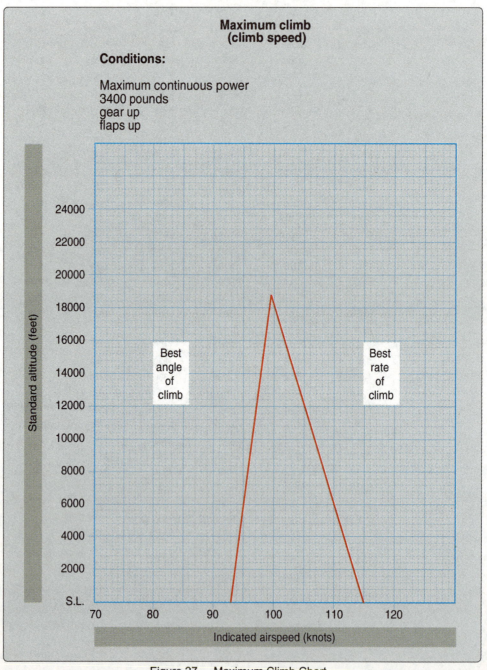

Figure 27. — Maximum Climb Chart.

SU 2: Airplane Performance

32. (Refer to Figure 27 on page 76.) What indicated airspeed at 3,000 feet would result in the greatest increase in altitude for a given distance?

A. 94 KIAS.
B. 113 KIAS.
C. 115 KIAS.

Answer (A) is correct. *(PHAK Chap 11)*
DISCUSSION: By definition, the best angle-of-climb speed provides the greatest increase in altitude for a given distance. Locate 3,000 ft. on the left margin of the chart and move horizontally to the right to the "Best Angle of Climb" diagonal line. Then move vertically down to determine an indicated airspeed of 94 kt.
Answer (B) is incorrect. The best rate-of-climb speed at 2,400 ft. is 113 KIAS. The best rate of climb provides the greatest increase in altitude in a unit of time, not a given distance. Answer (C) is incorrect. The best rate-of-climb speed at sea level (S.L.), not 3,000 ft., is 115 KIAS. The best rate of climb provides the greatest increase in altitude in a unit of time, not a given distance.

33. (Refer to Figure 27 on page 76.) To maintain the best rate of climb, the indicated speed should be

A. maintained at a constant value during the climb.
B. adjusted to maintain the specified rate of climb.
C. reduced approximately .8 knots per 1,000 feet of altitude.

Answer (C) is correct. *(PHAK Chap 11)*
DISCUSSION: The question requires the change in indicated airspeed for the best rate of climb. The best rate of climb is the reference line farthest to the right. Optimal airspeed decreases with altitude. Note that airspeed goes from 115 kt. at sea level to 107 kt. at 10,000 ft. Find the intersection of the second reference line with 10,000 ft. Move down and find 107 kt. Therefore, there is a decrease of 8 kt. for 10,000 ft. or 0.8 kt. for every 1,000 ft. [(115 − 107) ÷ 10].
Answer (A) is incorrect. The indicated airspeed decreases with altitude. Answer (B) is incorrect. The rate of climb decreases with altitude.

2.4 True Airspeed

34. An aircraft is flying at a constant power setting and constant indicated altitude. If the outside air temperature (OAT) decreases, true airspeed will

A. decrease and true altitude will decrease.
B. increase and true altitude will increase.
C. increase and true altitude will decrease.

Answer (A) is correct. *(PHAK Chap 8)*
DISCUSSION: True airspeed (TAS) decreases at a constant power setting as density altitude decreases. A decrease in outside air temperature results in a decrease in density altitude. An airplane flying at a constant indicated altitude is flying with reference to the pressure altimeter (i.e., a constant pressure surface), which does not sense temperature changes. Thus, when flying from a warmer column of air to a colder column of air, the airplane actually descends and true altitude decreases.
Answer (B) is incorrect. Both true altitude and TAS will decrease, not increase, if the OAT decreases. Answer (C) is incorrect. TAS will decrease, not increase, if the OAT decreases.

35. An aircraft is flying at a constant power setting and constant indicated altitude. If the outside air temperature (OAT) increases, true airspeed will

A. increase and true altitude will decrease.
B. increase and true altitude will increase.
C. decrease and true altitude will increase.

Answer (B) is correct. *(PHAK Chap 8)*
DISCUSSION: True airspeed (TAS) increases at a constant power setting as density altitude increases. An increase in outside air temperature results in an increase in density altitude. An airplane flying at a constant indicated altitude is flying with reference to the pressure altimeter (i.e., a constant pressure surface), which does not sense temperature changes. Thus, when flying from a colder column of air to a warmer column of air, the airplane actually climbs and true altitude increases.
Answer (A) is incorrect. True altitude will increase, not decrease, if the OAT increases. Answer (C) is incorrect. True airspeed will increase, not decrease, if the OAT increases.

36. As density altitude increases, which will occur if a constant indicated airspeed is maintained in a no-wind condition?

A. True airspeed increases; groundspeed decreases.
B. True airspeed decreases; groundspeed decreases.
C. True airspeed increases; groundspeed increases.

Answer (C) is correct. *(PHAK Chap 8)*
DISCUSSION: As density altitude increases, true airspeed increases. As true airspeed increases, groundspeed increases in a no-wind condition.
Answer (A) is incorrect. As density altitude increases, groundspeed increases, not decreases, in a no-wind condition. Answer (B) is incorrect. As density altitude increases, both TAS and groundspeed will increase, not decrease, in a no-wind condition.

37. In a propeller-driven airplane, maximum range occurs at

A. minimum drag required.
B. minimum power required.
C. maximum lift/drag ratio.

Answer (C) is correct. *(PHAK Chap 11)*
DISCUSSION: In a propeller-driven airplane, maximum range occurs where the proportion between speed and power required is greatest. This condition is obtained at maximum lift/drag ratio.
Answer (A) is incorrect. Minimum drag does not necessarily mean maximum lift/drag ratio. Answer (B) is incorrect. Maximum endurance, not range, occurs at the point of minimum power required.

2.5 Multi-Engine Performance

38. The critical engine on most light multiengine airplanes with clockwise rotating propellers is the

A. left engine, because of the P-factor of the left propeller.
B. right engine, because of the P-factor of the left propeller.
C. left engine, because of the P-factor of the right propeller.

Answer (C) is correct. *(AFH Chap 12)*
DISCUSSION: In most twin-engine airplanes, both engines rotate clockwise when viewed from the rear. At low airspeed and high power, the downward moving propeller of each engine develops more thrust than the upward moving blade. This asymmetric propeller thrust (P-factor) results in a center of thrust at the right side of each engine. The turning or yawing force of the right engine is greater than the left engine because the center of thrust is farther away from the center line of the fuselage. Thus, when the right engine is operative and the left engine is inoperative, the turning or yawing force would be greater than with an operative left engine and an inoperative right engine. In other words, directional control may be difficult when the left engine (i.e., the critical engine) is suddenly made inoperative.
Answer (A) is incorrect. The P-factor of the right, not left, propeller is farther from the airplane's centerline. Answer (B) is incorrect. The P-factor of the right, not left, propeller is farther from the airplane's centerline, thus making the left, not right, engine the critical engine.

39. On a multiengine airplane with engines which rotate clockwise, the critical engine is the

A. left engine, because the right engine center of thrust is closer to the centerline of the fuselage.
B. right engine, because the left engine center of thrust is closer to the centerline of the fuselage.
C. left engine, because the right engine center of thrust is farther away from the centerline of the fuselage.

Answer (C) is correct. *(AFH Chap 12)*
DISCUSSION: In most twin-engine airplanes, both engines rotate clockwise when viewed from the rear. At low airspeed and high power, the downward moving propeller of each engine develops more thrust than the upward moving blade. Asymmetric propeller thrust (P-factor) results in a center of thrust at the right side of each engine. The turning or yawing force of the right engine is greater than the left engine because the center of thrust is farther away from the center line of the fuselage. Thus, when the right engine is operative and the left engine is inoperative, the turning or yawing force would be greater than with an operative left engine and an inoperative right engine. In other words, directional control may be difficult when the left engine (i.e., the critical engine) is suddenly made inoperative.
Answer (A) is incorrect. The right engine thrust is farther from, not closer to, the fuselage centerline. Answer (B) is incorrect. Since the left engine's center of thrust is closer to the aircraft centerline, the left, not right, engine becomes the critical engine.

40. What is the significance of the blue radial line on the airspeed indicator of a light multiengine airplane and when is it to be used? It indicates the

A. minimum speed at which the airplane is controllable when the critical engine is suddenly made inoperative and should be used at all altitudes when an engine is inoperative.
B. speed which will provide the maximum altitude gain in a given time when one engine is inoperative and should be used for climb and final approach during engine-out operations.
C. speed which will provide the greatest height for a given distance of forward travel when one engine is inoperative and should be used for all climbs during engine-out operations.

Answer (B) is correct. *(AFH Chap 12)*
DISCUSSION: The blue radial line indicates the best rate-of-climb airspeed with one engine inoperative (V_{YSE}). This speed should be maintained while climbing with one engine inoperative and on the final approach to a single-engine landing.
Answer (A) is incorrect. V_{MC} is the minimum speed at which the airplane is controllable when the critical engine is suddenly made inoperative and is indicated by a red, not blue, radial line. The airplane should be operated well above, not at, this airspeed. Answer (C) is incorrect. V_{XSE} is the speed that will provide the greatest height for a given distance when one engine is inoperative and should be used during single-engine climb only when obstacles are present, not at all times. V_{XSE} is not marked on the airspeed indicator.

SU 2: Airplane Performance

41. On a multiengine airplane, where the propellers rotate in the same direction, why is the loss of power on one engine more critical than the loss of power on the other engine?

A. The corkscrew pattern of airflow from one propeller is less effective against the airflow from the critical engine.
B. The torque reaction from operation of the critical engine is more severe around the vertical axis as well as the longitudinal axis.
C. The asymmetric propeller thrust or P-factor results in the center of thrust from one engine being farther from the airplane centerline than the center of thrust from the other engine.

Answer (C) is correct. *(AFH Chap 12)*
DISCUSSION: In most twin-engine airplanes, both engines rotate clockwise when viewed from the rear. At low airspeed and high power, the downward moving propeller of each engine develops more thrust than the upward moving blade. Asymmetric propeller thrust (P-factor) results in a center of thrust at the right side of each engine. The turning or yawing force of the right engine is greater than the left engine because the center of thrust is farther away from the center line of the fuselage. Thus, when the right engine is operative and the left engine is inoperative, the turning or yawing force would be greater than with an operative left engine and an inoperative right engine. In other words, directional control may be difficult when the left engine (i.e., the critical engine) is suddenly made inoperative.
Answer (A) is incorrect. Airflow effective against airflow is a nonsense concept. Answer (B) is incorrect. The torque reaction from the critical engine would be less, not more, severe and would have no effect on the vertical axis.

42. For an airplane with reciprocating, nonturbo-charged engines, V_{MC}

A. decreases with altitude.
B. increases with altitude.
C. is not affected by altitude.

Answer (A) is correct. *(AFH Chap 12)*
DISCUSSION: For an airplane with nonturbo-charged engines, V_{MC} decreases as altitude is increased; i.e., directional control can be maintained at a lower indicated airspeed than at sea level. The reason for this is that, since power decreases with altitude, the thrust moment of the operating engine becomes less, thereby lessening the need for the rudder's yawing force.
Answer (B) is incorrect. V_{MC} decreases, not increases, with altitude. Answer (C) is incorrect. V_{MC} is always affected by altitude.

43. When one engine fails on a twin-engine airplane, the resulting performance loss

A. may reduce the rate of climb by 80 percent or more.
B. reduces cruise indicated airspeed by 50 percent or more.
C. is approximately 50 percent since 50 percent of the normally available thrust is lost.

Answer (A) is correct. *(AFH Chap 12)*
DISCUSSION: When one engine fails on a light twin-engine airplane, the climb performance loss is greater than 50% because climb performance is a function of thrust horsepower in excess of that required for level flight. When power is increased in both engines in level flight and airspeed is held constant, the airplane will climb at a rate depending on the power added. When one engine fails, however, it not only loses power but the drag increases considerably because of asymmetric thrust. The operating engine must carry the full burden alone, and climb performance may be reduced by 80% or more.
Answer (B) is incorrect. The power loss affects climb capability much more than it does cruise speed. Answer (C) is incorrect. Climb performance is a function of excess, not available, thrust.

44. Which is true regarding the operation of a multiengine airplane with one engine inoperative?

A. Banking toward the operating engine increases V_{MC}.
B. Banking toward the inoperative engine increases V_{MC}.
C. V_{MC} is a designed performance factor which must be proven during type certification and will not change as long as the ball is centered with appropriate rudder pressure.

Answer (B) is correct. *(AFH Chap 12)*
DISCUSSION: Flight tests have shown that holding the ball of the turn-and-slip indicator in the center while maintaining heading with wings level would increase V_{MC} as much as 20 kt. due to increased drag. Banking into the operative engine reduces V_{MC}, whereas banking into the inoperative engine increases V_{MC}. Banking 5° into the operating engine ensures the airplane will be controllable at any speed above the certified V_{MC}.
Answer (A) is incorrect. Banking toward the operating engine decreases, not increases, V_{MC}. Answer (C) is incorrect. Flying with the ball centered with one engine inoperative is never correct. If the ball is centered, the airplane will be in a sideslip toward the inoperative engine, which increases drag and increases V_{MC}.

45. In a twin-engine airplane, the single-engine service ceiling is the maximum density altitude at which V_{YSE} will produce

A. 50 feet per minute rate of climb.
B. 100 feet per minute rate of climb.
C. 500 feet per minute rate of climb.

Answer (A) is correct. *(AFH Chap 12)*
DISCUSSION: The single-engine service ceiling of a twin-engine airplane is the maximum density altitude at which the single-engine best rate-of-climb speed will produce a 50-fpm rate of climb.
Answer (B) is incorrect. One hundred fpm is the measure to determine the service ceiling for a multi-engine aircraft with both engines operating. Answer (C) is incorrect. Five hundred fpm is not a measure used for any performance figures.

46. When operating a light multiengine airplane at V_{MC}, the pilot should expect performance to be sufficient to maintain

A. heading.
B. heading and altitude.
C. heading, altitude, and be able to climb at 50 feet per minute.

Answer (A) is correct. *(AFH Chap 12)*
DISCUSSION: V_{MC} represents the minimum controllable airspeed with a critical engine inoperative. FAA regulations require that, in an airplane at V_{MC}, the pilot must at least be able to stop the turn that results when the critical engine is suddenly made inoperative within 20° of the original heading using maximum rudder deflection and a maximum bank of 5° into the operative engine. Also, after recovery, the pilot must be able to maintain the airplane in straight flight with not more than 5° bank wing lowered toward the operating engine. This does not mean that the airplane must be able to climb or even to hold altitude. It only means that a heading can be maintained.
Answer (B) is incorrect. To be able to maintain altitude is not a requirement of V_{MC}. Answer (C) is incorrect. To be able to hold altitude and climb are not requirements of V_{MC}.

47. Which condition causes V_{MC} to be the highest?

A. CG is at the most forward allowable position.
B. CG is at the most rearward allowable position.
C. Gross weight is at the maximum allowable value.

Answer (B) is correct. *(AFH Chap 12)*
DISCUSSION: V_{MC} is greater when the center of gravity is at the most rearward allowable position. Since the airplane rotates around its center of gravity, the moments are measured using that point as a reference. A rearward CG would not affect the thrust moment but would shorten the arm to the center of the rudder's horizontal lift, which would mean that a higher force or airspeed would be required to provide the necessary rudder effectiveness.
Answer (A) is incorrect. A forward CG increases rudder effectiveness and reduces, not increases, V_{MC}. Answer (C) is incorrect. Increased weight reduces, not increases, V_{MC}.

2.6 Glide Distance

48. (Refer to Figure 29 on page 81.) What is the approximate glide distance?

Height above terrain 7,500 ft
Headwind 30 kts

A. 11.5 miles.
B. 16.5 miles.
C. 21.5 miles.

Answer (A) is correct. *(AFH Chap 3)*
DISCUSSION: Fig. 29 presents the glide distance chart. To find the approximate glide distance:

1. Locate the height above terrain of 7,500 ft. on the left side of the chart.
2. Move to the right horizontally to the bold diagonal line.
3. Then move down vertically to the bottom of the chart to determine a glide distance of approximately 16.5 SM in a no-wind condition.
4. Note 2 (above the graph) indicates to decrease the glide distance approximately 10% for each 10 kt. of headwind. Thus, the approximate glide distance with a 30-kt. headwind is 11.5 SM (16.5 × 70%).

Answer (B) is incorrect. This is the approximate glide distance in a no-wind condition, not with a 30-kt. headwind. Answer (C) is incorrect. This is the approximate glide distance with a 30-kt. tailwind, not headwind.

49. (Refer to Figure 29 on page 81.) What is the approximate glide distance?

Height above terrain 10,500 ft
Tailwind 20 kts

A. 24 miles.
B. 26 miles.
C. 28 miles.

Answer (C) is correct. *(AFH Chap 3)*
DISCUSSION: Fig. 29 presents the glide distance chart. To find the approximate glide distance:

1. Locate the height above terrain of 10,500 ft. on the left side of the chart.
2. Move to the right horizontally to the bold diagonal line.
3. Then move down vertically to the bottom of the chart to determine a glide distance of approximately 23 SM, in a no-wind condition.
4. Note 1 (above the graph) indicates to increase the glide distance approximately 10% for each 10 kt. of tailwind. Thus, the approximate glide distance with a 20-kt. tailwind is 28 SM (23 × 120%).

Answer (A) is incorrect. This is the approximate glide distance in a no-wind condition, not a 20-kt. tailwind. Answer (B) is incorrect. This is the approximate glide distance with a 20-kt. tailwind from a height of 10,000 ft., not 10,500 ft.

50. (Refer to Figure 29 below.) What is the approximate glide distance?

Height above terrain	5,500 ft
Tailwind	10 kts

A. 11 miles.
B. 12 miles.
C. 13 miles.

Answer (C) is correct. *(AFH Chap 3)*
   DISCUSSION: Fig. 29 presents the glide distance chart. To find the approximate glide distance:

1. Locate the height above terrain of 5,500 ft. on the left side of the chart.
2. Move to the right horizontally to the bold diagonal line.
3. Then move down vertically to the bottom of the chart to determine a glide distance of approximately 12 SM, in a no-wind condition.
4. Note 1 (above the graph) indicates to increase the glide distance approximately 10% for each 10 kt. of tailwind. Thus, the approximate glide distance with a 10-kt. tailwind is 13 SM (12 × 110%).

   Answer (A) is incorrect. Eleven SM is the glide distance from a height of 5,000 ft., not 5,500 ft., in a no-wind condition. Answer (B) is incorrect. Twelve SM is the glide distance in a no-wind condition, not with a 10-kt. tailwind.

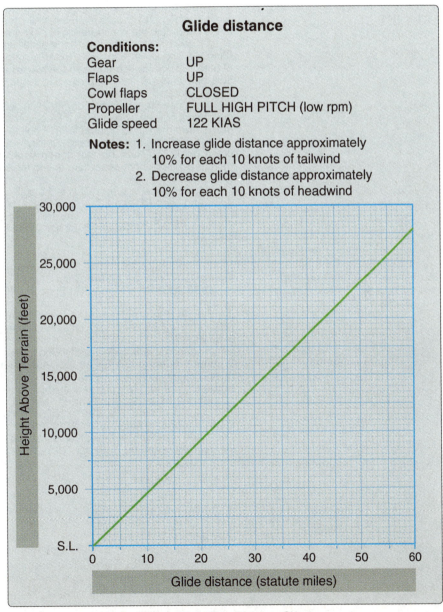

Figure 29. – Glide Distance Chart.

2.7 Stall Speed

51. (Refer to Figure 25 on page 83.) What would be the indicated stall speed in a 60° banked turn with the gear and flaps up?

A. 110 KIAS.
B. 117 KIAS.
C. 121 KIAS.

Answer (B) is correct. *(PHAK Chap 11)*
DISCUSSION: Use the Stall Speeds - KCAS chart (at the bottom of Fig. 25) to determine the stall speed. On the left side of the chart, find the configuration of gear and flaps up and move right to the 60° angle-of-bank column to determine a stall speed of 119 KCAS.
Next, use the Airspeed Calibration table (at the top of Fig. 25) to convert KCAS to KIAS. Find flaps 0° and move down the KCAS column; note that 122 KCAS is 120 KIAS, a difference of 2 kt. Thus, the indicated stall speed is 117 KIAS (119 – 2).
Answer (A) is incorrect. This is the approximate indicated stall speed if the bank angle is 60° with the gear down, not up, and the flaps set at 15°, not 0°. Answer (C) is incorrect. This is obtained when the correction of 2 kt. is incorrectly added to, not subtracted from, the 119 KCAS.

52. (Refer to Figure 25 on page 83.) What would be the indicated stall speed in a 30° banked turn with the gear down and flaps set at 15°?

A. 77 KIAS.
B. 82 KIAS.
C. 88 KIAS.

Answer (B) is correct. *(PHAK Chap 11)*
DISCUSSION: First, use the Stall Speeds - KCAS chart (bottom of Fig. 25) to determine the stall speed. On the left side of the chart, find the configuration of gear down and flaps 15°. Then move right to determine that the stall speed at 20° bank is 83 KCAS and at 40° bank is 92 KCAS. Interpolate for a 30° angle of bank. The difference between the two values is 9 kt. (92 – 83); 50% of 9 kt. is 4.5 kt. (rounded to 5 kt.). Add 5 kt. to 83 to get 88 kt. calibrated airspeed (KCAS).
Next, use the top portion of Fig. 25 to determine the knots indicated airspeed (KIAS). Find the column titled "Flaps 15°" and move down the KCAS column to 86. Look to the left, in the KIAS column to 80, meaning you must subtract 6 kt. from KCAS to determine KIAS. Thus, the stall speed would be 82 KIAS (88 – 6). Interpolation is not necessary due to the small difference of less than 1 kt.
Answer (A) is incorrect. This is the stalling speed with gear down and flaps 15° at a 20° angle of bank, not a 30° angle of bank. Answer (C) is incorrect. The stalling speed in a 30° banked turn with the gear down and flaps set at 15° is 88 KCAS, not 88 KIAS.

53. (Refer to Figure 25 on page 83.) What would be the indicated stall speed during a 40° banked turn with the gear down and flaps set at 45°?

A. 81 KIAS.
B. 83 KIAS.
C. 89 KIAS.

Answer (B) is correct. *(PHAK Chap 11)*
DISCUSSION: Use the Stall Speeds - KCAS chart (at the bottom of Fig. 25) to determine the stall speed. On the left side of the chart, find the configuration of gear down and flaps 45°; move right to the 40° angle-of-bank column to determine a stall speed of 87 KCAS.
Next, use the Airspeed Calibration table (at the top of Fig. 25) to convert KCAS to KIAS. Find flaps 45° and move down the KCAS column; note that, at a KCAS of 84 kt., the KIAS is 80 kt., a difference of 4 kt. Thus, the stall speed is 83 KIAS (87 – 4).
Answer (A) is incorrect. This is obtained by using the "Flaps 15°" column, not the "Flaps 45°" column, and applying a 6-kt., not a 4-kt., calibration factor to the 87 KCAS. Answer (C) is incorrect. This is the approximate indicated stall speed in a 40° bank with the gear down and the flaps set at 15°, not 45°.

Airspeed calibration—Normal system

Flaps 0°		Flaps 15°		Flaps 45°	
KIAS	KCAS	KIAS	KCAS	KIAS	KCAS
80	84	70	79	70	76
100	102	80	86	80	84
120	122	90	94	90	93
140	141	100	103	100	102
160	161	110	112	110	111
180	181	120	121	120	120
200	201	130	131	130	129
220	221	140	141	140	138
240	242	150	151		

KIAS—indicated airspeed in knots
KCAS—calibrated airspeed in knots

Stall speeds—KCAS   4,600 lb gross weight

Configuration	Angle of bank			
	0°	20°	40°	60°
Gear and flaps up	84	87	97	119
Gear down and flaps 15°	80	83	92	113
Gear down and flaps 45°	76	79	87	108

Figure 25. – Airspeed Calibration Stalls/Speeds Chart.

2.8 Landing Distance

54. What can a pilot expect when landing at an airport located in the mountains?

A. Higher true airspeed and longer landing distance.
B. Higher indicated airspeed and shorter landing distance.
C. Lower true airspeed and longer landing distance.

Answer (A) is correct. *(AIM Para 7-5-6)*
   DISCUSSION: In mountainous areas, you may assume that you will have a high density altitude, and because of this you will also have a higher true airspeed. A higher true airspeed will result in a higher groundspeed, which in turn results in a longer landing distance.
   Answer (B) is incorrect. Regardless of altitude, the indicated airspeed should remain the same and landing distance will be longer, not shorter. Answer (C) is incorrect. At higher altitudes, you will have a higher, not lower, true airspeed.

55. (Refer to Figure 31 on page 85.) What is the total landing distance over a 50-foot obstacle?

Temperature	15°C
Pressure altitude	4,000 ft
Weight	3,000 lb
Headwind	22 kts

A. 1,250 feet.
B. 1,175 feet.
C. 1,050 feet.

Answer (B) is correct. *(PHAK Chap 11)*
DISCUSSION: Begin at 15°C on the left side of the chart, and go up to the pressure altitude of 4,000 ft. Proceed horizontally to the right to the first reference line, and then up, parallel to the sloping line, to 3,000 lb. From that point, proceed horizontally to the second reference line. Since the headwind is 22 kt., follow parallel to the headwind line down to 22 kt. and then horizontally to the right edge of the chart to determine the landing distance of 1,175 ft.
Answer (A) is incorrect. This is the total landing distance with a headwind of 16 kt., not 22 kt. Answer (C) is incorrect. This is the total landing distance with a headwind of 30 kt., not 22 kt.

56. (Refer to Figure 31 on page 85.) Determine the approximate ground roll.

Temperature	33°C
Pressure altitude	6,000 ft
Weight	2,800 lb
Headwind	14 kts

A. 742 feet.
B. 1,280 feet.
C. 1,480 feet.

Answer (A) is correct. *(PHAK Chap 11)*
DISCUSSION: Begin at 33°C on the left side of the chart, and go up to the pressure altitude of 6,000 ft. Proceed horizontally to the right to the first reference line, and then up, parallel to the sloping line, to 2,800 lb. From that point, proceed horizontally to the second reference line. Since the headwind is 14 kt., follow parallel to the headwind line down to 14 kt. and then horizontally to the right edge of the chart to determine the landing distance of 1,400 ft. The chart note says that ground roll is approximately 53% of total landing distance. Therefore, calculate the ground roll to be 742 ft. (1,400 × .53).
Answer (B) is incorrect. This is the approximate total landing distance, not the ground roll, with a 22-kt., not a 14-kt., headwind. Answer (C) is incorrect. This is approximately the total landing distance, not the ground roll.

57. (Refer to Figure 31 on page 85.) What is the total landing distance over a 50-foot obstacle?

Temperature	35°C
Pressure altitude	2,000 ft
Weight	3,400 lb
Headwind	10 kts

A. 1,650 feet.
B. 1,575 feet.
C. 1,475 feet.

Answer (C) is correct. *(PHAK Chap 11)*
DISCUSSION: Begin at 35°C on the left side of the chart, and go up to the pressure altitude of 2,000 ft. Proceed horizontally to the right to the first reference line, and then up, parallel to the sloping line, to 3,400 lb. From that point, proceed horizontally to the second reference line. Since the headwind is 10 kt., follow parallel to the headwind line down to 10 kt. and then horizontally to the right edge of the chart to determine the landing distance of 1,475 ft.
Answer (A) is incorrect. This is the total landing distance when the wind is calm, not when there is a 10-kt. headwind. Answer (B) is incorrect. This is the approximate total landing distance with a 8-kt., not a 10-kt., headwind.

SU 2: Airplane Performance

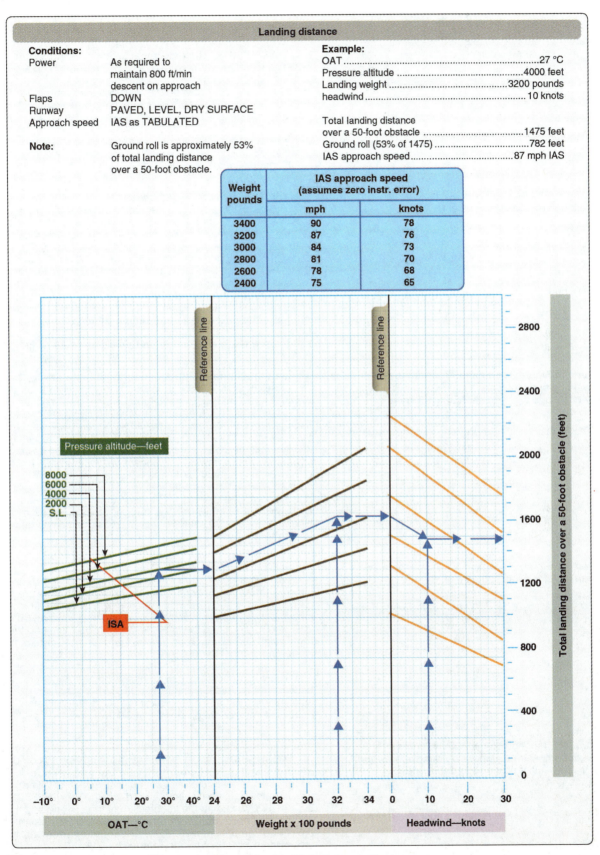

Figure 31. – Landing Distance Chart.

2.9 Crosswind/Headwind Components

58. (Refer to Figure 30 on page 87.) Determine the approximate crosswind component.

Landing Rwy 30
Wind 020° at 15 kts

A. 4 knots.
B. 15 knots.
C. 22 knots.

Answer (B) is correct. *(PHAK Chap 11)*
DISCUSSION: The requirement is the crosswind component, which is found on the horizontal axis of the graph. You are given a 15-kt. wind speed (the wind speed is shown on the arcs). First, calculate the angle between the wind and the runway (360° − 300° = 60°; 60° + 20° = 80°). Next, find the intersection of the 80° line and the 15-kt. wind speed arc. Then, proceed downward to determine the crosswind component of 15 kt.
Answer (A) is incorrect. Four kt. is approximately the headwind component. Answer (C) is incorrect. A 22-kt. crosswind component is impossible with a 15-kt. wind.

59. (Refer to Figure 30 on page 87.) Determine the approximate crosswind component.

Landing Rwy 03
Wind 060° at 35 kts

A. 12 knots.
B. 18 knots.
C. 22 knots.

Answer (B) is correct. *(PHAK Chap 11)*
DISCUSSION: The requirement is the crosswind component, which is found on the horizontal axis of the graph. You are given a 35-kt. wind speed (the wind speed is shown on the arcs). First, calculate the angle between the wind and the runway (60° − 30° = 30°). Next, find the intersection of the 30° line and the 35-kt. wind speed arc. Then, proceed downward to determine the crosswind component of 18 kt.
Answer (A) is incorrect. Twelve kt. is obtained if a wind speed of 25 kt. is used instead of 35 kt. Answer (C) is incorrect. A 22-kt. crosswind component can be obtained if a 40° angle between wind direction and flight path is used and wind speed of 35 kt., or by using a 30° angle and a wind speed of 45 kt.

60. (Refer to Figure 30 on page 87.) What is the crosswind component for a landing on Runway 18 if the tower reports the wind as 220° at 25 knots?

A. 16 knots.
B. 19 knots.
C. 22 knots.

Answer (A) is correct. *(PHAK Chap 11)*
DISCUSSION: The requirement is the crosswind component, which is found on the horizontal axis of the graph. You are given a 30-kt. wind speed (the wind speed is shown on the circular lines or arcs). First, calculate the angle between the wind and the runway (220° − 180° = 40°). Next, find the intersection of the 40° line and the 25-kt. headwind arc. Then, proceed downward to determine a crosswind component of 16 knots. NOTE: The crosswind component is on the horizontal axis, and the headwind component is on the vertical axis.
Answer (B) is incorrect. The headwind (not crosswind) component is 19 knots. Answer (C) is incorrect. The wind velocity would have to be 35 knots to have a crosswind component of 22 knots.

61. (Refer to Figure 30 on page 87.) Determine the approximate crosswind component.

Landing Rwy 22
Wind 260° at 23 kts

A. 10 knots.
B. 15 knots.
C. 17 knots.

Answer (B) is correct. *(PHAK Chap 11)*
DISCUSSION: The requirement is the crosswind component, which is found on the horizontal axis of the graph. You are given a 23-kt. wind speed (the wind speed is shown on the arcs). First calculate the angle between the wind and the runway (260° − 220° = 40°). Next find the intersection of the 40° line and the 23-kt. wind speed arc. Then proceed downward to determine the crosswind component of 15 kt.
Answer (A) is incorrect. A 10-kt. crosswind component results if you measure the 26-kt. headwind at a 23° angle between wind direction and flight path, rather than using the wind specified as 260° at 23 kt. Answer (C) is incorrect. It refers to the headwind component given the conditions.

62. (Refer to Figure 30 on page 87.) Using a maximum demonstrated crosswind component equal to 0.2 V_{SO}, what is a pilot able to determine?

V_{SO} 70 kts
Landing Rwy 35
Wind 300° at 20 kts

A. Headwind component is excessive.
B. Headwind component exceeds the crosswind component.
C. Maximum demonstrated crosswind component is exceeded.

Answer (C) is correct. *(PHAK Chap 11)*
DISCUSSION: The requirement is the crosswind component, which is found on the horizontal axis of the graph. You are given a 20-kt. wind speed (the wind speed is shown on the arcs). First, calculate the angle between the wind and the runway (350° − 300° = 50°). Next, find the intersection of the 50° line and the 20-kt. wind speed arc. Then, proceed downward to determine the crosswind component of 15.25 kt. The maximum demonstrated crosswind component is calculated to be 14 kt. (0.2 V_{SO} = 0.2 × 70). Therefore, the maximum safe crosswind component is exceeded.
Answer (A) is incorrect. A headwind is not a detrimental factor for landing. Answer (B) is incorrect. The headwind component is 13 kt., whereas the crosswind component is 15 kt.

SU 2: Airplane Performance

63. (Refer to Figure 30 below.) Using a maximum demonstrated crosswind component equal to 0.2 V_{SO}, what is a pilot able to determine?

V_{SO}	60 kts
Landing Rwy	12
Wind	150° at 20 kts

A. Headwind component exceeds recommended limits.

B. Crosswind component is within safe limits.

C. Maximum demonstrated crosswind component is exceeded.

Answer (B) is correct. *(PHAK Chap 11)*
DISCUSSION: The requirement is the crosswind component, which is found on the horizontal axis of the graph. You are given a 20-kt. wind speed (the wind speed is shown on the arcs). First, calculate the angle between the wind and the runway (150° – 120° = 30°). Next, find the intersection of the 30° line and the 20-kt. wind speed arc. Then, proceed downward to determine the crosswind component of 10 kt. The maximum demonstrated crosswind component is calculated to be 12 kt. (0.2 V_{SO} = 0.2 × 60 kt.). Therefore, the crosswind component is within safe limits.
Answer (A) is incorrect. A headwind is not a detrimental factor for landing. Answer (C) is incorrect. The crosswind component is within limits (10 kt. vs. maximum 12 kt.).

64. (Refer to Figure 30 below.) Using a maximum demonstrated crosswind component equal to 0.2 V_{SO}, what is a pilot able to determine?

V_{SO}	65 kts
Landing Rwy	17
Wind	200° at 30 kts

A. Crosswind component is within safe limits.

B. Crosswind component exceeds the headwind component.

C. Maximum demonstrated crosswind component is exceeded.

Answer (C) is correct. *(PHAK Chap 11)*
DISCUSSION: The requirement is the crosswind component, which is found on the horizontal axis of the graph. You are given a 30-kt. wind speed (the wind speed is shown on the arcs). First, calculate the angle between the wind and the runway (200° – 170° = 30°). Next find the intersection of the 30° line and the 30-kt. wind speed arc. Then proceed downward to determine the crosswind component of 15 kt. The maximum demonstrated crosswind component is calculated to be 13 kt. (0.2 V_{SO} = 0.2 × 65 kt.). Therefore, the maximum safe crosswind component is exceeded.
Answer (A) is incorrect. The crosswind component is exceeded by 2 kt. Answer (B) is incorrect. The headwind component is 26 kt., whereas the crosswind component is 15 kt.

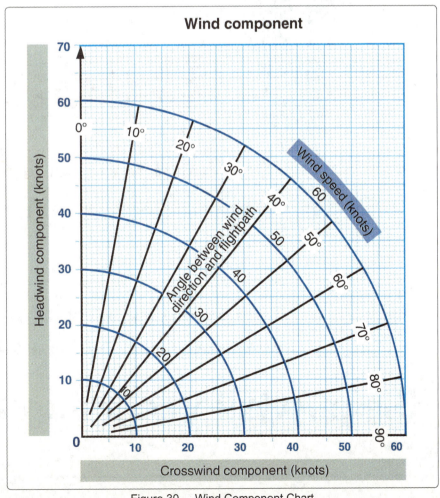

Figure 30. – Wind Component Chart.

STUDY UNIT THREE
AIRPLANE INSTRUMENTS, ENGINES, AND SYSTEMS

(7 pages of outline)

3.1	Compass Errors	(6 questions)	89, 96
3.2	Pitot-Static and Vacuum Systems	(6 questions)	90, 97
3.3	Airspeed Indicator	(5 questions)	90, 98
3.4	Altimeter	(3 questions)	91, 99
3.5	Engine Temperature	(10 questions)	91, 100
3.6	Propellers	(8 questions)	92, 102
3.7	Manifold Pressure Gauge	(1 question)	93, 103
3.8	Engine Ignition System	(4 questions)	93, 104
3.9	Carburetor and Fuel-Injection Systems	(3 questions)	93, 105
3.10	Carburetor Icing	(10 questions)	93, 105
3.11	Turbocharged Engines	(2 questions)	94, 107
3.12	Engine Cycle	(4 questions)	94, 108
3.13	Fuel/Air Mixture	(12 questions)	94, 108
3.14	Fuel Tank Vents	(2 questions)	95, 111
3.15	Detonation and Abnormal Combustion	(8 questions)	95, 111
3.16	Aviation Fuel Practices	(4 questions)	95, 113
3.17	Electrical System	(2 questions)	95, 114
3.18	Oxygen Systems	(4 questions)	95, 114
3.19	Cold Weather Operation	(3 questions)	95, 115

This study unit contains outlines of major concepts tested; sample test questions and answers regarding airplane instruments, engines, and systems; and an explanation of each answer. The table of contents above lists each subunit within this study unit, the number of questions pertaining to that particular subunit, and the pages on which the outlines and questions begin, respectively.

 Recall that the **sole purpose** of this book is to expedite your passing of the FAA pilot knowledge test for the CFI, BGI, or AGI certificate. Accordingly, all extraneous material (i.e., topics or regulations not directly tested on the FAA pilot knowledge test) is omitted, even though much more knowledge is necessary to become a proficient flight or ground instructor. This additional material is presented in *Pilot Handbook* and *Flight Instructor Flight Maneuvers and Practical Test Prep*, available from Gleim Publications, Inc. Order online at www.GleimAviation.com.

3.1 COMPASS ERRORS

1. The difference between the direction indicated by a magnetic compass not installed in an airplane and one installed in an airplane is called compass **deviation**.

    a. Magnetic fields produced by metals and electrical accessories in the airplane disturb the compass needles.
    b. Deviation varies for different headings of the same aircraft.

2. **Acceleration/deceleration error** occurs when on an easterly or westerly heading. In the Northern Hemisphere,

    a. A magnetic compass will indicate a turn toward the north during acceleration on an easterly or westerly heading, and
    b. A magnetic compass will indicate a turn toward the south during deceleration on an easterly or westerly heading.
    c. Acceleration/deceleration error does not occur when on a northerly or southerly heading.

3. **Turning error** occurs when turning from a northerly or southerly heading.

    a. When turning from a southerly heading in the Northern Hemisphere, the magnetic compass indicates the turn but at a faster rate than is actually occurring.

    b. When making a turn to a heading of south in the Northern Hemisphere, start the rollout after the compass indication passes south by a number of degrees approximately equal to the latitude minus the normal rollout lead.

3.2 PITOT-STATIC AND VACUUM SYSTEMS

1. In most airplanes, the vacuum system operates the gyroscopes of both the heading indicator and the attitude indicator.

    a. Thus, an excessively low pressure in the airplane's vacuum system would affect both the heading indicator and the attitude indicator.

2. The pitot system provides impact pressure for the airspeed indicator.

3. The pitot tube may become blocked by ice or debris, or you may forget to remove the pitot tube cover during preflight.

    a. If the pitot tube is clogged, only the airspeed indicator will be affected, as it is the only instrument dependent on the pitot tube in the pitot-static system.

    b. If both the ram-air input and the drain hole of the pitot system are blocked, the airspeed indication will not change in level flight even if large power changes are made.

4. Pitot-static system installation and instrument errors are generally the greatest at low airspeeds when the airplane is flying at a higher angle of attack.

    a. This higher angle of attack affects the airflow around the airplane and causes the greatest error in the static system (i.e., position, or installation, error) due to the position of the static vent(s).

    b. If, during a power-off stall with flaps full down, the stall occurs and the pointer on the airspeed indicator shows a speed less than the minimum limit of the white arc on the indicator, it is probably due to installation error in the pitot-static system.

3.3 AIRSPEED INDICATOR

1. Airspeed indicators have several color-coded markings (figure below).

- a. The **white arc** is the full flap operating range.
    1) The lower limit is the power-off stalling speed with wing flaps and landing gear in the landing configuration (V_{S0}).
    2) The upper limit is the maximum full flaps-extended speed (V_{FE}).
- b. The **green arc** is the normal operating range.
    1) The lower limit is the power-off stalling speed in a specified configuration (V_{S1}). This is normally wing flaps up and landing gear retracted.
    2) The upper limit is the maximum structural cruising speed (V_{NO}) for normal operation.
- c. The **yellow arc** indicates the airspeed that is safe in smooth air only.
    1) It is known as the caution range.
- d. The **red line** indicates the speed that should never be exceeded (V_{NE}).

2. **The most important airspeed limitation that is not color-coded is the design maneuvering speed** (V_A).
   - a. The design maneuvering speed is the speed below which you can move a single flight control, one time, to its full deflection, for one axis of airplane rotation only (pitch, roll, or yaw), in smooth air, without risk of damage to the airplane.
   - b. It is usually the maximum speed for flight in turbulent air.

3.4 ALTIMETER

1. If the static pressure tubes are broken inside a pressurized cabin during a high-altitude flight, the altimeter will probably indicate a lower-than-actual flight altitude because the pressure in the cabin is greater than the pressure outside the airplane.
   - a. Use of an emergency alternate static source inside the cabin of an unpressurized airplane may result in the altimeter indicating an altitude higher than that actually being flown because of the venturi effect of air flowing around the cabin, resulting in a slightly lower pressure inside the cabin.
2. Temperature variations expand or contract the atmosphere and raise or lower the pressure levels that the altimeter is designed to sense.
   - a. Thus, colder-than-standard temperatures will place the aircraft lower than the altimeter indicates.

3.5 ENGINE TEMPERATURE

1. Excessively high engine temperature either in the air or on the ground will cause excessive oil consumption, loss of power, and possible permanent internal engine damage.
   - a. Effective engine cooling is dependent on the circulation of lubricating oil.
2. Aircraft engines are either cooled by airflow, circulated coolant, or some combination of both.
   - a. Air-cooled engines rely on direct airflow of the engine's cylinders to dissipate collected heat.
   - b. Liquid-cooled engines rely on an air-cooled radiator, fluid lines, coolant, and a coolant pump to remove heat from engine components.

3. Engine oil and cylinder head temperatures can exceed their normal operating range because of (among other causes)

   a. Operating with too much power
   b. Climbing too steeply (at too low an airspeed) in hot weather
   c. Using fuel that has a lower-than-specified octane rating
   d. Operating with too lean a mixture
   e. Operating with the oil level too low

4. To cool an overheating engine, follow these steps:

   a. Open the cowl flaps, if equipped;
   b. Increase airspeed;
   c. Decrease engine RPM; and
   d. Richen the mixture.

      1) These steps need not be accomplished one by one. You may perform all the steps and then check the CHT indication for a change, or you may elect to perform each step individually, checking the CHT between each step for a change.
      2) If you are unable to cool the engine, seek an airport for landing without undue delay.

3.6 PROPELLERS

1. The advantage of a **constant-speed propeller** (also known as controllable-pitch) is that it permits the pilot to select the blade pitch setting that is suitable for each flight situation and power setting.

   a. Maximum engine power for maximum thrust is obtained by use of a small angle of attack, which results in a high RPM.

2. To avoid overstressing cylinders, high manifold pressure should not be used with low RPM settings.

   a. When reducing power, reduce manifold pressure before RPM.
   b. When increasing power, increase RPM before manifold pressure.

3. **Propeller efficiency** is the ratio of thrust horsepower to brake horsepower.

   a. **Geometric pitch** is the theoretical distance the propeller would move forward in a solid medium in one revolution.
   b. **Effective pitch** is the actual distance the propeller moves through the air in one revolution.
   c. **Propeller slip** is the difference between the geometric pitch and the effective pitch of the propeller.

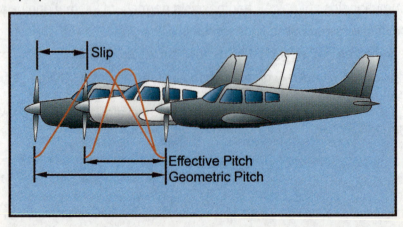

4. At high density altitudes, propeller efficiency is reduced because the propeller exerts less force at high density altitudes than at low density altitudes.
5. The **blade angle of a propeller** is the angle between the chord line and the plane of rotation.
6. The variation in geometric pitch (twisting) along the propeller blade permits a relatively constant angle of attack along its length when in cruising flight.

3.7 MANIFOLD PRESSURE GAUGE

1. The manifold pressure gauge measures the air pressure in the fuel/air induction manifold.
   a. When the engine is not running, the pressure in the induction manifold equals the local atmospheric pressure and is indicated on the manifold pressure gauge.

3.8 ENGINE IGNITION SYSTEM

1. Dual ignition systems, in addition to providing an additional safety factor, provide better combustion of the burning fuel/air mixture.
2. If the ground wire between the magneto and the ignition switch is disconnected, the engine cannot be shut down by turning the ignition switch off.
   a. It does not affect the operation of the engine while it is running.
   b. If the propeller is moved while fuel is in the engine cylinders, the engine could accidentally start.
3. After starting the engine, you should instruct your students to immediately adjust the throttle to 800 - 1,000 RPMs (or as specified by the aircraft manufacturer) and check engine gauges for adequate oil pressure.

3.9 CARBURETOR AND FUEL-INJECTION SYSTEMS

1. **Fuel-injection systems** are just as susceptible to impact icing as carburetor systems.
2. **Float-type carburetors** operate on the principle of increasing the air velocity in the throat of a venturi causing a decrease in air pressure, which draws the fuel from a fuel jet into the air.
3. **Fuel-injection systems** inject fuel directly into the cylinders, which results in a more even fuel distribution to each cylinder than in a carburetor system.

3.10 CARBURETOR ICING

1. The first indication of carburetor ice in an aircraft with a fixed-pitch propeller is a drop in RPM.
   a. When carburetor heat is applied, there will be a further decrease in RPM (due to the warmer, less dense air entering the engine). Generally, carburetor heat tends to decrease engine performance. If icing is present, there will be a gradual increase in RPM as the ice melts.
2. The first indication of carburetor icing in airplanes with constant-speed propellers is a decrease in manifold pressure.
3. Carburetor ice is likely to form when the outside air temperature is between –7°C (20°F) and 21°C (70°F), with visible moisture or high humidity.

4. The low temperature that causes carburetor ice in an engine equipped with a float-type carburetor is normally the result of the vaporization of fuel and expansion of air in the carburetor.
5. Leaving the carburetor heat on during takeoff will decrease engine performance and increase the takeoff roll.

3.11 TURBOCHARGED ENGINES

1. Engine exhaust gases drive the turbines of a turbocharged engine.
2. A turbocharged engine can maintain a constant manifold pressure until the engine's critical altitude is reached.
   a. Above the critical altitude, the turbine is rotating at its highest speed and can no longer compensate for the decreasing power (i.e., manifold pressure).

3.12 ENGINE CYCLE

1. For a reciprocating engine to complete one cycle, the piston must complete the following four strokes:
   a. Intake
   b. Compression
   c. Power
   d. Exhaust
2. Fuel and exhaust enter and exit a 4-cycle engine through intake and exhaust ports.
3. During the power stroke, the gaseous mixture is burned and expands within the cylinder to push the piston down.
4. Four-cycle engines are lubricated by forcing oil directly to the components requiring lubrication.

3.13 FUEL/AIR MIXTURE

1. The fuel/air ratio is the ratio between the weight of fuel and the weight of air entering the cylinder. This ratio should remain constant.
2. An exhaust gas temperature (EGT) gauge permits the mixture to be properly leaned so that the engine runs at the optimal temperature for better economy.
3. The mixture control knob adjusts the fuel flow to obtain the proper fuel/air ratio.
   a. The leaning process reduces the amount of fuel entering the combustion chamber.
   b. If this is not done as flight altitude increases, the density of air entering the carburetor will decrease while the amount of fuel remains constant.
      1) The purpose of adjusting the fuel/air mixture at altitude is to decrease fuel flow to compensate for decreased air density.
4. The best power mixture is the fuel/air ratio where the most power can be obtained for any given throttle setting.
5. If the mixture is too rich, excessive fuel consumption, rough engine operation, and loss of power will occur.
   a. Due to excessive fuel from a too-rich mixture, a cooling of the combustion chamber takes place, which leads to spark plug fouling.
   b. Fouling of spark plugs is more likely to occur if the aircraft gains altitude with no mixture adjustment.

3.14 FUEL TANK VENTS

1. The fuel tank vents must be open to allow proper air pressure within the fuel tanks so as to maintain a steady fuel flow to the engine.

3.15 DETONATION AND ABNORMAL COMBUSTION

1. Detonation is most likely to occur when the engine is operated under conditions that cause the fuel/air mixture to burn instantaneously rather than burning normally.
   a. At high power settings, detonation occurs when the fuel mixture explodes instead of burning evenly and progressively.
   b. The initial corrective action for detonation during climb-out would be to lower the nose. This will lessen the climb rate, increase airspeed, and increase cooling airflow through the engine compartment.
2. Use of a lower-than-specified grade of fuel may cause detonation.
3. Pre-ignition is the uncontrolled firing of the fuel/air charge in advance of the normal spark ignition.

3.16 AVIATION FUEL PRACTICES

1. All fuel strainer drains and fuel tank sumps should be drained before each flight to make sure there is no water in the fuel system.
2. The amount of water that can be absorbed by aviation fuels increases as the fuel temperature increases.
3. In an airplane equipped with fuel pumps, running a fuel tank dry before switching tanks while in the air is not a good practice because the fuel pump may draw air into the fuel system and cause vapor lock.
4. To prevent the potential hazard of static electricity when refueling aircraft, connect a ground wire between the aircraft, the fuel truck, the fuel nozzle, and the ground.

3.17 ELECTRICAL SYSTEM

1. Alternators provide more electrical power at lower engine RPM than generators do.
2. Electrical system failure (battery and alternator) usually results in avionics system failure.

3.18 OXYGEN SYSTEMS

1. Only use aviation breathing oxygen in airplane oxygen systems.
   a. Do not use industrial oxygen, which is not designed for human consumption.
2. A continuous-flow oxygen system is most commonly found in general aviation aircraft.
3. The rebreather bag in a continuous-flow oxygen system helps conserve oxygen by allowing part of the exhaled gases to be reused.

3.19 COLD WEATHER OPERATION

1. Low temperatures may cause a change in the viscosity of engine oils, batteries may lose a high percentage of their effectiveness, and instruments may stick.
   a. Thus, preheating of engines as well as the cockpit before starting is desirable in low temperatures.
2. In cold weather, crankcase breather lines should be inspected to determine whether they are blocked with ice from crankcase vapors that have condensed and frozen.

QUESTIONS AND ANSWER EXPLANATIONS: All of the AGI/CFI knowledge test questions chosen by the FAA for release as well as additional questions selected by Gleim relating to the material in the previous outlines are reproduced on the following pages. These questions have been organized into the same subunits as the outlines. To the immediate right of each question are the correct answer and answer explanation. You should cover these answers and answer explanations while responding to the questions. Refer to the general discussion in the Introduction on how to take the FAA knowledge test.

Remember that the questions from the FAA knowledge test bank have been reordered by topic and organized into a meaningful sequence. Also, the first line of the answer explanation gives the citation of the authoritative source for the answer.

QUESTIONS

3.1 Compass Errors

1. Deviation error of the magnetic compass is caused by

A. northerly turning error.
B. certain metals and electrical systems within the aircraft.
C. the difference in location of true north and magnetic north.

Answer (B) is correct. *(PHAK Chap 8)*
DISCUSSION: The difference between the direction indicated by a magnetic compass not installed in an airplane and one that is installed in an airplane is called compass deviation. Magnetic fields produced by metals and electrical accessories in the airplane disturb the compass needle and produce errors.
Answer (A) is incorrect. A northerly turning error is a compass error caused by magnetic dip, not deviation. Answer (C) is incorrect. It defines magnetic variation, not deviation.

2. Which statement is true about magnetic deviation of a compass?

A. Deviation is the same for all aircraft in the same locality.
B. Deviation varies for different headings of the same aircraft.
C. Deviation is different in a given aircraft in different localities.

Answer (B) is correct. *(PHAK Chap 8)*
DISCUSSION: Magnetic disturbances from magnetic fields produced by metals and electrical accessories in an aircraft disturb the compass needles to produce an error called deviation. As an aircraft turns, metallic and electrical equipment in the aircraft change their position relative to the compass's north-seeking magnetized needles. This causes their influence on the compass needles to change, which changes the amount of deviation error. Thus, deviation varies for different headings of the same aircraft.
Answer (A) is incorrect. Variation, not deviation, is the same for all aircraft in the same locality. Answer (C) is incorrect. Variation, not deviation, is different in a given aircraft in different localities.

3. In the Northern Hemisphere, a magnetic compass will normally indicate a turn toward the north if

A. a left turn is entered from a west heading.
B. an aircraft is decelerated while on an east or west heading.
C. an aircraft is accelerated while on an east or west heading.

Answer (C) is correct. *(PHAK Chap 8)*
DISCUSSION: In the Northern Hemisphere, a magnetic compass will normally indicate a turn toward the north if an airplane is accelerated while on an east or west heading.
Answer (A) is incorrect. On turns from west headings, the compass will not reflect turning errors; i.e., it will be accurate in smooth, coordinated turns. Answer (B) is incorrect. If an airplane is decelerated while on an east or west heading, the compass would indicate a turn to the south, not north.

4. In the Northern Hemisphere, if an aircraft is accelerated or decelerated, the magnetic compass will normally indicate

A. a turn momentarily, with changes in airspeed on any heading.
B. a turn toward the south while accelerating on a west heading.
C. correctly when on a north or south heading while either accelerating or decelerating.

Answer (C) is correct. *(PHAK Chap 8)*
DISCUSSION: Acceleration and deceleration errors on magnetic compasses do not occur when on north or south headings. These errors occur only on east and west headings.
Answer (A) is incorrect. Acceleration and deceleration errors occur only on easterly and westerly headings. Answer (B) is incorrect. The magnetic compass will normally indicate a turn toward the north, not south, while accelerating on a westerly heading.

5. In the Northern Hemisphere, which would be correct about starting the rollout from a turn using a magnetic compass? Start the rollout

A. after the compass indication passes south by a number of degrees approximately equal to the latitude minus the normal rollout lead.
B. before the compass indication reaches south by a number of degrees approximately equal to the latitude over which the turn is made plus the pilot's normal lead.
C. after the compass indication passes south by a number of degrees approximately equal to the magnetic variation of the area over which the turn is made plus the pilot's normal lead.

Answer (A) is correct. *(IFH Chap 5)*
DISCUSSION: When turning toward the south in the Northern Hemisphere, magnetic compasses lead the turn. With a standard-rate turn, the amount of lead is approximately equal to the latitude. Thus, during a turn to the south, roll out when the compass passes south by the number of degrees of your latitude, minus your normal rollout lead.
Answer (B) is incorrect. When turning to the south in the Northern Hemisphere, you start the rollout after, not before, the compass indication passes south by the number of degrees of approximate latitude minus, not plus, your normal rollout lead. Answer (C) is incorrect. You subtract, not add, the pilot's normal lead and the compass leads the turn by the number of degrees of latitude, not magnetic variation.

6. What should be the indication on the magnetic compass as you roll into a standard rate turn to the right from a south heading in the Northern Hemisphere?

A. The compass will initially indicate a turn to the left.
B. The compass will indicate a turn to the right, but at a faster rate than is actually occurring.
C. The compass will remain on south for a short time, then gradually catch up to the magnetic heading of the airplane.

Answer (B) is correct. *(IFH Chap 5)*
DISCUSSION: When on a southerly heading in the Northern Hemisphere and you roll into a standard rate turn to the right, the magnetic compass indication precedes the turn, showing a greater amount of turn than is actually occurring.
Answer (A) is incorrect. The magnetic compass will initially indicate a turn to the left when you roll into a standard rate turn from a north, not south, heading in the Northern Hemisphere. Answer (C) is incorrect. The magnetic compass indication will precede the turn, not remain constant, when you roll into a standard rate turn from a south heading in the Northern Hemisphere.

3.2 Pitot-Static and Vacuum Systems

7. Which instrument would be affected by excessively low pressure in the airplane's vacuum system?

A. Heading indicator.
B. Airspeed indicator.
C. Pressure altimeter.

Answer (A) is correct. *(PHAK Chap 8)*
DISCUSSION: The gyroscopic instruments are the heading indicator, attitude indicator, and the turn coordinator. The heading and attitude indicators are usually operated by a vacuum system.
Answer (B) is incorrect. The airspeed indicator does not have a gyroscope and is part of the pitot-static system. Answer (C) is incorrect. The pressure altimeter does not have a gyroscope and is part of the pitot-static system.

8. If both the ram-air input and drain hole of the pitot system are blocked, what airspeed indication can be expected?

A. Decrease of indicated airspeed during a climb.
B. Zero indicated airspeed until blockage is removed.
C. No variation of indicated airspeed in level flight even if large power changes are made.

Answer (C) is correct. *(AC 91-43)*
DISCUSSION: If the ram-air input plus the drain hole are blocked, the pressure is trapped in the system and the airspeed indicator will react as an altimeter. During level flight, airspeed indications will not change even if large power changes are made.
Answer (A) is incorrect. Indicated airspeed would increase, not decrease, in a climb. Answer (B) is incorrect. The airspeed would indicate zero if only the ram-air input was blocked while the drain hole remained open, not blocked.

9. The pitot system provides impact pressure for which instrument?

A. Altimeter.
B. Vertical-speed indicator.
C. Airspeed indicator.

Answer (C) is correct. *(PHAK Chap 8)*
DISCUSSION: The pitot tube provides impact, or dynamic pressure for the airspeed indicator.
Answer (A) is incorrect. Only static pressure is used by the altimeter. Answer (B) is incorrect. Only static pressure is used by the vertical-speed indicator.

10. Pitot-static system errors are generally the greatest in which range of airspeed?

A. Low airspeed.
B. High airspeed.
C. Maneuvering speed.

Answer (A) is correct. *(PHAK Chap 8)*
DISCUSSION: Pitot-static system errors are generally the greatest at low airspeeds when there is a high angle of attack. This higher angle of attack affects the airflow around the airplane and causes the most error in the static system (i.e., position error) due to the position of the static vent(s). The error in the pitot tube is relatively small compared with the position error.
Answer (B) is incorrect. High airspeed occurs when the angle of attack is low, i.e., normal, and the pitot-static system error is the smallest, not the greatest. Answer (C) is incorrect. Maneuvering speed is the airspeed for turbulent air penetration and occurs at a lower angle of attack than at low airspeeds. Thus, pitot-static system errors are less at maneuvering speed than at low airspeed.

11. During power-off stalls with flaps full down, the stall occurs and the pointer on the airspeed indicator shows a speed less than the minimum limit of the white arc on the indicator. This is most probably due to

A. a low density altitude.
B. a malfunction in the pitot-static system.
C. installation error in the pitot-static system.

Answer (C) is correct. *(PHAK Chap 8)*
DISCUSSION: At certain airspeeds with certain flap settings, the installation and instrument error in the pitot-static system may be several knots (or MPH). This error is generally greatest at low airspeeds and maximum flap settings. Thus, during a power-off stall with full flaps, the pointer on the airspeed indicator may show an airspeed less than the lower limit of the white arc.
Answer (A) is incorrect. The density altitude affects the stall speed and airspeed indicator in the same manner; i.e., airplanes stall at the same indicated airspeed at all altitudes. Answer (B) is incorrect. An airspeed indication of less than the lower limit of the white arc during a power-off stall with full flaps is probably due to installation error, not a malfunction, in the pitot-static system.

12. If a pitot tube is clogged, which instrument would be affected?

A. Altimeter.
B. Airspeed indicator.
C. Vertical speed indicator.

Answer (B) is correct. *(PHAK Chap 8)*
DISCUSSION: Only the airspeed indicator uses the pitot tube by measuring the differential pressure between pitot tube and static port to indicate airspeed.
Answer (A) is incorrect. The altimeter utilizes only the static port. Answer (C) is incorrect. The vertical speed indicator utilizes only the static port.

3.3 Airspeed Indicator

13. What does the lower limit of the white arc on an airspeed indicator represent?

A. Minimum controllable airspeed with flaps extended.
B. Power-off stall speed in a landing configuration.
C. Power-off stall speed in a specified configuration.

Answer (B) is correct. *(PHAK Chap 8)*
DISCUSSION: The lower limit of the white arc is the power-off stall speed in a landing configuration, i.e., with gear and flaps extended (V_{S0}).
Answer (A) is incorrect. Minimum controllable airspeed in any configuration is not indicated by color-coded markings on the airspeed indicator. Answer (C) is incorrect. The lower limit of the green, not white, arc represents the power-off stall speed in a specified configuration (V_{S1}).

14. What does the lower limit of the green arc on an airspeed indicator represent?

A. Power-off stall speed in a landing configuration.
B. Power-off stall speed in a specified configuration.
C. Minimum controllable airspeed with gear and flaps retracted.

Answer (B) is correct. *(PHAK Chap 8)*
DISCUSSION: The lower limit of the green arc indicates the power-off stall speed in a specified configuration, i.e., with the flaps and landing gear retracted (V_{S1}).
Answer (A) is incorrect. The lower limit of the white, not green, arc represents the power-off stall speed in the landing configuration (V_{S0}). Answer (C) is incorrect. Minimum controllable airspeed in any configuration is not indicated by color-coded markings on the airspeed indicator.

SU 3: Airplane Instruments, Engines, and Systems   99

15. What airspeed indicator marking identifies the maximum structural cruising speed of an aircraft?

A. Red radial line.
B. Upper limit of the green arc.
C. Upper limit of the yellow arc.

Answer (B) is correct. *(PHAK Chap 8)*
DISCUSSION: The upper limit of the green arc indicates the maximum structural cruising speed (V_{NO}) of the airplane.
Answer (A) is incorrect. The red radial line indicates the never-exceed speed (V_{NE}). Answer (C) is incorrect. The lower, not upper, limit of the yellow arc on the airspeed indicator indicates the maximum structural cruising speed.

16. Which airspeed is identified by color coding on an airspeed indicator?

A. Design maneuvering speed.
B. Maximum structural cruising speed.
C. Maximum gear operation or extended speed.

Answer (B) is correct. *(PHAK Chap 8)*
DISCUSSION: The upper limit of the green arc or the lower limit of the yellow arc is the maximum structural cruising speed (V_{NO}).
Answer (A) is incorrect. The design maneuvering speed (V_A) is not shown on the airspeed indicator. It is found in the operating handbook or on a placard. Answer (C) is incorrect. The maximum gear operation (V_{LO}) and extended speed (V_{LE}) are not shown on the airspeed indicator. They are found in the airplane's operating handbook or on a placard.

17. What is an important airspeed limitation not color coded on airspeed indicators?

A. Maneuvering speed.
B. Never-exceed speed.
C. Maximum flaps-extended speed.

Answer (A) is correct. *(PHAK Chap 8)*
DISCUSSION: The maneuvering speed (V_A) is not indicated on an airspeed indicator. It is the speed below which you can move a single flight control, one time, to its full deflection, for one axis of airplane rotation only (pitch, roll, or yaw), in smooth air, without risk of damage to the airplane. This is also the airspeed used when you encounter rough or turbulent air during flight.
Answer (B) is incorrect. The never-exceed speed (V_{NE}) is the red line at the upper limit of the yellow arc. Answer (C) is incorrect. The maximum flaps-extended speed (V_{FE}) is the upper limit of the white arc.

3.4 Altimeter

18. If the static pressure tubes are broken inside a pressurized cabin during a high-altitude flight, the altimeter would probably indicate

A. sea level.
B. lower than actual flight altitude.
C. higher than actual flight altitude.

Answer (B) is correct. *(PHAK Chap 8)*
DISCUSSION: The static pressure (in contrast to the impact pressure) provides the altimeter reading. As pressure increases, the altimeter indicates a lower altitude. Thus, if the static pressure tubes are broken inside a pressurized cabin, the altimeter would indicate cabin pressure altitude and thus a lower-than-actual flight altitude.
Answer (A) is incorrect. At high altitudes, pressurized aircraft cannot maintain a cabin pressure of sea level. Answer (C) is incorrect. The altimeter would probably indicate a higher than actual flight altitude if the static pressure tube were broken inside an unpressurized, not a pressurized, airplane.

19. Which statement is true about the effect of temperature changes on the indications of a sensitive altimeter?

A. Warmer-than-standard temperatures will place the aircraft lower than the altimeter indicates.
B. Colder-than-standard temperatures will place the aircraft lower than the altimeter indicates.
C. Colder-than-standard temperatures will place the aircraft higher than the altimeter indicates.

Answer (B) is correct. *(PHAK Chap 8)*
DISCUSSION: Variations in air temperature affect the difference between indicated and true altitude. On a cold day, the denser air is heavier in weight than on a warm day, so the pressure levels are lowered. For example, the true altitude at which the altimeter reads 10,000 ft. will be lower under colder-than-standard conditions.
Answer (A) is incorrect. Warmer-than-standard temperatures raise the pressure levels, and thus the aircraft is higher, not lower, than the altimeter indicates. Answer (C) is incorrect. Colder-than-standard temperatures lower the pressure levels, and thus the aircraft is lower, not higher, than the altimeter indicates.

20. A possible result of using the emergency alternate source of static pressure inside the cabin of an unpressurized airplane is the

   A. airspeed indicator may indicate less than normal.
   B. altimeter may indicate an altitude lower than the actual altitude being flown.
   C. altimeter may indicate an altitude higher than the actual altitude being flown.

Answer (C) is correct. *(PHAK Chap 8)*
DISCUSSION: The alternate static port is provided in airplanes for use when the static port becomes clogged. The source is usually vented to the pressure inside the cockpit. Because of the venturi effect of the flow of air over the cockpit, the alternate static pressure (inside the cabin) is lower than the pressure provided by the normal static source (outside). Accordingly, the altimeter may indicate higher than the actual altitude, the airspeed indicator may indicate greater than the actual airspeed, and the vertical speed indicator may indicate a momentary climb.
Answer (A) is incorrect. The airspeed indicator may indicate greater, not lower, than the actual airspeed due to the greater differential pressure between the pitot source and the alternate static source. Answer (B) is incorrect. The altimeter may indicate an altitude higher, not lower, than the actual altitude due to the decreased pressure from the alternate static source.

3.5 Engine Temperature

21. Excessively high engine temperatures, either in the air or on the ground, will

   A. increase fuel consumption and may increase power due to the increased heat.
   B. result in damage to heat-conducting hoses and warping of cylinder cooling fans.
   C. cause loss of power, excessive oil consumption, and possible permanent internal engine damage.

Answer (C) is correct. *(PHAK Chap 7)*
DISCUSSION: Operating the engine at excessively high temperatures will cause loss of power and excessive oil consumption, and can permanently damage engines.
Answer (A) is incorrect. Overheating can cause excessive oil, not fuel, consumption and a loss, not increase, of power. Answer (B) is incorrect. Hoses are not used to transfer heat in airplane engines. Also, it is extremely unlikely one could overheat an engine to an extent to warp the cylinder cooling fans.

22. What action can a pilot take to aid in cooling an engine that is overheating during a climb?

   A. Reduce rate of climb and increase airspeed.
   B. Reduce climb speed and increase RPM.
   C. Increase climb speed and increase RPM.

Answer (A) is correct. *(AFH Chap 16)*
DISCUSSION: Reducing the rate of climb by lowering the pitch attitude and increasing airspeed will increase airflow through the engine compartment, thus assisting you in cooling the engine.
Answer (B) is incorrect. Reducing the climb speed will limit airflow through the engine compartment, thus increasing engine temperature. Likewise, increasing RPM will increase engine temperature. Answer (C) is incorrect. Increasing RPM will increase engine temperature, not lower it.

23. Excessively high engine temperatures will

   A. cause damage to heat-conducting hoses and warping of the cylinder cooling fins.
   B. cause loss of power, excessive oil consumption, and possible permanent internal engine damage.
   C. not appreciably affect an aircraft engine.

Answer (B) is correct. *(PHAK Chap 7)*
DISCUSSION: Operating the engine at excessively high temperatures will cause loss of power, excessive oil consumption, and possible permanent internal engine damage.
Answer (A) is incorrect. Hoses are not used to transfer heat in an aircraft engine. Also, it is extremely unlikely that one could overheat an engine to the extent that it warps the cylinder cooling fins. Answer (C) is incorrect. Operating the engine at excessively high temperatures will cause loss of power, excessive oil consumption, and possible permanent internal engine damage.

24. An abnormally high engine oil temperature indication may be caused by

   A. the oil quantity being too low.
   B. operating with a too high viscosity oil.
   C. operating with an excessively rich mixture.

Answer (A) is correct. *(PHAK Chap 7)*
DISCUSSION: Oil temperature changes are registered more slowly than oil pressure changes. Oil temperature should be monitored periodically during flight. High oil temperature may indicate a plugged oil line, a low oil quantity, a blocked oil cooler, or a defective temperature gauge.
Answer (B) is incorrect. Using too high an oil viscosity rating may result in low, not high, oil temperatures. Answer (C) is incorrect. An excessively rich fuel mixture will result in slightly cooler engine operating temperatures.

25. For internal cooling, air-cooled engines are especially dependent on

  A. a properly functioning thermostat.
  B. air flowing over the exhaust manifold.
  C. the circulation of lubricating oil.

Answer (C) is correct. *(PHAK Chap 7)*
  DISCUSSION: The oil system is vital to the internal cooling of the engine.
  Answer (A) is incorrect. Air-cooled engines do not have thermostats installed in them. Answer (B) is incorrect. Air is circulated through the engine compartment and over the cylinder heads to aid in cooling, not the exhaust manifold.

26. If, during flight, you notice that the cylinder head temperature (CHT) indication exceeds the normal operating range, how would you proceed to cool the engine?

  A. Open the cowl flaps, increase airspeed, increase engine RPM, and lean the mixture.
  B. Open the cowl flaps, increase airspeed, decrease engine RPM, and richen the mixture.
  C. Open the cowl flaps, decrease airspeed, decrease engine RPM, and richen the mixture.

Answer (B) is correct. *(PHAK Chap 4)*
  DISCUSSION: To remedy an overheating engine, first open the cowl flaps (if equipped). Then, increase the airspeed by placing the airplane in a descent if possible. Next, decrease the engine RPM to reduce the amount of combustion inside the cylinders. Finally, richen the mixture to allow more fuel to flow into the cylinders and cool the operating temperature. These steps need not be accomplished one by one. You may perform all the steps and then check the CHT indication for a change, or you may elect to perform each step individually, checking the CHT between each step for a change. If you are unable to cool the engine, seek an airport for landing without undue delay.
  Answer (A) is incorrect. Increasing the engine RPM and leaning the mixture will increase, not decrease, engine operating temperature. Answer (C) is incorrect. Decreasing airspeed will limit airflow into the engine compartment and could prevent engine cooling.

27. If the engine oil temperature and cylinder head temperature gauges have exceeded their normal operating range, you may have been

  A. operating with the mixture set too rich.
  B. using fuel that has a higher-than-specified fuel rating.
  C. operating with too much power and with the mixture set too lean.

Answer (C) is correct. *(PHAK Chap 7)*
  DISCUSSION: Engine oil temperatures and cylinder head temperatures exceeding the normal operating range may indicate that you are operating with too much power and the mixture set too lean. An airplane engine runs warmer when it operates with the fuel mixture set too lean. Also, an engine that operates at a power setting that is too high will overheat.
  Answer (A) is incorrect. Rich mixtures have a tendency to lower, not raise, engine operating temperatures. Answer (B) is incorrect. Higher-than-specified fuel ratings have a tendency to lower, not raise, engine operating temperatures.

28. An abnormally high engine oil temperature indication may be caused by

  A. a defective bearing.
  B. the oil level being too low.
  C. operating with an excessively rich mixture.

Answer (B) is correct. *(PHAK Chap 7)*
  DISCUSSION: Oil temperature changes are registered more slowly than oil pressure changes. Oil temperature should be monitored periodically during flight. High oil temperature may indicate a plugged oil line, a low oil quantity, a blocked oil cooler, or a defective temperature gauge.
  Answer (A) is incorrect. A defective bearing would be caused by a low oil level and high oil temperature. Said another way, it is the result, not the cause, of high oil temperature. Answer (C) is incorrect. An excessively rich fuel mixture will result in slightly cooler engine operating temperatures.

29. Air cooled engines dissipate heat

  A. through cooling fins on the cylinder and head.
  B. by air flowing through the radiator fins.
  C. through the cylinder head temperature probe.

Answer (A) is correct. *(PHAK Chap 7)*
  DISCUSSION: Air cooled engines rely on direct airflow over the engine cylinders to dissipate heat. The addition of cooling fins increases the surface area of the cylinder to allow for better cooling.
  Answer (B) is incorrect. An air cooled engine would not employ a radiator. Radiators are found on liquid cooled engines. Answer (C) is incorrect. The cylinder head temperature (CHT) probe measures the temperature of the cylinder head, but it does not offer any help in cooling the cylinder.

30. Coolant in a liquid cooled engine is normally circulated by

A. capillary attraction.
B. an electric pump.
C. an engine driven pump.

Answer (C) is correct. *(PHAK Chap 7)*
  DISCUSSION: A liquid cooled engine relies on an engine-driven pump, similar to the oil pump, to circulate coolant through the system.
  Answer (A) is incorrect. While an effective circulation method, capillary attraction does not provide the rate of flow required to dissipate the heat produced by a liquid cooled engine. Answer (B) is incorrect. Because engine cooling is a required function at all times during engine operation, a coolant pump is driven by the engine itself, rather than by an auxiliary electric pump.

3.6 Propellers

31. What is the primary advantage of a constant-speed propeller?

A. To maintain a specific engine speed.
B. To obtain a pitch setting that is suitable for each flight situation and power setting.
C. To obtain and maintain a selected pitch angle of the blades regardless of the flight situation or power setting.

Answer (B) is correct. *(PHAK Chap 7)*
  DISCUSSION: A constant-speed propeller is a variable-pitch propeller. Accordingly, it can be adjusted to obtain a pitch setting that is suitable for each flight situation and power setting.
  Answer (A) is incorrect. The most efficient engine speed (RPM) will vary with different phases of flight. Answer (C) is incorrect. The advantage of a constant-speed propeller is that it maintains a selected angle of attack, not pitch angle, of the blade.

32. To absorb maximum engine power and to develop maximum thrust, a constant-speed propeller should be adjusted to a blade angle which will produce a

A. large angle of attack and low RPM.
B. large angle of attack and high RPM.
C. small angle of attack and high RPM.

Answer (C) is correct. *(PHAK Chap 7)*
  DISCUSSION: When using a constant-speed propeller, the maximum engine power for maximum thrust can be obtained by adjusting the propeller blade angle to produce a small angle of attack and high RPM.
  Answer (A) is incorrect. Low RPMs do not provide maximum power. Answer (B) is incorrect. A small, not large, angle of attack develops maximum thrust and maximum engine power.

33. When operating an aircraft with a constant-speed propeller, which procedure places the least stress on cylinder components?

A. When power settings are being increased, increase manifold pressure before RPM.
B. When power settings are being decreased, reduce manifold pressure before RPM.
C. Whether power settings are being increased or decreased, RPM is adjusted before manifold pressure.

Answer (B) is correct. *(PHAK Chap 7)*
  DISCUSSION: When using a constant-speed propeller, the best procedure is to reduce manifold pressure before RPM to preclude exceeding the maximum manifold pressure.
  Answer (A) is incorrect. The critical factor is getting manifold pressure too high for a specified RPM. Thus, one must increase RPM before adding manifold pressure when increasing power, and not vice versa. Answer (C) is incorrect. The critical factor is getting manifold pressure too high for a specified RPM. Thus, one must increase RPM before adding manifold pressure when increasing power, and decrease manifold pressure prior to decreasing RPM when reducing power.

34. Which statement is true regarding propeller efficiency? Propeller efficiency is the

A. ratio of thrust horsepower to brake horsepower.
B. actual distance a propeller advances in one revolution.
C. difference between the geometric pitch of the propeller and its effective pitch.

Answer (A) is correct. *(PHAK Chap 5)*
  DISCUSSION: Propeller efficiency is the ratio of useful power output to actual power output. Thus, propeller efficiency is the ratio of thrust horsepower to brake (engine) horsepower. Propeller efficiency generally varies between 50% and 87%, depending upon propeller slippage.
  Answer (B) is incorrect. Effective pitch, not propeller efficiency, is the actual distance a propeller advances in one revolution. Answer (C) is incorrect. Propeller slippage, not efficiency, is the difference between the geometric pitch of the propeller and its effective pitch.

35. The distance a propeller actually advances in one revolution is

A. twisting.
B. effective pitch.
C. geometric pitch.

Answer (B) is correct. *(PHAK Chap 7)*
   DISCUSSION: Effective pitch is the actual distance the propeller moves forward through the air in one revolution.
   Answer (A) is incorrect. Twisting is the change in blade angle from the hub to the tip. Answer (C) is incorrect. Geometric pitch is the theoretical, not actual, distance a propeller would advance in one revolution if it were rotated in a solid medium.

36. Propeller slip is the difference between the

A. geometric pitch and blade angle of the propeller.
B. geometric pitch and the effective pitch of the propeller.
C. plane of rotation of the propeller and forward velocity of the aircraft.

Answer (B) is correct. *(PHAK Chap 7)*
   DISCUSSION: Propeller slip is the difference between the geometric pitch of the propeller and its effective pitch.
   Answer (A) is incorrect. Propeller slip is the difference between the geometric pitch of the propeller and its effective pitch, not blade angle. Answer (C) is incorrect. The plane of rotation and the chord line of the blade determine the blade angle that, together with the forward velocity, determines the blade's angle of attack, not propeller slip.

37. Blade angle of a propeller is defined as the angle between the

A. angle of attack and chord line.
B. chord line and plane of rotation.
C. angle of attack and line of thrust.

Answer (B) is correct. *(PHAK Chap 7)*
   DISCUSSION: The blade angle of a propeller is the angle between the chord line of the blade and the propeller's plane of rotation.
   Answer (A) is incorrect. The chord line and the relative wind determine angle of attack. Answer (C) is incorrect. As the angle of attack changes, the resulting thrust changes.

38. The reason for variations in geometric pitch (twisting) along a propeller blade is that it

A. prevents the portion of the blade near the hub to stall during cruising flight.
B. permits a relatively constant angle of attack along its length when in cruising flight.
C. permits a relatively constant angle of incidence along its length when in cruising flight.

Answer (B) is correct. *(PHAK Chap 7)*
   DISCUSSION: A propeller is twisted because the outer parts of the propeller blades, like all things that turn about a central point, travel faster than the portions near the hub. The blade being twisted permits the propeller to operate with a relatively constant angle of attack along its length when in cruising flight. If the blades had the same geometric pitch throughout their lengths, then the portions near the hub, at cruise speed, could have negative angles of attack while the propeller tips would be stalled.
   Answer (A) is incorrect. Twisting prevents the portions of the blade near the tip, not hub, from stalling during cruise flight. Answer (C) is incorrect. Twisting means the angle of attack, not the angle of incidence, will remain constant along the length of the propeller.

3.7 Manifold Pressure Gauge

39. Prior to starting the engine, the manifold pressure gauge usually indicates approximately 29" Hg. This is because the

A. pointer on the gauge is stuck at the full-power indication.
B. throttle is closed, trapping high air pressure in the manifold.
C. pressure within the manifold is the same as atmospheric pressure.

Answer (C) is correct. *(PHAK Chap 7)*
   DISCUSSION: The manifold pressure gauge measures the air pressure in the fuel/air induction manifold. When the engine is not running, the pressure in the manifold equals atmospheric pressure (approximately 29 in. Hg at sea level).
   Answer (A) is incorrect. When the engine is stopped, the manifold pressure gauge reflects the local atmospheric pressure (approximately 29 in. Hg at sea level). Answer (B) is incorrect. The throttle position when the engine is stopped has no impact on the manifold pressure gauge. The manifold pressure gauge reflects the local atmospheric pressure (approximately 29 in. Hg at sea level).

3.8 Engine Ignition System

40. In addition to an added safety factor, dual ignition systems also provide

A. better combustion.
B. increased spark plug life.
C. shorter engine warmup periods.

Answer (A) is correct. *(PHAK Chap 7)*
DISCUSSION: Dual ignition systems provide a safety backup if one system fails. They also provide for two spark plugs on opposite sides of the cylinder top. When they fire simultaneously, they provide a more uniform ignition of the fuel/air mixture and thus better combustion.
Answer (B) is incorrect. Regardless of the number of spark plugs, their life is determined by other factors, such as engine condition, mixture, power settings, etc. Answer (C) is incorrect. Dual ignition systems, while providing better combustion and safety, do not shorten warmup periods for the engine.

41. If the ground wire between the magneto and the ignition switch becomes disconnected, the most noticeable result will be that the engine

A. will run very rough.
B. cannot be started with the switch in the ON position.
C. cannot be shut down by turning the switch to the OFF position.

Answer (C) is correct. *(PHAK Chap 7)*
DISCUSSION: If the ground wire from the magneto to the ignition switch becomes disconnected, it will be impossible to ground (turn off) the magneto with the switch.
Answer (A) is incorrect. Having the ground wire disconnected has no effect on the smooth operation of the engine. The only result is the magnetos will always be on. Answer (B) is incorrect. If the magneto ground wire is disconnected, the magnetos will be on.

42. What should be the first action after starting an aircraft engine?

A. Adjust for proper RPM and check for desired indications on the engine gauges.
B. Place the magneto or ignition switch momentarily in the OFF position to check for proper grounding.
C. Test each brake and the parking brake.

Answer (A) is correct. *(AFH Chap 2)*
DISCUSSION: It is recommended that pilots adjust the throttle to 800-1,000 RPM immediately following engine start. Allowing the engine to run at a higher speed may cause damage to the internal components, as insufficient lubrication exists until the oil pressure rises. As the engine warms, check the oil pressure gauge to ensure that the needle is rising to the manufacturer's specified value. If the oil pressure does not rise as expected, the engine should be shut down to prevent serious damage from occurring.
Answer (B) is incorrect. The magneto check is normally done during the run-up, prior to takeoff. Answer (C) is incorrect. The brake test is performed when the airplane begins its initial roll, not immediately after start-up.

43. If the ground wire between the magneto and the ignition switch becomes disconnected, the engine

A. will not operate on one magneto.
B. cannot be started with the switch in the on position.
C. could accidentally start if the propeller is moved with fuel in the cylinder.

Answer (C) is correct. *(PHAK Chap 7)*
DISCUSSION: With the grounding wire disconnected, both magnetos are in the ON position and cannot be turned off, even with the ignition switch. Because of this, if the propeller is turned so that the magnetos are engaged, a spark will be produced. If fuel is present in one or more cylinders, the engine could accidentally start.
Answer (A) is incorrect. If the magneto ground wire is disconnected, the magnetos will be on. Both magnetos will continue to run and run normally. Answer (B) is incorrect. If the magneto ground wire is disconnected, the magnetos will be on. You will have no trouble starting the engine should this situation occur.

3.9 Carburetor and Fuel-Injection Systems

44. Fuel injection systems, compared to carburetor systems, are generally considered to be

A. just as susceptible to impact icing.
B. more susceptible to evaporative icing.
C. less susceptible to icing unless visible moisture is present.

Answer (A) is correct. *(PHAK Chap 7)*
DISCUSSION: The fuel injection system is generally considered to be less susceptible to icing than the carburetor system. However, impact icing of the air intake is a possibility in either system. Impact icing occurs when ice forms on the exterior of the airplane and results in clogging openings such as the air intake.
Answer (B) is incorrect. The fuel injection system is less, not more, susceptible to evaporative icing than the carburetor system. Answer (C) is incorrect. Fuel injection systems are generally considered to be less susceptible to icing than carburetor systems, even when visible moisture is present.

45. The operating principle of float-type carburetors is based on the

A. measurement of the fuel flow into the induction system.
B. difference in air pressure at the venturi throat and the throttle valve.
C. increase in air velocity in the throat of a venturi causing a decrease in air pressure.

Answer (C) is correct. *(PHAK Chap 7)*
DISCUSSION: The increase in air velocity in the throat of a venturi causes a decrease in air pressure, which draws the fuel from the main fuel jet into the airstream where it is mixed with the flowing air.
Answer (A) is incorrect. Fuel flow is governed by a mixture control knob in the cockpit. Answer (B) is incorrect. The difference in air pressure is between the venturi throat and the air inlet, not the throttle valve.

46. One advantage of fuel injection systems over carburetor systems is

A. easier hot-engine starting.
B. better fuel distribution to the cylinders.
C. less difficulty with hot weather vapor locks during ground operations.

Answer (B) is correct. *(PHAK Chap 7)*
DISCUSSION: Fuel-injection systems inject fuel directly into the cylinders, in contrast to carburetor systems in which the fuel/air mixture flows from the carburetor through the intake manifold to the cylinders. Fuel-injection systems result in more even fuel distribution to each cylinder.
Answer (A) is incorrect. Due to vapor lock, fuel-injection systems are generally not easier to start when the engine is hot. Answer (C) is incorrect. Fuel-injection systems traditionally have had problems with vapor locks during ground operations.

3.10 Carburetor Icing

47. The presence of carburetor ice in an aircraft equipped with a fixed-pitch propeller can be verified by applying carburetor heat and noting

A. a decrease in RPM and then a constant RPM indication.
B. a decrease in RPM and then a gradual increase in RPM.
C. an increase in RPM and then a gradual decrease in RPM.

Answer (B) is correct. *(PHAK Chap 7)*
DISCUSSION: In an airplane equipped with a fixed-pitch propeller, the presence of carburetor ice can be verified by applying carburetor heat and noting a decrease in RPM and then a gradual increase in RPM as the ice is melted. The initial decrease occurs because the heated air is less dense than the outside air that had been entering the engine.
Answer (A) is incorrect. If, after applying carburetor heat, you note a decrease in RPM with no further changes, it indicates that there is no carburetor ice. Answer (C) is incorrect. The application of carburetor heat produces a decrease, not increase, in RPM because the heated air is less dense than the air that had been entering the engine before. If ice is present, the RPM will then increase, not decrease, as the ice is melted.

48. The first indication of carburetor ice in an aircraft with a fixed-pitch propeller is

A. a decrease in RPM.
B. a decrease in manifold pressure.
C. an increase in manifold pressure.

Answer (A) is correct. *(PHAK Chap 7)*
DISCUSSION: In airplanes with fixed-pitch propellers, the first indication of carburetor icing is a decrease or loss of RPM.
Answer (B) is incorrect. A decrease in manifold pressure is the first indication of carburetor ice in an airplane equipped with a constant-speed, not fixed-pitch, propeller. Answer (C) is incorrect. A decrease, not increase, in manifold pressure is the first indication of carburetor ice in an airplane equipped with a constant-speed, not fixed-pitch, propeller.

49. Which condition is most favorable to the development of carburetor icing?

A. Any temperature below freezing and a relative humidity of less than 50 percent.
B. Temperature between 32 and 50°F and low humidity.
C. Temperature between 20 and 70°F and high humidity.

Answer (C) is correct. *(PHAK Chap 7)*
DISCUSSION: The most favorable condition for carburetor icing is when the temperature is between 20°F and 70°F. Due to the sudden cooling that takes place in the carburetor, icing can occur even with temperatures as high as 100°F and humidity as low as 50%. During low or closed throttle settings, an engine is particularly susceptible to carburetor icing.
Answer (A) is incorrect. At temperatures below freezing with low humidity, carburetor icing is unlikely. Answer (B) is incorrect. The formation of carburetor ice depends on high humidity, not low humidity.

50. The first indication of carburetor icing in an aircraft equipped with a constant-speed propeller would most likely be a

A. decrease in RPM.
B. decrease in manifold pressure.
C. rough running engine followed by loss of RPM.

Answer (B) is correct. *(PHAK Chap 7)*
DISCUSSION: In airplanes equipped with constant-speed propellers, carburetor icing results in less power. Thus, the manifold pressure decreases and the engine runs rougher. The RPM does not change because the constant-speed propeller automatically adjusts to maintain a constant RPM during changes in power.
Answer (A) is incorrect. The first indication of carburetor ice in an airplane with a constant-speed propeller is a decrease in manifold pressure, not RPM. The propeller governor maintains a constant RPM. Answer (C) is incorrect. The first indication of carburetor ice is a decrease in manifold pressure, not a rough engine. Also, the RPM does not change because the constant-speed propeller automatically adjusts to maintain a constant RPM.

51. Concerning carburetor icing, which statement is true?

A. The first indication of carburetor icing, in an aircraft equipped with a fixed-pitch propeller, is a decrease in manifold pressure.
B. Carburetor icing will form in a carburetor whenever the ambient temperature is below freezing with a reduced or closed throttle setting.
C. Carburetor icing would most likely form when the air temperature is between -7°C and 21°C and visible moisture or high humidity is present.

Answer (C) is correct. *(PHAK Chap 7)*
DISCUSSION: Carburetor icing would most likely occur when the air temperature is between -7°C and 21°C, with visible moisture or high humidity. The vaporization of fuel, combined with the expansion of air as it flows through the carburetor, causes a sudden cooling of the mixture. The water vapor in the air may condense due to the cooling and, if the temperature in the carburetor is 0°C or colder, ice will form.
Answer (A) is incorrect. The first indication of carburetor icing, in an aircraft equipped with a fixed-pitch propeller, is a decrease in RPM, not manifold pressure. Answer (B) is incorrect. On dry days or when the ambient temperature is below freezing, the moisture content in the air is not generally enough to cause carburetor icing, even with a reduced or closed throttle setting.

52. The low temperature that causes carburetor ice in an engine equipped with a float-type carburetor is normally the result of the

A. compression of air at the carburetor venturi.
B. freezing temperature of the air entering the carburetor.
C. vaporization of fuel and expansion of air in the carburetor.

Answer (C) is correct. *(PHAK Chap 7)*
DISCUSSION: The low temperature that causes carburetor ice in an engine equipped with a float-type carburetor is normally the result of the vaporization of fuel and expansion of the air.
Answer (A) is incorrect. The low temperatures result from the expansion, not compression, of the air in the carburetor venturi. Answer (B) is incorrect. The low temperatures result from the vaporization of fuel and expansion of the air in the carburetor, not because the temperature of the air is freezing before entering the carburetor.

53. Generally speaking, the use of carburetor heat tends to

A. increase engine performance.
B. have no effect on engine performance.
C. decrease engine performance.

Answer (C) is correct. *(PHAK Chap 7)*
DISCUSSION: Use of carburetor heat tends to decrease the engine performance and also to increase the operating temperature. Warmer air is less dense, and engine performance decreases with density. Thus, carburetor heat should not be used when full power is required (as during takeoff) or during normal engine operation except as a check for the presence or removal of carburetor ice.
Answer (A) is incorrect. Carburetor heat decreases (not increases) engine performance. Answer (B) is incorrect. Carburetor heat does not have an effect on performance.

54. In an aircraft equipped with a fixed-pitch propeller and a float-type carburetor, the first indication of carburetor ice would most likely be

A. a drop in oil temperature and cylinder head temperature.
B. engine roughness.
C. loss of RPM.

Answer (C) is correct. *(PHAK Chap 7)*
DISCUSSION: In airplanes with fixed-pitch propellers, the first indication of carburetor icing is a decrease or loss of RPM.
Answer (A) is incorrect. A drop in oil and cylinder temperatures would happen just before the engine shutdown in this situation. Neither of these would be the first indication of carburetor icing. Answer (B) is incorrect. While engine roughness would eventually result, the first indication of carburetor icing in an airplane with a fixed-pitch propeller is a loss of RPM.

55. Carburetor ice

A. occurs mostly as a function of temperature.
B. can only form when the outside air temperature is near freezing with high relative humidity.
C. is more likely to form when outside air temperatures are below 70 degrees F and relative humidity is above 80%.

Answer (C) is correct. *(PHAK Chap 7)*
DISCUSSION: Carburetor icing is most likely to occur when temperatures are below 70°F and humidity is above 80%. These conditions are common in the eastern half of the United States during the late spring, throughout summer, and in the early portion of the fall. These conditions are especially prevalent at night.
Answer (A) is incorrect. There must be moisture present in order for ice to develop. Answer (B) is incorrect. Carburetor ice can form, and is most likely to do so, when outside air temperatures are below 70°F and relative humidity is above 80%.

56. Leaving the carburetor heat on during takeoff

A. leans the mixture for more power on takeoff.
B. will decrease the takeoff distance.
C. will increase the ground roll.

Answer (C) is correct. *(PHAK Chap 7)*
DISCUSSION: Carburetor heat routes heated, less dense air into the engine. This decreases engine power by up to 15%. This reduction in power will certainly lengthen the takeoff roll. As such, carburetor heat should never be used during takeoff.
Answer (A) is incorrect. The heated air routed into the engine enriches, not leans, the mixture. Answer (B) is incorrect. Takeoff distance will be increased due to the reduction in engine power when using carburetor heat.

3.11 Turbocharged Engines

57. What energy source is used to drive the turbine of a turbocharged airplane?

A. Ignition system.
B. Engine compressor.
C. Engine exhaust gases.

Answer (C) is correct. *(PHAK Chap 7)*
DISCUSSION: The turbocharger consists of a compressor to provide pressurized air to the engine and a turbine driven by exhaust gases of the engine to drive the compressor.
Answer (A) is incorrect. The turbine is driven by the energy taken from the exhaust gases, not the ignition system. Answer (B) is incorrect. The turbine is driven by the energy taken from the exhaust gases to drive the compressor.

58. During climbing flight using a turbocharged airplane, the manifold pressure will remain approximately constant until the

A. engine's critical altitude is reached.
B. airplane's service ceiling is reached.
C. waste gate is fully open and the turbine is operating at minimum speed.

Answer (A) is correct. *(PHAK Chap 7)*
DISCUSSION: During climbing flight using a turbocharged airplane, the manifold pressure will remain approximately constant until the engine's critical altitude is reached. At that altitude, the turbine is rotating at its highest speed and can no longer compensate for the decreasing power (i.e., manifold pressure) after that altitude is reached.
Answer (B) is incorrect. The airplane's service ceiling is the altitude at which the maximum rate of climb is 100 fpm. Answer (C) is incorrect. The waste gate (which is used to vent exhaust stream gases to prevent exceeding maximum allowable manifold pressure) is open at low, not high, altitudes.

3.12 Engine Cycle

59. During which stroke of a reciprocating engine is the gaseous mixture expanding within the cylinder?

A. Power.
B. Intake.
C. Compression.

Answer (A) is correct. *(PHAK Chap 7)*
DISCUSSION: Four-stroke engines have the following strokes: intake, compression, power, and exhaust. During the power stroke when the piston is approximately at the top of the cylinder, the spark plug ignites the mixture, which burns at a controlled rate. Expansion of the burning fuel/air mixture exerts pressure on the piston, forcing it downward.
Answer (B) is incorrect. During the intake stroke, the intake valve opens and the fuel/air mixture is drawn into the cylinder; no expansion of gases takes place. Answer (C) is incorrect. During the compression stroke, the piston returns to the top of the cylinder with both valves closed and the fuel/air mixture is compressed, not expanded.

60. Fuel and exhaust enter and exit a 4-cycle engine

A. through exhaust ports and reed valves.
B. through intake and exhaust valve ports.
C. through intake ports and reed valves.

Answer (B) is correct. *(PHAK Chap 7)*
DISCUSSION: In a 4-cycle engine, air and fuel are drawn into the cylinder through the intake valve ports. After the charge is ignited, it is expelled through exhaust valve ports.
Answer (A) is incorrect. Reed valves are used in 2-cycle engines. Answer (C) is incorrect. Reed valves are used in 2-cycle engines.

61. Four-cycle engines are lubricated by

A. mixing the lubricating oil in the fuel.
B. a vaporized mixture of fuel and oil.
C. forcing oil directly to the components requiring lubrication.

Answer (C) is correct. *(PHAK Chap 7)*
DISCUSSION: In 4-cycle engines, oil is transmitted through the crankshaft by an oil pump and slung around the crankcase.
Answer (A) is incorrect. Fuel and oil are mixed in 2-cycle engines but not 4-cycle engines. Answer (B) is incorrect. Fuel and oil are mixed in 2-cycle engines but not 4-cycle engines.

62. Many 4-cycle engines utilize what type of lubrication system?

A. Forced.
B. Gravity.
C. Fuel/oil mixture.

Answer (A) is correct. *(PHAK Chap 7)*
DISCUSSION: Due to the size and complexity of 4-cycle engines, a forced lubrication system, often including an engine-driven pump, is typically employed.
Answer (B) is incorrect. Many 4-cycle engines utilize a gravity feed system to sling oil from the crankshaft into the engine case. However, engine oil is still forced into the crankshaft using an engine-driven pump. Gravity-fed systems would feature an oil sump on top of the crank case, which is not common in 4-cycle engines, due mainly to the size of the engine block. Answer (C) is incorrect. A fuel/oil mixture lubrication system is common in 2-cycle, not 4-cycle, engines.

3.13 Fuel/Air Mixture

63. Which statement is true regarding fouling of the spark plugs of an aircraft engine?

A. Spark plug fouling results from operating with an excessively rich mixture.
B. Carbon fouling of the spark plugs is caused primarily by operating an engine at excessively high cylinder head temperatures.
C. Excessive heat in the combustion chamber of a cylinder causes oil to form on the center electrode of a spark plug and this fouls the plug.

Answer (A) is correct. *(PHAK Chap 7)*
DISCUSSION: Excessive fuel results in cooler and incomplete combustion. The residue from the incomplete combustion results in spark plug fouling.
Answer (B) is incorrect. Carbon fouling of the plugs is caused primarily by operating at low, not high, cylinder head temperatures. Answer (C) is incorrect. Excessive heat is caused by too lean, not too rich, a mixture, which does not foul spark plugs.

SU 3: Airplane Instruments, Engines, and Systems

64. Fuel/air ratio is the ratio between the

A. volume of fuel and volume of air entering the cylinder.
B. weight of fuel and weight of air entering the cylinder.
C. weight of fuel and weight of air entering the carburetor.

Answer (B) is correct. *(PHAK Chap 7)*
　DISCUSSION: The fuel/air ratio, by definition, is the ratio between the weight of fuel and weight of air entering the cylinder.
　Answer (A) is incorrect. The fuel/air ratio is the ratio between the weight of the fuel and the weight of the air, rather than the volume of the fuel and the volume of the air, entering the cylinder. Answer (C) is incorrect. The fuel/air ratio is the ratio between the weight of fuel and weight of air entering the cylinder, not the carburetor.

65. Proper mixture control and better economy in the operation of a fuel injected engine can be achieved best by use of

A. a fuel-flow gauge.
B. an exhaust gas temperature indicator.
C. the recommended manifold and RPM setting for a particular altitude.

Answer (B) is correct. *(PHAK Chap 7)*
　DISCUSSION: A proper mixture control and better economy in both fuel-injected and carbureted engines is achieved by reference to the exhaust gas temperature (EGT) gauge. Monitoring the temperature of the exhaust gases permits the mixture to be leaned so the engine runs at EGT temperatures recommended by the manufacturer.
　Answer (A) is incorrect. The fuel-flow gauge indicates how much fuel is, not how much should be, flowing to the engine. Answer (C) is incorrect. Manifold pressure and RPM setting do not affect mixture control.

66. The main purpose of the mixture control is to

A. increase the air supplied to the engine.
B. adjust the fuel flow to obtain the proper air/fuel ratio.
C. decrease the fuel supplied to the engine as the aircraft descends.

Answer (B) is correct. *(PHAK Chap 7)*
　DISCUSSION: The primary purpose of the mixture control is to adjust the fuel flow to obtain the proper fuel/air ratio.
　Answer (A) is incorrect. The fuel flow to the engine, not the air supply, is affected by the mixture control knob. Answer (C) is incorrect. The fuel supplied to the engine should be increased, not decreased, in a descent.

67. When the pilot leans the mixture control, what is being accomplished?

A. The volume of air entering the carburetor is being reduced.
B. The volume of air entering the carburetor is being increased.
C. The amount of fuel entering the combustion chamber is being reduced.

Answer (C) is correct. *(PHAK Chap 7)*
　DISCUSSION: As the mixture control is leaned, the amount of fuel entering the combustion chamber is reduced. This is necessary because, as altitude increases, the amount of air entering the combustion chamber is reduced. A reduction in the amount of fuel maintains a proper fuel/air ratio.
　Answer (A) is incorrect. The mixture control governs fuel, not air. Answer (B) is incorrect. The mixture control governs fuel, not air.

68. The best power mixture is that fuel/air ratio at which

A. cylinder head temperatures are the coolest.
B. the most power can be obtained for any given throttle setting.
C. a given power can be obtained with the highest manifold pressure or throttle setting.

Answer (B) is correct. *(PHAK Chap 11)*
　DISCUSSION: The best power mixture is obtained by leaning the engine to 100°F on the rich side of peak EGT. This setting will give you the most forward speed at any throttle setting.
　Answer (A) is incorrect. Cylinder head temperatures are actually cooler at 50°F lean of peak EGT than they are at 100°F rich of peak. Answer (C) is incorrect. Best power mixture can be obtained for any throttle setting, not just the maximum one.

69. As flight altitude increases, what will occur if no leaning is made with the mixture control?

A. The volume of air entering the carburetor decreases and the amount of fuel decreases.
B. The density of air entering the carburetor decreases and the amount of fuel increases.
C. The density of air entering the carburetor decreases and the amount of fuel remains constant.

Answer (C) is correct. *(PHAK Chap 7)*
　DISCUSSION: If the mixture is not leaned as altitude increases, the fuel/air ratio will increase because the density of air decreases with an increase in altitude, while the amount of fuel remains constant.
　Answer (A) is incorrect. The amount of fuel does not change if no adjustment is made to the mixture control. Also, the volume of air remains constant; it does not decrease. Answer (B) is incorrect. The amount of fuel does not change if no adjustment is made to the mixture control.

70. The basic purpose of adjusting the fuel/air mixture control at altitude is to

A. decrease the fuel flow to compensate for decreased air density.
B. decrease the amount of fuel in the mixture to compensate for increased air density.
C. increase the amount of fuel in the mixture to compensate for the decrease in pressure and density of the air.

Answer (A) is correct. *(PHAK Chap 7)*
DISCUSSION: Air density decreases as altitude increases. The mixture control in the cockpit allows the pilot to decrease the fuel flow in order to compensate for decreased air density.
Answer (B) is incorrect. Air density decreases, not increases, with altitude. Answer (C) is incorrect. The mixture control exists to allow the pilot to decrease, not increase, the amount of fuel in the mixture as altitude increases.

71. The pilot controls the air/fuel ratio with the

A. throttle.
B. manifold pressure.
C. mixture control.

Answer (C) is correct. *(PHAK Chap 6)*
DISCUSSION: The mixture control, color-coded red in the cockpit, allows the pilot to control the air/fuel ratio.
Answer (A) is incorrect. The throttle controls the amount of air introduced into the system, but the ratio of air/fuel is controlled by the mixture. Answer (B) is incorrect. Manifold pressure is controlled with the throttle, which controls the amount of air introduced into the system, but the ratio of air/fuel is controlled by the mixture.

72. At high altitudes, an excessively rich mixture will cause the

A. engine to overheat.
B. fouling of spark plugs.
C. engine to operate smoother even though fuel consumption is increased.

Answer (B) is correct. *(PHAK Chap 7)*
DISCUSSION: If the mixture is not leaned properly as the airplane climbs, the excessively rich mixture will leave carbon deposits behind that can foul the spark plugs.
Answer (A) is incorrect. An excessively rich mixture will lead to lower engine temperatures. Answer (C) is incorrect. An excessively rich engine at high altitudes will cause the engine to be sluggish due to having too much fuel in the fuel/air mixture. This condition could cause the engine to stumble, not operate smoother.

73. Unless adjusted, the fuel/air mixture becomes richer with an increase in altitude because the amount of fuel

A. decreases while the volume of air decreases.
B. remains constant while the volume of air decreases.
C. remains constant while the density of air decreases.

Answer (C) is correct. *(PHAK Chap 7)*
DISCUSSION: Without adjustment, the amount of fuel delivered to the engine remains constant, regardless of changes in altitude. When climbing, the density of the outside air decreases. If the pilot does not lean the mixture, it will become excessively rich.
Answer (A) is incorrect. The amount of fuel delivered to the engine will not decrease unless the pilot leans the mixture. Also, the density, not the volume, of air decreases with altitude. Answer (B) is incorrect. The density, not the volume, of air decreases with altitude.

74. Fouling of spark plugs is more apt to occur if the aircraft

A. gains altitude with no mixture adjustment.
B. descends from altitude with no mixture adjustment.
C. throttle is advanced very abruptly.

Answer (A) is correct. *(PHAK Chap 7)*
DISCUSSION: If no adjustment to the mixture is made while the airplane climbs, an excessively rich mixture will result. This condition can and will lead to fouled spark plugs.
Answer (B) is incorrect. If no adjustment to the mixture is made while the airplane descends, the mixture will become excessively lean. This can lead to detonation and engine overheating but not fouled spark plugs. Answer (C) is incorrect. The momentary enriching effects of abruptly advancing the throttle do not last long enough to cause fouling of the spark plugs.

3.14 Fuel Tank Vents

75. What is the main reason fuel tank vents must be open? To allow

A. proper air pressure within the tanks for maintaining a steady fuel flow.
B. excess fuel to drain overboard when heat expands the volume of fuel within the tanks.
C. fuel fumes to escape from the tanks, thus eliminating the possibility of the tanks exploding.

Answer (A) is correct. *(PHAK Chap 7)*
DISCUSSION: Fuel tank vents allow uniform air pressure within the fuel tanks so as not to disrupt the fuel flow to the engine. If the vents become clogged, a vacuum could develop within the fuel tank, which would result in an inadequate fuel flow.
Answer (B) is incorrect. While some fuel vents do permit excess fuel to drain, the primary reason for fuel tank vents is to allow proper air pressure within the tanks for maintaining a steady fuel flow. Answer (C) is incorrect. While vents do permit fuel fumes to escape, the primary reason for fuel tank vents is to allow proper air pressure within the tanks for maintaining a steady fuel flow.

76. During preflight, the fuel vent system should always be checked

A. to ensure the vent is closed.
B. to ensure the vent is open.
C. to ensure the vent system pressure is in the green range.

Answer (B) is correct. *(AFH Chap 2)*
DISCUSSION: During a preflight inspection, you should ensure that the fuel vent opening is open, meaning not blocked, to ensure proper air pressure within the tanks for maintaining a steady fuel flow. Some fuel loss may be observed during the preflight inspection. This is normal on hot days or immediately after the tank has been filled.
Answer (A) is incorrect. A closed fuel vent would cause a vacuum to develop inside the fuel tank. This could result in fuel flow indication errors and/or fuel starvation. Be sure that the fuel vent is unobstructed during the preflight inspection. Answer (C) is incorrect. There is no vent pressure indication in the cockpit to inspect during a preflight inspection. The fuel vent is located near the fuel tank(s) and serves to allow air to enter the tank as fuel is removed during flight. It also serves as an overflow valve in cases of fuel expansion or overfilling.

3.15 Detonation and Abnormal Combustion

77. Detonation in an aircraft engine is most likely to occur whenever the

A. fuel/air ratio is such that the mixture burns extremely slow.
B. engine is operated under conditions which cause the fuel mixture to burn instantaneously.
C. fuel being used is of a higher grade than recommended by the engine manufacturer.

Answer (B) is correct. *(PHAK Chap 7)*
DISCUSSION: Detonation occurs when the engine is operated under conditions that cause the fuel/air mixture in the cylinders to burn instantaneously instead of burning normally.
Answer (A) is incorrect. Detonation occurs when the fuel/air mixture burns instantaneously, not too slowly. Answer (C) is incorrect. Detonation is most likely to occur when the fuel being used is of a lower, not higher, grade than recommended by the engine manufacturer.

78. The uncontrolled firing of the fuel/air charge in advance of normal spark ignition is known as

A. instantaneous combustion.
B. pre-ignition.
C. detonation.

Answer (B) is correct. *(PHAK Chap 7)*
DISCUSSION: Pre-ignition is the ignition of the fuel prior to normal ignition or ignition before the electrical arcing occurs at the spark plug. Pre-ignition may be caused by excessively hot exhaust valves, carbon particles, or spark plugs and electrodes heated to an incandescent, or glowing, state. These hot spots are usually caused by high temperatures encountered during detonation. A significant difference between pre-ignition and detonation is that, if the conditions for detonation exist in one cylinder, they usually exist in all cylinders, but pre-ignition often takes place in only one or two cylinders.
Answer (A) is incorrect. Instantaneous combustion is another name for detonation, or an explosion of the fuel/air mixture inside the cylinder. Answer (C) is incorrect. Detonation is an uncontrolled, explosive ignition of the fuel/air mixture within the cylinder's combustion chamber caused by a combination of excessively high temperature and pressure in the cylinder.

79. If the grade of fuel used in an aircraft engine is lower than that specified, it may cause

A. detonation.
B. lower cylinder head temperatures.
C. a decrease in power which could overstress internal engine components.

Answer (A) is correct. *(PHAK Chap 7)*
DISCUSSION: Lower grades of fuel ignite at lower temperatures. A higher temperature engine (which should use a higher grade of fuel) may cause lower-grade fuel to explode (detonate) rather than burn evenly.
Answer (B) is incorrect. A lower grade of fuel will cause higher, not lower, cylinder head temperatures. Answer (C) is incorrect. A decrease in power leading to over-stressing of internal engine components is a product of detonation, not a lower fuel grade.

80. Detonation occurs at high power settings when the

A. fuel mixture explodes instead of burning progressively and evenly.
B. fuel mixture is ignited too early by red-hot carbon deposits in the cylinder.
C. intake valve opens before the previous charge of fuel has finished burning in the cylinder.

Answer (A) is correct. *(PHAK Chap 7)*
DISCUSSION: Detonation occurs when the fuel/air mixture in the cylinder explodes instead of burning progressively and evenly.
Answer (B) is incorrect. Pre-ignition, not detonation, occurs when the fuel/air mixture ignites too early. Answer (C) is incorrect. Backfiring, not detonation, will occur if the intake valves open before completion of the power stroke.

81. If a pilot suspects that the engine (with a fixed-pitch propeller) is detonating during climb-out after takeoff, the initial corrective action to take would be to

A. lean the mixture.
B. lower the nose slightly to increase airspeed.
C. apply carburetor heat.

Answer (B) is correct. *(PHAK Chap 7)*
DISCUSSION: Detonation refers to the explosion of the fuel/air mixture in the cylinders, rather than burning in a controlled manner. Detonation can be caused by extended, high power, steep climbs that cause the engine to run hotter than normal. Lowering the nose slightly will increase airspeed, while reducing the load on the engine (with a fixed pitch prop attached). The cooling effect of the additional airflow through the engine compartment will assist in remedying the detonation problem.
Answer (A) is incorrect. A leaner mixture could make the detonation problem worse rather than better. Answer (C) is incorrect. Although the warmer air introduced to the carburetor will cause a slightly enriched mixture, the cooling effects of this change will likely not be sufficient to stop the detonation.

82. Detonation occurs in a reciprocating aircraft engine when

A. the spark plugs are fouled or shorted out or the wiring is defective.
B. hot spots in the combustion chamber ignite the fuel/air mixture in advance of normal ignition.
C. the unburned charge in the cylinders explodes instead of burning normally.

Answer (C) is correct. *(PHAK Chap 5)*
DISCUSSION: Detonation occurs when the fuel/air mixture in the cylinder explodes instead of burning progressively and evenly.
Answer (A) is incorrect. Ignition (normal or abnormal, excluding pre-ignition) of the fuel/air mixture is not possible if the spark plugs cannot fire. Answer (B) is incorrect. Pre-ignition, not detonation, occurs when the fuel/air mixture ignites too early.

83. Detonation can be caused by

A. a short ground operation.
B. a 'rich' mixture.
C. using a lower grade of fuel than recommended.

Answer (C) is correct. *(PHAK Chap 7)*
DISCUSSION: Using a lower grade fuel type than that recommended by the manufacturer will result in increased engine operating temperatures and quite possibly detonation.
Answer (A) is incorrect. A short ground operation will result in a relatively cool overall engine temperature. This condition is unlikely to result in detonation. Answer (B) is incorrect. A rich mixture decreases engine operating temperatures, preventing detonation.

84. Detonation occurs in a reciprocating aircraft engine when

A. there is an explosive increase of fuel caused by too rich a fuel/air mixture.
B. the spark plugs receive an electrical jolt caused by a short in the wiring.
C. the unburned fuel/air charge in the cylinders is subjected to instantaneous combustion.

Answer (C) is correct. *(PHAK Chap 7)*
DISCUSSION: Detonation is the uncontrolled, explosive, and instantaneous consumption of the fuel/air charge in a cylinder.
Answer (A) is incorrect. Detonation does not result from too rich a fuel/air mixture. Answer (B) is incorrect. A short in the wiring would cause pre-ignition, not detonation.

3.16 Aviation Fuel Practices

85. To properly purge water from the fuel system of an aircraft equipped with fuel tank sumps and a fuel strainer quick drain, it is necessary to drain fuel from the

A. fuel strainer drain.
B. lowest point in the fuel system.
C. fuel strainer drain and the fuel tank sumps.

Answer (C) is correct. *(PHAK Chap 7)*
DISCUSSION: One should purge water from both the fuel strainer drain and all the fuel tank sumps on an airplane. This is the purpose of such drains. They are placed at low areas of the fuel system and should be drained prior to each flight.
Answer (A) is incorrect. All drains, not only the fuel strainer, should be checked for water. Answer (B) is incorrect. All fuel drains and sumps, not just the lowest point in the system, should be checked for water.

86. The amount of water absorbed in aviation fuels will

A. remain the same regardless of temperature changes.
B. increase as the temperature of the fuel increases.
C. increase as the temperature of the fuel decreases.

Answer (B) is correct. *(AC 20-43C)*
DISCUSSION: All fuels absorb moisture from the atmosphere. The warmer the fuel, the more water it can absorb (in the same way that air can hold more water at higher temperatures). Thus, as temperature increases, fuel draws and absorbs more water from the air.
Answer (A) is incorrect. The amount of water absorbed in aviation fuel will vary, not remain constant, with temperature changes. Answer (C) is incorrect. The amount of water absorbed in aviation fuel will decrease, not increase, as the temperature of the fuel decreases.

87. Running a fuel tank dry before switching tanks is not a good practice because

A. any foreign matter in the tank will be pumped into the fuel system.
B. the engine-driven fuel pump is lubricated by fuel and operating on a dry tank may cause pump failure.
C. the engine-driven fuel pump or electric fuel boost pump draw air into the fuel system and cause vapor lock.

Answer (C) is correct. *(PHAK Chap 7)*
DISCUSSION: Vapor lock may occur if fuel tanks are allowed to run dry due to air being pumped into the fuel lines by the engine-driven or electric fuel pump.
Answer (A) is incorrect. Any foreign matter should be filtered out by the fuel filter. Answer (B) is incorrect. Operating on a dry tank causes engine failure long before any damage can be done to the fuel pump.

88. When refueling aircraft, which precaution would be adequate for eliminating the potential hazard of static electricity?

A. Ensure that battery and ignition switches are off.
B. Connect a ground wire from the fuel truck to ground.
C. Connect a ground wire between the aircraft, fuel truck, fuel nozzle, and ground.

Answer (C) is correct. *(PHAK Chap 7)*
DISCUSSION: Static electricity, formed by the flow of fuel through the hose and nozzle, can result in sparks which can ignite fuel fumes and/or fuel. To adequately eliminate the potential for static electricity, connect a ground wire between the aircraft, fuel truck, fuel nozzle, and ground.
Answer (A) is incorrect. Simply eliminating electrical flow in the aircraft does not prevent static electricity from being produced during the fueling process. Answer (B) is incorrect. Although grounding the truck is a necessary step, the aircraft and fuel nozzle should also be grounded.

3.17 Electrical System

89. Concerning the advantages of an aircraft generator or alternator, select the true statement.

A. A generator always provides more electrical current than an alternator.

B. An alternator provides more electrical power at lower engine RPM than a generator.

C. A generator charges the battery during low engine RPM; therefore, the battery has less chance to become fully discharged, as often occurs with an alternator.

Answer (B) is correct. *(PHAK Chap 7)*
DISCUSSION: Alternators provide more electrical power output at lower engine RPM than generators. Aircraft equipped with generators commonly have no charging power when the engine is running at a low RPM.
Answer (A) is incorrect. An alternator, not a generator, provides more electrical power at lower RPM. Answer (C) is incorrect. The alternator, not the generator, charges the battery during low engine RPM, thereby decreasing the chance for the battery to become fully discharged, as often occurs with generators.

90. An electrical system failure (battery and alternator) occurs during flight. In this situation, you would

A. experience avionics equipment failure.

B. probably experience failure of the engine ignition system, fuel gauges, aircraft lighting system, and avionics equipment.

C. probably experience engine failure due to the loss of the engine-driven fuel pump and also experience failure of the radio equipment, lights, and all instruments that require alternating current.

Answer (A) is correct. *(PHAK Chap 7)*
DISCUSSION: A battery and alternator failure during flight inevitably results in avionics equipment failure due to the lack of electricity.
Answer (B) is incorrect. The engine ignition systems are based on magnetos, which generate their own electricity to operate the spark plugs. Answer (C) is incorrect. Engine-driven fuel pumps are mechanical and not dependent upon electricity.

3.18 Oxygen Systems

91. What precautions should be taken with respect to aircraft oxygen systems?

A. Ensure that only medical oxygen has been used to replenish oxygen containers.

B. Prohibit smoking while in an aircraft equipped with a portable oxygen system.

C. Ensure that industrial oxygen has not been used to replenish the system.

Answer (C) is correct. *(AC 61-107A)*
DISCUSSION: Industrial oxygen is not designed for breathing and should not be used in airplanes. Aircraft oxygen systems require aviation breathing oxygen, which is almost 100% pure oxygen, in contrast to medical oxygen, which contains water vapor that can freeze in the regulator when exposed to cold temperatures.
Answer (A) is incorrect. Aviation breathing oxygen, not medical oxygen, should be used in airplanes. Answer (B) is incorrect. Smoking must be prohibited when using oxygen, not necessarily in airplanes equipped with oxygen systems.

92. What type of oxygen should be used to replenish an aircraft oxygen system?

A. Medical.

B. Aviation.

C. Industrial.

Answer (B) is correct. *(AC 61-107A)*
DISCUSSION: Only aviator's breathing oxygen, which is nearly 100% oxygen, should be used to replenish an aircraft's oxygen supply.
Answer (A) is incorrect. Medical oxygen contains water vapor, which can freeze in the regulator when exposed to cold temperatures. Answer (C) is incorrect. Industrial oxygen is not intended for human consumption and may contain impurities.

93. What type of oxygen system is most commonly found in general aviation aircraft?

A. Demand.

B. Continuous flow.

C. Pressure demand.

Answer (B) is correct. *(AC 61-107A)*
DISCUSSION: Since most general aviation aircraft operate below 25,000 ft. MSL, the most common (and easiest to operate and maintain) oxygen system used is the continuous flow.
Answer (A) is incorrect. The demand system is for operations up to altitudes of 35,000 to 40,000 ft., which is well above the operating altitudes of most general aviation aircraft. Answer (C) is incorrect. The pressure demand system is used for operations at altitudes above 40,000 ft., which is well above the operating altitudes of most general aviation aircraft.

SU 3: Airplane Instruments, Engines, and Systems

94. What is the purpose of the rebreather bag on an oxygen mask in a continuous-flow system?

A. Helps to conserve oxygen.
B. Allows excess oxygen to be expelled during use.
C. Controls amount of oxygen that each individual breathes through the mask.

Answer (A) is correct. *(AC 61-107A)*
 DISCUSSION: The continuous-flow oxygen system's mask is designed so the oxygen can be diluted with ambient air by allowing the user to exhale around the face piece, and comes with a rebreather bag, which allows the individual to reuse part of the exhaled oxygen, thus helping to conserve the airplane's oxygen supply.
 Answer (B) is incorrect. The rebreather bag will retain, not expel, any oxygen that is not used when the individual inhales. Answer (C) is incorrect. The regulator, not the rebreather bag, controls the amount of oxygen that each individual breathes through the mask.

3.19 Cold Weather Operation

95. Which statement is true regarding preheating of an aircraft during cold-weather operations?

A. The cockpit, as well as the engine, should be preheated.
B. The cockpit area should not be preheated with portable heaters.
C. Hot air should be blown directly at the engine through the air intakes.

Answer (A) is correct. *(AC 91-13C)*
 DISCUSSION: Just as the engine becomes very stiff and inadequately lubricated when it is very cold, so do the communication and navigation instruments. Accordingly, the cockpit should be preheated as well as the engine.
 Answer (B) is incorrect. The cockpit area can and should be preheated with portable heaters if they are available and appropriate. Answer (C) is incorrect. The engine should be heated by blowing warm air on the entire engine surface, not through the air intake areas.

96. Crankcase breather lines of an aircraft engine should receive special attention during preflight in cold weather because they are susceptible to being clogged by

A. ice in the breather lines.
B. congealed oil from the crankcase.
C. moisture from the outside air which has frozen.

Answer (A) is correct. *(AC 91-13C)*
 DISCUSSION: Frozen crankcase breather lines prevent oil from circulating adequately in the engine and may even result in broken oil lines or oil being pumped out of the crankcase. Accordingly, you must always visually inspect to make sure that the crankcase breather lines are free of ice. The ice may have formed as a result of the crankcase vapors freezing in the lines after the engine has been turned off.
 Answer (B) is incorrect. Oil in the crankcase virtually never gets into the breather lines but rather remains in the bottom of the crankcase. Answer (C) is incorrect. Very cold outside air has a low moisture content.

97. During preflight in cold weather, crankcase breather lines should receive special attention because they are susceptible to being clogged by

A. congealed oil from the crankcase.
B. moisture from the outside air which has frozen.
C. ice from crankcase vapors that have condensed and subsequently frozen.

Answer (C) is correct. *(AC 91-13C)*
 DISCUSSION: Frozen crankcase breather lines prevent oil from circulating adequately in the engine and may even result in broken oil lines or oil being pumped out of the crankcase. Accordingly, you must always visually inspect to make sure that the crankcase breather lines are free of ice. The ice may have formed as a result of the crankcase vapors freezing in the lines after the engine has been turned off.
 Answer (A) is incorrect. Oil in the crankcase virtually never gets into the breather lines but rather remains in the bottom of the crankcase. Answer (B) is incorrect. Very cold outside air has a low moisture content.

STUDY UNIT FOUR
AIRPORTS, AIRSPACE, AND ATC

(9 pages of outline)

4.1	Runway Signs, Markings, and Lighting	(10 questions)	117, 126
4.2	Taxiway Signs and Markings	(8 questions)	118, 128
4.3	Airport Traffic Patterns	(3 questions)	119, 129
4.4	Wake Turbulence	(6 questions)	120, 130
4.5	Traffic Advisories at Uncontrolled Airports	(3 questions)	120, 132
4.6	Airport Beacons	(1 question)	121, 132
4.7	Visual Approach Slope Indicator (VASI)	(5 questions)	121, 132
4.8	Chart Supplements	(5 questions)	121, 133
4.9	ATIS	(2 questions)	122, 135
4.10	Special Use Airspace	(6 questions)	122, 136
4.11	Controlled Airspace	(6 questions)	123, 137
4.12	Class C Airspace	(9 questions)	123, 138
4.13	Radio Failure	(1 question)	123, 140
4.14	Transponder Codes	(2 questions)	123, 140
4.15	Collision Avoidance	(6 questions)	124, 140
4.16	Flight Plans	(4 questions)	124, 142
4.17	Notice to Airmen (NOTAM)	(5 questions)	125, 142

This study unit contains outlines of major concepts tested; sample test questions and answers regarding airports, airspace, and ATC; and an explanation of each answer. The table of contents above lists each subunit within this study unit, the number of questions pertaining to that particular subunit, and the pages on which the outlines and questions begin, respectively.

 Recall that the **sole purpose** of this book is to expedite your passing of the FAA pilot knowledge test for the CFI, BGI, or AGI certificate. Accordingly, all extraneous material (i.e., topics or regulations not directly tested on the FAA pilot knowledge test) is omitted, even though much more knowledge is necessary to become a proficient flight or ground instructor. This additional material is presented in *Pilot Handbook* and *Flight Instructor Flight Maneuvers and Practical Test Prep*, available from Gleim Publications, Inc. Order online at www.GleimAviation.com.

4.1 RUNWAY SIGNS, MARKINGS, AND LIGHTING

1. When runways have centerline lighting systems (lights that are flush with the runway centerline), all lights on the last 1,000 ft. of runway centerline are red.

2. The number at the end of each runway indicates the magnetic alignment rounded to the nearest 10° increment and divided by 10; e.g., Runway 26 indicates 260° magnetic, Runway 8 indicates 080° magnetic.

3. A displaced threshold is a threshold (marked as a broad solid white line across the runway) that is not at the beginning of the full-strength runway pavement. The remainder of the runway, following the displaced threshold, is the landing portion of the runway.

   a. The paved area before the displaced threshold (marked by arrows) is available for taxiing, the landing rollout, and takeoff of aircraft.

      1) It is not suitable for landing.

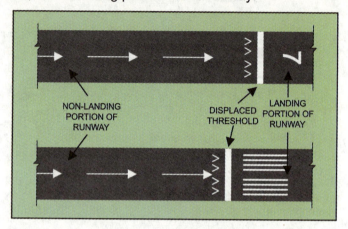

4. Runway hold position signs denote areas where aircraft should hold short of a runway.

   a. These signs can be located where taxiways intersect runways or where runways themselves intersect.

   b. Runway hold position markings on a taxiway denote where an aircraft should hold short of a runway.

5. A yellow demarcation bar is used to delineate a runway with a displaced threshold from a blast pad, stopway, or taxiway that precedes the runway.

   a. The demarcation bar is 3 feet wide, runs perpendicular across the entire width of the runway, and is yellow.

6. At airports with pilot-controlled lighting, the keying of the microphone is used to turn on and adjust the intensity of the lights.

   a. At airports without approach lighting systems but with MIRL (medium intensity runway lights), seven clicks of the microphone will turn on the MIRL at high intensity, five clicks for medium intensity, and three clicks for low intensity.

7. Runway exit signs show the designation and direction of exit taxiways from the runway.

   a. Like all direction signs, they have a yellow background with black lettering and always feature directional arrows.

8. An ILS critical area boundary sign is located adjacent to the pavement marking and is intended to provide pilots with another visual cue in deciding when they are "clear of the ILS critical area."

   a. At airports where these signs and markings are present and when the instrument landing system is being used, aircraft must hold at this line and not pass it unless authorized by ATC so as not to interfere with the signal from the ILS glide slope antenna installed at the airport.

4.2 TAXIWAY SIGNS AND MARKINGS

1. When leaving an airport ramp area, an outbound destination sign identifies the direction to the takeoff runways.

   a. These signs feature a yellow background with black lettering and directional arrows.

2. Taxiway location signs identify the taxiway on which an aircraft is currently located.

   a. Location signs feature a black background with yellow lettering and do not have directional arrows.

3. Taxiway directional signs indicate the designation and direction of a taxiway.
    a. When turning from one taxiway to another, a taxiway directional sign indicates the designation and direction of a taxiway leading out of the intersection.
    b. Taxiway directional signs feature a yellow background with black lettering and directional arrows.
4. When approaching taxiway holding lines from the side with continuous lines, the pilot should not cross the lines without an ATC clearance.
    a. Taxiway holding lines are painted across the width of the taxiway and are yellow.
5. Taxiway ending marker signs indicate that the taxiway in use does not continue beyond the sign.
    a. When placed in an intersection, the sign indicates that the taxiway in use does not continue beyond the intersection.
    b. Taxiway ending marker signs consist of alternating yellow and black diagonal stripes.
6. A "No Entry" sign is a mandatory instruction sign that identifies a paved area where aircraft are prohibited from entering.
    a. This sign has a white horizontal line surrounded by a white circle on a red background.
7. Hold position markings on a taxiway holding bay indicate an area where aircraft should hold when there is an operational need to do so and as instructed by ATC.

4.3 AIRPORT TRAFFIC PATTERNS

1. The segmented circle system provides traffic pattern information at airports without operating control towers. It consists of the
    a. Segmented circle -- located in a position for maximum visibility to pilots in the air and on the ground and providing a centralized point for the other elements of the system.
    b. Landing strip indicators -- show the alignment of landing runways (legs sticking out of the segmented circle).
    c. Traffic pattern indicators -- indicators at right angles to the landing strip indicator showing the direction of turn from base to final.
        1) In the example below, runways 22 and 36 use left traffic, while runways 4 and 18 use right traffic.
        2) The "X" indicates runways 4 and 22 are closed.
        3) The area behind the displaced thresholds of runways 18 and 36 (marked by arrows) can be used for taxiing and takeoff, but not for landing.

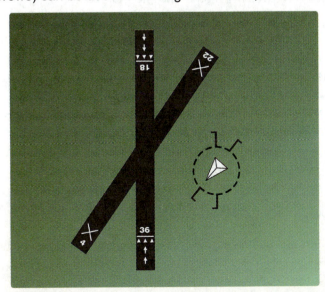

d. Wind direction indicator -- a wind cone, sock, or wind tee is installed near the runways to indicate wind direction.
e. Landing direction indicator -- a tetrahedron (as shown in the figure on the previous page) on a swivel is installed when conditions at the airport warrant its use. It is used to indicate the direction of takeoffs and landings. It should be located at the center of a segmented circle and may be lighted for night operations.
1) The small end points toward the direction in which a takeoff or landing should be made; i.e., the small end points into the wind.
2. If there is no segmented circle installed at the airport, traffic pattern indicators may be installed on or near the end of the runway.
3. Remember, you land
   a. In the same direction as the tip of the tetrahedron is pointing,
   b. As if you were flying out of the large (open) end of the wind cone, or
   c. Toward the cross-bar end of a wind "T" (visualize the "T" as an airplane with no nose, with the top of the "T" being the wings).
4. The recommended entry position to an airport traffic pattern is to enter 45° at the midpoint of the downwind leg at traffic pattern altitude.

4.4 WAKE TURBULENCE

1. **Wake turbulence vortices** circulate outward, upward, and around each wingtip.
2. A crosswind of 5 kt. or less would result in the upwind vortex remaining on the runway longer than the downwind vortex.
3. Due to the effects of wake turbulence, ATC will provide a minimum separation of 6 mi. for a small aircraft landing behind a heavy jet.
4. During a takeoff made behind a departing large jet airplane, you can minimize the hazard of wingtip vortices by being airborne prior to reaching the jet's flight path until able to turn clear of its wake.
5. When landing behind a large airplane, you should plan to land beyond the jet's touchdown point.
6. Vortices generated by helicopters in forward flight are similar to those generated by fixed-wing aircraft.

4.5 TRAFFIC ADVISORIES AT UNCONTROLLED AIRPORTS

1. The Common Traffic Advisory Frequency (CTAF) is designated for carrying out airport advisories when operating to/from an airport without an operating control tower.
   a. As a standard operating practice, pilots of inbound traffic to an airport without a control tower should continuously monitor and communicate as appropriate on the designated CTAF from 10 mi. to landing.
2. The CTAF may be a UNICOM, MULTICOM, FSS, or tower frequency and is identified in the Chart Supplement and aeronautical charts.
   a. In the absence of a tower, FSS, or UNICOM, use MULTICOM frequency 122.9 MHz as the CTAF to announce your intentions to all traffic in the area.
3. UNICOM stations can also be located at airports with a control tower.
   a. The frequency for these UNICOM stations is 122.95 MHz.

SU 4: Airports, Airspace, and ATC

4.6 AIRPORT BEACONS

1. Military airfields are identified by a green and dual-peaked white rotating beacon.
   a. Civilian fields have a green and single-flash white rotating beacon.
2. A white and green rotating beacon identifies a lighted land airport.

4.7 VISUAL APPROACH SLOPE INDICATOR (VASI)

1. Visual approach slope indicator (VASI) is a system of lights to provide visual descent information during an approach to landing.
2. **The standard VASI consists of a two-barred tier of lights.** You are
   a. Below the glide path if both light bars are red; i.e., "red means dead"
   b. On the glide path if the far (on top visually) lights are red and the near (on bottom visually) lights are white
   c. Above the glide path if both light bars are white
3. Remember, red over white (i.e., R before W alphabetically) is the desired sequence.
   a. White over red is impossible.
   b. As lights change from white to red or reverse, they may appear pink.
4. A **tri-color VASI** is a single light unit projecting three colors.
   a. The below glide path indicator is red.
   b. The above glide path indicator is amber.
   c. The on glide path indicator is green.
5. A **three-bar VASI** projects two glide paths. This is used to aid certain large aircraft.
   a. Below both glide paths, all three bars (near, middle, and far) are red.
   b. On the lower glide path, the near bar is white, while the middle and far bars are red.
   c. On the upper glide path, the near and middle bars are white, while the far bar is red.
   d. Above both glide paths is indicated by all three bars showing white.
6. The visual glide path of VASI provides safe obstruction clearance within ±10° of the extended runway centerline and to 4 NM from the runway threshold.
7. On a **precision approach path indicator (PAPI)**,
   a. Low is four red lights (less than 2.5°).
   b. Slightly low is one white and three red lights (2.8°).
   c. On glide path is two white and two red lights (3.0°).
   d. Slightly high is three white and one red light (3.2°).
   e. High is four white lights (more than 3.5°).

4.8 CHART SUPPLEMENTS

1. Chart Supplements are published by FAA Approved Print Providers every 56 days for each of the seven geographical districts of the U.S.
   a. Chart Supplements provide information on services available, runways, special conditions at the airport, communications, navigational aids, etc.
2. The airport name is the first item listed.
3. The hours of operation of a part-time control tower are found after the tower frequency in the "Communications" section.
   a. Hours of operation are expressed in Coordinated Universal Time (UTC) and are shown a "Z" time.
   b. To convert UTC to local time, use the time conversion factor shown as the third item on the first line, i.e., UTC – 6(–5DT).

4. The "Airport Remarks" section contains information on pilot-controlled lighting, i.e., types of lights, on which runways, and what frequency.

    a. LDIN means lead-in lighting system, which is a type of approach light.

5. Runway gradient is not shown in the runway data if it is less than 0.3%.

6. The "Radio Aids to Navigation" section lists all the facilities by name for an airport for which the FAA has approved an Instrument Approach Procedure.

    a. The last item listed for VOR, VORTAC, or VOR/DME is the elevation and magnetic variation at the site of the facility.

        1) EXAMPLE: 560/08E means an elevation of 560 ft. MSL and a magnetic variation of 08°E at the site.

7. The Chart Supplement also contains information concerning parachute jumping sites.

4.9 ATIS

1. **Automatic Terminal Information Service (ATIS)** is a continuous broadcast of recorded noncontrol information in selected high-activity terminal areas (i.e., busy airports).

2. ATIS broadcasts are updated upon the receipt of any official weather, regardless of content change or reported values.

    a. A new ATIS recording will also be made when there is a change in other pertinent data, such as runway change, instrument approach in use, etc.

3. Absence of the ceiling/sky condition, visibility, and obstructions to vision on an ATIS broadcast indicates that the ceiling is more than 5,000 ft. and the visibility is more than 5 SM.

4.10 SPECIAL USE AIRSPACE

1. **Restricted areas** denote the existence of unusual, often invisible, hazards to aircraft, such as artillery firing, aerial gunnery, or guided missiles.

    a. Flight into a restricted area should not be attempted unless the pilot has received prior authorization from the controlling agency.

2. A **warning area** is airspace of defined dimensions, extending from 3 NM outward from the coast of the U.S.

    a. A warning area may be located in domestic or international airspace, or both.

3. **Military operations areas** (MOAs) are designed to separate IFR traffic from certain military training activities.

    a. You may operate VFR in an MOA, but you should use extreme caution to look for military activity in progress and also seek information concerning those activities from a local FSS.

4. **Military Training Routes (MTRs)** are labeled on charts as IR or VR and have a three- or four-digit identifier.

    a. **IR** means flown with instrument flight rules.
    b. **VR** means flown with visual flight rules.
    c. **Four digits** mean the MTR has no segment above 1,500 ft. AGL.

        1) These are generally developed to be flown VR but may also be flown IR.

    d. **Three-digit identifiers** mean the MTR has one or more segments above 1,500 ft. AGL.

        1) These are developed, to the maximum extent possible, to be flown IR.

4.11 CONTROLLED AIRSPACE

1. Controlled airspace is a generic term that covers

    a. Class A
    b. Class B
    c. Class C
    d. Class D
    e. Class E

2. Class A airspace extends from 18,000 ft. MSL up to and including FL 600.

3. Class D airspace will normally extend from the surface up to and including 2,500 ft. AGL.

    a. When a part-time control tower in Class D airspace ceases operation for the day, the Class D airspace becomes Class E or a combination of Class E and Class G airspace during the hours the tower is not in operation.

4. Class E airspace will begin either at the surface, 700 ft. AGL, 1,200 ft. AGL, or 14,500 ft. MSL.

    a. Class E airspace extends vertically up to but not including the base of the overlying airspace. Unless obstructed vertically by Class B or Class C airspace, it continues up to the base of Class A airspace (i.e., up to but not including 18,000 ft. MSL).

4.12 CLASS C AIRSPACE

1. Class C airspace consists of a surface area and a shelf area.

    a. The surface area has a 5-NM radius from the primary airport.

        1) It extends from the surface to 4,000 ft. above the airport elevation.

    b. The shelf area is an area from 5 to 10 NM from the primary airport.

        1) It extends from 1,200 ft. AGL to 4,000 ft. above the airport elevation.

2. Surrounding the Class C airspace is the outer area. The outer area is not classified as Class C airspace.

    a. The normal radius of the outer area is 20 NM from the primary airport.

3. The minimum equipment needed to operate Class C airspace includes

    a. A 4096 code transponder
    b. Mode C (altitude encoding) capability
    c. Two-way radio communication capability with ATC

4. You must establish and maintain two-way radio communication with ATC prior to entering, and while operating within, Class C airspace.

    a. All operations within Class C airspace must be in compliance with ATC instructions.
    b. You are not required to have an ATC clearance to enter Class C airspace.

5. When departing from a satellite airport without an operating control tower, you must contact ATC as soon as practicable after takeoff.

4.13 RADIO FAILURE

1. If your radio fails, the procedure to land at a controlled airport is to observe the traffic flow, enter the pattern, and watch for a light signal from the tower.

4.14 TRANSPONDER CODES

1. Civil pilots never use transponder code 7777. It is for military intercept operations.

4.15 COLLISION AVOIDANCE

1. Most midair collisions occur on clear days when more traffic is flying and pilots, comfortable with the weather, become complacent and fail to use proper see-and-avoid techniques.
2. Because the eyes can focus on only a narrow viewing area, effective scanning is accomplished in daylight with a series of short, regularly spaced eye movements that bring successive areas of the sky into the central visual field.
   a. Each eye movement should not exceed 10°.
   b. Each area should be observed for at least 1 second to enable detection.
3. At night, off-center viewing is better than center viewing due to the physiology of the eye.
   a. Pilots should scan slowly at night to facilitate off-center viewing.
4. Traffic advisories, when issued by a controller, are based on a computer-generated ground track (i.e., magnetic course) of your aircraft.
   a. Thus, if a controller advises radar traffic utilizing the 12-hour clock, it is based upon your ground track, not your heading.
5. The most effective way to prevent collisions in the traffic pattern is to maintain the proper traffic pattern altitude and continually scan for traffic.
6. Pilots are encouraged to turn on their landing lights when operating below 10,000 ft., day or night, especially within 10 mi. of any airport.
7. ADS-B (Automatic Dependent Surveillance-Broadcast) is technology that allows air traffic controllers (and ADS-B equipped aircraft) to see traffic with more precision. Instead of relying on old radar technology, ADS-B uses highly accurate GPS signals. Because of this, ADS-B works where radar often will not.
   a. This system
      1) Works in remote areas such as mountainous terrain
      2) Functions at low altitudes and even on the ground
      3) Can be used to monitor traffic on the taxiways and runways
      4) Allows air traffic controllers as well as aircraft with certain equipment to receive ADS-B traffic
      5) Provides subscription-free weather information to all aircraft flying over the U.S.
   b. ADS-B will be required in 2020. This system helps make our skies safer. For more information, visit www.garmin.com/us/intheair/ads-b.

4.16 FLIGHT PLANS

NOTE: As of the publication date of this text, pilots may file flight plans in the U.S. under either the domestic or International Civil Aviation Organization (ICAO) format. The FAA is planning to exclusively use the ICAO format for civil aircraft in the fall of 2017. The FAA previously removed all questions from its test bank referring to flight plans; however, new questions regarding ICAO flight plans are expected to be added by June 2018.

1. When a VFR flight plan is filed, it will be held by the FSS until 1 hr. after the proposed departure time, unless
   a. The actual departure time is received,
   b. A revised proposed departure time is received, or
   c. At the time of the filing, the FSS is informed that the proposed time will be met, but actual time cannot be given because of inadequate communications (i.e., assumed departure).

SU 4: Airports, Airspace, and ATC 125

2. If you fail to report or cancel your flight plan within 1/2 hr. after your ETA, search and rescue procedures will be commenced.
3. Block 3 of a flight plan asks for your aircraft type/special equipment. Some of the special equipment codes used are
    a. A -- DME and transponder with altitude encoding capability
    b. I -- RNAV (no GNSS) and transponder with altitude encoding capability
    c. U -- Transponder with altitude encoding capability
    d. W -- RVSM, no GNSS, no RNAV, transponder with Mode C
        1) Reduced Vertical Separation Minimum (RVSM) in the United States requires prior authorization from the FAA or from the responsible authority, as appropriate.
    e. Y -- RNAV, no transponder

4.17 NOTICE TO AIRMEN (NOTAM)

1. The Notices to Airmen (NOTAM) system disseminates time-critical aeronautical information that either is of a temporary nature or is not sufficiently known in advance to permit publication on aeronautical charts or in other operational publications.
    a. NOTAM information is aeronautical information that could affect your decision to make a flight.
2. NOTAMs are grouped into five types:
    a. **NOTAMs (D)** include information such as airport or primary runway closures; changes in the status of navigational aids, ILSs, and radar service availability; and other information essential to planned en route, terminal, or landing operations. Also included is information on airport taxiways, aprons, ramp areas, and associated lighting.
    b. **FDC NOTAMs** are issued by the Flight Data Center and contain regulatory information such as amendments to published instrument approach charts and other current aeronautical charts. FDC NOTAMs are also used to broadcast the establishment of temporary flight restrictions (TFRs).
        1) TFRs are established to protect people and property on the ground and in the air during certain events.
    c. **Pointer NOTAMs** reduce total NOTAM volume by pointing to other NOTAMs (D) and FDC NOTAMs rather than duplicating potentially unnecessary information for an airport or NAVAID. They allow pilots to reference NOTAMs that might not be listed under a given airport or NAVAID identifier.
    d. **SAA NOTAMs** are issued when Special Activity Airspace (SAA) will be active outside the published schedule times and when required by the published schedule, although pilots must still check published times for SAA as well as any other NOTAMs for that airspace.
    e. **Military NOTAMs** reference military airports and NAVAIDs and are rarely of any interest to civilian pilots.
3. The *Notices to Airmen Publication (NTAP)* is issued every 28 days and is an integral part of the NOTAM system. Once a NOTAM is published in the NTAP, the NOTAM is not provided during pilot weather briefings unless specifically requested.
    a. The *NTAP* contains NOTAMs (D) that are expected to remain in effect for an extended period and FDC NOTAMs that are current at the time of publication.

QUESTIONS AND ANSWER EXPLANATIONS: All of the AGI/CFI knowledge test questions chosen by the FAA for release as well as additional questions selected by Gleim relating to the material in the previous outlines are reproduced on the following pages. These questions have been organized into the same subunits as the outlines. To the immediate right of each question are the correct answer and answer explanation. You should cover these answers and answer explanations while responding to the questions. Refer to the general discussion in the Introduction on how to take the FAA knowledge test.

Remember that the questions from the FAA knowledge test bank have been reordered by topic and organized into a meaningful sequence. Also, the first line of the answer explanation gives the citation of the authoritative source for the answer.

QUESTIONS

4.1 Runway Signs, Markings, and Lighting

1. A series of continuous red lights in the runway centerline lighting indicates

   A. 3,000 feet of runway remaining.
   B. 1,000 feet of runway remaining.
   C. the beginning of the runway overrun area.

Answer (B) is correct. *(AIM Para 2-1-5)*
   DISCUSSION: When runway centerline lighting is installed, only red lights are seen for the last 1,000 ft. of the runway.
   Answer (A) is incorrect. Alternate red and white lights are seen from the 3,000-ft. point to the 1,000-ft. point. Answer (C) is incorrect. The runway centerline lights are white and spaced at 50-ft. intervals until the last 3,000 ft. of runway.

2. The numbers 8 and 26 on the approach ends of the runway indicate that the runway is orientated approximately

   A. 008° and 026° true.
   B. 080° and 260° true.
   C. 080° and 260° magnetic.

Answer (C) is correct. *(AIM Para 2-3-3)*
   DISCUSSION: Runway numbers are determined from the approach direction. The runway number is the whole number nearest one-tenth the magnetic direction of the centerline. Thus, the numbers 8 and 26 on a runway indicate that the runway is oriented approximately 080° and 260° magnetic.
   Answer (A) is incorrect. The ending digit, not a leading zero, is dropped. Answer (B) is incorrect. Runways are numbered based on magnetic, not true, direction.

3. What does a series of arrows painted on the approach end of a runway signify?

   A. That area is restricted solely to taxi operations.
   B. That portion of the runway is not suitable for landing.
   C. That portion of the runway is the designated touchdown zone.

Answer (B) is correct. *(AIM Para 2-3-3)*
   DISCUSSION: A series of arrows to a solid white line across the approach end of a runway indicates that there is a displaced threshold. The portion of the runway before the displaced threshold is not suitable for landing.
   Answer (A) is incorrect. Although that portion is not suitable for landing, it may be used for taxiing, the landing rollout, and the takeoff of aircraft. Answer (C) is incorrect. Touchdown zone marks are a series of six lines, not arrows, parallel to the runway direction.

4. What is the purpose of the runway/runway hold position sign?

   A. Denotes entrance to runway from a taxiway.
   B. Denotes area protected for an aircraft approaching or departing a runway.
   C. Denotes intersecting runways.

Answer (C) is correct. *(AIM Para 2-3-8)*
   DISCUSSION: Runway/runway hold position signs are a type of mandatory instruction sign used to denote intersecting runways. These are runways that intersect and are being used for "Land, Hold Short" operations or are normally used for taxiing. These signs have a red background with white lettering. Runway/runway hold position signs are identical to the signs used for taxiway/runway intersections.
   Answer (A) is incorrect. A runway/runway hold position sign is located on a runway and denotes an intersecting runway, not the entrance to a runway from a taxiway. Answer (B) is incorrect. A runway approach area holding position sign protects an area from approaching or departing aircraft.

5. What is the purpose of the runway hold position sign?

   A. Denotes entrance to runway from a taxiway.
   B. Denotes area protected for an aircraft approaching or departing a runway.
   C. Denotes taxiway location.

Answer (A) is correct. *(AIM Para 2-3-5)*
   DISCUSSION: A runway hold position sign is located on a taxiway and denotes an entrance to a runway from a taxiway.
   Answer (B) is incorrect. A runway approach area holding position sign protects an area from approaching or departing aircraft. Answer (C) is incorrect. The taxiway direction sign, not the runway hold position sign, indicates the designation and direction of the taxiways leading out of an intersection.

SU 4: Airports, Airspace, and ATC

6. What is the purpose for the runway hold position markings on the taxiway?

A. Identifies area where aircraft are prohibited.
B. Allows an aircraft permission to taxi onto the runway.
C. Holds aircraft short of the runway.

Answer (C) is correct. *(AIM Para 2-3-5)*
DISCUSSION: Runway holding position markings on taxiways identify the location where you are supposed to stop when you do not have an ATC clearance to proceed at an airport with an operating control tower. At an airport without an operating control tower, you must verify adequate separation before crossing the holding position markings. These markings consist of four yellow lines--two solid and two dashed--spaced 6 inches apart and extending across the width of the taxiway, with the dashed lines nearest the runway. The solid lines are always on the side where the aircraft is to hold.
Answer (A) is incorrect. A no entry sign, not a runway hold position marking, identifies an area where aircraft are prohibited. Answer (B) is incorrect. Runway holding position markings indicate that aircraft should hold short of the runway, not taxi onto it, until a clearance to proceed onto the runway is received.

7. What is the purpose of the yellow demarcation bar marking?

A. Delineates entrance to runway from a taxiway.
B. Delineates beginning of runway available for landing when pavement is aligned with runway on approach side.
C. Delineates runway with a displaced threshold from a blast pad, stopway or taxiway that precedes the runway.

Answer (C) is correct. *(AIM Para 2-3-3)*
DISCUSSION: The demarcation bar delineates a runway with a displaced threshold from a blast pad, stopway, or taxiway that precedes the runway. The demarcation bar is 3 feet wide, runs perpendicular to the runway, and is yellow.
Answer (A) is incorrect. A runway holding position sign, not a demarcation bar, identifies the entrance to a runway from a taxiway. Runway holding position signs consist of a red background with white inscription. Answer (B) is incorrect. A runway threshold bar, not a demarcation bar, delineates the beginning of runway available for landing.

8. An airport has pilot controlled lighting but runways without approach lights. How many times should you key your microphone to turn on the MIRL at medium intensity?

A. 5 clicks.
B. 3 clicks.
C. None, the MIRL is left on all night.

Answer (A) is correct. *(AIM Para 2-1-7)*
DISCUSSION: At an airport with pilot-controlled lighting and no approach lights, you should key your microphone five clicks to turn on the MIRL at medium intensity.
Answer (B) is incorrect. Three clicks will turn on the MIRL at low, not medium, intensity. Answer (C) is incorrect. At airports with pilot-controlled lighting, the lights are usually off until activated by the pilot.

9. When exiting the runway, what is the purpose of the runway exit sign?

A. Indicates designation and direction of exit taxiway from runway.
B. Indicates designation and direction of taxiway leading out of an intersection.
C. Indicates direction to take-off runway.

Answer (A) is correct. *(AIM Para 2-3-3)*
DISCUSSION: The runway exit sign indicates the designation and direction of the taxiway that is used to exit the runway. These signs have black inscriptions on a yellow background and always contain arrows.
Answer (B) is incorrect. The taxiway direction sign, not the runway exit sign, indicates the designation and direction of the taxiways leading out of an intersection. Answer (C) is incorrect. Outbound destination signs, not runway exit signs, indicate the direction that must be taken out of an intersection in order to follow the preferred taxi route to a runway.

10. The "ILS critical area boundary" sign identifies

A. the area where an aircraft is prohibited from entering.
B. the edge of the ILS critical area.
C. the exit boundary for the runway protected area.

Answer (B) is correct. *(PHAK Chap 14)*
DISCUSSION: The ILS critical area boundary sign has a yellow background with two horizontal, parallel black lines and four sets of two vertical, parallel lines connecting the two horizontal lines. This sign is the same as the painted marking representing the ILS critical area boundary. When an ILS is in operation, aircraft must hold at this line and not pass it unless so authorized by ATC so as not to block or interfere with the signal from the ILS glide slope antenna installed at the airport. If taxiing off of a runway, the aircraft is not clear of the ILS critical area until all parts of the aircraft are past this sign and associated painted marking.
Answer (A) is incorrect. It describes the purpose of a no entry sign. Answer (C) is incorrect. It describes the purpose of a runway hold position sign.

4.2 Taxiway Signs and Markings

11. What does the outbound destination sign identify?

A. Identifies entrance to the runway from a taxiway.
B. Identifies runway on which an aircraft is located.
C. Identifies direction to take-off runways.

Answer (C) is correct. *(AIM Para 2-3-11)*
DISCUSSION: Outbound destination signs define taxiing directions to takeoff runways. Destination signs have a yellow background with a black inscription. Outbound destination signs always have an arrow showing the direction of the taxiing route to the takeoff runway.
Answer (A) is incorrect. A runway holding position sign, not an outbound destination sign, identifies the entrance to a runway from a taxiway. Runway holding position signs consist of a red background with white inscription. Answer (B) is incorrect. A runway location sign, not an outbound destination sign, identifies the runway on which the aircraft is currently located. Runway location signs consist of a black background with a yellow inscription and a yellow border.

12. What is the purpose of the taxiway ending marker sign?

A. Identifies area where aircraft are prohibited.
B. Indicates taxiway does not continue beyond intersection.
C. Provides general taxiing direction to named taxiway.

Answer (B) is correct. *(AIM Para 2-3-12)*
DISCUSSION: A taxiway ending marker sign consists of alternating yellow and black diagonal stripes. Taxiway ending marker signs indicate that the taxiway does not continue beyond the sign.
Answer (A) is incorrect. No entry signs, not taxiway ending marker signs, identify an area where aircraft are prohibited from entering. No entry signs consist of a white horizontal line surrounded by a white circle on a red background. Answer (C) is incorrect. A direction sign, not a taxiway ending marker sign, indicates the general direction to take out of an intersection in order to taxi onto the named taxiway. Direction signs consist of black lettering on a yellow background with an arrow indicating the direction of turn.

13. The "No Entry" sign identifies

A. paved area where aircraft entry is prohibited.
B. an area that does not continue beyond intersection.
C. the exit boundary for the runway protected area.

Answer (A) is correct. *(AIM Para 2-3-8)*
DISCUSSION: No entry signs consist of a white horizontal line surrounded by a white circle on a red background. These signs are posted at points where aircraft entry is prohibited. These signs are typically found on taxiways that are intended to be used in only one direction and at the intersection of vehicle roadways with runways, taxiways, or ramp areas where the roadway may be mistaken for a taxiway or other aircraft movement area.
Answer (B) is incorrect. A taxiway ending marker sign, not a no entry sign, indicates that a taxiway does not continue beyond the next intersection. Taxiway ending marker signs consist of alternating yellow and black diagonal stripes. Answer (C) is incorrect. A runway boundary sign, not a no entry sign, identifies the boundary of the runway protected area for aircraft leaving the runway. Runway boundary signs consist of a black depiction of a runway holding position marking on a yellow background.

14. When turning onto a taxiway from another taxiway, what is the purpose of the taxiway directional sign?

A. Indicates direction to take-off runway.
B. Indicates designation and direction of exit taxiway from runway.
C. Indicates designation and direction of taxiway leading out of an intersection.

Answer (C) is correct. *(AIM Para 2-3-10)*
DISCUSSION: Direction signs consist of black lettering on a yellow background. These signs identify the designations of taxiways leading out of an intersection. An arrow next to each taxiway designation indicates the direction that an aircraft must turn in order to taxi onto that taxiway.
Answer (A) is incorrect. Outbound destination signs, not direction signs, indicate the direction that must be taken out of an intersection in order to follow the preferred taxi route to a runway. Answer (B) is incorrect. The question specifies that you are turning onto a taxiway from another taxiway, not from a runway.

SU 4: Airports, Airspace, and ATC

15. What purpose does the taxiway location sign serve?

A. Provides general taxiing direction to named runway.
B. Denotes entrance to runway from a taxiway.
C. Identifies taxiway on which an aircraft is located.

Answer (C) is correct. *(AIM Para 2-3-9)*
DISCUSSION: Taxiway location signs are used to identify a taxiway on which the aircraft is currently located. Taxiway location signs consist of a black background with a yellow inscription and yellow border.
Answer (A) is incorrect. A runway destination sign, not a taxiway location sign, provides general taxiing information to a named runway. Answer (B) is incorrect. A runway holding position sign, not a taxiway location sign, identifies the entrance to a runway from a taxiway. Runway holding position signs consist of a red background with white inscription.

16. When approaching taxiway holding lines from the side with the continuous lines, the pilot

A. may continue taxiing.
B. should not cross the lines without ATC clearance.
C. should continue taxiing until all parts of the aircraft have crossed the lines.

Answer (B) is correct. *(AIM Para 2-3-5)*
DISCUSSION: When approaching taxiway holding lines, the solid (continuous) lines are always on the side where the aircraft is to hold. Therefore, do not cross the hold line without ATC clearance.
Answer (A) is incorrect. You cannot cross the hold line without ATC clearance. Answer (C) is incorrect. No part of the aircraft can cross the hold line without ATC clearance.

17. What does a destination sign identify?

A. Entrance to the runway from a taxiway.
B. Direction to takeoff runways.
C. Runway on which an aircraft is located.

Answer (B) is correct. *(AIM Para 2-3-11)*
DISCUSSION: Outbound destination signs define taxiing directions to takeoff runways. Destination signs have a yellow background with a black inscription. Outbound destination signs always have an arrow showing the direction of the taxiing route to the takeoff runway.
Answer (A) is incorrect. A runway holding position sign, not an outbound destination sign, identifies the entrance to a runway from a taxiway. Runway holding position signs consist of a red background with white inscription. Answer (C) is incorrect. A runway location sign, not an outbound destination sign, identifies the runway on which the aircraft is currently located. Runway location signs consist of a black background with a yellow inscription and a yellow border.

18. What is the purpose of the hold position markings on a holding bay?

A. Identifies the taxiway on which the aircraft is located.
B. Holds aircraft on the holding bay when there is an operational need.
C. Identifies an area where aircraft are prohibited from entering.

Answer (B) is correct. *(AIM Para 2-3-5)*
DISCUSSION: If necessary, an aircraft can be held in the holding bay to allow for another aircraft to taxi past. The hold position marking on a holding bay is only in effect when so instructed by ATC, but you should always communicate with ATC if there is any doubt over your holding status.
Answer (A) is incorrect. A taxiway location sign, not hold position markings, identifies the taxiway on which an aircraft is located. Answer (C) is incorrect. A no entry sign, not hold position markings, identifies an area where aircraft are prohibited from entering.

4.3 Airport Traffic Patterns

19. The recommended entry position to an airport traffic pattern is

A. 45° to the base leg just below traffic pattern altitude.
B. to enter 45° at the midpoint of the downwind leg at traffic pattern altitude.
C. to cross directly over the airport at traffic pattern altitude and join the downwind leg.

Answer (B) is correct. *(AIM Para 4-3-3)*
DISCUSSION: The recommended entry position to an airport traffic pattern is to enter 45° at the midpoint of the downwind leg at traffic pattern altitude.
Answer (A) is incorrect. The recommended entry to an airport traffic pattern is to enter 45° at the midpoint of the downwind, not base, leg and at traffic pattern altitude, not below. Answer (C) is incorrect. The recommended entry to an airport traffic pattern is to enter 45° at the midpoint of the downwind, not to cross directly over the airport and join the downwind leg. Also, flying at traffic pattern altitude directly over an airport is an example of poor judgment in collision avoidance precautions.

20. (Refer to Figure 54 below.) The segmented circle indicates that the airport traffic pattern is

A. left-hand for Rwy 17 and right-hand for Rwy 35.
B. right-hand for Rwy 35 and right-hand for Rwy 9.
C. left-hand for Rwy 35 and right-hand for Rwy 17.

Answer (C) is correct. *(AIM Para 4-3-3)*
DISCUSSION: A segmented circle is installed at uncontrolled airports to provide traffic pattern information. The landing runway indicators are shown coming out of the segmented circle to show the alignment of landing runways. In Fig. 54, given the north marker, the available runways are 17-35 and 9-27.
The traffic pattern indicators are at the end of the landing runway indicators and are angled out at 90°. These indicate the direction of turn from base to final. Thus, the airport traffic pattern is left-hand for Rwy 35 and right-hand for Rwy 17. It is also left-hand for Rwy 9 and right-hand for Rwy 27.
Answer (A) is incorrect. Rwy 17 traffic pattern is right-hand, not left-hand, and Rwy 35 is left-hand, not right-hand. Answer (B) is incorrect. Both Rwys 35 and 9 have left-hand, not right-hand, traffic patterns.

21. (Refer to Figure 54 below.) Which runway and traffic pattern should be used as indicated by the wind cone in the segmented circle?

A. Right-hand traffic on Rwy 17.
B. Left-hand traffic on Rwy 27 or Rwy 35.
C. Left-hand traffic on Rwy 35 or right-hand traffic on Rwy 27.

Answer (C) is correct. *(AIM Para 4-3-3)*
DISCUSSION: In Fig. 54, the large end of the wind cone is pointing to the direction from which the wind is coming, i.e., northwest. Thus, you could use either left-hand traffic on Rwy 35 or right-hand traffic on Rwy 27.
Answer (A) is incorrect. The wind is from the northwest and use of Rwy 17 would result in a tailwind landing. Answer (B) is incorrect. Rwy 27 has a right-hand, not left-hand, traffic pattern.

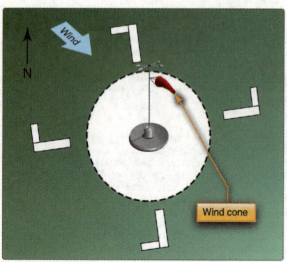

Figure 54. – Traffic Pattern Indicator.

4.4 Wake Turbulence

22. How does the wake turbulence vortex circulate around each wingtip?

A. Inward, upward, and around each tip.
B. Inward, upward, and counterclockwise.
C. Outward, upward, and around each tip.

Answer (C) is correct. *(AIM Para 7-3-4)*
DISCUSSION: Since the pressure differential is caused by a lower pressure above the wing and a higher pressure below the wing, the air from the bottom moves out, up, and around each wingtip.
Answer (A) is incorrect. The air moves out around the edge of the wing, not in underneath the wing. Answer (B) is incorrect. The air moves out around the edge of the wing. From behind, the left wingtip vortex is clockwise and the right wingtip vortex is counter-clockwise.

23. What effect would a crosswind of 5 knots or less have on the wingtip vortices generated by a large aircraft that had just taken off?

A. A light crosswind would rapidly dissipate the strength of both vortices.
B. The upwind vortex would tend to remain on the runway longer than the downwind vortex.
C. Both vortices would move downwind at a greater rate than if the surface wind was directly down the landing runway.

Answer (B) is correct. *(AIM Para 7-3-4)*
DISCUSSION: When vortices of large aircraft sink close to the ground (within about 200 ft.), they tend to move laterally over the ground at a speed of about 5 kt. in the direction of each generating wing. Thus, the downwind vortex in a light crosswind is blown away quickly, but the upwind vortex remains on the runway longer.
Answer (A) is incorrect. Strong winds rather than light winds would tend to dissipate vortex strength. Answer (C) is incorrect. The downwind vortex moves away at a faster rate than the upwind vortex.

24. Due to the effects of wake turbulence, what minimum separation does ATC provide for a small aircraft landing behind a heavy jet?

A. 4 miles.
B. 5 miles.
C. 6 miles.

Answer (C) is correct. *(AIM Para 7-3-9)*
DISCUSSION: Because of the possible effects of wake turbulence, controllers are required to provide a minimum separation for aircraft operating behind a heavy jet and, in certain instances, behind large non-heavy aircraft. For a small aircraft landing behind a heavy jet, ATC provides for a 6-mi. separation.
Answer (A) is incorrect. Four miles is the minimum separation of small aircraft landing behind large, not heavy jet, aircraft. Answer (B) is incorrect. Five miles is the minimum separation of small/large aircraft operating directly behind a heavy jet at the same altitude or less than 1,000 ft. below, not landing.

25. During a takeoff made behind a departing large jet airplane, the pilot can minimize the hazard of wingtip vortices by

A. remaining below the jet's flightpath until able to turn clear of its wake.
B. extending the takeoff roll and not rotating until well beyond the jet's rotation point.
C. being airborne prior to reaching the jet's flightpath until able to turn clear of its wake.

Answer (C) is correct. *(AIM Para 7-3-6)*
DISCUSSION: When taking off behind a large jet, you should be airborne prior to reaching the point of the jet's rotation. You also should turn to the right or left and make sure you do not fly through the jet's wingtip vortices (i.e., the jet will climb faster than a propeller airplane).
Answer (A) is incorrect. You should remain above, not below, the jet's flight path to avoid the sinking vortices. Answer (B) is incorrect. If you rotate beyond the jet's rotation point, you will be flying up into the jet's vortices.

26. When landing behind a large jet aircraft, at which point on the runway should you plan to land?

A. Beyond the jet's touchdown point.
B. At least 1,000 feet beyond the jet's touchdown point.
C. If any crosswind, land on the windward side of the runway and prior to the jet's touchdown point.

Answer (A) is correct. *(AIM Para 7-3-6)*
DISCUSSION: Since the vortices from a large landing jet extend downward and cease at the touchdown point, you should land beyond the jet's touchdown point to ensure that you are above the wingtip vortices at all times.
Answer (B) is incorrect. One ft. is as good as 1,000 ft.; i.e., no vortices are generated after touchdown. Answer (C) is incorrect. Prior to the jet's touchdown point, you may encounter the jet's wingtip vortices. After the jet lands, it no longer generates lift or vortices.

27. Which statement is true regarding wingtip vortices?

A. Helicopter rotors generate downwash turbulence only, not vortices.
B. Vortices generated by helicopters in forward flight are similar to those generated by fixed wing aircraft.
C. Vortices tend to remain level for a period of time before sinking below the generating aircraft's flightpath.

Answer (B) is correct. *(AIM Para 7-3-7)*
DISCUSSION: In forward flight, departing or landing helicopters produce a pair of strong, high-speed trailing vortices similar to wingtip vortices of larger fixed-wing aircraft.
Answer (A) is incorrect. Although helicopters generate downwash turbulence while hovering, they also create vortices in forward flight. Answer (C) is incorrect. Vortices begin sinking immediately at a rate of several hundred feet per minute.

4.5 Traffic Advisories at Uncontrolled Airports

28. As standard operating practice, all inbound traffic to an airport without a control tower should continuously monitor the appropriate facility from a distance of

A. 25 miles.
B. 20 miles.
C. 10 miles.

Answer (C) is correct. *(AIM Para 4-1-9)*
DISCUSSION: As a standard operating practice, pilots of inbound traffic to an airport without a control tower should continuously monitor and communicate, as appropriate, on the designated Common Traffic Advisory Frequency (CTAF) from 10 mi. to landing.
Answer (A) is incorrect. All inbound traffic to an airport without a control tower should continuously monitor the CTAF from a distance of 10 mi., not 25 mi. Answer (B) is incorrect. All inbound traffic to an airport without a control tower should continuously monitor the CTAF from a distance of 10 mi., not 20 mi.

29. When landing at an airport that does not have a tower, FSS, or UNICOM, you should broadcast your intentions on

A. 122.9 MHz.
B. 123.0 MHz.
C. 123.6 MHz.

Answer (A) is correct. *(AIM Para 4-1-9)*
DISCUSSION: Where there is no tower, FSS, or UNICOM station at the airport, use the MULTICOM frequency 122.9 MHz for self-announcing your position and intentions.
Answer (B) is incorrect. This is a UNICOM frequency. Answer (C) is incorrect. This is an FSS frequency.

30. The UNICOM frequency at airports with a control tower is

A. 123.0
B. 122.95
C. 122.8

Answer (B) is correct. *(AIM Para 4-1-11)*
DISCUSSION: The appropriate frequency for UNICOM at an airport with a control tower is 122.95.
Answer (A) is incorrect. This is a UNICOM frequency for airports without a control tower. Answer (C) is incorrect. This is a UNICOM frequency for airports without a control tower.

4.6 Airport Beacons

31. A military airfield can be identified by

A. a white and red rotating beacon.
B. white flashing sequence lights (strobes).
C. a green and dual-peaked white rotating beacon.

Answer (C) is correct. *(AIM Para 2-1-8)*
DISCUSSION: Military airport beacons flash dual-peaked (two quick) white flashes between each green flash.
Answer (A) is incorrect. A white and red rotating beacon is not used to identify any type of airfield. Answer (B) is incorrect. White flashing sequence lights (strobes) are part of an approach light system, not an airport beacon.

4.7 Visual Approach Slope Indicator (VASI)

32. A slightly below glidepath indication on a 2-bar VASI glidepath is indicated by

A. two red lights over two white lights.
B. two white lights over two red lights.
C. two red lights over two more red lights.

Answer (C) is correct. *(AIM Para 2-1-2)*
DISCUSSION: On a 2-bar VASI, whenever the aircraft is low, the lights are "red over red." An easy way to remember this is with the following memory aids: "White over white, you're out of sight," meaning you are too high, above the glidepath; "Red over white, you're alright," meaning you are on the glidepath; and "Red over red, you're dead," meaning you are too low, below the glidepath.
Answer (A) is incorrect. On a 2-bar VASI, whenever the aircraft is on the glidepath, the lights are "red over white." Answer (B) is incorrect. On a 2-bar VASI, there is no white over red indication.

33. Which indications would a pilot see while approaching to land on a runway served by a 2-bar VASI?

A. If below the glidepath, the near bars will be red and the far bars white.
B. If on the glidepath, the near bars will appear red and the far bars will appear white.
C. If departing to the high side of the glidepath, the far bars will change from red to pink to white.

Answer (C) is correct. *(AIM Para 2-1-2)*
DISCUSSION: The basic principle of the VASI is that of color differentiation. Each light unit projects a beam of light having a white segment in the upper part and a red segment in the lower part of the beam. As you move to the high side of a VASI glide path, the far bars will change from red to white. Pink occurs due to the momentary combination of red and white.
Answer (A) is incorrect. If you are below the glide path, both near and far bars are red. Answer (B) is incorrect. If on the glide path, the near bar is white and the far bar is red; the opposite is impossible.

34. When on the upper glidepath of a 3-bar VASI, what would be the colors of the lights?

A. All three sets of lights would be white.
B. The near bar is white and the middle and far bars are red.
C. The near and middle bars are white and the upper bar is red.

Answer (C) is correct. *(AIM Para 2-1-2)*
DISCUSSION: When on the upper glide path of a 3-bar VASI, the near and middle bars are white and the upper (far) bar is red.
Answer (A) is incorrect. All three sets of lights would be white when you are above both glide paths. Answer (B) is incorrect. With the near bar white and the middle and far bars red, you would be on the lower, not upper, glide path.

35. The visual glidepath of a 2-bar VASI provides safe obstruction clearance within plus or minus 10° of the extended runway centerline and to a distance of how many miles from the runway threshold?

A. 4 NM.
B. 6 NM.
C. 10 NM.

Answer (A) is correct. *(AIM Para 2-1-2)*
DISCUSSION: While VASI lights are visible from 3 to 5 mi. during the day and up to 20 mi. at night, safe obstruction clearance is only provided up to 4 NM from the runway threshold.
Answer (B) is incorrect. Safe obstruction clearance is provided up to 4 NM, not 6 NM, from the runway threshold. Answer (C) is incorrect. Safe obstruction clearance is provided up to 4 NM, not 10 NM, from the runway threshold.

36. A slightly low indication on a PAPI glidepath is indicated by

A. four red lights.
B. one red light and three white lights.
C. one white light and three red lights.

Answer (C) is correct. *(AIM Para 2-1-2)*
DISCUSSION: A precision approach path indicator (PAPI) has a row of four lights; each emits a red or white light. Above the glide path is indicated by four white lights. Slightly above glide path: three white and one red. On glide path: two white and two red. Slightly below glide path: one white and three red. Below the glide path: four red.
Answer (A) is incorrect. Four red lights is a low glide path. Answer (B) is incorrect. One red and three white lights is the indication for a slightly high, not slightly low, glide path.

4.8 Chart Supplements

37. Information concerning parachute jumping sites may be found in the

A. NOTAM's.
B. Chart Supplement.
C. Graphic Notices and Supplemental Data.

Answer (B) is correct. *(Chart Supplement)*
DISCUSSION: Information concerning parachute jump sites may be found in the Chart Supplement.
Answer (A) is incorrect. NOTAMs are only issued for special situations, not routine jump sites. Answer (C) is incorrect. Graphic Notices and Supplemental Data are no longer published.

TEXAS 239

DALLAS LOVE FLD (DAL) 5 NW UTC−6(−5DT) N32°50.83′ W96°51.11′ DALLAS−FT. WORTH
487 B S4 **FUEL** 100LL, JET A OX 1, 2, 3, 4 LRA Class I, ARFF Index B COPTER
NOTAM FILE DAL H−6H, L−17C, A
  RWY 13R−31L: H8800X150 (CONC−GRVD) S−100, D−200, 2S−175, 2D−350 HIRL CL IAP, AD
    RWY 13R: PAPI(P4R)—GA 3.0° TCH 52′. Thld dsplcd 490′. Rgt tfc.
    RWY 31L: MALSR. TDZL. Building.
  RWY 13L−31R: H7752X150 (CONC−GRVD) S−100, D−200, 2S−175, 2D−350 HIRL CL
    RWY 13L: MALSR. TDZL.
    RWY 31R: MALSR. PAPI(P4L)—GA 3.0° TCH 49′. Pole. Rgt tfc.
  RWY 18−36: H6147X150 (ASPH) S−50, D−74, 2S−93, 2D−138 HIRL
    RWY 18: VASI(V4L)—GA 3.0° TCH 52′. Tree. Rgt tfc.
    RWY 36: VASI(V4L)—GA 3.0° TCH 52′. REIL. Rgt tfc.
  RUNWAY DECLARED DISTANCE INFORMATION
    RWY 13L: TORA−7752 TODA−7752 ASDA−7752 LDA−7752
    RWY 13R: TORA−8800 TODA−8800 ASDA−8800 LDA−8310
    RWY 18: TORA−6147 TODA−6147 ASDA−6147 LDA−6147
    RWY 31L: TORA−8800 TODA−8800 ASDA−8000 LDA−8000
    RWY 31R: TORA−7752 TODA−7752 ASDA−7752 LDA−7752
    RWY 36: TORA−6147 TODA−6147 ASDA−6147 LDA−6147
  AIRPORT REMARKS: Attended continuously. Birds on and invof arpt. Ldg Rwy 18 & takeoff Rwy 36 not authorized to acft over 60,000 lbs gross weight unless crosswind NW−SE rwys exceed acft safe operating capability. Rwy 13R, 13L, 31L and Rwy 31R runway visual range touchdown avbl. Noise sensitive areas all quadrants, noise abatement procedures in effect for fixed and rotary wing tfc, for information call arpt ops 214−670−6610. Private pilot certificate or better required to takeoff or land. No student solo flights permitted. Twy K clsd thru traffic. Twy L clsd indef. PAPI Rwy 31R unusable byd 7° either side of centerline. Flight Notification Service (ADCUS) available.
  WEATHER DATA SOURCES: ASOS (214) 904−0251.
  COMMUNICATIONS: D−ATIS 120.15 (214) 358−5355 **UNICOM** 122.95
    DALLAS RCO 122.3 (FORT WORTH RADIO)
  ® **RGNL APP CON** 125.2 (South) 124.3 (North)
    LOVE TOWER 123.7 118.7 **GND CON** 121.75 **CLNC DEL** 127.9
  ® **RGNL DEP CON** 124.3 (North Props) 125.2 (South Props) 125.125 118.55 (Turbojets)
  AIRSPACE: CLASS B See VFR Terminal Area Chart.
  RADIO AIDS TO NAVIGATION: NOTAM FILE FTW.
    COWBOY (H) VORW/DME 116.2 CVE Chan 109 N32°53.42′ W96°54.24′ 128° 3.7 NM to fld. 450/6E.
    ILS/DME 111.5 I−DAL Chan 52 Rwy 13L. Class IT. LOC unusable byd 20° right of centerline.
    ILS/DME 111.1 I−DPX Chan 48 Rwy 13R. Class IT. LOC unusable beyond 25° right side of course.
    ILS/DME 111.1 I−LVF Chan 48 Rwy 31L. Class IB. LOC unusable byd 20° right of course.
    ILS/DME 111.5 I−OVW Chan 52 Rwy 31R. Class IE. Glide slope unusable for coupled apchs blo 636′ MSL.

DALLAS EXECUTIVE (RBD) 6 SW UTC−6(−5DT) N32°40.85′ W96°52.09′ DALLAS−FT. WORTH
660 B S4 **FUEL** 100LL, JET A OX 1, 2 NOTAM FILE RBD COPTER
  RWY 13−31: H6451X150 (ASPH−CONC) S−35, D−60, 2D−110 MIRL H−6H, L−17C, A
    RWY 13: REIL. VASI(V4L)—GA 3.0° TCH 50′. Trees. IAP, AD
    RWY 31: LDIN. VASI(V4L)—GA 3.0° TCH 47′. Road.
  RWY 17−35: H3800X150 (ASPH−CONC) S−35, D−60, 2D−110 MIRL
    RWY 17: REIL. PAPI(P4R)—GA 3.0° TCH 43′. Tree.
    RWY 35: REIL. Tree.
  AIRPORT REMARKS: Attended 1400−2300Z‡. 24 hr FBO. Fuel avbl 24 hr with major credit card. Birds on and invof arpt. Asphalt at rwy intersection. When twr closed ACTIVATE LDIN Rwy 31 and VASI Rwy 13 and Rwy 31−CTAF. PAPI Rwy 17 opr continuously.
  WEATHER DATA SOURCES: ASOS (214) 330−5317. LAWRS.
  COMMUNICATIONS: CTAF 127.25 **ATIS** 126.35 **UNICOM** 122.95
  ® **RGNL APP/DEP CON** 125.2
    EXECUTIVE TOWER 127.25 (1300−0300Z‡) **GND CON** 119.475
    CLNC DEL 118.625
  AIRSPACE: CLASS D svc 1300−0300Z‡ other times **CLASS G**.
  RADIO AIDS TO NAVIGATION: NOTAM FILE FTW.
    MAVERICK (H) VORW/DME 113.1 TTT Chan 78 N32°52.15′ W97°02.43′ 136° 14.3 NM to fld. 540/6E.
    ILS 108.5 I−RBD Rwy 31. Class IE. Unmonitored when tower closed.

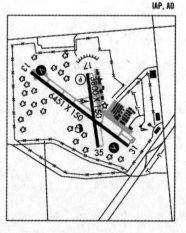

Figure 55. − Chart Supplements U.S. (formerly Airport/Facility Directory).

SU 4: Airports, Airspace, and ATC

38. (Refer to Figure 55 on page 134.) At what time of day does the tower shut down at Dallas Executive?

A. 0330Z.
B. 1400Z.
C. 2100 local.

Answer (C) is correct. *(Chart Supplement)*
DISCUSSION: In the Chart Supplement in Fig. 55, the information about the control tower at Dallas Executive is found on the third line under the section titled Communications. If the tower is operated on a part-time basis, the hours of operation are found next to the tower frequency. Dallas Executive tower operates from 1300-0300Z. To convert to local time, find the time conversion on the top line (UTC – 6). Thus, Dallas Executive tower will shut down at 2100 local time (0300 – 6).
Answer (A) is incorrect. The Chart Supplement indicates that the tower shuts down at 0300Z, not 0330Z. Answer (B) is incorrect. The tower opens, not closes, at 1400Z.

39. (Refer to Figure 55 on page 134.) On what frequency can a pilot activate the approach lights at Dallas Executive when the control tower is not in operation?

A. 120.15
B. 127.25
C. 122.95

Answer (B) is correct. *(Chart Supplement)*
DISCUSSION: In the Chart Supplement in Fig. 55, under Airport Remarks for Dallas Executive, it indicates that when the tower is closed, activate the lead-in lighting system (LDIN) for Rwy 31 on CTAF, which is 127.25.
Answer (A) is incorrect. This is the ATIS frequency for Dallas Love Field. Answer (C) is incorrect. This is the UNICOM frequency of Dallas Executive, which will not activate the approach lights.

40. (Refer to Figure 55 on page 134.) Select the correct statement concerning Dallas Love Field.

A. Right traffic is in effect for all runways.
B. The runway gradient for Rwy 18 is less than .3 percent.
C. The touchdown zone elevation for Rwy 13R is 52 feet.

Answer (B) is correct. *(Chart Supplement)*
DISCUSSION: This question requires you to evaluate each of the three answers because it asks for the correct statement. Runway gradient is not specified in the Chart Supplement if it is less than .3%. At Dallas Love Field, there is no mention of runway gradient for Rwy 18-36; therefore, it is less than .3%.
Answer (A) is incorrect. Rwy 31L and 13L dictate left traffic. Runways that use other than standard (left) traffic patterns will be listed in the Chart Supplement following the information for each such runway, i.e., rgt tfc. Answer (C) is incorrect. The threshold crossing height (TCH), not the touchdown zone elevation, is 52 ft. for Rwy 13R.

41. (Refer to Figure 55 on page 134.) What is the elevation of the Maverick VORTAC?

A. 450 feet MSL.
B. 540 feet MSL.
C. 660 feet MSL.

Answer (B) is correct. *(Chart Supplement)*
DISCUSSION: In the Chart Supplement in Fig. 55, information about the Maverick VORTAC is located under Radio Aids to Navigation for Dallas Executive. The elevation and variation are found at the end of the information, which is 540/6E. Thus, the Maverick VORTAC site elevation is 540 ft. MSL and a magnetic variation of 6°E.
Answer (A) is incorrect. The elevation of the Cowboy VORTAC is 450 ft. MSL. Answer (C) is incorrect. This is the elevation of Dallas Executive, not the Maverick VORTAC.

4.9 ATIS

42. When are ATIS broadcasts updated?

A. Only when the ceiling and/or visibility changes by a reportable value.
B. Every 30 minutes if weather conditions are below basic VFR; otherwise, hourly.
C. Upon receipt of any official weather, regardless of content change or reported values.

Answer (C) is correct. *(AIM Para 4-1-13)*
DISCUSSION: An ATIS broadcast shall be updated upon the receipt of any official (hourly or special) weather report, regardless of content change or reported values. A new recording will also be made when there is a change in other pertinent data, such as runway change, instrument approach in use, etc.
Answer (A) is incorrect. Whenever an official weather report is received, the recording will be updated. Answer (B) is incorrect. ATIS broadcasts are updated upon receipt of any official weather and do not differ under VFR or IFR weather conditions.

43. Absence of the sky condition and visibility on an ATIS broadcast indicates that

A. weather conditions are at or above VFR minimums.
B. the sky condition is clear and visibility is unrestricted.
C. the ceiling is at least 5,000 feet and visibility is 5 miles or more.

Answer (C) is correct. *(AIM Para 4-1-13)*
DISCUSSION: The ceiling/sky condition, visibility, and obstructions to vision may be omitted from the ATIS broadcast if the ceiling is above 5,000 ft. with visibility more than 5 SM.
Answer (A) is incorrect. The absence of the sky condition and visibility on an ATIS broadcast implies that the ceiling is above 5,000 ft. and the visibility is more than 5 SM. Answer (B) is incorrect. The absence of the sky condition and visibility on an ATIS broadcast implies that the ceiling is above 5,000 ft., not clear, and the visibility is more than 5 SM, not unrestricted.

4.10 Special Use Airspace

44. Flight through a restricted area should not be accomplished unless the pilot has

A. filed a IFR flight plan.
B. received prior authorization from the controlling agency.
C. received prior permission from the commanding officer of the nearest military base.

Answer (B) is correct. *(AIM Para 3-4-3)*
DISCUSSION: Before an aircraft penetrates a restricted area, authorization must be obtained from the controlling agency. Information pertaining to the agency controlling the restricted area may be found at the bottom of the En Route Chart appropriate to navigation.
Answer (A) is incorrect. The restriction is to all flight, not just flights without an IFR flight plan. Answer (C) is incorrect. The commanding officer is not necessarily in charge (i.e., controlling agency) of nearby restricted areas.

45. A warning area is airspace of defined dimensions established

A. for training purposes in the vicinity of military bases.
B. from three nautical miles outward from the coast of the U.S.
C. over either domestic or international waters for the purpose of separating military from civilian aircraft.

Answer (B) is correct. *(AIM Para 3-4-4)*
DISCUSSION: A warning area is airspace of defined dimensions extending from 3 NM outward from the U.S. coast and may be in domestic or international airspace.
Answer (A) is incorrect. Warning areas are established from 3 NM outward from the U.S. coast, not in the vicinity of military bases. Answer (C) is incorrect. A warning area is used to warn nonparticipating pilots of the potential danger of hazardous activities.

46. When operating VFR in a military operations area (MOA), a pilot

A. must operate only when military activity is not being conducted.
B. should exercise extreme caution when military activity is being conducted.
C. must obtain a clearance from the controlling agency prior to entering the MOA.

Answer (B) is correct. *(AIM Para 3-4-5)*
DISCUSSION: Pilots operating under VFR should exercise extreme caution while flying within an MOA when military activity is being conducted. Information regarding status (active/inactive) of MOAs may be obtained from a local FSS.
Answer (A) is incorrect. MOAs are designed to separate certain military training activities from IFR traffic. There is no prohibition or restriction for VFR activity within these areas. Answer (C) is incorrect. A VFR pilot must obtain a clearance from the controlling agency prior to entering a restricted area, not an MOA.

47. A military operations area (MOA) is airspace of defined vertical and lateral limits established for the purpose of

A. separating certain military training activities from IFR traffic.
B. military services conducting VFR low altitude navigation, tactical training, and flight testing.
C. denoting the existence of unusual hazards to aircraft, such as artillery firing, aerial gunnery, or guided missiles.

Answer (A) is correct. *(AIM Para 3-4-5)*
DISCUSSION: Military operations areas (MOAs) consist of airspace of defined vertical and lateral limits established for the purpose of separating certain military training activities from IFR traffic.
Answer (B) is incorrect. Although military aircraft may be conducting VFR low-altitude navigation, tactical training, and flight testing within an MOA, the purpose for establishing the MOA is to separate these activities from IFR traffic. Answer (C) is incorrect. Restricted or warning areas, not MOAs, are established for the purpose of denoting the existence of unusual hazards to aircraft, such as artillery firing, aerial gunnery, or guided missiles.

SU 4: Airports, Airspace, and ATC

48. If a military training route has flights operating at or below 1,500 feet AGL, it will be designated by

A. VR and a three digit number only.
B. IR or VR and a four digit number.
C. IR or VR and a three digit number.

Answer (B) is correct. *(AIM Para 3-5-2)*
DISCUSSION: Military training routes (MTRs) are labeled IR for instrument routes and VR for visual routes, followed by a three- or four-digit designator. A four-digit designator means the route has flights operating at or below 1,500 ft.
Answer (A) is incorrect. A three-digit designator means the MTR has one or more segments above 1,500 ft. AGL. Answer (C) is incorrect. A three-digit designator means the MTR has one or more segments above 1,500 ft. AGL.

49. Flight through a military operations area (MOA) is

A. never permitted.
B. permitted anytime, but caution should be exercised because of military activity.
C. permitted at certain times, but only with prior permission from the appropriate authority.

Answer (B) is correct. *(AIM Para 3-4-5)*
DISCUSSION: Pilots operating VFR are permitted to fly through an MOA at any time, but extreme caution should be exercised when military activity is being conducted.
Answer (A) is incorrect. A flight through a prohibited area, not an MOA, is never permitted. Answer (C) is incorrect. A flight through a restricted area, not an MOA, is permitted only with prior permission from the appropriate authority.

4.11 Controlled Airspace

50. When a control tower, located on an airport within Class D airspace ceases operation for the day, what happens to the airspace designation?

A. The airspace designation normally will not change.
B. The airspace remains Class D airspace as long as a weather observer or automated weather system is available.
C. The airspace reverts to Class E or a combination of Class E and G airspace during the hours the tower is not in operation.

Answer (C) is correct. *(AIM Para 3-2-5)*
DISCUSSION: When a tower ceases operation, the Class D airspace reverts to Class E or a combination of Class G and Class E.
Answer (A) is incorrect. Class D airspace is designated when there is an operating control tower. When the tower ceases operation for the day, the airspace reverts to Class E or a combination of Class G and Class E airspace. Answer (B) is incorrect. The airspace reverts to Class E, not Class D, when the tower ceases operation for the day and an approved weather observer or automated weather system is available.

51. Class E airspace within the contiguous United States extends upward from either 700 feet or 1,200 feet AGL to, but not including,

A. 3,000 feet MSL.
B. 14,500 feet MSL.
C. the base of the overlying controlled airspace.

Answer (C) is correct. *(AIM Para 3-2-6)*
DISCUSSION: Class E airspace extends up to, but not including, the base of the overlying controlled airspace.
Answer (A) is incorrect. Class E airspace extends not to a specific altitude (3,000 ft. MSL) but to the base of the overlying controlled airspace. Answer (B) is incorrect. Class E airspace extends not to a specific altitude (14,500 ft. MSL) but to the base of the overlying controlled airspace.

52. Within the contiguous United States, the floor of Class A airspace is

A. 14,500 feet MSL.
B. 18,000 feet MSL.
C. 18,000 feet AGL.

Answer (B) is correct. *(AIM Para 3-2-2)*
DISCUSSION: Within the contiguous U.S., Class A airspace begins at 18,000 ft. MSL and continues to FL 600.
Answer (A) is incorrect. Unless designated at a lower altitude, the floor of Class E, not Class A, airspace is 14,500 ft. MSL. Answer (C) is incorrect. Class A airspace begins at 18,000 ft. MSL, not AGL.

53. With certain exceptions, Class E airspace extends upward from either 700 feet or 1,200 feet AGL to, but does not include,

A. 10,000 feet MSL.
B. 14,500 feet MSL.
C. 18,000 feet MSL.

Answer (C) is correct. *(AIM Para 3-2-6)*
DISCUSSION: Beginning at either 700 ft. AGL or 1,200 ft. AGL, Class E airspace extends up to, but not including, the base of the overlying controlled airspace. With the exception of Class B and Class C airspace, Class E airspace extends up to, but not including, 18,000 ft. MSL, i.e., the floor of Class A airspace.
Answer (A) is incorrect. This is the base of increased VFR visibility and cloud distance requirements and the Mode C requirement. Answer (B) is incorrect. Class G, not Class E, airspace may extend from the surface up to, but not including, 14,500 ft. MSL.

54. The vertical limit of Class D airspace will normally be designated at

A. the base of the Class E airspace.
B. up to, and including, 2,500 feet AGL.
C. up to, but not including, 3,000 feet AGL.

Answer (B) is correct. *(AIM Para 3-2-5)*
DISCUSSION: Generally, the vertical limit of Class D airspace will be 2,500 ft. AGL.
Answer (A) is incorrect. At some locations, Class E airspace could overlie Class D airspace. Answer (C) is incorrect. The vertical limit of Class D airspace is normally 2,500 ft. AGL, not 3,000 ft. AGL.

55. Normally, the vertical limits of Class D airspace extend up to and including how many feet above the surface?

A. 2,500 feet.
B. 3,000 feet.
C. 4,000 feet.

Answer (A) is correct. *(AIM Para 3-2-5)*
DISCUSSION: Normally, the vertical limits of Class D airspace extend up to and include 2,500 ft. above the airport elevation.
Answer (B) is incorrect. Class D airspace normally extends up to and includes 2,500 ft., not 3,000 ft., above the airport elevation. Answer (C) is incorrect. Class C, not Class D, airspace normally extends up to and includes 4,000 ft. above the airport elevation.

4.12 Class C Airspace

56. (Refer to Figure 47 on page 139.) Which altitude (box 1) is applicable to the vertical extent of the surface and shelf areas of this Class C airspace?

A. 3,000 feet AGL.
B. 3,000 feet above airport.
C. 4,000 feet above airport.

Answer (C) is correct. *(AIM Para 3-2-4)*
DISCUSSION: Normally, the vertical extent of Class C airspace is 4,000 ft. above the airport elevation.
Answer (A) is incorrect. The vertical extent of Class C airspace is 4,000 ft. above the airport, not 3,000 ft. AGL. Answer (B) is incorrect. The vertical extent of Class C airspace is 4,000 ft. above the airport, not 3,000 ft. above the airport.

57. (Refer to Figure 47 on page 139.) What is the normal radius of the outer area (area B)?

A. 10 NM.
B. 20 NM.
C. 25 NM.

Answer (B) is correct. *(AIM Para 3-2-4)*
DISCUSSION: The normal radius of the outer area of Class C airspace is 20 NM from the airport.
Answer (A) is incorrect. Ten NM is the radius of the shelf area (formerly the outer circle) of Class C airspace. Answer (C) is incorrect. Twenty-five NM does not pertain to any set radius of Class C airspace.

58. (Refer to Figure 47 on page 139.) What is the radius of the shelf area (circle A)?

A. 5 miles.
B. 10 miles.
C. 15 miles.

Answer (B) is correct. *(AIM Para 3-2-4)*
DISCUSSION: The radius of the shelf area of Class C airspace is 10 NM from the airport.
Answer (A) is incorrect. Five NM is the radius of the surface, not shelf, area of Class C airspace. Answer (C) is incorrect. Fifteen NM is not established as the radius for any area of Class C airspace.

59. (Refer to Figure 47 on page 139.) What is the radius of the surface area (circle C)?

A. 5 miles.
B. 10 miles.
C. 15 miles.

Answer (A) is correct. *(AIM Para 3-2-4)*
DISCUSSION: The radius of the surface area of Class C airspace is 5 NM from the airport.
Answer (B) is incorrect. Ten NM is the radius of the shelf, not surface, area of Class C airspace. Answer (C) is incorrect. Fifteen NM is not established as the radius for any portion of Class C airspace.

60. (Refer to Figure 47 on page 139.) Which altitude (box 2) is applicable to the base of the shelf area?

A. 700 feet AGL.
B. 1,200 feet MSL.
C. 1,200 feet AGL.

Answer (C) is correct. *(AIM Para 3-2-4)*
DISCUSSION: The base of the shelf area of Class C airspace is 1,200 ft. above the airport elevation.
Answer (A) is incorrect. This is the base of a transition area, not the base of the shelf area. Answer (B) is incorrect. The base of the shelf area is 1,200 ft. AGL, not MSL.

SU 4: Airports, Airspace, and ATC

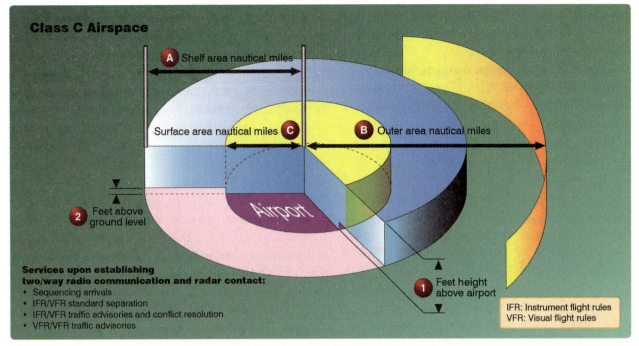

Figure 47. – Class C Airspace Diagram.

61. (Refer to Figure 47 above.) Class C airspace usually extends up to

A. 3,000 feet MSL.
B. 3,000 feet above airport.
C. 4,000 feet above airport.

Answer (C) is correct. *(AIM Para 3-2-4)*
    DISCUSSION: Class C airspace usually extends up to 4,000 ft. above the airport and is charted in MSL.
    Answer (A) is incorrect. Class C airspace usually extends up to 4,000 ft. above the airport (charted in MSL), not 3,000 ft. MSL. Answer (B) is incorrect. Class C airspace usually extends up to 4,000 ft. above the airport, not 3,000 ft. above the airport.

62. To operate an aircraft within Class C airspace from a satellite airport without an operating control tower, a pilot must

A. monitor ATC until clear of the Class C airspace.
B. contact ATC as soon as practicable after takeoff.
C. secure prior approval from ATC before takeoff at the airport.

Answer (B) is correct. *(AIM Para 3-2-4)*
    DISCUSSION: Aircraft departing from a satellite airport without an operating control tower within Class C airspace must contact ATC as soon as practicable after takeoff.
    Answer (A) is incorrect. The departing aircraft must establish, not just monitor, communications with ATC. Answer (C) is incorrect. Prior approval from ATC before takeoff at a satellite airport without an operating control tower is not required.

63. All operations within Class C airspace must be in

A. compliance with ATC clearances and instructions.
B. accordance with instrument flight rules.
C. an aircraft equipped with a transponder with automatic altitude reporting capability.

Answer (C) is correct. *(AIM Para 3-2-4)*
    DISCUSSION: Unless otherwise authorized by ATC, an operable radar beacon transponder with altitude reporting equipment is required.
    Answer (A) is incorrect. Clearances are not required to operate within Class C airspace areas. Answer (B) is incorrect. IFR operations are not required within Class C airspace and there is no minimum pilot certification required; i.e., student pilots may operate within Class C airspace.

64. What minimum avionics equipment is required for operation within Class C airspace?

A. Two-way communications.
B. Two-way communications and transponder with automatic altitude reporting capability.
C. Two-way communications, transponder with automatic altitude reporting capability, and VOR.

Answer (B) is correct. *(AIM Para 3-2-4)*
DISCUSSION: The equipment requirements for operating in Class C airspace are two-way communications and a transponder with altitude reporting capability.
Answer (A) is incorrect. A Mode C transponder is also required. Answer (C) is incorrect. A VOR is not required to operate in Class C airspace. This equipment is required for IFR operations in Class B airspace.

4.13 Radio Failure

65. If the aircraft's radio fails, what is the recommended procedure when landing at a controlled airport?

A. Select 7700 on your transponder, fly a normal traffic pattern, and land.
B. Flash your landing lights and make shallow banks in opposite directions while circling the airport.
C. Observe the traffic flow, enter the pattern, and look for a light signal from the tower.

Answer (C) is correct. *(AIM Para 4-2-13)*
DISCUSSION: If your radio fails and you wish to land at a controlled airport, remain outside or above the airport traffic pattern until you determine the direction and flow of traffic, then join the pattern and maintain visual contact with the tower to receive light signals.
Answer (A) is incorrect. The transponder frequency to indicate radio failure is 7600. The emergency code is 7700. Answer (B) is incorrect. The procedure to acknowledge light signals from the tower is to flash your landing lights at night and to rock your wings during the day.

4.14 Transponder Codes

66. Which transponder code should the pilot of a civilian aircraft never use?

A. 7500
B. 7600
C. 7777

Answer (C) is correct. *(AIM Para 4-1-19)*
DISCUSSION: Transponder code 7777 is for military interception operations and should never be used by civilian aircraft.
Answer (A) is incorrect. The hijack code is 7500, which civil aircraft may use if needed. Answer (B) is incorrect. The lost communications code is 7600, which civil aircraft may use if needed.

67. When making routine transponder code changes, pilots should avoid inadvertent selection of which codes?

A. 0700, 1700, 7000.
B. 1200, 1500, 7000.
C. 7500, 7600, 7700.

Answer (C) is correct. *(AIM Para 4-1-20)*
DISCUSSION: Some special codes set aside for emergencies should be avoided during routine VFR flights. They are 7500 for hijacking, 7600 for lost radio communications, and 7700 for a general emergency. Additionally, you should know that code 7777 is reserved for military interceptors.
Answer (A) is incorrect. Any of these may be assigned by ATC. Answer (B) is incorrect. The standard VFR code is 1200.

4.15 Collision Avoidance

68. Most midair collision accidents occur during

A. hazy days within the traffic pattern environment.
B. clear days in the vicinity of navigational aids.
C. night conditions during simulated instrument flight.

Answer (B) is correct. *(AC 90-48C)*
DISCUSSION: Most midair collision accidents and reported near midair collision incidents occur during good VFR weather conditions (i.e., clear days) and during the hours of daylight. This is when more aircraft are likely to be flying.
Answer (A) is incorrect. During hazy days, fewer pilots will be flying, and those who are will be more vigilant in their scanning for other traffic. Answer (C) is incorrect. During nights, fewer pilots will be flying, and those who are will be more vigilant in their scanning for other traffic.

69. Which technique should a student be taught to scan for traffic to the right and left during straight-and-level flight?

A. Continuous sweeping of the windshield from right to left.
B. Concentrate on relative movement detected in the peripheral vision area.
C. Systematically focus on different segments of the sky for short intervals.

Answer (C) is correct. *(AC 90-48C)*
DISCUSSION: The most effective way to scan for other aircraft is to use a series of short, regularly spaced eye movements that bring successive areas of the sky into your central vision field. Each movement should not exceed 10°, and each area should be observed for at least 1 second to enable detection.
Answer (A) is incorrect. A series of short, regularly spaced eye movements of not more than 10°, and each area observed for at least 1 second, is the most effective way to scan for other aircraft, not a continuous sweeping of the windshield. Answer (B) is incorrect. While peripheral vision detects movement, you must stop and focus your eyes on different segments of the sky in order to detect the movement.

70. The most effective technique to use for detecting other aircraft at night is to

A. turn the head and sweep the eyes rapidly over the entire visible region.
B. avoid staring directly at the point where another aircraft is suspected to be flying.
C. avoid scanning the region below the horizon so as to avoid the effect of ground lights on the eyes.

Answer (B) is correct. *(AC 90-48C)*
DISCUSSION: Visual search at night depends almost entirely on peripheral vision, or off-center viewing. In order to detect other aircraft at night, you should avoid staring directly at the point where the other aircraft is suspected to be flying, but scan the area adjacent to it. Short stops of a few seconds in each scan will help detect the light and its movement.
Answer (A) is incorrect. Sweeping your eyes rapidly over the entire visible region will not allow your peripheral vision the opportunity to detect motion. Answer (C) is incorrect. The ground lights usually do not have a great impact on the eyes, and you must be concerned with aircraft in all quadrants (i.e., above and below as well as at your altitude).

71. ATC advises traffic 12 o'clock. This advisory is relative to your

A. true course.
B. ground track.
C. magnetic heading.

Answer (B) is correct. *(AIM Para 4-1-14)*
DISCUSSION: When issuing radar traffic information, the controller will provide the direction of the traffic from your airplane in relation to the 12-hr. clock based on your ground track, or magnetic course.
Answer (A) is incorrect. The controller will issue radar traffic information in relation to the 12-hr. clock based on your airplane's magnetic, not true, course. Answer (C) is incorrect. The controller will issue radar traffic information in relation to the 12-hr. clock based on your airplane's ground track, not magnetic heading.

72. What is an effective way to prevent a collision hazard in the traffic pattern?

A. Enter the pattern in a descent.
B. Maintain the proper traffic pattern altitude and continually scan the area.
C. Rely on radio reports from other aircraft who may be operating in the traffic pattern.

Answer (B) is correct. *(AC 90-48C)*
DISCUSSION: The most effective way to prevent collisions in the traffic pattern is to maintain the proper altitude and continually scan the area for traffic.
Answer (A) is incorrect. One should enter the traffic pattern at the traffic pattern altitude, not in a descent. Answer (C) is incorrect. Not all other aircraft in the traffic pattern may be using a radio and/or your frequency.

73. Pilots are encouraged to turn on their landing lights when operating below 10,000 feet, day or night, and when operating within

A. Class B airspace.
B. 10 miles of any airport.
C. 5 miles of a controlled airport.

Answer (B) is correct. *(AIM Para 4-3-23)*
DISCUSSION: The FAA has a voluntary pilot safety program, Operation Lights On, to enhance the see-and-avoid concept. Pilots are encouraged to turn on their landing lights when operating below 10,000 ft., day or night, especially within 10 mi. of any airport.
Answer (A) is incorrect. Landing lights are recommended to be turned on within 10 mi. of any airport, not only in Class B airspace. Answer (C) is incorrect. Landing lights are recommended to be turned on within 10 mi., not 5 mi., of any airport, not only a controlled airport.

4.16 Flight Plans

74. If an aircraft has a transponder, encoding altimeter, and DME, the proper equipment suffix to be entered on a flight plan is

A. A.
B. I.
C. U.

Answer (A) is correct. *(AIM Para 5-1-8)*
DISCUSSION: The proper equipment suffix to be entered in Block 3 on a flight plan for an aircraft equipped with a transponder, encoding altimeter, and DME is A.
Answer (B) is incorrect. The suffix I indicates RNAV, not DME, and a transponder with altitude encoding capability. Answer (C) is incorrect. The suffix U indicates transponder with altitude encoding only.

75. How long will a Flight Service Station hold a VFR flight plan past the proposed departure time?

A. 30 minutes.
B. 1 hour.
C. 2 hours.

Answer (B) is correct. *(AIM Para 5-1-4)*
DISCUSSION: When a VFR flight plan is filed, it will be held by the FSS until 1 hr. after the proposed departure time, unless

1. The actual departure time is received.
2. A revised proposed departure time is received.
3. At the time of filing, the FSS is informed that the proposed time will be met, but actual time cannot be given because of inadequate communications (i.e., assumed departure).

Answer (A) is incorrect. An FSS will only hold a VFR flight plan for 1 hr., not 30 min., past the proposed departure time. Answer (C) is incorrect. An FSS will only hold a VFR flight plan for 1 hr., not 2 hr., past the proposed departure time.

76. If an aircraft has a transponder, encoding altimeter, and RNAV, the proper equipment suffix to be entered on a flight plan is

A. A.
B. I.
C. Y.

Answer (B) is correct. *(AIM Para 5-1-8)*
DISCUSSION: The proper equipment suffix to be entered in Block 3 on a flight plan for an aircraft equipped with a transponder, encoding altimeter, and RNAV is I.
Answer (A) is incorrect. The suffix A indicates DME, not RNAV, and a transponder with altitude encoding capability. Answer (C) is incorrect. The suffix Y designates RNAV but no transponder.

77. How much time do you have to close a VFR flight plan before search and rescue procedures are initiated?

A. One hour after your ATA.
B. One-half hour after landing.
C. One-half hour after your ETA.

Answer (C) is correct. *(AIM Para 5-1-14)*
DISCUSSION: It is the responsibility of the pilot to update (or cancel) a VFR flight plan within 1/2 hr. of his or her ETA with the nearest FSS; otherwise, search and rescue procedures are started.
Answer (A) is incorrect. It is 30 min., not 60 min., after your ETA, not ATA. Answer (B) is incorrect. Search and rescue procedures will be started 1/2 hr. after your ETA, not after landing, if you do not close a VFR flight plan.

4.17 Notice to Airmen (NOTAM)

78. When information is disseminated about a taxiway closure, it will be located in

A. FDC NOTAMs.
B. NOTAM (D) distribution.
C. The *Notices to Airmen Publication (NTAP)*.

Answer (B) is correct. *(AIM Para 5-1-3)*
DISCUSSION: NOTAMs (D), or distant, cover information such as taxiway closures and airport rotating beacon outages as well as more substantial items such as runway closures and issues that affect instrument approach availability.
Answer (A) is incorrect. FDC NOTAMs contain information that is regulatory in nature. A taxiway closure does not fit that description and thus would not be included. Answer (C) is incorrect. The *NTAP* contains published NOTAMs (D) and FDC NOTAMs. Notice of a taxiway closure would not appear in this publication until it was republished, provided the NOTAM was still effective.

79. When information is disseminated for a navigational facility, it will be located in

A. FDC NOTAMs.
B. NOTAM (D) distribution.
C. The *Notices to Airmen Publication (NTAP)*.

Answer (B) is correct. *(AIM Para 5-1-3)*
DISCUSSION: NOTAMs (D), or distant, are NOTAMs that are disseminated for all navigational facilities that are part of the National Airspace System (NAS) and for all public-use airports, seaplane bases, and heliports listed in the Chart Supplement. They include factors such as runway/taxiway closures, navigational facility failures, approach outages, etc.
Answer (A) is incorrect. FDC NOTAMs are regulatory in nature. A navigational facility outage does not fit that description and thus would not be included. Answer (C) is incorrect. The *NTAP* contains published NOTAMs (D) and FDC NOTAMs. Notice of a navigational facility outage would not appear in this publication until it was republished, provided the NOTAM was still effective.

80. When information is disseminated for a temporary flight restriction (TFR), it will be located in

A. FDC NOTAMs.
B. NOTAM (D) distribution.
C. The *Notices to Airmen Publication (NTAP)*.

Answer (A) is correct. *(AIM Para 5-1-3)*
DISCUSSION: FDC NOTAMs are regulatory in nature. FDC NOTAMs contain changes to instrument approach procedures, the establishment of TFRs, and important changes to aeronautical charts.
Answer (B) is incorrect. NOTAMs (D), or distant, cover issues related to airport operations and navigational aid availability. They do not contain regulatory material, such as the establishment of a TFR. Answer (C) is incorrect. The *NTAP* contains published NOTAMs (D) and FDC NOTAMs. Notice of a TFR would not appear in this publication until it was republished, provided the NOTAM was still effective.

81. What information is contained in the *Notices to Airmen Publication (NTAP)*?

A. Current NOTAM (D) and FDC NOTAMs.
B. All current NOTAMs (D) and military NOTAMs.
C. Pointer NOTAMs and FDC NOTAMs.

Answer (A) is correct. *(AIM Para 5-1-3)*
DISCUSSION: The *NTAP* contains NOTAMs (D) that are expected to remain in effect for an extended period and FDC NOTAMs that are current at the time of publication.
Answer (B) is incorrect. Military NOTAMs are not published in the *NTAP*. Answer (C) is incorrect. Although current FDC NOTAMs are published in the *NTAP*, pointer NOTAMs are issued by a flight service station to highlight or point out another NOTAM and are not published in the *NTAP*.

82. Public figures are protected by

A. special use airspace.
B. prohibited areas.
C. temporary flight restriction.

Answer (C) is correct. *(AIM Para 3-5-3)*
DISCUSSION: The purpose of temporary flight restrictions is to protect persons and property in the air or on the surface from airborne hazards. These are found in NOTAMs and on specialty TFR websites.
Answer (A) is incorrect. Special use airspace consists of airspace where activities have to be confined because of the nature of their activities. This airspace consists of prohibited and restricted areas, warning areas, military operations areas, alert areas, and controlled firing areas. Answer (B) is incorrect. Prohibited areas contain airspace that has defined dimensions on the ground over which a flight is prohibited.

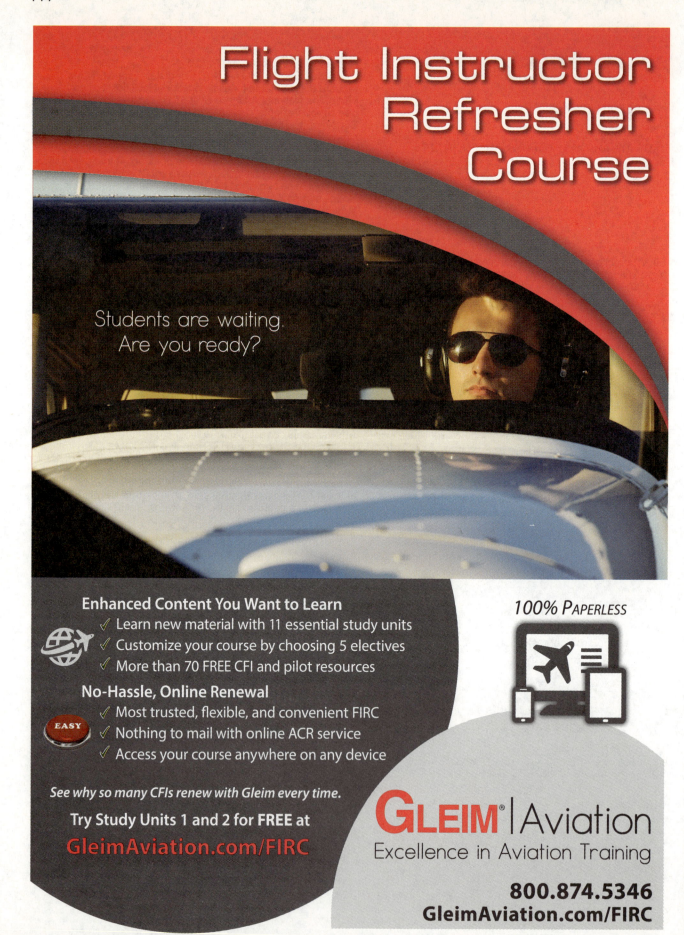

STUDY UNIT FIVE
WEIGHT AND BALANCE

(7 pages of outline)

5.1	Center of Gravity	(16 questions) 145, 152
5.2	Center of Gravity Calculations	(11 questions) 146, 155
5.3	Center of Gravity Tables	(5 questions) 148, 160
5.4	Weight Change Calculations	(12 questions) 150, 164

This study unit contains outlines of major concepts tested, sample test questions and answers regarding weight and balance, and an explanation of each answer. The table of contents above lists each subunit within this study unit, the number of questions pertaining to that particular subunit, and the pages on which the outlines and questions begin, respectively.

 Recall that the **sole purpose** of this book is to expedite your passing of the FAA pilot knowledge test for the CFI, BGI, or AGI certificate. Accordingly, all extraneous material (i.e., topics or regulations not directly tested on the FAA pilot knowledge test) is omitted, even though much more knowledge is necessary to become a proficient flight or ground instructor. This additional material is presented in *Pilot Handbook* and *Flight Instructor Flight Maneuvers and Practical Test Prep*, available from Gleim Publications, Inc. Order online at www.GleimAviation.com.

5.1 CENTER OF GRAVITY

1. The center of gravity (CG) of an airplane is computed along the longitudinal axis.

    a. The CG is determined by dividing the total moment by the total weight.

2. As CG moves aft, the following changes occur:

    a. Recovery from a stall becomes more difficult.
    b. Stalling speed decreases.
    c. Cruising speed increases.
    d. The airplane becomes less stable and less controllable.

3. As CG moves forward, the following changes occur:

    a. An additional download must be imposed on the horizontal stabilizer. This in turn produces an additional load which the wing must support.
    b. Stalling speed increases.

        1) Stalling speed will be at its highest with a high gross weight and forward CG.

    c. Cruising speed decreases.
    d. Longitudinal stability increases.

4. When an aircraft is loaded with the CG aft of the aft limit, stall and spin recovery may be difficult or impossible.

    a. A flat spin may develop if the CG is too far aft.

5. A forward CG is most critical on landing.

6. When the nosewheel of an airplane moves aft during gear retraction, the CG location also moves aft.

    a. If the landing gear on an airplane moves forward during retraction, the total moment will decrease.

5.2 CENTER OF GRAVITY CALCULATIONS

1. The basic formula for weight and balance is

    $$Weight \times Arm = Moment$$

    a. Arm is the distance of the weight from the datum (a fixed position on the longitudinal axis of the airplane).
    b. The weight/arm/moment calculation computes where the CG is.
        1) Multiply the weight of each item loaded into the airplane by its arm (distance from datum) to determine moment.
        2) Add moments.
        3) Divide total moments by total weight to obtain CG (expressed in distance from the datum).
    c. EXAMPLE: You have items A, B, and C in the airplane. Note the airplane's empty weight is given as 1,500 lb. with a 20-in. arm.

	Weight		Arm		Moment
Empty airplane	1,500	×	20	=	30,000
A (pilot and passenger?)	300	×	25	=	7,500
B (25 gal. of fuel × 6 lb./gal.?)	150	×	30	=	4,500
C (baggage?)	100	×	40	=	4,000
	2,050				46,000

    The total loaded weight of the airplane is 2,050 lb. Take the total moments of 46,000 in.-lb. divided by the total weight of 2,050 lb. to obtain the CG of 22.44 in.

    The weight and the CG are then checked to see whether they are within allowable limits.

2. The moment of an object is a measure of the force that causes a tendency of the object to rotate about a point or axis. It is usually expressed in pound·inches. In the figure below, assume that a weight of 50 lb. is placed on the board at a point (station) 100 in. from the datum (fulcrum). The downward force of the weight at that spot can be determined by multiplying 50 lb. by 100 in., which produces a moment of 5,000 lb.-in.

    a. To establish a balance, a total moment of 5,000 lb.-in. must be applied to the other end of the board. Any combination of weight and distance that, when multiplied, produces 5,000 lb.-in. moment to the left of the datum will balance the board.

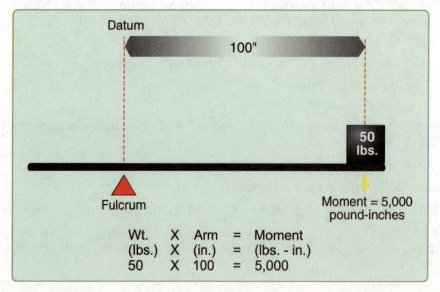

SU 5: Weight and Balance

b. If a 100-lb. weight is placed at a point (station) 25 in. on the other side of the datum and a second 50-lb. weight is placed at a point (station) 50 in. on the other side of the datum, the sum of the products of these two weights and their distances will total a moment of 5,000 lb.-in., which will balance the board (figure below).

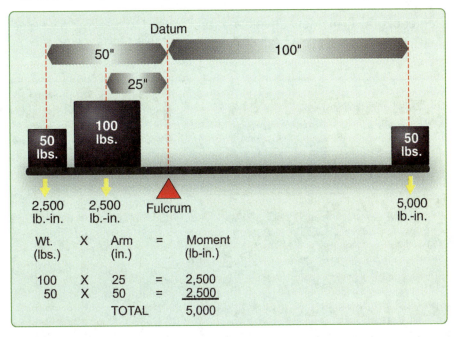

3. When asked to balance the plank on the fulcrum, compute and sum the moments left and right. Then set left and right equal to each other and solve for the desired variable.

   a. EXAMPLE: How should the 1,000-lb. weight in the following diagram be shifted to balance the plank on the fulcrum?

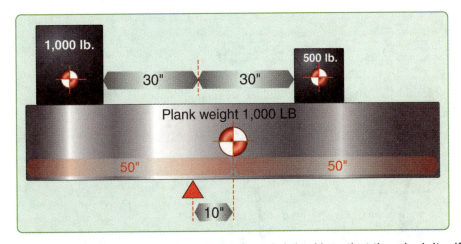

Compute and sum the moments left and right. Note that the plank itself weighs 1,000 lb. and that its CG is 10 in. right of the fulcrum. Set them equal to one another and solve for the desired variable:

$$\begin{aligned}
\text{Left} &= \text{Right} \\
1{,}000 \text{ lb.}(X) &= 500 \text{ lb.}(30 \text{ in.}) + 1{,}000 \text{ lb.}(10 \text{ in.}) \\
1{,}000 (X) &= 15{,}000 + 10{,}000 \\
1{,}000 (X) &= 25{,}000 \\
X &= 25 \text{ in.}
\end{aligned}$$

The 1,000-lb. weight must be 25 in. from the fulcrum to balance the plank. Thus, the weight should be shifted 5 in. to the right.

148   SU 5: Weight and Balance

5.3 CENTER OF GRAVITY TABLES

1. Tables and graphs are frequently used to compute center of gravity (illustrated in Figure 36, Weight and Balance Chart, below).

   a. Tables of moments -- used to compute the moment.
   b. Center of gravity moment envelope graph -- used to determine whether or not the airplane's moment or CG is within the acceptable range, given the gross weight of the airplane.

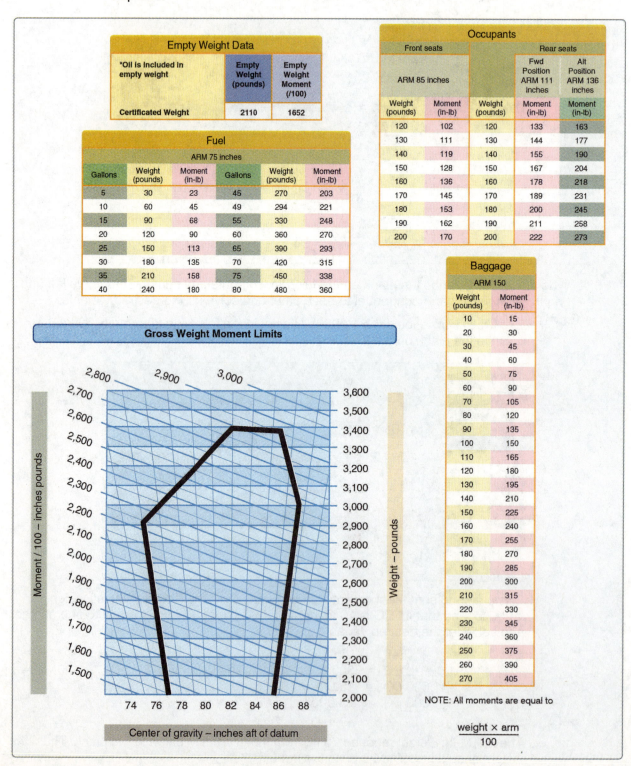

Figure 36. – Weight and Balance Chart.

2. First, determine total moment from the moment tables. Then check to see whether the total moment is within maximum and minimum limits on the moment limit graph, or divide the total moment by the total weight to determine the CG.

3. EXAMPLE: Determine the condition of the airplane given the following data and using Figure 36 on the previous page.

    Pilot and copilot   340lb.
    Aft passengers   160lb.
    Baggage   55lb.
    Fuel   45gal.

   a. As in most weight and balance problems, you should begin by setting up a schedule as below.

      1) Note that the empty weight (Figure 36) is given as 2,110 lb. with a moment/100 of 1,652 lb.-in. Note that empty weight includes the oil.

      2) Note that each moment shown on the table is actually a moment index, or moment/100. This reduces the moments to smaller, more manageable numbers.

	Weight (lb.)	Moment/100 (lb.-in.)
Empty weight (w/oil)	2,110	1,652
Pilot and copilot	340	289
Passengers (aft position)	160	218
Baggage	55	82.5
Fuel (45 gal.)	270	203
	2,935	2,444.5

   b. Next, compute the individual moments.

      1) The pilot and copilot's moment for 340 lb. can be calculated by adding the moments for 200 lb. (170 lb.-in.) and 140 lb. (119 lb.-in.). Thus, the moment/100 for 340 lb. is 289 lb.-in.

         a) Or, simply multiply the weight (340 lb.) by the arm shown in the table (85 in.) to find the moment (28,900 lb.-in.). Divide by 100 for moment/100 (289 lb.-in.).

      2) The passengers' (aft position) moment/100 for 160 lb. is 218 lb.-in., which is read directly from the table.

      3) The baggage moment/100 for 55 lb. can be calculated by interpolating between 50 lb. and 60 lb. The moment/100 for 50 lb. is 75 lb.-in. and the moment/100 for 60 lb. is 90 lb.-in. Thus, the moment/100 for 55 lb. is 82.5 lb.-in. [(75 + 90) ÷ 2].

         a) Or, simply multiply the weight (55 lb.) by the arm shown in the table (150 in.) to find the moment (8,250 lb.-in.). Divide by 100 for moment/100 (82.5 lb.-in.).

      4) Determine the weight and moment/100 for 45 gal. of fuel, which is read directly from the table. The weight is 270 lb. with a moment/100 of 203 lb.-in.

   c. Next, add the total weight and total moments.

   d. Last, go to the Gross Weight Moment Limits graph (bottom left of Figure 36 on the previous page).

      1) Find the weight of 2,935 lb. on the horizontal lines that begin on the right side of the graph.

      2) See that it is less than the maximum allowable gross weight of 3,400 lb.

      3) Find the moment/100 of 2,444.5 lb.-in. on the diagonal lines, which begin on the left side of the graph.

      4) See that the two lines intersect within the envelope.

5.4 WEIGHT CHANGE CALCULATIONS

1. Accurate weight and balance computations can be dependent on the understanding of certain specific terms.

    a. Basic empty weight includes the airplane's standard empty weight, plus any optional and/or special equipment that has been installed.
    b. Useful load is the difference after basic empty weight is subtracted from maximum allowable gross weight.
    c. Maximum allowable gross weight is the maximum permissible weight of the airplane.

2. The FAA provides two formulas for weight change and one formula for weight shift. They are not reproduced here because the following weight change and weight shift formula is much simpler and intuitively appealing. It is adapted from a class handout developed by Dr. Melville R. Byington at Embry-Riddle Aeronautical University (used with permission).

3. **Basic Theory** – The issue is: **If the CG started out there and certain changes occurred, where is it now?** It can be answered directly using the following formula:

    a. At **any** time, the CG is simply the sum of all moments divided by the sum of all weights.

    $$CG = \frac{\Sigma M}{\Sigma W}$$

    b. Since CG was known at some previous (#1) loading condition (with moment = M_1 and weight = W_1), it is logical that this becomes the point of departure. Due to weight addition, removal, or shift, the moment has changed by some amount, ΔM. The total weight has also changed **if**, and only if, weight has been added or removed. Therefore, the current CG is merely the current total moment divided by the current total weight. In equation format,

    $$CG = Current\ moment \div Current\ weight\ becomes\ CG = \frac{M_1 \pm \Delta M}{W_1 \pm \Delta W}$$

    c. This formula will accommodate any weight change and/or CG shift problem. Before proceeding, certain conventions deserve review:

        1) Any weight added causes a "+" moment change (weight removed is –).
        2) Weight **shifted** rearward causes a "+" moment change (forward is –).
        3) A weight **shift** changes only the moment ($\Delta W = 0$).

4. EXAMPLES:

    a. What is the maximum weight that could be added at Station 130.0 without exceeding the aft CG limit?

Total weight	2,900 lb.
CG location	Station 115.0
Aft CG limit	Station 116.0

    To rephrase the question, how much weight must be added to move the CG to the aft limit? Let X represent the added weight.

    $$New\ CG = \frac{M_1 \pm \Delta M}{W_1 \pm \Delta W}$$

    Where M_1 = Original moment and W_1 = Original weight.

$$116.0 = \frac{2{,}900(115.0) + 130.0(X)}{2{,}900 + X}$$

$$116.0(2{,}900 + X) = 2{,}900(115.0) + 130.0(X)$$
$$2{,}900(116.0) + 116.0(X) = 2{,}900(115.0) + 130.0(X)$$
$$336{,}400 + 116X = 333{,}500 + 130X$$
$$336{,}400 - 333{,}500 = 130X - 116X$$
$$2{,}900 = 14X$$
$$207.1 = X$$

Thus, 207.1 lb. can be added at Station 130.0 without exceeding the aft CG limit at Station 116.0.

b. What is the location of the CG if 90 lb. are removed from Station 140?

| Aircraft weight | 6,230 lb. |
| CG location | Station 79 |

$$\text{New CG} = \frac{M_1 \pm \Delta M}{W_1 \pm \Delta W}$$

Where M_1 = Original moment and W_1 = Original weight.

$$\text{New CG} = \frac{(6{,}230 \times 79) - (90 \times 140)}{6{,}230 - 90}$$

$$= \frac{492{,}170 - 12{,}600}{6{,}140} = \frac{479{,}570}{6{,}140} = 78.1$$

Thus, if 90 lb. are removed from Station 140, the new CG is located at Station 78.1.

NOTE: Weight removed causes a "–" moment change (weight added is +).

c. How much weight must be shifted from Station 150.0 to Station 30.0 to move the CG to exactly the aft limit?

Total weight	7,500 lb.
CG location	Station 80.5
Aft CG limit	Station 79.5

Let X represent the shifted weight.

$$\text{New CG} = \frac{M_1 \pm \Delta M}{W_1 \pm \Delta W}$$

Where M_1 = Original moment and W_1 = Original weight.

Since there is no change in weight, $\Delta W = 0$ and weight shifted forward causes a "–" moment change.

$$79.5 = \frac{7{,}500(80.5) - X(150.0 - 30.0)}{7{,}500}$$

$$7{,}500(79.5) = 7{,}500(80.5) - X(150.0 - 30.0)$$
$$596{,}250 = 603{,}750 - 120X$$
$$-7{,}500 = -120X$$
$$62.5 = X$$

Thus, 62.5 lb. must be shifted from Station 150.0 to Station 30.0 to move the CG to the aft CG limit at Station 79.5.

152 SU 5: Weight and Balance

QUESTIONS AND ANSWER EXPLANATIONS: All of the AGI/CFI knowledge test questions chosen by the FAA for release as well as additional questions selected by Gleim relating to the material in the previous outlines are reproduced on the following pages. These questions have been organized into the same subunits as the outlines. To the immediate right of each question are the correct answer and answer explanation. You should cover these answers and answer explanations while responding to the questions. Refer to the general discussion in the Introduction on how to take the FAA knowledge test.

Remember that the questions from the FAA knowledge test bank have been reordered by topic and organized into a meaningful sequence. Also, the first line of the answer explanation gives the citation of the authoritative source for the answer.

QUESTIONS

5.1 Center of Gravity

1. The center of gravity of an aircraft is computed along the

A. lateral axis.
B. vertical axis.
C. longitudinal axis.

Answer (C) is correct. *(AWBH Chap 1)*
DISCUSSION: Although the CG affects movements around both the lateral and longitudinal axes, the prime concern of aircraft balancing is longitudinal balance, or the fore and aft location of the CG along the longitudinal axis (from nose to tail).
Answer (A) is incorrect. Although balance along the lateral axis is very important, CG is only computed along the longitudinal axis. Answer (B) is incorrect. The CG along the vertical axis cannot normally be computed.

2. The center of gravity of an aircraft can be determined by

A. dividing total arm by total moment.
B. dividing total moment by total weight.
C. multiplying total arm by total weight.

Answer (B) is correct. *(AWBH Chap 1)*
DISCUSSION: Arm is the horizontal distance in inches of the weight from the datum. Moment is the product of arm times weight. Total moment is the sum of individual moments. CG is calculated by dividing the total moment by the total weight.
Answer (A) is incorrect. The CG is calculated by dividing the total moment, not total arm, by the total weight, not moment. Answer (C) is incorrect. The CG is calculated by dividing, not multiplying, the total moment, not total arm, by the total weight.

3. As the CG location is changed, recovery from a stall becomes progressively

A. less difficult as the CG moves rearward.
B. more difficult as the CG moves rearward.
C. more difficult as the CG moves either forward or rearward.

Answer (B) is correct. *(PHAK Chap 10)*
DISCUSSION: Generally speaking, an airplane becomes more unstable, especially at slow flight speeds, as the center of gravity is moved farther aft. An airplane that cleanly recovers from a stall with the CG at one position may fail completely to respond to normal recovery attempts when the CG is moved aft by 1 or 2 in.
Answer (A) is incorrect. Stall recovery becomes more (not less) difficult as the CG is moved rearward. Answer (C) is incorrect. Stall recovery becomes easier, not more difficult, as the CG is moved forward.

4. When an aircraft's forward CG limit is exceeded, it will affect the flight characteristics of the aircraft by producing

A. improved performance since it reduces the induced drag.
B. higher stalling speeds and more longitudinal stability.
C. very light elevator control forces which make it easy to inadvertently overstress the aircraft.

Answer (B) is correct. *(PHAK Chap 10)*
DISCUSSION: When an airplane's forward CG is exceeded, the airplane will stall at a higher airspeed because the critical angle of attack is reached at a higher airspeed due to increased wing loading. Also, the airplane will have more longitudinal stability because, as the CG moves forward of the center of lift, the tail surface is required to produce more negative lift to counteract the tendency to pitch down and provides an increase in stability (i.e., positive stability).
Answer (A) is incorrect. The airplane will cruise more slowly with a forward CG location due to an increase, not decrease, in induced drag arising from higher wing loadings. Answer (C) is incorrect. When an airplane's aft, not forward, CG limit is exceeded, it will affect the flight characteristics of the airplane by producing very light elevator control forces that make it easy to inadvertently overstress the airplane.

SU 5: Weight and Balance

5. An aircraft is loaded with the CG at the aft limit. What are the performance characteristics compared with the CG at the forward limit?

A. The aft CG provides the highest stall speed and cruising speed.
B. The aft CG provides the lowest stalling speed, the highest cruising speed, and least stability.
C. Cruising speed is lower because of more induced drag created by the elevator or stabilizer being required to provide more lift with an aft CG.

Answer (B) is correct. *(PHAK Chap 5)*
DISCUSSION: The airplane will stall at a lower speed with an aft CG loading. The airplane will cruise at a higher speed with an aft CG location because of reduced drag. The airplane will become less stable as the CG is moved rearward.
Answer (A) is incorrect. Aft CG provides the lowest, not highest, stall speed. Answer (C) is incorrect. Cruise speed increases with aft CG because of the decreased wing loading resulting in decreased drag.

6. An aircraft is loaded with the CG aft of the aft limit. What effect will this have on controllability?

A. Stall and spin recovery may be difficult or impossible.
B. A stall will occur at a lower airspeed, but recovery will be easier because of reduced wing loading.
C. A stall will occur at a higher indicated airspeed due to the greater downloading on the elevator.

Answer (A) is correct. *(PHAK Chap 10)*
DISCUSSION: Loading an aircraft with the CG aft of the CG limit has the most serious effect on longitudinal stability and can reduce the aircraft's capability to recover from stalls and spins.
Answer (B) is incorrect. While the stall will occur at a lower airspeed with the CG aft of the CG limit, recovery would be more difficult, not easier, because the pilot could generate higher, not lower, load factors (i.e., wing loading) due to very light back elevator control forces. Answer (C) is incorrect. A stall that occurs at a higher indicated airspeed due to the greater downloading on the elevator is caused by a forward, not aft, CG location.

7. What is the effect of center of gravity on the spin characteristics of an aircraft?

A. A flat spin may develop if the CG is too far aft.
B. If the CG is too far forward, spin entry will be difficult.
C. If the CG is too far aft, spins can become high-speed spirals.

Answer (A) is correct. *(PHAK Chap 5)*
DISCUSSION: CG location is particularly important in spin recovery, as there is a point in rearward loading of any airplane at which a flat spin will develop. A flat spin is one in which centrifugal force, acting through a CG located well to the rear, will pull the tail of the airplane out away from the axis of the spin, making it impossible to get the nose down and recover.
Answer (B) is incorrect. Stall speed is higher with a forward CG, making spin entry easier, not more difficult. Answer (C) is incorrect. The wings are no longer stalled in a high-speed spiral, and an aft CG makes stall/spin recovery more difficult, not easier.

8. What is the effect of center of gravity on the spin characteristics of a fixed-wing aircraft? If the CG is too far

A. aft, a flat spin may develop.
B. forward, spin entry will be difficult.
C. aft, spins can become high-speed spirals.

Answer (A) is correct. *(PHAK Chap 4)*
DISCUSSION: CG location is particularly important in spin recovery, as there is a point in rearward loading of any airplane at which a flat spin will develop. A flat spin is one in which centrifugal force, acting through a CG located well to the rear, will pull the tail of the airplane out away from the axis of the spin, making it impossible to get the nose down and recover.
Answer (B) is incorrect. Stall speed is higher with a forward CG, making spin entry easier, not more difficult. Answer (C) is incorrect. The wings are no longer stalled in a high-speed spiral, and an aft CG makes stall/spin recovery more difficult, not easier.

9. The stalling speed of an aircraft will be highest when the aircraft is loaded with a

A. high gross weight and aft CG.
B. low gross weight and forward CG.
C. high gross weight and forward CG.

Answer (C) is correct. *(PHAK Chap 5)*
DISCUSSION: An airplane will stall at a higher airspeed with a forward CG location because the critical angle of attack is reached at a higher speed due to increased wing loading. As the weight of an airplane is increased, the stall speed increases because the increased weight requires a higher angle of attack to produce additional lift to support the weight. Therefore, high gross weight and forward CG produce the highest stalling speed.
Answer (A) is incorrect. A forward, not aft, CG increases the stalling speed. Answer (B) is incorrect. High, not low, gross weight produces a high stall speed.

10. As the CG moves aft, an aircraft becomes

    A. less stable and less controllable.

    B. less stable, yet easier to control.

    C. more stable and controllable as long as the aft CG is not exceeded.

Answer (A) is correct. *(PHAK Chap 5)*
    DISCUSSION: Aft CG reduces the moment arm from the CG to the tail control surfaces, which decreases controllability. Stability decreases with aft CG due to the decreased downward lift being required by the horizontal stabilizer to balance the airplane as the CG moves aft toward the center of lift.
    Answer (B) is incorrect. Controllability decreases, not increases, as the CG moves aft. Answer (C) is incorrect. Stability and controllability both decrease, not increase, as the CG moves aft.

11. If the CG of an aircraft is moved from the aft limit to beyond the forward limit, how will it affect the cruising and stalling speed?

    A. Increase both the cruising speed and stalling speed.

    B. Decrease both the cruising speed and stalling speed.

    C. Decrease the cruising speed and increase the stalling speed.

Answer (C) is correct. *(PHAK Chap 10)*
    DISCUSSION: The airplane will stall at a higher speed with a forward CG location because the critical angle of attack is reached at a higher airspeed due to increased wing loading. Also, it will cruise more slowly with a forward CG location because of increased drag.
    Answer (A) is incorrect. Cruise speed is decreased, not increased, with a forward CG. Answer (B) is incorrect. Stalling speed is increased, not decreased, with a forward CG.

12. What is characteristic of the indicated airspeed if the CG is at the most forward allowable position and constant power and altitude are maintained?

    A. There is no relationship between CG location and indicated airspeed.

    B. Indicated airspeed will be less than it would be with the CG in the most rearward allowable position.

    C. Indicated airspeed will be greater than it would be with the CG in the most rearward allowable position.

Answer (B) is correct. *(PHAK Chap 5)*
    DISCUSSION: An airplane will cruise at a higher speed with an aft CG location due to reduced drag arising from the lower wing loading. The tail provides negative lift to balance CG in front of the center of pressure, and rearward CG reduces the need for negative lift, reducing the wing load. Therefore, an aircraft with forward loading is "heavier" and, consequently, slower than the same aircraft with the CG further aft.
    Answer (A) is incorrect. CG location affects indicated airspeed. Answer (C) is incorrect. The airspeed will be less, not greater, with a forward CG.

13. To maintain level flight in an airplane which is loaded with the CG at the forward limit, an additional download must be imposed on the horizontal stabilizer. This in turn produces

    A. an additional load which the wing must support.

    B. a lesser load that must be supported by the wing.

    C. a decrease in drag and results in a faster airspeed.

Answer (A) is correct. *(AWBH Chap 1)*
    DISCUSSION: With forward loading, nose-up trim is required in most airplanes to maintain level cruising flight. Nose-up trim involves setting the tail surfaces to produce a greater download on the aft portion of the fuselage, which adds to the wing loading and the total lift required from the wing if altitude is to be maintained. This in turn requires a higher angle of attack, which results in increased drag.
    Answer (B) is incorrect. Forward CG produces a higher, not lower, wing loading. Answer (C) is incorrect. Forward CG results in increased, not decreased, drag and a slower cruising speed.

14. Under which condition is a forward CG most critical?

    A. On takeoff.

    B. On landing.

    C. When in an unusual attitude.

Answer (B) is correct. *(PHAK Chap 10)*
    DISCUSSION: A forward CG location requires greater elevator back pressure. As the CG moves forward of the forward limit, the elevator may no longer be able to oppose any increase in nose downpitching. Adequate elevator control is needed to control the airplane throughout the airspeed range down to the stall for landing.
    Answer (A) is incorrect. On takeoff, the airplane will accelerate until there is adequate airflow over the horizontal stabilizer to rotate the aircraft. Answer (C) is incorrect. During a spin or in an unusual attitude, an aft CG, not forward, is more critical (i.e., more likely to produce an uncontrollable situation).

SU 5: Weight and Balance

15. If the nosewheel of an airplane moves aft during gear retraction, how would this aft movement affect the CG location of that airplane? It would

A. cause the CG location to move aft.
B. have no effect on the CG location.
C. cause the CG location to move forward.

Answer (A) is correct. *(AWBH Chap 1)*
DISCUSSION: The CG is not a fixed point. As variable load items are shifted or expanded, there is a shift in CG location. If the nosewheel retracts aft, weight is also being shifted aft and the CG moves aft.
Answer (B) is incorrect. The CG shifts aft, not remains the same, as weight is shifted aft. Answer (C) is incorrect. The CG shifts aft, not forward, as the weight is shifted aft.

16. If the landing gear on an airplane moves forward during retraction, the total moment will

A. increase.
B. decrease.
C. remain the same.

Answer (B) is correct. *(AWBH Chap 1)*
DISCUSSION: When weight is shifted from one location to another, the total moment changes in relation and proportion to the direction and distance the weight is moved. When weight is moved forward, the total moment decreases; when weight is moved aft, the total moment increases. Thus, if the landing gear on an airplane moves forward during retraction, the total moment will decrease.
Answer (A) is incorrect. Total moment increases when weight is shifted aft, not forward. Answer (C) is incorrect. Total moment decreases, not remains the same, when weight is shifted forward.

5.2 Center of Gravity Calculations

17. Based on this information, the CG would be located how far aft of datum?

Weight A	120 lb at 15" aft of datum
Weight B	200 lb at 117" aft of datum
Weight C	75 lb at 195" aft of datum

A. 100.8 inches.
B. 109.0 inches.
C. 121.7 inches.

Answer (A) is correct. *(PHAK Chap 10)*
DISCUSSION: To determine the CG, use a three-step process:

1. First, multiply the individual weights by their arms to get the individual moments.

	W	×	A	=	M
A =	120	×	15	=	1,800
B =	200	×	117	=	23,400
C =	75	×	195	=	14,625
	395				39,825

2. Compute total weights and total moments.
3. Divide total moments by total weight to get the CG.

$$CG = \frac{39,825}{395} = 100.8 \text{ in.}$$

Answer (B) is incorrect. The CG is 100.8 in. (not 109.0 in.). Answer (C) is incorrect. The CG is 100.8 in. (not 121.7 in.).

18. Based on this information, the CG would be located how far aft of datum?

Weight D	160 lb at 45" aft of datum
Weight E	170 lb at 145" aft of datum
Weight F	105 lb at 185" aft of datum

A. 86.0 inches aft of datum.
B. 117.8 inches aft of datum.
C. 125.0 inches aft of datum.

Answer (B) is correct. *(PHAK Chap 10)*
DISCUSSION: To determine the CG, use a three-step process:

1. First, multiply the individual weights by their arms to get the individual moments.

	W	×	A	=	M
A =	160	×	45	=	7,200
B =	170	×	145	=	24,650
C =	105	×	185	=	19,425
	435				51,275

2. Compute total weights and total moments.
3. Divide total moments by total weight to get the CG.

$$CG = \frac{51,275}{435} = 117.8 \text{ in.}$$

Answer (A) is incorrect. The CG is 117.8 in. (not 86.0 in.). Answer (C) is incorrect. The CG is 117.8 in. (not 125.0 in.).

19. Based on this information, the CG would be located how far aft of datum?

Weight X 130 lb at 17" aft of datum
Weight Y 110 lb at 110" aft of datum
Weight Z 75 lb at 210" aft of datum

A. 89.1 inches.
B. 95.4 inches.
C. 106.9 inches.

Answer (B) is correct. *(PHAK Chap 10)*
DISCUSSION: To determine the CG, use a three-step process:

1. First, multiply the individual weights by their arms to get the individual moments.

	W	×	A	=	M
A =	130	×	17	=	2,210
B =	110	×	110	=	12,100
C =	75	×	210	=	15,750
	315				30,060

2. Compute total weights and total moments.
3. Divide total moments by total weight to get the CG.

$$CG = \frac{30,060}{315} = 95.4 \text{ in.}$$

Answer (A) is incorrect. The CG is 95.4 in. (not 89.1 in.).
Answer (C) is incorrect. The CG is 95.4 in. (not 106.9 in.).

20. (Refer to Figure 32 on page 157.) How should the 1,000-pound weight A be shifted to balance the plank on the fulcrum? Weight B is 500 pounds.

A. 12.5 inches to the right.
B. 37.5 inches to the right.
C. 37.5 inches to the left.

Answer (B) is correct. *(PHAK Chap 9)*
DISCUSSION:

Left	Right
Weight × Arm = Moment	Weight × Arm = Moment
1,000 × –50 = –50,000	500 × 25 = 12,500

We know the left moment and right moment must sum to zero. Thus, we need to solve the desired location of where weight A should be located.

left = right
1,000 lb.(X) = 500 lb.(25 in.)
1,000X = 12,500
X = 12,500 ÷ 1,000
X = 12.5 inches

We know weight A needs to be located 12.5 inches from datum. We know weight A is 50 inches to the left. It needs to be moved 37.5 inches to the right, so the arm is at –12.5 inches.
Answer (A) is incorrect. The weight needs to be at –12.5 inches to the left, but the weight is currently –50 inches to the left. Thus, it needs to move 37.5 inches to the right. Answer (C) is incorrect. The weight needs to be moved to the right, not the left. If the weight moved 37.5 inches to the left, it would have an arm of –87.5, not –12.5.

21. (Refer to Figure 32 on page 157.) How should the 500-pound weight B be shifted to balance the plank on the fulcrum? Weight A is 1,000 pounds.

A. 75 inches to the left.
B. 75 inches to the right.
C. 100 inches to the right.

Answer (B) is correct. *(PHAK Chap 10)*
DISCUSSION:

Left	Right
Weight × Arm = Moment	Weight × Arm = Moment
1,000 × –50 = –50,000	500 × 25 = 12,500

We know the right and left moments must sum to zero. Thus, we need to solve the desired location of where weight B should be located.

left = right
1,000 lb.(50 in.) = 500 lb.(X)
50,000 = 500(X)
50,000 ÷ 500 = X
100 in. = X

We know weight B should be 100 inches from the fulcrum. We know weight B is currently 25 inches from the fulcrum. Thus, it must move 75 inches to the right.
Answer (A) is incorrect. The weight needs to be at 100 inches to the right, not the left. If you moved the weight 75 inches to the left, it would be on the left side of the fulcrum, not the right side. Answer (C) is incorrect. The weight is already 25 inches to the right, so it only needs to move 75 inches to the right, not 100 inches to the right.

SU 5: Weight and Balance

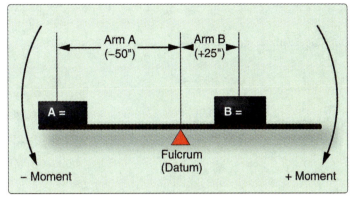

Figure 32. – The Law of the Lever.

22. (Refer to Figure 33 below.) All three weights are 10 pounds. How should weight C be shifted to balance the plank on the CG?

A. 36 inches to the left.
B. 36 inches to the right.
C. 64 inches to the right.

Answer (B) is correct. *(PHAK Chap 10)*
DISCUSSION: The datum is 72 inches from the CG, which means B is 8 inches (80 – 72) to the right of the CG. C is 28 inches (100 – 28) to the right of the CG.

left = right
10 × 72 = (10 × 8) + 10X
720 = 80 + 10X
640 = 10X
64 = X

Weight C needs to be located 64 inches to the right of the CG. It is currently sitting 28 inches to the right of the CG. Thus, it must move 36 inches more to the right, so it is 64 inches from the CG.
Answer (A) is incorrect. The weight needs to move to the right, not the left. Sixty-four inches from the CG means it must move further away to the right and away from weight A. Answer (C) is incorrect. Weight C is currently sitting 28 inches to the right of the CG. You need to subtract 28 inches from 64 inches to determine how far weight C should be shifted.

23. (Refer to Figure 33 below.) Weight A is 200 pounds and weight B is 250 pounds. How much weight should weight C equal to balance the plank on the fulcrum?

A. 56 pounds.
B. 586 pounds.
C. 443 pounds.

Answer (C) is correct. *(PHAK Chap 10)*
DISCUSSION:

left = right
72 × 200 = (8 × 250) + 28X
14,400 = 2,000 + 28X
12,400 = 28X
442.86 = X

The best answer choice is 443 pounds.
Answer (A) is incorrect. The objective is to balance the weights on the CG. Thus, you need to determine the arms based on the CG, not weight A. Answer (B) is incorrect. The moment of weight B should not be added to the left side. It should be added to the right side since it is to the right of the CG.

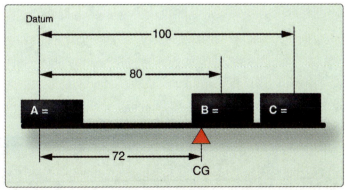

Figure 33. – Moving the CG of a Board by Shifting the Weights.

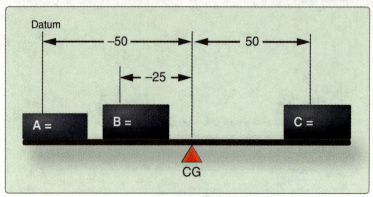

Figure 34. – Placement of Weight B to Cause the Board to Balance About Its Center.

24. (Refer to Figure 34 above.) Weight A is 500 pounds and weight B is 250 pounds. How much does weight C weigh?

A. 625 pounds.
B. 250 pounds.
C. 31,250 pounds.

Answer (A) is correct. *(PHAK Chap 10)*
DISCUSSION: To find the weight of C, compute and sum the moments left and right of the fulcrum. Set them equal to one another and solve for the desired variable:

$$\begin{aligned}
\text{left} &= \text{right} \\
(50 \times 500) + (25 \times 250) &= 50X \\
25{,}000 + 6{,}250 &= 50X \\
31{,}250 &= 50X \\
31{,}250 \div 50 &= X \\
625 &= X
\end{aligned}$$

Weight C equals 625 pounds.
    Answer (B) is incorrect. Weight B is on the left side, not the right side. Answer (C) is incorrect. The moment is 31,250, not the weight of weight C.

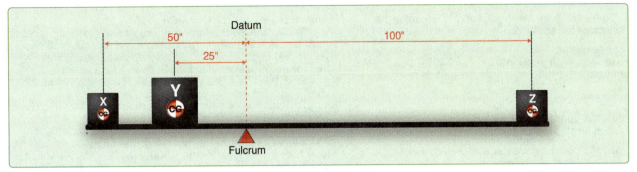

Figure 35. – Weight and Balance Diagram.

25. (Refer to Figure 35 above.) If 50 pounds of weight is located at point X and 100 pounds at point Z, how much weight must be located at point Y to balance the plank?

A. 30 pounds.
B. 50 pounds.
C. 300 pounds.

Answer (C) is correct. *(PHAK Chap 10)*
DISCUSSION: Compute and sum the moments left and right of the fulcrum. Set them equal to one another and solve for the desired variable:

$$\begin{aligned} \text{left} &= \text{right} \\ 50\ \text{lb.}(50\ \text{in.}) + Y(25\ \text{in.}) &= 100\ \text{lb.}(100\ \text{in.}) \\ 2{,}500 + 25Y &= 10{,}000 \\ 25Y &= 7{,}500 \\ Y &= 300\ \text{lb.} \end{aligned}$$

Answer (A) is incorrect. Thirty lb. in the place of Y would cause the plank to be heavier on the right side. Answer (B) is incorrect. Fifty lb. in the place of Y would cause the plank to be heavier on the right side.

26. (Refer to Figure 35 above.) If 50 pounds of weight is located at point X and 100 pounds at point Y, how much weight must be located at point Z to balance the plank?

A. 150 pounds.
B. 100 pounds.
C. 50 pounds.

Answer (C) is correct. *(PHAK Chap 10)*
DISCUSSION: Compute and sum the moments left and right of the fulcrum. Set them equal to one another and solve for the desired variable:

$$\begin{aligned} \text{left} &= \text{right} \\ 50\ \text{lb.}(50\ \text{in.}) + 100\ \text{lb.}(25\ \text{in.}) &= Z(100\ \text{in.}) \\ 2{,}500 + 2{,}500 &= 100Z \\ 5{,}000 &= 100Z \\ 50\ \text{lb.} &= Z \end{aligned}$$

Answer (A) is incorrect. Putting 150 lb. in the place of Z would cause the plank to be heavier on the right side. Answer (B) is incorrect. Putting 100 lb. in the place of Z would cause the plank to be heavier on the right side.

27. (Refer to Figure 35 above.) If 50-pound weights are located at points X, Y, and Z, how would point Z have to be shifted to balance the plank?

A. 25 inches to the left.
B. 2.5 inches to the left.
C. 2.5 inches to the right.

Answer (A) is correct. *(PHAK Chap 10)*
DISCUSSION: Compute and sum the moments left and right of the fulcrum. Set them equal to one another and solve for the desired variable:

$$\begin{aligned} \text{left} &= \text{right} \\ 50\ \text{lb.}(50\ \text{in.}) + 50\ \text{lb.}(25\ \text{in.}) &= 50\ \text{lb.}(Z) \\ 2{,}500 + 1{,}250 &= 50Z \\ 3{,}750 &= 50Z \\ 75\ \text{in.} &= Z \end{aligned}$$

The 50-lb. weight at Z must be 75 in. from the fulcrum to balance the plank. Thus, Z should be shifted 25 in. to the left.
Answer (B) is incorrect. Shifting 2.5 in. to the left would cause the plank to be heavier on the right side. Answer (C) is incorrect. Shifting 2.5 in. to the right would cause the plank to be heavier on the right side.

5.3 Center of Gravity Tables

28. (Refer to Figure 36 on page 161.) Determine the condition of the airplane:

Pilot and copilot	375 lb
Passengers -- aft position	245 lb
Baggage	65 lb
Fuel	70 gal

A. 185 pounds under allowable gross weight; CG is located within limits.

B. 162 pounds under allowable gross weight; CG is located within limits.

C. 162 pounds under allowable gross weight; CG is located aft of the aft limit.

Answer (A) is correct. *(PHAK Chap 10)*
DISCUSSION: Both the total weight and the total moment must be calculated. As in most weight and balance problems, you should begin by setting up a schedule as below. Note that the empty weight in Fig. 36 is given as 2,110 with a moment/100 in. of 1,652 (note the use of moment/100 on this chart), and that empty weight includes the oil.
The next step is to compute the moment/100 for each item. The pilot and copilot moment/100 is 318.75 lb.-in. (375 lb. × 85 in. ÷ 100). The passengers (aft position) moment/100 is 333.2 lb.-in. (245 lb. × 136 in. ÷ 100). The baggage moment/100 is 97.5 lb.-in. (65 lb. × 150 in. ÷ 100). The 70-gal. fuel weight is 420 lb., and the moment/100 is 315 lb.-in. (read directly from the table).

	Weight	Moment/100
Empty weight w/oil	2,110	1,652.00
Pilot and copilot	375	318.75
Passengers (aft position)	245	333.20
Baggage	65	97.50
Fuel (70 gal.)	420	315.00
	3,215	2,716.45

Note that the gross weight of 3,215 lb. is within the 3,400 lb. maximum allowable by 185 lb., and that the moment/100 of 2,716.45 is within the moment envelope at the intersection with 3,215 lb.
Answer (B) is incorrect. You are 185 lb., not 162 lb., under gross weight. Answer (C) is incorrect. You are 185 lb., not 162 lb., under gross weight, and you are within, not aft of, the allowable CG limits.

29. (Refer to Figure 36 on page 161.) Determine the condition of the airplane:

Pilot and copilot	400 lb
Passengers -- aft position	240 lb
Baggage	20 lb
Fuel	75 gal

A. 157 pounds under allowable gross weight; CG is located within limits.

B. 180 pounds under allowable gross weight; CG is located within limits.

C. 180 pounds under allowable gross weight, but CG is located aft of the aft limit.

Answer (B) is correct. *(PHAK Chap 10)*
DISCUSSION: Both the total weight and the total moment must be calculated. As in most weight and balance problems, you should begin by setting up a schedule as below. Note that the empty weight in Fig. 36 is given as 2,110 with a moment/100 in. of 1,652 (note the use of moment/100 on this chart), and that empty weight includes the oil.
The next step is to compute the moment/100 for each item. The pilot and copilot moment/100 is 340 lb.-in. (400 lb. × 85 in. ÷ 100). The passengers (aft position) moment/100 is 326.4 lb.-in. (240 lb. × 136 in. ÷ 100). The baggage moment/100 is 30 lb.-in. (read directly from the table). The 75-gal. fuel weight is 450 lb., and the moment/100 is 338 lb.-in. (read directly from the table).

	Weight	Moment/100
Empty weight w/oil	2,110	1,652.00
Pilot and copilot	400	340.00
Passengers (aft position)	240	326.40
Baggage	20	30.00
Fuel (75 gal.)	450	338.00
	3,220	2,686.40

Note that the gross weight of 3,220 lb. is within the 3,400 lb. maximum allowable by 180 lb., and that this moment/100 of 2,686.4 lb.-in. is within the moment envelope at the intersection with 3,220 lb.
Answer (A) is incorrect. The airplane is 180 lb., not 157 lb., under gross weight. Answer (C) is incorrect. The airplane is within, not aft of, allowable CG limits at 3,220 lb.

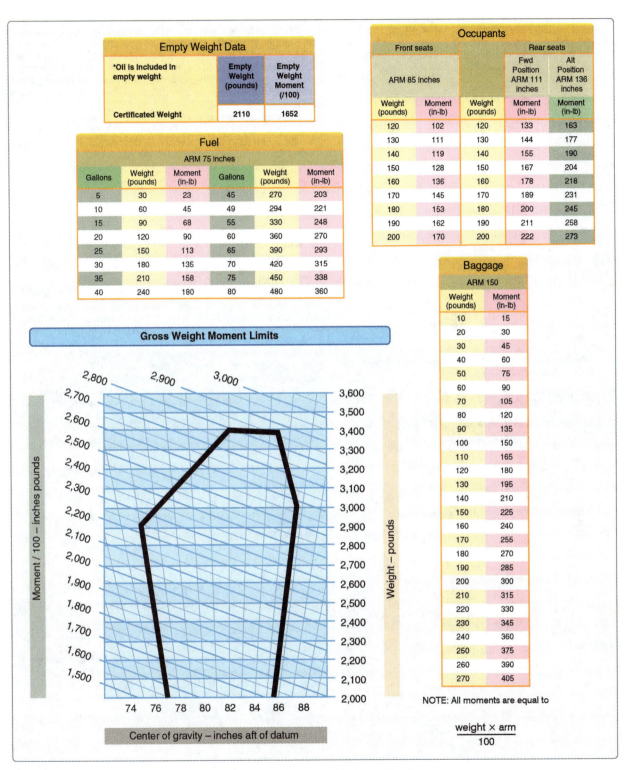

Figure 36. – Weight and Balance Chart.

30. (Refer to Figure 36 on page 163.) (Chart moments are divided by 100 but not labeled.) What effect does a 35-gallon fuel burn have on the weight and balance if the airplane weighed 2,890 pounds and the MOM/100 was 2,452 at takeoff?

A. Weight is reduced by 210 pounds and the CG moves aft.

B. Weight is reduced by 270 pounds and the CG is unaffected.

C. Weight is reduced to 2,680 pounds and the CG moves forward.

Answer (A) is correct. *(AWBH Chap 2)*
DISCUSSION: The effect of a 35-gal. fuel burn on weight and balance is required. Burning 35 gal. of fuel will reduce weight by 210 lb. and moment by 158. At 2,680 lb. (2,890 − 210), the 2,294 MOM/100 (2,452 − 158) is above the maximum moment of 2,287. Therefore, the CG is aft of limits. This is why weight and balance should always be computed for the beginning and end of each flight.
Answer (B) is incorrect. A fuel burn of 35 gal. is 210 lb. (35 gal. × 6 lb. per gal = 210 lb.), not 270 lb. Answer (C) is incorrect. Although the moment has decreased, the CG (moment divided by weight) has moved aft, not forward.

31. (Refer to Figure 36 on page 163.) Determine the condition of the airplane:

Pilot and copilot	316 lb
Passengers	
Fwd position	130 lb
Aft position	147 lb
Baggage	50 lb
Fuel	75 gal

A. 197 pounds under allowable gross weight; CG 83.6 inches aft of datum.

B. 163 pounds under allowable gross weight; CG 82 inches aft of datum.

C. 197 pounds under allowable gross weight; CG 84.6 inches aft of datum.

Answer (A) is correct. *(PHAK Chap 10)*
DISCUSSION: Both the total weight and the total moment must be calculated. As in most weight and balance problems, you should begin by setting up a schedule as below. Note that the empty weight in Fig. 36 is given as 2,110 with a moment/100 in. of 1,652 (note the use of moment/100 on this chart), and that empty weight includes the oil. Be aware that some table values do not result in an accurate mathematical answer. You should use the table as a guide, but do not neglect to check your math.

The next step is to compute the moment/100 for each item. The pilot and copilot together weigh 316 lb., and their moment/100 is 268.6 lb.-in. (316 lb. × 85 in. ÷ 100). The passengers (forward position) moment/100 is 144.3 lb.-in. (130 lb. × 111 in. ÷ 100). The passengers (aft position) moment/100 is 199.92 lb.-in. (147 lb. × 136 in. ÷ 100). The baggage moment/100 is 75 lb.-in. (read directly from the table). The 75-gal. fuel weight is 450 lb., and the moment/100 is 338 lb.-in. (read directly from the table).

	Weight	Moment/100
Empty weight w/oil	2,110	1,652.00
Pilot and copilot	316	268.60
Passengers		
Fwd position	130	144.30
Aft position	147	199.92
Baggage	50	75.00
Fuel (75 gal.)	450	338.00
	3,203	2,677.82

Note that the gross weight of 3,203 is within the 3,400-lb. maximum allowable by 197 lb., which is within the CG envelope.

$$CG = \frac{2,677.82}{3,203} \times 100 = 83.6 \text{ in. aft of datum}$$

Answer (B) is incorrect. The airplane is 197 lb., not 163 lb., under gross weight and the CG is 83.6 in., not 82.0 in., aft of datum. Answer (C) is incorrect. The airplane's CG is 83.6 in., not 84.6 in., aft of datum.

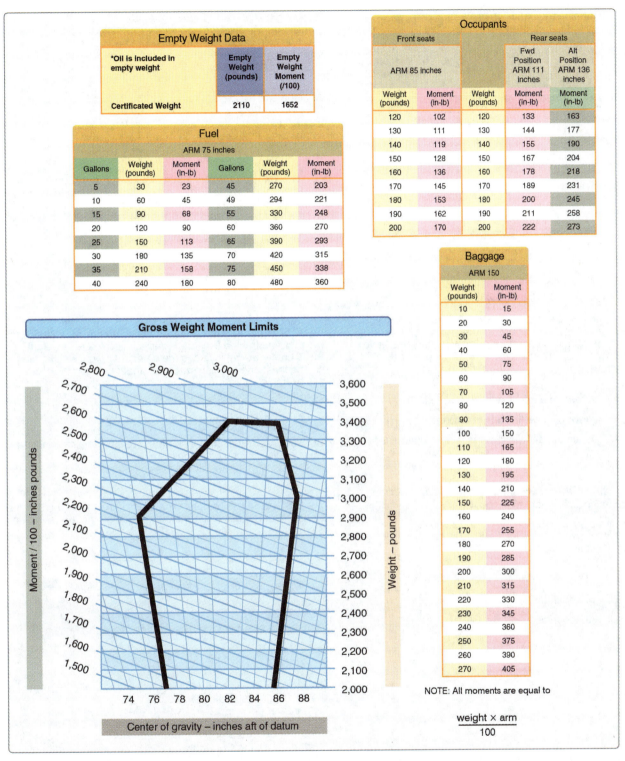

Figure 36. — Weight and Balance Chart.

32. Determine the condition of the aircraft:

Pilot	160 lb	26 inch arm
Passenger	120 lb	26 inch arm
Baggage	80 lb	62 inch arm
Fuel	24 gal	7 inch arm
Aircraft empty weight =	730.5 lbs	
Empty CG =	17 inches	
MAC =	59 inches	
MGTOW =	1,320 lbs	

A. The aircraft is slightly over MGTOW with the CG aft of the aft limit of 37% MAC.

B. The aircraft is under MGTOW with the CG at 35.2% MAC.

C. The CG is forward of the aft limit of 37% and the aircraft is 100 pounds under MGTOW.

Answer (B) is correct. *(PHAK Chap 10)*
DISCUSSION: Both the total weight and the total moment must be calculated. As in most weight and balance problems, you should begin by setting up a schedule as below.
The next step is to compute the moment for each item.

	Weight		Moment
Airplane empty weight	730.5	17	12,418.5
Pilot	160.0	26	4,160.0
Passenger	120.0	26	3,120.0
Baggage	80.0	62	4,960.0
Fuel (24 gal.)	144.0	7	1,008.0
	1,234.5		25,666.5

The loaded aircraft is 1,234.5 lb., which is 85.5 lb. under MGTOW, and the CG is 20.79 lb.-in. Loaded aircraft CG is 35.2% MAC (CG 20.79 lb.-in. ÷ MAC 59 lb.-in).
Answer (A) is incorrect. The aircraft is under MGTOW and forward of the aft limit of 37% MAC. Answer (C) is incorrect. The aircraft is 85.5 lb. under MGTOW.

5.4 Weight Change Calculations

33. With respect to using the weight information given in a typical aircraft owner's manual for computing gross weight, it is important to know that if items have been installed in the aircraft in addition to the original equipment, the

A. allowable useful load is decreased.

B. allowable useful load remains unchanged.

C. maximum allowable gross weight is increased.

Answer (A) is correct. *(PHAK Chap 10)*
DISCUSSION: Useful load is the difference after basic empty weight is subtracted from maximum allowable gross weight. Basic empty weight includes the standard empty weight, plus any optional and special equipment that has been installed. In this example, basic empty weight has increased, and maximum allowable gross weight remains a fixed number, which leaves a decreased useful load.
Answer (B) is incorrect. Given any addition of equipment, the useful load will decrease, not remain unchanged. Answer (C) is incorrect. Maximum allowable gross weight remains unchanged when additional equipment is installed.

34. What is the maximum weight that could be added at Station 130.0 without exceeding the aft CG limit?

Total weight	2,900 lb
CG location	Station 115.0
Aft CG limit	Station 116.0

A. 14 pounds.

B. 140 pounds.

C. 207 pounds.

Answer (C) is correct. *(PHAK Chap 10)*
DISCUSSION: To determine the maximum weight that may be added at Station 130.0 without exceeding the aft CG limit at Station 116.0, use the following formula:

$$\text{New CG} = \frac{M_1 \pm \Delta M}{W_1 \pm \Delta W}$$

Where M_1 = Original moment and W_1 = Original weight.

$$116.0 = \frac{2,900(115.0) + 130.0(X)}{2,900 + X}$$

$2,900(116.0) + 116.0(X) = 2,900(115.0) + 130.0(X)$
$336,400 + 116X = 333,500 + 130X$
$2,900 = 14X$
$207.1 = X$

Thus, 207 lb. could be added at Station 130.0 without exceeding the aft CG limit at Station 116.0.
Answer (A) is incorrect. If 14 lb. were added to Station 130.0, the CG would be 115.07, which is forward of the aft CG limit of 116.0. Answer (B) is incorrect. If 140 lb. were added to Station 130.0, the CG would be 115.69, which is forward of the aft CG limit of 116.0.

SU 5: Weight and Balance

35. What is the maximum weight that could be added at Station 150.0 without exceeding the aft CG limit?

Aircraft weight	5,000 lb
CG location	Station 80.0
Aft CG limit	Station 80.5

A. 70.0 pounds.
B. 69.5 pounds.
C. 35.9 pounds.

Answer (C) is correct. *(PHAK Chap 10)*
DISCUSSION: To determine the maximum weight that may be added, use the following formula:

$$\text{New CG} = \frac{M_1 \pm \Delta M}{W_1 \pm \Delta W}$$

Where M_1 = Original moment and W_1 = Original weight.

$$80.5 = \frac{5,000(80.0) + 150.0(X)}{5,000 + X}$$
$$5,000(80.5) + 80.5(X) = 5,000(80.0) + 150.0(X)$$
$$402,500 + 80.5X = 400,000 + 150X$$
$$2,500 = 69.5X$$
$$35.97 = X$$

Thus, 35.9 lb. could be added at Station 150.0 without exceeding the aft CG limit at Station 80.5.
Answer (A) is incorrect. If 70 lb. were added at Station 150.0, the CG would be 80.97, which is aft of the CG limit of 80.5. Answer (B) is incorrect. If 69.5 lb. were added at Station 150.0, the CG would be 80.96, which is aft of the CG limit of 80.5.

36. How much weight could be added at Station 160 without exceeding the aft CG limit?

Total weight	8,300 lb
CG location	Station 90.0
Aft CG limit	Station 90.5

A. 59.7 pounds.
B. 16.5 pounds.
C. 13.9 pounds.

Answer (A) is correct. *(PHAK Chap 10)*
DISCUSSION: To determine the maximum weight that may be added, use the following formula:

$$\text{New CG} = \frac{M_1 \pm \Delta M}{W_1 \pm \Delta W}$$

Where M_1 = Original moment and W_1 = Original weight.

$$90.5 = \frac{8,300(90.0) + 160.0(X)}{8,300 + X}$$
$$8,300(90.5) + 90.5(X) = 8,300(90.0) + 160.0(X)$$
$$751,150 + 90.5X = 747,000 + 160X$$
$$4,150 = 69.5X$$
$$59.7 = X$$

Thus, 59.7 lb. could be added at Station 160 without exceeding the aft CG limit at Station 90.5.
Answer (B) is incorrect. If 16.5 lb. were added at Station 160.0, the CG would be 90.14, which is forward of the aft CG limit of 90.5. Answer (C) is incorrect. If 13.9 lb. were added at Station 160.0, the CG would be 90.12, which is forward of the aft CG limit of 90.5.

37. How much weight could be added at Station 120 without exceeding the aft CG limit?

Total weight	9,500 lb
CG location	Station 90.0
Aft CG limit	Station 90.5

A. 61.0 pounds.
B. 110.5 pounds.
C. 161.0 pounds.

Answer (C) is correct. *(PHAK Chap 10)*
DISCUSSION: To determine the maximum weight that may be added, use the following formula:

$$\text{New CG} = \frac{M_1 \pm \Delta M}{W_1 \pm \Delta W}$$

Where M_1 = Original moment and W_1 = Original weight.

$$90.5 = \frac{9,500(90.0) + 120.0(X)}{9,500 + X}$$
$$9,500(90.5) + 90.5(X) = 9,500(90.0) + 120.0(X)$$
$$859,750 + 90.5X = 855,000 + 120X$$
$$4,750 = 29.5X$$
$$161.0 = X$$

Thus, 161.0 lb. could be added at Station 120 without exceeding the aft CG limit at Station 90.5.
Answer (A) is incorrect. If 61.0 lb. were added at Station 120.0, the CG would be 90.19, which is forward of the aft CG limit of 90.5. Answer (B) is incorrect. If 110.5 lb. were added at Station 120.0, the CG would be 90.34, which is forward of the aft CG limit of 90.5.

38. What is the location of the CG if 90 pounds are removed from Station 140?

Total weight	6,230 lb
CG location	Station 79

A. 79.9
B. 78.1
C. 77.9

Answer (B) is correct. *(PHAK Chap 10)*
DISCUSSION: To determine the new CG, use the following formula:

$$\text{New CG} = \frac{M_1 \pm \Delta M}{W_1 \pm \Delta W}$$

Where M_1 = Original moment and W_1 = Original weight.

$$\text{New CG} = \frac{(6{,}230 \times 79) - (90 \times 140)}{6{,}230 - 90}$$

$$= \frac{492{,}170 - 12{,}600}{6{,}140}$$

$$= \frac{479{,}570}{6{,}140}$$

$$= 78.1$$

Answer (A) is incorrect. Ninety lb. would have to be added, not removed, at Station 140 to move the CG from 79 to 79.9. Answer (C) is incorrect. Removing 112.0 lb., not 90 lb., from Station 140 would be necessary to move the CG from 79.0 to 77.9.

39. What is the location of the CG if 60 pounds are removed from Station 70?

Total weight	8,420 lb
CG location	Station 85

A. 85.1
B. 84.9
C. 84.1

Answer (A) is correct. *(PHAK Chap 10)*
DISCUSSION: To determine the new CG, use the following formula:

$$\text{New CG} = \frac{M_1 \pm \Delta M}{W_1 \pm \Delta W}$$

Where M_1 = Original moment and W_1 = Original weight.

$$\text{New CG} = \frac{(8{,}420 \times 85) - (60 \times 70)}{8{,}420 - 60}$$

$$= \frac{715{,}700 - 4{,}200}{8{,}360}$$

$$= \frac{711{,}500}{8{,}360}$$

$$= 85.1$$

Answer (B) is incorrect. Sixty lb. would have to be added, not removed, at Station 70 to move the CG from 85.0 to 84.9. Answer (C) is incorrect. Adding 540 lb. to Station 70 would be necessary to move the CG from 85.0 to 84.1.

SU 5: Weight and Balance

40. What is the location of the CG if 146 pounds are removed from Station 150?

Total weight	7,152 lb
CG location	Station 82

A. 83.4
B. 81.3
C. 80.6

Answer (C) is correct. *(PHAK Chap 10)*
DISCUSSION: To determine the new CG, use the following formula:

$$\text{New CG} = \frac{M_1 \pm \Delta M}{W_1 \pm \Delta W}$$

Where M_1 = Original moment and W_1 = Original weight.

$$\text{New CG} = \frac{(7{,}152 \times 82) - (146 \times 150)}{7{,}152 - 146}$$

$$= \frac{586{,}464 - 21{,}900}{7{,}006}$$

$$= \frac{564{,}564}{7{,}006}$$

$$= 80.6$$

Answer (A) is incorrect. To change the CG from 82 to 83.4, 146 lb. would have to be added to, not removed from, Station 150. Answer (B) is incorrect. Seventy-three lb., not 146 lb., would have to be removed to change the CG from 82 to 81.3.

41. What would be the new CG location if 135 pounds of weight were added at Station 109.0?

Total weight	2,340 lb
CG location	Station 103.0

A. Station 103.3.
B. Station 104.2.
C. Station 109.3.

Answer (A) is correct. *(PHAK Chap 10)*
DISCUSSION: To determine the new CG, use the following formula:

$$\text{New CG} = \frac{M_1 \pm \Delta M}{W_1 \pm \Delta W}$$

Where M_1 = Original moment and W_1 = Original weight.

$$\text{New CG} = \frac{(2{,}340 \times 103.0) + (135 \times 109.0)}{2{,}340 + 135}$$

$$= \frac{241{,}020 + 14{,}715}{2{,}475}$$

$$= \frac{255{,}735}{2{,}475}$$

$$= 103.3$$

Answer (B) is incorrect. Adding 585 lb. to Station 109.0 would be necessary to change the CG from 103.0 to 104.2. Answer (C) is incorrect. Weight would have to be added aft of Station 109.0 to change the CG from 103.0 to 109.3.

42. How much weight must be shifted from Station 150.0 to Station 30.0 to move the CG to exactly the aft CG limit?

Total weight	7,500 lb
CG location	Station 80.5
Aft CG limit	Station 79.5

A. 68.9 pounds.
B. 65.8 pounds.
C. 62.5 pounds.

Answer (C) is correct. *(PHAK Chap 10)*
DISCUSSION: To determine how much weight must be shifted, use the following formula:

$$\text{New CG} = \frac{M_1 \pm \Delta M}{W_1 \pm \Delta W}$$

Where M_1 = Original moment and W_1 = Original weight.

Since there is no change in weight, $\Delta W = 0$ and weight shifted forward causes a "−" moment change.

$$79.5 = \frac{(7{,}500 \times 80.5) - X(150.0 - 30.0)}{7{,}500}$$

$7{,}500 \times 79.5 = (7{,}500 \times 80.5) - X(150.0 - 30.0)$
$596{,}250 = 603{,}750 - 120X$
$-7{,}500 = 120X$
$62.5 = X$

Answer (A) is incorrect. Shifting 68.9 lb. moves the CG to 79.4, which is forward of the aft CG limit of 79.5. Answer (B) is incorrect. Shifting 65.8 lb. moves the CG to 79.45, which is forward of the aft CG limit of 79.5.

43. Could 100 pounds of weight be shifted from Station 130.0 to Station 30.0 without exceeding the forward CG limit?

Total weight	2,800 lb
CG location	Station 120.0
Forward CG limit	Station 117.0

A. No; the new CG would be located at Station 116.89.

B. No; the new CG would be located at Station 116.42.

C. Yes; the new CG would be located at Station 117.89.

Answer (B) is correct. *(PHAK Chap 10)*
DISCUSSION: To determine the new CG, use the following formula:

$$\text{New CG} = \frac{M_1 \pm \Delta M}{W_1 \pm \Delta W}$$

Where M_1 = Original moment and W_1 = Original weight.

Since there is no change in weight, $\Delta W = 0$, and weight shifted forward causes a "−" moment change.

$$\text{New CG} = \frac{(2,800 \times 120.0) - 100(130.0 - 30.0)}{2,800}$$

$$= \frac{336,000 - 10,000}{2,800}$$

$$= \frac{326,000}{2,800}$$

$$= 116.42$$

As this is forward of the indicated 117.0 forward CG limit, the 100 lb. cannot be shifted to Station 30 without exceeding the forward CG limit.
Answer (A) is incorrect. The new CG would be located at Station 116.89 if 87.1 lb., not 100 lb., was shifted from Station 130.0 to Station 30.0. Answer (C) is incorrect. The new CG would be located at Station 117.89 if 41 lb. was shifted from Station 30.0 to Station 130.0, not if 100 lb. was shifted from Station 130.0 to Station 30.0.

44. Could 100 pounds of weight be shifted from Station 30.0 to Station 120.0 without exceeding the aft CG limit?

Total weight	4,750 lb
CG location	Station 115.8
Aft CG limit	Station 118.0

A. Yes; the CG would remain at Station 115.8.

B. No; the new CG would be located at Station 118.15.

C. Yes; the new CG would be located at Station 117.69.

Answer (C) is correct. *(PHAK Chap 10)*
DISCUSSION: To determine the new CG, use the following formula:

$$\text{New CG} = \frac{M_1 \pm \Delta M}{W_1 \pm \Delta W}$$

Where M_1 = Original moment and W_1 = Original weight.

Since there is no change in weight, $\Delta W = 0$, and weight shifted aft causes a "+" moment change.

$$\text{New CG} = \frac{(4,750 \times 115.8) + 100(120.0 - 30.0)}{4,750}$$

$$= \frac{550,050 + 9,000}{4,750}$$

$$= \frac{559,050}{4,750}$$

$$= 117.69$$

As this is forward of the indicated 118.0 aft CG limit, the 100 lb. can be shifted.
Answer (A) is incorrect. When weight shifts in an airplane, the CG shifts. Answer (B) is incorrect. The new CG would be located at Station 118.15 if 124 lb., not 100 lb., was shifted from Station 30.0 to Station 120.0.

STUDY UNIT SIX
AVIATION WEATHER

(22 pages of outline)

6.1	Causes of Weather	(3 questions)	169, 191
6.2	The Earth's Atmosphere	(1 question)	170, 191
6.3	High-Low Pressure	(8 questions)	170, 191
6.4	Dew Point and Fog	(11 questions)	170, 193
6.5	Temperature Lapse Rate	(8 questions)	171, 195
6.6	Stability of Air Masses	(12 questions)	171, 196
6.7	Temperature Inversion	(3 questions)	172, 198
6.8	Weather Fronts	(4 questions)	172, 199
6.9	Turbulence and Wind Shear	(7 questions)	172, 200
6.10	Thunderstorms and Microbursts	(9 questions)	173, 201
6.11	Icing and Hail	(9 questions)	173, 203
6.12	Clouds	(4 questions)	173, 205
6.13	Aviation Routine Weather Report (METAR)	(10 questions)	174, 206
6.14	Pilot Weather Report (PIREP)	(5 questions)	175, 208
6.15	Radar Weather Report (SD/ROB) and Weather Advisories	(2 questions)	176, 209
6.16	Surface Analysis Chart	(8 questions)	177, 210
6.17	Ceiling and Visibility Chart	(3 questions)	178, 212
6.18	Constant Pressure Analysis Chart	(2 questions)	180, 213
6.19	Turbulence	(2 questions)	180, 214
6.20	Significant Weather Prognostic Chart	(1 question)	181, 216
6.21	Convective Weather Forecast Chart	(3 questions)	182, 216
6.22	Winds and Temperatures Aloft Forecast (FB)	(3 questions)	183, 218
6.23	Terminal Aerodrome Forecast (TAF)	(8 questions)	184, 218
6.24	Convective Outlook Chart	(4 questions)	185, 220
6.25	AIRMET and SIGMET	(4 questions)	185, 222
6.26	Current Icing Potential and Forecast Icing Potential	(2 questions)	188, 223

This study unit contains outlines of major concepts tested, sample test questions and answers regarding weather, and an explanation of each answer. The table of contents above lists each subunit within this study unit, the number of questions pertaining to that particular subunit, and the pages on which the outlines and questions begin, respectively.

 Recall that the **sole purpose** of this book is to expedite your passing of the FAA pilot knowledge test for the CFI, BGI, or AGI certificate. Accordingly, all extraneous material (i.e., topics or regulations not directly tested on the FAA pilot knowledge test) is omitted, even though much more knowledge is necessary to become a proficient flight or ground instructor. This additional material is presented in *Pilot Handbook* and *Flight Instructor Flight Maneuvers and Practical Test Prep*, available from Gleim Publications, Inc. Order online at www.GleimAviation.com.

6.1 CAUSES OF WEATHER

1. **The primary driving force of weather is the Sun.** The Sun's unequal heating of the Earth's surface causes changes in temperature and pressure that cause circulation and weather.

2. **Pressure differences** create a force from higher pressure to lower pressure that results in wind.

3. The **Coriolis force** deflects winds to the right in the Northern Hemisphere. It is caused by the Earth's rotation.

    a. The Coriolis force is less at the surface due to weaker wind.
    b. Wind is weaker at the surface due to friction between wind and the Earth's surface.

6.2 THE EARTH'S ATMOSPHERE

1. The **troposphere** is the part of the atmosphere where most weather occurs.
   a. It is the layer from the surface to an average altitude of 7 miles.

6.3 HIGH-LOW PRESSURE

1. **In the Northern Hemisphere, high-pressure air circulates (anticyclonic)**
   a. Outward,
   b. Downward, and
   c. Clockwise.
2. **Low-pressure air circulates in the opposite direction (cyclonic).**
   a. When flying toward a low pressure area, the wind velocity will be from the left (counterclockwise) and increasing (winds are greater in low-pressure systems than high-pressure systems).
3. When planning trips from east to west in the Northern Hemisphere, you would go south of a high and north of a low to find tailwinds.
4. A low-pressure area or trough is an area of rising air.
5. Development of convective circulation is caused by the cooler, denser air sinking to force the warm air upward.
   a. Convective circulation associated with sea breezes is caused by land absorbing and radiating heat faster than water.
6. Strong thermals have proportionally increased sink in the air between them.

6.4 DEW POINT AND FOG

1. **Relative humidity** is the ratio of existing water vapor in the air compared to the amount that could exist at a given temperature.
   a. High relative humidity is one condition necessary for the formation of fog.
2. **Dew point** is the temperature at which the air will have 100% relative humidity, i.e., be saturated.
   a. As relative humidity increases, the spread (i.e., difference) between the temperature and dew point decreases.
   b. As the temperature and dew point converge, fog, clouds, or rain should be anticipated. Therefore, one should be alert for the development of fog when temperature-dew point spread is 3°C (5°F) or less and decreasing.
3. **Sublimation** is the direct conversion of a solid to a vapor or vice versa (e.g., ice forming on a surface directly from water vapor on a cold, clear night).
4. **Radiation fog** is most likely to occur when there is high humidity during the early evening, cool cloudless nights with light winds, and favorable topography (such as low-lying areas, like mountain valleys).
5. **Advection fog** is formed as a result of moist air moving over a colder surface.
   a. It can appear suddenly during day or night and is more persistent than radiation fog.
6. **Precipitation-induced fog** is a result of saturation due to evaporation of precipitation.
   a. It is most commonly associated with warm fronts.
7. Fog occurs on the leeward side of a lake when warm air moves over the cold lake.

SU 6: Aviation Weather

6.5 TEMPERATURE LAPSE RATE

1. Standard temperature at mean sea level is 15°C (59°F).
2. Standard pressure at mean sea level is 29.92 in. Hg (1013.2 mb).
   a. "Hg" is the periodic symbol for mercury.
   b. "mb" is the abbreviation for millibar.
3. The **standard lapse rate** (cooling rate per increase in altitude) is 2°C per 1,000 ft. of increased altitude.
   a. To compute the approximate freezing level, add 1,000 ft. for each 2°C.
   b. EXAMPLE: If it is 12°C at 1,000 ft., the freezing level would be at 7,000 ft. (12° ÷ 2 = 6; 6,000 + 1,000 = 7,000 ft.).
4. A **temperature inversion** occurs when temperature increases as altitude increases (normally, temperature decreases as altitude increases).
   a. The most frequent type of ground- or surface-based temperature inversion is that produced by terrestrial radiation on a clear, relatively still night.
   b. When relative humidity is high beneath a low-level temperature inversion, one would expect smooth air and poor visibility due to fog, haze, or low clouds.
5. The **height of cumuliform cloud bases** can be estimated using surface temperature-dewpoint spread.
   a. Unsaturated air in a convective current cools at about 5.4°F (3.0°C) per 1,000 ft., and dewpoint decreases about 1°F (0.5°C) per 1,000 ft.
   b. Thus, temperature and dewpoint converge at about 4.4°F (2.5°C) per 1,000 ft.
   c. Cloud bases are at the altitude where the temperature and the dewpoint are the same.
6. The **average lapse rate** in the troposphere is 2.0°C per 1,000 ft.

6.6 STABILITY OF AIR MASSES

1. The **ambient lapse rate** is the rate of decrease in temperature with height.
   a. More than normal lapse rate (temperature decreases with altitude) encourages warm air from below to rise, i.e., increases instability.
   b. In a stable situation, there is less temperature decrease with altitude and there is little or no tendency for lifting.
   c. Thus, stability can be determined by measuring the ambient lapse rate.
2. Stable air characteristics:
   a. Stratiform clouds
   b. Smooth air
   c. Fog
   d. Continuous precipitation
   e. Restricted visibility in haze and smoke
3. When warm, moist air is cooled from below, it takes on the characteristics of stable air.
4. Unstable air characteristics:
   a. Cumuliform clouds
   b. Turbulent air
   c. Good visibility except in blowing sand or snow
   d. Showery precipitation
5. When moist, cold air is warmed from below, it takes on the characteristics of unstable air.
6. When very stable, moist air is forced to ascend a mountain slope, the clouds will be stratus type with little vertical development and little or no turbulence.

7. The formation of either predominantly stratiform or predominantly cumuliform clouds is dependent upon the stability of the air being lifted.

6.7 TEMPERATURE INVERSION

1. In the stratosphere, one commonly finds a temperature inversion. The stratosphere is the layer of Earth's atmosphere above the troposphere. The bottom of the stratosphere can be as low as 20,000 feet over the poles.
2. A stable layer of air is associated with a temperature inversion.
3. Poor visibility characterizes a ground-based inversion.
4. Terrestrial radiation on a clear, relatively calm night produces the most frequent type of ground- or surface-based temperature inversion.
5. A calm or light wind near the surface and a relatively strong wind just above the inversion are necessary conditions for the occurrence of low-level temperature inversion wind shear.

6.8 WEATHER FRONTS

1. Frontal waves normally form on slow-moving cold fronts or stationary fronts.
    a. If a frontal wave were to form on a stationary front running east and west across the U.S., the portion east of the wave would normally become a warm front and the portion west of the wave would become a cold front.
2. The weather associated with an advancing warm front that has moist, unstable air is cumuliform clouds, turbulent air, and showery-type precipitation.
3. In a cold front occlusion, the air ahead of the warm front is warmer than the air behind the overtaking cold front.
    a. An occlusion is composed of two fronts as a cold front overtakes a warm front.

6.9 TURBULENCE AND WIND SHEAR

1. In a mountain wave, the air dips sharply downward immediately to the lee (downwind) side of a ridge before rising and falling in a wave motion for a considerable distance downstream.
    a. If the air is humid and the wave is of large amplitude, lenticular (lens-shaped) clouds mark the wave's crest.
    b. One of the most dangerous features of mountain waves is the turbulence in and below rotor clouds, which may lie underneath each crest.
    c. **When flying over ridges or mountain ranges**, the greatest potential danger from turbulent air currents will be encountered on the leeward side when flying into the wind. You are flying into a downdraft, which may preclude your flying over the terrain.
    d. The conditions most favorable to wave formation over mountainous areas are a layer of stable air at mountaintop altitude and a wind of at least 15 to 25 kt. (depending on the height of the ridge) blowing across the ridge.
2. **Low-level wind shear**, which results in a sudden change of wind direction, may occur when there is a low-level temperature inversion with strong winds above the inversion.
    a. The possibility of a sudden loss of airspeed should be expected.
3. Expect and avoid areas of CAT (clear air turbulence) where horizontal wind shear exceeds 40 kt. per 150 NM.

6.10 THUNDERSTORMS AND MICROBURSTS

1. The minimum requirements for the formation of a thunderstorm are
   a. Sufficient moisture
   b. An unstable lapse rate
   c. A lifting action
2. A thunderstorm passes through three stages during its life cycle:
   a. **Cumulus:** The building stage of a thunderstorm when there are continuous updrafts.
   b. **Mature:** The beginning of rain on the Earth's surface indicates the mature stage of a thunderstorm.
   c. **Dissipating:** There are only downdrafts; i.e., the storm is raining itself out.
3. A squall line is usually associated with a fast-moving cold front.
4. Cumulonimbus mamma clouds are associated with violent turbulence and a tendency toward the production of funnel clouds.
5. Tornadoes are most likely to occur with steady-state thunderstorms associated with cold fronts or squall lines.
6. **Individual microbursts** seldom last longer than 15 min. from the time the burst strikes the ground until dissipation.
   a. Maximum downdrafts in a microburst encounter may be as strong as 6,000 fpm.
   b. Maximum intensity winds in a microburst usually last 2 to 4 min.

6.11 ICING AND HAIL

1. **Freezing rain** results from rain falling from air that has a temperature of more than 0°C into air having a temperature of 0°C or less.
2. **Large hail** is most commonly found in thunderstorms with strong updrafts and large liquid water content.
   a. Hail is usually produced during the mature stage of the thunderstorm's lifespan.
   b. Hailstones may be thrown upward and outward from a storm cloud for several miles.
   c. Hail is most likely to be associated with cumulonimbus clouds.
   d. Hail will most likely be encountered beneath the anvil of a large cumulonimbus.
3. **Ice pellets** usually indicate freezing rain at higher altitudes.
4. The most rapid accumulation of **clear ice** on an aircraft in flight may occur with temperatures between 0°C and –15°C in cumuliform clouds.
   a. In order for structural ice to form, the temperature at the point where moisture strikes the aircraft must be 0°C (32°F) or colder.
5. If inflight icing is encountered, the pilot should disengage the autopilot and hand-fly the airplane. Using the autopilot during icing conditions may mask important cues relating to control or systems.

6.12 CLOUDS

1. The height of the bases of the **middle clouds** in the middle latitudes ranges from 6,500 ft. to 23,000 ft.
2. **Nimbostratus** is a middle-level cloud characterized by rain, snow, or ice pellets, posing a serious icing problem if temperatures are near or below freezing.
3. A smooth **cumulus** cloud with a concave base is one of the best visual indications of a thermal.
4. **Virga** is streamers of precipitation that evaporate before reaching the ground.

6.13 AVIATION ROUTINE WEATHER REPORT (METAR)

1. Aviation routine weather reports (METARs) are actual weather observations at the time indicated on the report. There are two types of reports:

    a. METAR is an hourly routine observation (scheduled).
    b. SPECI is a special METAR observation (unscheduled).

2. Following the type of report are the elements listed below and on the next page.

    a. The four-letter ICAO station identifier

    1) In the contiguous 48 states, the three-letter domestic identifier is prefixed with a "K."

    b. Date and time of report. It is appended with a "Z" to denote Coordinated Universal Time (UTC).

    1) EXAMPLE: **301651Z** means the observation was taken on the 30th day at 1651 UTC (or Z).

    c. Modifier (if required)

    1) **AUTO** identifies the report as an automated weather report with no human intervention.

    d. Wind is reported as a five-digit group (six digits if the wind speed is greater than 99 kt.). It is appended with the abbreviation KT to denote the use of knots for wind speed.

    1) A calm wind (less than 3 kt.) is reported as **00000KT**.

    e. Visibility
    f. Runway visual range
    g. Weather phenomena

    1) Fog (FG) is used to indicate fog restricting visibility to less than 5/8 SM.
    2) Mist (BR) is used to indicate fog restricting visibility from 5/8 SM to 6 SM.

    h. Sky conditions

    1) The ceiling is the lowest broken or overcast layer, or vertical visibility into an obscuration.

        a) There are no provisions to report partial obscurations or thin layers in the body of the METAR.

            i) Partial obscurations are explained in the remarks section, which is not considered the body of the METAR.

    2) Cloud bases are reported with three digits in hundreds of feet AGL.

        a) EXAMPLE: **OVC007** means overcast cloud layer at 700 ft. AGL.

    3) Total obscurations are reported in the format "VVhhh" with "VV" meaning vertical visibility and "hhh" being the vertical visibility in hundreds of feet.

        a) EXAMPLE: **VV006** means vertical visibility of 600 ft.

    i. Temperature/dew point is reported in a two-digit form in whole degrees Celsius separated by a solidus, "/."

    1) EXAMPLE: 21/17 means the temperature is 21°C and the dew point is 17°C.

    j. Altimeter

k. Remarks (RMK)
 1) **RAB25** means rain began at 25 min. past the hour.
   a) If the time of the observation was at 1651 UTC, the duration of the rain is 26 min., i.e., from 1625 to 1651.
 2) A maintenance indicator sign **($)** is included when an automated weather reporting system is possibly in need of maintenance.
 3) **SLPNO** means that sea-level pressure is not available.

3. EXAMPLE: METAR KAUS 301651Z 12008KT 4SM –RA HZ BKN010 BKN023 OVC160 21/17 A3005 RMK RAB25
 a. **METAR** is a routine weather observation.
 b. **KAUS** is Austin, TX.
 c. **301651Z** is the date (30th day) and time (1651 UTC) of the observation.
 d. **12008KT** means the wind is from 120° true at 8 kt.
 e. **4SM** means the visibility is 4 statute miles.
 f. **–RA HZ** means light rain and haze.
 g. **BKN010 BKN023 OVC160** means broken cloud layers at 1,000 ft. and 2,300 ft. and an overcast cloud layer at 16,000 ft.
 h. **21/17** means the temperature is 21°C and the dew point is 17°C.
 i. **A3005** means the altimeter setting is 30.05 in. of Hg.
 j. **RMK RAB25** means remarks, rain began at 25 min. past the hour.

4. The Automated Surface Observation System (ASOS) will provide continuous observations and perform the basic observing functions necessary to generate METAR reports.

6.14 PILOT WEATHER REPORT (PIREP)

1. Pilot weather reports are reported in the "Remarks" section of hourly weather reports (SA). They consist of up to 12 sections:
 a. **UA -- Routine PIREP, UUA -- Urgent PIREP**
 b. **/OV -- Location:** Use three-letter NAVAID idents only.
   1) **Fix:** /OV ABC, /OV ABC 090025
   2) **Fix to fix:** /OV ABC-DEF, /OV ABC-DEF 120020, /OV ABC 045020-DEF 120005, /OV ABC-DEF-GHI
 c. **/TM -- Time:** Four digits in UTC: /TM 0915
 d. **/FL -- Altitude/Flight Level:** Three digits for hundreds of feet. If not known, use UNKN: /FL095, /FL310, FLUNKN.
 e. **/TP -- Type aircraft:** Four digits maximum. If not known, use UNKN: /TP L329, /TP B727. /TP UNKN.
 f. **/SK -- Cloud layers:** Describe as follows:
   1) Cloud cover symbol.
   2) Height of cloud base in hundreds of feet. If unknown, use UNKN.
   3) Height of cloud tops in hundreds of feet.
   4) Use a slash (/) to separate layers.
   5) EXAMPLES: /SK BKN 038, /SK OVC 038-TOP045, /SK BKN018-TOP055/OVC072-TOP089, /SK OVCUNKN.

g. **/WX -- Weather:** Flight visibility reported first. Use standard weather symbols. Intensity is reported with a "+" or "–" sign (no sign signifies moderate intensity): /WX FV02 +SHRA, /WX FV01 FU.

   1) When reporting flight visibility,

      a) Fog (FG) can be reported only if the visibility is less than 5/8 mile.
      b) Mist (BR) can be reported only if the visibility is greater than or equal to 5/8 statute mile.
      c) There is no provision to report partial obscurations.

h. **/TA -- Air temperature** in Celsius: If below zero, prefix with an "M": /TA 15, /TA M06.
i. **/WV -- Wind:** Direction and speed in five or six digits: /WV 27045, /WV 280110.
j. **/TB -- Turbulence:** Use standard contractions for intensity and type (use CAT or CHOP when appropriate). Include altitude only if different from /FL: /TB EXTRM, /TB LGT 055-072.
k. **/IC -- Icing:** Describe using standard intensity and type contractions. Include altitude only if different from /FL: /IC LGT-MOD RIME, /IC SVR CLR 028-045.
l. **/RM -- Remarks:** Use free form to clarify the report. Most hazardous element first: /RM LLWS -15KT SFC-003 DURGC RNWY 22 JFK.

2. EXAMPLE: **UA/OV CRP 180020 1629 FL050 /TP C182 /SK SCT 040-TOP050**

   a. This means that the pilot of a Cessna 182 reported scattered clouds with bases at 4,000 ft. MSL and tops at 5,000 ft. MSL at a point on the 180° radial 20 NM from Corpus Christi, Texas.
   b. Item-by-item translation of the PIREP:

   UA - Pilot report • **OV CRP** - Over Corpus Christi • **180020** - 180°, 020 NM • **1629** - 1629 UTC • **FL050** - 5,000 ft. MSL • **TP** - "Type of airplane" • **C182** - Cessna 182 • **SK** - Sky • **SCT** - Scattered • **040** - Bases at 4,000 ft. • **TOP050** - Tops at 5,000 ft.

6.15 RADAR WEATHER REPORT (SD/ROB) AND WEATHER ADVISORIES

1. SD/ROBs are of special interest to pilots because they report location of precipitation along with the type, intensity, and trend.

   a. In addition to transmission as a separate report, some SD/ROBs are included in scheduled weather broadcasts by Flight Service Stations.

2. EXAMPLE SD/ROB explained in the diagram on the next page.

   a. **Location identifier and time of radar observation.** In the example, Oklahoma City SD/ROB at 1934 UTC.
   b. **Echo pattern (LN).** The radar echo pattern or configuration may be a

      1) **Line (LN)** -- a line of precipitation echoes at least 30 NM long, at least four times as long as it is wide, and at least 25% coverage within the line.
      2) **Fine Line (FINE LN)** -- a unique clear air echo (usually precipitation-free and cloud-free) in the form of a thin or fine line on the radar scope. It represents a strong temperature/moisture boundary, such as an advancing dry cold front.
      3) **Area (AREA)** -- a group of echoes of similar type and not classified as a line.
      4) **Spiral Band Area (SPRL BAND AREA)** -- an area of precipitation associated with a hurricane that takes on a spiral band configuration around the center.
      5) **Single Cell (CELL)** -- a single isolated precipitation not reaching the ground.
      6) **Layer (LYR)** -- an elevated layer of stratiform precipitation not reaching the ground.

   c. **Coverage in tenths.** The 8 in the example is thus to be read as "8/10ths sky coverage."

SU 6: Aviation Weather

d. **Type, intensity, and intensity trend of weather.** In the example, the radar depicted thunderstorms (T) and very heavy rain showers (RW++) that are increasing in intensity (/+). Note that the intensity is separated from intensity trend by a slash.
e. **Azimuth (reference true N) and range in nautical miles (NM) of points defining the echo pattern.** 86/40 164/60 199/115 in the example.
f. **Dimension of echo pattern.** In the example, 15 NM wide. The dimension of an echo pattern is given when azimuth and range define only the center line of the pattern. In this example, "15W" means the line has a total width of 15 NM, 7 1/2 mi. either side of a center line drawn from the points given. "D15" would mean a convective echo is 15 mi. in diameter around a given center point.
g. **Pattern movement.** The LINE is moving from 240° at 25 kt. in the example. This element may also show movement of individual storms or cells with a "C" or movement of an area with an "A."
h. **Maximum top and location.** In the example, 57,000 ft. MSL on radial 159° at 65 NM.
i. **Remarks.** Self-explanatory using plain-language contractions.

3. **SD/ROB symbols**   **Example SD/ROB**

Intensity		Intensity Trend		OKC 1934 LN 8TRW++/+ 86/40 164/60 199/115 15W L2425 MT570 AT 159/65 2 INCH HAIL RPRTD THIS CELL MO1 NO2 ON3 PM34 QM3 RL2 SL9		
Symbol	Intensity	Symbol	Trend	OKC 1934 a.	LN b.	8 c.
–	Light	+	Increasing			
(none)	Moderate	–	Decreasing	TRW++/+ d.	86/40 164/60 199/115 e.	
+	Heavy	NC	No change	15W f.	L2425 g.	
++	Very Heavy	NEW	New echo			
X	Intense			MT 570 AT 159/65 h.		
XX	Extreme			2 INCH HAIL RPRTED THIS CELL i.		
U	Unknown			M01 N02 0N3 PM34 QM3 RL2 SL9 j.		

4. Below FL180, weather advisories can be obtained from an FSS on 122.2 MHz.

6.16 SURFACE ANALYSIS CHART

1. The surface analysis chart, often referred to as a surface weather chart, is the basic weather chart.

    a. It displays weather information such as

        1) Surface wind direction and speed,
        2) Temperature,
        3) Dew point,
        4) Position of fronts, and
        5) Areas of high or low pressure.

    b. On a surface analysis chart, isobars are solid lines depicting the sea-level pressure pattern and are usually spaced at intervals of 4 millibars (mb).
    c. You can also determine the intensity of a front as of chart time.

2. Types of fronts are characterized on surface analysis charts according to symbols (as illustrated below). Some stations color these symbols to facilitate use of the chart.
    a. Frontolysis refers to a dissipating front.
    b. Frontogenesis refers to the initial formation of a front.

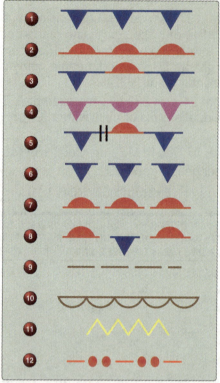

Figure 8. – Surface Analysis Chart Symbols.

1) Cold front
2) Warm front
3) Stationary front
4) Occluded front
5) Change of front type
6) Cold frontogenesis
7) Warm frontogenesis
8) Stationary frontogenesis
9) Trough (TROF) or Outflow boundary (OUTFLOW BNDRY)
10) Dryline
11) Ridge
12) Squall line

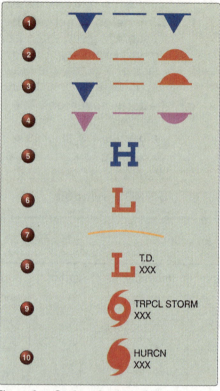

Figure 9. – Surface Analysis Chart Symbols.

1) Cold frontolysis
2) Warm frontolysis
3) Stationary frontolysis
4) Occluded frontolysis
5) High pressure center
6) Low pressure center
7) Tropical (TRPL) wave
8) Tropical depression
9) Tropical storm
10) Hurricane

6.17 CEILING AND VISIBILITY CHART

1. The ceiling and visibility chart helps pilots identify areas of VFR, MVFR, IFR, and LIFR conditions. This chart is found online at the Aviation Weather Center under Observations.
    a. The ceiling and visibility chart is intended to aid flight planning and is best used along with other weather products, such as METARs, AIRMETs, and TAFs.
    b. The ceiling and visibility chart can be viewed by region by using "Regional Ceiling and Vis Plots," which is located below the ceiling and visibility chart.
    c. Both charts use the following color coding:
        1) Orange suggests possible terrain obscuration.
        2) Yellow suggests IFR conditions.
        3) Teal (or blue/green) suggests VFR conditions.

SU 6: Aviation Weather   179

Once you use these charts to identify areas where IFR, VFR, and possible terrain obscuration conditions may exist, you must investigate these areas further by looking at more detailed FAA-approved weather products, such as METARs, AIRMETs, and TAFs.

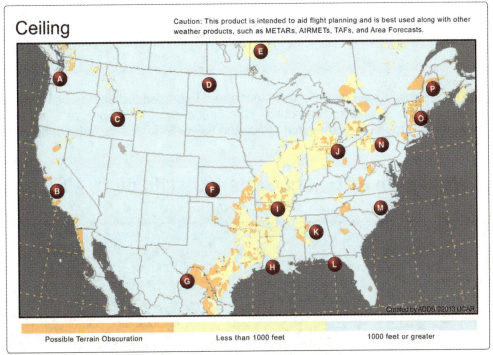

Figure 2. – CONUS Display of CVA Ceiling Analysis.

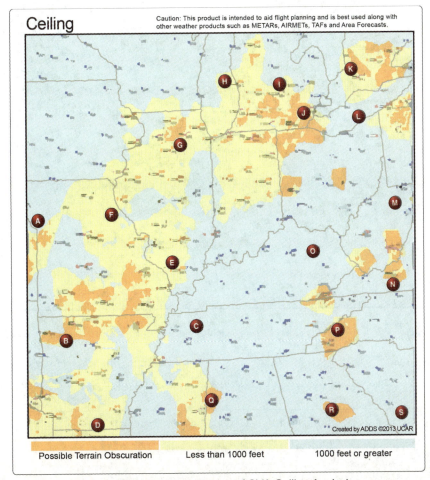

Figure 2A. – Regional Display of CVA Ceiling Analysis.

6.18 CONSTANT PRESSURE ANALYSIS CHART

1. Constant pressure charts can be used to determine the observed temperature, wind, and temperature/dewpoint spread at specified flight levels.

    a. For planning a flight at 10,000 ft. MSL, you should refer to the 700-mb analysis.

6.19 TURBULENCE

1. Pilots can find information about turbulence and expected turbulence by visiting the Aviation Weather Center online and selecting "Turbulence" under the Forecasts drop-down menu. The current Graphical Turbulence Guidance (GTG-3) forecasts turbulence from the surface to FL 500.

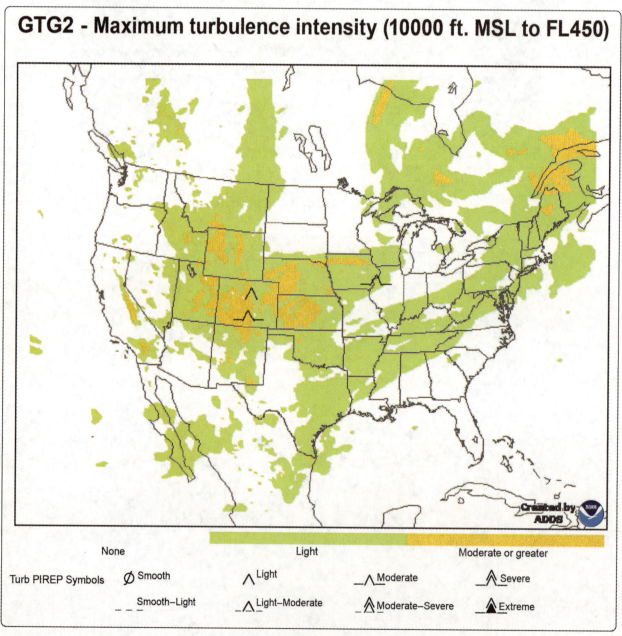

Figure 13A. – GTG Composite Example.

2. The figure on the previous page is a depiction of the GTG (version 2).

   a. GTG-2 forecasts turbulence from the surface to FL 450, with 0, 1, 2, 3, 6, 9, 12, 15, and 18 hour lead-times.

3. GTG provides computer-generated four-dimensional forecasts of information related to the expected intensity of atmospheric turbulence relating to clear air turbulence (CAT), mountain wave turbulence (MWT), and low-level terrain and thermally-induced turbulence sources.

   a. GTG is not intended to predict turbulence associated with convection and thunderstorm clouds but may provide some guidance in areas of properly predicted thunderstorms when the convection is widespread.

4. GTG is intended for flight planning purposes and should always be used in combination with turbulence information from all available sources including AIRMETs, SIGMETs, and PIREPs.

   a. Although the GTG product has been verified against thousands of turbulence reports by pilots, users should be aware that turbulence is a highly dynamic phenomenon and, in rapidly changing conditions, GTG may not accurately convey a significant hazard.

   b. GTG is a "snapshot" graphic intended to depict forecast turbulence conditions at the valid time (for example, at 1200Z). GTG does not depict turbulence for a valid time range (for example, from 1200Z to 1300Z).

   c. The graphics suite is automatically produced with no human modifications.

6.20 SIGNIFICANT WEATHER PROGNOSTIC CHART

1. Significant weather prognostic charts contain conditions forecast to exist at a valid time shown on the chart.

   a. The two panels forecast significant weather from the surface up to 24,000 ft.: one for 12 hr. and the other for 24 hr. from the time of issuance.

   b. Some service providers also include two lower panels with forecast surface conditions: one for 12 hr. and the other for 24 hr. from time of issuance.

2. The low-level significant prognostic charts depict

   a. Ceilings less than 1,000 ft. and/or visibility less than 3 SM (IFR) by a solid line around the area

   b. Ceilings 1,000 to 3,000 ft. and/or visibility 3 to 5 SM (MVFR) by a scalloped line around the area

   c. Moderate or greater turbulence by a broken line around the area

      1) A peaked hat ⁀⋀⁀ indicates moderate turbulence.
      2) Altitudes are indicated on the chart; e.g., 180 means from surface to 18,000 ft.

   d. Freezing levels, given by a dashed line corresponding to the height of the freezing level

3. The bottom panels show the location of

   a. Highs, lows, fronts
   b. Other areas of significant weather

      1) Unshaded outlined areas indicate precipitation covering half or less of the area.
      2) Shaded outlined areas indicate precipitation covering more than half of the area.

3) Precipitation type and intensity is reported with standard symbols. Some examples include the following:

a) ⋯ thunderstorms embedded in a larger area of continuous moderate rain

b) ⋯ thunderstorms embedded in a larger area of intermittent moderate rain

c) ✶✶/✶✶ continuous light snow

d) ✶✶/✶✶ continuous light to moderate snow

e) ✶/✶ intermittent light to moderate snow

4) Precipitation symbols may be connected to an area of precipitation by an arrow if there is not sufficient room to place them in that area.

4. These charts are used to determine areas to avoid (freezing levels and turbulence).

6.21 CONVECTIVE WEATHER FORECAST CHART

1. The convective weather forecast chart is taken from the National Convective Weather Forecast (NCWF). It is for selected hazardous convective conditions for the conterminous United States and is intended for use by general aviation, airline dispatchers, and Traffic Management Units. It has the following attributes:

   a. Near real-time
   b. High resolution display
   c. Current and 1-hour extrapolated forecasts

2. This forecast information is available at the Aviation Weather Center at www.aviationweather.gov/convection/.

3. The content of the NCWF displays

   a. Current convective hazard fields

      1) Level 1 - green (least hazardous)
      2) Level 2 - green
      3) Level 3 - yellow
      4) Level 4 - orange
      5) Level 5 - red
      6) Level 6 - red (most severe)

   b. One-hour extrapolated forecast polygons (blue semi-circular line)
   c. Forecast speed and directions (32/450 where 32 is the speed in knots, and the side the polygons are on is the direction of the hazard field)
   d. Echo tops plotted in hundreds of feet MSL (32/450 where 450 would be the echo tops of 45,000 ft. MSL)

4. Thunderstorms may contain any or all of the following hazards to flight:

   a. Severe turbulence,
   b. Severe icing,
   c. Hail,
   d. Frequent lightning,
   e. Tornadoes, and
   f. Low-level wind shear.

SU 6: Aviation Weather 183

5. The risk of hazardous weather increases with the levels on the NCWF hazard scale.

Radar Detection
35/500
Speed of MVMT (KTS)
32/450
Direction of Movement (Southeast)
25/450
ECHO Tops (cft MSL)
Blue Line 1-hr. Forecast Location

6.22 WINDS AND TEMPERATURES ALOFT FORECAST (FB)

1. Forecast winds and temperatures at specified altitudes for specific locations in the United States are presented in table form.

2. A four-digit group (used when temperatures are not forecast) shows wind direction with reference to true north and the wind speed in knots.

    a. The first two digits indicate the wind direction after you add a zero.
    b. The next two digits indicate the wind speed.

3. A six-digit group includes the forecast temperature aloft.

    a. The last two digits indicate the temperature in degrees Celsius.
    b. Plus or minus is indicated before the temperature, except at higher altitudes (above 24,000 ft. MSL), where it is always below freezing and the minus sign is dropped.

4. When the wind speed is less than 5 kt., the forecast is coded 9900, which means that the wind is light and variable.

5. Note that at some of the lower levels the wind and temperature information is omitted.

    a. Winds aloft are not forecast for levels within 1,500 ft. of the station elevation.
    b. No temperatures are forecast for the 3,000-ft. level or for a level within 2,500 ft. of the station elevation.

6.23 TERMINAL AERODROME FORECAST (TAF)

1. The terminal aerodrome forecast (TAF) is a concise statement of the expected meteorological conditions at an airport during a specified period. The TAF covers an area within 5 SM of the airport's center.

    a. TAFs are released four times daily and are valid for 24 hours.

2. The elements of a TAF are listed below:

    a. Type of report:

        1) TAF is a routine forecast.
        2) TAF AMD is an amended forecast.

    b. ICAO station identifier.
    c. Date and time the forecast is actually prepared.
    d. Valid period of the forecast.
    e. Forecast meteorological conditions. This is the body of the forecast and includes

        1) Wind.

            a) **00000KT** means a calm wind (3 kt. or less) is forecast.

        2) Visibility.

            a) **P6SM** means the forecast visibility is greater than 6 SM.

        3) Weather.

            a) Weather phenomena include precipitation, obscuring phenomena, thunderstorms, and other phenomena, such as tornadoes.
            b) The intensity symbol indicates the intensity of the precipitation.

        4) Sky condition.

            a) A ceiling is the lowest broken or overcast cloud layer or vertical visibility into a complete obscuration.
            b) Vertical visibility is shown on METAR/TAF reports when the sky is obscured.

3. EXAMPLE TAF
    KSJT 031745Z 0318/0418 12012KT 6SM HZ BKN016
    FM032000 17018KT BKN025
    FM032200 BKN030 OVC250 PROB40 0323/0403 1SM +TSRA OVC008CB
    FM040900 27020G34KT 2SM OVC010CB RA BR=

    a. **TAF** is a routine forecast issuance.
    b. **KSJT** is San Angelo, TX.
    c. **031745Z 0318/0418** means the TAF was issued on the third day of the month at 1745 UTC and is valid from the third day at 1800 UTC until the following day at 1800 UTC.
    d. **12012KT 6SM HZ BKN016** means the forecast from 1800 UTC to 2000 UTC on the third day, wind 120° true at 12 kt., visibility 6 SM in haze, broken cloud layer base at 1,600 ft.
    e. **FM032000 17018KT BKN025** means the forecast from 2000 UTC to 2200 UTC on the third day, wind 170° true at 18 kt., broken cloud layer base at 2,500 ft.
    f. **FM032200 BKN030 OVC250 PROB40 0323/0403 1SM +TSRA OVC008CB** means the forecast from 2200 UTC to 0900 UTC, broken cloud layer base at 3,000 ft., overcast cloud layer base at 25,000 ft. Between the hours of 2300 UTC and 0300 UTC, there is a 40% probability of visibility reduced to 1 SM, thunderstorm, heavy rain, and overcast cumulonimbus cloud layer base at 800 ft.

g. **FM040900 27020G34KT 2SM OVC010CB RA BR=** means the forecast from 0900 UTC until 1800 UTC on the fourth day, wind 270° true at 20 kt., gusts to 34 kt., visibility 2 SM in rain and mist, overcast cumulonimbus clouds at 1,000 ft. The equal sign (=) indicates the end of the TAF.

4. Be aware that the FAA figures relating to TAFs still use the old TAF format that did not include the date before the forecast time.

6.24 CONVECTIVE OUTLOOK CHART

1. The severe weather outlook chart, also referred to as a convective outlook chart, is a 48-hr. outlook for thunderstorm activity in two panels.
   a. The top panel covers the first 24-hr. period beginning at 1200Z and depicts areas of possible general thunderstorm activity as well as severe thunderstorms.
   b. The bottom panel covers the following day at 1200Z and is a forecast of severe thunderstorms only.
2. The contraction **APCHG** designating an area means that general thunderstorm activity may approach severe intensity. Approaching means
   a. Winds greater than or equal to 35 kt. but less than 50 kt. and/or
   b. Hail greater than or equal to 1/2 in. in diameter but less than 3/4 in.
3. Moderate (MDT) risk areas indicate 6-10% coverage.
4. Regarding convective outlook charts, when well-organized severe thunderstorms are expected but in small numbers and/or low coverage, the risk is referred to as slight (SLGT).

6.25 AIRMET AND SIGMET

1. AIRMETs and SIGMETs are issued to notify en route pilots of the possibility of encountering hazardous flying conditions.
   a. You should refer to an AIRMET or SIGMET to determine the freezing level and areas of probable icing aloft.
2. AIRMETs may be of significance to any pilot or aircraft and are issued for the following weather phenomena:
   a. Moderate icing
   b. Moderate turbulence
   c. Sustained winds of 30 kt. or more at the surface
   d. Widespread area of ceilings less than 1,000 ft. and/or visibility less than 3 SM
   e. Extensive mountain obscuration
3. SIGMETs are issued for the following weather phenomena, which are significant to the safety of all aircraft:
   a. Severe icing not associated with thunderstorms
   b. Severe or extreme turbulence or clear air turbulence (CAT) not associated with thunderstorms
   c. Duststorms, sandstorms, or volcanic ash lowering surface or in-flight visibilities to below 3 SM
   d. Volcanic eruption

4. Convective SIGMETs are issued for the following convective weather phenomena that are significant to the safety of all aircraft:

   a. Severe thunderstorms due to

      1) Surface winds greater than or equal to 50 kt.
      2) Hail at the surface greater than or equal to 3/4 in. in diameter
      3) Tornadoes

   b. Embedded thunderstorms
   c. A line of thunderstorms
   d. Thunderstorms greater than or equal to VIP level 4 affecting 40% or more of an area of at least 3,000 square miles

5. National Convective Weather Forecast (NCWF)

   a. The NCWF is a near real-time, high-resolution display of current and 1-hour extrapolated forecasts of selected hazardous convective conditions for the conterminous United States. The purpose of the NCWF is to produce a convective hazard field diagnostic and forecast product based on radar data, echo-top mosaics, and lightning data. The target audience includes the FAA.
   b. The NCWF is a supplement to, but does not substitute for, the report and forecast information contained within Convective SIGMETs.
   c. The NCWF is issued by the Aviation Weather Center and is updated every 5 minutes.
   d. The NCWF displays current convective hazard fields, 1-hour extrapolated forecast polygons, forecast speed and directions, and echo tops.
   e. The current convective hazard field is a high-resolution display that identifies selected hazards associated with convective precipitation. Reflectivity data with echo tops of less than 17,000 feet MSL are eliminated from the data. This process removes ground clutter and anomalous propagation as well as significantly reduces the amount of stratiform (non-convective) precipitation from the data.
   f. The convective hazard field scale uses six hazard levels to characterize hazardous convective conditions.

      1) The six hazard levels are determined by two factors:

         a) Intensities and maximum tops of radar reflectivity data and
         b) Frequencies of cloud-to-ground lightning.

      2) Higher hazard levels are associated with higher radar reflectivity intensities and higher frequencies of lightning strikes.
      3) The six hazard levels are reduced to four-color codes for display on the NCWF. The relationships between the six hazard levels and four-color codes are summarized below:

NCWF Hazard Scale		
Level	Color	Effect
6	RED	Thunderstorms may contain any or all
5	RED	of the following: severe turbulence, severe icing,
4	Orange	hail, frequent lightning, tornadoes, and low-level wind shear.
3	Yellow	The risk of hazardous weather generally increases
2	Green	with levels on the NCWF hazard scale
1	Green	

g. One-hour extrapolated forecast polygons.
   1) One-hour extrapolated forecast polygons are high-resolution polygons outlining areas expected to be filled by selected convective hazard fields in 1 hour.
   2) Extrapolated forecasts depict new locations for the convective hazard fields based on their past movements.
   3) Forecasts are provided only for convective hazard scale levels 3 or higher.
h. Forecast speed and direction.
   1) Forecast speed and direction are assigned to current convective hazard fields having a 1-hour extrapolated forecast.
   2) A line is used to depict the direction of movement.
i. Echo tops.
   1) Echo tops are assigned to current convective hazard fields having a 1-hour extrapolated forecast.
   2) Echo tops are depicted by a group of three numbers located near the current convective hazard field and are plotted in hundreds of feet MSL.
   3) The first number of the group identifies forecast speed of movement.
j. Previous performance polygons.
   1) Previous performance polygons are magenta polygons displaying the previous hour's extrapolated forecast polygons with the current convective hazard fields.
   2) A perfect forecast would have the polygons filled with convective hazard scale levels 3 or higher data.
   3) Levels 1 and 2 would be outside the polygons.
   4) The display of previous performance polygons allows the user to review the accuracy of the previous hour's forecast.
k. Strengths and limitations.
   1) Strengths of the NCWF include
      a) Convective hazard fields that agree very well with radar and lightning data,
      b) Updates every 5 minutes,
      c) High-resolution forecasts of convective hazards, and
      d) Long-lived convective precipitation is well forecast.

2) Limitations of the NCWF include the following:

   a) Initiation, growth, and decay of convective precipitation are not forecast.
   b) Short-lived or embedded convection may not be accurately displayed or forecast.
   c) Low-topped convection that contains little or no lightning may not be depicted.
   d) Erroneous motion vectors are occasionally assigned to storms.
   e) Convective hazard field scales are not identified within the forecast polygons.

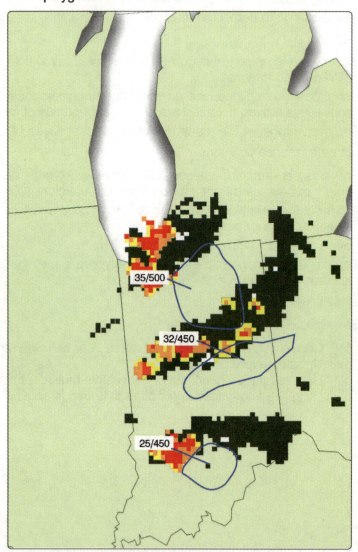

Figure 16. – Convective Weather Forecast.

6.26 CURRENT ICING POTENTIAL AND FORECAST ICING POTENTIAL

1. The current icing potential (CIP) and forecast icing potential (FIP) plots aid flight planning and situational awareness through graphical depiction of current and forecast icing conditions across an area or along a route of flight. This graphic can be found online at the Aviation Weather Center by selecting "Icing" in the Forecasts drop-down menu, then selecting the "Forecast Icing" image.

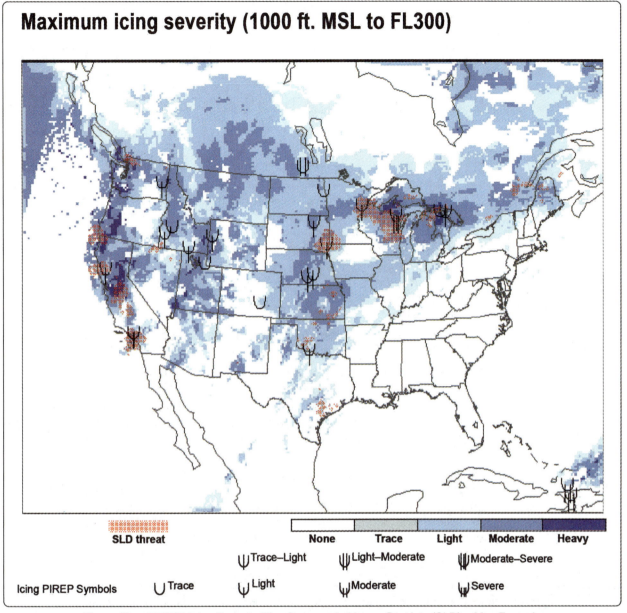

Figure 13. – CIP/FIP Icing Severity Plus Supercooled Large Droplets (SLD) – Max Example.

a. The figure above is a combined CIP and FIP plot. It is a graphics suite that consists of computer-generated three-dimensional analyses of information related to the likelihood of encountering icing conditions. In the combined graphic, the CIP represents the latest analysis of potential icing regions, and the FIP represents a forecast of anticipated icing conditions.

b. Information on the plot is determined from observational data, including radar, satellite, pilot weather reports, surface weather reports, lightning, and computer model output.

c. CIP/FIP is automatically produced with no human modifications. Thus, the information is intended for flight planning purposes only and always should be used in combination with icing information from all available sources including AIRMETs, SIGMETs, and PIREPs.

d. CIP/FIP provides information on expected icing severity in five categories: none, trace, light, moderate, and heavy.

1) The severity estimations are roughly based on the accretion rate of ice on an airplane, and the levels are determined by the time it would take for an airfoil to accrete 1/4 inch of ice:

   a) **Trace.** Ice becomes perceptible. Rate of accumulation slightly greater than sublimation. Expect 1/4 inch ice in **1 hour**. Deicing/anti-icing equipment is not expected to be utilized unless encountered for an extended period of time (over 1 hour).

   b) **Light.** The rate of accumulation to 1/4 inch of ice is expected between **15 minutes** and **1 hour**. The rate of accumulation may create a problem if flight is prolonged in this environment. Occasional use of deicing/anti-icing equipment removes/prevents accumulation. It does not present a problem if the deicing/anti-icing equipment is used.

   c) **Moderate.** The rate of accumulation (1/4 inch between **5 minutes to 15 minutes**) is such that even short encounters become potentially hazardous and use of deicing/anti-icing equipment or flight diversion is necessary.

   d) **Severe.** The rate of accumulation (1/4 inch in less than **5 minutes**) is such that deicing/anti-icing equipment fails to reduce or control the hazard. Immediate flight diversion is necessary.

2) The rates are estimated and are further tuned by nearby pilot reports of encountered severity.

3) These are relative values, the use of which should take into account the airframe and the level of icing protection provided by your specific aircraft. The ultimate safety factor is the vigilance demonstrated by you, the pilot, in potential icing situations.

4) Different aircraft and different flight configurations (airspeed, angle of attack, etc.) will experience variations in accretion rate. The rates above have been simulated for a range of aircraft and are a "broad brush" approach to severity prediction. They are presented here as guidance and supplement the primary forecasts produced as AIRMETs by the Aviation Weather Center.

QUESTIONS AND ANSWER EXPLANATIONS: All of the AGI/CFI knowledge test questions chosen by the FAA for release as well as additional questions selected by Gleim relating to the material in the previous outlines are reproduced on the following pages. These questions have been organized into the same subunits as the outlines. To the immediate right of each question are the correct answer and answer explanation. You should cover these answers and answer explanations while responding to the questions. Refer to the general discussion in the Introduction on how to take the FAA knowledge test.

Remember that the questions from the FAA knowledge test bank have been reordered by topic and organized into a meaningful sequence. Also, the first line of the answer explanation gives the citation of the authoritative source for the answer.

QUESTIONS

6.1 Causes of Weather

1. Which is the primary driving force of weather on the Earth?

A. The Sun.
B. Coriolis.
C. Rotation of the Earth.

Answer (A) is correct. *(AvW Chap 2)*
DISCUSSION: The primary driving force of weather is temperature variations. The Sun's unequal heating of the surface causes changes in temperature and pressure, which cause circulation and weather.
Answer (B) is incorrect. The Coriolis force describes the effect of the Earth's rotation on wind. Answer (C) is incorrect. The rotation of the Earth affects wind, but it is not the primary cause of weather.

2. What causes wind?

A. Coriolis force.
B. Pressure differences.
C. The rotation of the Earth.

Answer (B) is correct. *(AvW Chap 4)*
DISCUSSION: Wind is caused by pressure differences with wind flowing from high-pressure areas to low-pressure areas. These pressure differences arise from the different heating of the Earth's surface.
Answer (A) is incorrect. The Coriolis force describes the effect of the Earth's rotation on wind, which is to deflect it to the right in the Northern Hemisphere. Answer (C) is incorrect. The Earth's rotation is a factor in the Coriolis force, but does not cause wind.

3. Winds at 5,000 feet AGL on a particular flight are southwesterly while most of the surface winds are southerly. This difference in direction is primarily due to

A. local terrain effects on pressure.
B. stronger Coriolis force at the surface.
C. friction between the wind and the surface.

Answer (C) is correct. *(AvW Chap 4)*
DISCUSSION: Winds near the surface generally have a different direction from winds aloft. The surface friction slows the surface winds and decreases the Coriolis force, i.e., winds close to the surface generally flow more directly from areas of high pressure to areas of low pressure.
Answer (A) is incorrect. Pressure gradients are generally similar at low and higher altitudes. Answer (B) is incorrect. The Coriolis force is weaker, not stronger, at the surface since wind speeds are slowed by surface friction.

6.2 The Earth's Atmosphere

4. In what part of the atmosphere does most weather occur?

A. Tropopause.
B. Troposphere.
C. Stratosphere.

Answer (B) is correct. *(AvW Chap 1)*
DISCUSSION: The troposphere is the part of the atmosphere where most weather occurs. The troposphere is the layer from the surface to an average altitude of 7 mi.
Answer (A) is incorrect. The tropopause is the thin layer marking the boundary between the troposphere and the stratosphere. Answer (C) is incorrect. The stratosphere is characterized by relatively small changes in temperature with height. Little weather occurs at this level.

6.3 High-Low Pressure

5. The general circulation of air associated with a high-pressure area in the Northern Hemisphere is

A. inward, upward, and clockwise.
B. outward, downward, and clockwise.
C. outward, upward, and counterclockwise.

Answer (B) is correct. *(AvW Chap 4)*
DISCUSSION: In the Northern Hemisphere, winds in high-pressure systems flow clockwise while low-pressure systems have winds that flow counterclockwise. Also, in a high-pressure system, the air flow is downward and outward.
Answer (A) is incorrect. The general circulation of high-pressure air in the Northern Hemisphere is outward, not inward, and downward, not upward. Answer (C) is incorrect. The circulation of high-pressure air in the Northern Hemisphere is downward, not upward, and clockwise, not counterclockwise.

6. When flying from a high- to a low-pressure area in the Northern Hemisphere, the wind direction and velocity will be from the

   A. left and increasing.
   B. left and decreasing.
   C. right and increasing.

Answer (A) is correct. *(AvW Chap 4)*
DISCUSSION: When flying into a low-pressure area, the wind is flowing counterclockwise and thus will be from the left. Also, winds tend to be greater in low-pressure systems than high-pressure systems, so the velocity will increase as you fly into the area.
Answer (B) is incorrect. The wind is usually increasing, not decreasing, as you fly into a low-pressure area. Answer (C) is incorrect. The wind flow in a low-pressure area is counterclockwise and would be from the left, not right.

7. The windflow around a low pressure is

   A. cyclonic.
   B. adiabatic.
   C. anticyclonic.

Answer (A) is correct. *(AvW Chap 4)*
DISCUSSION: The wind around a low-pressure system blows counterclockwise, i.e., it is a cyclonic wind system.
Answer (B) is incorrect. Adiabatic relates to the cooling of air as it rises. Answer (C) is incorrect. Anticyclonic describes a high-pressure system.

8. In the Northern Hemisphere, a pilot making a long distance flight from east to west would most likely find favorable winds associated with high- and low-pressure systems by flying to the

   A. north of a high and a low.
   B. north of a high and to the south of a low.
   C. south of a high and to the north of a low.

Answer (C) is correct. *(AvW Chap 4)*
DISCUSSION: Because winds associated with a high-pressure system flow clockwise, you should fly south of a high when going east to west. Thus, you would be flying with a tailwind. Winds associated with a low-pressure system flow counterclockwise, so you would fly north of a low on an east to west flight to get a tailwind.
Answer (A) is incorrect. On an east to west flight, you should fly south, not north, of a high-pressure system. Answer (B) is incorrect. On a flight from west to east, not east to west, you would most likely find favorable winds by flying to the north of a high and to the south of a low.

9. Which is true regarding the development of convective circulation?

   A. Cool air must sink to force the warm air upward.
   B. Warm air is less dense and rises on its own accord.
   C. Cool air surrounding convective circulation sinks at a greater rate than the warmer air rises (within the thermal), thus forcing the warmer air upward.

Answer (A) is correct. *(AvW Chap 4)*
DISCUSSION: The cooler, denser air is drawn to the ground by its greater gravitational force, forcing the warm air upward.
Answer (B) is incorrect. Warm air rises because it is displaced by the heavier, colder air. Answer (C) is incorrect. Warm air rises at the same rate as cold air sinks.

10. Convective circulation patterns associated with sea breezes are caused by

    A. land absorbing and radiating heat faster than the water.
    B. warm and less dense air moving inland from over the water, causing it to rise.
    C. cool and less dense air moving inland from over the water, causing it to rise.

Answer (A) is correct. *(PHAK Chap 7)*
DISCUSSION: Sea breezes are caused by cooler and denser air moving inland off the water. Once over the warmer land, the air heats and rises. Currents push the hot air over the water where it cools and descends, starting the cycle over again.
Answer (B) is incorrect. The air over the water is cooler, not warmer, and denser, not less dense. Answer (C) is incorrect. The cool air moving inland is denser, not less dense, and it rises after it is warmed, not while it is cool.

11. Select the true statement concerning thermals.

    A. Strong thermals have proportionately increased sink in the air between them.
    B. Thermals will not develop unless the Sun's rays strike the Earth at a vertical angle.
    C. A thermal invariably remains directly above the surface area from which it developed.

Answer (A) is correct. *(AvW Chap 16)*
DISCUSSION: Thermals have proportionally increased sink in the air between them. Rising warm air displaces cooler air, which descends between the thermals.
Answer (B) is incorrect. Thermals develop whenever the Sun's rays warm the Earth unevenly. Answer (C) is incorrect. Thermals are moved by wind.

12. Which statement is true regarding high- or low-pressure systems?

A. A high-pressure area or ridge is an area of rising air.
B. A low-pressure area or trough is an area of rising air.
C. A high-pressure area is a trough of descending air.

Answer (B) is correct. *(AvW Chap 4)*
DISCUSSION: Low-pressure air rises because it weighs less than high-pressure air. Trough refers to an elongated area of low pressure.
Answer (A) is incorrect. High-pressure air descends, not rises. Answer (C) is incorrect. A trough is associated with a low-pressure area.

6.4 Dew Point and Fog

13. The ratio of the existing water vapor in the air, as compared to the maximum amount that could exist at a given temperature, is called

A. the dewpoint.
B. saturation point.
C. relative humidity.

Answer (C) is correct. *(AvW Chap 5)*
DISCUSSION: Air temperature determines how much water vapor can be held by the air. Warm air can hold more water vapor than cold air. The relative humidity is the amount of water being held by the air relative to the amount of water that could be held at that temperature.
Answer (A) is incorrect. The dewpoint is the temperature to which air must be cooled to become saturated. Answer (B) is incorrect. The saturation point is the condition of the atmosphere when actual water vapor present is the maximum possible at existing temperature, i.e., 100% humidity.

14. Which is an operational consideration regarding actual air temperature and dewpoint temperature spread?

A. The temperature spread decreases as the relative humidity decreases.
B. The temperature spread decreases as the relative humidity increases.
C. The temperature spread increases as the relative humidity increases.

Answer (B) is correct. *(AvW Chap 5)*
DISCUSSION: Air is saturated with moisture when its temperature declines to its dewpoint. Thus, as the temperature spread decreases, the relative humidity increases.
Answer (A) is incorrect. When the relative humidity decreases, the temperature spread between temperature and dewpoint increases, not decreases. Answer (C) is incorrect. As relative humidity increases, the temperature spread between dewpoint and temperature decreases, not increases.

15. One condition necessary for the formation of fog is

A. calm air.
B. visible moisture.
C. high relative humidity.

Answer (C) is correct. *(AvW Chap 12)*
DISCUSSION: Fog is moisture-saturated air, i.e., high relative humidity.
Answer (A) is incorrect. Wind is necessary to form advection fog and upslope fog. Answer (B) is incorrect. The humidity is invisible until the fog forms, when it becomes visible.

16. Fog associated with a warm front is a result of saturation due to

A. nocturnal cooling.
B. evaporation of precipitation.
C. evaporation of surface moisture.

Answer (B) is correct. *(AvW Chap 12)*
DISCUSSION: A warm front describes a situation whereby warm air overrides cooler air. When relatively warm rain or drizzle falls through cool air, evaporation from the precipitation saturates the cool air and forms fog.
Answer (A) is incorrect. Nocturnal cooling generally produces radiation fog. Answer (C) is incorrect. Evaporation of surface moisture can help create the conditions for radiation fog by adding moisture to the air.

17. You may anticipate fog when the temperature-dew point spread is

A. 15°F or less and decreasing.
B. 15°F or more and increasing.
C. 5°F or less and decreasing.

Answer (C) is correct. *(AvW Chap 12)*
DISCUSSION: The temperature-dew point spread provides the difference in temperature between the air temperature and the dew point. The dew point is the point where air is cooled enough to become saturated by water vapor that is already present in that air. As the temperature and dew point converge, fog, clouds, or rain should be anticipated. Therefore, one should be alert for the development of fog when temperature-dew point spread is 3°C (5°F) or less and decreasing.
Answer (A) is incorrect. A 15°F difference between the air temperature and dew point for the air to become saturated by the water vapor is not enough to be concerned about the development of fog. This is especially true if the temperature-dew point spread is 15°F and increasing. Answer (B) is incorrect. A 15°F difference between the air temperature and dew point for the air to become saturated by the water vapor is not enough to be concerned about the development of fog. While this temperature-dew point spread is 15°F and decreasing, the temperature needs to decrease by more than 10°F to become concerned about the development of fog.

18. What is the process by which ice can form on a surface directly from water vapor on a cold, clear night?

A. Sublimation.
B. Condensation.
C. Supersaturation.

Answer (A) is correct. *(AvW Chap 5)*
DISCUSSION: Although deposition is the changing of ice into water vapor, the FAA sometimes incorrectly interchanges sublimation for deposition.
Answer (B) is incorrect. Condensation is the conversion of gas into liquid. Answer (C) is incorrect. Supersaturation is the existence of excess water in the air.

19. Radiation fog is most likely to occur under what conditions?

A. Warm, moist air being forced upslope by light winds resulting in the air being cooled and condensed.
B. High humidity during the early evening, cool cloudless night with light winds, and favorable topography.
C. Low temperature/dewpoint spread, calm wind conditions, the presence of hydroscopic nuclei, low overcast, and favorable topography.

Answer (B) is correct. *(AvW Chap 12)*
DISCUSSION: When the air near the ground is 4°F or 5°F above dewpoint, the water vapor condenses and becomes fog. Radiation fog most often occurs when there is high humidity, cool cloudless nights with light winds, and favorable topography (such as low-lying areas, like mountain valleys).
Answer (A) is incorrect. Upslope, not radiation, fog is most likely to occur when warm, moist air is forced upslope by light winds, resulting in the air being cooled and condensed. Answer (C) is incorrect. A low overcast would preclude the ground from cooling sufficiently to cool the air at the surface.

20. Advection fog is formed as a result of

A. moist air moving over a colder surface.
B. the addition of moisture to a mass of cold air as it moves over a body of water.
C. the ground cooling adjacent air to the dewpoint temperature on clear, calm nights.

Answer (A) is correct. *(AvW Chap 12)*
DISCUSSION: Advection fog can appear suddenly during the day or night and is more persistent than radiation fog. It forms as a result of moist air moving over a colder surface.
Answer (B) is incorrect. Advection fog is formed as already moist air moves over a colder surface (body of water or the ground), not by the addition of moisture to a mass of cold air. Answer (C) is incorrect. Radiation, not advection, fog is formed as a result of the ground cooling adjacent air to the dewpoint temperature on clear, calm nights.

21. With respect to advection fog, which statement is true?

A. It forms almost exclusively at night or near daybreak.
B. It forms when unstable air is cooled adiabatically.
C. It can appear suddenly during day or night, and it is more persistent than radiation fog.

Answer (C) is correct. *(AvW Chap 12)*
DISCUSSION: Advection fog is usually more extensive and much more persistent than radiation fog. Advection fog can form rapidly regardless of the time of day or night.
Answer (A) is incorrect. Radiation, not advection, fog forms almost exclusively at night or near daybreak. Answer (B) is incorrect. Upslope, not advection, fog forms when stable, not unstable, air is cooled adiabatically as it moves up sloping terrain.

SU 6: Aviation Weather

22. Which in-flight hazard is most commonly associated with warm fronts?

A. Ground fog.
B. Advection fog.
C. Precipitation-induced fog.

Answer (C) is correct. *(AvW Chap 12)*
DISCUSSION: Precipitation-induced fog arises from drops of warm rain or drizzle evaporating as it falls through cool air. This evaporation saturates the cool air and forms fog. This kind of fog can become quite dense and continue for an extended period of time. It is most commonly associated with warm fronts.
Answer (A) is incorrect. Ground fog is a type of radiation fog that occurs on cool, still, cloudless nights. Answer (B) is incorrect. Advection fog results from the transport of warm, humid air over a colder surface.

23. When warm air moves over a cold lake, what weather phenomenon is likely to occur on the leeward side of the lake?

A. Fog.
B. Showers.
C. Cloudiness.

Answer (A) is correct. *(AvW Chap 5)*
DISCUSSION: When warm air moves over a cold lake, the air next to the surface is cooled to its dewpoint and fog forms. Fog often becomes extensive and dense to the leeward (downwind) side of the lake.
Answer (B) is incorrect. Showers develop over the leeward side of a lake when cold air moves over the warm lake. Answer (C) is incorrect. The warm air moving over a cold lake cools, and there is no convective development that would produce clouds.

6.5 Temperature Lapse Rate

24. What are the standard temperature and pressure values for mean sea level?

A. 15°F and 29.92" Hg.
B. 59°C and 29.92 mb.
C. 59°F and 1013.2 mb.

Answer (C) is correct. *(AvW Chap 3)*
DISCUSSION: The standard temperature and pressure at mean sea level are 15°C and 29.92 in. Hg, which is the same as 59°F and 1013.2 mb.
Answer (A) is incorrect. The 15° should be Celsius, not Fahrenheit. Answer (B) is incorrect. The 59° should be Fahrenheit, not Celsius, and 29.92 should be inches of mercury, not millibars.

25. If the air temperature is +6°C at an elevation of 700 feet and a standard (average) temperature lapse rate exists, what will be the approximate freezing level?

A. 6,700 feet MSL.
B. 3,700 feet MSL.
C. 2,700 feet MSL.

Answer (B) is correct. *(AvW Chap 2)*
DISCUSSION: If the air temperature is +6°C at 700 ft., the freezing level is expected to be 3,700 ft. because the standard lapse rate is 2°C per 1,000 ft. Thus, at another 3,000 ft., the freezing level of 0°C will be reached.
Answer (A) is incorrect. The standard lapse rate is 2°C per 1,000 ft., not 1°C per 1,000 ft. Answer (C) is incorrect. The standard lapse rate is 2°C per 1,000 ft., not 3°C per 1,000 ft.

26. If the air temperature is +12°C at an elevation of 1,250 feet and a standard (average) temperature lapse rate exists, what will be the approximate freezing level?

A. 7,250 feet MSL.
B. 5,250 feet MSL.
C. 4,250 feet MSL.

Answer (A) is correct. *(AvW Chap 2)*
DISCUSSION: With a standard lapse rate of 2°C per 1,000 ft., an additional 6,000 ft. will reduce the temperature from +12°C to 0°C. Given that it is +12°C at 1,250 ft., the approximate freezing level would be 7,250 ft.
Answer (B) is incorrect. The standard lapse rate is 2°C per 1,000 ft., not 3°C per 1,000 ft. Answer (C) is incorrect. The standard lapse rate is 2° per 1,000 ft., not 4° per 1,000 ft.

27. The most frequent type of ground- or surface-based temperature inversion is that produced by

A. terrestrial radiation on a clear, relatively still night.
B. warm air being lifted rapidly aloft in the vicinity of mountainous terrain.
C. the movement of colder air under warm air or the movement of warm air over cold air.

Answer (A) is correct. *(AvW Chap 2)*
DISCUSSION: A temperature inversion occurs when the temperature becomes warmer with increases in altitude rather than cooler. A ground- or surface-based temperature inversion is produced when the air near the surface is cooled as a result of radiation of surface heat on a clear, still night. Thus, the air very close to the surface becomes cooler than the air a few hundred feet above.
Answer (B) is incorrect. When warm air is lifted rapidly aloft in mountainous terrain, upslope fog is produced. Answer (C) is incorrect. It describes temperature inversions aloft, not ground-based.

28. Which weather conditions should be expected beneath a low-level temperature inversion layer when the relative humidity is high?

A. Light wind shear and poor visibility due to light rain.
B. Smooth air and poor visibility due to fog, haze, or low clouds.
C. Turbulent air and poor visibility due to fog, low stratus type clouds, and showery precipitation.

Answer (B) is correct. *(AvW Chap 6)*
DISCUSSION: Low-level inversions mean that there is cool air near the surface beneath warmer air so there is no lifting; i.e., conditions are stable. The result is smooth air with poor visibility, especially fog given high relative humidity and smog when pollutants are trapped.
Answer (A) is incorrect. Wind shear would be found near the top of, not beneath, a low-level temperature inversion. Answer (C) is incorrect. Turbulent air and showery precipitation occur when there is instability, not in the stable conditions produced by a temperature inversion.

29. At approximately what altitude above the surface would you expect the base of cumuliform clouds if the surface air temperature is 77°F and the dewpoint is 53°F?

A. 9,600 feet AGL.
B. 8,000 feet AGL.
C. 5,500 feet AGL.

Answer (C) is correct. *(AvW Chap 6)*
DISCUSSION: The height of cumuliform cloud bases can be estimated using surface temperature/dewpoint spread. Unsaturated air in a convective current cools at about 5.4°F per 1,000 ft., and dewpoint decreases about 1°F per 1,000 ft. This means that temperature and dewpoint converge at about 4.4°F per 1,000 ft. (2.5°C per 1,000 ft.). Thus, if the temperature/dewpoint spread were 24°F (77° − 53°), temperature and dewpoint would converge at about 5,500 ft. AGL, causing the formation of cumuliform clouds.
Answer (A) is incorrect. This is determined by incorrectly using a temperature and dewpoint convergence of 2.5°F, not 2.5°C, per 1,000 ft. Answer (B) is incorrect. The base of cumuliform clouds would be expected at 8,000 ft. AGL if the temperature/dewpoint spread were 35°F, not 24°F.

30. At approximately what altitude above the surface would you expect the base of cumuliform clouds if the surface air temperature is 33°C and the dewpoint is 15°C?

A. 4,100 feet AGL.
B. 6,000 feet AGL.
C. 7,200 feet AGL.

Answer (C) is correct. *(AvW Chap 6)*
DISCUSSION: The height of cumuliform cloud bases can be estimated using surface temperature/dewpoint spread. Unsaturated air in a convective current cools at about 5.4°F per 1,000 ft., and dewpoint decreases about 1°F per 1,000 ft. This means that temperature and dewpoint converge at about 4.4°F per 1,000 ft. (2.5°C per 1,000 ft.). Thus, if the temperature/dewpoint spread were 18°C (33° − 15°), temperature and dewpoint would converge at about 7,200 ft. AGL (18°C ÷ 2.5°C per 1,000 ft.), causing the formation of cumuliform clouds.
Answer (A) is incorrect. This is determined by incorrectly using a temperature and dewpoint convergence of 4.4°C, not 4.4°F, per 1,000 ft. Answer (B) is incorrect. The base of cumuliform clouds would be expected at 6,000 ft. AGL if the temperature/dewpoint spread were 15°C, not 18°C.

31. The average lapse rate in the troposphere is

A. 2.0°C per 1,000 feet.
B. 3.0°C per 1,000 feet.
C. 5.4°C per 1,000 feet.

Answer (A) is correct. *(AvW Chap 2)*
DISCUSSION: The average lapse rate in the troposphere is 2°C per 1,000 ft.
Answer (B) is incorrect. The dry, not average, adiabatic rate of temperature change is 3.0°C. Answer (C) is incorrect. The dry, not average, adiabatic rate is 5.4°F, not °C.

6.6 Stability of Air Masses

32. From which measurement of the atmosphere can stability be determined?

A. Ambient lapse rate.
B. Atmospheric pressure.
C. Difference between standard temperature and surface temperature.

Answer (A) is correct. *(AvW Chap 6)*
DISCUSSION: The ambient lapse rate is the rate of decrease in temperature with height. A great decrease encourages warm air from below to rise. This lifting action creates instability. In a stable situation, there is less temperature decrease with altitude and little or no tendency for lifting.
Answer (B) is incorrect. Atmospheric pressure relates to larger air masses and their horizontal components. Answer (C) is incorrect. Stability relates to changes in temperatures between altitudes, not actual vs. standard temperature at the surface.

SU 6: Aviation Weather

33. What is a characteristic of stable air?

A. Excellent visibility.
B. Restricted visibility.
C. Showery-type precipitation.

Answer (B) is correct. *(AvW Chap 8)*
DISCUSSION: Stable air means there is no vertical development, and fog, haze, smoke, or steady precipitation may restrict visibility.
Answer (A) is incorrect. Excellent visibility is a characteristic of an unstable, not a stable, air mass. Answer (C) is incorrect. Showery-type precipitation is a characteristic of an unstable, not a stable, air mass.

34. What is a typical characteristic of a stable air mass?

A. Cumuliform clouds.
B. Showery precipitation.
C. Continuous precipitation.

Answer (C) is correct. *(AvW Chap 8)*
DISCUSSION: Stable air results in no vertical development, i.e., clouds form in horizontal levels. As entire layers are cooled to their dewpoint, steady and continuous precipitation usually occurs.
Answer (A) is incorrect. Cumuliform clouds are a characteristic of an unstable, not a stable, air mass. Answer (B) is incorrect. Showery precipitation is a characteristic of an unstable, not a stable, air mass.

35. A moist, warm air mass that is being cooled from below is characterized, in part, by

A. smooth air.
B. cumuliform clouds.
C. showers and thunderstorms.

Answer (A) is correct. *(AvW Chap 8)*
DISCUSSION: A warm, moist air mass that is being cooled from below generates stability and produces smooth air. The cooling inhibits rising air (vertical development).
Answer (B) is incorrect. Cumuliform clouds are a characteristic of an unstable, not a stable, air mass. Answer (C) is incorrect. Showers and thunderstorms are characteristics of an unstable, not a stable, air mass.

36. A moist, cold air mass that is being warmed from below is characterized, in part, by

A. fog and drizzle.
B. showers and thunderstorms.
C. continuous heavy precipitation.

Answer (B) is correct. *(AvW Chap 8)*
DISCUSSION: A moist, cold air mass being warmed from below is an unstable air mass and results in showers and thunderstorms.
Answer (A) is incorrect. Fog and drizzle are characteristics of a stable, not an unstable, air mass. Answer (C) is incorrect. Continuous precipitation, whether heavy or not, is a characteristic of a stable, not an unstable, air mass.

37. Cool air moving over a warm surface is generally characterized by

A. instability and showers.
B. stability, fog, and drizzle.
C. instability and continuous precipitation.

Answer (A) is correct. *(AvW Chap 8)*
DISCUSSION: Cool air moving over a warm surface becomes warmed from below and is therefore an unstable air mass characterized by showery precipitation, good visibility, turbulent air, and cumuliform clouds.
Answer (B) is incorrect. Stability, fog, and drizzle are characteristics of a stable, not an unstable, air mass. Answer (C) is incorrect. Continuous precipitation is a characteristic of a stable, not an unstable, air mass.

38. Consider the following air mass characteristics:
1. Cumuliform clouds.
2. Stable lapse rate.
3. Unstable lapse rate.
4. Stratiform clouds and fog.
5. Smooth air (above the friction level) and poor visibility.
6. Turbulence up to about 10,000 feet and good visibility except in areas of precipitation.

A moist air mass, which is colder than the surface over which it passes, frequently has which of the above characteristics?

A. 1, 3, and 6.
B. 3, 4, and 5.
C. 2, 4, and 5.

Answer (A) is correct. *(AvW Chap 8)*
DISCUSSION: If a moist air mass moves over a warm surface, lifting action is induced, which results in instability, turbulence, and cumulus clouds. These are all indications of an unstable air mass.
Answer (B) is incorrect. Stratiform clouds and fog and smooth air and poor visibility are characteristics of stable, not unstable, air. Answer (C) is incorrect. Stable lapse rate, stratiform clouds, and fog and smooth air and poor visibility are characteristics of a moist air mass that is warmer, not colder, than the surface over which it passes.

39. The weather condition normally associated with unstable air is

A. stratiform clouds.
B. fair to poor visibility.
C. good visibility.

Answer (C) is correct. *(AvW Chap 8)*
DISCUSSION: Unstable air means there is a lifting action. Thus, warmer air near the surface rises and mixes up or carries away inhibitors to good visibility like fog, smoke, and haze.
Answer (A) is incorrect. Stratiform clouds are characteristics of stable, not unstable, air conditions. Answer (B) is incorrect. Fair to poor visibility is a characteristic of stable, not unstable, air conditions.

40. A moist, unstable air mass is characterized by

A. poor visibility and smooth air.
B. cumuliform clouds and showery precipitation.
C. stratiform clouds and continuous precipitation.

Answer (B) is correct. *(AvW Chap 8)*
DISCUSSION: Moist, unstable air forms vertically developed clouds (cumuliform), resulting in showery precipitation.
Answer (A) is incorrect. Poor visibility and smooth air are characteristics of a stable, not an unstable, air mass. Answer (C) is incorrect. Stratiform clouds and continuous precipitation are characteristics of a stable, not an unstable, air mass.

41. What type weather can one expect from moist, unstable air and very warm surface temperature?

A. Fog and low stratus clouds.
B. Continuous heavy precipitation.
C. Strong updrafts and cumulonimbus clouds.

Answer (C) is correct. *(AvW Chap 8)*
DISCUSSION: Moist air moving over a warm surface that is heated from below produces updrafts. Cumulonimbus clouds can form under these circumstances and produce both strong updrafts and strong downdrafts.
Answer (A) is incorrect. Fog and low stratus clouds are characteristics of a stable, not an unstable, air mass. Answer (B) is incorrect. Continuous precipitation, whether heavy or not, is a characteristic of a stable, not an unstable, air mass.

42. If clouds form as a result of very stable, moist air being forced to ascend a mountain slope, the clouds will be

A. cirrus type with no vertical development or turbulence.
B. cumulonimbus with considerable vertical development and heavy rains.
C. stratus type with little vertical development and little or no turbulence.

Answer (C) is correct. *(AvW Chap 6)*
DISCUSSION: Very stable air flowing upslope produces stratified clouds as it cools. Stable air resists upward movement and thus there would be very little vertical development and no turbulence.
Answer (A) is incorrect. Cirrus clouds are high clouds. Answer (B) is incorrect. Cumulonimbus clouds with vertical development indicate unstable, not stable, air.

43. The formation of either predominantly stratiform or predominantly cumuliform clouds is dependent upon the

A. source of lift.
B. stability of the air being lifted.
C. percent of moisture content of the air being lifted.

Answer (B) is correct. *(AvW Chap 6)*
DISCUSSION: Clouds formed by vertical currents in unstable air are cumulus clouds. Clouds formed by cooling of a stable layer are stratus clouds. Thus, the stability of the air, i.e., the absence or presence of lifting action, determines whether clouds are cumuliform or stratiform.
Answer (A) is incorrect. Stratiform clouds can form without a source of lift. Answer (C) is incorrect. Stratiform clouds can form without being lifted.

6.7 Temperature Inversion

44. Convective SIGMETs are issued for which weather conditions?

A. Any thunderstorm with a severity level of VIP 2 or more.
B. Cumulonimbus clouds with tops above the tropopause and thunderstorms with 1/2-inch hail or funnel clouds.
C. Embedded thunderstorms, lines of thunderstorms, and thunderstorms with 3/4 inch hail or tornadoes.

Answer (C) is correct. *(AWS Sect 3)*
DISCUSSION: Convective SIGMETs are issued for (1) severe thunderstorm due to surface winds greater than 50 kt., hail at the surface equal to or greater than 3/4 in. in diameter, or tornadoes; (2) embedded thunderstorms; (3) line of thunderstorms; or (4) thunderstorms greater than or equal to VIP level 4 affecting 40% or more of an area at least 3,000 square mi.
Answer (A) is incorrect. Thunderstorms must be at least VIP level 4, not level 2. Answer (B) is incorrect. Cumulonimbus clouds with tops above the tropopause is not a weather condition covered in a convective SIGMET.

SU 6: Aviation Weather

45. A surface inversion can

   A. indicate the chance of gusty winds.
   B. produce poor visibility.
   C. mean an unstable air mass.

Answer (B) is correct. *(AvW Chaps 2, 6)*
   DISCUSSION: A temperature inversion is defined as an increase in temperature with height; i.e., the normal lapse rate is inverted. Thus, any warm air rises to its own temperature and forms a stable layer of air. Inversions may occur at any altitude and are common in the stratosphere. An inversion often develops near the ground on clear, cool nights when the wind is relatively calm. The ground radiates heat and cools much faster than the overlying air. Air in contact with the ground becomes cold, while the temperature a few hundred feet above changes very little. A ground-based inversion is characterized by poor visibility as a result of trapping fog, smoke, and other restrictions into low levels of the atmosphere.
   Answer (A) is incorrect. Gusty winds result from instability. They do not occur when there is a temperature inversion. Answer (C) is incorrect. Instability occurs when the temperature decreases, not increases as in a temperature inversion, with an increase in altitude and continuing rising air.

46. An increase in temperature with an altitude increase

   A. is indication of an inversion.
   B. denotes the beginning of the stratosphere.
   C. means a cold front passage.

Answer (A) is correct. *(AvW Chap 2)*
   DISCUSSION: A temperature inversion is simply any time the correlation of altitude and temperature changes. That is, if temperature at first increases when altitude increases, and later temperature decreases when altitude increases, an inversion has occurred, and vice versa.
   Answer (B) is incorrect. The stratosphere layer is typified by relatively small changes in temperature with height except for a warming trend near the top. Answer (C) is incorrect. A cold front passage is usually indicated by a colder temperature and an increase in pressure, not an altitude increase.

6.8 Weather Fronts

47. Frontal waves normally form on

   A. stationary or occluded fronts.
   B. slow-moving warm fronts or occluded fronts.
   C. slow-moving cold fronts or stationary fronts.

Answer (C) is correct. *(AvW Chap 8)*
   DISCUSSION: Frontal waves and cyclones (areas of low pressure) usually form on slow-moving cold fronts or on stationary fronts.
   Answer (A) is incorrect. An occluded front is comprised of two fronts as a cold front overtakes a warm front. It normally does not result in a frontal wave. Answer (B) is incorrect. An occluded front is comprised of two fronts as a cold front overtakes a warm front. It normally does not result in a frontal wave, nor do frontal waves form on slow-moving warm fronts.

48. If a wave were to form on a stationary front running east and west across the United States, that portion east of the wave would normally

   A. remain stationary with that portion west of the wave becoming a cold front.
   B. become a warm front and that portion west of the wave would become a cold front.
   C. become a cold front and that portion west of the wave would become a warm front.

Answer (B) is correct. *(AvW Chap 8)*
   DISCUSSION: When a wave occurs on a stationary front, it is a low that circulates counterclockwise; the front to the west of the low forms a cold front; and the front to the east becomes a warm front.
   Answer (A) is incorrect. The front to the east of the wave becomes a warm front rather than remaining stationary. Answer (C) is incorrect. The front to the east becomes a warm front, not a cold front, and the portion west of the wave becomes a cold front, not a warm front.

49. What type weather is associated with an advancing warm front that has moist, unstable air?

   A. Stratiform clouds, lightning, steady precipitation.
   B. Cumuliform clouds, smooth air, steady precipitation.
   C. Cumuliform clouds, turbulent air, showery-type precipitation.

Answer (C) is correct. *(AvW Chap 8)*
   DISCUSSION: Unstable moist air produces cumuliform clouds, turbulent air, and showery-type precipitation.
   Answer (A) is incorrect. Stratiform clouds and steady precipitation are characteristics of stable, not unstable, air. Answer (B) is incorrect. Smooth air and steady precipitation are characteristics of stable, not unstable, air.

50. Which statement is true regarding a cold front occlusion?

A. The air ahead of the warm front is warmer than the air behind the overtaking cold front.
B. The air ahead of the warm front has the same temperature as the air behind the overtaking cold front.
C. The air between the warm front and cold front is colder than either the air ahead of the warm front or the air behind the overtaking cold front.

Answer (A) is correct. *(AvW Chap 8)*
DISCUSSION: A cold front occlusion occurs when the air behind the cold front is colder than the air in advance of the warm front. This lifts the warm air aloft.
Answer (B) is incorrect. The air ahead of the warm front must be warmer than the air behind the overtaking cold front. Answer (C) is incorrect. The air between the warm front and the cold front must be warmer than the air behind the overtaking cold front.

6.9 Turbulence and Wind Shear

51. Consider the following statements about mountain waves:

1. Mountain waves always develop in a series on the upwind (windward) side of mountain ridges.
2. In a mountain wave, the air dips sharply downward immediately to the lee side of a ridge, before rising and falling in a wave motion for a considerable distance downstream.
3. If the air is humid and the wave is of large amplitude, lenticular (lens-shaped) clouds mark the wave's crest.
4. In a typical wave, the greatest amplitude is seldom more than 1,000 feet above the ridge crest elevation.

From the statements above, select those that are true.

A. 2 and 3.
B. 1, 2, and 3.
C. 1, 3, and 4.

Answer (A) is correct. *(AvW Chap 9)*
DISCUSSION: Mountain waves describe the movement when a strong wind passes over a mountain causing a good deal of turbulence on the downwind side. The turbulence may be marked by stationary, lens-shaped clouds known as standing lenticular clouds. The wave crest can extend well above the highest mountain, sometimes into the lower stratosphere.
Answer (B) is incorrect. Mountain waves develop on the downwind, not upwind, side of mountain ridges. Answer (C) is incorrect. Mountain waves always develop on the downwind, not upwind, side of mountains, and the wave crest may extend into the lower stratosphere.

52. One of the most dangerous features of mountain waves is the turbulent areas in and

A. below rotor clouds.
B. above rotor clouds.
C. below lenticular clouds.

Answer (A) is correct. *(AvW Chap 9)*
DISCUSSION: Mountain waves create wave crests that can extend downwind for 100 mi. or more from the mountain. Underneath each wave crest is a rotary circulation called a rotor. This rotor can create violent turbulence. If you get into a rotor downdraft and you are below a rotor cloud, you can be forced down to the surface.
Answer (B) is incorrect. While the turbulence above rotor clouds can be very dangerous, you are not threatened with a crash into the surface. Answer (C) is incorrect. While the turbulence below lenticular clouds can be very dangerous, you are not threatened with a crash into the surface.

53. When flying low over hilly terrain, ridges, or mountain ranges, the greatest potential danger from turbulent air currents will usually be encountered on the

A. leeward side when flying with the wind.
B. leeward side when flying into the wind.
C. windward side when flying into the wind.

Answer (B) is correct. *(AvW Chap 9)*
DISCUSSION: When wind flows over ridges or mountain ranges, it flows up the windward side and down the leeward side. Thus, a pilot who approaches mountainous terrain from the leeward side may be forced into the side of the mountain by the downward-flowing air.
Answer (A) is incorrect. When flying with the wind, you are flying away from the obstruction. Answer (C) is incorrect. When flying into the wind on the windward side, you are flying away from the obstruction.

54. The conditions most favorable to wave formation over mountainous areas are a layer of

A. unstable air at mountaintop altitude and a wind of at least 15 to 25 knots blowing across the ridge.
B. stable air at mountaintop altitude and a wind of at least 15 to 25 knots blowing across the ridge.
C. moist, unstable air at mountaintop altitude and a wind of less than 5 knots blowing across the ridge.

Answer (B) is correct. *(AvW Chap 16)*
DISCUSSION: The conditions most favorable to wave formation over mountainous areas are a layer of stable air at mountaintop altitude and a wind of at least 15 to 25 kt. (depending on the height of the ridge) blowing across the ridge.
Answer (A) is incorrect. The air must be stable, not unstable. Answer (C) is incorrect. The air must be stable, not unstable, and the wind must be at least 15 to 25 kt.

55. Low-level wind shear, which results in a sudden change of wind direction, may occur

A. after a warm front has passed.
B. when surface winds are light and variable.
C. when there is a low-level temperature inversion with strong winds above the inversion.

Answer (C) is correct. *(AvW Chap 9)*
DISCUSSION: A low-level wind shear may occur when a temperature inversion forms near the surface, with strong winds above the inversion.
Answer (A) is incorrect. Low-level wind shear is usually associated with cold, not warm, fronts. Answer (B) is incorrect. There must be a temperature inversion with strong winds above the inversion, not only light and variable surface winds.

56. Which condition could be expected if a strong temperature inversion exists near the surface?

A. Strong, steady downdrafts and an increase in OAT.
B. A wind shear with the possibility of a sudden loss of airspeed.
C. An OAT increase or decrease with a constant wind condition.

Answer (B) is correct. *(AvW Chap 9)*
DISCUSSION: A low-level temperature inversion results in relatively calm air near the surface. When there are strong winds above the inversion, there is a strong wind shear between the calm air and the high winds just above. Because surface wind is calm or very light, takeoff or landing can be in any direction. If takeoff is in the direction of the wind above the inversion, the aircraft encounters a sudden tailwind and corresponding loss of airspeed.
Answer (A) is incorrect. A temperature inversion does not have updrafts or downdrafts. Answer (C) is incorrect. In a temperature inversion, the outside air temperature increases, not decreases, and the wind may well differ on both sides of the inversion.

57. In reference to clear air turbulence (CAT), areas to be avoided are those where horizontal wind shear exceeds

A. 40 knots per 150 miles.
B. 10 knots per 50 miles.
C. 6 knots per 1,000 feet.

Answer (A) is correct. *(AvW Chap 13)*
DISCUSSION: Severe CAT is considered likely when the vertical wind shear is 6 kt. per 1,000 ft. and/or the horizontal wind shear exceeds 40 kt. per 150 mi.
Answer (B) is incorrect. It is not a CAT criterion. Answer (C) is incorrect. This is the vertical, not horizontal, wind shear associated with severe CAT.

6.10 Thunderstorms and Microbursts

58. What are the minimum requirements for the formation of a thunderstorm?

A. Sufficient moisture and a lifting action.
B. Sufficient moisture, an unstable lapse rate, and lifting action.
C. Towering cumulus clouds, sufficient moisture, and a frontal zone.

Answer (B) is correct. *(AvW Chap 11)*
DISCUSSION: Thunderstorms form when there is sufficient water vapor, an unstable lapse rate, and an initial lifting action to start the process.
Answer (A) is incorrect. An unstable lapse rate is also required. Answer (C) is incorrect. A frontal zone is not needed. Also, towering cumulus clouds usually are signs of a developing thunderstorm.

59. Select the true statement pertaining to the life cycle of a thunderstorm.

A. The initial stage of a thunderstorm is always indicated by the development of a nimbus cloud.
B. The beginning of rain at the Earth's surface indicates the mature stage of the thunderstorm.
C. The beginning of rain at the Earth's surface indicates the dissipating stage of the thunderstorm.

Answer (B) is correct. *(AvW Chap 11)*
DISCUSSION: Thunderstorms have three stages in their life cycle: cumulus, mature, and dissipating. The mature stage means downdrafts have developed and precipitation has begun to fall to the Earth's surface.
Answer (A) is incorrect. The cumulus stage is the building stage when there are updrafts, generally without rain. Answer (C) is incorrect. The dissipating stage of thunderstorms means the thunderstorm is raining itself out.

60. What feature is associated with the cumulus stage of a thunderstorm?

A. Frequent lightning.
B. Continuous updrafts.
C. Beginning of rain at the surface.

Answer (B) is correct. *(AvW Chap 11)*
DISCUSSION: During the cumulus stage of a thunderstorm, the cumulus cloud is building and there are continuous updrafts.
Answer (A) is incorrect. Frequent lightning occurs after the downdrafts have developed and produced static electricity, causing lightning. Answer (C) is incorrect. The beginning of rain at the surface marks the beginning of the mature stage.

61. A squall line is usually associated with a

A. stationary front.
B. fast-moving cold front.
C. fast-moving warm front.

Answer (B) is correct. *(AvW Chap 11)*
DISCUSSION: A squall line is a nonfrontal, narrow band of active thunderstorms that develops ahead of a cold front. A squall line is usually associated with a fast-moving cold front and may proceed well ahead of the front's leading edge.
Answer (A) is incorrect. A stationary front does not produce a squall line. Answer (C) is incorrect. A fast-moving warm front does not produce a squall line.

62. Which type of cloud is associated with violent turbulence and a tendency toward the production of funnel clouds?

A. Cumulonimbus mamma.
B. Standing lenticular.
C. Altocumulus castellanus.

Answer (A) is correct. *(AvW Chap 11)*
DISCUSSION: Cumulonimbus mamma is a cumulonimbus cloud having hanging protuberances like pouches, testes, or udders on the underside of the cloud, usually indicative of severe turbulence. This is the type of cloud that can produce a tornado.
Answer (B) is incorrect. Standing lenticular clouds mark mountain waves that are the product of stable air flowing over an obstruction. Answer (C) is incorrect. Altocumulus castellanus is a middle cloud that indicates instability and turbulence but does not produce tornadoes.

63. Tornadoes are most likely to occur with which type of thunderstorms?

A. Tropical thunderstorms during the mature stage.
B. Squall line thunderstorms that form ahead of warm fronts.
C. Steady-state thunderstorms associated with cold fronts or squall lines.

Answer (C) is correct. *(AvW Chap 11)*
DISCUSSION: Tornadoes are more likely to occur in the vicinity of steady-state thunderstorms associated with cold fronts or squall lines. These storms are intense, often violent, and prolonged. In a steady-state thunderstorm, rain falls outside the updraft, which permits the updrafts to continue and the storm to persist.
Answer (A) is incorrect. Tropical thunderstorms usually do not reach the steady-state situation. Answer (B) is incorrect. A squall line forms ahead of a cold, not warm, front.

64. What is the expected duration of an individual microburst?

A. One microburst may continue for as long as an hour.
B. Five minutes with maximum winds lasting approximately 2 to 4 minutes.
C. Seldom longer than 15 minutes from the time the burst strikes the ground until dissipation.

Answer (C) is correct. *(AIM Para 7-1-27)*
DISCUSSION: An individual microburst will seldom last longer than 15 min. from the time it strikes the ground until dissipation.
Answer (A) is incorrect. Microbursts seldom last in excess of 15 min. Answer (B) is incorrect. Horizontal winds, which are only a portion of a microburst, continue to increase for the first 5 min., with the maximum intensity winds lasting approximately 2 to 4 min.

65. Maximum downdrafts in a microburst encounter may be as strong as

A. 6,000 feet per minute.
B. 4,500 feet per minute.
C. 1,500 feet per minute.

Answer (A) is correct. *(AIM Para 7-1-27)*
DISCUSSION: The downdrafts can be as strong at 6,000 fpm. Horizontal winds near the surface can be as strong as 45 kt., resulting in a 90-kt. shear (headwind to tailwind change for a traversing aircraft) across the microburst.
Answer (B) is incorrect. The maximum downdraft is 6,000 fpm, not 4,500 fpm. Answer (C) is incorrect. The maximum downdraft is 6,000 fpm, not 1,500 fpm.

66. How long do the maximum intensity winds last in an individual microburst?

A. 2 to 4 minutes.
B. 5 to 10 minutes.
C. 15 minutes.

Answer (A) is correct. *(AIM Para 7-1-27)*
DISCUSSION: While individual microbursts seldom last longer than 15 min. from the time they strike the ground to dissipation, the horizontal winds may continue to increase during the first 5 min. Note that the maximum intensity horizontal winds in a microburst last approximately 2 to 4 min.
Answer (B) is incorrect. A microburst intensifies for about the first 5 min. after it strikes the ground. Answer (C) is incorrect. Fifteen min. is the normal maximum duration of an individual microburst.

6.11 Icing and Hail

67. Which situation would most likely result in freezing rain?

A. Rain falling from air which has a temperature of more than 0°C into air having a temperature of 0°C or less.
B. Rain falling from air which has a temperature of 0°C or less into air having a temperature of more than 0°C.
C. Rain which has a supercooled temperature of 0°C or less falling into air having a temperature of more than 0°C.

Answer (A) is correct. *(AvW Chap 10)*
DISCUSSION: Freezing rain at your flight altitude indicates that there is a layer of warm air (above 0°C) above where it is raining and the rain has supercooled as it falls through a layer of colder air (at or below 0°C).
Answer (B) is incorrect. The rain must begin in temperatures of 0°C or warmer and fall through a layer of below-freezing temperatures. Answer (C) is incorrect. The rain must begin in temperatures of 0°C or warmer and fall through a layer of below-freezing temperatures.

68. Consider the following statements regarding hail as an in-flight hazard and select those which are correct.

1. There is a correlation between the visual appearance of thunderstorms and the amount of hail within them.
2. Large hail is most commonly found in thunderstorms which have strong updrafts and large liquid water content.
3. Hail may be found at any level within a thunderstorm but not in the clear air outside of the storm cloud.
4. Hail is usually produced during the mature stage of the thunderstorm's lifespan.
5. Hailstones may be thrown upward and outward from a storm cloud for several miles.

The true statements are:

A. 2, 4, and 5.
B. 1, 2, and 3.
C. 1, 2, 4, and 5.

Answer (A) is correct. *(AvW Chap 11)*
DISCUSSION: Large hail is commonly produced in the mature stage of thunderstorms that have strong updrafts and large liquid water content. The hailstones may be thrown upward and outward from the storm cloud for several miles.
Answer (B) is incorrect. There is no correlation between the visual appearance of thunderstorms and the amount of hail within them, and the hail may be thrown out of the storm cloud for several miles. Answer (C) is incorrect. There is no correlation between the visual appearance of thunderstorms and the amount of hail within them.

69. Which statement is true concerning the in-flight hazard of hail?

A. Hail is usually produced by altocumulus clouds.
B. Rain at the surface indicates the absence of hail aloft.
C. Hailstones may be thrown outward from a storm cloud for several miles.

Answer (C) is correct. *(AvW Chap 11)*
DISCUSSION: The maximum possible flight distance should be kept from intense thunderstorms as hail can be thrown several miles outward from the cell.
Answer (A) is incorrect. Hail is generated by cumulonimbus, not altocumulus, clouds. Answer (B) is incorrect. Rain at the surface does not mean absence of hail aloft. As hail falls through the freezing level, it begins to melt and can reach the ground as hail or rain.

70. Hail, an in-flight hazard, is most likely to be associated with

A. cumulus clouds.
B. stratocumulus clouds.
C. cumulonimbus clouds.

Answer (C) is correct. *(AvW Chap 11)*
DISCUSSION: Cumulonimbus clouds are formed by rising air currents and are extremely turbulent. Such clouds frequently contain large hailstones capable of severely damaging an airplane.
Answer (A) is incorrect. Cumulus clouds do not produce hail. Answer (B) is incorrect. Stratocumulus clouds normally do not produce hail.

71. Hail will most likely be encountered

A. beneath the anvil cloud of a large cumulonimbus.
B. during the dissipating stage of the cumulonimbus.
C. above the cumulonimbus cloud well above the freezing level.

Answer (A) is correct. *(AvW Chap 11)*
DISCUSSION: Cumulonimbus clouds are formed by rising air currents and are extremely turbulent. Such clouds frequently contain large hailstones, especially beneath the anvil, which are thrown outward and can severely damage an airplane.
Answer (B) is incorrect. During the dissipating stage, the storm is lessening and the hazards are diminishing. Answer (C) is incorrect. Above the cloud, you are usually safe from hail.

72. Which precipitation type usually indicates freezing rain at higher altitudes?

A. Snow.
B. Hail.
C. Ice pellets.

Answer (C) is correct. *(AvW Chap 5)*
DISCUSSION: Ice pellets always indicate freezing rain at a higher altitude. Rain falling through colder air may become supercooled, freezing on impact as freezing rain, or it may freeze during its descent, falling as ice pellets.
Answer (A) is incorrect. Snow indicates that the temperature of the air aloft is well below freezing. Answer (B) is incorrect. Hail indicates instability of the air aloft where supercooled droplets above the freezing level begin to freeze. Once a drop has frozen, other drops latch on to it, and the hailstone grows.

73. The most rapid accumulation of clear ice on an aircraft in flight may occur with temperatures between 0°C to –15°C in

A. cumuliform clouds.
B. stratiform clouds.
C. any clouds or dry snow.

Answer (A) is correct. *(AvW Chap 10)*
DISCUSSION: Rapid accumulation of clear ice most frequently occurs in cumuliform clouds because they have larger water droplets.
Answer (B) is incorrect. Stratiform clouds are generally associated with rime, not clear, ice. Answer (C) is incorrect. Dry snow will not accumulate as ice on the airplane.

74. Which is an operational consideration regarding aircraft structural icing?

A. It is unnecessary for an aircraft to fly through rain or cloud droplets for structural ice to form.
B. Clear ice is most likely to form on an airplane when flying through stratified clouds or light drizzle.
C. In order for structural ice to form, the temperature at the point where moisture strikes the aircraft must be 0°C (32°F) or colder.

Answer (C) is correct. *(AvW Chap 10)*
DISCUSSION: Ice will not form on the airplane structure unless the temperature at the point where the moisture strikes the airplane is 0°C (32°F) or colder.
Answer (A) is incorrect. Visible moisture must be encountered by the airplane before icing can occur. Answer (B) is incorrect. Rime ice, not clear ice, is most frequently encountered when flying through stratified clouds or light drizzle.

75. A generally recommended practice for autopilot usage during cruise flight in icing conditions is

A. keeping the autopilot engaged while monitoring the system.
B. periodically disengaging the autopilot and hand flying the airplane.
C. periodically disengaging and immediately reengaging the altitude hold function.

Answer (B) is correct. *(AC 91-74B)*
DISCUSSION: The autopilot can mask changes in handling characteristics. The recommended procedure is, when possible, for pilots to periodically disengage the autopilot and hand fly the airplane to detect changes in handling characteristics due to aerodynamic effects of icing. But if this is not desirable because of cockpit workload levels, pilots should monitor the autopilot closely for abnormal trim, trim rate, or airplane attitude.
Answer (A) is incorrect. The autopilot can mask changes in handling characteristics due to aerodynamic effects of icing that would be detected by the pilot if the airplane were being hand flown. The recommended procedure is to periodically disengage the autopilot and hand fly the airplane to detect any handling changes, not just keep the autopilot engaged while monitoring the system. Answer (C) is incorrect. The pilot should disengage the autopilot and hand fly the airplane for the amount of time necessary to detect any changes in the handling characteristics due to aerodynamic effects of icing, not periodically disengage and immediately reengage the altitude hold function.

6.12 Clouds

76. The height of the bases of the middle clouds in the middle latitudes ranges from

A. 1,000 to 10,000 feet.
B. 6,500 to 23,000 feet.
C. 16,500 to 45,000 feet.

Answer (B) is correct. *(AvW Chap 7)*
DISCUSSION: The height of middle clouds in the middle latitudes ranges from 6,500 ft. to 23,000 ft.
Answer (A) is incorrect. The height range of cumuliform, not middle, cloud bases is from 1,000 to 10,000 ft. Answer (C) is incorrect. The height range of high, not middle, clouds is from 16,500 to 45,000 ft.

77. Which middle level clouds are characterized by rain, snow, or ice pellets posing a serious icing problem if temperatures are near or below freezing?

A. Nimbostratus.
B. Altostratus lenticular.
C. Altocumulus castellanus.

Answer (A) is correct. *(AvW Chap 7)*
DISCUSSION: Nimbostratus is a gray or dark massive cloud layer diffused by more or less continuous rain, snow, or ice pellets. This is a middle cloud, although it may merge into very low stratus or stratocumulus. It usually contains very little turbulence but can pose a serious icing problem if temperatures are near or below freezing.
Answer (B) is incorrect. Altostratus clouds are a bluish veil or layer of clouds. They pose only a moderate threat of ice. Answer (C) is incorrect. Altocumulus castellanus are middle level convective clouds. They are characterized by billowing tops and comparatively high bases. They are a good indication of mid-level instability, i.e., turbulence with some icing.

78. One of the best visual indications of a thermal is a

A. smooth cumulus cloud with a concave base.
B. broken to overcast sky with cumulus clouds.
C. fragmented cumulus cloud with a concave base.

Answer (A) is correct. *(AvW Chap 16)*
DISCUSSION: Cumulus clouds are positive signs of thermals. A growing cumulus has an outline that is firm and sharp, and indicates a strong thermal. The warmest and most rapidly rising air is in the center of the thermal, giving a concave shape to the cloud base.
Answer (B) is incorrect. A broken to overcast sky shades the surface, cutting off surface heating and convective thermals. Answer (C) is incorrect. A fragmented cumulus cloud with a concave base indicates the thermal has ceased.

79. Streamers of precipitation trailing beneath clouds but evaporating before reaching the ground are known as

A. virga.
B. sublimation.
C. evaporation.

Answer (A) is correct. *(AvW Chap 5)*
DISCUSSION: Virga is ice or water particles falling from a cloud, usually in wisps or streaks, and evaporating before reaching the ground.
Answer (B) is incorrect. Sublimation is the changing of ice directly to water vapor. Answer (C) is incorrect. Evaporation is the changing of liquid water to water vapor.

6.13 Aviation Routine Weather Report (METAR)

80. (Refer to Figure 3 below.) Which station is reporting the lowest ceiling?

A. KAMA.
B. KFTW.
C. KDAL.

Answer (B) is correct. *(AWS Sect 3)*
DISCUSSION: The ceiling is the lowest broken or overcast layer, or vertical visibility into an obscuration. KAMA is reporting 700 ft. overcast (OVC007); KFTW is reporting indefinite ceiling (vertical visibility) of 600 ft. (VV006); and KDAL is reporting 900 ft. overcast (OVC009). Thus, the lowest ceiling is reported at KFTW.
Answer (A) is incorrect. KAMA is reporting a ceiling of 700 ft. overcast (OVC007), but KFTW is reporting an indefinite ceiling (vertical visibility) of 600 ft. (VV006). Answer (C) is incorrect. KDAL is reporting a ceiling of 900 ft. overcast (OVC009), but KFTW is reporting an indefinite ceiling (vertical visibility) of 600 ft. (VV006).

81. (Refer to Figure 3 below.) Which station is reporting the wind as calm?

A. KDAL.
B. KFTW.
C. KTYR.

Answer (A) is correct. *(AWS Sect 3)*
DISCUSSION: The wind element is reported as a five-digit group (six-digit if the wind speed is over 99 kt.) and follows the date/time or modifier element. If the wind speed is less than 1 knot, the wind is reported as calm and is coded as 00000KT. KDAL is reporting a calm wind.
Answer (B) is incorrect. KFTW is reporting a wind from 090° at 4 kt. (09004KT), but KDAL is reporting a calm wind (00000KT). Answer (C) is incorrect. KTYR is reporting a wind from 080° at 4 kt. (08004KT), but KDAL is reporting a calm wind (00000KT).

82. (Refer to Figure 3 below.) In the report for KBRO, what is the reported ceiling?

A. 2,000 feet.
B. 13,000 feet.
C. 25,000 feet.

Answer (C) is correct. *(AWS Sect 3)*
DISCUSSION: The ceiling is the lowest broken or overcast layer, or vertical visibility into an obscuration. KBRO is reporting the sky cover as 2,000 ft. scattered, 13,000 ft. scattered towering cumulus, ceiling 25,000 ft. overcast (SCT020 SCT130TCU OVC250).
Answer (A) is incorrect. There is a scattered layer at 2,000 ft. (SCT020). The ceiling is the lowest broken or overcast layer, not a scattered layer. Answer (B) is incorrect. There is a scattered towering cumulus layer at 13,000 ft. (SCT130TCU). The ceiling is the lowest broken or overcast layer, not a scattered layer.

```
METAR KAMA 301651Z 05016KT 5/8SM R04/3000FT BR
OVC007 11/9 A3013 RMK DZB26DZE40

METAR KAUS 301651Z 12008KT 4SM -RAHZ BKN010
BKN023 OVC160 21/17 A3005 RMK RAB25

METAR KBRO 301655Z 15015G20KT 7SM SCT020 SCT130
TCU OVC250 29/19 A2997 RMK RAB19RAE25

METAR KDAL 301649Z 00000KT 3SM BRHZ OVC009 22/17
A3010

METAR KFTW 301654Z 09004KT 1/2SM HZFU VV006 21/17
A3010

METAR KTYR 301650Z AUTO 08004KT 3SM BR SCT015
24/19 A2999
```

Figure 3. – Aviation Routine Weather Reports (METAR).

83. (Refer to Figure 3 on page 206.) The temperature/dewpoint spread at KAUS is

A. 4°C.
B. 4°F.
C. 7°C.

Answer (A) is correct. *(AWS Sect 3)*
DISCUSSION: The temperature/dewpoint group follows the sky conditions and is reported in a two-digit form in whole degrees Celsius. At KAUS, the reported temperature is 21°C, and the dewpoint is 17°C (21/17). Thus, the temperature/dewpoint spread at KAUS is 4°C.
Answer (B) is incorrect. The temperature/dewpoint spread at KAUS is 4°C, not 4°F. Answer (C) is incorrect. The temperature/dewpoint spread at KAUS is 4°C, not 7°C.

84. (Refer to Figure 3 on page 206.) What is the reported duration of the rain at the time of the observation at KAUS?

A. 25 minutes.
B. 26 minutes.
C. 36 minutes.

Answer (B) is correct. *(AWS Sect 3)*
DISCUSSION: At AUS, the observation was taken at 1651Z. The remarks (RMK) section states that the rain began at 25 min. past the hour (RAB25), and at the observation, there is still light rain (-RA). The duration of the rain at AUS is 26 min. (1625 to 1651).
Answer (A) is incorrect. The 25 refers to the time after the hour at which it began to rain. Answer (C) is incorrect. The rain began at 25 min. after the hour, and the next observation was taken at 51 min. after the hour, the difference being 26 min., not 36 min.

85. (Refer to Figure 3 on page 206.) What is the reported duration of the rain at the time of the observation at KBRO?

A. 25 minutes.
B. 6 minutes.
C. 19 minutes.

Answer (B) is correct. *(AWS Sect 3)*
DISCUSSION: Refer to Fig. 3, the third paragraph is the METAR for KBRO. The observation was taken at 1655Z. The remarks section (RMK) indicates that the precipitation began at 19 hr. (RAB19) and ended at 25 minutes past the hour (RAE25). The rain lasted 6 minutes (25 − 19 = 6).
Answer (A) is incorrect. RAE25 indicates the rain ended 25 minutes past the hour, not the reported duration of the rain. Answer (C) is incorrect. RAB19 indicates the rain started at 19 minutes past the hour, not the reported duration of the rain.

86. GIVEN: METAR KOUN 151355Z AUTO 22010KT 10SM CLR BLO 120 13/10 A2993 RMK A02 $.

The ASOS report indicates that the location is

A. reporting a temperature of 45°F.
B. possibly in need of maintenance.
C. augmented with a weather observer.

Answer (B) is correct. *(AWS Sect. 3)*
DISCUSSION: A maintenance indicator sign, $, is included when an automated weather reporting system detects that the system is possibly in need of maintenance.
NOTE: In an automated METAR report, CLR (not CLR BLO 120) will be used when no clouds below 12,000 ft. are reported. The FAA may update this question in the future.
Answer (A) is incorrect. The METAR reports a temperature of 13°C (13/10), not 45°F. Answer (C) is incorrect. If this automated report had human augmentation or backup, the modifier AUTO would be removed from the report; i.e., AUTO means no human intervention.

87. Consider the following statements regarding an Aviation Routine Weather Report (METAR).

1. A vertical visibility entry does not constitute a ceiling.
2. Fog (FG) can be reported only if the visibility is less than 5/8 mile.
3. The ceiling layer will be designated by a "C."
4. Mist (BR) can be reported only if the visibility is 5/8 mile up to six miles.
5. Temperatures reported below zero will be prefixed with a "−."
6. There is no provision to report partial obscurations.

Select the true statements.

A. 2, 4, and 6.
B. 2, 3, and 5.
C. 1, 2, 5, and 6.

Answer (A) is correct. *(AWS Sect 3)*
DISCUSSION: In the METAR code, fog (FG) is reported only when the visibility is less than 5/8 SM; mist (BR) is used to indicate mist (fog) restricting visibility from 5/8 to 6 SM; and there is no provision to report partial obscurations in the body of a METAR (it is done by use of remarks).
Answer (B) is incorrect. A ceiling layer is not designated by the letter "C" in the METAR code, and temperatures reported below zero will be prefixed with "M," not "−." Answer (C) is incorrect. A ceiling is defined as the lowest broken or overcast layer, or vertical visibility into an obscuration. Also, temperatures reported below zero will be prefixed with "M," not "−."

88. Which statement is true concerning ASOS/AWOS weather reporting systems?

A. Each AWOS station is part of a nationwide network of weather reporting stations.
B. ASOS locations perform weather observing functions necessary to generate METAR reports.
C. Both ASOS and AWOS have the capability of reporting density altitude, as long as it exceeds the airport elevation by more than 1,000 feet.

Answer (B) is correct. *(AIM Para 7-1-10)*
DISCUSSION: The ASOS is the primary automated surface weather observing system of the U.S. and is designed to support aviation operations and weather forecast activities. Each ASOS will provide continuous minute-by-minute observations and perform the basic observing functions necessary to generate a METAR report and other aviation weather reports.
Answer (A) is incorrect. Selected individual AWOS sites, not all, may be incorporated into nationwide data collection and dissemination networks in the future. Answer (C) is incorrect. Only the AWOS has the capability of reporting density altitude when it exceeds the field elevation by more than 1,000 ft.

89. GIVEN: METAR KPNC 131215 AUTO 33025KT 1/2SM OVC005 00/M03 A2990 RMK A02 SLPNO.

This ASOS report indicates that the

A. temperature is missing.
B. station reports every 15 minutes.
C. sea level pressure is not available.

Answer (C) is correct. *(AWS Sect 3)*
DISCUSSION: At designated stations that report sea-level pressure, the remark begins with SLP followed by three digits. SLPNO indicates that sea-level pressure is not available.
Answer (A) is incorrect. The indication 00/M03 means that the temperature is 0°C and the dewpoint is –3°C, not that the temperature is missing. Answer (B) is incorrect. The time at which the report was recorded is 1215Z; it does not mean that the station reports every 15 min.

6.14 Pilot Weather Report (PIREP)

```
UA/OV  KOKC-KTUL/TM  1800/FL120/TP  BE90//SK  BKN0
18-TOP055/OVC072-TOP089/CLR ABV/TA M7/WV 08021/
TB  LGT  055-072/IC  LGT-MOD  RIME  072-089
```

Figure 4. – Pilot Weather Report.

90. (Refer to Figure 4 above.) The base and tops of the overcast layer reported by a pilot are

A. 1,800 feet MSL and 5,500 feet MSL.
B. 5,500 feet AGL and 7,200 feet MSL.
C. 7,200 feet MSL and 8,900 feet MSL.

Answer (C) is correct. *(AWS Sect 3)*
DISCUSSION: The base and top of the overcast (OVC) layer reported by a pilot are 7,200 ft. MSL and 8,900 ft. MSL (OVC 072-TOP089).
Answer (A) is incorrect. The base and top of the broken (BKN), not the overcast (OVC), layer reported by the pilot are 1,800 ft. MSL and 5,500 ft. MSL. Answer (B) is incorrect. The area between 5,500 ft. MSL, not AGL, and 7,200 ft. is the clear area between the broken layer (1,800 ft. to 5,500 ft. MSL) and the overcast layer (7,200 ft. to 8,900 ft. MSL).

91. (Refer to Figure 4 above.) The wind and temperature at 12,000 feet MSL as reported by a pilot are

A. 090° at 21 knots and –9°.
B. 090° at 21 MPH and –9° F.
C. 080° at 21 knots and –7° C.

Answer (C) is correct. *(AWS Sect 3)*
DISCUSSION: The wind and temperature reported by a pilot at 12,000 ft. MSL are 080° at 21 kt. (WV 08021) and –7°C (TA M7).
Answer (A) is incorrect. The wind is reported as 080° at 21 kt. (WV 08021), not 090° at 21 kt., and the temperature is –7°C (TA M7), not –9° (temperature is reported in degrees Celsius). Answer (B) is incorrect. The wind is reported at 080° at 21 kt. (WV 08021), not 090° at 21 MPH, and the temperature is –7°C (TA M7), not –9°F. Wind speed is reported in knots and temperature is reported in degrees Celsius.

92. (Refer to Figure 4 above.) The intensity of the turbulence reported at a specific altitude is

A. moderate from 5,500 feet to 7,200 feet.
B. moderate at 5,500 feet and at 7,200 feet.
C. light from 5,500 feet to 7,200 feet.

Answer (C) is correct. *(AWS Sect 3)*
DISCUSSION: A pilot reported light turbulence from 5,500 ft. to 7,200 ft. MSL (TB LGT 055-072).
Answer (A) is incorrect. Turbulence is reported as light, not moderate, from 5,500 ft. to 7,200 ft. MSL (TB LGT 055-072). Answer (B) is incorrect. Turbulence is reported as light, not moderate. Additionally, the turbulence is reported from 5,500 ft. to 7,200 ft. MSL, not only at 5,500 ft. and 7,200 ft. MSL.

93. (Refer to Figure 4 on page 208.) If the terrain elevation is 1,295 feet MSL, what is the height above ground level of the base of the ceiling?

A. 505 feet AGL.
B. 6,586 feet AGL.
C. 1,295 feet AGL.

Answer (A) is correct. *(AWS Sect 3)*
DISCUSSION: A ceiling is defined as the height above ground of the lowest broken or overcast layer aloft or the vertical visibility into a surface-based obstruction. A pilot reported the base of a broken layer at 1,800 ft. MSL (SK BKN018). Subtract the terrain elevation from the reported cloud base in order to find the ceiling height of 505 ft. AGL (1,800 – 1,295).
Answer (B) is incorrect. This is the approximate height above ground of the overcast layer, but a ceiling is the lowest broken or overcast layer. The base of a broken layer is reported at 1,800 ft. MSL or 505 ft. AGL. Answer (C) is incorrect. The terrain elevation is 1,295 ft. MSL, not AGL. The base of the broken layer is reported at 1,800 ft. MSL, which is 505 ft. AGL (1,800 – 1,295).

94. Consider the following statements regarding a Pilot Weather Report (PIREP).

1. A vertical visibility entry does not constitute a ceiling.
2. Fog (FG) can be reported only if the visibility is less than 5/8 mile.
3. The ceiling layer will be designated by a "C."
4. Mist (BR) can be reported only if the visibility is greater than or equal to 5/8 statute mile.
5. Temperatures reported below zero will be prefixed with a "–."
6. There is no provision to report partial obscurations.

Select the true statements.

A. 2, 4, and 6.
B. 2, 3, and 5.
C. 1, 2, 5, and 6.

Answer (A) is correct. *(AWS Sect 3)*
DISCUSSION: Fog and mist are similar in their ability to obscure in-flight visibility. Fog should be reported when visibility is below 5/8 statute mile, and mist should be reported when visibility is greater than or equal to 5/8 statute mile. There is no provision in a PIREP to report partial obscurations.
Answer (B) is incorrect. Ceilings are not designated with a "C" in a PIREP, and temperatures below freezing are prefixed with the letter "M," not a minus sign (–). Answer (C) is incorrect. Vertical visibility does constitute a ceiling. As well, temperatures below freezing are prefixed with the letter "M," not a minus sign (–).

6.15 Radar Weather Report (SD/ROB) and Weather Advisories

95. Interpret the following radar weather report:

LIT 1133 AREA 4TRW 22/100 88/170 196/180 220/115 C2425 MT 310 AT 162/110

A. There are four cells with tops at 10,000 feet, 17,000 feet, and 11,500 feet.
B. The maximum top of the cells is located 162° and 110 NM from the station (LIT).
C. The visibility is 4 miles in thunderstorms and the intensity of thunderstorms remains unchanged.

Answer (B) is correct. *(AWS Sect 3)*
DISCUSSION: "LIT 1133" is the location identifier and time of observation. "AREA 4TRW" means an area of thunderstorms and rain showers covering 4/10 of the sky. The following four sets of numbers are the corners of the AREA; e.g., "22/100" is 22°, 100 NM. "C2425" means the cells are moving from 240° at 25 kt. "MT 310 at 162/110" means the maximum top of the cells is 31,000 ft. MSL and is located 162° and 110 NM from LIT.
Answer (A) is incorrect. The numbers 100, 170, and 115 refer to NM from LIT, not cloud tops. Answer (C) is incorrect. The 4 refers to 4/10 sky coverage, not visibility.

96. Which statement is true concerning this radar weather report for OKC?

OKC 1934 LN 8TRW / 86/ 40 164/60 199/115 15W 2425MT 570 AT 159/65 2 INCH HAIL RPRTD THIS ECHO.

A. The visibility is 8 miles in rain showers.
B. There are three cells with tops at 11,500, 40,000, and 60,000 feet.
C. The maximum top of the cells is 57,000 feet located 65 NM south-southeast of the station.

Answer (C) is correct. *(AWS Sect 3)*
DISCUSSION: "OKC 1934" is the location identifier and time of observation. "LN 8TRW" means a line of thunderstorms and rain showers covering 8/10 of the sky. The following three sets of numbers delineate the center of the line; e.g., "86/40" is 86°, 40 NM. The "15W" means the line is 15 NM wide. The "2425" means the line is moving from 240° at 25 kt. The "MT 570 at 159/65" means the maximum top of the cells is 57,000 ft. and is located 159° and 65 NM from OKC.
Answer (A) is incorrect. The 8 refers to 8/10 sky coverage, not visibility. Answer (B) is incorrect. The numbers 40, 60, and 115 refer to NM from OKC, not cloud tops.

6.16 Surface Analysis Chart

97. The intensity trend of a front (as of chart time) is best determined by referring to a

A. Surface Analysis Chart.
B. Prognostic Chart.
C. Weather Depiction Chart.

Answer (A) is correct. *(AWS Sect 5)*
DISCUSSION: The surface analysis chart indicates the movement of fronts by the pips on the front line, which indicate the type of front and point in the direction in which the front is moving. Pips on both sides of the front suggest little or no movement.
Answer (B) is incorrect. A prognostic chart displays the likely weather forecast for a future time. Answer (C) is incorrect. The weather depiction chart is computer-prepared from METAR reports to give a broad overview of observed flying conditions valid at the time of the chart. This product is being phased out by the FAA.

98. On a Surface Analysis Weather Chart, isobars are usually spaced at intervals of

A. 4 millibars.
B. 2 millibars.
C. 6 millibars.

Answer (A) is correct. *(AWS Sect 5)*
DISCUSSION: On a surface analysis chart, isobars are solid lines depicting the sea level pressure patterns. They are usually spaced at intervals of 4 millibars (mb).
Answer (B) is incorrect. Isobars on a surface analysis chart are usually spaced at intervals of 4 mb, not 2 mb. Answer (C) is incorrect. Isobars on a surface analysis chart are usually spaced at intervals of 4 mb, not 6 mb.

99. The strength and position of a front (as of chart time) is best determined by referring to a

A. Surface Analysis Chart.
B. Prognostic Chart.
C. Weather Depiction Chart.

Answer (A) is correct. *(AWS Sect 5)*
DISCUSSION: The surface analysis chart indicates both the current position and the movement of the fronts. Pips on one or both sides of the front indicate frontal movement. A three-digit number along the front indicates type, intensity, and character.
Answer (B) is incorrect. A prognostic chart displays the likely weather forecast for a future time. Answer (C) is incorrect. The weather depiction chart is computer-prepared from METAR reports to give a broad overview of observed flying conditions valid at the time of the chart. This product is being phased out by the FAA.

100. (Refer to Figure 8 on page 211.) Which symbol is used when there is a change in the front type?

A. 1
B. 5
C. 8

Answer (B) is correct. *(AWS Sect 5)*
DISCUSSION: Whenever there is a change in a front type, the symbol in illustration 5 will be seen.
Answer (A) is incorrect. Illustration 1 is the symbol for a cold front. Answer (C) is incorrect. Illustration 8 is the symbol for a stationary frontogenesis.

101. (Refer to Figure 8 on page 211.) (Refer to illustration 12.) What does this symbol mean on a Surface Analysis Weather Chart?

A. Squall line.
B. Occluded front.
C. High-pressure ridge.

Answer (A) is correct. *(AWS Sect 5)*
DISCUSSION: The dashed line alternating with two dots on a Surface Analysis map indicates a squall line.
Answer (B) is incorrect. An occluded front is indicated by a line with alternating semicircular and triangular pips. Answer (C) is incorrect. A high-pressure ridge is indicated by a sawtoothed line.

SU 6: Aviation Weather

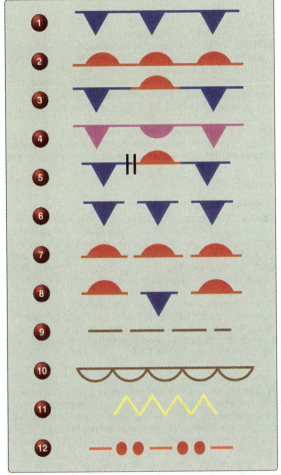

Figure 8. – Surface Analysis Chart Symbols.

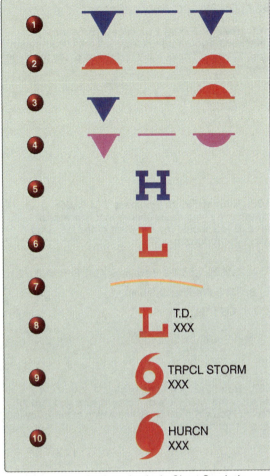

Figure 9. – Surface Analysis Chart Symbols.

102. (Refer to Figure 9 above.) What type of front is show in illustration 4?

A. Cold frontolysis.
B. Warm frontolysis.
C. Occluded frontolysis.

Answer (C) is correct. *(AWS Sec 5)*
DISCUSSION: An occluded frontolysis symbol is shown in illustration 4.
Answer (A) is incorrect. The symbol for a cold frontolysis is show in illustration 1. Answer (B) is incorrect. The symbol for a warm frontolysis is shown in illustration 2.

103. (Refer to Figure 9 above.) Which illustration indicates a tropical wave?

A. 7
B. 8
C. 9

Answer (A) is correct. *(AWS Sec 5)*
DISCUSSION: A tropical wave is shown by the symbol in illustration 7.
Answer (B) is incorrect. Illustration 8 is the symbol for a tropical depression. Answer (C) is incorrect. Illustration 9 is the symbol for a tropical storm, not a tropical wave.

104. (Refer to Figure 9 above.) Which symbol used on a Surface Analysis Weather Chart represents a dissipating warm front?

A. 1
B. 2
C. 3

Answer (B) is correct. *(AWS Sect 5)*
DISCUSSION: A warm front is indicated by half-circles on the same side of a line. As the front is forming, it is known as warm frontogenesis and is indicated by spaces between the underlined half-circles. When the warm front is dissipating, it is known as frontolysis and there are broken straight lines between each underlined half-circle.
Answer (A) is incorrect. Symbol 1 illustrates a cold frontolysis, which is a dissipating cold front. Answer (C) is incorrect. Symbol 3 depicts the dissipating stationary front, which is called stationary frontolysis.

6.17 Ceiling and Visibility Chart

105. (Refer to Figure 2 on page 213.) After determining your route of flight will take you through area L, you will most likely find which of the following weather conditions?

A. Marginal VFR.
B. VFR.
C. IFR.

Answer (B) is correct. *(Aviation Weather Center)*
DISCUSSION: Area L is in an area with blue/green coloring. Therefore, this area is most likely VFR. This should be confirmed by reviewing the METARs and TAF for area L.
Answer (A) is incorrect. Area L is in an area with blue/green coloring. This indicates VFR conditions are most likely the conditions. However, you should always confirm the actual conditions by reviewing the TAF or METAR. Answer (C) is incorrect. Area L is in an area with blue/green coloring. This indicates VFR conditions are most likely the conditions. However, you should always confirm the actual conditions by reviewing the TAF or METAR.

106. (Refer to Figure 2 on page 213.) After determining your destination is in the vicinity of area J, you should review which of the following weather products next?

A. Winds and Temperatures Aloft Forecast (FB).
B. The Weather Channel.
C. METAR.

Answer (C) is correct. *(Aviation Weather Center)*
DISCUSSION: In regards to weather, METARs provide the most useful information for determining if you can arrive safely at your destination airport. In the event that your destination airport does not have a METAR, you should review the TAF for the area your destination airport is located.
Answer (A) is incorrect. The winds and temperatures aloft forecast (FB) provides wind and temperature information at specified altitudes, times, and locations. It is generally used for enroute planning, not evaluating current conditions at your destination. Answer (B) is incorrect. Although The Weather Channel is a great source of weather information, it is not considered an official source by the FAA.

107. (Refer to Figure 2 on page 213.) After determining your route of flight will take you through area E, you will most likely find which of the following weather conditions?

A. IFR.
B. VFR.
C. LIFR.

Answer (A) is correct. *(Aviation Weather Center)*
DISCUSSION: Area E is in an area with yellow coloring. This suggests the area has 1,000 feet or less in obscuration, but not terrain obscuration. Therefore, this area is most likely IFR. This should be confirmed by reviewing the METARs, TAF, and AIRMET for area E.
Answer (B) is incorrect. Area E is in an area with yellow coloring. This suggests the area has 1,000 feet or less in obscuration, but not terrain obscuration. This indicates IFR conditions are most likely the conditions. However, you should always confirm the actual conditions by reviewing the METARs, TAF, and AIRMETs for the area. Answer (C) is incorrect. Area E is in an area with yellow coloring. This suggests the area has 1,000 feet or less in obscuration, but not terrain obscuration. LIFR conditions would be shown in orange. Yellow indicates IFR conditions are most likely the conditions. However, you should always confirm the actual conditions by reviewing the METAR, TAF, and AIRMETs for the area.

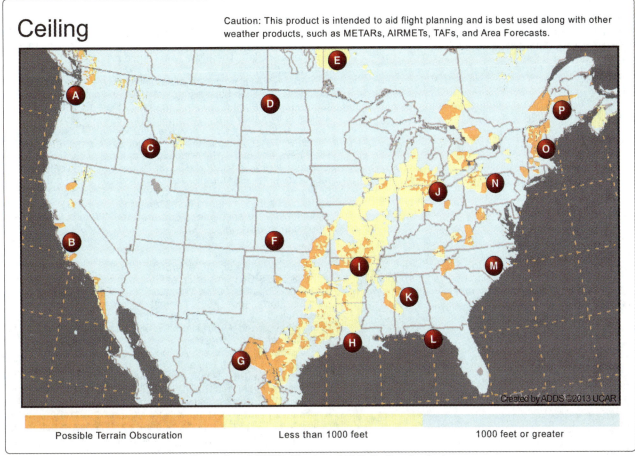

Figure 2. – CONUS Display of CVA Ceiling Analysis.

6.18 Constant Pressure Analysis Chart

108. When using a Constant Pressure Analysis Chart for planning a flight at 10,000 feet MSL, a pilot should refer to the

A. 850-millibar analysis.
B. 700-millibar analysis.
C. 500-millibar analysis.

Answer (B) is correct. *(AWS Sect 5)*
DISCUSSION: A constant pressure analysis chart is an upper-air weather map depicting certain observed data at specified pressure altitudes. The 700-mb analysis corresponds to the 10,000-ft. pressure altitude.
Answer (A) is incorrect. The 850-mb analysis is equal to about 5,000 ft. Answer (C) is incorrect. The 500-mb analysis is equal to 18,000 ft.

109. From which of the following can the observed temperature, wind, and temperature/dewpoint spread be determined at specified flight levels?

A. Stability Charts.
B. Winds Aloft Forecasts.
C. Constant Pressure Charts.

Answer (C) is correct. *(AWS Sect 5)*
DISCUSSION: The temperature/dewpoint spread and winds aloft at specified flight levels are shown on constant pressure analysis charts. They are published for pressure altitudes of 5,000, 10,000, 18,000, 30,000 and 39,000 ft.
Answer (A) is incorrect. Stability Charts indicate the stability of upper air, which assists in forecasting the type of clouds and precipitation that will form. Answer (B) is incorrect. The Winds Aloft Forecast includes only the forecast, not observed, wind and temperature.

6.19 Turbulence

110. (Refer to Figure 13A on page 215.) For a flight between Denver, CO, and Las Vegas, NV, you should expect the following turbulent conditions:

A. None.
B. Light.
C. Moderate or greater.

Answer (C) is correct. *(AC 00-45G)*
DISCUSSION: The GTG graphic indicates moderate or greater clear air turbulence (CAT) (yellow) in most of Colorado and parts of Utah. Therefore, you should expect moderate or greater turbulence.
Answer (A) is incorrect. According to the GTG graphic, Colorado and Utah have an almost 100% indication of turbulence (shown by green and yellow) and the southern tip of Nevada indicates light turbulence (in green). Therefore, a flight from Denver to Las Vegas should expect turbulence. Answer (B) is incorrect. According to the GTG graphic, Colorado and Utah have an almost 100% indication of turbulence. Most of Colorado's turbulence is shown as yellow, which indicates moderate or greater turbulence. Utah also has areas of moderate or greater turbulence (indicated as yellow). Therefore, you should not expect light turbulence from Denver to Las Vegas. You should expect to encounter moderate to severe turbulence at times during your flight.

111. (Refer to Figure 13A on page 215.) After analyzing your flight path through northwestern Illinois and eastern Iowa, you should continue your flight planning by examining

A. AIRMET.
B. SIGMET.
C. PIREP.

Answer (C) is correct. *(AC 00-45G)*
DISCUSSION: This route of flight is forecast to be light turbulence, but there is an indication of a PIREP calling for moderate turbulence. In the interest of flight safety, your next step would be to review the PIREP to see if you would be in the same location and if your aircraft is of similar size (737 vs. C-152) to the aircraft in the PIREP.
Answer (A) is incorrect. Although you should review any AIRMETs for your route of flight, your next step should be to review the PIREP that reports moderate turbulence to determine whether this PIREP is applicable to your specific route. Answer (B) is incorrect. Although you should definitely review any SIGMETs for your route of flight, your next step should be to review the PIREP that reports moderate turbulence to determine whether this PIREP is applicable to your specific route.

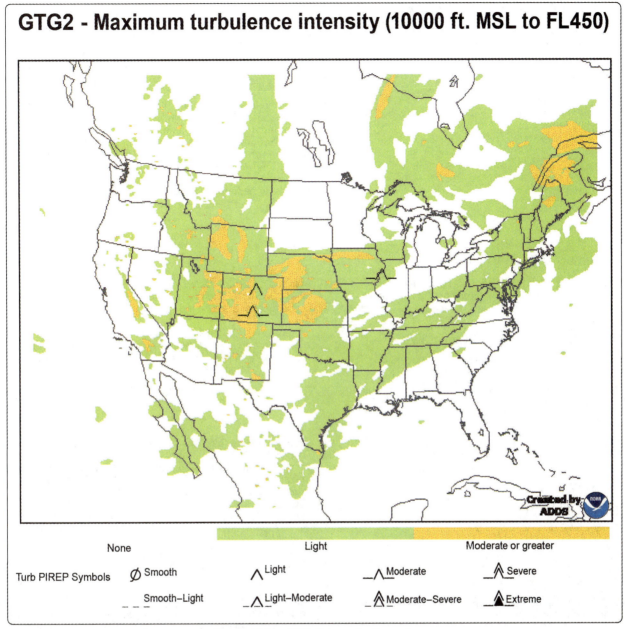

Figure 13A. – GTG Composite Example.

6.20 Significant Weather Prognostic Chart

112. Which weather chart depicts the conditions forecast to exist at a specific time in the future?

A. Prognostic.
B. Surface Analysis.
C. Weather Depiction.

Answer (A) is correct. *(AWS Sect 8)*
DISCUSSION: Significant weather prognostic charts (called "progs") forecast weather that may influence flight planning. On the low-level prog, the two panels forecast significant weather from the surface up to 24,000 ft.: one for 12 hr. and the other for 24 hr. from the time of issuance. If a service provider includes two lower panels, these panels forecast surface conditions: one for 12 hr. and the other for 24 hr. from time of issuance.
Answer (B) is incorrect. The surface analysis chart analyzes weather data that have already been observed and is not a forecast of weather conditions in the future. Answer (C) is incorrect. The weather depiction chart analyzes weather data that have already been observed and is not a forecast of weather conditions in the future. This product is being phased out by the FAA.

6.21 Convective Weather Forecast Chart

113. (Refer to Figure 16 on page 217.) What do the blue colored semi-circular polygons located southeast of each cell indicate?

A. The distance between the hazard fields.
B. The location of the hazard field at the last report.
C. The forecast of where the hazard field will be in 1 hour.

Answer (C) is correct. *(AWS Sect 9)*
DISCUSSION: The blue-colored semi-circular polygons show the locations where the hazard fields are expected to be in 1 hour.
Answer (A) is incorrect. Distance between the hazard fields is not measured on this chart. Answer (B) is incorrect. The blue-colored semi-circular polygons show where the hazard fields should be, not where they have been.

114. (Refer to Figure 16 on page 217.) At what speed is the most southern hazard field moving?

A. 45 kts.
B. 25 kts.
C. 45 mph.

Answer (B) is correct. *(AWS Sect 9)*
DISCUSSION: The numbers to the top left of the hazard field are separated by a slash. This indicates the speed at which the hazard field is moving. The number "25/450" means that the hazard field is moving at 25 kts. and that the echo tops are 45,000 ft. MSL.
Answer (A) is incorrect. The group of numbers to the top left of the hazard field are 25/450, indicating the hazard field is moving at 25, not 45, kts. Answer (C) is incorrect. The group of numbers the the top left of the hazard field are 25/450, indicating the hazard field is moving at 25 kts., not 45 mph.

115. (Refer to Figure 16 on page 217.) What direction are the hazard fields moving?

A. Northwest.
B. Southeast.
C. Cannot determine without movement arrows.

Answer (B) is correct. *(AWS Sect 9)*
DISCUSSION: The blue-lined polygons to the southeast of each hazard field indicate a 1-hour extrapolated forecast of the hazard fields.
Answer (A) is incorrect. The blue-lined polygons indicate the direction in which the hazard field is moving. The majority of the blue-lined polygons are located to the southeast of the storm cells. Answer (C) is incorrect. The blue-lined polygons indicate the direction in which the hazard field is moving.

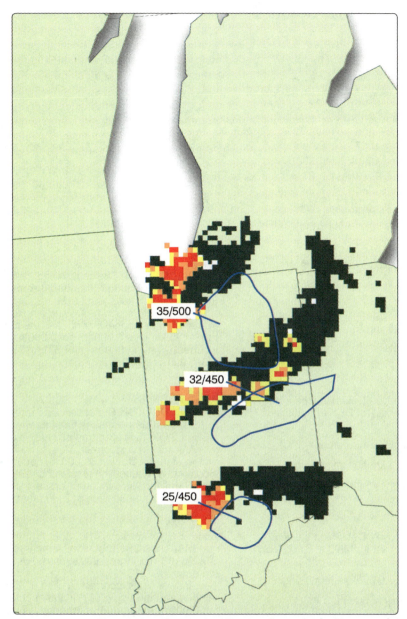

Figure 16. – Convective Weather Forecast.

6.22 Winds and Temperatures Aloft Forecast (FB)

```
FB WBC 151745
DATA BASED ON 151200Z
VALID 1600Z FOR USE 1800-0300Z. TEMPS NEG ABV 24000
```

FT	3000	6000	9000	12000	18000	24000	30000	34000	39000
ALS			2420	2635-08	2535-18	2444-30	245945	246755	246862
AMA		2714	2725+00	2625-04	2531-15	2542-27	265842	256352	256762
DEN			2321-04	2532-08	2434-19	2441-31	235347	236056	236262
HLC		1707-01	2113-03	2219-07	2330-17	2435-30	244145	244854	245561
MKC	0507	2006+03	2215-01	2322-06	2338-17	2348-29	236143	237252	238160
STL	2113	2325+7	2332+02	2339-04	2356-16	2373-27	239440	730649	731960

Figure 7. – Winds and Temperatures Aloft Forecast (FB).

116. (Refer to Figure 7 above.) What wind is forecast for STL at 9,000 feet?

A. 230° true at 32 knots.
B. 230° magnetic at 25 knots.
C. 230° true at 25 knots.

Answer (A) is correct. *(AWS Sect 7)*
DISCUSSION: The coded wind forecast for STL at 9,000 ft. is 2332+02. This means the wind is from 230° true at 32 kt., and the temperature is forecast to be +2°C.
Answer (B) is incorrect. Wind direction is referenced to true north, not magnetic north, and the forecast wind of 230° true at 25 kt. is for 6,000 ft., not 9,000 ft., at STL. Answer (C) is incorrect. The wind forecast at STL of 230° true at 25 kt. is for 6,000 ft., not 9,000 ft.

117. (Refer to Figure 7 above.) Determine the wind and temperature aloft forecast for DEN at 9,000 feet.

A. 230° true at 53 knots, temperature –47°C.
B. 230° magnetic at 53 knots, temperature 47°C.
C. 230° true at 21 knots, temperature –4°C.

Answer (C) is correct. *(AWS Sect 7)*
DISCUSSION: The coded wind forecast for DEN at 9,000 ft. is 2321-04. This means the forecast wind and temperature for DEN at 9,000 ft. is 230° true at 21 kt., temperature –4°C.
Answer (A) is incorrect. This is the forecast wind and temperature for DEN at 30,000 ft., not 9,000 ft. Answer (B) is incorrect. Wind direction is referenced to true north, not magnetic north. Additionally, the coded forecast for DEN at 9,000 ft. is 2321-04 or wind 230° true at 21 kt., temperature –4°C.

118. (Refer to Figure 7 above.) Determine the wind and temperature aloft forecast for MKC at 6,000 feet.

A. 050° true at 7 knots, temperature missing.
B. 200° true at 6 knots, temperature +3°C.
C. 200° magnetic at 6 knots, temperature +3°C.

Answer (B) is correct. *(AWS Sect 7)*
DISCUSSION: The coded forecast for MKC at 6,000 ft. is 2006+03. This translates to a wind of 200° true at 6 kt., temperature +3°C.
Answer (A) is incorrect. A wind of 050° true at 7 kt., temperature missing (0507) is the forecast for MKC at 3,000 ft., not 6,000 ft. Answer (C) is incorrect. Wind direction is referenced to true north, not magnetic north.

6.23 Terminal Aerodrome Forecast (TAF)

119. Which primary source should be used to obtain forecast weather information at your destination for the planned ETA?

A. Winds Aloft Chart.
B. Weather Depiction Charts.
C. Terminal Aerodrome Forecast (TAF).

Answer (C) is correct. *(AWS Sect 4)*
DISCUSSION: The TAF is a concise statement of the expected meteorological conditions at an airport during a specified period of time. The TAF usually covers an area within 5SM of the airport's center.
Answer (A) is incorrect. Winds and Temperatures Aloft Forecasts (FB) are computer-prepared forecasts of wind direction, wind speed, and temperature at specified times, altitudes, and locations. Answer (B) is incorrect. Weather depiction charts display information on current weather conditions and do not provide an indication of expected weather conditions at a point in the future. This product is being phased out by the FAA.

SU 6: Aviation Weather

120. (Refer to Figure 5 below.) In the TAF for KMCO, what does "SHRA" stand for?

KMCO 021136Z 0212/0312 22005KT P6SM VCSH
FEW026 FEW045 SCT180 TEMPO 0212/0214
3SM SHRA BKN020 OVC040 FM021400 27009KT
P6SM VCTS SCT020CB BKN035 OVC050 TEMPO
0214/0217 2SM TSRA BKN015CB OVC030
FM021800 34009KT P6SM SCT025 BKN060
FM022100 04010KT P6SM SCT040 BKN080
FM030000 09008KT P6SM SCT040 BKN120

A. Rain showers.
B. A shift in wind direction is expected.
C. A significant change in precipitation is possible.

Answer (A) is correct. *(AWS Sect 7)*
DISCUSSION: Expected weather is coded in TAF reports using the same format and contractions as METAR reports. "SHRA" means rain (RA) showers (SH).
Answer (B) is incorrect. "SHRA" means rain showers, not a shift in wind direction, is expected. Answer (C) is incorrect. "SHRA" means rain showers are forecast, not that a significant change in precipitation is possible.

TAF	
KMEM	121720Z 121818 20012KT 5SM HZ BKN030 PROB40 2022 1SM TSRA OVC008CB FM2200 33015G20KT P6SM BKN015 OVC025 PROB40 2202 3SM SHRA FM0200 35012KT OVC008 PROB40 0205 2SM-RASN BECMG 0608 02008KT BKN012 BECMG 1012 00000KT 3SM BR SKC TEMPO 1214 1/2SM FG FM1600 VRB06KT P6SM SKC=
KOKC	051130Z 051212 14008KT 5SM BR BKN030 TEMPO 1316 1 1/2SM BR FM1600 18010KT P6SM SKC BECMG 2224 20013G20KT 4SM SHRA OVC020 PROB40 0006 2SM TSRA OVC008CB BECMG 0608 21015KT P6SM SCT040=

Figure 5. – Terminal Aerodrome Forecasts (TAF).

121. (Refer to Figure 5 above.) What is the valid period for the TAF for KMEM?

A. 1800Z to 1800Z.
B. 1200Z to 1800Z.
C. 1200Z to 1200Z.

Answer (A) is correct. *(AWS Sect 7)*
DISCUSSION: The valid period of the forecast is a two-digit date followed by the two-digit beginning hour and two-digit ending hour in UTC (or Z). The valid period for the TAF for KMEM is shown as "121818" or the 12th day beginning at 1800Z and ending at 1800Z on the following day.
Answer (B) is incorrect. The first two digits are the date, so the TAF for KMEM is valid on the 12th day beginning at 1800Z, not 1200Z, to 1800Z on the following day. Answer (C) is incorrect. A valid period of 1200Z to 1200Z is for the TAF for KOKC, not KMEM.

122. (Refer to Figure 5 above.) In between 1000Z and 1200Z the visibility at KMEM is forecast to be

A. 6 statute miles.
B. ½ statute mile.
C. 3 statute miles.

Answer (C) is correct. *(AWS Sect 7)*
DISCUSSION: In the fourth line of the TAF for KMEM, it states that between 1000Z and 1200Z, conditions are forecast to become a calm wind with 3 SM visibility in mist and a clear sky.
Answer (A) is incorrect. The TAF for KMEM does not forecast any period where the visibility will be 6 SM. Answer (B) is incorrect. There is an occasional chance (temporary conditions) of 1/2 SM visibility between 1200Z and 1400Z, not between 1000Z and 1200Z.

123. (Refer to Figure 5 above.) In the TAF from KOKC, the clear sky becomes

A. overcast at 200 feet with the probability of becoming 400 feet overcast during the forecast period between 2200Z and 2400Z.
B. overcast at 2,000 feet during the forecast period between 2200Z and 2400Z.
C. overcast at 200 feet with a 40% probability of becoming overcast at 600 feet during the forecast period between 2200Z and 2400Z.

Answer (B) is correct. *(AWS Sect 7)*
DISCUSSION: In the TAF for KOKC, the clear sky (SKC) becomes overcast at 2,000 ft. (OVC020) during the forecast period between 2200Z and 2400Z (BECMG 2224).
Answer (A) is incorrect. Between 2200Z and 2400Z, the clear sky (SKC) will become overcast at 2,000 ft. (OVC020), not 200 ft. During the period between 2200Z and 2400Z, there is no probability forecast. Answer (C) is incorrect. Between 2200Z and 2400Z, the clear sky (SKC) will become overcast at 2,000 ft. (OVC020), not 200 ft. The probability forecast (PROB40) is for the period between 0000Z and 0600Z.

124. Vertical visibility is shown on Terminal Aerodrome Forecasts (TAF) reports when the sky is

A. overcast.
B. obscured.
C. partially obscured.

Answer (B) is correct. *(AWS Sect 7)*
DISCUSSION: When the sky is obscured due to a surface-based phenomenon, vertical visibility (VV) into the obscuration is reported/forecast.
Answer (A) is incorrect. Vertical visibility (VV) is shown on METAR/TAF reports when the sky is obscured. An overcast sky is shown as OVC on METAR/TAF reports. Answer (C) is incorrect. There is no provision in the body of METAR/TAF reports to indicate a partially obscured sky.

125. When the visibility is greater than 6 SM on a TAF it is expressed as

A. 6PSM.
B. P6SM.
C. 6SMP.

Answer (B) is correct. *(AWS Sect 7)*
DISCUSSION: When the forecast visibility is greater than 6 SM, it will be coded as P6SM.
Answer (A) is incorrect. Forecast visibility greater than 6 SM will be coded as P6SM, not 6PSM. Answer (C) is incorrect. Forecast visibility greater than 6 SM will be coded as P6SM, not 6SMP.

126. What is the wind shear forecast in the following TAF?

TAF
KCVG 231051Z 231212 12012KT 4SM –RA BR OVC008
  WS005/27050KT TEMPO 1719 1/2SM –RA FG
FM1930 09012KT 1SM –DZ BR VV003 BECMG
  2021 5SM HZ=

A. 5 feet AGL from 270° at 50 KT.
B. 50 feet AGL from 270° at 50 KT.
C. 500 feet AGL from 270° at 50 KT.

Answer (C) is correct. *(AIM Para 7-1-31)*
DISCUSSION: Wind shear in a TAF is a forecast of nonconvective low-level wind shear (up to 2,000 ft. AGL) and is entered after the sky condition when wind shear is expected. The wind shear forecast for KCVG is coded as **WS005/27050KT**, which means low-level wind shear at 500 ft. AGL, wind from 270° true at 50 kt.
Answer (A) is incorrect. The height of the wind shear (WS005) is 500 ft. AGL, not 5 ft. AGL. Answer (B) is incorrect. The height of the wind shear (WS005) is 500 ft. AGL, not 50 ft. AGL.

6.24 Convective Outlook Chart

127. (Refer to Figure 15 on page 221.) The bottom panel on this Convective Outlook Chart indicates

A. areas of AIRMETs and SIGMETs.
B. general thunderstorm activity.
C. forecast severe thunderstorm areas.

Answer (C) is correct. *(AWS Sect 6)*
DISCUSSION: On the bottom panel of the convective outlook chart, only areas of possible severe thunderstorms are forecast
Answer (A) is incorrect. Convective outlook charts forecast the risk of severe thunderstorms and tornadoes; the convective outlook chart does not indicate the specific locations of AIRMETs or SIGMETs. Answer (B) is incorrect. General thunderstorm activity is depicted on the top, not bottom, panel of the convective outlook chart.

128. (Refer to Figure 15 on page 221.) What percent coverage of severe thunderstorms is forecast to occur in the area of moderate risk in the north-central United States?

A. 6 to 10.
B. 10 to 50.
C. 50 to 90.

Answer (A) is correct. *(AWS Sect 6)*
DISCUSSION: The convective outlook area on the top panel shows that the moderate risk area is surrounded by a slight risk area. The moderate risk means 6-10% coverage and the slight risk is 2-5% coverage.
Answer (B) is incorrect. A forecast of 10-50% coverage is said to be high, not moderate, risk. Answer (C) is incorrect. Moderate risk on the convective outlook chart is forecast to be a 6-10% chance of occurrence, not 50-90%.

129. (Refer to Figure 15 on page 221.) Regarding Convective Outlook Charts, when well-organized severe thunderstorms are expected, but in small numbers and/or low coverage, the risk is referred to as

A. POSSIBLE.
B. MDT.
C. SLGT.

Answer (C) is correct. *(AWS Sect 6)*
DISCUSSION: When a slight (SLGT) risk of severe thunderstorms is indicated on a convective outlook chart, this implies that well organized severe thunderstorms are expected, but in small numbers and/or low coverage of the affected area.
Answer (A) is incorrect. "POSSIBLE" is not a term used on convective outlook charts to describe the risk of severe thunderstorm activity. Answer (B) is incorrect. A moderate (MDT) risk of severe thunderstorms implies a greater concentration of severe thunderstorms and, in most situations, a greater magnitude of severe weather.

SU 6: Aviation Weather

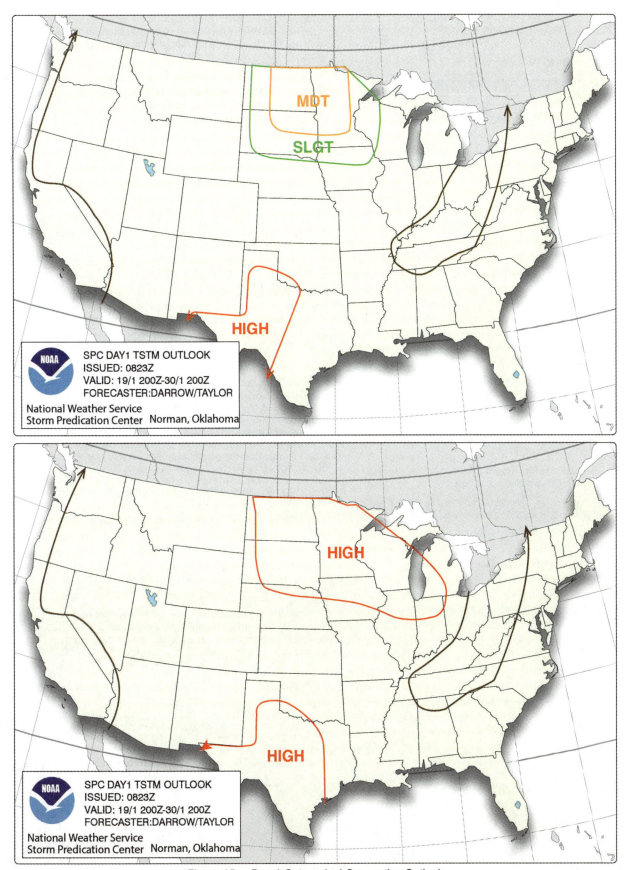

Figure 15. – Day 1 Categorical Convective Outlook.

130. If an area on a Convective Outlook Chart is labeled APCHG, this indicates

A. possible tornadoes.

B. thunderstorm activity may approach extreme intensity.

C. winds greater than or equal to 35 knots but less than 50 knots.

Answer (C) is correct. *(AWS Sect 6)*
DISCUSSION: APCHG means that thunderstorm activity may approach severe intensity, having surface winds greater than or equal to 35 kt. but less than 50 kt. and/or hail greater than or equal to 1/2 in. in diameter but less than 3/4 in. at the surface.
Answer (A) is incorrect. Tornadoes are associated with severe thunderstorms, and APCHG means severe thunderstorm but does not meet severe thunderstorm criteria. Answer (B) is incorrect. There is no special symbol to signify extreme thunderstorm intensity.

6.25 AIRMET and SIGMET

131. To determine the freezing level and areas of probable icing aloft, you should refer to

A. an Area Forecast.

B. an AIRMET or SIGMET.

C. a Weather Depiction Chart.

Answer (B) is correct. *(AWS Sect 6)*
DISCUSSION: In-flight aviation weather advisories (e.g., AIRMETs or SIGMETs) provide information on freezing levels and areas of probable icing aloft.
Answer (A) is incorrect. In-flight weather advisories, not an area forecast, provide information on freezing levels and icing conditions for a specific region. This product is being phased out by the FAA. Answer (C) is incorrect. A weather depiction chart is prepared from METAR reports and gives only a broad overview of the observed condition at the valid time of the chart. It does not provide any information on freezing levels and icing conditions for a specific region. This product is being phased out by the FAA.

132. What information is contained in a CONVECTIVE SIGMET in the conterminous United States?

A. Moderate thunderstorms and surface winds greater than 40 knots.

B. Tornadoes, embedded thunderstorms, and hail 3/4 inch or greater in diameter.

C. Severe icing, severe turbulence, or widespread dust storms lowering visibility to less than 3 miles.

Answer (B) is correct. *(AWS Sect 6)*
DISCUSSION: Convective SIGMETs notify pilots of the development of severe thunderstorms, including those due to tornadoes, lines of thunderstorms, embedded thunderstorms, and hail at the surface of 3/4 in. or greater.
Answer (A) is incorrect. A convective SIGMET is issued when thunderstorms produce surface winds greater than 50 kt., not 40 kt. Answer (C) is incorrect. Severe icing, severe turbulence, or widespread dust storms lowering visibility to less than 3 SM would be contained in a SIGMET, not a convective SIGMET.

133. Which in-flight advisory would contain information on severe icing?

A. PIREP.

B. SIGMET.

C. CONVECTIVE SIGMET.

Answer (B) is correct. *(AWS Sect 6)*
DISCUSSION: SIGMETs specifically forecast severe icing, severe or extreme turbulence, and obstructions (e.g., dust, etc.) lowering visibility to less than 3 SM.
Answer (A) is incorrect. A PIREP is a pilot report of in-flight weather, not an in-flight advisory message forecasting development of potentially dangerous weather. Answer (C) is incorrect. A convective SIGMET only implies possible severe icing in conjunction with forecast severe thunderstorms.

134. What information would be covered in an AIRMET?

A. Severe turbulence.

B. Extensive mountain obscurement.

C. Hail of 3/4 inch or greater diameter.

Answer (B) is correct. *(AWS Sect 6)*
DISCUSSION: AIRMETs specifically forecast moderate icing, moderate turbulence, sustained winds of 30 kt. or greater at the surface, extensive areas of IFR weather, and extensive mountain obscurement.
Answer (A) is incorrect. Severe turbulence would be covered in a SIGMET, not an AIRMET. Answer (C) is incorrect. Hail of 3/4 in. in diameter would be covered in a convective SIGMET.

6.26 Current Icing Potential and Forecast Icing Potential

135. (Refer to Figure 13 below.) For a flight between San Francisco, CA, and Seattle, WA, you should expect icing to accumulate to 1/4 inch thickness within:

A. 1 hour.
B. between 15 minutes and 1 hour.
C. less than 15 minutes.

Answer (C) is correct. *(Aviation Weather Center)*
DISCUSSION: The CIP/FIP indicates moderate to heavy icing between San Francisco and Seattle. Moderate icing indicates 1/4 inch accumulation between 5 minutes to 15 minutes, and severe icing indicates 1/4 inch accumulation at less than 5 minutes. Therefore, you should expect 1/4 inch accumulation in 15 minutes or less time.
Answer (A) is incorrect. Trace icing is expected to produce 1/4 inch thickness of ice in 1 hour. Most of the airspace between San Francisco and Seattle is moderate to severe, not trace. Answer (B) is incorrect. Light icing is expected to produce 1/4 inch thickness of ice between 15 minutes and 1 hour. Most of the airspace between San Francisco and Seattle is moderate to severe, not light. The best answer choice is accumulation of 1/4 inch of ice in less than 15 minutes.

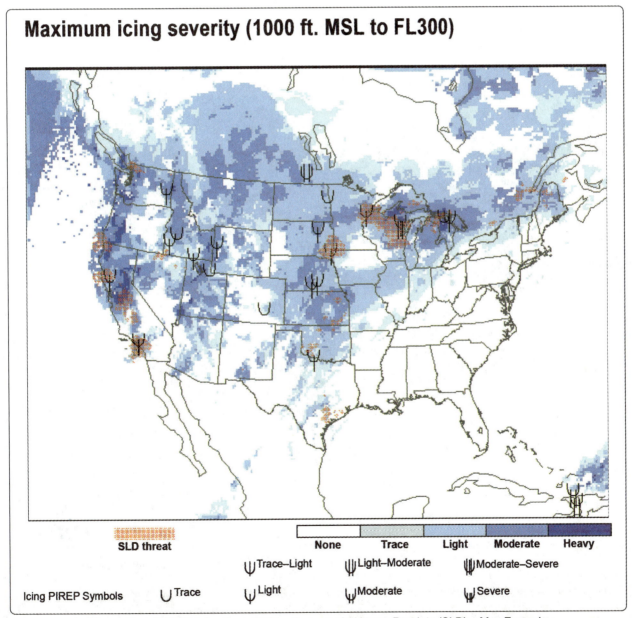

Figure 13. – CIP/FIP Icing Severity Plus Supercooled Large Droplets (SLD) – Max Example.

136. (Refer to Figure 13 below.) After identifying areas of potential icing, you should review which of the following weather products?

A. AIRMETs.
B. TAF.
C. METAR.

Answer (A) is correct. *(Aviation Weather Center)*
DISCUSSION: CIP/FIP is intended for flight planning purposes and should always be used in combination with icing information from all available sources including AIRMETs, SIGMETs, and PIREPs.
Answer (B) is incorrect. Although a TAF provides official information on the conditions for airports in a geographical area, it does not provide information concerning icing enroute. CIP/FIP is intended for flight planning purposes and should always be used in combination with icing information from all available sources including AIRMETs, SIGMETs, and PIREPs. Answer (C) is incorrect. METARs provide the most useful information for determining if you can arrive safely at your destination airport. It does not provide information concerning icing enroute. CIP/FIP is intended for flight planning purposes and should always be used in combination with icing information from all available sources including AIRMETs, SIGMETs, and PIREPs.

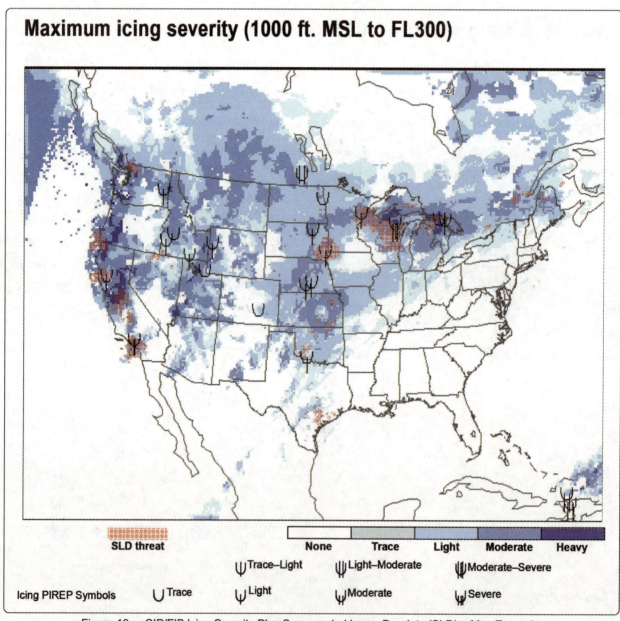

Figure 13. – CIP/FIP Icing Severity Plus Supercooled Large Droplets (SLD) – Max Example.

STUDY UNIT SEVEN
FEDERAL AVIATION REGULATIONS

(15 pages of outline)

7.1	14 CFR Part 1			
	1.2	Abbreviations and Symbols	(1 question)	227, 241
7.2	14 CFR Part 23			
	23.3	Airplane Categories	(1 question)	227, 241
7.3	14 CFR Part 61			
	61.3	Requirement for Certificates, Ratings, and Authorizations	(3 questions)	227, 241
	61.13	Issuance of Airman Certificates, Ratings, and Authorizations	(1 question)	227, 242
	61.15	Offenses Involving Alcohol or Drugs	(1 question)	227, 242
	61.19	Duration of Pilot and Instructor Certificates	(2 questions)	227, 242
	61.23	Medical Certificates: Requirement and Duration	(3 questions)	228, 243
	61.31	Type Rating Requirements, Additional Training, and Authorization Requirements	(5 questions)	228, 244
	61.35	Knowledge Test: Prerequisites and Passing Grades	(1 question)	228, 245
	61.37	Knowledge Tests: Cheating or Other Unauthorized Conduct	(2 questions)	228, 245
	61.39	Prerequisites for Practical Tests	(5 questions)	229, 246
	61.43	Practical Tests: General Procedures	(1 question)	229, 247
	61.45	Practical Tests: Required Aircraft and Equipment	(1 question)	229, 247
	61.49	Retesting after Failure	(6 questions)	229, 247
	61.51	Pilot Logbooks	(1 question)	229, 249
	61.56	Flight Review	(4 questions)	229, 249
	61.57	Recent Flight Experience: Pilot in Command	(3 questions)	230, 250
	61.60	Change of Address	(2 questions)	230, 251
	61.63	Additional Aircraft Ratings (other than for ratings at the airline transport pilot certification level)	(1 question)	230, 251
	61.69	Glider Towing: Experience and Training Requirements ...	(1 question)	230, 251
	61.83	Eligibility Requirements for Student Pilots	(1 question)	230, 252
	61.85	Application for a Student Pilot Certificate	(1 question)	230, 252
	61.87	Solo Requirements for Student Pilots	(6 questions)	230, 252
	61.93	Solo Cross-Country Flight Requirements	(4 questions)	231, 253
	61.95	Operations in Class B Airspace and at Airports Located within Class B Airspace	(2 questions)	231, 254
	61.101	Recreational Pilot Privileges and Limitations	(3 questions)	231, 255
	61.109	Aeronautical Experience	(5 questions)	231, 255
	61.123	Eligibility Requirements: General	(1 question)	231, 256
	61.129	Aeronautical Experience	(3 questions)	231, 257
	61.133	Commercial Pilot Privileges and Limitations	(1 question)	232, 257
	61.189	Flight Instructor Records	(2 questions)	232, 258
	61.191	Additional Flight Instructor Ratings	(1 question)	232, 258
	61.195	Flight Instructor Limitations and Qualifications	(7 questions)	232, 258
	61.197	Renewal of Flight Instructor Certificates	(1 question)	232, 260
	61.199	Expired Flight Instructor Certificates and Ratings	(4 questions)	232, 260
	61.315	Sport Pilot Privileges and Limitations: Pilot in Command ..	(4 questions)	233, 261
	61.325	Required Endorsements for Class B, C, and D Airspaces	(2 questions)	233, 262
7.4	14 CFR Part 91			
	91.3	Responsibility and Authority of the Pilot in Command	(1 question)	234, 262
	91.9	Civil Aircraft Flight Manual, Marking, and Placard Requirements	(1 question)	234, 262
	91.17	Alcohol or Drugs	(3 questions)	234, 263
	91.103	Preflight Action	(2 questions)	234, 263
	91.107	Use of Safety Belts, Shoulder Harnesses, and Child Restraint Systems	(1 question)	234, 264

	91.109	Flight Instruction; Simulated Instrument Flight and Certain Flight Tests	(1 question)	234, 264
	91.111	Operating near Other Aircraft	(1 question)	234, 264
	91.113	Right-of-Way Rules: Except Water Operations	(5 questions)	235, 264
	91.117	Aircraft Speed	(4 questions)	235, 265
	91.119	Minimum Safe Altitudes: General	(3 questions)	235, 266
	91.123	Compliance with ATC Clearances and Instructions	(1 question)	235, 267
	91.125	ATC Light Signals	(3 questions)	236, 267
	91.127	Operating on or in the Vicinity of an Airport in Class E Airspace	(1 question)	236, 268
	91.129	Operations in Class D Airspace	(2 questions)	236, 268
	91.131	Operations in Class B Airspace	(3 questions)	236, 268
	91.135	Operations in Class A Airspace	(1 question)	236, 269
	91.151	Fuel Requirements for Flight in VFR Conditions	(2 questions)	236, 269
	91.153	VFR Flight Plan: Information Required	(1 question)	236, 270
	91.155	Basic VFR Weather Minimums	(7 questions)	237, 270
	91.157	Special VFR Weather Minimums	(3 questions)	237, 271
	91.159	VFR Cruising Altitude or Flight Level	(2 questions)	237, 272
	91.203	Civil Aircraft: Certifications Required	(1 question)	237, 273
	91.205	Powered Civil Aircraft with Standard Category U.S. Airworthiness Certificates: Instrument and Equipment Requirements	(2 questions)	237, 273
	91.207	Emergency Locator Transmitters	(4 questions)	238, 273
	91.209	Aircraft Lights	(4 questions)	238, 274
	91.211	Supplemental Oxygen	(2 questions)	238, 275
	91.213	Inoperative Instruments and Equipment	(3 questions)	238, 276
	91.215	ATC Transponder and Altitude Reporting Equipment and Use	(4 questions)	238, 277
	91.307	Parachutes and Parachuting	(1 question)	239, 278
	91.403	General (Maintenance, Preventive Maintenance, and Alterations)	(2 questions)	239, 278
	91.405	Maintenance Required	(1 question)	239, 279
	91.407	Operation after Maintenance, Preventive Maintenance, Rebuilding, or Alteration	(1 question)	239, 279
	91.409	Inspections	(3 questions)	239, 279
	91.413	ATC Transponder Tests and Inspections	(2 questions)	239, 280
	91.417	Maintenance Records	(1 question)	239, 280
	91.421	Rebuilt Engine Maintenance Records	(1 question)	239, 280
7.5	NTSB Part 830			
	830.2	Definitions	(1 question)	240, 281
	830.5	Immediate Notification	(3 questions)	240, 281
	830.15	Reports and Statements to Be Filed	(2 questions)	240, 282

This study unit contains outlines of major concepts tested, sample questions and answers regarding pertinent Federal Aviation Regulations, and an explanation of each answer. The table of contents above lists each subunit within this study unit, the number of questions pertaining to that particular subunit, and the pages on which the outlines and questions begin, respectively.

Recall that the **sole purpose** of this book is to expedite your passing of the FAA pilot knowledge test for the CFI, BGI, or AGI certificate. Accordingly, all extraneous material (i.e., topics or regulations not directly tested on the FAA pilot knowledge test) is omitted, even though much more knowledge is necessary to become a proficient flight or ground instructor. This additional material is presented in *Pilot Handbook* and *Flight Instructor Flight Maneuvers and Practical Test Prep*, available from Gleim Publications, Inc. Order online at www.GleimAviation.com.

SU 7: Federal Aviation Regulations

NOTE: The FAA now refers to the Federal Aviation Regulations as "14 CFR" rather than "FAR." CFR stands for Code of Federal Regulations, and the Federal Aviation Regulations are in Title 14. For example, FAR Part 1 and FAR 61.109 are now referred to as 14 CFR Part 1 and 14 CFR Sec. 61.109, respectively.

7.1 14 CFR PART 1

1.2 Abbreviations and Symbols

1. V_s means the minimum steady flight speed at which an airplane is controllable.

7.2 14 CFR PART 23

23.3 Airplane Categories

1. If the certification category of an airplane is listed as "utility," it means the airplane is intended for all nonacrobatic maneuvers plus limited acrobatics, including spins, lazy eights, chandelles, and steep turns between 60° and 90°.

7.3 14 CFR PART 61

61.3 Requirement for Certificates, Ratings, and Authorizations

1. While operating as pilot in command (PIC) of an aircraft, you must have an appropriate pilot certificate and a current medical certificate in your personal possession.
2. A flight instructor is required to have a current and valid pilot certificate and flight instructor certificate to provide instruction to any student pilot.
   a. A flight instructor, other than a flight instructor with a sport pilot rating, must also have a current medical certificate to provide primary training to a student pilot who cannot legally act as PIC of the airplane.
   b. A flight instructor with a sport pilot rating must also have a valid state-issued driver's license or a medical certificate when conducting flight instruction to a sport pilot applicant.

61.13 Issuance of Airman Certificates, Ratings, and Authorizations

1. A person whose flight instructor certificate has been suspended may not apply for any rating, certificate, or authorization to be added to that certificate during the period of suspension.

61.15 Offenses Involving Alcohol or Drugs

1. Conviction of an offense involving alcohol or drugs is grounds for
   a. Suspension or revocation of any certificate or rating issued under 14 CFR Part 61
   b. The denial of an application for any certificate or rating issued under 14 CFR Part 61 for a period of up to 1 year after the final conviction date

61.19 Duration of Pilot and Instructor Certificates

1. Student Pilot Certificates: The new student pilot application requirements went into effect on April 1, 2016. Student pilots are now issued a separate permanent plastic certificate instead of a combined medical and student pilot certificate on paper. The plastic certificate does not have an expiration date.
   a. If a student was issued a combined medical/student pilot certificate prior to this change, his or her certificate is valid until the existing expiration date. After expiration, the student pilot must submit a new application under the new process.

2. The duration of a flight instructor certificate is valid for 24 calendar months from the month in which it was issued or renewed.
3. A ground instructor certificate is issued without a specific expiration date.

61.23 Medical Certificates: Requirement and Duration

1. For those operations requiring a commercial pilot certificate, a second-class medical certificate expires at the end of the last day of the month 12 months after the date of examination.
2. For private, recreational, flight instructor, student pilot, or sport pilot operations (when not using a U.S. driver's license as medical qualification), any class of medical certificate expires at the end of the last day of the month either
    a. 60 months after the date of examination, if you are less than 40 years old on the date of your examination, or
    b. 24 months after the date of examination, if you are 40 years old or older on the date of your examination.

61.31 Type Rating Requirements, Additional Training, and Authorization Requirements

1. To act as pilot in command, a person is required to receive and log ground and flight training and obtain a logbook endorsement of proficiency in each of the following airplanes:
    a. High-performance airplane, which is an airplane with an engine of more than 200 horsepower
    b. Complex airplane, which is an airplane that has retractable landing gear, flaps, and a controllable pitch propeller
2. No person may act as pilot in command of a pressurized airplane with a service ceiling or maximum operating altitude, whichever is lower, above 25,000 ft. MSL unless that person has received ground and flight training in high-altitude operations and a logbook endorsement certifying this training.
3. A private pilot with ASEL ratings who has never flown a tailwheel airplane must have received instruction and a logbook endorsement before acting as PIC in such an airplane.
4. The pilot in command must hold a type rating when operating a turbojet-powered airplane.

61.35 Knowledge Test: Prerequisites and Passing Grades

1. According to 14 CFR 61.183, Eligibility Requirements (flight instructor), flight instructor applicants are not required to have a knowledge test endorsement to take the knowledge test, unless the applicant has previously failed the test.
    a. Flight instructor applicants must still receive and log the appropriate aeronautical knowledge training found in 14 CFR 61.185, Aeronautical Knowledge (flight instructor).
2. The minimum documentation required to take any flight instructor knowledge test is proper identification, which contains your photograph, signature, actual address, and date of birth showing you meet the age requirements to take the tests.

61.37 Knowledge Tests: Cheating or Other Unauthorized Conduct

1. A person who has cheated or committed any unauthorized act during a knowledge test may not take another knowledge test within 1 year.
    a. Also, any certificate or rating (s)he holds may be suspended or revoked.

61.39 Prerequisites for Practical Tests

1. To be eligible for a practical test under 14 CFR Part 61, an applicant is required to have passed the appropriate knowledge test (when required) within the preceding 24 calendar months.
2. A written statement from an authorized instructor certifying that an applicant has received the required training in preparation for a practical test must be dated within 2 calendar months preceding the month of application.
3. An applicant must hold at least a third-class medical certificate for any practical test.
    a. EXAMPLE: If an applicant who holds a commercial pilot certificate with airplane, single-engine land (ASEL) ratings, and who is seeking a multiengine land (MEL) rating at the commercial level, has a second-class medical certificate issued 19 months ago, (s)he may still take the practical test.

61.43 Practical Tests: General Procedures

1. If all increments of a practical test for a certificate or rating are not completed on the same date, all remaining increments must be satisfactorily completed no later than 60 days from the date of the test.
    a. Otherwise, the entire test must be repeated.

61.45 Practical Tests: Required Aircraft and Equipment

1. One requirement for an aircraft furnished for a practical test is that it must have no prescribed operating limitations that prohibit its use in any required area of operation.

61.49 Retesting after Failure

1. A person who fails a knowledge or practical test may immediately reapply for the test only after (s)he has received
    a. The necessary training from an authorized instructor who has determined that the person is proficient to pass the test
    b. An endorsement from the instructor who gave the person the additional training
2. A flight instructor applicant must demonstrate spins in an airplane or glider when the applicant is being retested for deficiencies in instructional proficiency on stall awareness or spins demonstrated during an initial practical test.
3. A flight instructor recommendation is not required for an ATP applicant except when applying for a retest.

61.51 Pilot Logbooks

1. A pilot exercising the privileges of a commercial certificate need only record the flight time necessary to meet the recent flight experience requirements.

61.56 Flight Review

1. A flight review consists of a minimum of 1 hr. of ground training and 1 hr. of flight training. The review must include
    a. The current general operating and flight rules of Part 91
    b. Those maneuvers and procedures necessary for the pilot to demonstrate the appropriate pilot privileges

2. No pilot may fly solo who has not satisfactorily accomplished a flight review in any aircraft for which (s)he is rated within the preceding 24 calendar months.

   a. A flight review is not required if a pilot has completed, within the time specified, a pilot proficiency check conducted by the FAA.

   b. A flight instructor who has satisfactorily completed a renewal of a flight instructor certificate under 14 CFR 61.197 does not need to accomplish the 1 hour of ground training.

61.57 Recent Flight Experience: Pilot in Command

1. To meet the recent flight experience requirements for acting as PIC carrying passengers at night, a pilot must have made within the preceding 90 days and from 1 hr. after sunset to 1 hr. before sunrise three takeoffs and landings to a full stop in the same category, class, and type (if a type rating is required) of aircraft to be used.

   a. If this requirement is not met, no passengers may be carried beginning 1 hr. after sunset.

2. To meet the recent flight experience requirements for acting as PIC carrying passengers in a tailwheel airplane, a pilot must have made, within the preceding 90 days, three takeoffs and landings to a full stop in a tailwheel airplane.

61.60 Change of Address

1. To exercise pilot privileges, one must report a change of permanent mailing address to the FAA Airman Certification branch within 30 days of a move.

61.63 Additional Aircraft Ratings (other than for ratings at the airline transport pilot certification level)

1. To add a category rating to your certificate, you do not have to take an additional knowledge test if you hold an airplane, rotorcraft, powered-lift, or airship rating at the same certificate level.

   a. EXAMPLE: If a private pilot (airplane) wishes to obtain a private certificate (glider), (s)he is not required to sit for a knowledge test.

61.69 Glider Towing: Experience and Training Requirements

1. A private pilot with an ASEL rating may act as PIC of an airplane towing a glider if, within the preceding 12 months, this pilot has made three flights as PIC of a glider towed by an aircraft.

61.83 Eligibility Requirements for Student Pilots

1. To be eligible for a student pilot certificate limited to airplanes, an applicant is required to be at least 16 years old.

61.85 Application for a Student Pilot Certificate

1. Student pilot certificate applications can be accepted by a Certificated Flight Instructor (CFI), Airman Certification Representative (ACR) at a Part 141 flight school, designated pilot examiner (DPE), or FAA Aviation Safety Inspector.

61.87 Solo Requirements for Student Pilots

1. Prior to operating an aircraft in solo flight, a student pilot must have received a flight instructor endorsement in their logbook, within the preceding 90 days, stating that instruction was given in the same make and model aircraft to be flown and that the student is competent to make a safe solo flight.

2. Prior to solo flight, each student pilot is required to take a knowledge test that is administered by the student's authorized instructor.

   a. The test must include applicable sections of 14 CFR Parts 61 and 91, airspace rules and procedures for the airport where the solo flight will be conducted, and flight characteristics and operational limitations of make and model aircraft to be flown.

3. Prior to solo flight, a student must have received (among other things) flight training in ground reference maneuvers.

61.93 Solo Cross-Country Flight Requirements

1. A student pilot whose logbook is not endorsed by a flight instructor to make solo cross-country flights is prohibited from flying solo beyond 25 NM from the point of departure.
2. One requirement for a student pilot to be authorized to make a solo cross-country flight is an endorsement in the student's logbook that the preflight planning and preparation has been reviewed and the student is prepared to make the flight safely.

   a. However, students may make repeated solo cross-country flights without each flight being logbook-endorsed provided the flights take place under the following stipulated conditions:

      1) The route is no more than 50 NM from the point of departure.
      2) Instruction was given in both directions over the route.

61.95 Operations in Class B Airspace and at Airports Located within Class B Airspace

1. To operate an aircraft on a solo flight within Class B airspace, a student must have a logbook endorsement showing that (s)he has received ground training on and flight training in that specific Class B airspace area for which solo flight is authorized within the 90-day period preceding the date of the flight.

   a. Only the flight instructor who conducted the training is authorized to make this endorsement.

61.101 Recreational Pilot Privileges and Limitations

1. A recreational pilot certificate may be issued for airplanes, gyroplanes, and helicopters.
2. A recreational pilot is required to carry a logbook with the required endorsements on all flights when serving as pilot in command.
3. A recreational pilot with less than 400 hr. flight time may not act as PIC unless the pilot has logged PIC time in the last 180 days.

61.109 Aeronautical Experience

1. A student must receive 3 hr. of night flight training that includes

   a. One cross-country flight of more than 100 NM total distance
   b. 10 takeoffs and 10 landings to a full stop at an airport

2. A student must log at least 3 hr. of cross-country training (dual) and 5 hr. of solo cross-country flight.

61.123 Eligibility Requirements: General

1. The minimum age required to be eligible for a commercial pilot certificate is 18 years.

61.129 Aeronautical Experience

1. For a commercial pilot certificate with an airplane rating, an applicant must have at least 250 hr. of flight time as pilot.

   a. The flight time may include up to 50 hr. of instruction in a simulator.

      1) Thus, only 200 hr. of actual flight time in an aircraft are required.

b. All time logged as second in command (SIC) while acting as safety pilot for another pilot flying "under the hood" counts toward total time, as long as the other requirements of 100 hr. PIC and 50 hr. instruction received are met.

2. The applicant is required to have a minimum of 50 hr. of cross-country experience.

61.133 Commercial Pilot Privileges and Limitations

1. If a commercial pilot does not have an instrument rating, the carrying of passengers for hire on cross-country flights of more than 50 NM or at night is prohibited.

61.189 Flight Instructor Records

1. All flight training, flight simulator training, and ground training time must be certified by the instructor from whom it was received.
2. The name, type, and date of each student pilot endorsement given shall be retained by each flight instructor for a period of at least 3 years.

61.191 Additional Flight Instructor Ratings

1. A flight instructor who applies for an additional rating on that certificate must have a minimum of 15 hr. as PIC in the category and class of aircraft appropriate to the rating sought.

61.195 Flight Instructor Limitations and Qualifications

1. In order for a certificated flight instructor to prepare an applicant for an initial flight instructor certificate, the flight instructor must have held a flight instructor certificate for at least 24 months and given a minimum of 200 hr. of flight training.
2. During any 24 consecutive hr., an instructor is limited to 8 hr. of flight training.
3. To endorse a student for solo cross-country privileges, an instructor is required, in part, to have given that student the required cross-country flight training.
4. To endorse a student pilot's logbook for solo flight, an instructor is required, in part, to have given that student flight training in the type (make and model) of aircraft involved.
5. Sample endorsement templates for instructors to use can be found in FAA Advisory Circular 61-65, Appendix 1.
6. If flight training is being given in a helicopter or multi-engine airplane, the instructor is required to have at least 5 hr. of experience as PIC in the same make and model of aircraft involved.

61.197 Renewal of Flight Instructor Certificates

1. A flight instructor certificate may be renewed by
   a. Taking a practical test,
   b. Providing a record of instruction showing evidence the instructor is a competent flight instructor, or
   c. Completing a flight instructor refresher course within 3 calendar months of the application for renewal.

61.199 Expired Flight Instructor Certificates and Ratings

1. The holder of an expired flight instructor certificate may exchange that certificate for a new one by passing the appropriate practical test.
2. To reinstate an expired flight instructor certificate and all ratings on it, you may pass a flight instructor certification practical test for one of the ratings held on the expired flight instructor certificate or add a new flight instructor rating to the certificate.

61.315 Sport Pilot Privileges and Limitations: Pilot in Command

NOTE: This section is only tested on the Flight Instructor with a Sport Pilot Rating (SIA) FAA Knowledge Test.

1. Sport pilots may not act as pilot in command of a light-sport aircraft while carrying more than one passenger.
2. As a sport pilot, you must pay at least half of the operating expenses of a flight. The operating expenses that may be shared with a passenger involve only fuel, oil, airport expenses, or aircraft rental fees.
3. Sport pilots may not operate
    a. For compensation or hire
    b. In furtherance of a business
    c. In Class A airspace
    d. In Class B, C, and D airspace or at an airport or through airspace having an operational control tower without CFI training and logbook endorsement
    e. Aircraft in flight to a prospective buyer
    f. In a passenger-carrying airlift sponsored by a charitable organization
    g. Above 10,000 ft. MSL or above 2,000 ft. AGL, whichever is higher
    h. Without visual reference to the surface
    i. In less than 3 statute miles
    j. At night
    k. Contrary to any aircraft, flight instructor, or other limitations
    l. While towing any object
    m. In aircraft with V_H above 87 KCAS without CFI training and logbook endorsement
    n. Outside the United States unless you have prior authorization from the country in which you seek to operate
    o. In aircraft requiring more than one pilot

61.325 Required Endorsements for Class B, C, and D Airspaces

NOTE: This section is only tested on the Flight Instructor with a Sport Pilot Rating (SIA) FAA Knowledge Test.

1. A sport pilot must receive and log ground and flight training to operate a light-sport aircraft at an airport in airspace within Class B, C, and D airspace or in other airspace with an airport that has an operational control tower.
    a. The CFI who provides the training must provide the pilot with a logbook endorsement that certifies proficiency in the following aeronautical knowledge areas and areas of operation:
        1) The use of radios, communications, navigation system/facilities, and radar services.
        2) Operations at airports with an operating control tower to include three takeoffs and three landings to a full stop, with each landing involving a flight in the traffic pattern at an airport with an operating control tower.
        3) Applicable flight rules of 14 CFR Part 91 for operations in Class B, C, and D airspace and air traffic control clearances.

7.4 14 CFR PART 91

91.3 Responsibility and Authority of the Pilot in Command

1. If an in-flight emergency requires immediate action, a PIC may deviate from the 14 CFRs to the extent required to meet that emergency.

91.9 Civil Aircraft Flight Manual, Marking, and Placard Requirements

1. An airplane's operating limitations may be found in

    a. The airplane's flight manual,
    b. Approved manual material,
    c. Markings and placards, or
    d. Any combination thereof.

91.17 Alcohol or Drugs

1. A person may not act as a crewmember of a civil airplane if alcoholic beverages have been consumed by that person within the preceding 8 hr., or if his or her blood alcohol level is .04% or more.

2. A pilot may allow a person who is obviously under the influence of intoxicating liquors or drugs to be carried aboard an aircraft only if the person is a medical patient under proper care or in an emergency.

91.103 Preflight Action

1. Pilots are required to familiarize themselves with all available information concerning the flight prior to every flight, and specifically to determine,

    a. For any flight, runway lengths at airports of intended use and the airplane's takeoff and landing requirements
    b. For IFR flights or any flight not in the vicinity of an airport,

        1) Weather reports and forecasts
        2) Fuel requirements for the flight
        3) Alternatives available if the planned flight cannot be completed
        4) Any known traffic delays

91.107 Use of Safety Belts, Shoulder Harnesses, and Child Restraint Systems

1. The pilot in command must ensure that each person on board an aircraft is briefed on how to fasten and unfasten seatbelts and, if installed, shoulder harnesses.

91.109 Flight Instruction; Simulated Instrument Flight and Certain Flight Tests

1. If a pilot in a multi-engine land airplane is planning to practice IFR procedures under a hood in VMC conditions, the safety pilot must have at least a private pilot certificate, with airplane multi-engine land rating.

    a. Since the safety pilot is assigned certain duties, (s)he is considered to be a required flight crewmember and must also possess a current medical certificate.

91.111 Operating near Other Aircraft

1. An airplane may not be operated in formation flight while passengers are carried for hire.

91.113 Right-of-Way Rules: Except Water Operations

1. When two aircraft, regardless of category, approach each other at the same altitude and on a head-on collision course, both should give way to the right.
2. When aircraft of the same category are converging at approximately the same altitude, except head-on or nearly so, the aircraft to the other's right has the right-of-way.
    a. EXAMPLE: On a night flight, the pilot of aircraft A observes only the green navigation light of aircraft B, and the aircraft are converging. Aircraft A has the right-of-way because it is to the right of aircraft B.
3. When aircraft of different categories are converging, an airship has the right-of-way over an airplane or a rotorcraft, regardless of their relative positions.
    a. However, an aircraft towing or refueling another aircraft has the right-of-way over all other engine-driven aircraft.
4. When two or more aircraft are approaching an airport for the purpose of landing, the right-of-way belongs to the aircraft at the lower altitude, but it shall not take advantage of this rule to cut in front of or to overtake another.

91.117 Aircraft Speed

1. Unless otherwise authorized or required by ATC, the maximum indicated airspeed at which a person may operate an aircraft below 10,000 ft. MSL or in Class B airspace is 250 kt.
2. The maximum indicated airspeed permitted when operating an aircraft at or below 2,500 ft. AGL within 4 NM of the primary airport in Class C or Class D airspace is 200 kt.
3. When flying beneath the lateral limits, or through a VFR corridor, of Class B airspace, the maximum indicated airspeed authorized is 200 kt.

91.119 Minimum Safe Altitudes: General

1. To operate an aircraft over any congested area, a pilot should maintain an altitude of at least 1,000 ft. above the highest obstacle within a horizontal radius of 2,000 ft. of the aircraft.
2. The minimum distance at which an airplane may be operated over a structure that is located in a sparsely populated area is 500 ft. from the structure.
3. Except when necessary for takeoff or landing, the minimum safe altitude for a pilot to operate an aircraft anywhere is an altitude allowing, if a power unit fails, an emergency landing without undue hazard to persons or property on the surface.

91.123 Compliance with ATC Clearances and Instructions

1. If you deviate from an ATC instruction during an emergency and are given priority you must, if requested, submit a detailed report within 48 hr. to the manager of the ATC facility.

91.125 ATC Light Signals

1. ATC light signals have the meanings shown below.

Light Signal	On the Ground	In the Air
Steady Green	Cleared for takeoff	Cleared to land
Flashing Green	Cleared to taxi	Return for landing *(to be followed by steady green at proper time)*
Steady Red	Stop	Give way to other aircraft and continue circling
Flashing Red	Taxi clear of landing area (runway) in use	Airport unsafe -- Do not land
Flashing White	Return to starting point on airport	Not applicable
Alternating Red and Green	General warning signal -- Exercise extreme caution	General warning signal -- Exercise extreme caution

91.127 Operating on or in the Vicinity of an Airport in Class E Airspace

1. The correct departure procedure at a noncontrolled airport is the FAA-approved departure procedure for that airport.

91.129 Operations in Class D Airspace

1. A turbine-powered or large airplane is required to enter an airport traffic pattern at an altitude of at least 1,500 ft. AGL.
2. When an airport without a control tower lies within the controlled airspace of an airport with an operating tower, two-way radio communications with ATC are required for landing clearance at the tower-controlled airport only, as well as to fly through the area.

91.131 Operations in Class B Airspace

1. Solo student pilots are authorized to fly in Class B airspace if they meet certain requirements that are specified in 14 CFR 61.95 (e.g., logbook endorsement).
    a. However, there are specified primary Class B airports at which student pilots may not take off or land.
2. The minimum equipment requirement when operating an aircraft within Class B airspace is two-way radio communications and transponder with encoding altimeter.

91.135 Operations in Class A Airspace

1. VFR flights are prohibited in Class A airspace.

91.151 Fuel Requirements for Flight in VFR Conditions

1. The minimum fuel requirement for flight under VFR at night in an airplane is enough to fly to the first point of intended landing and to fly after that for 45 min. at normal cruise speed.
    a. During daylight hours, you must have enough fuel to fly to the point of intended landing and to fly after that for 30 min. at normal cruise speed.

91.153 VFR Flight Plan: Information Required

1. On your flight plan, you should enter the true airspeed at the planned cruise altitude.

91.155 Basic VFR Weather Minimums

Airspace	Flight Visibility	Distance from Clouds
Class A	Not Applicable	Not applicable
Class B	3 SM	Clear of Clouds
Class C	3 SM	500 ft. below 1,000 ft. above 2,000 ft. horiz.
Class D	3 SM	500 ft. below 1,000 ft. above 2,000 ft. horiz.
Class E:		
Less than 10,000 ft. MSL	3 SM	500 ft. below 1,000 ft. above 2,000 ft. horiz.
At or above 10,000 ft. MSL	5 SM	1,000 ft. below 1,000 ft. above 1 SM horiz.

Airspace	Flight Visibility	Distance from Clouds
Class G:		
1,200 ft. or less above the surface (regardless of MSL altitude)		
Day	1 SM	Clear of clouds
Night, except as in 1. below	3 SM	500 ft. below 1,000 ft. above 2,000 ft. horiz.
More than 1,200 ft. above the surface but less than 10,000 ft. MSL		
Day	1 SM	500 ft. below 1,000 ft. above 2,000 ft. horiz.
Night	3 SM	500 ft. below 1,000 ft. above 2,000 ft. horiz.
More than 1,200 ft. above the surface and at or above 10,000 ft. MSL	5 SM	1,000 ft. below 1,000 ft. above 1 SM horiz.

1. An airplane may be operated clear of clouds in Class G airspace at night below 1,200 ft. AGL when the visibility is less than 3 SM but more than 1 SM in an airport traffic pattern and within 1/2 NM of the runway.

91.157 Special VFR Weather Minimums

1. When operating an airplane under special VFR, the flight visibility is required to be at least 1 SM.
2. At an airport at which ground visibility is not reported, takeoffs and landings of airplanes under special VFR are authorized if the flight visibility is at least 1 SM.
3. No person may operate an airplane between sunset and sunrise under special VFR unless the airplane is equipped (and the pilot is certified) for instrument flight.

91.159 VFR Cruising Altitude or Flight Level

1. When operating under VFR at more than 3,000 ft. AGL, cruising altitudes to be maintained are based upon the magnetic course being flown.
   a. 0° to 179° inclusive, odd thousands plus 500 ft.
   b. 180° to 359° inclusive, even thousands plus 500 ft.
   c. As a memory aid, the "E" in even does not indicate east; i.e., on easterly heading of 0° through 179°, use odd rather than even.

91.203 Civil Aircraft: Certifications Required

1. No person may operate an aircraft unless it has within it an airworthiness certificate, registration certificate, and approved flight manual.

91.205 Powered Civil Aircraft with Standard Category U.S. Airworthiness Certificates: Instrument and Equipment Requirements

1. A magnetic compass is required for powered aircraft during VFR night flight.

2. If an aircraft is operated for hire over water and beyond power-off gliding distance from shore, approved flotation gear and at least one pyrotechnic signaling device must be readily available to each occupant.

91.207 Emergency Locator Transmitters

1. ELT batteries must be replaced or recharged after 1 cumulative hr. of use or after 50% of their useful life expires.
2. ELTs are required to be inspected every 12 months for proper installation, battery corrosion, operation of the controls and crash sensor, and the presence of a sufficient signal radiated from its antenna.
3. Airplanes may be operated for training purposes within 50 NM of the originating airport without an ELT.
4. No person may operate an aircraft more than 90 days after the ELT is initially removed for maintenance.

91.209 Aircraft Lights

1. From sunset to sunrise, no person may park or move an aircraft in a night-flight operations area of an airport unless the aircraft is
    a. Clearly illuminated,
    b. Equipped with lighted position lights, or
    c. Operated in an area that is marked by obstruction lights.
2. Position lights are required to be displayed on all aircraft in flight from sunset to sunrise.
    a. Thus, an aircraft not equipped with position lights must terminate flight at sunset.
    b. EXAMPLE: If official sunset is 1730 EST, the latest time a pilot may operate that aircraft is 1729 EST.

91.211 Supplemental Oxygen

1. Unless each occupant is provided with supplemental oxygen, no person may operate a civil aircraft of U.S. registry above a cabin pressure altitude of 15,000 ft. MSL.
2. At cabin pressure altitudes above 12,500 ft. MSL, up to and including 14,000 ft. MSL, the required minimum flight crew must use supplemental oxygen after 30 min. at those altitudes.
    a. EXAMPLE: A cabin pressure altitude of 12,600 ft. MSL would allow a pilot to operate an aircraft up to 30 min. without supplemental oxygen.

91.213 Inoperative Instruments and Equipment

1. The primary purpose of a minimum equipment list (MEL) is to list the equipment that can be inoperative and still not affect the airworthiness of an aircraft.
2. Authority for approval of an MEL must be obtained from the FAA district office, i.e., FSDO.
3. If an aircraft operating under 14 CFR Part 91, and for which a Master MEL has not been developed, is determined to have an inoperative instrument or piece of equipment that does not constitute a hazard to the aircraft, the item should be deactivated and placarded "Inoperative," but repairs can be deferred indefinitely.

91.215 ATC Transponder and Altitude Reporting Equipment and Use

1. A coded transponder with altitude reporting capability (Mode C) is required
    a. For all controlled airspace at or above 10,000 ft. MSL and below the floor of Class A airspace, excluding airspace at or below 2,500 ft. AGL.
    b. When operating within 30 NM of the primary Class B airport.

SU 7: Federal Aviation Regulations

2. To overfly Class C airspace, a transponder with automatic altitude reporting capability is required upward to 10,000 ft. MSL.
3. To operate without a required altitude reporting transponder, a request must be submitted to the controlling ATC facility at least 1 hr. before the proposed operation.

91.307 Parachutes and Parachuting

1. Each occupant of an aircraft must wear an approved parachute when an intentional maneuver that exceeds 30° nose-up or nose-down or a bank of 60° relative to the horizon is made.

91.403 General (Maintenance, Preventive Maintenance, and Alterations)

1. The owner or operator of an aircraft is primarily responsible for maintaining that aircraft in an airworthy condition.
    a. This includes ensuring compliance with Airworthiness Directives.
2. An operator is a person who uses, causes to use, or authorizes to use an aircraft for the purpose of air navigation, including the piloting of an aircraft, with or without the right of legal control (i.e., owner, lessee, or otherwise).
    a. Thus, the pilot in command is also responsible for ensuring the aircraft is maintained in an airworthy condition and that all Airworthiness Directives are complied with.

91.405 Maintenance Required

1. Completion of an annual inspection and the return of an aircraft to service should always be indicated by the appropriate entries in the aircraft maintenance records.

91.407 Operation after Maintenance, Preventive Maintenance, Rebuilding, or Alteration

1. If an aircraft's operation in flight was substantially affected by an alteration or repair, the aircraft documents must show that it was test-flown and approved for return to service by an appropriately rated pilot with at least a private pilot certificate prior to being flown with passengers aboard.

91.409 Inspections

1. Annual inspections expire on the last day of the 12th calendar month after the previous annual inspection.
2. 100-hr. inspections are required of aircraft carrying passengers for hire or giving flight instruction for hire.
    a. If an aircraft has a 100-hr. inspection after only 90 hr. in service, the next inspection is still due 100 hr. after that inspection.

91.413 ATC Transponder Tests and Inspections

1. The maximum time period during which a person may use an ATC transponder after it has been tested and inspected is 24 calendar months.

91.417 Maintenance Records

1. Aircraft maintenance records must include the current status of life-limited parts of each airframe, engine, propeller, rotor, and appliance.

91.421 Rebuilt Engine Maintenance Records

1. A new maintenance record being used for an aircraft engine rebuilt by the manufacturer must include the previous changes required by airworthiness directives.

7.5 NTSB PART 830

830.2 Definitions

1. Aircraft accident -- an occurrence that takes place between the time any person boards an aircraft with the intention of flight until such time as all such persons have disembarked, and in which

    a. Any person suffers death or serious injury as a result of being in or upon the aircraft or by direct contact with the aircraft or anything attached thereto, or

    b. The aircraft receives substantial damage.

2. Serious injury -- any injury that

    a. Requires hospitalization for more than 48 hr., commencing within 7 days from the date the injury was received

    b. Results in a fracture of any bone (except simple fractures of fingers, toes, or nose)

    c. Causes severe hemorrhages, nerve, muscle, or tendon damage

    d. Involves injury to any internal organ

    e. Involves second- or third-degree burns, or any burns affecting more than 5% of the body surface

3. Substantial damage -- damage or failure that adversely affects the structural strength, performance, or flight characteristics of the aircraft, and that would normally require major repair or replacement of the affected component

    a. Engine failure, damage limited to an engine, bent fairings or cowling, dented skin, small puncture holes in the skin or fabric, ground damage to rotor or propeller blades, and damage to landing gear, wheels, tires, flaps, engine accessories, brakes, or wingtips are not considered "substantial damage."

830.5 Immediate Notification

1. Even when no injuries occur to occupants, an airplane accident resulting in substantial damage must be reported to the nearest National Transportation Safety Board (NTSB) field office immediately.

2. The following incidents must also be reported immediately to the NTSB:

    a. Inability of any required crewmember to perform normal flight duties because of in-flight injury or illness

    b. In-flight fire

    c. Flight control system malfunction or failure

    d. An overdue airplane that is believed to be involved in an accident

    e. An airplane collision in flight

    f. Turbine (jet) engine failures

830.15 Reports and Statements to Be Filed

1. The operator of an aircraft that has been involved in an accident is required to file a report within 10 days.

    a. A report must be filed within 7 days if an overdue aircraft is still missing.

2. The operator of an aircraft that has been involved in an incident is required to submit a report only if requested to do so.

SU 7: Federal Aviation Regulations 241

QUESTIONS AND ANSWER EXPLANATIONS: All of the AGI/CFI knowledge test questions chosen by the FAA for release as well as additional questions selected by Gleim relating to the material in the previous outlines are reproduced on the following pages. These questions have been organized into the same subunits as the outlines. To the immediate right of each question are the correct answer and answer explanation. You should cover these answers and answer explanations while responding to the questions. Refer to the general discussion in the Introduction on how to take the FAA knowledge test.

Remember that the questions from the FAA knowledge test bank have been reordered by topic and organized into a meaningful sequence. Also, the first line of the answer explanation gives the citation of the authoritative source for the answer.

QUESTIONS

7.1 14 CFR Part 1

1.2 Abbreviations and Symbols

1. Which is the correct symbol for the minimum steady flight speed at which an airplane is controllable?

A. V_S.
B. V_{S1}.
C. V_{S0}.

Answer (A) is correct. *(14 CFR 1.2)*
DISCUSSION: V_S means the stalling speed or the minimum steady flight speed at which the airplane is controllable (in any configuration).
Answer (B) is incorrect. V_{S1} means the stalling speed or the minimum steady flight speed obtained in a specific (usually clean) configuration. Answer (C) is incorrect. V_{S0} means the stalling speed or the minimum steady flight speed in the landing configuration.

7.2 14 CFR Part 23

23.3 Airplane Categories

2. If the certification category of an airplane is listed as "utility," it means the airplane is intended for which maneuvers?

A. Any type of acrobatic maneuver.
B. All nonacrobatic maneuvers plus limited acrobatics including spins.
C. Any maneuver incident to normal flying except acrobatics or spins.

Answer (B) is correct. *(14 CFR 23.3)*
DISCUSSION: Airplanes certificated in the utility category may be used in any nonacrobatic operations and in limited acrobatic operations, which include (1) spins (if approved for the particular type of airplane), and (2) lazy eights, chandelles, and steep turns in which the angle of bank is between 60° and 90°.
Answer (A) is incorrect. An acrobatic, not utility, category airplane means the airplane is intended to perform any type of acrobatic maneuver. Answer (C) is incorrect. A normal, not utility, category airplane means the airplane is intended to perform any maneuver incident to normal flying except acrobatics or spins.

7.3 14 CFR Part 61

61.3 Requirement for Certificates, Ratings, and Authorizations

3. What document(s) must you have with you while operating as pilot in command of an aircraft?

A. An appropriate pilot certificate and a current medical certificate.
B. A certificate showing accomplishment of a checkout in the aircraft and a current flight review.
C. A pilot logbook with endorsements showing accomplishment of a current flight review and recency of experience.

Answer (A) is correct. *(14 CFR 61.3)*
DISCUSSION: No one may act as pilot in command or in any other capacity as a required flight crewmember of a U.S. registered civil aircraft unless (s)he has in his or her personal possession or readily accessible in the aircraft a current pilot certificate issued under Part 61 and an appropriate current medical certificate issued under Part 67.
Answer (B) is incorrect. Flight reviews and airplane checkouts do not result in certificates; they are simply logbook endorsements. Answer (C) is incorrect. A pilot is not required to have the logbook in his or her possession during the flight.

4. What documents must a flight instructor have on board when conducting instruction for a private pilot applicant?

A. Pilot certificate, flight instructor certificate, medical certificate.
B. Flight instructor certificate and medical certificate.
C. Pilot certificate and flight instructor certificate.

Answer (A) is correct. *(14 CFR 61.3)*
DISCUSSION: Any flight instructor providing flight instruction must have a current and valid pilot certificate and flight instructor certificate. Because a private pilot applicant cannot legally act as PIC, the instructor must also have a valid medical certificate.
Answer (B) is incorrect. A flight instructor certificate is only valid when accompanied by a pilot certificate. Answer (C) is incorrect. Because a private pilot applicant cannot legally act as PIC, the flight instructor must act as PIC; thus, the instructor must have a valid medical certificate.

5. What documents must a flight instructor have on board when conducting instruction for a commercial pilot applicant who is current and appropriately rated in the aircraft?

A. Pilot certificate, flight instructor certificate, medical certificate.
B. Flight instructor certificate and medical certificate.
C. Pilot certificate, flight instructor certificate, photo identification.

Answer (C) is correct. *(14 CFR 61.3)*
DISCUSSION: Any flight instructor providing flight instruction must have a current and valid pilot certificate, flight instructor certificate, and photo identification. Because a current and appropriately rated commercial pilot applicant can legally act as PIC, the instructor need not have a valid medical certificate.
Answer (A) is incorrect. Because a commercial pilot applicant can legally act as PIC, the instructor need not have a valid medical certificate. Answer (B) is incorrect. A flight instructor certificate is only valid when accompanied by a pilot certificate.

61.13 Issuance of Airman Certificates, Ratings, and Authorizations

6. A person whose Flight Instructor Certificate has been suspended may not

A. give flight instruction, but may apply for a rating to be added to that certificate.
B. apply for any rating to be added to that certificate during the period of suspension.
C. apply for any Flight Instructor Certificate for a period of 1 year after the date of the suspension.

Answer (B) is correct. *(14 CFR 61.13)*
DISCUSSION: Unless authorized by the FAA, a person whose pilot, flight instructor, or ground instructor certificate is suspended may not apply for any flight instructor certificate or rating during the period of suspension.
Answer (A) is incorrect. A person whose flight instructor certificate has been suspended cannot apply for any rating to be added to the flight instructor certificate during the period of suspension. Answer (C) is incorrect. A person whose flight instructor certificate is revoked, not suspended, may not apply for any flight instructor certificate for 1 year from the date of revocation, not suspension.

61.15 Offenses Involving Alcohol or Drugs

7. Conviction of an offense involving alcohol or drugs is grounds for

A. permanent revocation of all certificates and ratings.
B. suspension or revocation of any certificate or rating issued under 14 CFR Part 61.
C. denial of an application for any certificate or rating issued under 14 CFR Part 61 for a period of up to 24 months after date of conviction.

Answer (B) is correct. *(14 CFR 61.15)*
DISCUSSION: Conviction of an offense involving alcohol or drugs is grounds for denial of application for any pilot certificate or rating for a period of up to 1 year, or suspension or revocation of any certificate or rating.
Answer (A) is incorrect. A permanent revocation of all certificates and ratings is not provided for in the 14 CFR. Answer (C) is incorrect. The denial of application is for a period of up to 12 months, not 24 months, after date of conviction.

61.19 Duration of Pilot and Instructor Certificates

8. What is the duration of a student pilot certificate for a 45-year-old pilot seeking a sport pilot-airplane certificate?

A. Indefinite.
B. 24 calendar months from the month in which it was issued.
C. 60 calendar months from the month in which it was issued.

Answer (A) is correct. *(14 CFR 61.19)*
DISCUSSION: Student pilot certificates issued after April 1, 2016, do not expire.
Answer (B) is incorrect. Student pilot certificates issued after April 1, 2016, do not expire. Answer (C) is incorrect. Student pilot certificates issued after April 1, 2016, do not expire.

SU 7: Federal Aviation Regulations

9. What is the duration of a Student Pilot Certificate for an individual who is 35 years of age?

A. Indefinite.
B. 12 calendar months from the month in which it was issued or renewed.
C. 60 calendar months from the month in which it was issued or renewed.

Answer (A) is correct. *(14 CFR 61.19)*
DISCUSSION: Student pilot certificates issued after April 1, 2016, do not expire.
Answer (B) is incorrect. Student pilot certificates issued after April 1, 2016, do not expire. Answer (C) is incorrect. Student pilot certificates issued after April 1, 2016, do not expire.

61.23 Medical Certificates: Requirement and Duration

10. A Second-Class Medical Certificate issued January 18 of this year will expire

A. January 18 of next year for private pilot privileges.
B. January 31 of next year for commercial pilot privileges.
C. January 31, 2 years later for commercial pilot privileges.

Answer (B) is correct. *(14 CFR 61.23)*
DISCUSSION: A second-class medical certificate expires at the end of the last day of the 12th month after the month of the date of examination shown on the certificate for operations requiring a commercial pilot certificate. Thus, a second-class medical certificate issued January 18 of this year will expire January 31 of next year for commercial pilot privileges.
Answer (A) is incorrect. Medical certificates expire on the last day of the month, not the exact anniversary. Answer (C) is incorrect. A second-class medical certificate expires at the end of the 12th, not 24th, month for commercial pilot privileges.

11. A Third-Class Medical Certificate was issued on May 3 to a person over 40 years of age. To exercise the privileges of a Private Pilot Certificate, the medical certificate will be valid through

A. May 3, 24 months later.
B. May 31, 24 months later.
C. May 31, 60 months later.

Answer (B) is correct. *(14 CFR 61.23)*
DISCUSSION: A pilot may exercise the privileges of a private pilot certificate under his or her third-class medical certificate until it expires at the end of the last day of the month 24 months (2 yr.) after it was issued, for pilots 40 years of age or older on the date of the medical examination. A third-class medical certificate issued to a person over 40 years of age on May 3 will be valid through May 31, 24 months later.
Answer (A) is incorrect. Medical certificates expire at the end of the last day of the month. Thus, a medical certificate issued on May 3 would expire on May 31, not May 3. Answer (C) is incorrect. A pilot may exercise the privileges of a private pilot certificate under a third-class medical certificate until it expires on the last day of the month, 60 months later if the pilot was less than 40 years of age, not 40 years of age or older, on the date of the medical examination.

12. If a Second-Class Medical Certificate was issued to a commercial pilot 13 months ago, during the next 11 months this pilot may

A. not act as pilot in command or carry passengers or property.
B. act as pilot in command and carry passengers or property, but not for compensation or hire.
C. act as pilot in command for compensation or hire, but may not carry passengers or property for compensation or hire.

Answer (B) is correct. *(14 CFR 61.23)*
DISCUSSION: A second-class medical certificate expires at the end of the last day of

1. The 12th month after the month of the date of examination shown on the certificate for operations requiring a commercial pilot certificate; and
2. The 24th or 60th month for operations requiring only a private, recreational, or student pilot certificate.

Thus, for the last 11 months, this pilot may act as pilot in command and carry passengers or property, but not for compensation or hire.
Answer (A) is incorrect. For the last 11 months, this pilot may act as pilot in command and carry passengers or property, but not for compensation or hire. Answer (C) is incorrect. For the last 11 months, this pilot may act as pilot in command and carry passengers or property, but not for compensation or hire.

61.31 Type Rating Requirements, Additional Training, and Authorization Requirements

13. To act as pilot in command of an airplane that has more than 200 horsepower, a person holding a Private or Commercial Pilot Certificate is required to

A. successfully complete a practical test in such an airplane.
B. receive ground and flight training in an airplane that has more than 200 horsepower.
C. make three takeoffs and landings with an authorized instructor in an airplane of the same make and model.

Answer (B) is correct. *(14 CFR 61.31)*
DISCUSSION: A person holding a private or commercial pilot certificate may not act as pilot in command of a high-performance airplane (an airplane that has more than 200 horsepower) unless (s)he has received ground and flight training from an authorized flight instructor who has certified in his or her log that (s)he is proficient to operate a high-performance airplane.
Answer (A) is incorrect. Ground and flight training and a logbook endorsement, not successful completion of a practical test, are required for a person to act as pilot in command in an airplane that has more than 200 horsepower. Answer (C) is incorrect. Ground and flight training and a logbook endorsement, not three solo takeoffs and landings with an authorized instructor in the same make and model, are required for a person to act as pilot in command in an airplane that has more than 200 horsepower.

14. Which of the following normally requires the pilot in command to hold a type rating?

A. Any turbojet-powered aircraft.
B. Any airplane which has a gross weight of 6,000 pounds or more.
C. Any multi-engine airplane which is operated under interstate commerce.

Answer (A) is correct. *(14 CFR 61.31)*
DISCUSSION: The pilot in command must hold a type rating when operating turbojet-powered airplanes, large aircraft (more than 12,500 lb. maximum certificated takeoff weight), and other aircraft specified by the FAA through aircraft type certificate procedures.
Answer (B) is incorrect. The pilot in command must hold a type rating when operating an aircraft that has a maximum certificated takeoff weight of more than 12,500 lb. (large aircraft), not a gross weight of 6,000 lb. or more. Answer (C) is incorrect. The pilot in command must hold a type rating when operating a turbojet-powered airplane, large airplane, or any aircraft specified by the FAA through aircraft type certificate procedures, not any multi-engine airplane operated under interstate commerce.

15. To act as pilot in command of an airplane with retractable landing gear, flaps, and controllable propeller, a person holding a Private or Commercial Pilot Certificate is required to

A. complete a practical test in such an airplane.
B. have made at least three takeoffs and landings in such an airplane in the last 90 days.
C. receive ground and flight training in such an airplane, and obtain a logbook endorsement of proficiency.

Answer (C) is correct. *(14 CFR 61.31)*
DISCUSSION: A person holding a private or a commercial pilot certificate may not act as pilot in command of a complex airplane (an airplane that has retractable landing gear, flaps, and a controllable pitch propeller) unless (s)he has received ground and flight training from an authorized flight instructor who has certified in his or her log that (s)he is proficient to operate a complex airplane.
Answer (A) is incorrect. Ground and flight training and a logbook endorsement, not successful completion of a practical test, are required for a person to act as pilot in command of a complex airplane. Answer (B) is incorrect. Ground and flight training and a logbook endorsement, not three takeoffs and landings in the last 90 days, are required for a person to act as pilot in command of a complex airplane.

16. No person may act as pilot in command of a pressurized airplane with a service ceiling or maximum operating altitude, whichever is lower, above 25,000 feet unless that person has

A. completed a physiological training program conducted by the FAA or a military service.
B. received ground and flight training in high altitude operations and a logbook endorsement certifying this training.
C. completed a pilot proficiency check for a pilot or instructor pilot certificate or rating conducted by the FAA after April 15, 1991.

Answer (B) is correct. *(14 CFR 61.31)*
DISCUSSION: With certain exceptions, no person may act as pilot in command of a pressurized airplane that has a service ceiling or maximum operating altitude, whichever is lower, above 25,000 ft. MSL unless that person has received ground and flight training in high altitude operations and has received a logbook or training record endorsement from an authorized instructor certifying satisfactory completion of the training. This training is not required if a person has completed a pilot proficiency check for a pilot certificate or rating conducted by the FAA in such an airplane prior to April 15, 1991.
Answer (A) is incorrect. While completing a physiological training program is suggested for all pilots, both ground and flight training are required to act as PIC in a high-altitude airplane. Answer (C) is incorrect. The proficiency check must have been completed before, not after, April 15, 1991.

17. Which is applicable to a private pilot with ASEL ratings who has never flown a tailwheel airplane? The pilot

A. may fly solo with no instruction required.
B. must have received instruction and have a logbook endorsement before acting as pilot in command.
C. must have received at least 1 hour of instruction and have a logbook endorsement before carrying passengers.

Answer (B) is correct. *(14 CFR 61.31)*
DISCUSSION: No person may act as pilot in command of a tailwheel airplane unless that pilot has received flight instruction from an authorized flight instructor who has found the pilot competent to operate a tailwheel airplane and has made a one-time endorsement so stating in the pilot's logbook.
Answer (A) is incorrect. The pilot must have received instruction regardless of whether passengers are carried. Answer (C) is incorrect. The pilot must have received instruction regardless of whether passengers are carried, and there is no minimum amount of instruction required.

61.35 Knowledge Test: Prerequisites and Passing Grades

18. What minimum documentation is required to take an FAA knowledge test for any flight instructor rating?

A. Proper identification.
B. Proof of satisfactory completion of the appropriate ground training or home study course.
C. Authorization from an FAA inspector who has verified and endorsed the applicant's training record.

Answer (A) is correct. *(14 CFR 61.35)*
DISCUSSION: The minimum documentation required to take any flight instructor knowledge test is proper identification, which contains your photograph, signature, actual address, and date of birth showing that you meet the age requirement to take the test. 14 CFR 61.183, Eligibility Requirements (flight instructor), does not require an instructor endorsement to take the knowledge test. Thus, an endorsement is not required for any flight instructor knowledge test.
Answer (B) is incorrect. An endorsement from an authorized instructor certifying that the person has completed a ground training or home study course is required for the recreational, private, instrument, or commercial knowledge test, not for any flight instructor knowledge test. Answer (C) is incorrect. A person must have an authorization (endorsement) from an authorized instructor, not an FAA inspector, to take the recreational, private, instrument, or commercial knowledge test, not any flight instructor test.

61.37 Knowledge Tests: Cheating or Other Unauthorized Conduct

19. A person who the Administrator finds has cheated or committed any unauthorized act during a knowledge test may not take another knowledge test within

A. 90 days.
B. 1 year.
C. 2 years.

Answer (B) is correct. *(14 CFR 61.37)*
DISCUSSION: Anyone who cheats or commits any unauthorized act during a knowledge test is not eligible for any pilot or instructor certificate or rating, and may not take any test therefor for a period of 1 year after the date of the act. In addition, the commission of that act is a basis for suspending or revoking any pilot or instructor certificate or rating held by that person.
Answer (A) is incorrect. Such a person may not take another test within 1 year, not 90 days. Answer (C) is incorrect. Such a person may not take another test within 1 year, not 2 years.

20. What action may be taken against a person whom the Administrator finds has cheated on a knowledge test?

A. That person will be required to wait 24 months before taking another knowledge test.
B. Any certificate or rating held by the person may be suspended or revoked.
C. That person may be required to wait a maximum of 6 months before applying for any other certificate or rating.

Answer (B) is correct. *(14 CFR 61.37)*
DISCUSSION: Anyone who cheats or commits any unauthorized act during a knowledge test is not eligible for any pilot or instructor certificate or rating, and may not take any test therefor for a period of 1 year after the date of the act. In addition, the commission of that act is a basis for suspending or revoking any pilot or instructor certificate or rating held by that person.
Answer (A) is incorrect. That person will be required to wait 12 months, not 24 months. Answer (C) is incorrect. That person will be required to wait 1 year, not 6 months, before applying for any other certificate or rating.

61.39 Prerequisites for Practical Tests

21. To be eligible for a practical test under 14 CFR Part 61, an applicant must have passed the appropriate knowledge test (when required) within the preceding

A. 6 calendar months.
B. 12 calendar months.
C. 24 calendar months.

Answer (C) is correct. *(14 CFR 61.39)*
DISCUSSION: To be eligible for a practical test for a certificate, or an aircraft or instrument rating, the applicant must have passed any required knowledge test since the beginning of the 24th month before the month in which (s)he takes the practical test.
Answer (A) is incorrect. The knowledge test must have been passed within the preceding 24, not 6, calendar months. Answer (B) is incorrect. The knowledge test must have been passed within the preceding 24, not 12, calendar months.

22. A written statement from an authorized instructor certifying that an applicant has received the required training in preparation for a practical test must be dated within what period of time preceding the date of application?

A. 2 calendar months.
B. 90 days.
C. 120 days.

Answer (A) is correct. *(14 CFR 61.39)*
DISCUSSION: To be eligible for a practical test for a certificate, or an aircraft or instrument rating, the applicant must have a written statement from an authorized flight instructor certifying that (s)he has given the applicant flight training in preparation for the practical test within 2 calendar months preceding the month of application and finds him or her competent to pass the test and to have satisfactory knowledge of the subject areas in which (s)he is shown to be deficient by his or her FAA knowledge test report.
Answer (B) is incorrect. The written statement must be dated within 60, not 90, days preceding the application. Answer (C) is incorrect. The written statement must be dated within 60, not 120, days preceding the application.

23. An applicant who holds a Commercial Pilot Certificate with ASEL ratings is seeking a MEL rating at the commercial level. On August 1, 2007, the applicant shows you a second-class medical dated January 2, 2006. May the applicant take the practical test?

A. No.
B. Yes.
C. Yes, but at the private pilot skill level.

Answer (B) is correct. *(14 CFR 61.39)*
DISCUSSION: To be eligible for a practical test for a certificate or rating, the applicant must hold at least a current third-class medical certificate issued since the beginning of the 24th or 60th month (depending on age) before the month in which (s)he takes the practical test.
Answer (A) is incorrect. Although a second-class medical certificate is required for commercial operations, only a third-class certificate is required for a practical test. Answer (C) is incorrect. Although a second-class medical certificate is required for the commercial operations, only a third-class certificate is required for a practical test.

24. What class medical certificate, if any, is required for a person adding a rating to a pilot certificate?

A. None.
B. Second-Class.
C. Third-Class.

Answer (C) is correct. *(14 CFR 61.39)*
DISCUSSION: To be eligible for a practical test for a certificate or rating, a pilot must hold at least a third-class medical certificate.
Answer (A) is incorrect. Medical certificates are required of all powered-aircraft pilots except those flying gliders. Answer (B) is incorrect. A pilot must hold a third-class, not second-class, medical certificate to take a practical test.

25. To be eligible for a Commercial Pilot Certificate, one of the requirements is for the applicant to hold at least a valid

A. First-Class Medical Certificate.
B. Second-Class Medical Certificate.
C. Third-Class Medical Certificate.

Answer (C) is correct. *(14 CFR 61.39)*
DISCUSSION: To be eligible to take the practical test for a commercial pilot certificate, an applicant must hold at least a valid third-class medical certificate.
If this question were stated "to exercise the privileges of a commercial pilot," the correct answer would be a second-class medical certificate (14 CFR 61.23).
Answer (A) is incorrect. A first-class medical certificate is required for a pilot to exercise the privileges of an ATP certificate, not to be eligible for a commercial pilot certificate. Answer (B) is incorrect. A second-class medical certificate is required for a pilot to exercise the privileges of a commercial pilot certificate, not to be eligible for the certificate.

61.43 Practical Tests: General Procedures

26. If all increments for a practical test for a certificate or rating are not completed on one date, all remaining increments must be satisfactorily completed no later than

A. 90 days from the date of the test.
B. 120 days from the date of the test.
C. 60 days from the date of the test.

Answer (C) is correct. *(14 CFR 61.43)*
DISCUSSION: According to 14 CFR 61.43, if a practical test is discontinued, the applicant is entitled to receive credit for those areas of operation that were passed only if (s)he passes the remainder of the practical test within the 60-day period after the practical test was discontinued.
Answer (A) is incorrect. Satisfactory completion must be within 60 days, not 90 days. Answer (B) is incorrect. Satisfactory completion must be within 60 days, not 120 days.

61.45 Practical Tests: Required Aircraft and Equipment

27. What is one requirement for an aircraft furnished for a practical test?

A. All flight instruments must be fully functioning.
B. Must have no prescribed operating limitations that prohibit its use in any required area of operation.
C. Dual flight controls and engine power controls must be operable and easily reached by both pilots in a normal manner.

Answer (B) is correct. *(14 CFR 61.45)*
DISCUSSION: Aircraft furnished for a practical test must have

1. The equipment for each area of operation required for the practical test;
2. No prescribed operating limitations that prohibit its use in any area of operation required on the practical test; and
3. Engine power controls and flight controls that are easily reached and operated in a normal manner by both pilots, unless the examiner determines that the practical test can be conducted safely without them.

Answer (A) is incorrect. Only those instruments required for the practical test must be fully functional. Answer (C) is incorrect. Dual controls are not required if the examiner determines that the practical test can be conducted safely without them.

61.49 Retesting after Failure

28. A flight instructor recommendation is not required for an ATP applicant except when applying for

A. a retest.
B. a type rating.
C. the addition of a category rating.

Answer (A) is correct. *(14 CFR 61.49)*
DISCUSSION: An ATP applicant does not need to have the "Instructor's Recommendation" block on the back of his or her 8710-1 form (Airman Certificate and/or Rating Application) completed unless (s)he has previously failed an ATP practical test.
Answer (B) is incorrect. An ATP does not require an instructor recommendation when applying for a type rating. Answer (C) is incorrect. An ATP does not require an instructor recommendation when applying for the addition of an aircraft category rating.

29. An applicant has failed a knowledge test for the second time. With training and an endorsement from an authorized instructor, when may the applicant apply for a retest?

A. After 5 days.
B. After 30 days.
C. Immediately.

Answer (C) is correct. *(14 CFR 61.49)*
DISCUSSION: A person who fails a knowledge or practical test may take the test again immediately after (s)he has received the necessary training from an authorized instructor who has determined that (s)he is proficient to pass the test. Additionally, the instructor must provide the person with an endorsement that the training was given.
Answer (A) is incorrect. A person can retake the test immediately, not 5 days, after (s)he receives additional training and an endorsement from an authorized instructor. Answer (B) is incorrect. A person can retake the test immediately, not 30 days, after (s)he receives additional training and an endorsement from an authorized instructor.

30. An applicant who fails a knowledge test for the first time may apply for retesting after

A. waiting for a period of 20 days.
B. receiving 5 hours of ground instruction from an authorized ground instructor.
C. presenting an endorsement from an authorized instructor certifying that additional training has been given and the applicant is competent to pass the test.

Answer (C) is correct. *(14 CFR 61.49)*
DISCUSSION: A person who fails a knowledge or practical test may retake that test after (s)he has received the necessary training from an authorized instructor who provides that person with an endorsement that additional training was provided and that the person is proficient to pass the test.
Answer (A) is incorrect. There is no minimum time requirement between tests. The only requirement is that the person have an endorsement from an instructor that additional training was given and that (s)he is proficient to pass the test. Answer (B) is incorrect. There is no specified minimum amount of instruction required prior to retesting.

31. An applicant who fails a practical test for the second time may apply for retesting after

A. 30 days have passed.
B. presenting a letter of competency to the examiner signed by an authorized flight instructor who conducted the training.
C. receiving the necessary instruction and an endorsement from an authorized instructor who gave the training.

Answer (C) is correct. *(14 CFR 61.49)*
DISCUSSION: A person who fails a knowledge or practical test may retake that test after (s)he has received additional training from an authorized instructor and that instructor has provided an endorsement that the additional training was given and the person is proficient to pass the test.
Answer (A) is incorrect. A person may apply for retesting after receiving additional training and an endorsement from the authorized instructor who gave the training. There is no minimum number of days required between tests. Answer (B) is incorrect. A person may apply for retesting after receiving additional training and an endorsement from the authorized instructor who gave the training, not a letter of competency to the examiner.

32. Your student took a practical test for a pilot certificate on January 10 and failed to meet standards. After being retested on January 13 and failing to meet standards again, when is your student eligible to retest?

A. January 13.
B. February 12.
C. February 13.

Answer (A) is correct. *(14 CFR 61.49)*
DISCUSSION: If your student fails a practical test on January 13, (s)he is eligible to retest immediately after you provide him or her with the necessary training and with an endorsement stating that you have provided him or her with the training and determined that (s)he is proficient to pass the test. Thus, if your student fails a practical test on January 13 and you provide the additional training and endorsement, your student may be eligible to retest on the same day, January 13.
Answer (B) is incorrect. Your student is eligible to retest immediately after you provide additional training and an endorsement of that training. There is no minimum time between tests. Answer (C) is incorrect. Your student is eligible to retest immediately after you provide additional training and an endorsement of that training. There is no minimum time between tests.

33. A flight instructor applicant must demonstrate spins in an airplane or glider when

A. the practical test for initial certification is being given.
B. being retested for deficiencies in instructional proficiency on stall awareness or spins demonstrated during an initial test.
C. the airplane or glider to be used for the practical test is certificated for spins and the applicant is being given an initial practical test.

Answer (B) is correct. *(14 CFR 61.49)*
DISCUSSION: A flight instructor applicant must demonstrate spins in an airplane when being retested due to deficiencies in instructional proficiency on stall awareness, spin entry, spins, or spin recovery during the initial practical test.
Answer (A) is incorrect. A flight instructor applicant must demonstrate spins in an airplane only when being retested for deficiencies in instructional proficiency on stall awareness or spins during the initial practical test. Answer (C) is incorrect. A flight instructor applicant must demonstrate spins in an airplane only when being retested for deficiencies in instructional proficiency on stall awareness or spins during the initial practical test.

61.51 Pilot Logbooks

34. What flight time must be recorded by a pilot exercising the privileges of a commercial certificate?

A. All flight time.
B. Only the flight time necessary to meet the recent flight experience requirements.
C. All flight time flown for hire with passengers and/or cargo aboard the aircraft.

Answer (B) is correct. *(14 CFR 61.51)*
DISCUSSION: The aeronautical training and experience used to meet the requirements for a certificate or rating, and the recent flight experience requirements must be shown by a reliable record (e.g., logbook). The logging of other flight time is not required.
Answer (A) is incorrect. Only the flight time necessary to meet the recent experience requirements is required of commercial pilots. Answer (C) is incorrect. Only the flight time necessary to meet the recent experience requirements is required of commercial pilots.

61.56 Flight Review

35. A flight review is not required if a pilot has completed, within the time specified,

A. an industry-sponsored refresher clinic.
B. a pilot proficiency check conducted by the FAA.
C. an instrument proficiency check conducted by an instructor with the Armed Forces.

Answer (B) is correct. *(14 CFR 61.56)*
DISCUSSION: A person who has, within the prior 24 calendar months, satisfactorily completed a pilot proficiency check conducted by the FAA, an approved pilot check airman, or a U.S. Armed Force, for a pilot certificate, rating, or operating privilege, need not accomplish a flight review.
Answer (A) is incorrect. A refresher clinic can be used to renew a flight instructor certificate, but not to substitute for a flight review. Answer (C) is incorrect. An instrument proficiency check can by prior arrangement, but will not normally, include a review of the rules, maneuvers, and procedures necessary for a flight review.

36. A flight instructor who has not satisfactorily accomplished a flight review or passed a required proficiency check within the prescribed time is

A. not authorized to fly solo.
B. authorized to fly solo only.
C. not authorized to give instruction except to holders of Recreational Pilot Certificates.

Answer (A) is correct. *(14 CFR 61.56)*
DISCUSSION: A flight instructor who has not satisfactorily accomplished a flight review or passed a required proficiency check within the preceding 24 calendar months may not act as pilot in command of an aircraft, i.e., (s)he is not authorized to fly solo.
Answer (B) is incorrect. A flight instructor may not act as PIC (even solo) unless (s)he has satisfied the flight review requirement. Answer (C) is incorrect. A flight instructor may give instruction to any pilot who is appropriately rated in the aircraft being used, as long as the flight instructor does not act as PIC.

37. What recent flight experience must be met before a commercial airplane pilot may fly solo in an airplane?

A. Three takeoffs and three landings within the preceding 90 days in an airplane.
B. Satisfactorily accomplished a flight review in any aircraft for which rated within the preceding 24 calendar months.
C. Satisfactorily accomplished a flight review within the preceding 24 calendar months, but this review must be in an airplane.

Answer (B) is correct. *(14 CFR 61.56)*
DISCUSSION: A person may act as pilot in command of an aircraft if they have accomplished a flight review given in an aircraft for which that pilot is rated, by an appropriately rated instructor or other persons designated by the FAA, within the preceding 24 calendar months.
Answer (A) is incorrect. The three takeoffs and landings in 90 days is a requirement to carry passengers, not to fly solo. Answer (C) is incorrect. The flight review may be accomplished in any aircraft for which the pilot is rated, not only an airplane.

38. A flight review will consist of

A. a minimum of 1 hour ground training and 1 hour flight training.
B. at least 1 hour of flight time to include at least three takeoffs and landings.
C. three takeoffs and landings and a review of those maneuvers necessary for the pilot to demonstrate the appropriate pilot privileges.

Answer (A) is correct. *(14 CFR 61.56)*
DISCUSSION: A flight review consists of a minimum of 1 hr. of ground training and 1 hr. of flight training. The review must include
1. The current general operating and flight rules of Part 91; and
2. Those maneuvers and procedures that, in the discretion of the person giving the review, are necessary for the pilot to demonstrate the safe exercise of the privileges of the pilot certificate.

Answer (B) is incorrect. The flight review must consist of 1 hr. of ground training and 1 hr. of flight training. The number of takeoffs and landings are at the discretion of the CFI conducting the review. Answer (C) is incorrect. The flight review must consist of 1 hr. of ground training and 1 hr. of flight training, which must include, in part, those maneuvers necessary to demonstrate the appropriate pilot privileges. The number of takeoffs and landings are at the discretion of the CFI conducting the review.

61.57 Recent Flight Experience: Pilot in Command

39. If recency of experience requirements for night flight are not met and official sunset is 1830, the latest time passengers may be carried is

A. 1829
B. 1859
C. 1929

Answer (C) is correct. *(14 CFR 61.57)*
DISCUSSION: No person may act as pilot in command of an aircraft carrying passengers during the period beginning 1 hr. after sunset and ending 1 hr. before sunrise unless, within the preceding 90 days, (s)he has made at least three takeoffs and three landings to a full stop during that period in the category, class, and type (if a type rating is required) of aircraft to be used. Thus, if official sunset is 1830, the latest that passengers may be carried is 1929.

Answer (A) is incorrect. The latest time passengers may be carried is 1 hr. after, not at, sunset. Answer (B) is incorrect. Passengers may no longer be carried 1 hr., not 30 min., after sunset.

40. To meet the recent flight experience requirements for acting as pilot in command carrying passengers at night, a pilot must have made, within the preceding 90 days and from 1 hour after sunset to 1 hour before sunrise, three takeoffs and three landings to a full stop in

A. the same category of aircraft to be used.
B. the same category and class of aircraft to be used.
C. the same category, class, and type (if a type rating is required).

Answer (C) is correct. *(14 CFR 61.57)*
DISCUSSION: No person may act as pilot in command of an aircraft carrying passengers during the period beginning 1 hr. after sunset and ending 1 hr. before sunrise within the preceding 90 days unless (s)he has made at least three takeoffs and three landings to a full stop during that period in the category, class, and type (if a type rating is required) of aircraft to be used.

Answer (A) is incorrect. The takeoffs and landings must be in the same category, class, and type (if a type rating is required) of aircraft. Answer (B) is incorrect. The takeoffs and landings must also be in the same type of aircraft, if a type rating is required.

41. A private pilot has completed three takeoffs and three landings to a full stop within the preceding 90 days in a tricycle-gear airplane, single-engine land, and decides to take a passenger for a flight in a tailwheel airplane, single-engine land. Since these aircraft are of the same category and class, the pilot is current in

A. both airplanes.
B. the tricycle-gear airplane.
C. the tailwheel airplane.

Answer (B) is correct. *(14 CFR 61.57)*
DISCUSSION: No person may act as pilot in command of an airplane carrying passengers unless, within the preceding 90 days, (s)he has made three takeoffs and three landings as sole manipulator of the controls in an aircraft of the same category and class and, if a type rating is required, the same type. If the aircraft is a tailwheel airplane, the landings must have been to a full stop in a tailwheel airplane.

Answer (A) is incorrect. The takeoffs and landings must have been made in a tailwheel airplane for the pilot to be current in such an airplane. Answer (C) is incorrect. The takeoffs and landings must have been made in a tailwheel airplane for the pilot to be current in such an airplane.

61.60 Change of Address

42. The holder of a pilot or instructor certificate who fails to notify the FAA Airmen Certification Branch in writing of a change in permanent mailing address may exercise the privileges of that certificate for how many days after date of change?

A. 30
B. 60
C. 90

Answer (A) is correct. *(14 CFR 61.60)*

DISCUSSION: The holder of a pilot or instructor certificate who has made a change in his or her permanent mailing address may not, after 30 days from the date (s)he moved, exercise the privileges of his or her certificate unless (s)he has notified the FAA in writing.

Note: While you must notify the FAA if your address changes, you are not required to carry a certificate that shows your current address. The FAA will not issue a new certificate upon receipt of your new address unless you also send a request (written or online) and a $2 fee.

Answer (B) is incorrect. (S)he may exercise his or her pilot privileges for 30, not 60, days after the change. Answer (C) is incorrect. (S)he may exercise his or her pilot privileges for 30, not 90, days after the change.

43. When a permanent change of address occurs, pilot or instructor privileges may not be exercised unless the FAA Airmen Certification Branch is notified, in writing, within

A. 30 days.
B. 60 days.
C. 90 days.

Answer (A) is correct. *(14 CFR 61.60)*

DISCUSSION: The holder of a pilot or instructor certificate who has made a change in his or her permanent mailing address may not, after 30 days from the date (s)he moved, exercise the privileges of his or her certificate unless (s)he has notified the FAA in writing.

Note: While you must notify the FAA if your address changes, you are not required to carry a certificate that shows your current address. The FAA will not issue a new certificate upon receipt of your new address unless you also send a request (written or online) and a $2 fee.

Answer (B) is incorrect. The FAA must be notified within 30, not 60, days. Answer (C) is incorrect. The FAA must be notified within 30, not 90, days.

61.63 Additional Aircraft Ratings (other than for ratings at the airline transport pilot certification level)

44. You do not have to take a Private Pilot Glider Knowledge Test if

A. In the preceding 24 months, you passed a knowledge test for a powered aircraft.
B. You already hold an airplane powered certificate.
C. You already hold any powered aircraft certificate.

Answer (C) is correct. *(14 CFR 61.63)*

DISCUSSION: According to 14 CFR 61.63(b)(5), to add a category rating to your certificate, you do not have to take an additional knowledge test it you hold an airplane, rotorcraft, powered-lift, or airship rating at the same certificate level.

Answer (A) is incorrect. You do not have to have passed a powered aircraft knowledge test in the preceding 24 months. As long as you hold a powered certificate at the same level, it does not matter how long ago you took the knowledge test. Answer (B) is incorrect. Any powered aircraft certificate at the same level is sufficient, not just airplane.

61.69 Glider Towing: Experience and Training Requirements

45. A private pilot with an airplane single-engine land rating may act as pilot in command of an airplane towing a glider if, within the preceding 24 months, this pilot has made

A. ten actual or simulated glider tows.
B. three flights as pilot in command of a glider towed by an aircraft.
C. at least six flights as pilot in command of an airplane towing a glider.

Answer (B) is correct. *(14 CFR 61.69)*

DISCUSSION: No person may act as pilot in command of an aircraft towing a glider unless (among other requirements), within the preceding 24 months, (s)he has made at least three actual or simulated glider tows while accompanied by a qualified pilot, or made at least three flights as pilot in command of a glider towed by an aircraft.

Answer (A) is incorrect. The pilot must have made three, not 10, actual or simulated glider tows in the last 24 months. Answer (C) is incorrect. The pilot must have made three, not six, actual or simulated glider tows in the last 24 months.

61.83 Eligibility Requirements for Student Pilots

46. To be eligible for a Student Pilot Certificate limited to airplanes, an applicant is required to be at least how old?

A. 14 years.
B. 16 years.
C. 17 years.

Answer (B) is correct. *(14 CFR 61.83)*
DISCUSSION: To be eligible for a student pilot certificate, a person must be at least 16 years of age.
Answer (A) is incorrect. Fourteen is the minimum age for a student pilot certificate limited to the operation of a glider or free balloon. Answer (C) is incorrect. Seventeen is the minimum age for a private pilot, not student pilot, certificate.

61.85 Application for a Student Pilot Certificate

47. Student pilot certificate applications can be accepted by

A. an AME, a DPE, and an FAA inspector.
B. a DPE, an FAA inspector, and a military flight surgeon.
C. an FAA inspector, a CFI, ACR, and DPE.

Answer (C) is correct. *(14 CFR 61.85)*
DISCUSSION: Student pilot certificate applications may be accepted by an FAA inspector, CFI, ACR, or DPE.
Answer (A) is incorrect. An AME cannot accept student pilot certificate applications. Answer (B) is incorrect. A military flight surgeon is not authorized to accept student pilot certificate applications.

61.87 Solo Requirements for Student Pilots

48. Who is responsible for administering the required knowledge test to a student pilot prior to solo flight?

A. Any certificated ground instructor.
B. Any certificated flight instructor.
C. The student's authorized instructor.

Answer (C) is correct. *(14 CFR 61.87)*
DISCUSSION: The knowledge test is to be administered by the student's authorized instructor.
Answer (A) is incorrect. The knowledge test must be administered by the student's authorized flight instructor, not by any certificated ground instructor. Answer (B) is incorrect. The knowledge test must be administered by the student's authorized flight instructor, not by any certificated flight instructor.

49. What subjects must be covered on the presolo knowledge test?

A. Principles of flight, weather, and aircraft systems.
B. Applicable regulations, flight characteristics, and operational limitations of make and model aircraft to be flown.
C. Density altitude, operations from a controlled airport, and radio communications with appropriate air traffic control facilities.

Answer (B) is correct. *(14 CFR 61.87)*
DISCUSSION: The presolo knowledge test must include questions on the applicable sections of 14 CFR Parts 61 and 91, the airspace rules and procedures at the airport where the solo flight will be conducted, and the flight characteristics and operational limitations of the make and model aircraft to be flown.
Answer (A) is incorrect. Only Federal Aviation Regulations, airspace rules and procedures at the airport where the solo flight will be conducted, flight characteristics, and operating limitations are required on the presolo knowledge test. Answer (C) is incorrect. Only Federal Aviation Regulations, airspace rules and procedures at the airport where the solo flight will be conducted, flight characteristics, and operating limitations are required on the presolo knowledge test.

50. Prior to a first solo flight, the flight instructor is required to endorse the student's

A. logbook.
B. pilot certificate.
C. logbook and pilot certificate.

Answer (A) is correct. *(14 CFR 61.87)*
DISCUSSION: All endorsements are made in the student pilot's logbook. No student pilot may operate an aircraft in solo flight unless that student's logbook has been endorsed for the specific make and model aircraft to be flown within the 90 days prior to the student operating in solo flight, by an authorized flight instructor who has flown with the student. The instructor's endorsement must certify that the instructor

1. Has given the student instruction in the make and model aircraft in which the solo flight is to be made;
2. Finds that the student has met the flight training requirements; and
3. Finds that the student is competent to make safe solo flight in that aircraft.

Answer (B) is incorrect. All endorsements are made in the student pilot's logbook. Answer (C) is incorrect. All endorsements are made in the student pilot's logbook.

51. Prior to solo flight, a student must have received flight instruction in

A. ground reference maneuvers.
B. unusual attitude recoveries.
C. basic radio navigation procedures.

Answer (A) is correct. *(14 CFR 61.87)*
DISCUSSION: Prior to being authorized to conduct solo flight, a student must have received instruction in, among other maneuvers, ground reference maneuvers.
Answer (B) is incorrect. A student must have received flight instruction in unusual attitude recoveries prior to the private pilot practical test, not prior to a first solo flight. Answer (C) is incorrect. Basic radio navigation procedures are required prior to solo cross-country, not solo, flight.

52. Which is a required endorsement by an authorized flight instructor for a student pilot to operate an aircraft in solo flight?

A. An endorsement that instruction was given in the make and model of aircraft to be soloed within the preceding 6 months.
B. An endorsement within the preceding 90 days stating that instruction was given in the make and model aircraft to be flown and the student is competent to make a safe solo flight.
C. An endorsement made within the preceding 180 days that instruction was given in the make of aircraft to be soloed and that the instructor found the applicant competent to make a safe flight in that aircraft.

Answer (B) is correct. *(14 CFR 61.87)*
DISCUSSION: No student pilot may operate an aircraft in solo flight unless that student's logbook has been endorsed for the specific make and model aircraft to be flown by an authorized flight instructor, and the student's logbook has been endorsed, within the 90 days prior to the student operating in solo flight, by an authorized flight instructor who has flown with the student. The instructor's endorsement must certify that the instructor

1. Has given the student instruction in the make and model aircraft in which the solo flight is to be made;
2. Finds that the student has met the flight training requirements; and
3. Finds that the student is competent to make safe solo flight in that aircraft.

Answer (A) is incorrect. The endorsement must have been within the preceding 90 days, not 6 months, and it must state that the student is competent to make safe solo flight. Answer (C) is incorrect. Endorsement must be within the preceding 90 days, not 180 days.

53. A student is required to receive a logbook endorsement

A. for each solo flight.
B. to make repeated solo cross-country flights to an airport more than 50 NM from the point of departure.
C. for solo flight each 90 days.

Answer (C) is correct. *(14 CFR 61.87)*
DISCUSSION: A student pilot must receive three logbook endorsements for solo flight including

1. Presolo aeronautical knowledge: 14 CFR 61.87(b),
2. Presolo flight training: 14 CFR 61.87(c),
3. Solo flight (first 90-day period): 14 CFR 61.87(n)

A student pilot must receive an updated solo flight endorsement every 90 days according to 14 CFR 61.87(p). Additional endorsements are required for flight in Class B airspace, solo cross-country flight, and solo flight at night (not common).
Answer (A) is incorrect. A student pilot is not required to receive an endorsement for each flight. Answer (B) is incorrect. A student pilot may receive a logbook endorsement for repeated specific solo cross-country flights to another airport that is within (not more than) 50 NM of the airport from which the flight originated.

61.93 Solo Cross-Country Flight Requirements

54. Are students authorized to make repeated solo cross-country flights without each flight being logbook endorsed?

A. No; each solo cross-country flight requires a logbook endorsement.
B. Yes; provided the flights take place under stipulated conditions.
C. Yes; but only if the flights remain within 25 NM of the point of departure.

Answer (B) is correct. *(14 CFR 61.93)*
DISCUSSION: A flight instructor may endorse a student's logbook for repeated specific solo cross-country flights that are not greater than 50 NM from the point of departure, after giving that student flight instruction in both directions over the route, including takeoffs and landings at the airports to be used, and has specified the conditions for which the flights can be made.
Answer (A) is incorrect. An endorsement can be made for repeated specific cross-country flights within 50 NM. Answer (C) is incorrect. The flight must remain within 50 NM, not 25 NM, of the point of departure.

55. One requirement for a student pilot to be authorized to make a solo cross-country flight is an endorsement

A. in the student's logbook that the instructor has given the student cross-country instruction in the model of aircraft to be used.

B. in the student's logbook that the preflight planning and preparation has been reviewed and the student is prepared to make the flight safely.

C. on the Student Pilot Certificate stating the student is competent to make cross-country flights in the category, class, and type of aircraft involved.

Answer (B) is correct. *(14 CFR 61.93)*
DISCUSSION: An instructor endorses the student's logbook for each solo cross-country flight, after reviewing the student's preflight planning and preparation, attesting that the student is prepared to make the flight safely under known circumstances on the conditions listed by the instructor in the logbook.
Answer (A) is incorrect. The instruction must be in the make and model, not just the model, of aircraft to be used. Answer (C) is incorrect. The student pilot's certificate is endorsed by the instructor for the category, not class or type, of aircraft to be flown.

56. A student pilot whose logbook is not endorsed by a flight instructor to make solo cross-country flights is prohibited from flying solo beyond what distance from the point of departure?

A. 20 NM.

B. 25 NM.

C. 50 NM.

Answer (B) is correct. *(14 CFR 61.93)*
DISCUSSION: No student pilot may operate an aircraft in a solo cross-country flight, nor may that student, except in an emergency, make a solo flight landing at any point other than the airport of takeoff, unless the student has met the requirements for solo cross-country flight. However, an authorized flight instructor may allow the student to practice solo takeoffs and landings at another airport within 25 NM from the airport at which the student receives instruction if the instructor finds that the student pilot is competent. A solo cross-country flight is defined as one beyond a radius of 25 NM from the takeoff point.
Answer (A) is incorrect. Cross-country flight, as used here, means a flight of more than 25 NM, not 20 NM. Answer (C) is incorrect. Cross-country flight, as used here, means a flight of more than 25 NM, not 50 NM.

57. May repeated solo cross-country flights over the same route be made by a student without receiving an endorsement from a flight instructor for each flight?

A. No; an endorsement is required for each solo cross-country flight.

B. Yes; if the route is no more than 50 NM from the point of departure and instruction was given in both directions over the route.

C. Yes; if the total route is no more than 25 NM from the point of departure and the student has received at least 3 hours of cross-country instruction and logged at least 5 hours of solo cross-country flight.

Answer (B) is correct. *(14 CFR 61.93)*
DISCUSSION: A flight instructor may endorse a student's logbook for repeated specific solo cross-country flights that are not greater than 50 NM from the point of departure, after giving that student flight instruction in both directions over the route, including takeoffs and landings at the airports to be used, and has specified the conditions for which the flights can be made.
Answer (A) is incorrect. An endorsement can be made for repeated specific cross-country flights within 50 NM. Answer (C) is incorrect. The flight must remain within 50 NM, not 25 NM, of the point of departure.

61.95 Operations in Class B Airspace and at Airports Located within Class B Airspace

58. Who is authorized to endorse a student pilot logbook authorizing flight in Class B airspace?

A. Any flight instructor.

B. Only the flight instructor who conducted the training.

C. Any flight instructor who has personal knowledge of the flight training received.

Answer (B) is correct. *(14 CFR 61.95)*
DISCUSSION: A student pilot may not operate an aircraft on a solo flight in Class B airspace unless his or her logbook has been endorsed within the preceding 90 days for conducting solo flight in that Class B airspace area by the instructor who gave the flight training, specifying that the student has received the required ground and flight instruction and has been found competent to conduct solo flight in that specific Class B airspace area.
Answer (A) is incorrect. Only the flight instructor who gave the student training in that specific Class B airspace area may endorse the student's logbook. Answer (C) is incorrect. Only the flight instructor who gave the student training in that specific Class B airspace area may endorse the student's logbook.

59. To operate an aircraft on a solo flight within Class B airspace, a student must have a logbook endorsement showing that (s)he has

- A. received flight instruction from any authorized flight instructor on operating within Class B airspace.
- B. received ground instruction on and flight instruction in that specific airspace for which solo flight is authorized.
- C. within the preceding 90 days, been found to be competent by any flight instructor having knowledge of the student's experience in that specific airspace.

Answer (B) is correct. *(14 CFR 61.95)*
DISCUSSION: A student pilot may not operate an aircraft on a solo flight in Class B airspace unless his or her logbook has been endorsed within the preceding 90 days for conducting solo flight in that Class B airspace area by the instructor who gave the flight training, specifying that the student has received the required ground and flight instruction and has been found competent to conduct solo flight in that specific Class B airspace area.
Answer (A) is incorrect. The flight instruction must have been given by the instructor who endorses the logbook, in that specific Class B airspace area. Answer (C) is incorrect. The logbook must be endorsed by the flight instructor who gave the ground and flight instruction within that specific Class B airspace area.

61.101 Recreational Pilot Privileges and Limitations

60. A Recreational Pilot Certificate may be issued for

- A. airships, gliders, and balloons.
- B. airplanes, gyroplanes, and helicopters.
- C. airplanes, gliders, helicopters, and gyroplanes.

Answer (B) is correct. *(14 CFR 61.101)*
DISCUSSION: A recreational pilot certificate may be issued for airplanes, helicopters, and gyroplanes. A recreational pilot may not act as pilot in command of a glider, airship, or balloon.
Answer (A) is incorrect. A recreational pilot may not act as pilot in command of a glider, airship, or balloon. Answer (C) is incorrect. A recreational pilot may not act as pilot in command of a glider.

61. When is a recreational pilot required to carry a logbook with the required endorsements?

- A. Any flight up to 50 miles from the airport at which instruction was received.
- B. When flying during the hours between sunrise and sunset.
- C. On all flights when serving as pilot in command.

Answer (C) is correct. *(14 CFR 61.101)*
DISCUSSION: A recreational pilot is required to carry his or her logbook with the required endorsements on all flights when serving as pilot in command.
Answer (A) is incorrect. A recreational pilot is required to carry a logbook with the required endorsements only on flights in which (s)he is serving as pilot in command, not on any flight (which may include training) up to 50 NM from the airport at which instruction was received. Answer (B) is incorrect. A recreational pilot must carry a logbook with the required endorsements only on flights in which (s)he is serving as pilot in command between sunrise and sunset (day), not any flight during the day.

62. A recreational pilot with less than 400 hours' flight time may not act as pilot in command unless the pilot has

- A. logged pilot-in-command time in the last 90 days.
- B. logged pilot-in-command time in the last 180 days.
- C. received flight instruction from an instructor who certifies the pilot is competent to conduct flights beyond 50 miles.

Answer (B) is correct. *(14 CFR 61.101)*
DISCUSSION: A recreational pilot who has logged fewer than 400 flight hr. and who has not logged pilot-in-command time in an aircraft within the preceding 180 days may not act as pilot in command of an aircraft until the pilot has received flight training from an authorized flight instructor who certifies in the pilot's logbook that the pilot is competent to act as pilot in command of the aircraft.
Answer (A) is incorrect. The pilot must have logged PIC time in the last 180, not 90, days. Answer (C) is incorrect. If the pilot has not logged PIC time in the last 180 days, (s)he must receive flight training from a CFI who certifies that (s)he is competent to act as PIC, not fly beyond 50 NM.

61.109 Aeronautical Experience

63. Your student, who is preparing for a Private Pilot practical test in a single-engine airplane, received 3.5 hours of cross-country flight training including flights of 1.9 hours, 1.0 hours, and .6 hours. Is your student eligible to take the practical test?

- A. No.
- B. Yes.
- C. Yes, but if test is satisfactory, certificate will have an ICAO limitation on it.

Answer (B) is correct. *(14 CFR 61.109)*
DISCUSSION: For a private pilot certificate in a single-engine airplane, a student must receive at least 3 hr. of cross-country flight training.
Answer (A) is incorrect. A student must receive at least 3 hr. of cross-country flight training. Answer (C) is incorrect. A student must have received at least 3 hr. of cross-country flight training. The certificate will not have an ICAO limitation on it.

64. Your student is not interested in flying at night. May he/she take the practical test for a Private Pilot Certificate without any night flight training?

A. No, your student must have logged some night flight training in order to be eligible.
B. No, your student must have logged at least 3 hours of night flight training in order to be issued a certificate.
C. Yes, but after satisfactory completion of the practical test, the certificate will be issued with the limitation "Night Flying Prohibited."

Answer (B) is correct. *(14 CFR 61.109)*
DISCUSSION: For a private pilot certificate, a student must receive 3 hr. of night flight training that includes one cross-country flight of over 100 NM total distance and 10 takeoffs and 10 landings to a full stop at an airport.
Answer (A) is incorrect. Your student must receive at least 3 hr. of night training, not "some" night flight training. Answer (C) is incorrect. Your student must complete 3 hr. of night flight training in order to be issued a certificate.

65. What night flight training is required for an unrestricted Private Pilot Certificate with an airplane rating?

A. 3 hours to include five takeoffs and five landings (each landing from a traffic pattern).
B. 3 hours to include 10 takeoffs and 10 landings and one cross-country flight of over 100 nautical miles.
C. 1 hour to include three takeoffs and three landings.

Answer (B) is correct. *(14 CFR 61.109)*
DISCUSSION: An applicant for a private pilot certificate with an airplane rating must have had at least 3 hr. of night flight training, including one cross-country flight of over 100 NM total distance and 10 takeoffs and landings to a full stop at an airport.
The FAA may remove the word "unrestricted" since there are no restricted private pilot certificates issued, except specific cases in the state of Alaska.
Answer (A) is incorrect. Three hr. of night flight training, including one cross-country flight of over 100 NM total distance and 10, not 5, takeoffs and landings, are required. Answer (C) is incorrect. Three hr., not 1 hr., of night flight training, including one cross-country flight of over 100 NM total distance and 10, not 3, takeoffs and landings, are required.

66. Your student has received 3.0 hours of night flight training including five takeoffs and landings. Is your student eligible to take the Private Pilot practical test?

A. Yes, but the pilot certificate would bear the limitation "Night Flying Prohibited."
B. No.
C. Yes, but the pilot certificate would bear the restriction, "Holder does not meet ICAO requirements."

Answer (B) is correct. *(14 CFR 61.109)*
DISCUSSION: The 3 hr. of night flight training must also include one cross-country flight of over 100 NM total distance and 10 takeoffs and landings to a full stop at an airport. Thus, your student needs five additional night takeoffs and landings and one night cross-country flight of over 100 NM.
Answer (A) is incorrect. The 3 hr. of night flight training must also include one night cross-country flight of over 100 NM and 10, not 5, takeoffs and landings. Answer (C) is incorrect. The 3 hr. of night flight training must also include one night cross-country flight of over 100 NM and 10, not 5, takeoffs and landings.

67. With respect to day cross-country experience requirements, a private pilot-airplane applicant must have a minimum of

A. 3 hours' dual and 5 hours' solo.
B. 3 hours' dual and 10 hours' solo.
C. 5 hours' dual and 10 hours' solo.

Answer (A) is correct. *(14 CFR 61.109)*
DISCUSSION: An applicant for a private pilot (airplane) certificate must have had at least 3 hr. of cross-country flight training and at least 5 hr. of solo cross-country time.
Answer (B) is incorrect. A private pilot-airplane applicant must have at least 5 hr., not 10 hr., of solo cross-country flight training. Answer (C) is incorrect. A private pilot-airplane applicant must have at least 3 hr., not 5 hr., dual cross-country and 5 hr., not 10 hr., of solo cross-country flight training.

61.123 Eligibility Requirements: General

68. What is the minimum age required to be eligible for a Commercial Pilot Certificate?

A. 17
B. 18
C. 21

Answer (B) is correct. *(14 CFR 61.123)*
DISCUSSION: To be eligible for a commercial pilot certificate, a person must be at least 18 years of age.
Answer (A) is incorrect. Seventeen is the minimum age for a private, not commercial, pilot certificate. Answer (C) is incorrect. Twenty-one is not an age requirement for any pilot certificate.

61.129 Aeronautical Experience

69. As pilot, what is the minimum flight time in an aircraft an applicant must have for a Commercial Pilot Certificate with an airplane rating?

A. 250 hours.
B. 200 hours.
C. 150 hours.

Answer (B) is correct. *(14 CFR 61.129)*
DISCUSSION: An applicant for a commercial pilot certificate with an airplane rating must have a total of at least 250 hr. of flight time as pilot, which may include not more than 50 hr. of instruction from an authorized instructor in an approved flight simulator or flight training device. Thus, the minimum flight time in an aircraft is 200 hr. (250 – 50).
Answer (A) is incorrect. Although a total of 250 hr. is required, up to 50 hr. may be instruction in a simulator. Answer (C) is incorrect. A total of 250 hr. is required, and up to 50 hr., not 100 hr., may be instruction in a simulator.

70. An applicant for a Commercial Pilot Certificate with ASEL ratings presents a logbook with 254 hours' total time. Of that, 20 hours are logged as SIC in single-engine airplanes certificated for single pilot operations. You determine this time was accumulated as safety pilot with another pilot who was flying "under the hood." Does the applicant have enough total time to be eligible for the practical test?

A. Yes.
B. No, because SIC time does not count towards hours for certification requirements.
C. No, only one-half of the SIC time can be counted towards certification requirements.

Answer (A) is correct. *(14 CFR 61.129)*
DISCUSSION: An applicant for a commercial pilot certificate with an airplane rating must have a total of at least 250 hr. of flight time as pilot, including

1. 100 hr. in powered aircraft
2. 20 hr. of flight instruction
3. 100 hr. of pilot-in-command time

Answer (B) is incorrect. SIC time does count toward the total time as long as the requirements of 20 hr. of instruction and 100 hr. of PIC are met. Answer (C) is incorrect. All of the SIC time counts toward the total time as long as the requirements of 20 hr. of instruction and 100 hr. of PIC are met.

71. Under 14 CFR Part 61, a commercial pilot-airplane applicant is required to have a minimum of how much cross-country experience?

A. 30 hours.
B. 40 hours.
C. 50 hours.

Answer (C) is correct. *(14 CFR 61.129)*
DISCUSSION: An applicant for a commercial pilot certificate with an airplane rating must have at least 50 hr. of cross-country flights as pilot in command, each flight with a landing at a point more than 50 NM from the original departure point.
Answer (A) is incorrect. The minimum required cross-country flight time is 50 hr., not 30 hr. Answer (B) is incorrect. The minimum required cross-country flight time is 50 hr., not 40 hr.

61.133 Commercial Pilot Privileges and Limitations

72. What limitation is imposed on a newly certificated commercial airplane pilot if that person does not hold an instrument pilot rating?

A. The carrying of passengers for hire on cross-country flights of more than 50 NM or at night is prohibited.
B. The carrying of passengers for hire on cross-country flights is limited to 50 NM for night flights, but not limited for day flights.
C. The carrying of passengers or property for hire on cross-country flights is limited to 50 NM and the carrying of passengers for hire at night is prohibited.

Answer (A) is correct. *(14 CFR 61.133)*
DISCUSSION: An applicant for a commercial pilot certificate with an airplane rating must hold an instrument rating (airplane), or the commercial pilot certificate that is issued is endorsed with a limitation prohibiting the carriage of passengers for hire in airplanes on cross-country flights of more than 50 NM or at night.
Answer (B) is incorrect. Without an instrument rating, carrying passengers for hire at night is not permitted. Answer (C) is incorrect. Carrying freight (property) is not limited.

61.189 Flight Instructor Records

73. Which training time must be certified by the instructor from whom it was received?

A. Flight training.

B. Flight training and training in a flight training device.

C. All flight training, flight simulator training, and ground training.

Answer (C) is correct. *(14 CFR 61.189)*
DISCUSSION: A flight instructor must sign the logbook of each person to whom (s)he has given flight training, flight simulator training, and ground training and specify in that book the amount of time and the date on which it was given.
Answer (A) is incorrect. All ground and flight simulator training, as well as flight training time, must be certified by the instructor. Answer (B) is incorrect. All ground training, as well as flight training and flight simulator training, time must be certified by the instructor.

74. The name, type, and date of each student pilot endorsement given shall be maintained by each flight instructor. For what period of time is this record required to be retained?

A. 1 year.

B. 2 years.

C. 3 years.

Answer (C) is correct. *(14 CFR 61.189)*
DISCUSSION: Each certificated flight instructor shall maintain a record in his or her flight instructor logbook or in a separate document containing the name of each person whose logbook or student pilot certificate he has endorsed for solo flight privileges. The record must include the type and date of each endorsement, and it shall be retained by the flight instructor for at least 3 years.
Answer (A) is incorrect. The record must be retained for 3 years, not 1 year. Answer (B) is incorrect. The records must be retained for 3 years, not 2 years.

61.191 Additional Flight Instructor Ratings

75. A flight instructor who applies for an additional rating on that certificate must have a minimum of how many hours as pilot in command in the category and class of aircraft appropriate to the rating sought?

A. 15.

B. No minimum number of hours.

C. 5.

Answer (A) is correct. *(14 CFR 61.191)*
DISCUSSION: The holder of a flight instructor certificate who applies for an additional rating on that certificate must have had at least 15 hr. as pilot in command in the category and class of aircraft appropriate to the rating sought.
Answer (B) is incorrect. The flight instructor must have a minimum of 15 hr. as pilot in command in the category and class of aircraft appropriate to the rating sought. Answer (C) is incorrect. The flight instructor must have 15 hr., not 5 hr., as pilot in command in the category and class of aircraft appropriate to the rating sought.

61.195 Flight Instructor Limitations and Qualifications

76. What requirement(s) must an authorized instructor meet in order to prepare an applicant for an initial Flight Instructor Certificate?

A. Logged a minimum of 80 hours of flight training time.

B. Held a Flight Instructor Certificate for at least 12 months immediately preceding the date the training is given.

C. Held a Flight Instructor Certificate for at least 24 months and given a minimum of 200 hours of flight training.

Answer (C) is correct. *(14 CFR 61.195)*
DISCUSSION: A flight instructor who provides training to an applicant for an initial flight instructor certificate must hold the appropriate flight instructor certificate and rating; have held a flight instructor certificate for at least 24 months; and, for training in preparation for an airplane rating, have given at least 200 hr. of flight training as an instructor.
Answer (A) is incorrect. The flight instructor must have held a flight instructor certificate for 24 months. The 80 hr. requirement is for gliders, while, for an airplane rating, the flight instructor must have given at least 200 hr. of flight training. Answer (B) is incorrect. The flight instructor must have held the flight instructor certificate for at least 24 months, not 12 months, and, in preparation for an airplane rating, must have given at least 200 hr. of flight training as an instructor.

77. During any 24 consecutive hours, an instructor is limited to how many hours of flight training?

A. 8

B. 10

C. 12

Answer (A) is correct. *(14 CFR 61.195)*
DISCUSSION: The holder of a flight instructor certificate may not conduct more than 8 hr. of flight training in any period of 24 consecutive hours.
Answer (B) is incorrect. The limitation as to flight training within a 24-hr. period is 8 hr., not 10 hr. Answer (C) is incorrect. The limitation as to flight training within a 24-hr. period is 8 hr., not 12 hr.

78. To endorse a student pilot's logbook for solo flight, an instructor is required, in part, to have

A. given that student cross-country flight training.
B. given that student flight training in the type of aircraft involved.
C. at least 5 hours of experience as pilot in command in the aircraft involved.

Answer (B) is correct. *(14 CFR 61.195)*
   DISCUSSION: The holder of a flight instructor certificate may not endorse a student pilot's logbook for solo flight unless (s)he has given that student flight training required for the endorsement and considers that student prepared to conduct the flight safely with the type of aircraft involved.
   Answer (A) is incorrect. Cross-country flight training is not required prior to solo flight. Answer (C) is incorrect. Five hr. of PIC experience in the aircraft involved are required only to give instruction in a multi-engine airplane.

79. To endorse a student pilot for solo cross-country privileges, an instructor is required, in part, to have

A. determined that the student's preparation, planning, and procedures are adequate for the proposed flight under the existing conditions.
B. assurance from another instructor that the student is prepared to conduct the flight safely under current conditions.
C. given that student the required cross-country flight training and checked the flight planning.

Answer (A) is correct. *(14 CFR 61.195)*
   DISCUSSION: To endorse a student pilot for solo cross-country privileges, an instructor is required, in part, to have determined that the student's flight preparation, planning, equipment, and proposed procedures are adequate for the proposed flight under the existing conditions and within any limitations listed in the logbook that the instructor considers necessary for the safety of the flight.
   Answer (B) is incorrect. The instructor who endorses the student's logbook for a solo cross-country flight must check the student's preparation, not have assurance from another instructor that the student is properly prepared. Answer (C) is incorrect. While the instructor who endorses the student's pilot certificate and logbook for solo cross-country privileges must have given the student the required flight training, that instructor is not required to check the flight planning for each solo cross-country flight personally.

80. Certain flight training is required for the issuance of a certificate. If that training is in a helicopter or multi-engine airplane, the instructor is required, in part, to have

A. given at least 200 hours of flight training
B. given at least 25 hours of flight training in the particular make and model aircraft.
C. at least 5 hours of experience as pilot in command in the make and model of aircraft involved.

Answer (C) is correct. *(14 CFR 61.195)*
   DISCUSSION: The holder of a flight instructor certificate may not give flight training required for the issuance of a certificate or a category or class rating in a multi-engine airplane or a helicopter unless (s)he has at least 5 hr. of experience as pilot in command in the make and model of aircraft involved.
   Answer (A) is incorrect. Two-hundred hr. of flight training experience is required to provide instruction to initial flight instructor applicants. Answer (B) is incorrect. The instructor needs to have only 5 hr. of experience as PIC, not to have given 25 hr. of flight training in the make and model of aircraft involved.

81. The minimum pilot-in-command time requirement for a flight instructor with multi-engine privileges to give flight training to a student for a multi-engine rating is

A. 5 hours in the make and model of aircraft in which training is to be given.
B. 10 hours in the make of aircraft in which the training is to be given.
C. 15 hours in the make and model of aircraft in which training is to be given.

Answer (A) is correct. *(14 CFR 61.195)*
   DISCUSSION: The holder of a flight instructor certificate may not give flight training required for the issuance of a certificate or a category or class rating in a multi-engine airplane unless (s)he has at least 5 hr. of experience as pilot in command in the make and model of that airplane.
   Answer (B) is incorrect. The minimum PIC time requirement is 5 hr., not 10 hr., and it must be in not only the make, but also the model of aircraft to be used. Answer (C) is incorrect. Fifteen is the number of hours required as pilot in command in the category and class of aircraft appropriate to an additional rating sought by a flight instructor.

82. Where can you find templates of sample endorsements to provide to your students?

A. AC 65-61, Appendix 1.
B. AC 61-65, Appendix 1.
C. AC 91-67, Appendix 1.

Answer (B) is correct. *(AC 61-65)*
   DISCUSSION: Advisory Circular 61-65 contains a great deal of information about pilot and instructor certification. Appendix 1 of this AC contains sample endorsements that an instructor can issue to student pilots.
   Answer (A) is incorrect. There is no FAA Advisory Circular 65-61. Answer (C) is incorrect. Advisory Circular 91-67 describes acceptable methods for the operation of aircraft under Part 91 with certain inoperative instruments and equipment, not instructor endorsements for student pilots.

61.197 Renewal of Flight Instructor Certificates

83. A Flight Instructor Certificate may be renewed by

A. providing a record of training showing evidence the applicant has given at least 80 hours of flight training in the last 24 months.
B. successfully completing a flight instructor refresher course within 3 calendar months prior to renewal.
C. passing both a knowledge and a practical test.

Answer (B) is correct. *(14 CFR 61.197)*
DISCUSSION: A person who holds a flight instructor certificate that has not expired may renew that certificate for an additional 24 calendar months by successfully completing a flight instructor refresher course (FIRC) within 3 calendar months prior to the expiration month of his or her flight instructor certificate.
Answer (A) is incorrect. A flight instructor certificate may be renewed by providing a record of training students that shows that within the last 24 months, the instructor has endorsed at least five students for a practical test and at least 80% have passed on the first attempt, not that the instructor has given 80 hr. of flight training. Answer (C) is incorrect. A flight instructor certificate may be renewed by passing a practical test for the renewal of the flight instructor certificate or an additional flight instructor rating, not by passing any knowledge and practical test.

61.199 Expired Flight Instructor Certificates and Ratings

84. The holder of an expired Flight Instructor Certificate may exchange that certificate for a new one by

A. passing the appropriate practical test.
B. presenting a satisfactory record of flight training.
C. successfully completing a flight instructor refresher course.

Answer (A) is correct. *(14 CFR 61.199)*
DISCUSSION: The holder of an expired flight instructor certificate may exchange that certificate for a new certificate by passing the appropriate practical test.
Answer (B) is incorrect. A practical test is required after a flight instructor certificate has expired. Answer (C) is incorrect. A practical test is required after a flight instructor certificate has expired.

85. If you hold an expired flight instructor certificate with instrument and multi-engine ratings,

A. you must pass a flight instructor practical test for all ratings to reinstate your certificate.
B. you must pass a practical test for any certificate or rating to reinstate your certificate.
C. you must pass a flight instructor practical test for only one of your existing ratings to reinstate your certificate.

Answer (C) is correct. *(14 CFR 61.199)*
DISCUSSION: The holder of an expired flight instructor certificate may reinstate that flight instructor certificate and ratings by passing a flight instructor certification practical test for one of the ratings held on the expired flight instructor certificate.
Answer (A) is incorrect. You are only required to pass a flight instructor practical test for one rating on your CFI certificate, not all ratings on the certificate. Answer (B) is incorrect. You must pass a flight instructor practical test, not just any practical test, for one of your existing flight instructor ratings or add a new flight instructor rating to reinstate your expired flight instructor certificate.

86. You have an expired CFI certificate and you pass a practical test to add a seaplane rating to your flight instructor certificate. Which of the following is true regarding your flight instructor certificate?

A. You must pass practical tests for the other ratings on your certificate before your certificate can be reinstated.
B. Your flight instructor certificate, including all ratings previously held, is renewed.
C. You must pass a proficiency check with a designated pilot examiner before your certificate can be renewed.

Answer (B) is correct. *(14 CFR 61.199)*
DISCUSSION: The holder of an expired flight instructor certificate may reinstate that flight instructor certificate and ratings by passing a flight instructor certification practical test for one of the ratings held on the expired flight instructor certificate or by adding a new rating to the flight instructor certificate.
Answer (A) is incorrect. To reinstate an expired CFI certificate, you are only required to pass a flight instructor practical test for one rating on your CFI certificate or add a new rating to your flight instructor certificate. Answer (C) is incorrect. A proficiency check or flight review will not reinstate an expired CFI certificate.

87. To reinstate an expired flight instructor certificate, you must

A. pass a practical test for one of your existing flight instructor ratings or pass a practical test for an additional flight instructor rating.
B. pass a practical test for an additional flight instructor rating not currently on your flight instructor certificate.
C. complete a flight review with a flight instructor or designated pilot examiner.

Answer (A) is the best answer. *(14 CFR 61.199)*
   DISCUSSION: The holder of an expired flight instructor certificate may reinstate that flight instructor certificate and ratings by passing a flight instructor certification practical test for one of the ratings held on the expired flight instructor certificate or by adding a new rating to the flight instructor certificate.
   Answer (B) is incorrect. While this is one option for CFI certificate reinstatement, it is not the only avenue for reinstatement. You can pass a practical test for one of your existing flight instructor ratings or add a new rating to your certificate. Answer (C) is incorrect. A flight review will not reinstate an expired CFI certificate.

61.315 Sport Pilot Privileges and Limitations: Pilot in Command

NOTE: Questions 88 - 91 are only tested on the Flight Instructor with a Sport Pilot Rating (SIA) FAA Knowledge Test.

88. How many passengers is a sport pilot allowed to carry on board?

A. One.
B. Two.
C. Three.

Answer (A) is correct. *(14 CFR 61.315)*
   DISCUSSION: As a sport pilot, you may not act as a pilot in command of a light-sport aircraft while carrying more than one passenger.
   Answer (B) is incorrect. As a sport pilot, you are not permitted to carry any more than one passenger. Answer (C) is incorrect. As a sport pilot, you are not permitted to carry any more than one passenger.

89. According to regulations pertaining to privileges and limitations, a sport pilot may

A. be paid for the operating expenses of a flight if at least three takeoffs and three landings were made by the pilot within the preceding 90 days.
B. not pay less than half of the share of the operating expenses of a flight with passengers provided the expenses involve only fuel, oil, airport expenditures, or rental fees.
C. not be paid in any manner for the operating expenses of a flight.

Answer (B) is correct. *(14 CFR 61.315)*
   DISCUSSION: A sport pilot may not pay less than an equal (pro rata) share of the operating expenses of a flight with passengers. These expenses may involve only fuel, oil, airport expenditures (e.g., landing fees, tie-down fees, etc.), or rental fees.
   Answer (A) is incorrect. A sport pilot may be paid for the operating expenses of a flight in connection with any business or employment if the flight is only incidental to that business or employment and no passengers or property are carried for compensation or hire, not if the pilot has made three takeoffs and three landings in the preceding 90 days. Answer (C) is incorrect. A sport pilot may equally share the operating expenses of a flight with his or her passengers.

90. As a sport pilot, you may carry no more than

A. one passenger.
B. two passengers.
C. three passengers.

Answer (A) is correct. *(14 CFR 61.315)*
   DISCUSSION: Sport pilots may not act in command of a light-sport aircraft while carrying more than one passenger.
   Answer (B) is incorrect. Sport pilots may not act as pilot in command of a light-sport aircraft while carrying more than one, not two, passengers. Answer (C) is incorrect. Sport pilots may not act as pilot in command of a light-sport aircraft while carrying more than one, not three, passengers.

91. The highest altitude at which sport pilots may operate is

A. 18,000 ft. MSL or 2,000 ft. AGL, whichever is higher.
B. 10,000 ft. MSL or 2,000 ft. AGL, whichever is higher.
C. 12,000 ft. MSL or 2,000 ft. AGL, whichever is higher.

Answer (B) is correct. *(14 CFR 61.315)*
   DISCUSSION: Sport pilots are restricted to operating within a number of limitations, including not above 10,000 ft. MSL or 2,000 ft. AGL, whichever is higher.
   Answer (A) is incorrect. Sport pilots may not operate at altitudes from 18,000 ft. MSL or 2,000 ft. AGL, whichever is higher. Answer (C) is incorrect. Sport pilots may not operate at altitudes from 12,000 ft. MSL or 2,000 ft. AGL, whichever is higher.

61.325 Required Endorsements for Class B, C, and D Airspaces

92. Which is true regarding flight operations to a satellite airport, without an operating tower, within Class C airspace?

A. Prior to entering that airspace, a sport pilot must contact the FSS.

B. Prior to entering that airspace, a sport pilot must contact the primary airport tower.

C. Prior to entering that airspace, a sport pilot must receive the appropriate logbook endorsement.

Answer (C) is correct. *(14 CFR 61.325)*
DISCUSSION: A sport pilot must receive and log ground and flight training to operate a light-sport aircraft at an airport or in airspace within Class B, C, and D airspace, or in another airspace with an airport that has an operational control tower. Therefore, a sport pilot must receive the appropriate logbook endorsement prior to entering Class C airspace.
Answer (A) is incorrect. FSS does not have authority to control Class C airspace. Only ATC has this authority. Answer (B) is incorrect. The sport pilot, after (s)he has received the appropriate logbook endorsement, should contact ATC and establish two-way radio communications prior to entering Class C airspace.

93. In order to operate a light-sport aircraft at an airport within, or in airspace within, Class B, C, and D airspace, a sport pilot

A. does not have to meet any additional requirements.

B. must receive ground training on operations within Class B, C, and D airspace.

C. must receive and log ground and flight training on operations within Class B, C, and D airspace.

Answer (C) is correct. *(14 CFR 61.325)*
DISCUSSION: A sport pilot must receive and log ground and flight training to operate a light-sport aircraft at an airport or in airspace within Class B, C, and D airspace, or in other airspace with an airport that has an operational control tower.
Answer (A) is incorrect. Sport pilots do have to meet the additional requirements of receiving and logging ground and flight training on operations within Class B, C, and D airspace. Answer (B) is incorrect. Sport pilots must not only receive ground training on operations within Class B, C, and D airspace, but also must receive and log ground and flight training on operations within Class B, C, and D airspace.

7.4 14 CFR Part 91

91.3 Responsibility and Authority of the Pilot in Command

94. If an in-flight emergency requires immediate action, a pilot in command may

A. deviate from 14 CFR's to the extent required to meet that emergency.

B. not deviate from 14 CFR's unless permission is obtained from air traffic control.

C. deviate from 14 CFR's to the extent required to meet the emergency, but must submit a written report to the Administrator within 24 hours.

Answer (A) is correct. *(14 CFR 91.3)*
DISCUSSION: In an in-flight emergency requiring immediate action, the pilot in command may deviate from any rule to the extent required to meet that emergency. Each pilot who does so deviate shall, upon request, send a written report of that deviation to the FAA.
Answer (B) is incorrect. In an emergency, deviation from the 14 CFRs is permitted without approval. Answer (C) is incorrect. A written report to the FAA is required only upon request.

91.9 Civil Aircraft Flight Manual, Marking, and Placard Requirements

95. An aircraft's operating limitations may be found in the

A. FAA-approved aircraft flight manual.

B. owner's handbook published by the aircraft manufacturer.

C. aircraft flight manual, approved manual material, markings, and placards, or any combination thereof.

Answer (C) is correct. *(14 CFR 91.9)*
DISCUSSION: No one may operate a civil aircraft without complying with the operating limitations specified in the approved Airplane Flight Manual, markings, and placards. No one may operate a U.S. civil aircraft unless there is available in the aircraft a current approved flight manual, approved manual material, markings, and placards, or any combination thereof.
Answer (A) is incorrect. Several sources set forth the operating limitations; i.e., not just one is specified. Answer (B) is incorrect. Several sources set forth the operating limitations; i.e., not just one is specified.

91.17 Alcohol or Drugs

96. A person may not act as a crewmember of a civil aircraft if alcoholic beverages have been consumed by that person within the preceding

A. 8 hours.
B. 12 hours.
C. 24 hours.

Answer (A) is correct. *(14 CFR 91.17)*
DISCUSSION: No person may act or attempt to act as a crew member of a civil aircraft within 8 hr. after the consumption of any alcoholic beverage.
Answer (B) is incorrect. The required waiting time after consumption of alcoholic beverages is 8 hr., not 12 hr. Answer (C) is incorrect. The required waiting time after consumption of alcoholic beverages is 8 hr., not 24 hr.

97. No person may act as a crewmember of a civil aircraft with a minimum blood alcohol level of

A. any detectable amount.
B. 0.04 percent or greater.
C. 0.2 percent or greater.

Answer (B) is correct. *(14 CFR 91.17)*
DISCUSSION: No person may act or attempt to act as a crew member of a civil aircraft while having 0.04% by weight, or more, alcohol in the blood.
Answer (A) is incorrect. Pilots may have up to 0.04% blood alcohol level and still be legal. Answer (C) is incorrect. The limit is 0.04% blood alcohol level, not 0.2%.

98. Under what condition, if any, may a pilot allow a person who is obviously under the influence of intoxicating liquors or drugs to be carried aboard an aircraft?

A. Under no condition.
B. Only if a second pilot is aboard.
C. Only if the person is a medical patient under proper care or in an emergency.

Answer (C) is correct. *(14 CFR 91.17)*
DISCUSSION: Except in an emergency, no pilot of a civil aircraft may allow a person who appears to be intoxicated or who demonstrates by manner or physical indications that (s)he is under the influence of drugs (except a medical patient under proper care) to be carried in that aircraft.
Answer (A) is incorrect. If under medical care or in emergency, passengers under the influence of alcohol or drugs can be carried. Answer (B) is incorrect. The number of pilots is irrelevant.

91.103 Preflight Action

99. Which preflight action is required for every flight?

A. Check weather reports and forecasts.
B. Determine runway length at airports of intended use.
C. Determine alternatives if the flight cannot be completed.

Answer (B) is correct. *(14 CFR 91.103)*
DISCUSSION: Each pilot in command shall, before a flight, become familiar with all available information concerning that flight. This information must include, for any flight, runway lengths at airports of intended use and the required takeoff and landing distance data.
Answer (A) is incorrect. Weather reports and forecasts are not required to be referred to for local VFR flights, even though it is a good operating practice. Answer (C) is incorrect. Determining alternative airports is not required for local VFR flights, even though it is a good operating practice.

100. The preflight action required by regulations relative to alternatives available, if the planned flight cannot be completed, is applicable to

A. IFR flights only.
B. any flight not in the vicinity of an airport.
C. any flight conducted for hire or compensation.

Answer (B) is correct. *(14 CFR 91.103)*
DISCUSSION: Each pilot in command shall, before a flight, become familiar with all available information concerning that flight. This information must include, for a flight not in the vicinity of an airport, weather reports and forecasts, fuel requirements, alternatives available if the planned flight cannot be completed, and any known traffic delays.
Answer (A) is incorrect. VFR flights not in the vicinity of an airport as well as IFR flights require this information. Answer (C) is incorrect. VFR flights not in the vicinity of an airport as well as IFR flights require this information, regardless of whether the flight is for compensation or hire.

91.107 Use of Safety Belts, Shoulder Harnesses, and Child Restraint Systems

101. Which statement is true regarding the use of seatbelts and shoulder harnesses?

A. Crewmembers must keep seatbelts and shoulder harnesses fastened at all times during movement on the surface.

B. The pilot in command must ensure that each person on board an aircraft is briefed on how to fasten and unfasten seatbelts.

C. Passengers must keep seatbelts fastened at all times during movement on the surface but use of shoulder harnesses is optional.

Answer (B) is correct. *(14 CFR 91.107)*
DISCUSSION: No pilot may take off a U.S.-registry civil aircraft unless the pilot in command ensures that each person on board is briefed on how to fasten and unfasten that person's safety belt and, if installed, shoulder harness. Each person on board must occupy an approved seat with a safety belt, and shoulder harness if installed, properly secured about him or her during movement on the surface, takeoff, and landing.
Answer (A) is incorrect. Crewmembers are only required to keep seatbelts and shoulder harnesses fastened during takeoff and landing. Passengers must keep both fastened during taxi. Answer (C) is incorrect. Passengers must keep both seatbelts and shoulder harnesses fastened during taxi.

91.109 Flight Instruction; Simulated Instrument Flight and Certain Flight Tests

102. A pilot in a multi-engine land airplane is planning to practice IFR procedures under a hood in VMC conditions. The safety pilot must possess at least a

A. Recreational Pilot Certificate with an airplane rating.

B. Private Pilot Certificate with airplane multi-engine land rating and a current medical certificate.

C. Private Pilot Certificate with airplane and instrument ratings, but a current medical certificate is not required.

Answer (B) is correct. *(14 CFR 91.109)*
DISCUSSION: No person may operate a civil aircraft in simulated instrument flight unless the other control seat is occupied by a safety pilot who possesses at least a private pilot certificate with category (airplane) and class (multi-engine land) ratings. Additionally, since the safety pilot is assigned certain duties, the safety pilot is considered a required flight crewmember and must also possess a current medical certificate.
Answer (A) is incorrect. A safety pilot must possess at least a private pilot certificate, not a recreational pilot certificate. Answer (C) is incorrect. A safety pilot must have the category and class ratings appropriate to the aircraft flown (airplane, multi-engine land), not only the appropriate category. Additionally, since the safety pilot is a required flight crewmember, (s)he must hold a current medical certificate.

91.111 Operating near Other Aircraft

103. May an airplane be operated in formation flight while passengers are carried for hire?

A. No; this is not authorized.

B. Yes; if the passengers approve.

C. Yes; provided arrangements have been made with the other pilot(s).

Answer (A) is correct. *(14 CFR 91.111)*
DISCUSSION: No person may operate an aircraft carrying passengers for hire in formation flight.
Answer (B) is incorrect. Formation flight is not permitted when passengers are carried for hire, even if the passengers approve. Answer (C) is incorrect. Formation flight is not permitted when passengers are carried for hire, even if arrangements have been made with the other pilot(s).

91.113 Right-of-Way Rules: Except Water Operations

104. If on a night flight, the pilot of aircraft A observes only the green navigation light of aircraft B, and the aircraft are converging, which aircraft has the right-of-way?

A. Aircraft A; it is to the left of aircraft B.

B. Aircraft B; it is to the right of aircraft A.

C. Aircraft A; it is to the right of aircraft B.

Answer (C) is correct. *(14 CFR 91.113)*
DISCUSSION: When aircraft of the same category are converging at approximately the same altitude (except head-on or nearly so), the aircraft to the other's right has the right-of-way. Since the green light is on aircraft B's right wing, aircraft A must be to the right of aircraft B and thus has the right-of-way.
Answer (A) is incorrect. The green navigation light is on aircraft B's right wing, thus aircraft A is to the right, not left, of aircraft B. Answer (B) is incorrect. Aircraft B is to the left, not right, of aircraft A, and A has the right-of-way.

105. What action should be taken if a glider and an airplane approach each other at the same altitude and on a head-on collision course?

A. Both should give way to the right.
B. The airplane should give way because it is more maneuverable.
C. The airplane should give way because the glider has the right-of-way.

Answer (A) is correct. *(14 CFR 91.113)*
DISCUSSION: When aircraft are approaching each other head-on or nearly so, each pilot of each aircraft shall alter course to the right.
Answer (B) is incorrect. When approaching head-on, both aircraft should alter their course to the right. Answer (C) is incorrect. When approaching head-on, both aircraft should alter their course to the right.

106. When two or more aircraft are approaching an airport for the purpose of landing, the right-of-way belongs to the aircraft

A. that is the least maneuverable.
B. that is either ahead of or to the other's right regardless of altitude.
C. at the lower altitude, but it shall not take advantage of this rule to cut in front of or to overtake another.

Answer (C) is correct. *(14 CFR 91.113)*
DISCUSSION: When two or more aircraft are approaching an airport for the purpose of landing, the aircraft at the lower altitude has the right-of-way, but it shall not take advantage of this rule to cut in front of another that is on final approach to land or to overtake that aircraft.
Answer (A) is incorrect. On a landing approach, the aircraft at the lower altitude has the right-of-way. Answer (B) is incorrect. On a landing approach, the aircraft at the lower altitude has the right-of-way.

107. An airplane and an airship are converging. If the airship is left of the airplane's position, which aircraft has the right-of-way?

A. The airship.
B. The airplane.
C. Each should alter course to the right.

Answer (A) is correct. *(14 CFR 91.113)*
DISCUSSION: When aircraft of different categories are converging at approximately the same altitude (except head-on, or nearly so), an airship has the right-of-way over an airplane or rotorcraft.
Answer (B) is incorrect. When aircraft of different categories are converging, an airship has the right-of-way over an airplane, regardless of their relative positions. Answer (C) is incorrect. Each should alter course to the right if they are approaching head-on, or nearly so, not converging.

108. An airship has the right-of-way over which aircraft?

A. Glider.
B. Gyroplane.
C. Aircraft towing another aircraft.

Answer (B) is correct. *(14 CFR 91.113)*
DISCUSSION: When aircraft of different categories are converging at approximately the same altitude (except head-on, or nearly so), an airship has the right-of-way over an airplane or rotorcraft. However, an aircraft towing or refueling other aircraft has the right-of-way over all other engine-driven aircraft.
Answer (A) is incorrect. A glider has the right-of-way over an airship, airplane, or rotorcraft. Answer (C) is incorrect. An aircraft towing or refueling other aircraft has the right-of-way over all other engine-driven aircraft.

91.117 Aircraft Speed

109. Unless otherwise authorized, what is the maximum indicated airspeed at which an aircraft may be flown in a satellite airport traffic pattern located within Class B airspace?

A. 200 MPH.
B. 200 knots.
C. 250 knots.

Answer (C) is correct. *(14 CFR 91.117)*
DISCUSSION: Unless otherwise authorized, no person may operate an aircraft within Class B airspace at an indicated airspeed of more than 250 kt. (288 MPH).
Answer (A) is incorrect. No person may operate an aircraft at or below 2,500 ft. AGL within 4 NM of the primary airport of a Class C or Class D airspace area at an indicated airspeed of more than 200 kt., not 200 MPH. Answer (B) is incorrect. No person may operate an aircraft at or below 2,500 ft. AGL within 4 NM of the primary airport of a Class C or Class D airspace area, not within Class B airspace, at an indicated airspeed of more than 200 kt.

110. When flying beneath the lateral limits of Class B airspace, the maximum indicated airspeed authorized is

A. 156 knots.
B. 200 knots.
C. 250 knots.

Answer (B) is correct. *(14 CFR 91.117)*
DISCUSSION: No person may operate an aircraft in the airspace underlying a Class B airspace area designated for an airport, or in a VFR corridor designated through such a Class B airspace area, at an indicated airspeed of greater than 200 kt. (230 MPH).
Answer (A) is incorrect. This is the old speed limit in airport traffic areas for reciprocating-engine aircraft. Answer (C) is incorrect. This is the speed limit of aircraft within, not beneath the lateral limits of, Class B airspace.

111. Unless otherwise authorized or required by air traffic control, what is the maximum indicated airspeed at which a person may operate an aircraft below 10,000 feet MSL?

A. 200 knots.
B. 250 MPH.
C. 250 knots.

Answer (C) is correct. *(14 CFR 91.117)*
DISCUSSION: Unless otherwise authorized, no person may operate an aircraft below 10,000 ft. MSL at an indicated airspeed of more than 250 kt. (288 MPH).
Answer (A) is incorrect. This is the speed limit 2,500 ft. AGL or below within 4 NM of a Class C or Class D primary airport; and the speed limit beneath, or in a VFR corridor through, Class B airspace. Answer (B) is incorrect. The speed limit below 10,000 ft. MSL is 250 kt., not 250 MPH.

112. The maximum indicated airspeed permitted when operating an aircraft within 4 NM of the primary airport in Class D airspace is

A. 200 MPH.
B. 200 knots.
C. 250 knots.

Answer (B) is correct. *(14 CFR 91.117)*
DISCUSSION: Unless otherwise authorized or required by ATC, no person may operate an aircraft at or below 2,500 ft. AGL within 4 NM of the primary airport of a Class C or Class D airspace area at an indicated airspeed of more than 200 kt. Note that Class D airspace generally extends upward from the surface to 2,500 ft. AGL.
Answer (A) is incorrect. The speed limit within 4 NM of a primary Class D airport is 200 kt., not 200 MPH. Answer (C) is incorrect. The general speed limit below 10,000 ft. MSL or in Class B airspace is 250 kt., but not within 4 NM of a primary Class C or Class D airport.

91.119 Minimum Safe Altitudes: General

113. To operate an aircraft over any congested area, a pilot should maintain an altitude of at least

A. 500 feet above the highest obstacle within a horizontal radius of 1,000 feet.
B. 1,000 feet above the highest obstacle within a horizontal radius of 2,000 feet.
C. 2,000 feet above the highest obstacle within a horizontal radius of 1,000 feet.

Answer (B) is correct. *(14 CFR 91.119)*
DISCUSSION: Except when necessary for takeoff or landing, no person may operate an aircraft below, over any congested area of a city, town, or settlement, or over any open air assembly of persons, an altitude of 1,000 ft. above the highest obstacle within a horizontal radius of 2,000 ft. from the aircraft.
Answer (A) is incorrect. The minimum distance above the highest obstacle in a congested area is 1,000 ft., not 500 ft., within a horizontal radius of 2,000 ft., not 1,000 ft. Answer (C) is incorrect. The minimum distance above the highest obstacle in a congested area is 1,000 ft., not 2,000 ft., within a horizontal radius of 2,000 ft., not 1,000 ft.

114. Except when necessary for takeoff or landing, what is the minimum safe altitude for a pilot to operate an aircraft anywhere?

A. An altitude of 1,000 feet above the highest obstacle within a horizontal radius of 2,000 feet.
B. An altitude of 500 feet above the surface and no closer than 500 feet to any person, vessel, vehicle, or structure.
C. An altitude allowing, if a power unit fails, an emergency landing without undue hazard to persons or property on the surface.

Answer (C) is correct. *(14 CFR 91.119)*
DISCUSSION: Except when necessary for takeoff or landing, no person may operate an aircraft anywhere below an altitude allowing, if a power unit fails, an emergency landing without undue hazard to persons or property on the surface.
Answer (A) is incorrect. An altitude of 1,000 ft. above the highest obstacle within a horizontal radius of 2,000 ft. is the minimum altitude over a congested area. Answer (B) is incorrect. An altitude of 500 ft. above the surface and no closer than 500 ft. to any person, vessel, vehicle, or structure is the minimum altitude over other than congested areas and open water or sparsely populated areas.

115. The minimum distance at which an airplane may be operated over a structure which is located in a sparsely populated area is

A. 500 feet above the ground.
B. 500 feet from the structure.
C. 1,000 feet from the structure.

Answer (B) is correct. *(14 CFR 91.119)*
DISCUSSION: Except when necessary for takeoff or landing, no person may operate an aircraft below, over other than congested areas, an altitude of 500 ft. above the surface, except over open water or sparsely populated areas. In those cases, the aircraft may not be operated closer than 500 ft. to any person, vessel, vehicle, or structure.
Answer (A) is incorrect. It is 500 ft. from the structure, not above the ground. Answer (C) is incorrect. The requirement is 500 ft., not 1,000 ft., from the structure.

91.123 Compliance with ATC Clearances and Instructions

116. What action is appropriate if you deviate from an air traffic control instruction during an emergency and are given priority?

A. Submit a report to the nearest FAA regional office within 48 hours.
B. Submit a report to the manager of the air traffic control facility within 24 hours.
C. If requested, submit a detailed report within 48 hours to the manager of the air traffic control facility.

Answer (C) is correct. *(14 CFR 91.123)*
DISCUSSION: Each pilot in command who (though not deviating from a rule) is given priority by ATC in an emergency, shall submit a detailed report of that emergency within 48 hr. to the manager of that ATC facility, if requested by ATC.
Answer (A) is incorrect. A report, if requested, should be made to the manager of the ATC facility, not the FAA. Answer (B) is incorrect. A report, if requested, should be made within 48, not 24, hr.

91.125 ATC Light Signals

117. While in flight, a steady red light directed at you from the control tower means

A. continue flight; airport unsafe, do not land.
B. give way to other aircraft; continue circling.
C. return for landing; expect steady green light at the appropriate time.

Answer (B) is correct. *(14 CFR 91.125)*
DISCUSSION: With respect to an aircraft in flight, a steady red light means give way to other aircraft and continue circling.
Answer (A) is incorrect. While in flight, a flashing, not steady, red light means the airport is unsafe, do not land. Answer (C) is incorrect. While in flight, a flashing green, not steady red, light means to return for landing; expect steady green light at the appropriate time.

118. While in flight, an alternating red and green light directed at you from the control tower means

A. exercise extreme caution.
B. give way to other aircraft; continue circling.
C. return for landing; expect steady green light at proper time.

Answer (A) is correct. *(14 CFR 91.125)*
DISCUSSION: Whether with respect to an aircraft on the surface or in flight, an alternating red and green light means exercise extreme caution.
Answer (B) is incorrect. While in flight, a steady red, not alternating red and green, light means to give way to other aircraft; continue circling. Answer (C) is incorrect. While in flight, a flashing green, not alternating red and green, light means return for landing; expect steady green light at proper time.

119. You receive a flashing white light from the control tower during run-up prior to takeoff; what action should you take?

A. Taxi clear of the runway in use.
B. Return to your starting point on the airport.
C. None; this light signal is applicable only to aircraft in flight.

Answer (B) is correct. *(14 CFR 91.125)*
DISCUSSION: With respect to an aircraft on the surface, a flashing white light means return to starting point on the airport. The signal is not applicable to aircraft in flight.
Answer (A) is incorrect. While on the surface, a flashing red, not steady white, light means to taxi clear of the runway in use. Answer (C) is incorrect. A flashing white light is applicable only to aircraft on the surface, not in flight.

91.127 Operating on or in the Vicinity of an Airport in Class E Airspace

120. What is the correct departure procedure at a noncontrolled airport?

A. The FAA-approved departure procedure for that airport.
B. Make all left turns, except a 45° right turn on the first crosswind leg.
C. Departure in any direction consistent with safety, after crossing the airport boundary.

Answer (A) is correct. *(14 CFR 91.127)*
DISCUSSION: With respect to departures from an airport in Class E airspace, each pilot of an aircraft must comply with any traffic patterns established for that airport.
Answer (B) is incorrect. FAA-approved departure procedures should be followed at each airport. Answer (C) is incorrect. FAA-approved departure procedures should be followed at each airport.

91.129 Operations in Class D Airspace

121. A turbine-powered or large airplane is required to enter an airport traffic pattern at an altitude of at least

A. 1,000 feet AGL.
B. 1,500 feet AGL.
C. 2,000 feet AGL.

Answer (B) is correct. *(14 CFR 91.129)*
DISCUSSION: When operating at an airport in Class D airspace, each pilot of a large or turbine-powered airplane must, unless otherwise required by the applicable distance-from-cloud criteria, enter the traffic pattern at an altitude of at least 1,500 ft. above the elevation of the airport and maintain at least 1,500 ft. until further descent is required for a safe landing.
Answer (A) is incorrect. Large and turbine-powered airplanes are required to enter the traffic pattern of an airport in Class D airspace at an altitude of at least 1,500 ft. AGL, not 1,000 ft. AGL. Answer (C) is incorrect. Large and turbine-powered airplanes are required to enter the traffic pattern of an airport in Class D airspace at an altitude of at least 1,500 ft. AGL, not 2,000 ft. AGL.

122. An airport without a control tower lies within the controlled airspace of an airport with an operating tower. According to regulations, two-way radio communications with ATC are required for landing clearance at

A. both airports, as well as to fly through the area.
B. the tower-controlled airport only, as well as to fly through the area.
C. the tower-controlled airport only, but not required to fly through the area.

Answer (B) is correct. *(14 CFR 91.129)*
DISCUSSION: Each person operating an aircraft in Class D airspace must establish two-way radio communications with ATC prior to entering that airspace and thereafter maintain those communications while within that airspace. In addition, no person may, at any airport with an operating control tower, land an aircraft, unless an appropriate clearance is received from ATC. No clearance is required to land at a satellite airport without a control tower. However, every person must establish two-way radio communications with ATC as soon as practicable after departing such an airport.
Answer (A) is incorrect. One does not need ATC authorization to land at a noncontrolled airport. Answer (C) is incorrect. Radio communications with ATC is required to fly through the Class D airspace area.

91.131 Operations in Class B Airspace

123. What minimum pilot certificate will permit a pilot to enter all Class B airspace?

A. Private Pilot Certificate.
B. Commercial Pilot Certificate.
C. Student Pilot Certificate with an appropriate logbook endorsement.

Answer (C) is correct. *(14 CFR 91.131)*
DISCUSSION: 14 CFR 91.131, Pilot Requirements, state that no person may take off or land a civil aircraft at an airport within a Class B airspace area or operate a civil aircraft within a Class B airspace area unless

1. The pilot in command holds at least a private pilot certificate; or
2. The aircraft is operated by a sport pilot or recreational pilot who seeks additional pilot certification and has met certain requirements, i.e., 14 CFR 61.95; or
3. The aircraft is operated by a student pilot who has met the requirements of 14 CFR 61.94 or 14 CFR 61.95. Meeting the requirements of 61.94 or 61.95 allows the privilege to operate within Class B airspace and at airports located in Class B airspace.

Answer (A) is incorrect. A private pilot certificate is required to takeoff or land at the busiest primary airports of Class B airspace (e.g., Atlanta, Chicago, etc.), not all Class B airspace. Answer (B) is incorrect. Only a student pilot certificate with an appropriate logbook endorsement, not a commercial pilot certificate, is required to enter all Class B airspace.

SU 7: Federal Aviation Regulations

124. Which is true regarding VFR operations in Class B airspace?

A. An operating VOR is required.
B. A Private Pilot Certificate is required for all flight within this airspace.
C. Solo student pilots are authorized to fly in Class B airspace if they meet certain requirements.

Answer (C) is correct. *(14 CFR 91.131)*
DISCUSSION: No person may take off or land a civil aircraft at an airport within a Class B airspace area or operate a civil aircraft within a Class B airspace area unless

1. The pilot in command holds at least a private pilot certificate; or
2. The aircraft is operated by a student pilot or recreational pilot who seeks private pilot certification and has met certain requirements, i.e., 14 CFR 61.95.

Answer (A) is incorrect. An operating VOR is required for IFR, not VFR, operations in Class B airspace. Answer (B) is incorrect. Student pilots may operate in Class B airspace provided they have met certain requirements.

125. Which equipment is required when operating an aircraft within Class B airspace?

A. A VOR or TACAN receiver.
B. Two-way radio communications.
C. Two-way radio communications and transponder with encoding altimeter.

Answer (C) is correct. *(14 CFR 91.131)*
DISCUSSION: Unless otherwise authorized by ATC, no person may operate an aircraft within a Class B airspace area unless that aircraft is equipped with

1. For IFR operation, an operable VOR or TACAN receiver;
2. An operable two-way radio capable of communications with ATC on appropriate frequencies for the Class B airspace area; and
3. An operating transponder and automatic altitude reporting equipment.

Answer (A) is incorrect. A VOR or TACAN receiver is only required when operating under IFR in Class B airspace. Answer (B) is incorrect. A transponder with encoding altimeter is also required when operating in Class B airspace.

91.135 Operations in Class A Airspace

126. In which type of airspace are VFR flights prohibited?

A. Class A.
B. Class B.
C. Class C.

Answer (A) is correct. *(14 CFR 91.135)*
DISCUSSION: Unless authorized by ATC, each person operating an aircraft in Class A airspace must conduct that operation under IFR.
Answer (B) is incorrect. VFR flights are routinely conducted in Class B airspace. Answer (C) is incorrect. VFR flights are routinely conducted in Class C airspace.

91.151 Fuel Requirements for Flight in VFR Conditions

127. What is the minimum fuel requirement for flight under VFR at night in an airplane? Enough to fly to

A. the first point of intended landing and to fly after that for 20 minutes at normal cruise speed.
B. the first point of intended landing and to fly after that for 30 minutes at normal cruise speed.
C. the first point of intended landing and to fly after that for 45 minutes at normal cruise speed.

Answer (C) is correct. *(14 CFR 91.151)*
DISCUSSION: No person may begin a flight in an airplane under VFR conditions unless (considering wind and forecast weather conditions) there is enough fuel to fly to the first point of intended landing and, assuming normal cruising speed during the day, to fly after that for at least 30 min.; or, at night, to fly after that for at least 45 min.
Answer (A) is incorrect. The minimum VFR night fuel requirement is to fly to the first point of intended landing and to fly after that for 45 min., not 20 min., at normal cruise. Answer (B) is incorrect. To fly to the first point of intended landing and to fly after that for 30 min. at normal cruise speed is the VFR fuel requirement during the day, not at night.

128. What is the minimum fuel requirement for flight under VFR during daylight hours in an airplane? Enough to fly to

A. the first point of intended landing and to fly after that for 20 minutes at normal cruise speed.
B. the first point of intended landing and to fly after that for 30 minutes at normal cruise speed.
C. the first point of intended landing and to fly after that for 45 minutes at normal cruise speed.

Answer (B) is correct. *(14 CFR 91.151)*
　　DISCUSSION: No person may begin a flight in an airplane under VFR conditions unless (considering wind and forecast weather conditions) there is enough fuel to fly to the first point of intended landing and, assuming normal cruising speed during the day, to fly after that for at least 30 min.; or, at night, to fly after that for at least 45 min.
　　Answer (A) is incorrect. The minimum VFR day fuel requirement is to fly to the first point of intended landing and to fly after that for 30 min., not 20 min., at normal cruise. Answer (C) is incorrect. To fly to the first point of intended landing and to fly after that for 45 min. at normal cruise speed is the VFR fuel requirement at night, not during the day.

91.153 VFR Flight Plan: Information Required

129. What type airspeed at the planned cruise altitude should be entered on a flight plan?

A. True airspeed.
B. Indicated airspeed.
C. Estimated groundspeed.

Answer (A) is correct. *(14 CFR 91.153)*
　　DISCUSSION: Unless otherwise authorized by ATC, each person filing a VFR flight plan shall include in it the true airspeed at cruising altitude.
　　Answer (B) is incorrect. True, not indicated, airspeed should be entered on a flight plan. Answer (C) is incorrect. True airspeed, not estimated groundspeed, should be entered on a flight plan.

91.155 Basic VFR Weather Minimums

130. During operations within controlled airspace at altitudes of more than 1,200 feet AGL, but less than 10,000 feet MSL, the minimum horizontal distance from clouds requirement for VFR flight is

A. 1 mile.
B. 2,000 feet.
C. 1,000 feet.

Answer (B) is correct. *(14 CFR 91.155)*
　　DISCUSSION: In controlled (Class C, Class D, or Class E, but not Class B) airspace, when below 10,000 ft. MSL, the minimum distance from clouds for VFR flight is 500 ft. below, 1,000 ft. above, and 2,000 ft. horizontal.
　　Note: AGL altitudes are no longer used in controlled airspace. In Class E airspace, the visibility and distance from clouds are given for (1) below 10,000 ft. MSL and (2) at or above 10,000 ft. MSL.
　　Answer (A) is incorrect. One SM is the horizontal requirement at or above, not below, 10,000 ft. MSL. Answer (C) is incorrect. This is the vertical, not horizontal, distance above the clouds.

131. When operating VFR in Class B airspace, what are the visibility and cloud clearance requirements?

A. 3 SM visibility and clear of clouds.
B. 3 SM visibility, 500 feet below, 1,000 feet above, and 2,000 feet horizontal distance from clouds.
C. 1 SM visibility, 500 feet below, 1,000 feet above, and 2,000 feet horizontal distance from clouds.

Answer (A) is correct. *(14 CFR 91.155)*
　　DISCUSSION: In Class B airspace, the minimum in-flight visibility and cloud clearance requirements for VFR flight are 3 SM visibility and clear of clouds.
　　Answer (B) is incorrect. In Class C, Class D, or Class E airspace (below 10,000 ft. MSL), not Class B airspace, the cloud clearance requirement is 500 ft. below, 1,000 ft. above, and 2,000 ft. horizontal. Answer (C) is incorrect. The visibility and cloud clearance requirements are 1 SM visibility, 500 ft. below, 1,000 ft. above, and 2,000 ft. horizontal in Class G airspace during the day when above 1,200 ft. AGL and below 10,000 ft. MSL, not in Class B airspace.

132. The minimum visibility for VFR flight in Class E airspace increases from 3 to 5 SM beginning at an altitude of

A. 10,000 feet MSL.
B. 14,500 feet MSL.
C. 1,200 feet AGL and at or above 10,000 feet MSL.

Answer (A) is correct. *(14 CFR 91.155)*
　　DISCUSSION: The minimum visibility for VFR flight increases from 3 SM to 5 SM beginning at an altitude of 10,000 ft. MSL in Class E airspace.
　　Answer (B) is incorrect. This is not an altitude related to visibility minimums. Answer (C) is incorrect. In Class G airspace, the minimum visibility increases from 3 SM to 5 SM at 1,200 ft. AGL and at or above 10,000 ft. MSL, but only at night (in the day, it increases from 1 SM to 5 SM).

133. While in Class G airspace in VFR conditions, what minimum distance from clouds should be maintained when flying more than 1,200 feet AGL, and at or above 10,000 feet MSL?

A. 500 feet below; 1,000 feet above; 1 mile horizontal.
B. 1,000 feet below; 1,000 feet above; 1 mile horizontal.
C. 500 feet below; 1,000 feet above; 2,000 feet horizontal.

Answer (B) is correct. *(14 CFR 91.155)*
DISCUSSION: In Class G airspace, when above 1,200 ft. AGL and at or above 10,000 ft. MSL, the minimum distance from clouds for VFR flight is 1,000 ft. above and below and 1 SM horizontal.
Answer (A) is incorrect. These figures are not a distance from clouds requirement at any altitude. Answer (C) is incorrect. These figures are the distance from clouds requirement above 1,200 ft. AGL but less than, not at or above, 10,000 ft. MSL.

134. An airplane may be operated in uncontrolled airspace at night below 1,200 feet above the surface under the following conditions:

A. Clear of clouds and 1 mile visibility.
B. Clear of clouds and 3 miles visibility.
C. Less than 3 miles but more than 1 mile visibility in an airport traffic pattern and within one-half mile of the runway.

Answer (C) is correct. *(14 CFR 91.155)*
DISCUSSION: In uncontrolled (Class G) airspace below 1,200 ft. AGL, when the visibility is less than 3 SM but not less than 1 SM during night hours, an airplane may be operated clear of clouds in an airport traffic pattern within 1/2 mi. of the runway.
Answer (A) is incorrect. The operation must be within 1/2 mi. of the runway. Answer (B) is incorrect. The visibility must be 1 SM, not 3 SM, and the operation must be within 1/2 mi. of the runway.

135. While in Class G airspace under day VFR conditions, what in-flight visibility is required when flying more than 1,200 feet AGL and less than 10,000 feet MSL?

A. 5 SM.
B. 3 SM.
C. 1 SM.

Answer (C) is correct. *(14 CFR 91.155)*
DISCUSSION: In Class G airspace, when above 1,200 ft. AGL and less than 10,000 ft. MSL, the minimum in-flight visibility for day VFR flight is 1 SM.
Answer (A) is incorrect. Five SM is the visibility required in Class G airspace above 1,200 ft. AGL and at or above, not less than, 10,000 ft. MSL. Answer (B) is incorrect. Three SM is the visibility required in Class G airspace above 1,200 ft. AGL and less than 10,000 ft. MSL at night, not during the day.

136. While in Class E airspace in VFR conditions, what in-flight visibility is required when flying more than 1,200 feet AGL and at or above 10,000 feet MSL?

A. 5 SM.
B. 3 SM.
C. 1 SM.

Answer (A) is correct. *(14 CFR 91.155)*
DISCUSSION: In Class E airspace, when at or above 10,000 ft. MSL, the minimum in-flight visibility for VFR flight is 5 SM.
Note: AGL altitudes are no longer used in conjunction with controlled airspace VFR weather minimums.
Answer (B) is incorrect. Three SM is the visibility required in Class E airspace below, not at or above, 10,000 ft. MSL. Answer (C) is incorrect. One SM is the visibility required in Class G, not Class E, airspace when flying more than 1,200 ft. AGL and below, not at or above, 10,000 ft. MSL at night.

91.157 Special VFR Weather Minimums

137. No person may operate an airplane within Class D and E airspace between sunset and sunrise under special VFR unless the

A. flight visibility is at least 3 miles.
B. airplane is equipped for instrument flight.
C. flight can be conducted 500 feet below the clouds.

Answer (B) is correct. *(14 CFR 91.157)*
DISCUSSION: Special VFR operations may be conducted only, except for helicopters, between sunrise and sunset unless

1. That person meets the applicable requirements for instrument flight, and
2. The aircraft is equipped as required under IFR.

Answer (A) is incorrect. A flight visibility of 1 SM, not 3 SM, is required under special VFR. Answer (C) is incorrect. Flight may be conducted clear of clouds under special VFR.

138. When operating an airplane within Class D airspace under special VFR, the flight visibility is required to be at least

A. 3 SM.
B. 2 SM.
C. 1 SM.

Answer (C) is correct. *(14 CFR 91.157)*
DISCUSSION: Except for helicopters, special VFR operations may be conducted only when flight visibility is at least 1 SM.
Answer (A) is incorrect. Three SM is the normal, not special, VFR visibility minimum in Class D airspace. Answer (B) is incorrect. Two SM is not a visibility requirement.

139. Regulations stipulate that, at an airport located within Class E airspace and at which ground visibility is not reported, takeoffs and landings of airplanes under special VFR are

A. not authorized.
B. authorized if the flight visibility is at least 1 SM.
C. authorized only if another airport in that designated airspace reports a ground visibility of at least 1 SM.

Answer (B) is correct. *(14 CFR 91.157)*
DISCUSSION: No person may take off or land an aircraft (other than a helicopter) under special VFR

1. Unless ground visibility at that airport is at least 1 SM, or
2. If ground visibility is not reported, unless flight visibility during landing and takeoff is at least 1 SM.

Answer (A) is incorrect. Flight visibility may be used if ground visibility is not reported. Answer (C) is incorrect. The visibility relates to the airport of intended operations, not any other airport.

91.159 VFR Cruising Altitude or Flight Level

140. When operating under VFR at more than 3,000 feet AGL, cruising altitudes to be maintained are based upon the

A. true course being flown.
B. magnetic course being flown.
C. magnetic heading being flown.

Answer (B) is correct. *(14 CFR 91.159)*
DISCUSSION: Except while holding in a holding pattern of 2 min. or less, or while turning, each person operating an aircraft under VFR in level cruising flight more than 3,000 ft. AGL shall maintain the appropriate altitude or flight level prescribed below, unless otherwise authorized by ATC. When operating below 18,000 ft. MSL and on a magnetic course of

1. 0° through 179°, any odd 1,000-ft. MSL altitude + 500 ft. (e.g., 3,500, 5,500, or 7,500); or
2. 180° through 359°, any even 1,000 ft. MSL altitude + 500 ft. (e.g., 4,500, 6,500, or 8,500).

Answer (A) is incorrect. VFR cruising altitudes are determined by magnetic course, not true course. Answer (C) is incorrect. VFR cruising altitudes are determined by magnetic course, not heading.

141. Which courses and altitudes are appropriate for VFR aircraft operating more than 3,000 feet AGL, but below 18,000 feet MSL?

A. True course 0° to 179° inclusive, odd thousands plus 500 feet.
B. Magnetic course 0° to 179° inclusive, even thousands plus 500 feet.
C. Magnetic course 180° to 359° inclusive, even thousands plus 500 feet.

Answer (C) is correct. *(14 CFR 91.159)*
DISCUSSION: Except while holding in a holding pattern of 2 min. or less, or while turning, each person operating an aircraft under VFR in level cruising flight more than 3,000 ft. AGL shall maintain the appropriate altitude or flight level prescribed below, unless otherwise authorized by ATC. When operating below 18,000 ft. MSL and on a magnetic course of

1. 0° through 179°, any odd 1,000-ft. MSL altitude + 500 ft. (e.g., 3,500, 5,500, or 7,500); or
2. 180° through 359°, any even 1,000 ft. MSL altitude + 500 ft. (e.g., 4,500, 6,500, or 8,500).

Answer (A) is incorrect. VFR cruising altitudes are determined by magnetic course, not true course. Answer (B) is incorrect. Easterly magnetic courses (0°-179°) require odd, not even, 1,000-ft. MSL altitudes.

SU 7: Federal Aviation Regulations

91.203 Civil Aircraft: Certifications Required

142. Regarding certificates and documents, no person may operate an aircraft unless it has within it an

A. Airworthiness Certificate and minimum equipment list (MEL).
B. Airworthiness Certificate, aircraft and engine logbooks, and owner's handbook.
C. Airworthiness Certificate, Registration Certificate, and approved flight manual.

Answer (C) is correct. *(14 CFR 91.203)*
DISCUSSION: No person may operate a civil aircraft unless it has within it the following:

1. An appropriate and current airworthiness certificate
2. An effective U.S. registration certificate issued to its owner
3. A current, approved airplane or rotorcraft flight manual

Answer (A) is incorrect. A minimum equipment list is not required for all aircraft. Answer (B) is incorrect. Aircraft and engine logbooks are not required to be in the aircraft.

91.205 Powered Civil Aircraft with Standard Category U.S. Airworthiness Certificates: Instrument and Equipment Requirements

143. Which is required equipment for powered aircraft during VFR night flights?

A. Magnetic compass.
B. Sensitive altimeter and landing light.
C. VHF radio communications equipment.

Answer (A) is correct. *(14 CFR 91.205)*
DISCUSSION: For VFR flight at night, the following instruments and equipment are required:

1. Instruments and equipment required for VFR flight during the day, which includes a magnetic compass
2. Approved position lights
3. An approved aviation red or aviation white anticollision light system on all U.S.-registered civil aircraft
4. If the aircraft is operated for hire, one electric landing light
5. An adequate source of electrical energy for all installed electrical and radio equipment
6. One spare set of fuses, or three spare fuses of each kind that are required, that are accessible to the pilot in flight

Answer (B) is incorrect. A sensitive altimeter is required for IFR flight, not VFR night flight. Additionally, a landing light is required only if the airplane is operated for hire. Answer (C) is incorrect. VHF radio communications equipment is required for IFR, not VFR, flight.

144. When an aircraft is being flown over water, under what circumstance must approved flotation gear be readily available to each occupant?

A. At night and beyond gliding distance from shore.
B. Any time the aircraft is beyond power-off gliding distance from shore.
C. When operating for hire beyond power-off gliding distance from shore.

Answer (C) is correct. *(14 CFR 91.205)*
DISCUSSION: If an aircraft is operated for hire over water and beyond power-off gliding distance from shore, approved flotation gear readily available to each occupant and at least one pyrotechnic signaling device must be on board.
Answer (A) is incorrect. The approved flotation gear is only required on flights operated for hire. Answer (B) is incorrect. The approved flotation gear is only required on flights operated for hire.

91.207 Emergency Locator Transmitters

145. When are emergency locator transmitter batteries required to be replaced or recharged?

A. Every 24 months.
B. After 1 cumulative hour of use.
C. After 75 percent of their useful life has expired.

Answer (B) is correct. *(14 CFR 91.207)*
DISCUSSION: Batteries used in emergency locator transmitters must be replaced (or recharged if the batteries are rechargeable)

1. When the transmitter has been in use for more than 1 cumulative hr., or
2. When 50% of their useful life (or, for rechargeable batteries, 50% of their useful life of charge) has expired.

Answer (A) is incorrect. Batteries need to be replaced or recharged after 50% of their useful life has expired, not every 24 months. Answer (C) is incorrect. Batteries need to be replaced or recharged after 50%, not 75%, of their useful life has expired.

146. How often are emergency locator transmitters required to be inspected?

A. Every 12 months.
B. Every 24 months.
C. After every 100 hours of flight time.

Answer (A) is correct. *(14 CFR 91.207)*
DISCUSSION: Emergency locator transmitters are required to be inspected every 12 months for proper installation, battery corrosion, operation of the controls and crash sensor, and the presence of a sufficient signal radiated from its antenna.
Answer (B) is incorrect. A transponder, not an emergency locator transmitter, is required to be inspected every 24 months. Answer (C) is incorrect. An emergency locator transmitter is required to be inspected every 12 months, not after every 100 hr. of flight time.

147. What is the maximum distance from an airport that an aircraft engaged in training operations may be operated without an emergency locator transmitter?

A. 25 NM.
B. 50 NM.
C. 100 NM.

Answer (B) is correct. *(14 CFR 91.207)*
DISCUSSION: The rule requiring an emergency locator transmitter does not apply to aircraft while engaged in training operations conducted entirely within a 50-NM radius of the airport from which such local flight operations began.
Answer (A) is incorrect. The maximum distance from the airport that a training aircraft can operate without an ELT is 50 NM, not 25 NM. Answer (C) is incorrect. The maximum distance from the airport that a training aircraft can operate without an ELT is 50 NM, not 100 NM.

148. How long may an aircraft be operated after the emergency locator transmitter has been initially removed for maintenance?

A. 90 days.
B. 30 days.
C. 7 days.

Answer (A) is correct. *(14 CFR 91.207)*
DISCUSSION: The rule requiring an emergency locator transmitter does not apply to an aircraft during any period for which the transmitter has been temporarily removed for inspection, repair, modification, or replacement. However, no person may operate the aircraft more than 90 days after the ELT is initially removed from the aircraft.
Answer (B) is incorrect. An aircraft may be operated for 90 days, not 30 days, after the ELT is initially removed for maintenance. Answer (C) is incorrect. An aircraft may be operated for 90 days, not 7 days, after the ELT is initially removed for maintenance.

91.209 Aircraft Lights

149. From sunset to sunrise, no person may park or move an aircraft in a night-flight operations area of an airport unless the aircraft

A. is in an area marked by obstruction lights.
B. is equipped with an electric landing or taxi light.
C. has lighted aviation red or white anticollision lights.

Answer (A) is correct. *(14 CFR 91.209)*
DISCUSSION: No person may, from sunset to sunrise, park or move an aircraft in, or in dangerous proximity to, a night flight operations area of an airport unless the aircraft is clearly illuminated, has lighted position lights, or is in an area that is marked by obstruction lights.
Answer (B) is incorrect. Landing and/or taxi lights are not required for taxiing at night. Answer (C) is incorrect. Anticollision lights are not required for taxiing at night.

150. Position lights are required to be displayed on all aircraft in flight from

A. sunset to sunrise.
B. 1 hour before sunset to 1 hour after sunrise.
C. 30 minutes before sunrise to 30 minutes after sunset.

Answer (A) is correct. *(14 CFR 91.209)*
DISCUSSION: No person may, from sunset to sunrise, operate an aircraft unless it has lighted position lights.
Answer (B) is incorrect. Position lights are only required between sunset and sunrise, not before sunset and after sunrise. Answer (C) is incorrect. Position lights are only required between sunset and sunrise, not before sunset and after sunrise.

151. An aircraft not equipped with the required position lights must terminate flight

A. at sunset.
B. 30 minutes after sunset.
C. 1 hour after sunset.

Answer (A) is correct. *(14 CFR 91.209)*
DISCUSSION: No person may, from sunset to sunrise, operate an aircraft unless it has lighted position lights.
Answer (B) is incorrect. Lighted position lights are required at, not 30 min. after, sunset. Answer (C) is incorrect. Lighted position lights are required at, not 1 hr. after, sunset.

152. If an aircraft is not equipped for night flight and official sunset is 1730 EST, the latest a pilot may operate that aircraft without violating regulations is

A. 1629 EST.
B. 1729 EST.
C. 1829 EST.

Answer (B) is correct. *(14 CFR 91.209)*
DISCUSSION: No person may, from sunset to sunrise, operate an aircraft unless it is equipped for night flight. If the official sunset is 1730 EST, the latest a pilot may operate an aircraft not equipped for night flight is 1729 EST.
Answer (A) is incorrect. The latest time that a pilot may operate an aircraft that is not equipped for night flight is at sunset. Answer (C) is incorrect. The latest time a pilot may log a flight as day-VFR is an hour after sunset. An aircraft not equipped for night flight cannot legally be operated from sunset to sunrise.

91.211 Supplemental Oxygen

153. Unless each occupant is provided with supplemental oxygen, no person may operate a civil aircraft of U.S. registry above a cabin pressure altitude of

A. 12,500 feet MSL.
B. 14,000 feet MSL.
C. 15,000 feet MSL.

Answer (C) is correct. *(14 CFR 91.211)*
DISCUSSION: No person may operate a civil aircraft of U.S. registry

1. At cabin pressure altitudes above 12,500 ft. MSL up to and including 14,000 ft. MSL unless the required minimum flight crew is provided with and uses supplemental oxygen for that part of the flight at those altitudes that is of more than 30 min. duration;
2. At cabin pressure altitudes above 14,000 ft. MSL unless the required minimum flight crew is provided with and uses supplemental oxygen during the entire flight time at those altitudes; and
3. At cabin pressure altitudes above 15,000 ft. MSL unless each occupant of the aircraft is provided with supplemental oxygen.

Answer (A) is incorrect. Above 12,500 ft. MSL only the minimum flight crew, not each occupant, must use oxygen after 30 min. Answer (B) is incorrect. Above 14,000 ft. MSL only the minimum flight crew, not each occupant, must use oxygen.

154. Which cabin pressure altitude allows a pilot to operate an aircraft up to 30 minutes without supplemental oxygen?

A. 12,500 feet MSL.
B. 12,600 feet MSL.
C. 14,100 feet MSL.

Answer (B) is correct. *(14 CFR 91.211)*
DISCUSSION: No person may operate a civil aircraft of U.S. registry

1. At cabin pressure altitudes above 12,500 ft. MSL up to and including 14,000 ft. MSL unless the required minimum flight crew is provided with and uses supplemental oxygen for that part of the flight at those altitudes that is more than 30 min. duration;
2. At cabin pressure altitudes above 14,000 ft. MSL unless the required minimum flight crew is provided with and uses supplemental oxygen during the entire flight time at those altitudes; and
3. At cabin pressure altitudes above 15,000 ft. MSL unless each occupant of the aircraft is provided with supplemental oxygen.

Answer (A) is incorrect. A pilot must use oxygen after 30 min. above, not at, 12,500 ft. MSL. Answer (C) is incorrect. A pilot must use oxygen the entire time, not after 30 min., above 14,000 ft. MSL.

91.213 Inoperative Instruments and Equipment

155. The primary purpose of a minimum equipment list (MEL) is to

A. provide a list of equipment that must be operational at all times on the aircraft.
B. list the equipment that can be inoperative and still not affect the airworthiness of an aircraft.
C. list the minimum equipment that must be installed in all aircraft as required by airworthiness directives.

Answer (B) is correct. *(14 CFR 91.213)*
DISCUSSION: No person may take off an aircraft with inoperative instruments or equipment installed unless the following conditions are met:

1. An approved minimum equipment list exists for that aircraft.
2. The aircraft has within it a letter of authorization, issued by the FAA Flight Standards District Office having jurisdiction over the area in which the operator is located, authorizing operation of the aircraft under the minimum equipment list.
3. The approved minimum equipment list must provide for the operation of the aircraft with the instruments and equipment in an inoperable condition.

Answer (A) is incorrect. This information is covered by regulations for each condition of flight and the aircraft flight manual. Answer (C) is incorrect. This information is covered by the governing airworthiness directive.

156. Authority for approval of a minimum equipment list (MEL) must be obtained from the

A. Administrator.
B. FAA district office.
C. aircraft manufacturer.

Answer (B) is correct. *(14 CFR 91.213)*
DISCUSSION: No person may take off an aircraft with inoperative instruments or equipment installed unless the following conditions are met:

1. An approved minimum equipment list exists for that aircraft.
2. The aircraft has within it a letter of authorization, issued by the FAA Flight Standards District Office having jurisdiction over the area in which the operator is located, authorizing operation of the aircraft under the minimum equipment list.
3. The approved minimum equipment list must provide for the operation of the aircraft with the instruments and equipment in an inoperable condition.

Answer (A) is incorrect. Authority for approval of an MEL comes from the local FSDO, not the FAA Administrator. Answer (C) is incorrect. Authority for approval of an MEL comes from the local FSDO, not the aircraft manufacturer.

157. Which action is appropriate if an aircraft, operating under 14 CFR Part 91 and for which a master minimum equipment list has not been developed, is determined to have an inoperative instrument or piece of equipment that does not constitute a hazard to the aircraft? The item should be

A. removed and repaired prior to the next flight.
B. placarded "inoperative" and repaired during the next inspection.
C. deactivated and placarded "inoperative" but repairs can be deferred indefinitely.

Answer (C) is correct. *(14 CFR 91.213)*
DISCUSSION: A person may take off an aircraft for which a master minimum equipment list has not been developed under Part 91 with inoperative instruments and equipment provided

1. The item is not required by the aircraft's equipment list or kinds of operations list.
2. The item is not required by the VFR-day type certification requirements prescribed in the airworthiness certification regulations.
3. The item is not required by an airworthiness directive, 14 CFR 91.205, 14 CFR 91.207, or any other 14 CFR.
4. The item is either removed or deactivated and placarded "Inoperative."
5. A determination is made that the inoperative instrument or equipment does not constitute a hazard to the anticipated operation.

While the operator should have all inoperative items repaired at the next inspection, the operator may elect to defer the repairs indefinitely.

Answer (A) is incorrect. The item does not need to be removed and/or repaired until the next inspection, not the next flight. Answer (B) is incorrect. In addition to being placarded, the item must also be either removed or deactivated. While it is recommended that repairs be done at the next inspection, it is not required.

91.215 ATC Transponder and Altitude Reporting Equipment and Use

158. How long before the proposed operation should a request be submitted to the controlling ATC facility to operate in Class C airspace without the required altitude reporting transponder?

A. 1 hour.
B. 8 hours.
C. 24 hours.

Answer (A) is correct. *(14 CFR 91.215)*
DISCUSSION: Requests for ATC authorized deviations from the requirement for transponder having Mode C capability must be made to the ATC facility having jurisdiction over the concerned airspace. For operation of an aircraft that is not equipped with a transponder, the request must be made at least 1 hr. before the proposed operation.
Answer (B) is incorrect. One must notify the appropriate ATC facility at least 1 hr., not 8 hr., before the proposed operation. Answer (C) is incorrect. One must notify the appropriate ATC facility at least 1 hr., not 24 hr., before the proposed operation.

159. A coded transponder with altitude reporting capability is required for all controlled airspace

A. below 14,500 feet MSL.
B. above 12,500 feet MSL (excluding airspace at or below 2,500 feet AGL).
C. at and above 10,000 feet MSL (excluding airspace at or below 2,500 feet AGL).

Answer (C) is correct. *(14 CFR 91.215)*
DISCUSSION: The requirement for an operable transponder having Mode C capability applies

1. In Class A, Class B, and Class C airspace areas;
2. In all airspace within 30 NM of a Class B primary airport from the surface upward to 10,000 ft. MSL;
3. In all airspace above the ceiling and within the lateral boundaries of a Class B or Class C airspace area upward to 10,000 ft. MSL;
4. In all airspace of the 48 contiguous states and the District of Columbia at and above 10,000 ft. MSL, excluding the airspace at and below 2,500 ft. AGL; and
5. In the airspace from the surface to 10,000 ft. MSL within a 10-NM radius of any airport listed in the regulations, excluding the airspace below 1,200 ft. outside of the lateral boundaries of the surface area of the airspace designated for that airport.

Answer (A) is incorrect. A Mode C transponder is required at and above 10,000 ft. MSL, not below 14,500 ft. MSL. Answer (B) is incorrect. A Mode C transponder is required at and above 10,000 ft. MSL, not above 12,500 ft. MSL.

160. An altitude reporting coded transponder is required for all airspace

A. from the surface to 10,000 feet MSL within a 10 NM radius of any airport traffic pattern.
B. at and above 10,000 feet MSL and below the floor of Class A airspace (excluding airspace at or below 2,500 feet AGL).
C. within 25 NM of a Class B primary airport from the surface upward to 10,000 feet MSL (excluding airspace below 1,200 feet AGL).

Answer (B) is correct. *(14 CFR 91.215)*
DISCUSSION: The requirement for an operable transponder having Mode C capability applies

1. In Class A, Class B, and Class C airspace areas;
2. In all airspace within 30 NM of a Class B primary airport from the surface upward to 10,000 ft. MSL;
3. In all airspace above the ceiling and within the lateral boundaries of a Class B or Class C airspace area upward to 10,000 ft. MSL;
4. In all airspace of the 48 contiguous states and the District of Columbia at and above 10,000 ft. MSL, excluding the airspace at and below 2,500 ft. AGL; and
5. In the airspace from the surface to 10,000 ft. MSL within a 10-NM radius of any airport listed in the regulations, excluding the airspace below 1,200 ft. outside of the lateral boundaries of the surface area of the airspace designated for that airport.

Answer (A) is incorrect. A Mode C transponder is only required within 10 NM of specifically designated airports, not any airport traffic pattern. Answer (C) is incorrect. A Mode C transponder is required within 30 NM, not 25 NM, of a Class B primary airport.

161. What are the requirements, if any, to overfly Class C airspace?

A. None, provided the flight remains above the airspace ceiling.
B. Transponder with automatic altitude reporting capability is required above the airspace ceiling and upward to 10,000 feet MSL.
C. Two-way radio communications must be established with ATC and transponder must be operating at all times.

Answer (B) is correct. *(14 CFR 91.215)*
DISCUSSION: Unless otherwise authorized or directed by ATC, no person may operate an aircraft in the airspace above the ceiling and within the lateral boundaries of a Class C airspace area upward to 10,000 ft. MSL without an operable transponder with Mode C capability.
Answer (A) is incorrect. A transponder with Mode C capability is required to overfly Class C airspace below 10,000 ft. MSL. Answer (C) is incorrect. Two-way radio communications need to be established with ATC only when flying within, not overflying, Class C airspace.

91.307 Parachutes and Parachuting

162. When must each occupant of an aircraft wear an approved parachute?

A. When flying over water beyond gliding distance to the shore.
B. When practicing spins or other flight maneuvers for any certificate or rating.
C. When an intentional maneuver that exceeds 30° noseup or nosedown relative to the horizon is made.

Answer (C) is correct. *(14 CFR 91.307)*
DISCUSSION: Unless each occupant of the aircraft is wearing an approved parachute, no pilot of a civil aircraft carrying any person (other than a crewmember) may execute any intentional maneuver that exceeds

1. A bank of 60° relative to the horizon; or
2. A nose-up or nose-down attitude of 30° relative to the horizon.

This does not apply to

1. Flight tests for pilot certification or rating; or
2. Spins and other flight maneuvers required by the regulations for any certificate or rating when given by a certified flight instructor.

Answer (A) is incorrect. Approved flotation devices, not parachutes, are required when flying for hire over water beyond gliding distance to shore. Answer (B) is incorrect. Spins and other flight maneuvers may be performed without parachutes when being performed for a certificate or rating when given by a flight instructor.

91.403 General (Maintenance, Preventive Maintenance, and Alterations)

163. Who is primarily responsible for maintaining an aircraft in an airworthy condition?

A. Mechanic.
B. Pilot in command.
C. Owner or operator of the aircraft.

Answer (C) is correct. *(14 CFR 91.403)*
DISCUSSION: The owner or operator of an aircraft is primarily responsible for maintaining that aircraft in an airworthy condition. The term "operator" includes the pilot in command.
Answer (A) is incorrect. Although a mechanic will perform inspections and maintenance, the primary responsibility for an aircraft's airworthiness lies with its owner or operator. Answer (B) is incorrect. The owner or operator, not only the pilot in command, of an aircraft is primarily responsible for an aircraft's airworthiness.

164. Assuring compliance with airworthiness directives is the responsibility of the

A. FAA certificated mechanic.
B. pilot in command of the aircraft.
C. owner or operator of the aircraft.

Answer (C) is correct. *(14 CFR 91.403)*
DISCUSSION: Compliance with airworthiness directives is a part of maintaining an aircraft in an airworthy condition. Thus, it is primarily the responsibility of the owner or operator of the aircraft. The term "operator" includes the pilot in command.
Answer (A) is incorrect. Although a mechanic will perform the maintenance required to comply with an airworthiness directive, assuring compliance is the responsibility of the owner or operator. Answer (B) is incorrect. The owner or operator, not only the pilot in command, is responsible for assuring compliance with airworthiness directives.

91.405 Maintenance Required

165. Completion of an annual inspection and the return of an aircraft to service should always be indicated by

A. conduct of a test flight and the appropriate logbook entry.
B. the appropriate entries in the aircraft maintenance records.
C. the relicensing date on the Registration Certificate.

Answer (B) is correct. *(14 CFR 91.405)*
DISCUSSION: Each owner or operator of an aircraft

1. Shall have that aircraft inspected as prescribed and shall between required inspections have discrepancies repaired; and
2. Shall ensure that maintenance personnel make appropriate entries in the aircraft maintenance records indicating the aircraft has been approved for return to service.

Answer (A) is incorrect. A test flight is only required when alterations or repairs change the flight characteristics. Answer (C) is incorrect. Registration certificates are not reissued after annual inspections.

91.407 Operation after Maintenance, Preventive Maintenance, Rebuilding, or Alteration

166. If an aircraft's operation in flight was substantially affected by an alteration or repair, the aircraft documents must show that it was test flown and approved for return to service by an appropriately rated pilot prior to being flown

A. with passengers aboard.
B. for compensation or hire.
C. by instructors and students.

Answer (A) is correct. *(14 CFR 91.407)*
DISCUSSION: No person may carry any person (other than crewmembers) in an aircraft that has been maintained, rebuilt, or altered in a manner that may have appreciably changed its flight characteristics or substantially affected its operation in flight until an appropriately rated pilot with at least a private pilot certificate flies the aircraft, makes an operational check of the maintenance performed or alteration made, and logs the flight in the aircraft records.

Answer (B) is incorrect. Property, but not passengers, could be carried for compensation or hire before a flight test was flown. Answer (C) is incorrect. Instructors and students are not considered passengers of each other, i.e., they are each required crewmembers.

91.409 Inspections

167. Which is prohibited if the aircraft being used has not had a 100-hour inspection or annual inspection within the preceding 100 hours of time in service?

A. Giving flight instruction for hire.
B. Conducting any commercial operation.
C. Carrying passengers, either for hire or not for hire.

Answer (A) is correct. *(14 CFR 91.409)*
DISCUSSION: With certain exceptions, no person may operate an aircraft carrying any person (other than a crewmember) for hire, and no person may give flight instruction for hire in an aircraft which that person provides, unless within the preceding 100 hr. of time in service the aircraft has received an annual or 100-hr. inspection and been approved for return to service, or received an inspection for the issuance of an airworthiness certificate.

Answer (B) is incorrect. The 100-hr. inspection is required only when carrying passengers or giving flight instruction for hire, not when conducting any commercial operation. Answer (C) is incorrect. The 100-hr. inspection is required only when carrying passengers for hire.

168. An aircraft's last annual inspection was performed on July 12, this year. The next annual inspection will be due no later than

A. July 13, next year.
B. July 31, next year.
C. 12 calendar months after the date shown on the Airworthiness Certificate.

Answer (B) is correct. *(14 CFR 91.409)*
DISCUSSION: With certain exceptions, no person may operate an aircraft unless, within the preceding 12 calendar months, it has had

1. An annual inspection and has been approved for return to service by an authorized person; or
2. An inspection for the issuance of an airworthiness certificate.

Answer (A) is incorrect. Annual inspections expire on the last day of the month, not the exact anniversary. Answer (C) is incorrect. An airworthiness certificate is not reissued after an annual inspection.

169. An aircraft operated for hire with passengers aboard has a 100-hour inspection performed after 90 hours in service. The next 100-hour inspection would be due after

A. 90 hours' time in service.
B. 100 hours' time in service.
C. 110 hours' time in service.

Answer (B) is correct. *(14 CFR 91.409)*
DISCUSSION: With certain exceptions, no person may operate an aircraft carrying any person (other than a crewmember) for hire, and no person may give flight instruction for hire in an aircraft which that person provides, unless within the preceding 100 hr. of time in service the aircraft has received an annual or 100-hr. inspection and been approved for return to service, or received an inspection for the issuance of an airworthiness certificate.
Answer (A) is incorrect. A 100-hr. inspection is due after 100 hr., not 90 hr. Answer (C) is incorrect. A 100-hr. inspection is due after 100 hr., not 110 hr., and no credit is given if the prior 100-hr. inspection was done early.

91.413 ATC Transponder Tests and Inspections

170. What is the maximum time period during which a person may use an ATC transponder after it has been tested and inspected?

A. 12 calendar months.
B. 24 calendar months.
C. 36 calendar months.

Answer (B) is correct. *(14 CFR 91.413)*
DISCUSSION: No person may use an ATC transponder unless, within the preceding 24 calendar months, the ATC transponder has been tested and inspected and found to comply with the regulations.
Answer (A) is incorrect. Transponders must be tested and inspected every 24, not 12, calendar months. Answer (C) is incorrect. Transponders must be tested and inspected every 24, not 36, calendar months.

171. If an ATC transponder installed in an aircraft has not been tested, inspected, and found to comply with regulations within a specified period, what is the limitation on its use?

A. Its use is not permitted.
B. It may be used anywhere except in Class A and B airspace.
C. It may be used for VFR flight but not for IFR flight.

Answer (A) is correct. *(14 CFR 91.413)*
DISCUSSION: No person may use an ATC transponder unless, within the preceding 24 calendar months, the ATC transponder has been tested and inspected and found to comply with the regulations.
Answer (B) is incorrect. Transponders must be inspected every 24 months or they may not be used in any operation. Answer (C) is incorrect. Transponders must be inspected every 24 months or they may not be used in any operation.

91.417 Maintenance Records

172. Aircraft maintenance records must include the current status of

A. all appropriate Airworthiness Certificates.
B. life-limited parts of only the engine and airframe.
C. life-limited parts of each airframe, engine, propeller, rotor, and appliance.

Answer (C) is correct. *(14 CFR 91.417)*
DISCUSSION: Each owner or operator of an aircraft shall keep the following records:

1. The maintenance and inspections performed.
2. The current status of life-limited parts of each airframe, engine, propeller, rotor, and appliance.
3. The current status of applicable airworthiness directives.

Answer (A) is incorrect. The current status of applicable airworthiness directives, not certificates, must be included. Answer (B) is incorrect. The current status of life-limited parts of each propeller, rotor, and appliance must also be included.

91.421 Rebuilt Engine Maintenance Records

173. A new maintenance record being used for an aircraft engine rebuilt by the manufacturer must include the previous

A. operating hours of the engine.
B. annual inspections performed on the engine.
C. changes required by airworthiness directives.

Answer (C) is correct. *(14 CFR 91.421)*
DISCUSSION: The owner or operator of an aircraft may use a new maintenance record, without previous operating history, for an aircraft engine rebuilt by the manufacturer. The new record must include each change made as required by airworthiness directives and service bulletins.
Answer (A) is incorrect. No previous operating history, including operating hours, need be included in the new record of a rebuilt engine. Answer (B) is incorrect. No previous operating history, including previous annual inspections, need be included in the new record of a rebuilt engine.

SU 7: Federal Aviation Regulations

7.5 NTSB Part 830

830.2 Definitions

174. The NTSB defines a serious injury as any injury which

A. causes severe tendon damage.
B. results in a simple fracture of the nose.
C. involves first degree burns over 5 percent of the body.

Answer (A) is correct. *(NTSB 830.2)*
    DISCUSSION: Serious injury means any injury that (1) requires hospitalization for more than 48 hr., commencing within 7 days from the date the injury was received; (2) results in a fracture in any bone (except simple fractures of the fingers, toes, or nose); (3) causes severe hemorrhages, nerve, muscle, or tendon damage; (4) involves any internal organ; or (5) involves second- or third-degree burns, or any burns covering more than 5% of the body surface.
    Answer (B) is incorrect. Simple fractures, such as of the finger, toe, or nose, are not considered a serious injury. Answer (C) is incorrect. Only second- and third-degree burns or any burns over more than 5%, not just 5%, of the body are defined as a serious injury. First-degree burns are less serious than second- and third-degree burns.

830.5 Immediate Notification

175. Notification to the NTSB is required when there has been substantial damage which

A. adversely affects aircraft performance.
B. causes small puncture holes in the skin or fabric.
C. results in more than $25,000 for repairs to the aircraft.

Answer (A) is correct. *(NTSB 830.5)*
    DISCUSSION: The operator of an aircraft shall immediately and by the most expeditious means available notify the nearest NTSB field office when an aircraft accident occurs. Aircraft accident means an occurrence associated with the operation of an aircraft that takes place between the time any person boards the aircraft with the intention of flight and all such persons have disembarked, and in which any person suffers death or serious injury, or in which the aircraft receives substantial damage. Substantial damage means damage or failure that adversely affects the structural strength, performance, or flight characteristics of the aircraft.
    Answer (B) is incorrect. Small puncture holes do not constitute substantial damage. Answer (C) is incorrect. Notification must be made if more than $25,000 damage is done to property other than the aircraft.

176. NTSB Part 830 requires an immediate notification as a result of which incident?

A. Aircraft collide on the ground.
B. Flight control system malfunction.
C. Damage to property, other than the aircraft, estimated to exceed $10,000.

Answer (B) is correct. *(NTSB 830.5)*
    DISCUSSION: The operator of an aircraft shall immediately, and by the most expeditious means available, notify the nearest NTSB field office when any of the following listed incidents occur:

1. Flight control system malfunction or failure;
2. Inability of any required flight crewmember to perform normal flight duties as a result of injury or illness;
3. Failure of structural components of a turbine engine excluding compressor and turbine blades and vanes;
4. In-flight fire; or
5. Aircraft collide in flight.

    Answer (A) is incorrect. An in-flight, not ground, collision would require immediate notification. Answer (C) is incorrect. More than $25,000 (not $10,000) damage to property would require immediate notification.

177. If an aircraft is involved in an accident which results in substantial damage to the aircraft, the nearest NTSB field office shall be notified

A. immediately.
B. within 7 days.
C. within 10 days.

Answer (A) is correct. *(NTSB 830.5)*
    DISCUSSION: The operator of an aircraft shall immediately, and by the most expeditious means available, notify the nearest NTSB field office when an aircraft accident occurs.
    Answer (B) is incorrect. A report is required after 7 days if an overdue aircraft is still missing, not after an accident. Answer (C) is incorrect. A written report, not a notification, is required within 10 days after an accident.

830.15 Reports and Statements to Be Filed

178. The operator of an aircraft that has been involved in an accident is required to file a report within how many days?

A. 3
B. 7
C. 10

Answer (C) is correct. *(NTSB 830.15)*
DISCUSSION: The operator of an aircraft shall file a report within 10 days after an accident.
Answer (A) is incorrect. A report is required within 10 days, not 3 days, after an accident. Answer (B) is incorrect. A report is required after 7 days if an overdue aircraft is still missing, not after an accident.

179. The operator of an aircraft that has been involved in an incident is required to submit a report to the nearest field office of the NTSB

A. within 7 days.
B. within 10 days.
C. only if requested to do so.

Answer (C) is correct. *(NTSB 830.15)*
DISCUSSION: The operator of an aircraft shall file a report on an incident for which notification is required only as requested.
Answer (A) is incorrect. A report is required after 7 days if an overdue aircraft is still missing, not after an incident. Answer (B) is incorrect. A report must be filed within 10 days after an accident, not an incident.

STUDY UNIT EIGHT
NAVIGATION

(13 pages of outline)

8.1	Sectional Charts	(42 questions) 283, 296
8.2	Climb Calculations	(2 questions) 289, 314
8.3	Speed, Distance, and Fuel Calculations	(21 questions) 290, 315
8.4	Off-Course Corrections	(3 questions) 292, 320
8.5	Estimating Wind	(3 questions) 292, 321
8.6	Distance Measuring Equipment (DME)	(4 questions) 292, 322
8.7	VHF Omnidirectional Range (VOR)	(12 questions) 292, 323
8.8	Global Positioning Systems (GPS)	(5 questions) 295, 326

This study unit contains outlines of major concepts tested, sample test questions and answers regarding navigation, and an explanation of each answer. The table of contents above lists each subunit within this study unit, the number of questions pertaining to that particular subunit, and the pages on which the outlines and questions begin, respectively.

Recall that the **sole purpose** of this book is to expedite your passing of the FAA pilot knowledge test for the CFI, BGI, or AGI certificate. Accordingly, all extraneous material (i.e., topics or regulations not directly tested on the FAA pilot knowledge test) is omitted, even though much more knowledge is necessary to become a proficient flight or ground instructor. This additional material is presented in *Pilot Handbook* and *Flight Instructor Flight Maneuvers and Practical Test Prep*, available from Gleim Publications, Inc. Order online at www.GleimAviation.com.

8.1 SECTIONAL CHARTS

Important Note about FAA Charts

The FAA prints the charts published in their Airman Knowledge Testing Supplements to the wrong scale. If you were to measure a distance on one of these charts with the plotter, do the calculations based on that information, and enter that answer, you would be wrong every time.

Accurately calculating distance is a part of the testing process. By printing the charts to the wrong scale, the FAA is testing to see if you checked your plotter to the scale printed on the chart to make sure the chart is accurate. Because our goal at Gleim is to prepare you for your Knowledge Test, our reproductions of the charts are also not to scale.

To answer questions related to these charts, you must transfer the chart's scale to a scrap of paper, which is supplied to you at the testing site. You will use this scale as an accurate measuring tool in place of your plotter.

1. **The front page of each sectional chart contains a legend.** Obtain one and read through it, noting
    a. Airports and airport identifiers
    b. Radio Aids to Navigation box
    c. Communications box
    d. Airspace information
    e. Obstructions
    f. Topographical information
    g. Miscellaneous

2. **Sectional charts are divided by horizontal lines of latitude and vertical lines of longitude**, both of which are identified by short tick marks along the entire line.
    a. Lines of longitude (meridians) cross the equator at right angles.
        1) They are not parallel, however, because they converge at the poles.
        2) When using a meridian to determine a true course measurement on a sectional chart, you should attempt to make the measurement near the midpoint of the course because the angles formed by meridians and the course line vary from point to point.
    b. **Each quadrangle bounded by lines of latitude and longitude contains a pair of numbers in large, bold print to indicate the height of the maximum elevation of terrain or obstructions within that area of latitude and longitude.**
        1) The larger number to the left is thousands of feet MSL.
        2) The smaller number to the right is hundreds of feet MSL.
    c. **The angular difference between true north and magnetic north is called magnetic variation.**
    d. **When converting true course to magnetic heading,**
        1) East magnetic variation is subtracted (east is least),
        2) West magnetic variation is added (west is best),
        3) Left wind correction is subtracted, and
        4) Right wind correction is added.
    e. **When converting from magnetic course to true course**, you correct for magnetic variation only:
        1) Subtract westerly variation and
        2) Add easterly variation.
    f. **When correcting true heading (TH) to true course (TC)**, subtract right wind correction angle (the opposite of going from TC to TH).
3. **When diverting to an alternate airport due to an emergency**, use rule-of-thumb computations, estimates, and other appropriate shortcuts to divert to the new course as soon as possible.
4. **Obstruction altitude** in bold (not in parentheses) is the elevation of the top above MSL. The lighter number in parentheses just below the bold number is the height AGL.
    a. A series of lightning bolts emanating from the tip of an obstruction symbol indicates high-intensity lights.
5. **Airport identifiers** consist of a block of information near the airport symbol, e.g.,

> San Antonio Intl
> CT 119.8
> ATIS 118.9
> 809 L 85 122.95

   a. Note **ATIS** indicates Automatic Terminal Information Service.
   b. One line has **elevation MSL** in bold followed by an **"L"** if lighted, followed by the **length of the longest paved runway**, followed by the **UNICOM frequency**.
6. **VHF Omnidirectional Range (VOR) symbols**
    a. A VORTAC is depicted as a hexagon with a dot in the center and a small solid rectangle attached to three of the six sides.
    b. A VOR/DME is depicted as a hexagon within a square.
    c. A VOR is depicted as a hexagon with a dot in the center.

SU 8: Navigation

7. **VORs** without voice capability have a line under the VHF frequency, e.g., 116.8.

8. **Alert areas** are marked in magenta and labeled as to the hazards, e.g., "Alert A-632C, Concentrated Student Jet Training."

   a. Alert areas are depicted to inform nonparticipating pilots of areas that may contain a high volume of pilot training or an unusual type of aerial activity.

   b. There are no operating requirements, but pilots should be extremely cautious due to extensive student training.

9. Controlled airspace is designated as Class A, B, C, D, and E airspace.

   a. Class G airspace is considered to be uncontrolled.

10. Special VFR (SVFR) operations are permitted within Class B, C, D, or E surface areas, provided the airport identifier does not indicate NO SVFR.

11. **Class B airspace** is an area of controlled airspace, as well as a 30-NM ring (or veil) encircling the primary Class B airport.

    a. Class B airspace is depicted by heavy blue lines on sectional charts.

       1) The vertical limits of each section are shown in hundreds of feet MSL.

    b. The 30-NM veil is marked by a thin magenta circle.

    c. Class B airspace is shown on the chart as in the example below.

       1) Class B vertical limits in this example are

          a) From the surface (SFC) to 7,000 ft. MSL (70) in the inner circle
          b) From 2,000 ft. MSL (20) to 7,000 ft. MSL (70) in the middle circle
          c) From 4,000 ft. MSL (40) to 7,000 ft. MSL (70) in the outer circle

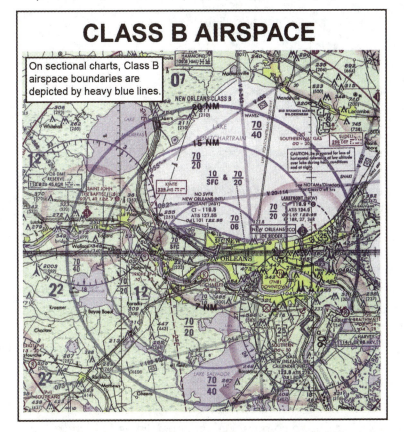

d. Satellite airports underlying Class B airspace may have different floor and ceiling altitude limitation markings, such as those indicated in the red circles in the figure below. These markings and their explanations can be found in the FAA Aeronautical Chart User's Guide. They may not be on all sectional chart legends.

1) For Class B airspace, these markings are numbers in light blue and appear to be written as a fraction. An example can be seen between the two floor and ceiling altitude limitation markings (circled in red) above area 6 in the figure below.

2) There may be what appears to be a "T" substituted for a number in the altitude.

a) This symbol is not actually a "T" but a line going from the lower, indicated altitude, up to the bottom of the overlying Class B airspace. The horizontal line represents the bottom of the overlying airspace. For example, the markings (circled in red) in the upper-left and bottom-right of the figure below are from 1,500 MSL up to the bottom (or floor) of the overlying Class B airspace of 2,100 MSL.

b) It may be easier to remember this as the "Top of the bottom" of the overlying airspace.

Excerpt from Figure 46.

NOTE: These red circles have been added to the figure excerpt for ease of reference and instructive purposes only. They will not appear on the actual Figure 46.

e. Two-way radio communication capability is required.
f. An ATC clearance to enter and operate within Class B airspace is mandatory.

1) The phrase "Radar contact, standby" is not an authorization to enter a Class B airspace area.

g. A Mode C transponder (i.e., a transponder with altitude encoding capability) is required within and above Class B airspace and also within the 30-NM veil.

12. **Class C airspace** is an area of controlled airspace that consists of a surface area and a shelf area.

a. Class C airspace is depicted by solid magenta lines on sectional charts.

1) The vertical limits of each circle are shown in hundreds of feet MSL.

b. Two-way radio communication must be maintained with ATC while within Class C airspace.

1) Two-way radio communication capability is required.

- c. A Mode C transponder is required within and above Class C airspace.
- d. Class C airspace is shown on the chart as in the example below.
  1) Class C airspace vertical limits in the example extend
     a) From the surface (SFC) to 4,000 ft. MSL (40) in the surface area
     b) From 1,200 ft. MSL (12) to 4,000 ft. MSL (40) in the shelf area
  2) The shaded magenta line in the example shows an area of Class E airspace extending upward from 700 feet AGL to the overlying Class C airspace.

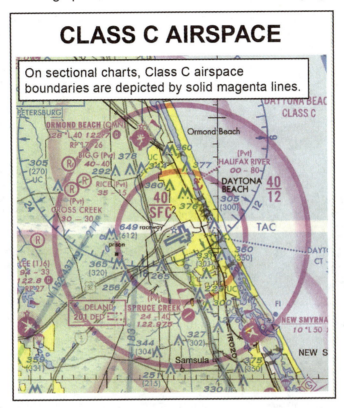

13. **Class D airspace** is an area of controlled airspace surrounding an airport with an operating control tower.
    - a. This area extends upward from the surface to a specified altitude (normally 2,500 ft. above the airport elevation).
    - b. Class D airspace is depicted by dashed blue lines on sectional charts.
      1) The ceiling is shown in a box within the circle in hundreds of feet MSL.
      2) A minus ceiling value indicates the Class D airspace extends from the surface up to, but not including, that value.

c. Class D airspace is shown on the chart as in the example below.

1) The ceilings of Class D airspace in the examples are 2,700 ft. MSL.
2) You may be within the lateral boundaries of Class D airspace while still remaining clear of the airspace by being above the ceiling.
3) On sectional charts, a dashed magenta line (see right side of the following example) illustrates an area of Class E airspace extending upward from the surface.

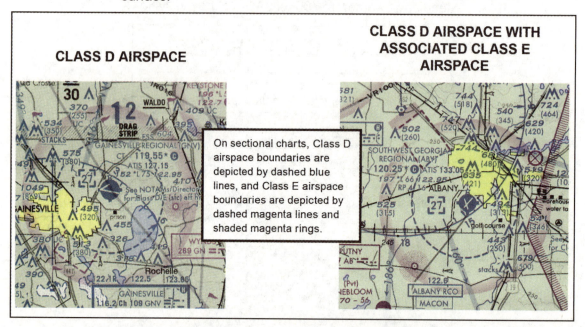

d. Two-way radio communication must be maintained with ATC while within Class D airspace.

1) Two-way radio communication capability is required.

14. **Class E airspace** is simply an area of controlled airspace.

a. This area begins at 1,200 ft. AGL unless otherwise indicated, or unless superseded by Class B, C, or D airspace, and extends upward to the base of the overlying airspace.

1) A dashed magenta line around an airport indicates Class E airspace extending upward from the surface to the base of the overlying airspace (often Class A airspace).

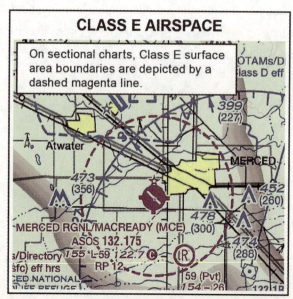

SU 8: Navigation

2) A light magenta-shaded line indicates Class E airspace extending upward from 700 ft. AGL to the base of the overlying airspace.

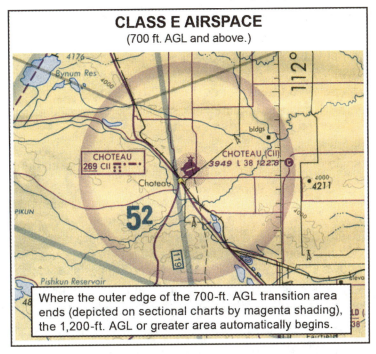

CLASS E AIRSPACE
(700 ft. AGL and above.)

Where the outer edge of the 700-ft. AGL transition area ends (depicted on sectional charts by magenta shading), the 1,200-ft. AGL or greater area automatically begins.

    b. There is no two-way radio communication requirement under VFR in Class E airspace.

15. **Class G airspace** is airspace that is not controlled airspace.

    a. It exists beneath the floor of controlled airspace in areas where that airspace does not extend down to the surface.

        1) Class G airspace that underlies Class B, C, D, or E airspace is implied -- it is not indicated on the chart.

    b. There is no two-way radio communication requirement in Class G airspace.

    c. When conducting night operations at an airport in Class G airspace, you must remain clear of the clouds and have 1 SM visibility if remaining within 1/2 mi. of the airport.

        1) See Study Unit 7, 14 CFR 91.155, "Basic VFR Weather Minimums," on page 237.

8.2 CLIMB CALCULATIONS

1. Questions that require the distance and time for a climb given the rate of climb and the amount of climb can be solved by dividing the amount of climb by the rate of climb.

2. Given the amount of time to reach a certain altitude, you can estimate the distance by multiplying the estimated groundspeed per minute by the number of minutes to make the climb.

 It is essential for each student to own an approved E6B flight computer (manual or electronic) and a navigation plotter. These tools are necessary to answer some questions on the knowledge test and to use during your check ride. Go to www.GleimAviation.com/E6B to access complete instructions on the use of the Gleim E6B flight computer.

8.3 SPEED, DISTANCE, AND FUEL CALCULATIONS

1. The FAA knowledge test database has several questions that require you **to determine a required indicated airspeed to maintain a cross-country flight schedule**, i.e., to get to a second point by a specified time.
    - Compute the required groundspeed based on the distance between the two points and the time required to reach the second point on schedule.
    - Compute the true airspeed, given the groundspeed and wind conditions.
    - Determine indicated airspeed by adjusting your true airspeed for pressure altitude and ambient temperature.

    a. To compute desired groundspeed, place the distance between the two points on the outer scale of the flight computer adjacent to the required number of minutes to fly to the second point.
        1) Then the number on the outer scale, which is adjacent to the solid triangular pointer (i.e., at 60 min.), is your groundspeed.
        2) EXAMPLE: If you travel 3 NM in 3 min., you are going 60 kt. (or 60 NM/hr.) Place 30 on the outer scale adjacent to 30 on the inner scale. Then the outer scale shows 60 kt. (or 60 NM/hr.) above the solid triangular pointer.
    b. To compute the true airspeed, place the wind direction under the true index (wind-side of computer) and place a mark indicating the wind speed up from the grommet.
        1) Place the true course direction under the true index and place the grommet over the groundspeed.
        2) True airspeed is indicated by the mark.
    c. To determine the required indicated airspeed, you must make corrections for pressure altitude and ambient temperature.
        1) On your flight computer, set the ambient (air) temperature adjacent to the pressure altitude (in the window on the right center of flight computer side).
        2) On the outer scale, locate your true airspeed and read your indicated airspeed adjacent to it on the inner scale.

2. **To compute fuel/distance problems**, determine the total flight time available.
    a. Place the fuel consumption rate over the true index of your flight computer.
    b. Then find the amount of usable fuel at takeoff on the outer scale and determine the total flight time on the inner scale.
    c. Then subtract the flight time since takeoff and any reserve time required by the Federal Aviation Regulations from the total flight time.
    d. Then either multiply the groundspeed and time to determine distance
        1) Or place the true index on the flight computer under the groundspeed and locate the time remaining on the inner scale; then read the distance on the outer scale.
    e. 14 CFR 91.151 states that under VFR conditions and given wind and forecast weather conditions, you must have enough fuel to fly to the first point of intended landing and, assuming normal cruising speed,
        1) Fly after that for 30 min. during the day or
        2) Fly after that for 45 min. during the night.

3. **To determine distance traveled**, place the groundspeed over the true index on your flight computer.
    a. Locate the time on the inner scale and read the distance above on the outer scale.
    b. Alternatively, multiply the groundspeed by the time (in min.).

c. EXAMPLE: How far will an aircraft travel in 2 1/2 min. with a groundspeed of 96 kt.? 96 kt. is 1.6 NM/min. (96 ÷ 60 = 1.6). The aircraft will travel 4 NM in 2 1/2 min. (1.6 × 2.5 = 4).

4. **To compute true or magnetic heading and groundspeed**, you must adjust for winds.

   a. To compute wind effect, use the wind side of the computer.

   1) Align the wind direction on the inner scale under the true index (top of the computer) on the outer scale.
   2) Slide the grid through the computer until the grommet (the hole in the center) is on the 100 kt. wind line. Measure up the vertical line the amount of wind speed in knots and put a pencil mark on the plastic.
   3) Rotate the inner scale so the true course is under the true index.
   4) Slide the grid so that your pencil dot is superimposed over the true airspeed. The location of the grommet will indicate the groundspeed.
   5) The pencil mark will indicate the wind correction angle (if to the left, it is a negative wind correction; if to the right, a positive wind correction).

   b. True heading is found by adjusting the true course heading for the wind correction.

   1) Add the number of degrees the pencil mark is to the right of the centerline or subtract the number of degrees to the left.

   c. Magnetic heading is found by adjusting the true heading for magnetic variation.

   1) Add the number of degrees of westerly magnetic variation or subtract the number of degrees of easterly magnetic variation.

5. **Some problems require the use of a wind triangle to compute speed, distance, and wind corrections.**

   a. The line connecting Point A to Point B represents the true heading and airspeed line.
   b. The line connecting Point C to Point A represents the wind direction and velocity line.
   c. The line connecting Point C to Point B represents the true course and groundspeed line.

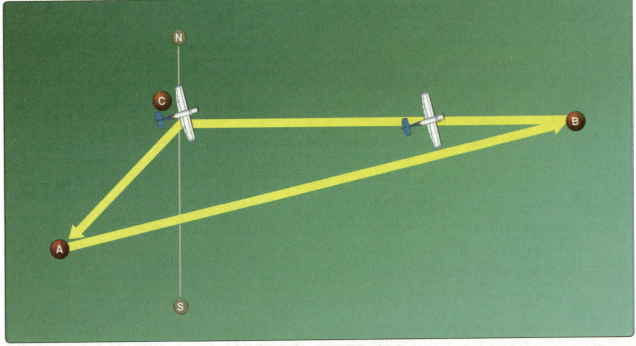

Figure 40. – Wind Triangle.

8.4 OFF-COURSE CORRECTIONS

1. To determine the correction to converge on the destination, use the following formulas and add the results:

$$\frac{\text{Miles off course}}{\text{Miles flown}} \times 60 = °\text{ to parallel}$$

$$\frac{\text{Miles off course}}{\text{Miles remaining}} \times 60 = °\text{ to intercept}$$

2. EXAMPLE: You are 140 NM from your departure point and determine that you are 11 NM off course. If 71 NM remain to be flown, the approximate total correction to be made to converge on the destination is 14°, as computed below.

$$(11 \div 140) \times 60 = 4.7°$$
$$(11 \div 71) \times 60 = 9.3°$$
$$\overline{14.0°}$$

8.5 ESTIMATING WIND

1. Given true heading and a ground track, you can estimate your wind on the wind side of the computer.
2. Place the groundspeed under the grommet with the ground track under the true index.
3. Then, on the true airspeed arc, place a pencil mark reflecting right or left deviation based upon your ground track relative to true heading.
   a. Subtract ground track from true heading.
      1) A positive number indicates a right deviation.
      2) A negative number indicates a left deviation.
4. Rotate the inner scale such that the pencil mark is on the centerline under the true index and the wind will be indicated under the true index.
5. The distance up from the grommet is the wind speed.

8.6 DISTANCE MEASURING EQUIPMENT (DME)

1. DME (distance measuring equipment) displays slant-range distance in nautical miles.
   a. The slant range error is greatest at high altitudes directly over the facility.
   b. EXAMPLE: If you are 6,000 ft. directly above a VOR, your DME will read 1.0 NM.
2. The DME coded identification is transmitted once for each three or four times that the VOR coded identification is transmitted.
3. Up to 199 NM at line-of-sight altitudes, the accuracy of DME systems is better than 1/2 mi. or 3% of the distance, whichever is greater.

8.7 VHF OMNIDIRECTIONAL RANGE (VOR)

1. **L class VORs** normally have a usable range of 40 NM below 18,000 ft.
   a. **T class VORs** normally have a usable range of 25 NM below 12,000 ft.
2. A VORTAC is a VOR facility that also has distance measuring equipment.
   a. When VORTACs are undergoing maintenance, the identification feature is not broadcast.
   b. The three individual navigation services provided by a VORTAC are VHF VOR azimuth, UHF TACAN azimuth, and UHF TACAN distance information.

SU 8: Navigation

3. When using a VOT to check the accuracy of a VOR receiver, the needle should be centered with a 180° TO indication or a 360° FROM indication.

4. A series of questions in the FAA knowledge test database requires you to identify the position of your airplane relative to a VOR given the omnibearing setting, the TO-FROM indicator, and the course deviation indicator (CDI).

   a. First, remember that the CDI needle does not point to the VOR. It indicates the position of the airplane relative to VOR radials.

      1) Irrespective of your direction of flight, the CDI needle always points toward the imaginary course line through the VOR determined by your omnibearing selector.

         a) This assumes that you are on a heading in the general direction of your omnibearing course.

         b) If you are heading opposite your omnibearing course, the CDI needle will point away from the imaginary course line through the VOR determined by your omnibearing selector.

   b. The TO-FROM indicator also operates independently of the heading of your airplane. Irrespective of your direction of flight, the TO-FROM indicator shows you whether you are before, on, or past a line 90° (perpendicular) to the course line determined by your omnibearing setting.

   c. Thus, the VOR display only shows your location (not your heading) with respect to the VOR.

      1) Solve all VOR problems by imagining yourself in an airplane heading in the general direction of the omnibearing setting.

   d. The following diagram explains the TO-FROM indicator and the CDI needle.

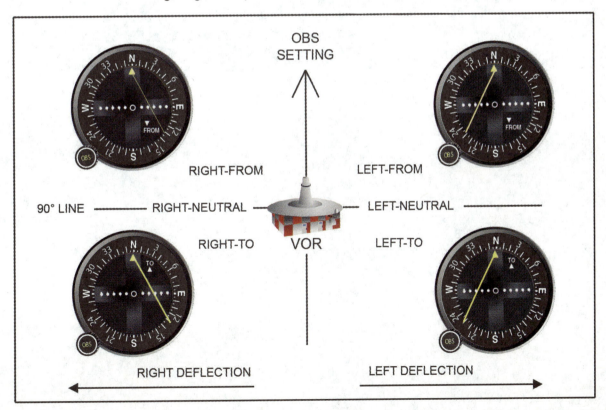

Figure 42 below assumes the OBS is set to 180°. Thus, you must imagine your airplane with a 180° heading irrespective of your **actual** heading. The "Left-TO" indication would mean you were to the northwest of the VOR irrespective of your heading. **BUT** you can visualize your relationship to the VOR by imagining a 180° heading -- then a "Left" indication means you are west of your desired course and a "TO" indication means you are north of the 270° and 090° radials.

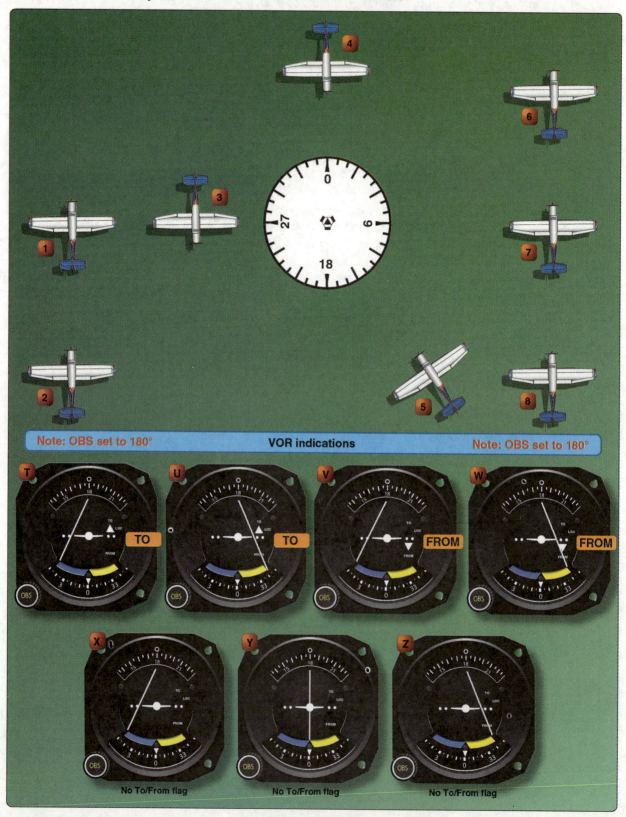

Figure 42. – VOR Indicators.

5. In the RNAV mode of a navigation system, the system acts very similar to normal VORs, except the CDI shows guidance to the waypoint rather than the VOR.

   a. Also, the lateral deflection of the CDI indicates NM left or right of course, not degrees.

8.8 GLOBAL POSITIONING SYSTEMS (GPS)

1. To effectively navigate by means of GPS, pilots should

   a. Determine the GPS unit is approved for their planned flight.

   b. Determine the status of the databases.

      1) The current status of navigational databases, weather databases, NOTAMs, and signal availability should be ensured prior to takeoff.

   c. Understand how to make and cancel all appropriate entries.

      1) Stressful situations, heavy workloads, and turbulence make data entry errors real problems; pilots should know how to recover basic aircraft controls quickly.

   d. Program and review the planned route.

      1) Because each GPS layout can vary widely in type and function (knobs, switches, etc.), programming of the units should be verified for accuracy.

      2) Name changes or spelling mistakes contribute to errors in flying appropriate routes.

   e. Ensure the track flown is approved by ATC.

2. One of the primary benefits of GPS navigation is that it permits aircraft to fly optimum routes and altitudes.

   a. The "Direct To," or ➲, key is a primary function key on most GPS units. A user hits the button and, using a series of knobs or switches, programs the intended waypoint or airport using the proper identifier. This feature shows the quickest way to fly to any given point, which is usually in a straight line.

   b. The "nearest" button, abbreviated on most units as NRST, will show the closest airports in relation to the aircraft's current location.

      1) This is very beneficial in emergency situations. A pilot simply presses this button to see the name, location, and direction to the nearest airport for landing.

      2) Information such as navigation and communication frequencies, runway numbers and lengths, and other pertinent data is also provided.

3. Due to the use of and reliance on GPS systems for navigation, it is easy for pilots to lose proficiency in performing manual calculations on courses, times, distances, headings, etc.

   a. Emergency situations (e.g., electrical failures) make it important to maintain proficiency in these calculations.

QUESTIONS AND ANSWER EXPLANATIONS: All of the AGI/CFI knowledge test questions chosen by the FAA for release as well as additional questions selected by Gleim relating to the material in the previous outlines are reproduced on the following pages. These questions have been organized into the same subunits as the outlines. To the immediate right of each question are the correct answer and answer explanation. You should cover these answers and answer explanations while responding to the questions. Refer to the general discussion in the Introduction on how to take the FAA knowledge test.

Remember that the questions from the FAA knowledge test bank have been reordered by topic and organized into a meaningful sequence. Also, the first line of the answer explanation gives the citation of the authoritative source for the answer.

296   SU 8: Navigation

QUESTIONS

8.1 Sectional Charts

1. (Refer to Figure 44 on page 297.) Where does the floor of positively controlled ATC airspace begin over Hicks Airport (area 1)?

A. Surface.
B. 700 feet AGL.
C. 4,000 feet MSL.

Answer (C) is correct. *(ACL)*
　DISCUSSION: Area 1 is in the center of the left-hand side of Fig. 44. Hicks Airport is outside of the blue dashed line that encircles both Ft. Worth Meacham and Ft. Worth Alliance. This indicates Class B airspace extending upward from 4,000 ft. MSL.
　Answer (A) is incorrect. Hicks is outside of the dashed lines. Answer (B) is incorrect. Although Class E airspace extending upward from 700 ft. AGL is indicated by the magenta shading, it is not actively controlled by ATC.

2. (Refer to Figure 44 on page 297.) The airspace overlying Addison Airport (area 4) is classified as

A. Class D below 3,000 feet.
B. Class B from the surface to 10,000 feet.
C. Class D from the surface up to and including 3,000 feet.

Answer (A) is correct. *(ACL)*
　DISCUSSION: Area 4 is northeast of Dallas-Ft. Worth Airport. The Class D airspace ceiling is charted as −30. A minus ceiling value indicates surface up to, but not including, that value. Thus, the Class D airspace at Addison Airport extends from the surface up to, but not including, 3,000 ft. MSL.
　Answer (B) is incorrect. The Class B airspace overlying Addison Airport extends from 3,000 ft. MSL, not the surface, to 11,000 ft. MSL. Answer (C) is incorrect. The Class D airspace overlying Addison Airport does NOT include 3,000 ft. MSL, as indicated by the −30 ceiling value.

3. (Refer to Figure 44 on page 297.) An aircraft takes off from Hicks Airport (area 1) and flies northeast towards Northwest Airport (area 2). What maximum elevation figure would assure obstruction clearance during the flight?

A. 3,200 feet MSL.
B. 1,700 feet MSL.
C. 1,900 feet MSL.

Answer (A) is correct. *(ACL)*
　DISCUSSION: The maximum elevation figure (MEF) is shown in each quadrangle bounded by ticked lines of latitude and longitude. The MEF in the quadrangle that contains Hicks Airport is shown just below and to the right of the name Fort Worth. The large "1" and somewhat smaller "9" mean the MEF is 1,900 ft. MSL. In the quadrangle containing Northwest Airport, the MEF is in the upper left corner of the figure. The large "3" and somewhat smaller "2" mean the MEF is 3,200 ft. MSL. Thus, on a flight from Hicks Airport to Northwest Airport, the maximum elevation figure that would ensure obstacle clearance is 3,200 ft. MSL.
　Answer (B) is incorrect. This is not an MEF for a flight from Hicks Airport to Northwest Airport. The MEF that ensures obstacle clearance is 3,200 ft. MSL, not 1,700 ft. MSL. Answer (C) is incorrect. This is the MEF for the quadrangle that contains Hicks Airport, but the MEF for the quadrangle that contains Northwest Airport is 3,200 ft. MSL.

4. (Refer to Figure 44 on page 297.) Where does the floor of controlled airspace begin over Ft. Worth Meacham (area 1)?

A. Surface.
B. 700 feet AGL.
C. 4,000 feet MSL.

Answer (A) is correct. *(ACL)*
　DISCUSSION: Area 1 is in the center of the left-hand side of Fig. 44. Ft. Worth Meacham is encircled by a blue dashed line. This indicates Class D airspace, extending upward from the surface to a specified altitude (here, 3,200 ft. MSL).
　Answer (B) is incorrect. Although Class E airspace extending upward from 700 ft. AGL is indicated by the magenta shading, it is superseded by Class D airspace extending upward from the surface, as indicated by the blue dashed line. Answer (C) is incorrect. Although Class B airspace extending upward from 4,000 ft. MSL is indicated by the blue solid lines, Class D airspace extends upward from the surface, as indicated by the blue dashed line.

5. (Refer to Figure 44 on page 297.) Select the correct statement concerning the obstruction 7 SM west of McKinney Airport (area 5).

A. The obstruction is unlighted.
B. The obstruction has high-intensity lights.
C. The elevation of the top of the obstruction is 729 feet AGL.

Answer (B) is correct. *(ACL)*
　DISCUSSION: Area 5 is in the upper right-hand corner of the chart. The group obstruction 7 SM west of McKinney Airport has a series of lightning bolts emanating from the top of the obstruction symbol. This indicates high-intensity lights.
　Answer (A) is incorrect. The lightning bolts emanating from the top of the obstruction symbol indicate high-intensity lights. Answer (C) is incorrect. The height of the top of the obstruction is 813 ft. AGL, not 729 ft. AGL, as indicated by the lower number in parentheses.

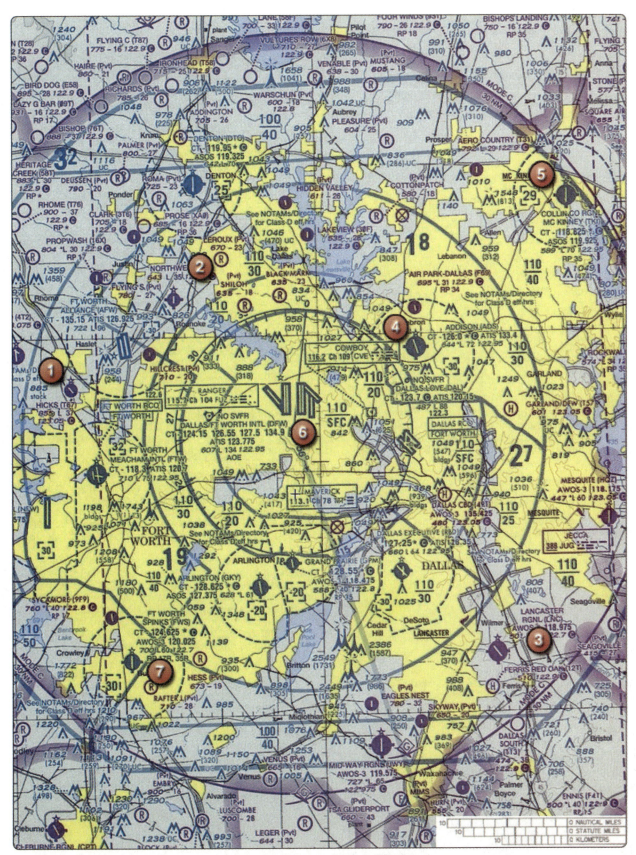

Figure 44. – Sectional Chart Excerpt.
NOTE: Chart is not to scale and should not be used for navigation. Use associated scale.

6. (Refer to Figure 44 on page 299.) Select the correct statement concerning special VFR operations at Addison Airport (area 4).

A. Special VFR operations are not permitted.
B. These operations are permitted at all times.
C. Airplanes are prohibited from conducting special VFR operations.

Answer (B) is correct. *(ACL)*
DISCUSSION: Refer to Fig. 44. Area 4 is northeast of Dallas/Ft. Worth. Addison Airport is encircled by a blue dashed line. This indicates Class D airspace extending upward from the surface to a specified altitude (here up to, but not including, 3,000 ft. MSL). Special VFR operations are permitted at all times (subject to certain restrictions at night) within surface-based areas of Class B, C, D, or E airspace, unless the notation NO SVFR appears above the airport identifier.
Answer (A) is incorrect. The NO SVFR notation below Addison Airport refers to Dallas-Love Airport, not Addison. Answer (C) is incorrect. The NO SVFR notation below Addison Airport refers to Dallas-Love Airport, not Addison.

7. (Refer to Figure 44 on page 299.) What altitude should be selected to avoid operating in Class B airspace on a flight from Northwest Airport (area 2) to McKinney Airport (area 5)?

A. 2,500 feet MSL.
B. 3,000 feet MSL.
C. 3,500 feet MSL.

Answer (A) is correct. *(ACL)*
DISCUSSION: Area 2 is northwest of Dallas/Ft. Worth, and area 5 is to the east-northeast, at the edge of the chart. A flight from Northwest Airport to McKinney Airport would pass through an area encircled by blue solid lines. Note also the "110" above the "30" (separated by a line) found between the two airports. These indicate Class B airspace extending upward from 3,000 ft. MSL to 11,000 ft. MSL. Thus, to avoid operating in Class B airspace, an altitude of 2,500 ft. MSL should be selected.
Answer (B) is incorrect. The Class B airspace extends upward from 3,000 ft. MSL, as indicated by the "110" above the "30" (separated by a line) between the two airports. Answer (C) is incorrect. The Class B airspace extends upward from 3,000 ft. MSL, as indicated by the "110" above the "30" (separated by a line) between the two airports.

8. (Refer to Figure 44 on page 299.) When, if ever, are two-way radio communications required while en route from Lancaster Airport (area 3) direct to McKinney Airport (area 5) at 2,700 feet MSL?

A. None required.
B. Before entering the Class B airspace.
C. Immediately after takeoff since the airport is located within Class B airspace.

Answer (B) is correct. *(ACL)*
DISCUSSION: Area 3 is in the lower right-hand corner, and area 5 is in the upper right-hand corner of the chart. The Class B airspace over Lancaster Airport extends upward from 4,000 ft. MSL to 11,000 ft. MSL, as indicated by the "110" above the "40" (separated by a line) southeast of the airport. However, a flight from Lancaster Airport to McKinney Airport would just enter a segment of Class B airspace extending upward from 2,500 ft. MSL, as indicated by the "110" above the "25" (separated by a line) north of Lancaster Airport. Two-way radio communication and ATC authorization are required prior to entering Class B airspace.
Answer (A) is incorrect. A flight from Lancaster Airport to McKinney Airport would just enter a segment of Class B airspace extending upward from 2,500 ft. MSL. Two-way radio communication and ATC authorization are required prior to entering Class B airspace. Answer (C) is incorrect. The Class B airspace over Lancaster Airport extends upward from 4,000 ft. MSL to 11,000 ft. MSL, as indicated by the "110" above the "25" (separated by a line) southwest of the airport.

9. (Refer to Figure 44 on page 299.) Select the correct statement concerning the Maverick VOR (area 6).

A. The VOR has voice capability.
B. Hazardous In-flight Weather Advisory Service (HIWAS) is not available over the VOR.
C. A pilot may receive transmissions from Fort Worth Flight Service Station over the VOR frequency.

Answer (B) is correct. *(ACL)*
DISCUSSION: Refer to Fig. 44. The Maverick VOR communication box is just to the right of the area 6 label (center of chart). HIWAS is not available over the VOR since there is no dark blue square at the lower right-hand corner of the communication box.
Answer (A) is incorrect. The underline indicates no voice transmission on this frequency. Answer (C) is incorrect. The frequency of the Maverick VOR (113.1) is underlined, indicating no voice capability.

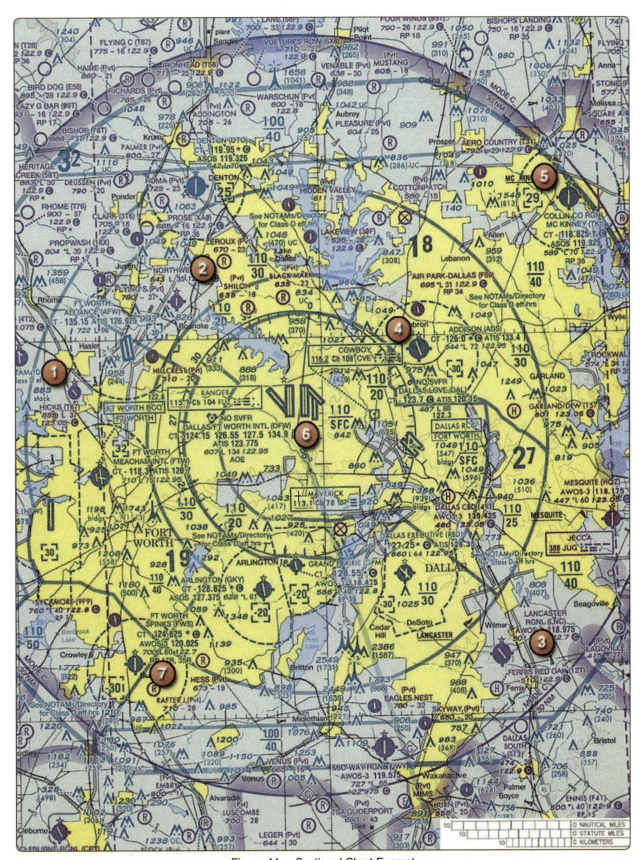

Figure 44. – Sectional Chart Excerpt.
NOTE: Chart is not to scale and should not be used for navigation. Use associated scale.

10. When converting from true course to magnetic heading, a pilot should

A. subtract easterly variation and right wind correction angle.
B. add westerly variation and subtract left wind correction angle.
C. subtract westerly variation and add right wind correction angle.

Answer (B) is correct. *(PHAK Chap 16)*
DISCUSSION: When converting true course to magnetic heading, you should remember two rules. With magnetic variation, east variation is subtracted and west variation is added. With wind corrections, left correction is subtracted and right correction is added.
Answer (A) is incorrect. Right wind correction is added, not subtracted. Answer (C) is incorrect. Westerly variation is added, not subtracted.

11. What are the visibility and cloud clearance requirements at an airport in Class G airspace when conducting takeoffs and landings at night?

A. 3 SM visibility and clear of clouds.
B. 1 SM visibility and clear of clouds if remaining within 1/2 mile of the airport.
C. Remain clear of clouds and operate at a speed that allows adequate opportunity to see other traffic and obstructions in time to avoid a collision.

Answer (B) is correct. *(ACL, 14 CFR 91.155)*
DISCUSSION: 14 CFR 91.155(b)(2) states that if visibility is less than 3 SM but not less than 1 SM during night hours and you are operating in an airport traffic pattern within 1/2 mile of the runway, you may operate an airplane clear of clouds.
Answer (A) is incorrect. The visibility requirement at a Class G airport at night is 1 SM, not 3 SM. Answer (C) is incorrect. Traffic pattern speed limits are not related to visibility requirements.

12. The angular difference between true north and magnetic north is

A. magnetic deviation.
B. magnetic variation.
C. compass acceleration error.

Answer (B) is correct. *(PHAK Chap 16)*
DISCUSSION: The angular difference between true and magnetic north is referred to as magnetic variation.
Answer (A) is incorrect. Deviation is the deflection of the compass needle in the airplane because of magnetic influences within the airplane. Answer (C) is incorrect. Compass acceleration error results from accelerating the aircraft.

13. (Refer to Figure 44 on page 301.) An aircraft takes off from Hicks Airport (area 1) and flies northeast towards Northwest Airport (area 2). What maximum altitude could be flown to remain under the Class B airspace?

A. 4,000 feet MSL.
B. 2,500 feet MSL.
C. 3,200 feet MSL.

Answer (B) is correct. *(PHAK Chap 14)*
DISCUSSION: Class B airspace begins at 4,000 ft. MSL above Hicks Airport. Class B airspace begins at 3,000 ft. MSL above Northwest Airport. Therefore, 2,500 ft. MSL could be flown to remain under the Class B airspace.
Answer (A) is incorrect. Class B airspace begins at 4,000 ft. MSL above Hicks Airport. Class B airspace begins at 3,000 ft. MSL above Northwest Airport. Answer (C) is incorrect. Class B airspace begins at 3,000 ft. MSL above Northwest Airport.

14. (Refer to Figure 44 on page 301.) What minimum avionics equipment is necessary to operate in the airspace up to 3,000 feet MSL over Northwest Airport (area 2)?

A. None required.
B. Transponder and encoding altimeter.
C. Two-way radio communications equipment, transponder, and encoding altimeter.

Answer (B) is correct. *(ACL)*
DISCUSSION: Area 2 is northwest of Dallas/Ft. Worth. The airspace over Northwest Airport is Class G extending upward from the surface to 700 ft. AGL and Class E from 700 ft. AGL to 2,999 ft. MSL, as indicated by the magenta shading. Extending upward from 3,000 ft. MSL is Class B airspace, indicated by the blue solid lines surrounding the airport and the "110" above the "30" (separated by a line), seen 5 NM northeast of the airport.
There is no communication requirement in either Class E or Class G airspace. However, a transponder and encoding altimeter (Mode C) are required within 30 NM of the primary Class B airport, as indicated by the thin magenta circle labeled Mode C 30 NM in the upper right-hand corner of the chart.
Answer (A) is incorrect. A transponder and encoding altimeter (Mode C) are required within 30 NM of the primary Class B airport, as indicated by the thin magenta circle labeled Mode C 30 NM in the upper right-hand corner of the chart. Answer (C) is incorrect. Two-way radio communications equipment is not required in either Class E or Class G airspace.

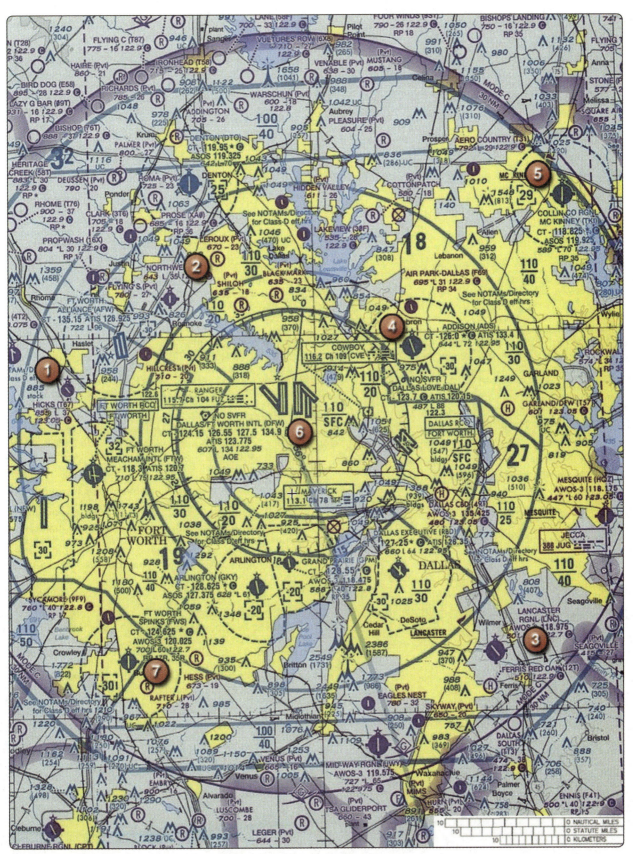

Figure 44. – Sectional Chart Excerpt.
NOTE: Chart is not to scale and should not be used for navigation. Use associated scale.

15. (Refer to Figure 45 on page 303.) Where does the floor of controlled airspace begin over McCampbell Airport (area 1)?

A. Surface.
B. 718 feet MSL.
C. 1,218 feet MSL.

Answer (B) is correct. *(ACL)*
DISCUSSION: Refer to Fig. 45 and locate McCampbell Airport, just southwest of area 1. There is a magenta-shaded area extending from the northeast down and around to the southwest of Campbell Airport and beyond. The figure cuts off the magenta-shaded area northwest of McCampbell Airport and southeast of Corpus Christi NAS/Truax, so we can assume that the magenta-shaded area goes around McCampbell Airport. We can also assume that McCampbell Airport is within a magenta-shaded area, as seen on the FAA's chart. This would indicate that the floor of that Class E (controlled) airspace extends upward from 700 ft. AGL to the base of the overlying airspace (here, Class A airspace at 18,000 ft.). The airport identifier shows the field elevation to be 18 ft. MSL. Thus, Class E airspace extends upward from 718 ft. MSL.
NOTE: There are issues with this question: (1) the actual airport is named McCampbell-Porter Airport, not McCampbell Airport; and (2) the shaded area actually extends into the Gulf of Mexico and then northwest before coming back southbound around to the northwest side of McCampbell-Porter Airport.
Answer (A) is incorrect. A magenta-shaded area indicates that Class E airspace extends upward from 700 ft. AGL, not the surface. Answer (C) is incorrect. A magenta-shaded area indicates that Class E airspace extends upward from 700 ft. AGL, not 1,218 ft. MSL.

16. (Refer to Figure 45 on page 303.) What are the visibility and cloud clearance requirements in an airplane at night when conducting takeoffs and landings at McCampbell Airport (area 1)?

A. 3 SM visibility and 500 feet below and 2,000 feet horizontal from clouds.
B. 1 SM visibility and 2,000 feet horizontal from clouds.
C. 1 SM visibility and clear of clouds.

Answer (A) is correct. *(14 CFR 91.155)*
DISCUSSION: Refer to Fig. 45 area 1 in the upper right-hand corner of the chart. McCampbell Airport lies within a shaded magenta area, which indicates Class E airspace from 700 feet AGL upward to the overlying controlled airspace. Basic VFR weather minimums in Class E airspace during the day are 3 SM visibility and 500 feet below, 1,000 feet above, and 2,000 feet horizontal distance from clouds. Below the shaded magenta area is Class G airspace, which extends from the surface up to 700 feet AGL. Operating in the pattern would place the aircraft at an altitude within Class E airspace, so Class E weather minimums apply.
Answer (B) is incorrect. VFR weather minimums during the day in Class G airspace more than 1,200 feet above the surface but less than 10,000 feet MSL are 1 SM visibility and 500 feet below, 1,000 feet above, and 2,000 feet horizontal distance from clouds. Answer (C) is incorrect. VFR weather minimums during the day in Class G airspace 1,200 feet or less above the surface (regardless of MSL altitude) are 1 SM visibility and clear of clouds.

17. (Refer to Figure 45 on page 303.) The controlled airspace located at the Corpus Christi VORTAC (area 5) begins at

A. the surface.
B. 700 feet AGL.
C. 1,200 feet MSL.

Answer (B) is correct. *(ACL)*
DISCUSSION: Refer to Fig. 45. Area 5 is 8 NM north of Corpus Christi. The Corpus Christi VORTAC is just inside the magenta-shaded area. This indicates that Class E (controlled) airspace extends upward from 700 ft. AGL to the base of the overlying airspace (here Class C airspace at 1,200 ft. MSL, as indicated by the magenta solid lines and the "40" above the "12" (separated by a line), 5 NM west of the VORTAC).
Answer (A) is incorrect. A magenta-shaded area indicates that Class E extends upward from 700 ft. AGL, not the surface. Answer (C) is incorrect. Although Class C airspace extending upward from 1,200 ft. MSL to 4,000 ft. MSL is indicated by the magenta solid lines, Class E airspace extends upward from 700 ft. AGL, as indicated by the magenta shading.

SU 8: Navigation

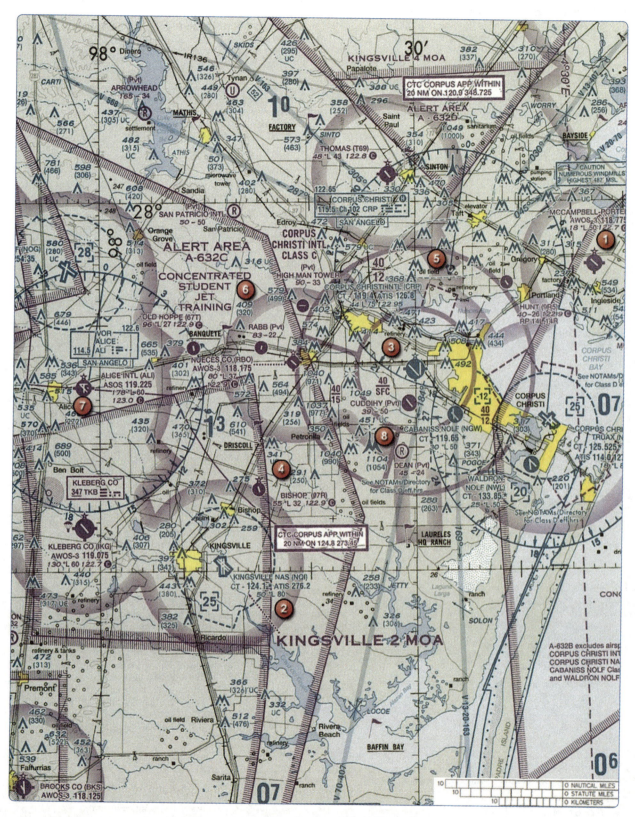

Figure 45. — Sectional Chart Excerpt.
NOTE: Chart is not to scale and should not be used for navigation. Use associated scale.

18. (Refer to Figure 45 on page 305.) When are two-way radio communications required on a flight from Bishop Airport (area 4) to McCampbell Airport (area 1) at an altitude of 2,000 feet MSL?

A. Entering the Corpus Christi Class C airspace.
B. Leaving and entering the alert areas and entering the Corpus Christi Class C airspace.
C. Leaving and entering the alert areas, entering the Corpus Christi Class C airspace, and passing through the Cabaniss Field Class D airspace.

Answer (A) is correct. *(ACL)*
DISCUSSION: Refer to Fig. 45. Area 4 is near the center and area 1 is in the upper right-hand corner of the chart. A flight from Bishop Airport to McCampbell Airport at 2,000 ft. MSL will pass through the Corpus Christi Class C airspace. Two-way radio communications and transponder with encoding altimeter are required when operating within Class C airspace.
Answer (B) is incorrect. Two-way radio communication is not required in alert areas. Answer (C) is incorrect. Two-way radio communication is not required in alert areas, and a direct flight will not pass through the Cabaniss Field Class D airspace.

19. (Refer to Figure 45 on page 305.) While on a flight from Alice Airport (area 7) to McCampbell Airport (area 1) at 5,500 feet MSL, when, if ever, is a transponder required?

A. Transponder is not required.
B. Required when overflying the Corpus Christi Class C airspace.
C. Required when leaving and entering the alert areas and overflying the Corpus Christi Class C airspace.

Answer (B) is correct. *(ACL)*
DISCUSSION: Refer to Fig. 45. Area 7 is in the center of the left-hand side of the chart, and area 1 is near the top of the right-hand side of the chart. A flight from Alice Airport to McCampbell Airport will overfly the Corpus Christi Class C airspace, as indicated by the magenta solid lines. A transponder with encoding altimeter is required when operating within, or overflying, Class C airspace.
Answer (A) is incorrect. A transponder with encoding altimeter is required when operating within, or overflying, Class C airspace. Answer (C) is incorrect. A transponder is not required when leaving or entering an Alert Area.

20. (Refer to Figure 45 on page 305.) Assuming owner permission, what minimum avionics equipment is required for operation into Cuddihy Airport (area 8)?

A. Two-way radio communications equipment.
B. None, if altitude remains at or below 1,200 feet MSL.
C. Two-way radio communications equipment and transponder with encoding altimeter.

Answer (C) is correct. *(ACL)*
DISCUSSION: Refer to Fig. 45. Area 8 is in the center of the chart, just below Corpus Christi. Cuddihy Airport is 4 NM south of Corpus Christi, and is located within the surface area of the Class C airspace, depicted by the first magenta circle around Corpus Christi. Thus, the Class C airspace extends upward from the surface at Cuddihy Airport. Two-way radio communications and a transponder with encoding altimeter are required when operating in Class C airspace.
Answer (A) is incorrect. The airport lies within the surface area of Class C airspace. A transponder with encoding altimeter is also required. Answer (B) is incorrect. The Class C airspace over the airport extends upward from the surface, not 1,200 ft. MSL, since the airport lies within the surface area of Class C airspace.

21. (Refer to Figure 45 on page 305.) The airspace beginning at the surface overlying NAS Kingsville (area 2) is

A. an Alert Area.
B. Class D airspace.
C. a military operations area (MOA).

Answer (B) is correct. *(ACL)*
DISCUSSION: Refer to Fig. 45. Area 2 is in the lower left-hand portion of the chart. NAS Kingsville is encircled by a blue dashed line. This indicates Class D airspace extending upward from the surface to a specified altitude (here, 2,500 ft. MSL).
Answer (A) is incorrect. While Alert Area A-632C does surround NAS Kingsville, the vertical limits are not known. Also, the blue dashed lines definitely indicate Class D airspace extending upward from the surface. Answer (C) is incorrect. The vertical limits of the Kingsville 2 MOA are not indicated, but MOAs rarely extend upward from the surface. Also, the blue dashed lines definitely indicate Class D airspace extending upward from the surface.

22. (Refer to Figure 45 on page 305.) What is the elevation of the Thomas (T69) Airport (area 5)?

A. 122.8 feet MSL.
B. 43 feet MSL.
C. 48 feet MSL.

Answer (C) is correct. *(ACL)*
DISCUSSION: Northwest of 5, note that the second line of the airport identifier for Thomas Airport reads "48 L 43 122.8 C." The first number, in bold type, is the altitude of the airport above MSL. It is followed by the L for lighted runway(s), the 43 for the length of the longest runway (4,300 ft.), and the CTAF frequency (122.8 MHz).
Answer (A) is incorrect. The CTAF, not elevation, of Thomas Airport is 122.8 MHz. This is indicated on the chart by the letter "C" immediately following 122.8. Answer (B) is incorrect. The number "43" is the length of the longest runway in hundreds of feet (4,300 ft.), not the elevation of the airport.

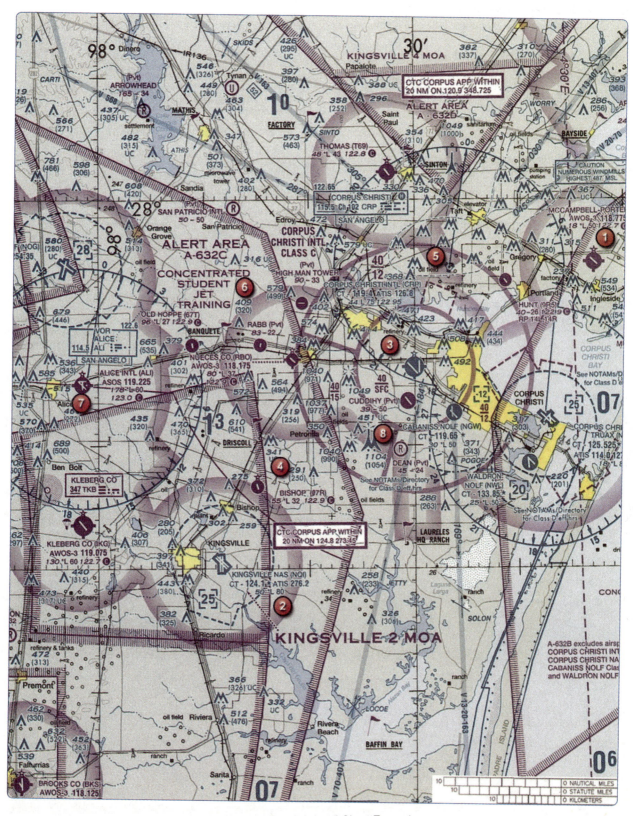

Figure 45. – Sectional Chart Excerpt.
NOTE: Chart is not to scale and should not be used for navigation. Use associated scale.

23. When converting from magnetic course to true course, a pilot should

A. add easterly variation regardless of heading.
B. add westerly variation regardless of heading.
C. subtract easterly variation when on a heading of 360°.

Answer (A) is correct. *(PHAK Chap 16)*
DISCUSSION: When converting from true course to magnetic course, you correct for magnetic variation. If the variation is east, you subtract, and if the variation is west, you add. Here the requirement is from MC to TC, not TC to MC. Thus, you add east and subtract west.
Answer (B) is incorrect. Westerly variation is added when converting from TC to MC, not MC to TC. Answer (C) is incorrect. Easterly variation is added to MC to get TC, regardless of heading.

24. When converting from true heading to true course, a pilot should

A. add right wind correction angle.
B. add left deviation correction angle.
C. subtract right wind correction angle.

Answer (C) is correct. *(PHAK Chap 16)*
DISCUSSION: When converting from true course to true heading, you correct for wind. If the wind is from the right, you add, and if the wind is from the left, you subtract. Here the requirement is from TH to TC (not TC to TH). Thus, you must subtract right wind correction angle.
Answer (A) is incorrect. This right wind correction angle is added when converting from TC to TH. Answer (B) is incorrect. Deviation refers to compass errors that concern compass heading, not TC and TH.

25. (Refer to Figure 45 on page 307.) What are the requirements for operating in the alert area (area 6) just west of Corpus Christi International Airport (area 3)?

A. Contact with approach control on frequency 120.9 is required.
B. Prior permission must be obtained from the controlling agency.
C. There are no requirements, but pilots should be extremely cautious due to extensive student training.

Answer (C) is correct. *(ACL)*
DISCUSSION: Refer to Fig. 45. Area 6 is near the center of the chart, just west of the Corpus Christi Class C airspace. Although pilots should be extremely cautious due to extensive student training in an Alert Area, there are no operating requirements unless you enter the Corpus Christi Class C airspace.
Answer (A) is incorrect. If you planned to enter the Class C airspace while within the Alert Area, you would use 124.8, not 120.9, to contact approach control, as indicated by the magenta box below the Class C airspace. Answer (B) is incorrect. No permission is required prior to operating in an Alert Area.

26. (Refer to Figure 45 on page 307.) What is the elevation of the top of the obstruction located approximately 3 NM northwest of McCampbell Airport (area 1)?

A. 237 feet AGL.
B. 367 feet MSL.
C. 315 feet MSL.

Answer (C) is correct. *(ACL)*
DISCUSSION: Area 1 is on the right side of Fig. 45. A group of obstructions is located 3 NM northwest of McCampbell Airport. The elevation of the top of the obstruction is the bold number, and it is expressed in feet above mean sea level. The elevation of the top of the obstruction is 315 ft. MSL.
Answer (A) is incorrect. This is the height above ground of the obstruction approximately 5 NM west-northwest, not 3 NM northwest, of McCampbell Airport. Answer (B) is incorrect. The height of the obstruction 3 NM northwest of McCampbell Airport is 315 ft. MSL. An obstacle 3 NM northwest of point 1 on the chart is 367 ft. MSL. The question is asking for the height of the obstacle 3 NM northwest of McCampbell Airport.

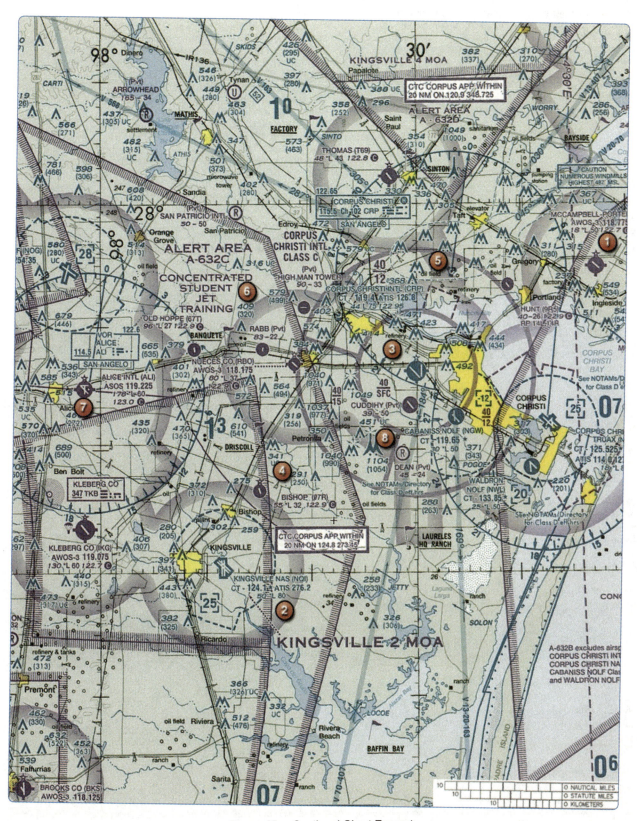

Figure 45. – Sectional Chart Excerpt.
NOTE: Chart is not to scale and should not be used for navigation. Use associated scale.

27. (Refer to Figure 46 on page 309.) An aircraft takes off from Gnoss Airport (area 4) and flies eastward to Rio Vista Airport (area 7). What maximum elevation figure would assure obstruction clearance during the flight?

A. 2,200 feet MSL.
B. 4,200 feet MSL.
C. 3,200 feet MSL.

Answer (C) is correct. *(ACL)*
DISCUSSION: The maximum elevation figure (MEF) is shown in each quadrangle bounded by latitude and longitude tick marks. The MEF in the quadrangle that is just east of Gnoss Airport consists of a large "3" and a somewhat smaller "2," which mean the MEF is 3,200 ft. MSL. In the quadrangle that contains Rio Vista Airport, the MEF is northwest of the airport. The large "2" and the somewhat smaller "2" mean the MEF is 2,200 ft. MSL. Thus, on a flight from Gnoss Airport to Rio Vista Airport, the MEF that would ensure obstacle clearance is 3,200 ft.
Answer (A) is incorrect. This is the MEF for the quadrangle that contains Rio Vista Airport, but the next quadrangle to the west has a higher MEF of 3,200 ft. Answer (B) is incorrect. This would be the MEF to ensure obstruction clearance on a flight from Gnoss Airport to Livermore Airport (area 5), not on a flight from Gnoss Airport to Rio Vista Airport.

28. (Refer to Figure 46 on page 309.) When are two-way radio communications required on a flight from Gnoss Airport (DVO) (area 4) to Livermore Airport (LVK) (area 5) at an altitude of 3,500 ft. AGL? When entering

A. the Class B airspace.
B. the Livermore Airport Class D airspace.
C. both the Class B airspace and the Livermore Airport Class D airspace.

Answer (B) is correct. *(ACL)*
DISCUSSION: Area 4 is in the upper left hand-corner, and area 5 is in the center of the right-hand side of Fig. 46. A flight from Gnoss Airport (DVO) to Livermore Airport (LVK) will pass beneath the sections of Class B airspace extending upward from 4,000 ft. MSL and 6,000 ft. MSL, as indicated by the "100" above the "40" (separated by a line) and the "100" above the "60" (separated by a line), respectively. (Note that the cruising altitude is given as 3,500 ft. AGL, not MSL, and that the terrain elevation along the route of flight appears to be 500 ft. MSL or less.)
Livermore Airport is encircled by blue dashed lines, indicating Class D airspace extending upward from the surface to a specified altitude (here 2,900 ft. MSL). Two-way radio communications must be established prior to entry and thereafter maintained while in Class D airspace.
Answer (A) is incorrect. The flight will pass beneath the Class B airspace, and two-way radio communications must be established prior to entry and thereafter maintained while in Class D airspace. Answer (C) is incorrect. The flight will pass beneath the Class B airspace.

29. (Refer to Figure 46 on page 309.) Where does the floor of controlled airspace begin over Half Moon Bay Airport (area 1)?

A. Surface.
B. 700 feet AGL.
C. 5,000 feet MSL.

Answer (B) is correct. *(ACL)*
DISCUSSION: Refer to Fig. 46. Area 1 is 9 NM southwest of San Francisco. Half Moon Bay Airport is inside a magenta-shaded area. This indicates Class E (controlled) airspace, extending upward from 700 ft. AGL to the base of the overlying airspace [here Class B airspace at 4,000 ft. MSL, as indicated by the blue solid lines and the "100" above the "40" (separated by a line)].
Answer (A) is incorrect. A magenta-shaded area indicates Class E airspace extending upward from 700 ft. AGL, not the surface. Answer (C) is incorrect. Class E airspace extends upward from 700 ft. AGL, as indicated by the magenta shading. Class B airspace, beginning at 5,000 ft. MSL, is to the southwest of Half Moon Bay Airport.

30. (Refer to Figure 46 on page 309.) What is the height of the Class D airspace over Livermore Airport (area 5)?

A. 2,900 feet MSL.
B. 3,000 feet AGL.
C. Base of the overlying Class B airspace.

Answer (A) is correct. *(ACL)*
DISCUSSION: Area 5 is in the center of the right-hand side of Fig. 46. Livermore Airport is encircled by a blue dashed line. Note also the 29 in the box just northwest of the airport. This indicates that Class D airspace extends upward from the surface to 2,900 ft. MSL.
Answer (B) is incorrect. Class D airspace generally extends upward from the surface to 2,500 ft. AGL, not 3,000 ft. AGL. Answer (C) is incorrect. Although the airport does lie within the 30-NM Mode-C veil, there is no overlying Class B airspace.

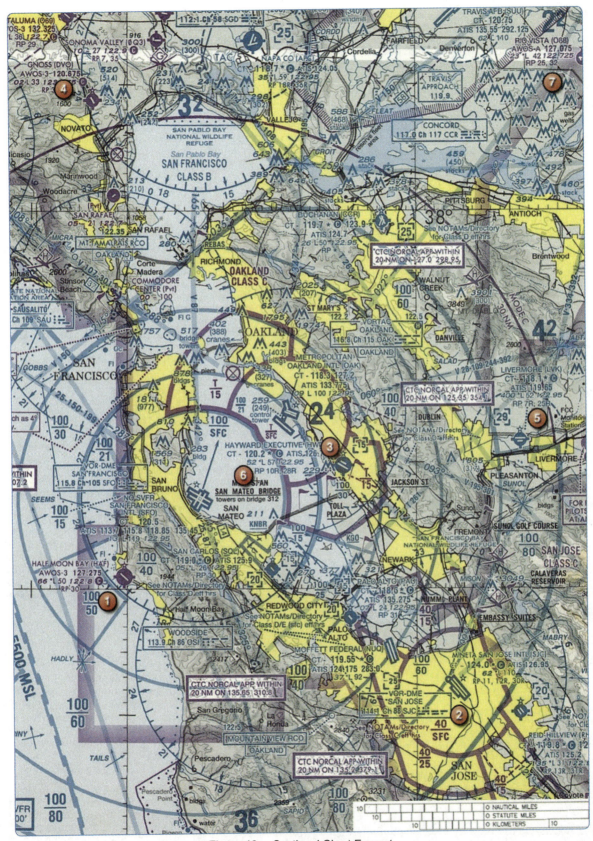

Figure 46. – Sectional Chart Excerpt.
NOTE: Chart is not to scale and should not be used for navigation. Use associated scale.

31. (Refer to Figure 46 on page 311.) While on a flight from Livermore Airport (area 5) to Gnoss Airport (area 4), you contact San Francisco Approach Control and request clearance through the Class B airspace. The controller states "Radar contact, standby." What are you authorized to do?

A. You may enter the airspace since the controller advised you "Radar contact."
B. You may enter the airspace since you have established two-way radio communications.
C. You may not enter the airspace until you have received authorization from ATC.

Answer (C) is correct. *(ACL)*
DISCUSSION: Refer to Fig. 46. Area 5 is in the center of the right-hand side, and area 4 is in the upper left-hand corner of the chart. A flight from Livermore Airport to Gnoss Airport will pass through the San Francisco Class B airspace, as indicated by the blue solid lines (depending, of course, on your cruising altitude). You may not enter Class B airspace without specific authorization from ATC.
Answer (A) is incorrect. You may not enter Class B airspace without specific authorization from ATC. Answer (B) is incorrect. You may not enter Class B airspace without specific authorization from ATC.

32. (Refer to Figure 46 on page 311.) At what altitude does the Class B airspace begin over Hayward Airport (area 3)?

A. Surface.
B. 1,500 feet MSL.
C. 3,000 feet MSL.

Answer (C) is correct. *(ACL)*
DISCUSSION: Refer to Fig. 46. Area 3 is in the center of the chart. Hayward Airport lies beneath an area of Class B airspace extending upward from 3,000 ft. MSL to 10,000 ft. MSL, as indicated by the blue solid lines and the blue "100" above the "30" (separated by a line) just south of the airport.
Answer (A) is incorrect. The Hayward Class D airspace, not Class B airspace, begins at the surface when the control tower is open. Answer (B) is incorrect. The Class C, not Class B, airspace over Hayward Airport extends upward from 1,500 ft. MSL, as indicated by the magenta solid lines and the magenta "T" above the "15" (separated by a line) southeast of the airport.

33. (Refer to Figure 46 on page 311.) At what altitude does the Class D airspace terminate over Hayward Airport (area 3)?

A. 1,500 feet MSL.
B. 1,499 feet MSL.
C. 3,000 feet MSL.

Answer (B) is correct. *(PHAK Chap 15)*
DISCUSSION: Refer to Fig. 46. Hayward Airport is located just to the southeast of area 3. To the northeast is the number 15 inside a square box with a "-" minus sign before the ceiling number. When a Class D airspace lies under a higher class airspace, the published ceiling is part of the higher class of airspace. In this figure, the ceiling of Hayward Airport extends to, but does not include, 1,500 feet MSL.
Answer (A) is incorrect. Hayward Airport is located just to the southeast of area 3. To the northeast is the number 15 inside a square box with a "-" minus sign before the ceiling number. When a Class D airspace lies under a higher class airspace, the published ceiling is part of the higher class of airspace. In this figure, the ceiling of Hayward Airport extends to, but does not include, 1,500 feet MSL. Answer (C) is incorrect. The 100/30 indicates that Class B airspace in the area of Hayward Airport is from 3,000 feet to 10,000 feet. The 30 does not indicate the termination of Hayward Airport's Class D airspace.

34. (Refer to Figure 46 on page 311.) The airport immediately northwest of Metropolitan Oakland International (OAK) (area 3) is a

A. seaplane base.
B. closed airport.
C. private airport.

Answer (B) is correct. *(ACL)*
DISCUSSION: The symbol of an open circle with an X over it means the airport is abandoned and closed.
Answer (A) is incorrect. A seaplane base is depicted on a sectional chart using an anchor symbol. Answer (C) is incorrect. A private airport is depicted on a sectional chart using a solid magenta circle and a runway symbol. Additionally, the designation "(Pvt)" will follow the airport name.

35. (Refer to Figure 46 on page 311.) What is the ceiling of the Class C airspace surrounding San Jose International Airport (area 2)?

A. 2,500 feet AGL.
B. 4,000 feet MSL.
C. 6,000 feet MSL.

Answer (B) is correct. *(ACL)*
DISCUSSION: Refer to Fig. 46. Area 2 is in the lower right-hand corner of the chart. San Jose International Airport is encircled by magenta solid lines. Note also the magenta "40" above the "SFC" (separated by a line) south of the airport. These indicate Class C airspace extending upward from the surface to 4,000 ft. MSL.
Answer (A) is incorrect. This many feet MSL, not AGL, is the floor, not ceiling, of the Class C airspace shelf area to the southwest of the airport. Answer (C) is incorrect. This is the floor of the Class B airspace just northwest of the airport, not the ceiling of the San Jose Class C airspace.

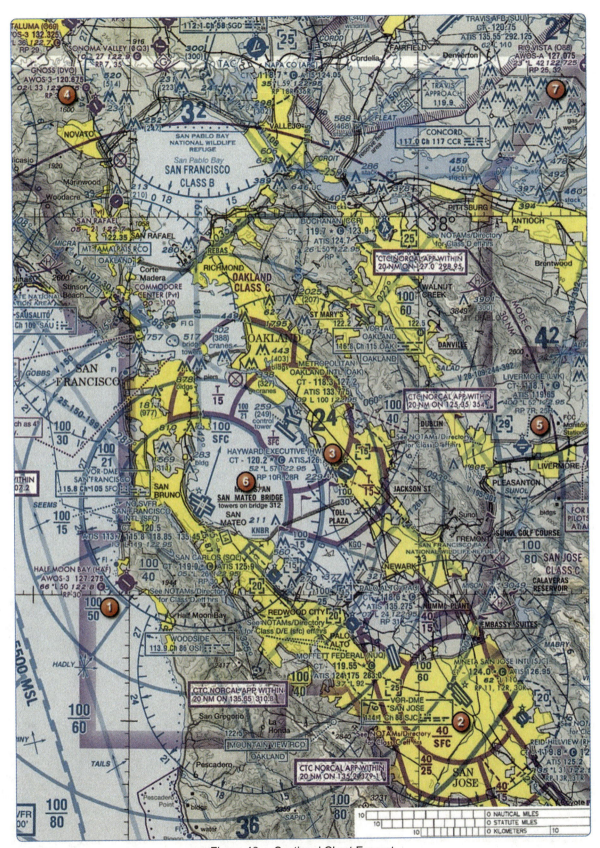

Figure 46. – Sectional Chart Excerpt.
NOTE: Chart is not to scale and should not be used for navigation. Use associated scale.

36. (Refer to Figure 46 on page 313.) What does the figure 2^4 (area 6) indicate?

A. Maximum elevation figure for that quadrangle.
B. Minimum safe altitude when approaching San Francisco.
C. Height above ground of the tallest obstruction for that quadrangle.

Answer (A) is correct. *(ACL)*
DISCUSSION: Refer to Fig. 46. Area 6 is near the center toward the left-hand side of the chart. The figure 2^4 northeast of San Francisco International Airport is the maximum elevation figure (MEF) for that quadrangle bounded by lines of latitude and longitude. The MEF is given in ft. MSL and is based on information available concerning the highest known feature in each quadrangle, including terrain and obstructions.
Answer (B) is incorrect. Minimum safe altitudes are shown on IFR approach plates, not VFR sectionals. Answer (C) is incorrect. The MEF is given above MSL, not AGL, and is based on terrain and obstructions, not just obstructions.

37. (Refer to Figure 46 on page 313.) The minimum avionics equipment necessary to operate in the airspace above 10,000 feet MSL over San Francisco International Airport (area 6) is

A. transponder and encoding altimeter.
B. two-way radio communications equipment.
C. two-way radio communications equipment, transponder, and encoding altimeter.

Answer (A) is correct. *(ACL)*
DISCUSSION: Refer to Fig. 46. Area 6 is near the center toward the left-hand side of the chart. San Francisco International Airport is encircled by blue solid lines. Note also the "100" above the "SFC" (separated by a line) northeast of the airport. These indicate Class B airspace extending upward from the surface to 10,000 ft. MSL. Class E airspace extends upward from 10,000 ft. MSL to the base of the overlying airspace (here, Class A airspace at 18,000 ft. MSL).
A transponder with encoding altimeter is required when operating above the ceiling and within the lateral boundaries of a Class B airspace area up to 10,000 ft. MSL in all airspace of the 48 contiguous United States and the District of Columbia at and above 10,000 ft. MSL, excluding airspace within 2,500 ft. AGL.
Answer (B) is incorrect. This airspace is Class E, where there is no minimum avionics equipment requirement. However, a transponder with encoding altimeter is required when operating within 30 NM of the primary Class B airport, as indicated by the thin magenta circle labeled Mode C 30 NM. Answer (C) is incorrect. This airspace is Class E, where there is no minimum avionics equipment requirement. However, a transponder with encoding altimeter is required when operating within 30 NM of the primary Class B airport, as indicated by the thin magenta circle labeled Mode C 30 NM.

38. (Refer to Figure 46 on page 313.) The minimum avionics equipment necessary to operate in the airspace above 8,000 feet MSL over San Francisco International Airport (area 6) is

A. transponder and encoding altimeter.
B. two-way radio communications equipment.
C. two-way radio communications equipment, transponder, and encoding altimeter.

Answer (C) is correct. *(ACL)*
DISCUSSION: Refer to Fig. 46. Area 6 is near the center toward the left-hand side of the chart. San Francisco International Airport is encircled by blue solid lines. Note also the "100" above the "SFC" (separated by a line) northeast of the airport. These indicate Class B airspace extending upward from the surface to 10,000 ft. MSL.
A transponder with encoding altimeter as well as two-way radio communications equipment are required when operating in a Class B airspace area.
Answer (A) is incorrect. Two-way radio communications equipment is required in Class B airspace. Answer (B) is incorrect. A Mode C transponder and encoding altimeter are also required to operate in Class B airspace.

39. (Refer to Figure 46 on page 313.) The area around Sonoma Valley (0Q3) (area 4) is a

A. parachute jumping area.
B. glider operating area.
C. hot air balloon launch area.

Answer (B) is correct. *(ACL)*
DISCUSSION: A glider operating area is depicted on a sectional chart using a glider image with the letter G above it enclosed in a diamond.
Answer (A) is incorrect. A parachute symbol near an airport means that parachute jumping operations are conducted there. You should consult the Chart Supplement for active jumping times. Answer (C) is incorrect. Hot air balloon launch areas are not specifically depicted on sectional aeronautical charts.

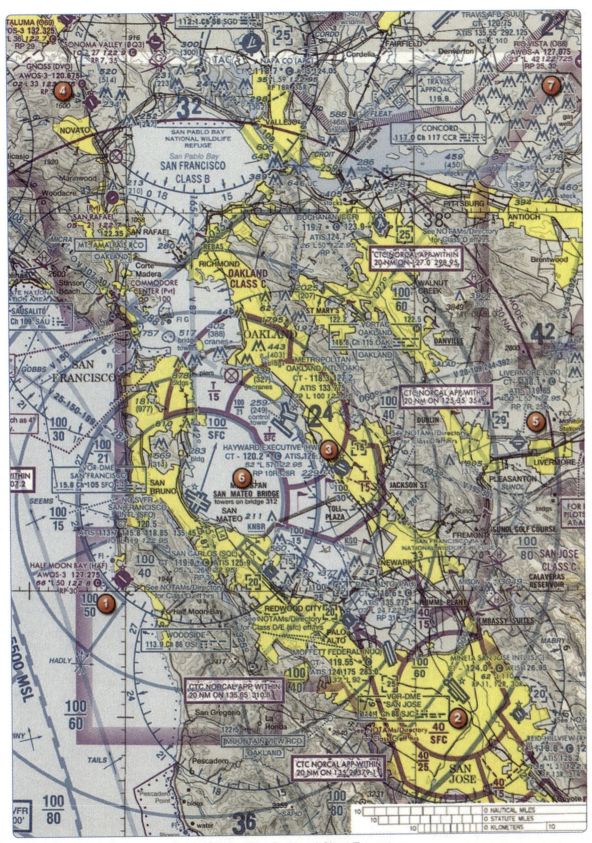

Figure 46. – Sectional Chart Excerpt.
NOTE: Chart is not to scale and should not be used for navigation. Use associated scale.

40. Which statement about longitude and latitude is true?

A. Lines of longitude are parallel to the Equator.
B. Lines of longitude cross the Equator at right angles.
C. The 0° line of latitude passes through Greenwich, England.

Answer (B) is correct. *(PHAK Chap 16)*
DISCUSSION: Lines of longitude are drawn from the north pole to the south pole and cross the equator at right angles. They indicate the number of degrees east and west of the 0° line of longitude, which passes through Greenwich, England.
Answer (A) is incorrect. Lines of latitude, not longitude, are parallel to the equator. Answer (C) is incorrect. The 0° line of longitude, not latitude, passes through Greenwich, England.

41. When diverting to an alternate airport because of an emergency, pilots should

A. rely upon radio as the primary method of navigation.
B. complete all plotting, measuring, and computations involved before diverting.
C. apply rule-of-thumb computations, estimates, and other appropriate shortcuts to divert to the new course as soon as possible.

Answer (C) is correct. *(PHAK Chap 16)*
DISCUSSION: When diverting to an alternate airport because of an emergency, time is usually of the essence. Accordingly, you should divert to the new course ASAP. Rule-of-thumb computations, estimates, and any other shortcuts are appropriate.
Answer (A) is incorrect. Any appropriate means of navigation is satisfactory. Answer (B) is incorrect. In an emergency, there is not time to complete all plotting, measuring, and computations before diverting.

42. When planning a distance flight, true course measurements on a Sectional Aeronautical Chart should be made at a meridian near the midpoint of the course because the

A. values of isogonic lines change from point to point.
B. angles formed by lines of longitude and the course line vary from point to point.
C. angles formed by isogonic lines and lines of latitude vary from point to point.

Answer (B) is correct. *(PHAK Chap 16)*
DISCUSSION: When measuring a true course on a Sectional Aeronautical Chart using a meridian, one should make the measurement at the midpoint of the course. While lines of latitude are parallel to one another, lines of longitude (meridians) (going from pole to pole) are not. Therefore, to obtain the best average measure of true course, one should measure the course at the midpoint and on a meridian.
Answer (A) is incorrect. Isogonic lines are lines of magnetic variation. Answer (C) is incorrect. Isogonic lines are lines of magnetic variation.

8.2 Climb Calculations

43. GIVEN:

Departure path	straight out
Takeoff time	1030 DST
Winds during climb	180° at 30 kts
True course during climb	160°
Airport elevation	1,500 ft
True airspeed	125 kts
Rate of climb	500 ft/min

What would be the distance and time upon reaching 8,500 feet MSL?

A. 20 NM and 1047 DST.
B. 23 NM and 1044 DST.
C. 25 NM and 1047 DST.

Answer (B) is correct. *(PH SU 9)*
DISCUSSION: Given the rate of climb of 500 fpm and a climb from 1,500 ft. to 8,500 ft., you will climb 7,000 ft. in 14 min. (7,000 ÷ 500). The time will be 1044 DST. Since the wind is from the south, almost a headwind at 30 kt., the groundspeed will be 96 kt. In 14 min., you would go about 23 NM.
Note that this problem should normally be worked out on a flight computer, but you can do it intuitively and logically with simple math much more quickly.
Answer (A) is incorrect. The time required for the climb is 14 min., not 17 min. Answer (C) is incorrect. The time required for the climb is 14 min., not 17 min.

44. GIVEN:

Departure path	straight out
Takeoff time	1435Z
Winds during climb	175° at 25 kts
True course during climb	155°
Airport elevation	2,000 ft
True airspeed	130 kts
Rate of climb	500 ft/min

What would be the distance and time upon reaching 8,000 feet MSL?

A. 27 NM and 1455Z.

B. 24 NM and 1452Z.

C. 21 NM and 1447Z.

Answer (C) is correct. *(PH SU 9)*
DISCUSSION: Given the rate of climb of 500 fpm and a climb from 2,000 ft. to 8,000 ft., you will climb 6,000 ft. in 12 min. (6,000 ÷ 500). The time will be 1447Z. Since the wind is from the south, almost a headwind at 25 kt., the groundspeed will be slightly more than 100 kt. In 12 min., you would go about 20 NM.
  Note that this problem should normally be worked out on a flight computer, but you can do it intuitively and logically with simple math much more quickly.
  Answer (A) is incorrect. The time required for the climb is 12 min., not 20 min. Answer (B) is incorrect. The time required for the climb is 12 min., not 17 min.

8.3 Speed, Distance, and Fuel Calculations

45. GIVEN:

Distance	300 NM
True course	260°
Wind	245° at 45 kts
True airspeed	119 kts
Rate of fuel consumption	12.7 gal/hr

What would be the approximate groundspeed and amount of fuel consumed?

A. 84 knots; 46.1 gallons.

B. 75 knots; 50.8 gallons.

C. 75 knots; 49.1 gallons.

Answer (B) is correct. *(PH SU 9)*
DISCUSSION: On the wind side of your flight computer, place the wind direction of 245 under the true index. Then measure up from the grommet and mark 45 kt. with a pencil. Next, place the true course of 260° under the true index. Then slide the scale such that the pencil mark is on the true airspeed of 119 kt. and read the groundspeed to be 75 kt. (under the grommet). On the other side of the computer, put 75 kt. on the outer scale under the index of 60 min. Find 300 NM on the outer scale and read 240 min., or 4 hr., under it. Four hr. (240 min.) at 12.7 GPH would require 50.8 gal. of fuel.
  Answer (A) is incorrect. A groundspeed of 84 kt. would require a TAS of 128 kt., not 119 kt. Answer (C) is incorrect. A fuel consumption of 49.1 gal. would require the rate of fuel consumption to be 12.3 gal./hr., not 12.7 gal./hr.

46. GIVEN:

Distance	200 NM
True course	320°
Wind	215° at 25 kts
True airspeed	116 kts
Rate of fuel consumption	19 gal/hr

What would be the approximate groundspeed and amount of fuel consumed?

A. 120 knots; 31.7 gallons.

B. 132 knots; 28.9 gallons.

C. 115 knots; 33.1 gallons.

Answer (A) is correct. *(PH SU 9)*
DISCUSSION: On the wind side of your flight computer, place the wind direction of 215 under the true index. Then measure up from the grommet and mark 25 kt. with a pencil. Next, put the true course of 320° under the true index. Then slide the scale such that the pencil mark is on the true airspeed of 116 kt. and read the groundspeed to be 120 kt. (under the grommet). On the other side of the computer, put 120 kt. on the outer scale under the index of 60 min. Find 200 NM on the outer scale, under which is 100 min., or 1 hr. and 40 min. At 19 GPH, this would require 31.7 gal.
  Answer (B) is incorrect. A groundspeed of 132 kt. would require a TAS of 128 kt., not 116 kt. Answer (C) is incorrect. A groundspeed of 115 kt. would require a TAS of 111 kt., not 116 kt.

47. GIVEN:

Usable fuel at takeoff	36 gal
Fuel consumption rate	12.4 gal/hr
Constant groundspeed	140 kts
Flight time since takeoff	48 min

According to 14 CFR Part 91, how much farther can an airplane be flown under night VFR?

A. 189 NM.

B. 224 NM.

C. 294 NM.

Answer (A) is correct. *(PH SU 9)*
DISCUSSION: Place 12.4 GPH on the outer scale over the index of your flight computer. Then find 36 on the outer scale and determine that the usable fuel at takeoff would last for 2 hr. and 54 min. Subtract the 48 min. already flown to get 2 hr. and 6 min.; 2 hr. and 6 min. minus the Part 91 night VFR fuel reserve of 45 min. leaves 1 hr. and 21 min. (1.35 hr.). Flying 1.35 hr. at 140 kt. is sufficient to travel 189 NM.
  Answer (B) is incorrect. This is the remaining distance the airplane can be flown under day VFR (a 30-min. fuel reserve), not night VFR. Answer (C) is incorrect. This is the remaining distance the aircraft can be flown with no fuel reserve.

48. (Refer to Figure 40 below.) The line from point A to point B of the wind triangle represents

A. true heading and airspeed.
B. true course and groundspeed.
C. groundspeed and true heading.

Answer (A) is correct. *(PHAK Chap 16)*
DISCUSSION: The line connecting point A to point B on the wind triangle represents the true heading and airspeed line.
Answer (B) is incorrect. The line from point B to point C, not point A, represents the true course and groundspeed line. Answer (C) is incorrect. These are values obtained through using a wind triangle. Groundspeed is obtained by measuring the length of the TC line using the same scale as the chart (point B to point C). True heading is the direction, measured in degrees clockwise from true north, in which the nose of the plane should point to make good the desired course (point A to point B).

49. (Refer to Figure 40 below.) The line from point C to point B of the wind triangle represents

A. airspeed and heading.
B. groundspeed and true course.
C. true heading and groundspeed.

Answer (B) is correct. *(PHAK Chap 16)*
DISCUSSION: The line from point C to point B on the wind triangle represents the true course and groundspeed line.
Answer (A) is incorrect. The line from point A, not point C, to point B represents the true heading and airspeed line. Answer (C) is incorrect. These are values obtained through using a wind triangle. Groundspeed is obtained by measuring the length of the TC line using the same scale as the chart (point C to point B). True heading is the direction, measured in degrees clockwise from true north, in which the nose of the plane should point to make good the desired course (point A to point B).

50. (Refer to Figure 40 below.) The line from point C to point A of the wind triangle represents

A. wind direction and velocity.
B. true course and groundspeed.
C. true heading and groundspeed.

Answer (A) is correct. *(PHAK Chap 16)*
DISCUSSION: The line from point C to point A on the wind triangle represents the wind direction and velocity line.
Answer (B) is incorrect. The line from point C to point B, not point A, represents the true course and groundspeed line. Answer (C) is incorrect. These are values obtained through using a wind triangle. Groundspeed is obtained by measuring the length of the TC line using the same scale as the chart (point C to point B). True heading is the direction, measured in degrees clockwise from true north, in which the nose of the plane should point to make good the desired course (point A to point B).

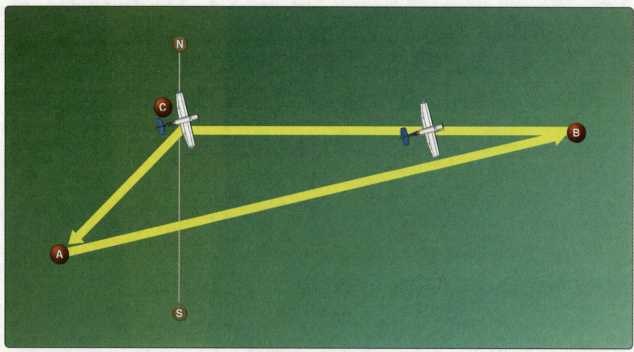

Figure 40. – Wind Triangle.

SU 8: Navigation

51. GIVEN:

Usable fuel at takeoff	36 gal
Fuel consumption rate	12.4 gal/hr
Constant groundspeed	140 kts
Flight time since takeoff	48 min

According to 14 CFR Part 91, how much farther can an airplane be flown under day VFR?

A. 294 NM.
B. 224 NM.
C. 189 NM.

Answer (B) is correct. *(PH SU 9)*
   DISCUSSION: Place 12.4 GPH on the outer scale over the index of your flight computer. Then find 36 on the outer scale and determine that the usable fuel at takeoff would last for 2 hr. and 54 min. Subtract the 48 min. already expired to get 2 hr. and 6 min.; 2 hr. and 6 min. minus the Part 91 day VFR fuel reserve of 30 min. leaves 1 hr. and 36 min. (1.6 hr.). Flying 1.6 hr. at 140 kt. is sufficient to travel 224 NM.
   Answer (A) is incorrect. This is the remaining distance the airplane can be flown with no fuel reserve. Answer (C) is incorrect. This is the remaining distance the airplane can be flown under night VFR (a 45-min. fuel reserve), not day VFR.

52. On a cross-country flight, point A is crossed at 1500 hours and the plan is to reach point B at 1530 hours. Use the following information to determine the indicated airspeed required to reach point B on schedule.

Distance between A and B	70 NM
Forecast wind	310° at 15 kts
Pressure altitude	8,000 ft
Ambient temperature	−10°C
True course	270°

The required indicated airspeed would be approximately

A. 126 knots.
B. 137 knots.
C. 152 knots.

Answer (B) is correct. *(PH SU 9)*
   DISCUSSION: First determine the required groundspeed to reach point B at 1530 by placing 70 NM on the outer scale over 30 min. on the inner scale to determine a groundspeed of 140 kt. On the wind side of the computer, put the wind direction of 310° under the true index and put a pencil mark 15 kt. up from the grommet. Next, turn the inner scale so the 270° true course is under the true index and put the grommet over the groundspeed. Note that to obtain the 140-kt. groundspeed, you need a 152-kt. true airspeed. Next, on the computer side, put the air temperature of −10°C over 8,000 ft. altitude. Then find the true airspeed of 152 kt. on the outer scale, which lies over approximately 137 kt. indicated airspeed on the inner scale.
   Answer (A) is incorrect. This would be your indicated airspeed if you had a true airspeed of 140 kt. Note that 140 kt. is your groundspeed, not true airspeed. Answer (C) is incorrect. This is your required true airspeed, not indicated airspeed.

53. GIVEN:

Usable fuel at takeoff	40 gal
Fuel consumption rate	12.2 gal/hr
Constant groundspeed	120 kts
Flight time since takeoff	1 hr 30 min

According to 14 CFR Part 91, how much farther can an airplane be flown under night VFR?

A. 216 NM.
B. 156 NM.
C. 121 NM.

Answer (C) is correct. *(PH SU 9)*
   DISCUSSION: Place 12.2 GPH on the outer scale over the index of your flight computer. Then find 40 on the outer scale and determine that the usable fuel at takeoff would last for 3 hr. and 17 min. Subtract the 1 hr. and 30 min. already flown to get 1 hr. and 47 min.; 1 hr. and 47 min. minus the Part 91 night VFR fuel reserve of 45 min. leaves 1 hr. and 2 min. (1.03 hr.). Flying 1.03 hr. at 120 kt. is sufficient to travel 124 NM.
   Answer (A) is incorrect. This is the remaining distance the airplane can be flown with no fuel reserve. Answer (B) is incorrect. This is the remaining distance the airplane can be flown under day VFR (a 30-min. fuel reserve), not night VFR.

54. If fuel consumption is 15.3 gallons per hour and groundspeed is 167 knots, how much fuel is required for an aircraft to travel 620 NM?

A. 63 gallons.
B. 60 gallons.
C. 57 gallons.

Answer (C) is correct. *(PH SU 9)*
   DISCUSSION: Divide 620 NM by 167 kt. to obtain 3.7 hr. Then multiply 3.7 hr. by 15.3 GPH to obtain 57 gal.
   Answer (A) is incorrect. Sixty-three gal. would require a groundspeed of 151 kt. and traveling 620 NM, or traveling 688 NM at a groundspeed of 167 kt. Answer (B) is incorrect. Sixty gal. would require a groundspeed of 158 kt. and traveling 620 NM, or traveling 655 NM at a groundspeed of 167 kt.

55. If an aircraft is consuming 91 pounds of fuel per hour and groundspeed is 168 knots, how much fuel is required to travel 457 NM?

A. 291 pounds.
B. 265 pounds.
C. 248 pounds.

Answer (C) is correct. *(PH SU 9)*
   DISCUSSION: Divide 457 NM by 168 kt. to obtain 2.72 hr. Then multiply 2.72 hr. by 91 PPH to obtain 248 lb.
   Answer (A) is incorrect. This would require the groundspeed to change to 143 kt. or the distance to increase to 537 NM. Answer (B) is incorrect. This would require the groundspeed to decrease to 157 kt. or the distance to increase to 489 NM.

56. How far will an aircraft travel in 2-1/2 minutes with a groundspeed of 98 knots?

A. 2.45 NM.
B. 3.35 NM.
C. 4.08 NM.

Answer (C) is correct. *(PH SU 9)*
DISCUSSION: To determine the distance traveled in 2 1/2 min. at 98 kt., note that 98 kt. is 1.6 NM/min. (98 ÷ 60 = 1.633). Thus, in 2 1/2 min., you will have traveled a total of 4.08 NM (1.633 × 2.5 = 4.08).
Alternatively, put 98 on the outer scale of your flight computer over the index on the inner scale. Find 2.5 min. on the inner scale, above which is 4.1 NM.
Answer (A) is incorrect. For 2.45 NM to be true, you would need a groundspeed of approximately 59 kt. Answer (B) is incorrect. For 3.35 NM to be true, you would need a groundspeed of approximately 80 kt.

57. How far will an aircraft travel in 3-1/2 minutes if its groundspeed is 165 knots?

A. 5.8 NM.
B. 9.6 NM.
C. 12.8 NM.

Answer (B) is correct. *(PH SU 9)*
DISCUSSION: To determine the distance traveled in 3 1/2 min. at 165 kt., note that 165 kt. is 2.75 NM/min. (165 ÷ 60 = 2.75). Thus, in 3 1/2 min., you will have traveled a total of 9.6 NM (2.75 × 3.5 = 9.6).
Alternatively, put 165 on the outer scale of your flight computer over the index on the inner scale. Find 3.5 min. on the inner scale, above which is 9.6 NM.
Answer (A) is incorrect. For 5.8 NM to be true, you would require a groundspeed of approximately 99 kt. Answer (C) is incorrect. For 12.8 NM to be true, you would require a groundspeed of approximately 219 kt.

58. How far will an aircraft travel in 3-1/2 minutes if its groundspeed is 65 knots?

A. 3.8 NM.
B. 3.3 NM.
C. 2.2 NM.

Answer (A) is correct. *(PH SU 9)*
DISCUSSION: To determine the distance traveled in 3 1/2 min. at 65 kt., note that 65 kt. is 1.08 NM/min. (65 ÷ 60 = 1.08). Thus, in 3 1/2 min., you will have traveled a total of 3.8 NM (1.08 × 3.5 = 3.78).
Answer (B) is incorrect. Traveling 3.3 NM would require a speed of 55 kt. Answer (C) is incorrect. Traveling 2.2 NM would require a speed of 38 kt.

59. How far will an aircraft travel in 3-1/2 minutes if its groundspeed is 55 knots?

A. 3.2 NM.
B. 3.6 NM.
C. 4.2 NM.

Answer (A) is correct. *(PH SU 9)*
DISCUSSION: To determine the distance traveled in 3 1/2 min. at 55 kts., note that 55 kts. is 0.9 NM/min. (55 ÷ 60 = 0.9). Thus, in 3 1/2 min., you will have traveled a total of 3.2 NM (0.9 × 3.5 = 3.2).
Answer (B) is incorrect. Traveling 3.6 NM would require 3 minutes 55 seconds. Answer (C) is incorrect. Traveling 4.2 NM would require 4 minutes 45 seconds.

60. On a cross-country flight, point X is crossed at 1015 and arrival at point Y is expected at 1025. Use the following information to determine the indicated airspeed required to reach point Y on schedule.

Distance between X and Y	27 NM
Forecast wind	240° at 30 kts
Pressure altitude	5,500 ft
Ambient temperature	+05°C
True course	100°

The required indicated airspeed would be approximately

A. 162 knots.
B. 140 knots.
C. 128 knots.

Answer (C) is correct. *(PH SU 9)*
DISCUSSION: First determine the required groundspeed to reach point Y at 1025 by placing 27 NM on the outer scale over 10 min. on the inner scale to determine a groundspeed of 162 kt. On the wind side of the computer, put the wind direction of 240° under the true index and put a pencil mark 30 kt. up from the grommet. Next, turn the inner scale so the 100° true course is under the true index and put the grommet over the groundspeed. Note that to obtain the 162-kt. groundspeed, you need a 140-kt. true airspeed. Next, on the computer side, put the air temperature of +05°C over 5,500 ft. altitude. Then find the true airspeed of 140 kt. on the outer scale, which lies over approximately 128 kt. indicated airspeed on the inner scale.
Answer (A) is incorrect. This is your required groundspeed, not indicated airspeed. Answer (B) is incorrect. This is your required true airspeed, not indicated airspeed.

61. On a cross-country flight, point X is crossed at 1550 and the plan is to reach point Y at 1620. Use the following information to determine the indicated airspeed required to reach point Y on schedule.

Distance between X and Y	70 NM
Forecast wind	115° at 25 kts
Pressure altitude	9,000 ft
Ambient temperature	–05°C
True course	088°

The required indicated airspeed would be approximately

    A. 138 knots.

    B. 143 knots.

    C. 162 knots.

Answer (B) is correct. *(PH SU 9)*
    DISCUSSION: First determine the required groundspeed to reach point Y at 1620 by placing 70 NM on the outer scale over 30 min. on the inner scale to determine a groundspeed of 140 kt. On the wind side of the computer, put the wind direction of 115° under the true index and put a pencil mark 25 kt. up from the grommet. Next, turn the inner scale so the 088° true course is under the true index and put the grommet over the groundspeed. Note that to obtain the 140-kt. groundspeed, you need a 162-kt. true airspeed. Next, on the computer side, put the air temperature of –05°C over 9,000 ft. altitude. Then find the true airspeed of 161 kt. on the outer scale, which lies over approximately 143 kt. indicated airspeed on the inner scale.
    Answer (A) is incorrect. This is your approximate groundspeed, not indicated airspeed. Answer (C) is incorrect. This is your required true airspeed, not indicated airspeed.

62. GIVEN:

True course	258°
Variation	10°E
Indicated airspeed	142 kts
Ambient temperature	+05°C
Pressure altitude	6,500 ft
Forecast wind	350° at 30 kts

Under these conditions, the magnetic heading and groundspeed would be approximately

    A. 260° and 155 knots.

    B. 270° and 157 knots.

    C. 280° and 155 knots.

Answer (A) is correct. *(PH SU 9)*
    DISCUSSION: First compute the true airspeed by using the right-hand side of the inner window scale of your flight computer. Put the temperature of +05°C over the pressure altitude of 6,500 ft. Then note the indicated airspeed of 142 kt. on the inner scale to be 157 kt. true airspeed on the outer scale. Second, on the wind side of your flight computer, put the wind direction of 350° under the true index and mark the wind velocity of 30 kt. up from the center grommet with a pencil. Then turn the computer so that the true course of 258° is under the true index and the pencil mark is on the true airspeed of 157 kt. The wind correction is 12° to the right, so add 12° to 258° to get a true heading of 270°. Next, subtract the magnetic variation of 10°E to obtain a magnetic heading of 260°. Note that the grommet is on 155 kt., which is the groundspeed.
    Answer (B) is incorrect. The true heading, not magnetic heading, is 270°. Answer (C) is incorrect. To obtain a magnetic heading of 280°, the magnetic variation of 10°E was incorrectly added to instead of subtracted from the true heading.

63. GIVEN:

True course	330°
Variation	15°E
Indicated airspeed	160 kts
Ambient temperature	–10°C
Pressure altitude	4,500 ft
Forecast wind	090° at 25 kts

Under these conditions, the magnetic heading and groundspeed would be approximately

    A. 323° and 177 knots.

    B. 332° and 166 knots.

    C. 340° and 177 knots.

Answer (A) is correct. *(PH SU 9)*
    DISCUSSION: First compute the true airspeed by using the right-hand side of the inner window scale of your flight computer. Put the temperature of –10°C over the pressure altitude of 4,500 ft. Then note the indicated airspeed of 160 kt. on the inner scale to be 166 kt. true airspeed on the outer scale. Second, on the wind side of your flight computer, put the wind direction of 090° under the true index and mark the wind velocity of 25 kt. up from the center grommet with a pencil. Then turn the computer so that the true course of 330° is under the true index and the pencil mark is on the true airspeed of 166 kt. The wind correction is 8° to the right, so add 8° to 330° to get a true heading of 338°. Next, subtract the magnetic variation of 15E° to obtain a magnetic heading of 323°. Note that the grommet is on 177 kt., which is the groundspeed.
    Answer (B) is incorrect. The computed true airspeed, not groundspeed, is 166 kt. Answer (C) is incorrect. The true heading is approximately 340°. The magnetic variation of 15°E must be subtracted from true heading to determine the magnetic heading.

64. GIVEN:

True course	238°
Variation	3°W
Indicated airspeed	160 kts
Ambient temperature	–15°C
Pressure altitude	8,500 ft
Forecast wind	160° at 25 kts

Under these conditions, the magnetic heading and groundspeed would be approximately

A. 224° and 171 knots.
B. 233° and 171 knots.
C. 241° and 178 knots.

Answer (B) is correct. *(PH SU 9)*
DISCUSSION: First compute the true airspeed by using the right-hand side of the inner window scale of your flight computer. Put the temperature of –15°C over the pressure altitude of 8,500 ft. Then note the indicated airspeed of 160 kt. on the inner scale to be 177 kt. true airspeed on the outer scale. Second, on the wind side of your flight computer, put the wind direction of 160° under the true index and mark the wind velocity of 25 kt. up from the center grommet with a pencil. Then turn the computer so that the true course of 238° is under the true index and the pencil mark is on the true airspeed of 177 kt. The wind correction is 8° to the left, so subtract 8° from 238° to get a true heading of 230°. Next, add the magnetic variation of 3°W to obtain a magnetic heading of 233°. Note that the grommet is on 171 kt., which is the groundspeed.
Answer (A) is incorrect. To obtain a magnetic heading of 224°, the magnetic variation of 3°W was incorrectly subtracted twice instead of added to the true heading. Answer (C) is incorrect. The magnetic variation was added to the true course of 238° to obtain 241°, and no correction was made for the wind correction angle. Also, 178 kt. is the approximate true airspeed, not groundspeed.

65. On a cross-country flight, point X is crossed at 1015 local. What is your expected arrival time at point Y? Use the following information to determine your ETA.

Distance between X and Y = 32 NM
Forecast wind = 240° at 25 kts
Pressure altitude = 5,500 ft
Ambient temperature = +05°C
True course = 100°
The indicated airspeed is 110 knots.

A. 1040 local.
B. 1059 local.
C. 1029 local.

Answer (C) is correct. *(PH SU 9)*
DISCUSSION: First compute the true airspeed by using the right-hand side of the inner window scale of your flight computer. Put the temperature of +05°C over the pressure altitude of 5,500 ft. Then note the indicated airspeed of 110 kt. on the inner scale to be 120 kt. true airspeed on the outer scale. Second, on the wind side of your flight computer, place the wind direction of 240 under the true index. Then measure up from the grommet and mark 25 kt. with a pencil. Next, put the true course of 100° under the true index. Then slide the scale such that the pencil mark is on the true airspeed of 120 kt. and read the groundspeed to be 138 kt. (under the grommet).
On the E6B side of the computer, put 138 kt. on the outer scale over rate triangle. Find 32 NM on the outer scale. Read the estimated time en route (ETE) time as 14 minutes on the inner scale under the distance. Add the ETE to the time crossing point X to get the arrival time at point Y (1015 + 14 = 1029).
Answer (A) is incorrect. An elapsed time of 25 minutes requires a groundspeed of 77 kt. The groundspeed is 138 kt. Answer (B) is incorrect. An elapsed time of 44 minutes requires a groundspeed of 44 kt. The groundspeed is 138 kt.

8.4 Off-Course Corrections

66. After 141 miles are flown from the departure point, the aircraft's position is located 11 miles off course. If 71 miles remain to be flown, what approximate total correction should be made to converge on the destination?

A. 8°.
B. 11°.
C. 14°.

Answer (C) is correct. *(IFH Chap 9)*
DISCUSSION: To determine the correction to converge on the destination, use these formulas:

$$\frac{\text{Miles Off Course}}{\text{Miles Flown}} \times 60 = ° \text{ to parallel}$$

$$\frac{\text{Miles Off Course}}{\text{Miles Remaining}} \times 60 = ° \text{ to intercept}$$

Given 141 mi. flown and 71 mi. to go, you are 11 mi. off course. Plug these figures into the above formulas to obtain the results below, indicating a correction of 14°.

$$(11 \div 141) \times 60 = 4.7°$$
$$(11 \div 71) \times 60 = \underline{9.3°}$$
$$14.0°$$

Answer (A) is incorrect. For an 8° total correction to converge on the destination, the aircraft's position would need to be a little more than 6 mi. off course. Answer (B) is incorrect. For an 11° total correction to converge on the destination, the aircraft's position would need to be approximately 9 mi. off course.

67. After 150 miles are flown from the departure point, the aircraft's position is located 8 miles off course. If 160 miles remain to be flown, what approximate total correction should be made to converge on the destination?

A. 6°.
B. 9°.
C. 12°.

Answer (A) is correct. *(IFH Chap 9)*
DISCUSSION: To determine the correction to converge on the destination, use these formulas:

$$\frac{\text{Miles Off Course}}{\text{Miles Flown}} \times 60 = °\text{ to parallel}$$

$$\frac{\text{Miles Off Course}}{\text{Miles Remaining}} \times 60 = °\text{ to intercept}$$

Given 150 mi. flown and 160 mi. to go, you are 8 mi. off course. Plug these figures into the above formulas to obtain the results below, indicating a correction of 6.2°.

$$(8 \div 150) \times 60 = 3.2°$$
$$(8 \div 160) \times 60 = \underline{3.0°}$$
$$6.2°$$

Answer (B) is incorrect. For a 9° total correction to converge on the destination, the aircraft's position would need to be approximately 12 mi. off course. Answer (C) is incorrect. For a 12° total correction to converge on the destination, the aircraft's position would need to be approximately 16 mi. off course.

68. After 240 miles are flown from the departure point, the aircraft's position is located 25 miles off course. If 100 miles remain to be flown, what approximate total correction should be made to converge on the destination?

A. 15°.
B. 21°.
C. 30°.

Answer (B) is correct. *(IFH Chap 9)*
DISCUSSION: To determine the correction to converge on the destination, use these formulas:

$$\frac{\text{Miles Off Course}}{\text{Miles Flown}} \times 60 = °\text{ to parallel}$$

$$\frac{\text{Miles Off Course}}{\text{Miles Remaining}} \times 60 = °\text{ to intercept}$$

Given 240 mi. flown and 100 mi. to go, you are 25 mi. off course. Plug these figures into the above formulas to obtain the results below, indicating a correction of 21.25°.

$$(25 \div 240) \times 60 = 6.25°$$
$$(25 \div 100) \times 60 = \underline{15.00°}$$
$$21.25°$$

Answer (A) is incorrect. For a 15° total correction to converge on the destination, the aircraft's position would need to be approximately 18 mi. off course. Answer (C) is incorrect. For a 30° total correction to converge on the destination, the aircraft's position would need to be a little more than 35 mi. off course.

8.5 Estimating Wind

69. If a true heading of 135° results in a ground track of 130° and a true airspeed of 135 knots results in a groundspeed of 140 knots, the wind would be from

A. 019° and 12 knots.
B. 200° and 13 knots.
C. 246° and 13 knots.

Answer (C) is correct. *(PH SU 9)*
DISCUSSION: To estimate your wind given true heading and a ground track, place the groundspeed under the grommet (140 kt.) with the ground track of 130° under the true index. Then find the true airspeed on the true airspeed arc of 135 kt., and put a pencil mark for a 5° right deviation (135° – 130° = +5°). Place the pencil mark on the centerline under the true index and note a wind from 246° under the true index. The pencil mark is now on 153 kt., which is about 13 kt. up from the grommet (153 – 140).
Answer (A) is incorrect. These would be your approximate wind and velocity for a 5° left wind correction, not right. Answer (B) is incorrect. These would be your approximate wind and velocity when at a true airspeed of 140 kt., not 135 kt., and a groundspeed of 135 kt., not 140 kt.

70. If a true heading of 350° results in a ground track of 335° and a true airspeed of 140 knots results in a groundspeed of 115 knots, the wind would be from

    A. 015° and 30 knots.
    B. 035° and 40 knots.
    C. 290° and 40 knots.

Answer (B) is correct. *(PH SU 9)*
    DISCUSSION: To estimate your wind given true heading and a ground track, place the groundspeed under the grommet (115 kt.) with the ground track of 335° under the true index. Then find the true airspeed on the true airspeed arc of 140 kt., and put a pencil mark for a 15° right deviation (350° – 335° = +15°). Place the pencil mark on the centerline under the true index and note a wind from 035° under the true index. The pencil mark is now on 155 kt., which is about 40 kt. up from the grommet (155 – 115).
    Answer (A) is incorrect. With the winds at 015° at 30 kt., it would be more of a headwind and less right wind correction would be needed to maintain a ground track of 335°. Answer (C) is incorrect. With the winds at 290° at 40 kt., it would require a left wind correction angle to maintain a ground track of 335° and the groundspeed would decrease.

71. If a true heading of 230° results in a ground track of 250° and a true airspeed of 160 knots results in a groundspeed of 175 knots, the wind would be from

    A. 135° and 59 knots.
    B. 165° and 60 knots.
    C. 343° and 60 knots.

Answer (A) is correct. *(PH SU 9)*
    DISCUSSION: To estimate your wind given true heading and a ground track, place the groundspeed under the grommet (175 kt.) with the ground track of 250° under the true index. Then find the true airspeed on the true airspeed arc of 160 kt., and put a pencil mark for a 20° left deviation (230° – 250° = –20°). Place the pencil mark on the centerline under the true index and note a wind from 135° under the true index. The pencil mark is now on 234 kt., which is about 59 kt. up from the grommet (234 – 175).
    Answer (B) is incorrect. With the winds at 165° at 60 kt., it would be a quartering headwind, which would decrease groundspeed by a considerable amount. Answer (C) is incorrect. With the winds at 343° at 60 kt., it would be a crosswind, but one that would require a right wind correction, not left.

8.6 Distance Measuring Equipment (DME)

72. Which distance is commonly displayed by a DME indicator?

    A. Slant-range distance in statute miles.
    B. Slant-range distance in nautical miles.
    C. The distance from the aircraft to a point at the same altitude directly above the VORTAC.

Answer (B) is correct. *(IFH Chap 9)*
    DISCUSSION: Distance measuring equipment (DME) measures the distance of the DME receiver from a VORTAC based upon the time it takes to transmit radio signals back and forth. Thus, it provides a slant-range distance. The calculations are commonly in nautical miles rather than in statute miles.
    Answer (A) is incorrect. The display is in nautical miles, not statute miles. Answer (C) is incorrect. The DME unit cannot determine the altitude AGL in order to find the horizontal rather than slant-range distance.

73. Which DME indication should you receive when you are directly over a VORTAC site at approximately 6,000 feet AGL?

    A. 0.
    B. 1.
    C. 1.3.

Answer (B) is correct. *(IFH Chap 9)*
    DISCUSSION: When you are 6,000 ft. AGL and the DME indicates 1 NM between the receiver and the station, you are directly over the station; i.e., 1 NM is approximately equal to 6,000 ft.
    Answer (A) is incorrect. Even directly over the station, you will receive slant-range distance. Six thousand ft. AGL is equal to 1 NM. Answer (C) is incorrect. Six thousand ft. is equal to 1 NM, not 1.3 NM.

74. Which statement is true concerning the operation of DME?

    A. DME operates in the VHF frequency band.
    B. Distance information received from DME is the actual horizontal distance from the station.
    C. DME coded identification is transmitted once for each three or four times that the VOR coded identification is transmitted.

Answer (C) is correct. *(AIM Para 1-1-7)*
    DISCUSSION: The DME-coded identification is transmitted once for each three or four times the VOR- or localizer-coded identification is transmitted. When either the VOR or the DME is inoperative, it is important to recognize which identifier is retained for the operating facility. A single coded identification with a repetitive interval of approximately 30 sec. indicates that the DME is operative.
    Answer (A) is incorrect. DME operates in the UHF spectrum between 962 and 1213 MHz. Answer (B) is incorrect. DME measures slant, not horizontal, distance.

75. The slant-range error of a DME is greatest at

A. low altitude directly over the facility.
B. high altitude directly over the facility.
C. high altitude and high range from the facility.

Answer (B) is correct. *(IFH Chap 9)*
DISCUSSION: The greatest slant-range error of DMEs occurs at high altitudes directly over the VOR facility. For example, if one were at 12,000 ft. AGL immediately over the VORTAC, the DME would show a distance from the VORTAC of approximately 2 NM.
Answer (A) is incorrect. At low altitude, the error is minimal. Answer (C) is incorrect. The farther you get from the VORTAC, the smaller the slant-range error is.

8.7 VHF Omnidirectional Range (VOR)

76. A particular VORTAC station is undergoing routine maintenance. This is evidenced by

A. removal of the identification feature.
B. removal of the voice feature of the TACAN.
C. transmitting a series of dashes after each identification signal.

Answer (A) is correct. *(AIM Para 1-1-3)*
DISCUSSION: When VORTACs are undergoing maintenance, the identification feature is not broadcast.
Answer (B) is incorrect. VORs, not TACANs, have voice units. Answer (C) is incorrect. Although the station may radiate a T-E-S-T code, the normal identification signal is removed.

77. When using a VOT to check the accuracy of a VOR receiver, with the CDI centered, what should the OBS indicate if no error exists?

A. 360° TO, 270° FROM.
B. 180° FROM, 360° TO.
C. 180° TO, 360° FROM.

Answer (C) is correct. *(AIM Para 1-1-4)*
DISCUSSION: A VOT transmits only the 360° radial. Thus, when using a VOT to check the accuracy of a VOR receiver the needle should be centered with either a 180° and (TO) indication or a 360° and (FROM) indication.
Answer (A) is incorrect. A VOT only transmits the 360° radial; thus, an indication of 270° FROM is not possible. If no error exists, the CDI should center with 180° TO or 360° FROM. Answer (B) is incorrect. The CDI will be centered, if no error exists, with 180° TO, not FROM, or 360° FROM, not TO.

78. The normal usable range of an L class VOR below 18,000 feet is

A. 25 NM.
B. 40 NM.
C. 100 NM.

Answer (B) is correct. *(PHAK Chap 16)*
DISCUSSION: L class VORs normally have a usable range of 40 NM below 18,000 ft.
Answer (A) is incorrect. This is the range for a T class VOR below 12,000 ft. Answer (C) is incorrect. This is the range of an H class VOR above 45,000 ft.

79. The normal usable range of a T class VOR below 12,000 feet is

A. 100 NM.
B. 40 NM.
C. 25 NM.

Answer (C) is correct. *(PHAK Chap 16)*
DISCUSSION: The range of a T class VOR below 12,000 ft. is 25 NM.
Answer (A) is incorrect. One hundred NM is the range of an H class VOR above 45,000 ft. Answer (B) is incorrect. Forty NM is the range of an L class VOR below 18,000 ft.

80. While maintaining a magnetic heading of 060° and a true airspeed of 130 knots, the 150° radial of a VOR is crossed at 1137 and the 140° radial at 1145. The approximate time and distance to the station would be

A. 38 minutes and 82 NM.
B. 42 minutes and 91 NM.
C. 48 minutes and 104 NM.

Answer (C) is correct. *(IFH Chap 9)*
DISCUSSION: Time to station is given by the following formula:

$$\frac{\text{Min. for bearing change}}{\text{Bearing change in degrees}} \times 60$$

$$\frac{8}{10} \times 60 = 48 \text{ min.}$$

At an airspeed of 130 kt., the airplane would fly 104 NM in 48 min.
Answer (A) is incorrect. For this to be true, the time for the 10° bearing change would have to be 6 min. 20 sec., not 8 min. Answer (B) is incorrect. For this to be true, the time for the 10° bearing change would have to be 7 min., not 8 min.

81. While maintaining a magnetic heading of 180° and a true airspeed of 130 knots, the 270° radial of a VOR is crossed at 1037 and the 260° radial at 1042. The approximate time and distance to the station would be

A. 30 minutes and 65 NM.
B. 42 minutes and 104 NM.
C. 44 minutes and 96 NM.

Answer (A) is correct. *(IFH Chap 9)*
DISCUSSION: Time to station is given by the following formula:

$$\frac{\text{Min. for bearing change}}{\text{Bearing change in degrees}} \times 60$$

$$\frac{5}{10} \times 60 = 30 \text{ min.}$$

At an airspeed of 130 kt., the airplane would fly 65 NM in 30 min.
Answer (B) is incorrect. For this to be true, the time for the 10° bearing change would be 7 min., and the true airspeed would need to be approximately 149 kt. Answer (C) is incorrect. For this to be true, the time for the 10° bearing change would be 7 min. 20 sec.

82. (Refer to Figure 42 on page 325.) At which aircraft position(s) would you receive OMNI indication V?

A. 2 only.
B. 6 only.
C. 5 and 8.

Answer (A) is correct. *(PHAK Chap 16)*
DISCUSSION: Note that the OBS is set to 180°. The FROM flag means that the airplane is south of the 270°/090° radial. The left deflection means that you are to the west of the 180° radial, so airplane 2 would have indication V.
Answer (B) is incorrect. Airplane 6 would have a TO, not FROM, indication and a right deflection, not left. Answer (C) is incorrect. Airplanes 5 and 8 would have right deflections, not left.

83. (Refer to Figure 42 on page 325.) At which aircraft position(s) would you receive OMNI indication X?

A. 1 and 3.
B. 3 and 7.
C. 7 only.

Answer (A) is correct. *(PHAK Chap 16)*
DISCUSSION: Note that OBS is set to 180°. The neutral flag means that the aircraft is on the 270°/090° radial. The left deflection means that you are west of the VOR, so airplanes 1 and 3 would have indication X.
Answer (B) is incorrect. Airplane 7 would have a right, not left, deflection. Answer (C) is incorrect. Airplane 7 would have a right, not left, deflection.

84. (Refer to Figure 42 on page 325.) At which aircraft position(s) would you receive OMNI indication U?

A. 1 and 2.
B. 2 only.
C. 6 only.

Answer (C) is correct. *(PHAK Chap 16)*
DISCUSSION: Note that the OBS is set to 180°. The TO flag means that the airplane is north of the 270°/090° radial. Since there is a right deflection, you are to the east of the 360° radial, so airplane 6 would have indication U.
Answer (A) is incorrect. Airplane 1 would have a neutral, not TO, flag and left, not right, deflection and airplane 2 would have a FROM, not TO, indication and a left, not right, deflection. Answer (B) is incorrect. Airplane 2 would have a FROM, not TO, indication and a left, not right, deflection.

85. (Refer to Figure 42 on page 325.) Which OMNI indication would you receive for aircraft 8?

A. T.
B. V.
C. W.

Answer (C) is correct. *(PHAK Chap 16)*
DISCUSSION: Note that the OBS is set to 180°. Airplane 8 is south of the 090° radial and thus would have a FROM indication. Because the airplane is to the east of the 180° radial, it would have a right deflection as shown in indication W.
Answer (A) is incorrect. Indication T has a TO, not FROM, indication and a left, not right, needle deflection. Answer (B) is incorrect. V indicates a left, not a right, deflection.

86. (Refer to Figure 42 on page 325.) Which OMNI indications would you receive for aircraft 5 and 7?

A. T and X.
B. V and X.
C. W and Z.

Answer (C) is correct. *(PHAK Chap 16)*
DISCUSSION: Note that the OBS is set to 180°. Airplane 5 is south of the 270°/090° radial and would have a FROM indication. It is to the east of the 180° radial and accordingly would have a right deflection. Indicator W has FROM with a right deflection. Aircraft 7 would have a neutral flag because it is on the 090° radial. Also, since it is east of the VOR, it would have a right deflection. Indicator Z has a right deflection with a neutral flag.
Answer (A) is incorrect. Indication T has a TO, not FROM, indication and a left, not right, deflection. Indication X has a left, not right, deflection. Answer (B) is incorrect. Both indications V and X have left, not right, needle deflections.

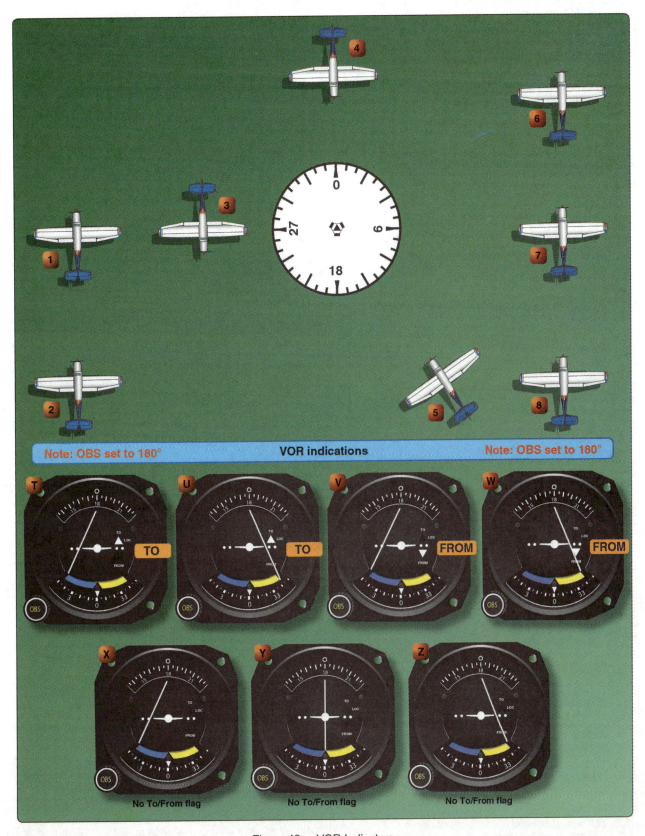

Figure 42. – VOR Indicators.

87. The three individual navigation services provided by a VORTAC facility are

A. UHF VOR azimuth, VHF TACAN azimuth, and VHF TACAN distance information.
B. VHF VOR azimuth, UHF TACAN azimuth, and UHF TACAN distance information.
C. VHF VOR azimuth, VHF TACAN azimuth, and UHF TACAN distance information.

Answer (B) is correct. *(AIM Para 1-1-6)*
DISCUSSION: A VORTAC is a facility consisting of two components, VOR and TACAN, which provide three individual services: VOR azimuth, TACAN azimuth, and TACAN (DME) distance at one site. TACAN operates in the UHF band.
Answer (A) is incorrect. VOR azimuth operates on a VHF band and TACAN operates on a UHF band. Answer (C) is incorrect. TACAN azimuth is given on a UHF band.

8.8 Global Positioning Systems (GPS)

88. The primary purpose of the direct-to button is to

A. provide waypoints to a given runway.
B. give routing to the nearest airport.
C. show the quickest way to fly to any given point.

Answer (C) is correct. *(AAH Chap 3)*
DISCUSSION: The "direct-to" feature shows the quickest way to fly to any given point, whether an airport or waypoint.
Answer (A) is incorrect. A pilot would not use the "direct-to" function to see all the waypoints to a given airport. The "flight plan" feature should be used to see this information. Answer (B) is incorrect. The "nearest," or NRST, button provides information about the closest airport at any given time.

89. Which button/feature provides information on the closest airport at any given time?

A. Direct-to.
B. Nearest.
C. Flight plan.

Answer (B) is correct. *(AAH Chap 3)*
DISCUSSION: The "nearest," or NRST, button will provide information including frequencies, direction, and distance to the closest airport. It is especially beneficial in emergency situations because very few keystrokes are needed to gather information.
Answer (A) is incorrect. The "direct-to" button shows the quickest way to fly to any given point, whether an airport or waypoint, but does not necessarily provide airport information. Answer (C) is incorrect. The "flight plan" button shows all waypoints to a given airport. A pilot has to program all the information manually.

90. Effective navigation by means of GPS includes

A. determining the current status of all databases.
B. assurance that ATC approves your planned route.
C. relying solely on the GPS for course information.

Answer (A) is correct. *(AAH Chap 3)*
DISCUSSION: A pilot must determine the status of all appropriate databases. If a database is not current, the pilot must use an alternate means of navigation.
Answer (B) is incorrect. Pilots may be, and frequently are, given changes to their requested planned route by ATC. A pilot must ensure that the route flown is approved by ATC whether it was the requested plan or not. Answer (C) is incorrect. All systems have the possibility of failing at some point, and it would not be effective to rely solely on a GPS unit for navigation. It is wise to have another means (paper charts, approach plates, etc.) from which to navigate.

91. Why should pilots understand how to cancel entries made on a GPS?

A. Because GPS units frequently provide wrong or false information.
B. Because heavy workloads and turbulence can increase data entry errors.
C. Because published route names commonly change.

Answer (B) is correct. *(AAH Chap 3)*
DISCUSSION: Stressful situations, heavy workloads, and turbulence make data entry errors real problems, and pilots should know how to recover basic aircraft controls quickly.
Answer (A) is incorrect. GPS units provide a high degree of accuracy and are unreliable very infrequently. Answer (C) is incorrect. It is not common for names of published routes to change.

92. Reliance on GPS units

A. can cause pilots to lose proficiency in performing manual calculations of time, distance, and heading.
B. will increase a pilot's skill in navigating by visual reference.
C. increases pilot workload.

Answer (A) is correct. *(AAH Chap 3)*
DISCUSSION: Due to the reliance on GPS systems for navigation, it is easy for pilots to lose proficiency in performing manual calculations on courses, times, distances, headings, etc.
Answer (B) is incorrect. Reliance on GPS units for navigation does not increase skill in navigating by outside references. Answer (C) is incorrect. Navigation by GPS decreases, not increases, pilot workload.

STUDY UNIT NINE
FLIGHT MANEUVERS

(11 pages of outline)

9.1	Taxiing	(4 questions)	327, 337
9.2	Fundamentals of Flight	(1 question)	327, 338
9.3	Takeoffs	(3 questions)	328, 338
9.4	Turns	(10 questions)	328, 339
9.5	Landings	(13 questions)	329, 341
9.6	Rectangular Course	(6 questions)	330, 343
9.7	Turns around a Point	(6 questions)	331, 345
9.8	S-Turns across a Road	(4 questions)	332, 347
9.9	Eights-on-Pylons	(5 questions)	333, 349
9.10	Stalls, Spins, and Slow Flight	(10 questions)	333, 350
9.11	Steep Turns	(4 questions)	334, 352
9.12	Chandelles	(5 questions)	335, 353
9.13	Lazy Eights	(9 questions)	336, 353
9.14	Flight by Reference to Instruments	(10 questions)	336, 355
9.15	Teaching Methods	(3 questions)	337, 357

This study unit contains outlines of major concepts tested, sample test questions and answers regarding flight maneuvers, and an explanation of each answer. The table of contents above lists each subunit within this study unit, the number of questions pertaining to that particular subunit, and the pages on which the outlines and questions begin, respectively.

Recall that the **sole purpose** of this book is to expedite your passing of the FAA pilot knowledge test for the CFI, BGI, or AGI certificate. Accordingly, all extraneous material (i.e., topics or regulations not directly tested on the FAA pilot knowledge test) is omitted, even though much more knowledge is necessary to become a proficient flight or ground instructor. This additional material is presented in *Pilot Handbook* and *Flight Instructor Flight Maneuvers and Practical Test Prep*, available from Gleim Publications, Inc. Order online at www.GleimAviation.com.

9.1 TAXIING

1. To help prevent overturning when taxiing light tricycle-gear airplanes (especially high-wing type) in strong quartering tailwinds, the elevator should be placed in the down position.

    a. The aileron should be down on the side from which the wind is blowing.

2. In a strong quartering headwind, the aileron should be up on the side from which the wind is blowing.

3. An airplane should be headed into the wind for the pretakeoff check to obtain more accurate operating indications and to minimize engine overheating during run-up.

9.2 FUNDAMENTALS OF FLIGHT

1. The four fundamentals involved in maneuvering an aircraft are

    a. Straight-and-level,
    b. Turns,
    c. Climbs, and
    d. Descents.

9.3 TAKEOFFS

1. During soft-field takeoffs, liftoff should be made as soon as possible.
2. The lift-off airspeed for short-field takeoffs is usually at V_X (the best angle-of-climb speed).
   a. This is greater than the lift-off speed for soft-field takeoffs, which is the earliest possible airspeed that will allow the airplane to get off the ground.
3. An immediate turn to downwind after takeoff is not a good practice because it
   a. Could create a traffic conflict
   b. Increases the risk of a low-altitude stall/spin incident
   c. Could violate noise abatement procedures at some airports
   d. Creates ground structure collision hazards

9.4 TURNS

1. Increasing the rate of turn without using rudder would likely result in a **slipping turn**.
2. In a **right descending turn**, if excessive left rudder is applied to compensate for the decreased torque effect, a slip will result.
3. During **level turns** in side-by-side airplanes, the student pilot typically makes diving left turns because the nose appears to rise during entry into these turns.
4. If during the entry to a right turn the nose of the aircraft swings slightly to the left before it swings to the right, it is a **slipping entry**.
   a. More right rudder pressure should have been applied for the amount of aileron pressure being used.
5. If the nose of an aircraft moves in the direction of turn before the bank starts, the rudder has been applied too soon.
6. During a constant banked turn, a reduction in airspeed will cause the rate of turn to increase and the radius of turn to decrease.
   a. Thus, the displacement of the turn needle will increase as airspeed decreases.
7. During a level turn, increasing the airspeed while maintaining a constant bank (constant load factor) will result in an increase in the radius of turn.
8. Instruction in level turns should begin with medium turns, so that the student has an opportunity to grasp the fundamentals of turning flight without having to deal with overbanking tendency or the inherent stability of the airplane attempting to level the wings.
   a. The instructor should not ask the student to roll the airplane from bank to bank, but to change its attitude from level to bank, bank to level, and so on, with a slight pause at the termination of each phase.
      1) This pause allows the airplane to free itself from the effects of any misuse of the controls and ensures a correct start for the next turn.
   b. During these exercises, the idea of control forces, rather than movement, should be emphasized by pointing out the resistance of the controls to varying forces applied to them.
   c. The beginning student should be encouraged to use the rudder freely.
      1) Skidding in this phase indicates positive control use and may be easily corrected later.
      2) On the other hand, the use of too little rudder, or rudder use in the wrong direction, at this stage of training indicates a lack of proper conception of coordination.

9. Common mistakes made by student pilots during their first attempts at level turns include
   a. Failure to adequately clear the area before beginning the turn
   b. Attempting to execute the turn solely by instrument reference
   c. Attempting to sit up straight, in relation to the ground, during a turn, rather than riding with the airplane
   d. Insufficient feel for the airplane as evidenced by the inability to detect slips/skids without reference to flight instruments
   e. Attempting to maintain a constant bank angle by referencing the "cant" of the airplane's nose
   f. Fixating on the nose reference while excluding wingtip reference
   g. "Ground shyness" – making "flat turns" (skidding) while operating at low altitudes in a conscious or subconscious effort to avoid banking close to the ground
   h. Holding rudder in the turn
   i. Gaining proficiency in turns in only one direction (usually the left)
   j. Failure to coordinate the use of throttle with other controls
   k. Altitude gain/loss during the turn

9.5 LANDINGS

1. Under normal conditions, a proper crosswind landing on a runway requires that, at the moment of touchdown, the direction of motion of the aircraft and its longitudinal axis be parallel to the runway.
   a. This minimizes the side loads placed on the landing gear during touchdown.
2. During a power approach to a **short-field landing**, the correct airspeed may be verified by little or no floating during the landing flare.
3. If an emergency situation requires a **downwind landing**, pilots should expect a higher groundspeed at touchdown, a longer ground roll, and the likelihood of overshooting the desired touchdown point.
   a. When making an off-field landing, it is recommended that the landing be accomplished in pastures that are seldom cultivated.
4. On final approach to landing, a faster-than-normal indicated airspeed should be used when turbulent conditions exist.
5. During go-arounds from a full-flap approach in conventional airplanes, unless the flight manual specifies differently, start retracting the flaps first, then retract the gear.
   a. A go-around from a poor landing approach should generally be preferable to last-minute attempts to prevent a bad landing.
   b. If poor aircraft controllability is experienced during an emergency go-around with full flaps, the cause is most probably due to the high-power, low-airspeed situation with the airplane trimmed for a full-flap configuration.
6. A student tends to **round out high** during a landing because (s)he is focusing on references that are too close or looking directly down.
7. Excessive speed on final approach usually results in **floating**.
8. Misjudging the rate of sink during a landing usually results in **ballooning**.
   a. To correct for slight ballooning during landing, you should hold a constant landing attitude.
9. If a student focuses too far ahead during a landing approach, (s)he will have difficulty in judging the closeness of the ground, resulting in a **nose-first touchdown**.

9.6 RECTANGULAR COURSE

1. When beginning a rectangular course, the determining factor in deciding the distance from the field boundary at which an aircraft should be flown is the steepness of the bank desired in the turns.

2. The same techniques of a rectangular course apply when flying an airport traffic pattern.

    a. On the turn from downwind to base, one goes from a steep to a medium bank.
    b. On the turn from base to final, one goes from a medium to a shallow bank.
    c. On a turn from upwind to crosswind, one goes from a shallow to a medium bank.
    d. On a turn from crosswind to downwind, one goes from a medium to a steep bank.

3. The corners that require **less** than a 90° turn in a rectangular course are

    a. The turn to final and
    b. The turn to crosswind.

4. The corners that require **more** than a 90° turn in a rectangular course are

    a. The turn to downwind and
    b. The turn to base.

5. To properly compensate for a crosswind during straight-and-level cruising flight, the pilot should establish a proper heading into the wind by coordinated use of the controls.

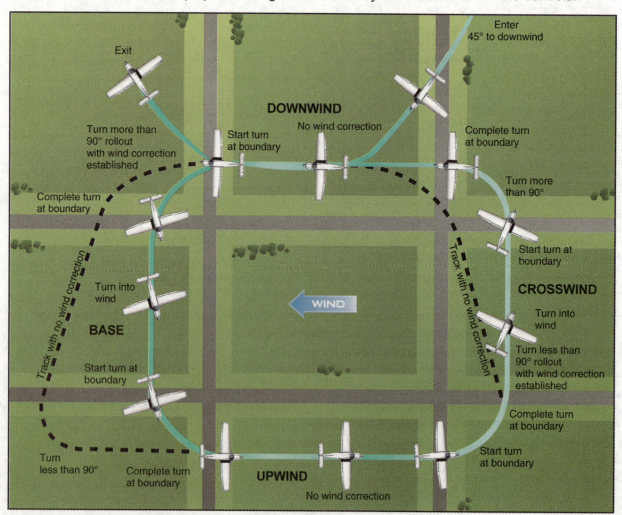

9.7 TURNS AROUND A POINT

1. During turns about a point, an imaginary line from the pilot's eye and parallel to the lateral axis should point to the pylon when the aircraft is abeam the point headed directly upwind or downwind.

2. It is best to enter turns around a point while flying downwind because that is where the bank will be at its maximum.

3. Groundspeed will be equal when the headwind or tailwind components are the same, e.g., direct crosswind, downwind just out of crosswind and just into crosswind, and the same for upwind.

4. Bank will be most nearly equal when flying crosswind, i.e., at the farthest upwind point and the farthest downwind point.

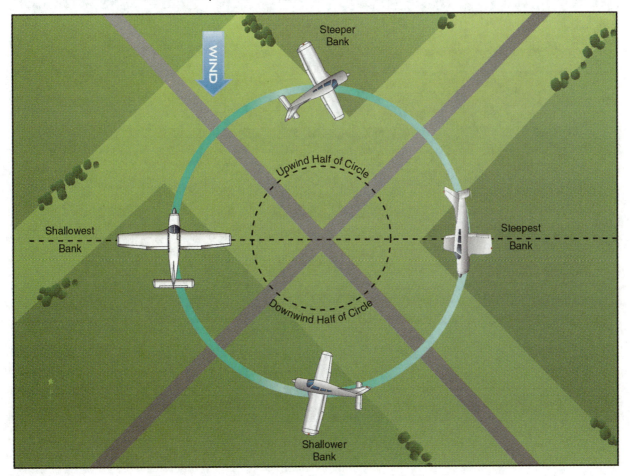

9.8 S-TURNS ACROSS A ROAD

1. Groundspeed will be equal when the headwind or tailwind components are the same, e.g., direct crosswind, downwind just out of crosswind and just into crosswind, and the same for upwind.
2. The angle of bank will be steepest when flying in a tailwind.
3. In S-turns, you must be crabbed into the wind the most when you have a full crosswind component.
4. In S-turns, a consistently smaller half-circle will be made on the upwind side of the road when the bank is increased too rapidly during the early part of the turn.

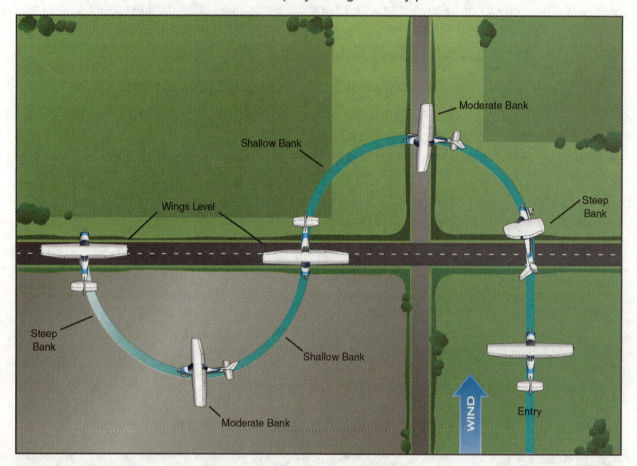

9.9 EIGHTS-ON-PYLONS

1. In proper coordinated eights-on-pylons, if the reference point is or moves behind the pylon, it means the airplane is above the pivotal altitude.
2. The pivotal altitude for eights-on-pylons is dependent primarily upon the groundspeed.
3. Misuse of rudder in attempting to hold the pylon during the performance of eights-on-pylons will result in a slip if above pivotal altitude and a skid if below pivotal altitude.
    a. Thus, if the ball is to the outside of the turn, the pilot must increase altitude to obtain the correct pivotal altitude, and correct the skidding turn.

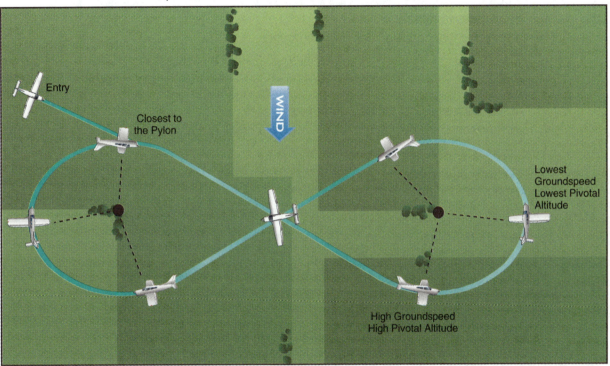

9.10 STALLS, SPINS, AND SLOW FLIGHT

1. Either a power-on or power-off stall must be performed during a flight instructor-airplane practical test.
2. The objective of a cross-control stall demonstration is to show the effect of improper control technique and emphasize the importance of coordinated control when making turns.
    a. If inadequate right rudder is used during a climbing right turn and the airplane stalls, a spin to the left may occur.
3. **Secondary stalls** may occur after a recovery from a preceding stall.
    a. They are caused by attempting to hasten the completion of a stall recovery before the airplane has regained sufficient flying speed.
    b. When this stall occurs, the back-elevator pressure should again be released just as in a normal stall recovery. When sufficient airspeed has been regained, the airplane can then be returned to straight-and-level flight.
    c. This stall usually occurs when the pilot uses abrupt control input to return to straight-and-level flight after a stall or spin recovery.
        1) It also occurs when the pilot fails to reduce the angle of attack sufficiently during stall recovery by not lowering pitch attitude sufficiently or by attempting to break the stall by using power only.

4. Common mistakes made by student pilots during their first attempts at intentional stalls include
    a. Failure to adequately clear the area
    b. Inability to recognize an approaching stall condition through feel for the airplane
    c. Premature recovery
    d. Over-reliance on the airspeed indicator while excluding other cues
    e. Inadequate scanning resulting in an unintentional wing-low condition during entry
    f. Excessive back-elevator pressure resulting in an exaggerated nose-up attitude during entry
    g. Inadequate rudder control
    h. Inadvertent secondary stall during recovery
    i. Failure to maintain a constant bank angle during turning stalls
    j. Excessive forward-elevator pressure during recovery resulting in negative load on the wings
    k. Excessive airspeed buildup during recovery
    l. Failure to take timely action to prevent a full stall during the conduct of imminent stalls
5. The correct spin recovery technique is as follows:
    a. Reduce power to idle.
    b. Apply opposite rudder to slow rotation.
    c. Apply positive forward elevator movement to break the stall.
    d. Neutralize rudder as rotation stops.
    e. Return to level flight.
6. The **primary purpose** of practicing operations at reduced airspeeds is to enable students to develop proficiency in their sense of feeling and their ability to use the controls properly at various speeds.
    a. When operating in the region of reverse command, i.e., behind the power curve, increased nose-up pitch can cause increased rate of descent.
    b. Thus, if an aircraft is in the region of reverse command during a landing approach, i.e., low and slow, the correct procedure is to decrease angle of attack and increase power.
7. The two distinct flight situations to be covered when teaching slow flight are
    a. Airspeeds appropriate for landing approaches.
    b. Flight at reduced airspeeds.

9.11 STEEP TURNS

1. If an accelerated stall occurs in a steep turn, the direction of roll depends upon whether the airplane is slipping, skidding, or in coordinated flight.
    a. In a slip, the high wing stalls first.
    b. In a skid, the low wing stalls first.
    c. In coordinated flight, both wings stall at the same time.
2. Students should be taught that throughout a level, steep turn, the rudder is normally used to prevent yawing.
3. To correct for a nose-low attitude during a steep turn, a student should be taught to reduce the angle of bank, then apply back elevator pressure to attain the desired pitch attitude.

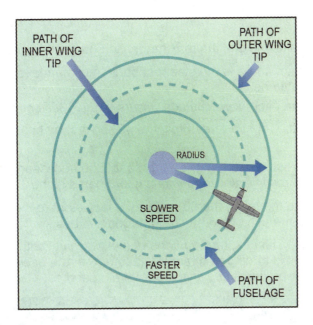

9.12 CHANDELLES

1. Pilots who initiate a chandelle with a bank that is too steep will most likely perform a comparatively level steep turn with a nose-high rollout at the 180° point.

    a. If the initial bank is too shallow when performing a chandelle, stalling the aircraft may occur before reaching the 180° point.

2. During the first 90° of a chandelle, there is constant bank and changing pitch.

    a. The maximum pitch occurs at the 90° point.

3. During the second 90° of a chandelle, there is constant pitch and changing bank.

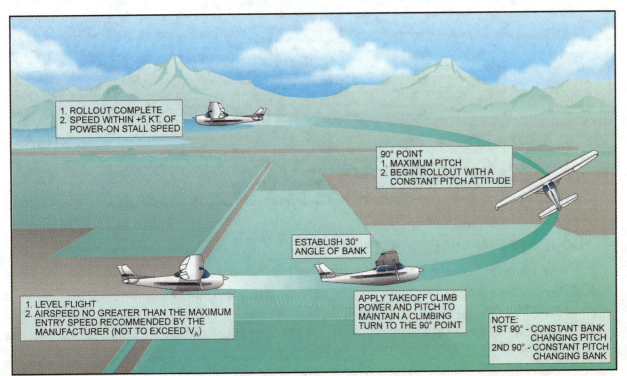

9.13 LAZY EIGHTS

1. When performing a lazy eight, the maximum pitch-up attitude occurs at the 45° point.
   a. At the 90° point, there is the steepest bank, minimum airspeed, maximum altitude, and level pitch attitude.
   b. The maximum pitch-down attitude occurs at the 135° point.
2. If one begins with too rapid a rate of roll, the 45° point may be reached before the maximum pitch-up attitude.
3. At the point of slowest speed (90°), it will probably be necessary to exert opposing aileron and rudder pressures in order to maintain coordinated flight.
   a. If the ball is to the left at the 90° point of a lazy eight to the left, the probable cause of this error is the use of too much right rudder pressure.
4. If a pilot initiates the climbing turn portions of the lazy eight with banks that are too steep, the probable result is turning at a rate too fast for the rate of climb and therefore completing each 180° change of direction with excessive airspeed.

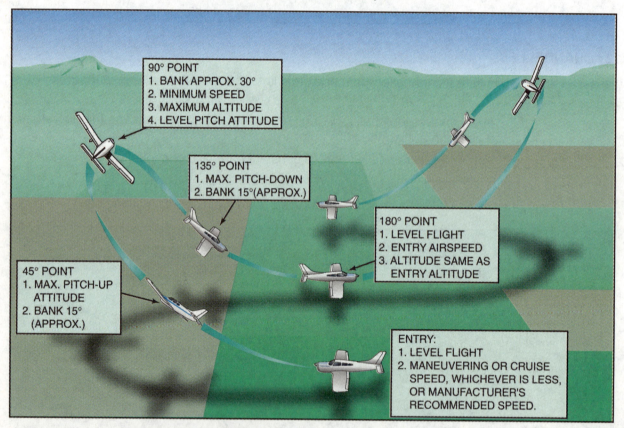

9.14 FLIGHT BY REFERENCE TO INSTRUMENTS

1. The altimeter is the primary flight instrument for pitch control during straight-and-level flight.
2. The attitude indicator and turn coordinator are supporting bank instruments when entering a constant airspeed climb from straight-and-level flight.
3. To establish a level standard rate turn, the attitude indicator and turn coordinator are primary and secondary flight instruments, respectively.
4. If the attitude indicator is inoperative in an unusual flight attitude, a nose-low or nose-high attitude can be determined by the airspeed indicator and altimeter.

SU 9: Flight Maneuvers

5. The recovery from a spiraling, nose-low, increasing airspeed, unusual flight attitude is to reduce power, correct bank attitude, and raise the nose to a level attitude.

9.15 TEACHING METHODS

1. To develop the high degree of aircraft control needed to fly safely, instructors are encouraged to use distractions to divert the attention of the student.
   a. The function of distractions is to determine whether the student can maintain aircraft control while his or her attention is diverted.
   b. During S-turn practice, an acceptable example of interjecting distractions is to request the student to identify objects on the ground (e.g., roads, buildings, lakes, etc.).
2. The objective of the Practical Test Standards (PTS) is to ensure the certification of pilots at a high level of performance and proficiency, consistent with safety.
   a. In addition, the Airman Certification Standards (ACS), built on the existing PTS, explicitly define the knowledge elements, flight proficiency performance metrics and tolerances, and risk management elements to ensure a high level of performance and proficiency, consistent with safety.

QUESTIONS AND ANSWER EXPLANATIONS: All of the AGI/CFI knowledge test questions chosen by the FAA for release as well as additional questions selected by Gleim relating to the material in the previous outlines are reproduced on the following pages. These questions have been organized into the same subunits as the outlines. To the immediate right of each question are the correct answer and answer explanation. You should cover these answers and answer explanations while responding to the questions. Refer to the general discussion in the Introduction on how to take the FAA knowledge test.

Remember that the questions from the FAA knowledge test bank have been reordered by topic and organized into a meaningful sequence. Also, the first line of the answer explanation gives the citation of the authoritative source for the answer.

QUESTIONS

9.1 Taxiing

1. To help prevent overturning when taxiing light tricycle-gear airplanes (especially high-wing type) in strong quartering tailwinds, the

    A. elevator should be placed in the up position.
    B. elevator should be placed in the down position.
    C. aileron on the downwind side should be placed in the down position.

Answer (B) is correct. *(AFH Chap 2)*
   DISCUSSION: When there is a strong quartering tailwind, the elevator should be held down to help keep the wind from getting under the tail and flipping the airplane tail over nose.
   Answer (A) is incorrect. The elevator should be in the down, not up, position. Answer (C) is incorrect. The aileron on the downwind side should be placed in the up, not down, position.

2. When taxiing with strong quartering tailwinds, which aileron position should be used?

    A. Neutral.
    B. Aileron up on the side from which the wind is blowing.
    C. Aileron down on the side from which the wind is blowing.

Answer (C) is correct. *(AFH Chap 2)*
   DISCUSSION: When there is a strong quartering tailwind, the aileron should be held down on the side from which the wind is blowing to exert pressure on the lowered aileron, which forces the wing down and prevents the wind from tipping the airplane over.
   Answer (A) is incorrect. If the ailerons are held in the neutral position or parallel to the ground, they are not being used to counteract the possible impact of a quartering tailwind. Answer (B) is incorrect. The aileron should be down, not up, on the side from which the wind is blowing.

3. Which aileron position should you generally use when taxiing in strong quartering headwinds?

A. Neutral.
B. Aileron up on the side from which the wind is blowing.
C. Aileron down on the side from which the wind is blowing.

Answer (B) is correct. *(AFH Chap 2)*
DISCUSSION: When there is a strong quartering headwind, the aileron should be up on the side from which the wind is blowing to exert pressure on the raised aileron, which forces the wing down and prevents the wind from tipping the airplane over. The elevator should be held neutral.
Answer (A) is incorrect. If the ailerons are held in the neutral position or parallel to the ground, they are not being used to counteract the possible impact of a quartering headwind. Answer (C) is incorrect. The aileron should be up, not down, on the windward side in a quartering headwind.

4. Why should an airplane be headed into the wind for the pretakeoff check?

A. To prevent the need for more brake pressure to keep the airplane from moving forward.
B. To obtain more accurate operating indications and to minimize engine overheating during run-up.
C. To prevent excessive load factors which could occur during run-up if a crosswind condition exists.

Answer (B) is correct. *(AFH Chap 2)*
DISCUSSION: Years ago, when airplanes used radial engines, which were more subject to overheating than current airplane engines, run-ups were done into the wind to help cool the engine. Today, airplanes are pointed into the wind to provide more accurate operating indications and better control responses and also to preclude prop blast on any airplanes behind the airplane.
Answer (A) is incorrect. The wind will not prevent the airplane from moving forward if the parking brake slips or if application of the toe brakes is inadequate for the amount of power applied. Answer (C) is incorrect. No load factors except gravity exist on the airplane when it is on the ground.

9.2 Fundamentals of Flight

5. Select the four flight fundamentals involved in maneuvering an aircraft.

A. Aircraft power, pitch, bank, and trim.
B. Starting, taxiing, takeoff, and landing.
C. Straight-and-level flight, turns, climbs, and descents.

Answer (C) is correct. *(AFH Chap 3)*
DISCUSSION: Maneuvering an airplane is generally divided into four flight fundamentals: straight-and-level flight, turns, climbs, and descents. All controlled flight consists of one or a combination of more than one of these basic maneuvers.
Answer (A) is incorrect. It lists variable factors necessary for the performance of the flight fundamentals. Answer (B) is incorrect. It lists a combination of basic maneuvers, not flight fundamentals.

9.3 Takeoffs

6. When explaining the techniques used for making short- and soft-field takeoffs, it would be correct to state that

A. during soft-field takeoffs, lift-off should be made as soon as possible.
B. during soft-field takeoffs, lift-off should be made only when best angle-of-climb speed is attained.
C. during short-field takeoffs, lift-off should be attempted only after best rate-of-climb speed is attained.

Answer (A) is correct. *(AFH Chap 5)*
DISCUSSION: Takeoffs and climbs from soft fields require the use of operational techniques for getting the airplane airborne as quickly as possible to eliminate the drag caused by tall grass, soft sand, mud, snow, etc.
Answer (B) is incorrect. Liftoff at best angle-of-climb speed should be used for short-field takeoffs, not soft-field takeoffs. Answer (C) is incorrect. For short-field takeoffs, liftoff should be attempted only when best angle-of-climb (V_X), not rate-of-climb (V_Y), speed is attained.

7. The indicated lift-off airspeed for short-field takeoffs in a particular aircraft will normally be

A. the same as for soft- or rough-field takeoffs.
B. greater than for soft- or rough-field takeoffs.
C. greater under tailwind conditions than required under headwind conditions.

Answer (B) is correct. *(AFH Chap 5)*
DISCUSSION: Takeoffs and climbs from soft fields require the use of operational techniques for getting the airplane airborne as quickly as possible to eliminate the drag caused by tall grass, soft sand, mud, snow, etc. This is in contrast to short-field takeoffs, where the weight is left on the wheels until V_X is attained, at which time the airplane is rotated, while V_X is maintained to clear any obstacles.
Answer (A) is incorrect. Lift-off speed for short-field takeoffs is V_X. For soft-field takeoffs, one lifts off as soon as possible, i.e., before V_X. Answer (C) is incorrect. One should not attempt takeoffs in soft- and short-field situations with tailwind conditions.

8. Immediately after takeoff, a downwind turn close to the ground is not good practice because it

A. could cause a traffic conflict.
B. decreases the risk of a low-altitude stall/spin.
C. violates noise abatement regulations.

Answer (A) is correct. *(AIM Para 4-3-5)*
DISCUSSION: Unexpected, non-standard maneuvers in the traffic pattern are unwise because you may not be aware of the positions of other aircraft in the pattern. If those aircraft are complying with standard traffic pattern guidance, you could cause a traffic conflict or a potential collision hazard.
Answer (B) is incorrect. A downwind turn near the ground increases, not decreases, the risk of a low-altitude stall/spin. Answer (C) is incorrect. Noise abatement procedures are not regulatory in nature, and not all airports have noise abatement procedures in effect.

9.4 Turns

9. Which would likely result in a slipping turn?

A. Not holding bottom rudder in a turn.
B. Increasing the rate of turn without using rudder.
C. Increasing the rate of turn without increasing bank.

Answer (B) is correct. *(AFH Chap 3)*
DISCUSSION: To increase the rate of turn, you would normally increase the bank. Rolling into a steeper bank using ailerons and no rudder will result in adverse yaw opposite the direction of turn. Thus, the ball will move to the inside of the turn, indicating a slip.
Answer (A) is incorrect. It is normally not necessary to hold bottom (inside) rudder in a turn to maintain coordinated flight. Answer (C) is incorrect. In order to increase rate of turn without increasing bank, either more rudder would have to be applied, resulting in a skidding, not slipping, turn or the airspeed would have to be reduced, resulting in a coordinated, not slipping, turn.

10. Choose the true statement pertaining to a slip or skid in an airplane.

A. A skid occurs when the rate of turn is too slow for the amount of bank being used.
B. In a left climbing turn, if insufficient right rudder is applied to compensate for the increased torque effect, a slip will result.
C. In a right descending turn, if excessive left rudder is applied to compensate for the decreased torque effect, a slip will result.

Answer (C) is correct. *(AFH Chap 3)*
DISCUSSION: A slip occurs when the ball of a turn-and-slip indicator is to the inside of the turn. Excessive rudder pressure pushes the ball to the opposite side. Thus, in a right turn, if excessive left rudder is applied, the ball will be on the right side and a slip will result.
Answer (A) is incorrect. A skid occurs when the rate of turn is too fast, not too slow, for the amount of bank being used; i.e., a skid occurs when centrifugal force exceeds the horizontal component of lift. Answer (B) is incorrect. Insufficient right rudder (i.e., excessive left rudder) in a climbing left turn will result in a skid, not a slip.

11. During level turns in side-by-side airplanes, which is characteristic of student performance?

A. Diving during right turns because the nose appears to rise during entry into these turns.
B. Diving during left turns because the nose appears to rise during entry into these turns.
C. Climbing during left turns because the nose appears to descend during entry into these turns.

Answer (B) is correct. *(AFH Chap 3)*
DISCUSSION: In airplanes that have side-by-side seats, the pilot is seated to the left of the longitudinal axis about which the airplane rolls. This makes the nose appear to rise when making a correct left turn and descend, not rise, in correct right turns. Thus, student pilots tend to dive when making left turns because the nose appears to rise during entry.
Answer (A) is incorrect. The nose appears to descend, not rise, when entering correct right turns. Answer (C) is incorrect. During a left turn, the nose appears to rise. Thus, one descends rather than climbs.

12. During the entry to a right turn, the nose of the aircraft swings slightly to the left before it swings along the horizon to the right. This is a

A. slipping entry, caused by excessive right rudder pressure.
B. skidding entry; more right rudder pressure and less right aileron pressure should have been applied.
C. slipping entry; more right rudder pressure should have been applied for the amount of aileron pressure being used.

Answer (C) is correct. *(AFH Chap 3)*
DISCUSSION: When entering a right turn, if the nose of the aircraft swings slightly to the left before it swings to the right, insufficient rudder has been applied, resulting in the airplane slipping to the inside of the turn. The correction is to apply more right rudder and to apply it sooner on the turn entry.
Answer (A) is incorrect. The slipping entry was caused by insufficient, not excessive, right rudder pressure and/or not applying the rudder soon enough. Answer (B) is incorrect. It is a slipping entry, not a skidding entry.

13. During a 30° banked turn, what effect would a reduction in airspeed have on the rate and radius of turn?

A. The rate would increase; the radius would decrease.
B. The rate would decrease; the radius would increase.
C. The rate would decrease; the radius would decrease.

Answer (A) is correct. *(AFH Chap 4)*
DISCUSSION: At a constant bank, the rate of turn increases with reductions in airspeed and the radius of the turn decreases.
Answer (B) is incorrect. The rate of turn increases, not decreases, and the radius of turn decreases, not increases. Answer (C) is incorrect. The rate of turn increases, not decreases.

14. What will cause the nose of an aircraft to move in the direction of the turn before the bank starts in a turn entry?

A. Rudder being applied too late.
B. Rudder being applied too soon.
C. Failure to apply back elevator pressure.

Answer (B) is correct. *(AFH Chap 3)*
DISCUSSION: If the nose starts to move in a turn before the bank starts, rudder is being applied too soon.
Answer (A) is incorrect. Rudder is being applied too soon, not too late. Answer (C) is incorrect. The back elevator pressure relates to whether the nose is moving up or down, not left or right.

15. While holding a constant angle of bank in a coordinated turn, the displacement of the turn needle will

A. increase as airspeed decreases.
B. increase as airspeed increases.
C. remain constant regardless of airspeed.

Answer (A) is correct. *(AFH Chap 3)*
DISCUSSION: The turn needle indicates the rate of turn. At a constant angle of bank, the rate of turn increases as airspeed decreases. Thus, the turn needle displacement will increase with the decrease in airspeed.
Answer (B) is incorrect. Displacement of the turn needle decreases, not increases, as airspeed increases. Answer (C) is incorrect. The turn needle showing the rate of turn will move as changes in airspeed change the turn rate.

16. During a level turn, increasing the airspeed while maintaining a constant load factor would result in

A. a decrease in radius of turn.
B. an increase in radius of turn.
C. an increase in centrifugal force.

Answer (B) is correct. *(AFH Chap 4)*
DISCUSSION: When maintaining a constant load factor, the airplane has the same angle of bank. An increase in airspeed with a constant angle of bank results in an increase of the radius of the turn and a decrease in the turn rate.
Answer (A) is incorrect. The radius of the turn increases, not decreases. Answer (C) is incorrect. The relationship of centrifugal force remains constant and is totally offset by the horizontal component of lift if the turn remains coordinated.

17. The best way to introduce turns and banking to a new student pilot is with

A. shallow turns.
B. medium turns.
C. steep turns.

Answer (B) is correct. *(AFH Chap 3)*
DISCUSSION: Instruction in level turns should begin with medium turns, so that the student has an opportunity to grasp the fundamentals of turning flight without having to deal with overbanking tendency.
Answer (A) is incorrect. Shallow turns do not provide adequate introduction to the use of the rudder during turning flight. Answer (C) is incorrect. Steep turns are too overwhelming for a beginning student because of the overbanking tendency of the airplane and the increased need for additional pitch control.

18. What is a common mistake new students make when performing turns?

A. Attempting to turn using only instrument references.
B. Overuse of rudder.
C. Riding with the airplane rather than sitting straight in reference to the ground.

Answer (A) is correct. *(AFH Chap 3)*
DISCUSSION: Students should keep their eyes outside during turns to ensure collision avoidance. The flight instruments should only be referenced as necessary to verify what the student interprets from outside observation.
Answer (B) is incorrect. New students often fail to use adequate rudder when initially performing turns. Answer (C) is incorrect. This behavior is actually the correct way to perform turns. Students often try to sit straight in reference to the ground, which makes it harder to interpret their relative position in space.

9.5 Landings

19. To minimize the side loads placed on the landing gear during touchdown, the pilot should keep the

A. direction of motion of the aircraft parallel to the runway.
B. longitudinal axis of the aircraft parallel to the direction of its motion.
C. downwind wing lowered sufficiently to eliminate the tendency for the aircraft to drift.

Answer (B) is correct. *(AFH Chap 8)*
 DISCUSSION: At touchdown when landing, the longitudinal axis of the airplane should be parallel to the direction of its motion, i.e., no side loads to stress the landing gear.
 Answer (A) is incorrect. It is important that the longitudinal axis also parallels the runway to avoid side loads on the landing gear. Answer (C) is incorrect. The upwind wing, not the downwind wing, needs to be lowered.

20. Under normal conditions, a proper crosswind landing on a runway requires that, at the moment of touchdown, the

A. direction of motion of the aircraft and its longitudinal axis be parallel to the runway.
B. downwind wing be lowered sufficiently to eliminate the tendency for the aircraft to drift.
C. direction of motion of the aircraft and its lateral axis be perpendicular to the runway.

Answer (A) is correct. *(AFH Chap 8)*
 DISCUSSION: At touchdown when landing, the longitudinal axis of the airplane should be parallel to the direction of its motion, i.e., no side loads to stress the landing gear.
 Answer (B) is incorrect. The upwind, not downwind, wing must be lowered. Answer (C) is incorrect. Although the lateral axis of the airplane should be perpendicular to the runway for landing, the direction of motion of the airplane would have to be parallel for this statement to be true.

21. During a power approach to a short-field landing, the correct airspeed may be verified by

A. the ability to land on a predetermined spot.
B. little or no floating during the landing flare.
C. the ability to maintain a constant angle of descent.

Answer (B) is correct. *(AFH Chap 8)*
 DISCUSSION: Short-field landings are usually done with a power approach at a steep approach angle and close to the airplane's stalling speed. A lack of floating during the flare with sufficient control to touch down properly is one verification that the approach speed was correct.
 Answer (A) is incorrect. The objective is to clear obstacles and land with little or no floating during the roundout, which permits the airplane to be stopped in the shortest possible distance. Answer (C) is incorrect. The objective is to clear obstacles and land with little or no floating during the roundout, which permits the airplane to be stopped in the shortest possible distance.

22. If an emergency situation requires a downwind landing, pilots should expect a faster

A. airspeed at touchdown, a longer ground roll, and better control throughout the landing roll.
B. groundspeed at touchdown, a longer ground roll, and the likelihood of overshooting the desired touchdown point.
C. groundspeed at touchdown, a shorter ground roll, and the likelihood of undershooting the desired touchdown point.

Answer (B) is correct. *(AFH Chap 8)*
 DISCUSSION: A downwind landing in an emergency or other situation will result in a faster groundspeed at touchdown, which means a longer ground roll, which in turn increases the likelihood of overshooting the desired touchdown point.
 Answer (A) is incorrect. The airspeed will probably be the same even though the groundspeed is greater, and the control during the landing roll will be less due to the high groundspeed. Answer (C) is incorrect. The ground roll is longer, not shorter, and there is a greater likelihood of overshooting, not undershooting, the touchdown point due to the faster groundspeed.

23. On final approach to landing, a faster-than-normal indicated airspeed should be used when

A. turbulent conditions exist.
B. ambient temperatures are above 90°F.
C. landing at airports above 5,000 feet MSL with above standard temperature conditions.

Answer (A) is correct. *(AFH Chap 8)*
 DISCUSSION: A faster-than-normal indicated airspeed is used when turbulent conditions exist. Faster airspeed gives a more positive control response and also provides a greater safety margin against stalls due to wind shears.
 Answer (B) is incorrect. Indicated airspeed adjusts itself to temperature, i.e., use the same indicated airspeed. Answer (C) is incorrect. The indicated airspeed should be the same regardless of the actual or density altitude.

24. If poor aircraft controllability is experienced during an emergency go-around with full flaps, the cause is most probably due to

A. excessive airspeed with full flaps extended.
B. the high-power, low-airspeed situation with the airplane trimmed for a full-flap configuration.
C. a reduction in the angle of attack with full flaps to the point where the aircraft control is greatly impaired.

Answer (B) is correct. *(AFH Chap 8)*
DISCUSSION: Since the airplane has been trimmed for the approach at a low-power and low-airspeed condition, the nose will tend to rise sharply and veer to the left when power is added during an emergency go-around unless firm control pressures are applied. Forward elevator pressure must be applied to hold the nose at a safe climbing attitude. Right rudder pressure must be increased to counteract the torque or P-factor and to keep the nose straight. This usually occurs before the retrimming process, i.e., just after full power is initiated on the go-around.
Answer (A) is incorrect. Increased airspeed provides increased control response. Answer (C) is incorrect. The angle of attack increases, not decreases, with the addition of full power during an emergency go-around when flaps are down.

25. A go-around from a poor landing approach should

A. not be attempted unless circumstances make it absolutely necessary.
B. generally be preferable to last minute attempts to prevent a bad landing.
C. not be attempted after the landing flare has been initiated regardless of airspeed.

Answer (B) is correct. *(AFH Chap 8)*
DISCUSSION: Regardless of the height above the ground at which it is begun, a safe go-around may be accomplished if an early decision is made, a sound plan is followed, and the procedure is performed properly. The earlier the dangerous situation is recognized and the sooner the landing is rejected and the go-around is started, the safer the procedure will be. Thus, it is a better procedure than last-minute attempts to prevent a bad landing.
Answer (A) is incorrect. A go-around should be attempted whenever unfavorable conditions exist. Answer (C) is incorrect. The go-around can be started any time in the landing process, including during the landing flare.

26. During go-arounds from a full-flap approach in conventional airplanes, which procedure should be used if the flight manual does not specify differently?

A. Start retracting the flaps first, then retract the gear.
B. Retract the gear first and adjust flaps only after reaching a safe altitude.
C. Retract the gear first since it has a far greater adverse effect on aircraft performance than do flaps.

Answer (A) is correct. *(AFH Chap 8)*
DISCUSSION: When initiating a go-around from a full-flap approach, you should retract the flaps at least partially first because they usually have much more drag than the extended landing gear. Also, in the event the airplane does settle onto the ground, you want the landing gear down.
Answer (B) is incorrect. The gear should not be retracted until you have established a positive rate of climb and there is insufficient runway or other landing area to make a safe landing. Also, the airplane will climb better with the flaps retracted at least partially. Answer (C) is incorrect. The gear should not be retracted until you have established a positive rate of climb and there is insufficient runway or other landing area to make a safe landing. Also, flaps usually create more drag than the landing gear.

27. One reason a student tends to round out high during landing is

A. changing focus gradually.
B. focusing on references too far ahead.
C. focusing on references that are too close or looking directly down.

Answer (C) is correct. *(AFH Chap 8)*
DISCUSSION: If the pilot attempts to focus on references that are too close or looks directly down, the references will become blurred and reactions will be either too abrupt or too late. The pilot's tendency will be to overcontrol, round out high, and make full-stall, drop-in landings.
Answer (A) is incorrect. By changing focus gradually as speed is reduced, the pilot can reduce the time between reaction and action and the whole landing process will smooth out. Answer (B) is incorrect. When the pilot focuses too far ahead, accuracy in judging closeness to the ground is less. Consequent reactions will be too slow, resulting in flying the airplane into the ground nose first.

28. What procedure should be used to correct for slight ballooning during landing?

A. Decrease power.
B. Decrease angle of attack.
C. Hold a constant landing attitude.

Answer (C) is correct. *(AFH Chap 8)*
DISCUSSION: When ballooning is slight, a constant landing attitude should be held and the airplane allowed to gradually decelerate and settle onto the runway.
Answer (A) is incorrect. By decreasing power, you may further decrease directional control, increase sink rate, and when pitch changes are initiated, the airplane may stall or sink rapidly, causing a hard impact with the ground. Answer (B) is incorrect. Decreasing the angle of attack will result in flying the airplane into the runway nose first.

29. What normally results from excessive airspeed on final approach?

A. Bouncing.
B. Floating.
C. Ballooning.

Answer (B) is correct. *(AFH Chap 8)*
DISCUSSION: If the airspeed on final approach is excessive, it will usually result in the airplane floating. Before a touchdown can be made, the airplane will be well past the desired landing point and remaining available runway may be insufficient.
Answer (A) is incorrect. Bouncing is the result of an improper attitude or an excessive rate of sink. Answer (C) is incorrect. Ballooning occurs when the pilot misjudges the rate of sink during a landing and thinks the airplane is descending faster than it should. There is a tendency to increase the pitch attitude and angle of attack too rapidly.

30. What normally results from misjudging the rate of sink during a landing?

A. Floating.
B. Ballooning.
C. Poor directional control.

Answer (B) is correct. *(AFH Chap 8)*
DISCUSSION: When the pilot misjudges the rate of sink during a landing and thinks the airplane is descending faster than it should, there is a tendency to increase the pitch attitude and angle of attack too rapidly. This not only stops the descent, but actually starts the airplane climbing, which is known as ballooning.
Answer (A) is incorrect. Floating results from excessive airspeed on final approach. Answer (C) is incorrect. Poor directional control results from lack of coordination of aileron and rudder controls as well as excessively slow approach speed.

31. What could be a result of a student focusing too far ahead during a landing approach?

A. Reactions will be either too abrupt or too late.
B. Rounding out too high and developing an excessive sink rate.
C. Difficulty in judging the closeness of the ground resulting in a nose-first touchdown.

Answer (C) is correct. *(AFH Chap 8)*
DISCUSSION: When the pilot focuses too far ahead, accuracy in judging the closeness of the ground is less. Consequent reactions will be slow since there will appear to be no necessity for any action, resulting in the airplane flying into the ground nose first.
Answer (A) is incorrect. Abrupt or delayed reactions may cause the airplane to balloon, bounce, or enter an accelerated stall. Answer (B) is incorrect. Rounding out too high and developing an excessive sink rate is a result of focusing too close, not too far ahead.

9.6 Rectangular Course

32. When beginning a rectangular course, the determining factor in deciding the distance from the field boundary at which an aircraft should be flown is the

A. windspeed.
B. size of the rectangular area chosen.
C. steepness of the bank desired in the turns.

Answer (C) is correct. *(AFH Chap 6)*
DISCUSSION: The closer the ground track of the airplane is to the field boundary, the steeper the bank necessary at the turning points.
Answer (A) is incorrect. The wind speed will determine the drift correction and the rate of turn necessary. Answer (B) is incorrect. The size of the rectangular area should not affect the distance from the field boundary.

33. To properly compensate for a crosswind during straight-and-level cruising flight, the pilot should

A. hold rudder pressure toward the wind.
B. establish a proper heading into the wind by coordinated use of the controls.
C. hold aileron pressure toward the wind and hold opposite rudder pressure to prevent a turn.

Answer (B) is correct. *(AFH Chap 6)*
DISCUSSION: In straight-and-level cruising flight, one compensates for crosswinds by crabbing into the wind, i.e., using a heading different from one's course such that the airplane continues to travel along the desired course.
Answer (A) is incorrect. One always uses coordinated flight in cruising flight. Answer (C) is incorrect. One always uses coordinated flight in cruising flight.

34. (Refer to Figure 48 on page 345.) In flying the rectangular course, when would the aircraft be turned less than 90°?

A. Corners 1 and 4.
B. Corners 1 and 2.
C. Corners 2 and 4.

Answer (A) is correct. *(AFH Chap 6)*
DISCUSSION: When doing a rectangular course, think in terms of traffic pattern descriptions of the various legs. In Fig. 48, note that the airplane is going counterclockwise about the rectangular pattern. While on the base leg (between corners 3 and 4), the airplane is crabbed to the inside of the course. Thus, on corner 4, less than a 90° turn is required. Similarly, when the airplane proceeds through corner 1, it should roll out such that it is crabbed into the wind, and again, a less-than-90° angle is required.
Answer (B) is incorrect. On corner 2, you would have to turn more than 90° (you must roll out of your crab angle plus 90° to be heading downwind). Answer (C) is incorrect. Corner 2 is more than 90° (you start with the airplane crabbed to the outside of the rectangular course).

35. (Refer to Figure 48 on page 345.) In flying the rectangular course, when would the aircraft be turned more than 90°?

A. Corners 2 and 3.
B. Corners 1 and 3.
C. Corners 2 and 4.

Answer (A) is correct. *(AFH Chap 6)*
DISCUSSION: When doing a rectangular course, think in terms of traffic pattern descriptions of the various legs. In Fig. 48, note that the airplane is going counterclockwise about the rectangular pattern. When on the crosswind leg approaching corner 2, the airplane is crabbed to the outside of the corner. When turning to downwind, the airplane must make more than a 90° angle to become aligned downwind. Similarly, when turning from downwind to base on corner 3, the airplane must turn a full 90° plus some crab into the wind.
Answer (B) is incorrect. Corner 1 would require less than a 90° turn. Answer (C) is incorrect. Corner 4 would require less than a 90° turn.

36. (Refer to Figure 48 on page 345.) In flying the rectangular course, when should the aircraft bank vary from a steep bank to a medium bank?

A. Corner 1.
B. Corner 3.
C. Corners 2 and 3.

Answer (B) is correct. *(AFH Chap 6)*
DISCUSSION: When doing a rectangular course, think in terms of traffic pattern descriptions of the various legs. In Fig. 48, note that the airplane is going counterclockwise about the rectangular pattern. When on the downwind leg, one has a high groundspeed. On the turn to base, the corner must initially be steep. As the airplane gets away from the tailwind and into the crosswind, one reduces the bank, such as in corner 3.
Answer (A) is incorrect. In corner 1, one begins with a shallow bank (due to a slow groundspeed) and increases it to a medium as one encounters the crosswind. Answer (C) is incorrect. At corner 2, the bank is begun at medium and then increased to steep as groundspeed increases due to the tailwind.

37. (Refer to Figure 48 on page 345.) In flying the rectangular course, which would describe the proper angle of bank?

A. Corner 1 shallow, corner 2 medium, corner 3 steep, and corner 4 shallow.
B. Corner 1 shallow, corner 2 medium to steep, corner 3 steep, and corner 4 medium to shallow.
C. Corner 1 shallow to medium, corner 2 medium to steep, corner 3 steep to medium, and corner 4 medium to shallow.

Answer (C) is correct. *(AFH Chap 6)*
DISCUSSION: Entering corner 1, the pilot has a headwind and a slow groundspeed so the pilot begins with a shallow bank and increases it to a medium bank as the headwind component decreases and groundspeed increases due to the crosswind. In entering corner 2, the pilot uses a medium bank initially and increases it to a steeper bank as groundspeed increases due to the tailwind. In corner 3, the pilot starts with a steep bank initially due to the tailwind and a high groundspeed and then decreases it to a medium as the tailwind component decreases, which causes a decrease in groundspeed. In corner 4, the pilot starts with a medium in the crosswind and decreases it to a shallow as the pilot encounters the headwind and a slow groundspeed.
Answer (A) is incorrect. There has to be a change in bank at all four corners. Answer (B) is incorrect. At corner 1, the bank must increase from a shallow to a medium bank and at corner 3 the steep bank must be decreased to a medium bank.

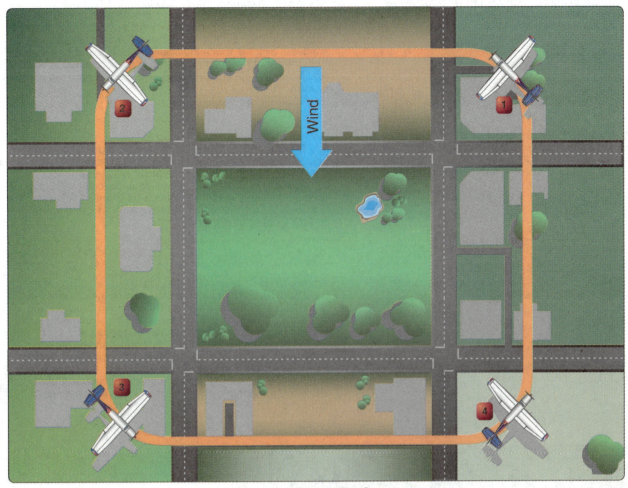

Figure 48. – Rectangular Course.

9.7 Turns around a Point

38. During turns around a point, an imaginary line from the pilot's eye and parallel to the lateral axis should point to the pylon when the aircraft is abeam the point headed directly

A. crosswind.
B. downwind only.
C. upwind or downwind.

Answer (C) is correct. *(AFH Chap 6)*
DISCUSSION: When directly into the wind or with the wind, no crabbing is needed and an extension of the airplane's lateral axis should intersect the "point" being flown around.
Answer (A) is incorrect. When flying crosswind, a crab angle will be needed in order to maintain the radius; therefore, the lateral axis does not point to the reference when viewed from the cockpit. Answer (B) is incorrect. No crab angle is needed when headed upwind or downwind, not only downwind.

39. (Refer to Figure 49 below.) At which points will the wing (lateral axis) be in alignment with the pylon during turns around a point?

A. 1 and 5.
B. 3 and 7.
C. 1, 3, 5, and 7.

Answer (B) is correct. *(AFH Chap 6)*
DISCUSSION: When directly into the wind or with the wind, no crabbing is needed and an extension of the airplane's lateral axis should intersect the "point" being flown around. Thus, the wing is in alignment with the pylon at points 3 and 7.
Answer (A) is incorrect. A crab angle is required at points 1 and 5. Answer (C) is incorrect. A crab angle is required at points 1 and 5.

40. (Refer to Figure 49 below.) If you instruct a student to practice turns around a point using a bank that is not to exceed 45° at its steepest point, it would be best to start at which of the positions shown?

A. 3.
B. 7.
C. 3 or 7.

Answer (B) is correct. *(AFH Chap 6)*
DISCUSSION: To enter turns around a point, the airplane should be flown on a downwind heading as at point 7, so that the maneuver is begun with the steepest bank, i.e., 45°.
Answer (A) is incorrect. Turns around a point should be entered downwind (point 7), not upwind (point 3). Answer (C) is incorrect. Turns around a point should be entered downwind (point 7), not upwind (point 3).

41. (Refer to Figure 49 below.) The groundspeed will be equal in which positions?

A. 1 and 5.
B. 1 and 5, 2 and 4, 6 and 8.
C. 1 and 5, 2 and 8, 4 and 6.

Answer (B) is correct. *(AFH Chap 6)*
DISCUSSION: In turns around a point, the groundspeed is equal wherever there is a direct crosswind on the circle, e.g., at 1 and 5. It is also equal whenever the same component of tailwind or headwind exists, such as at points 2 and 4, or 6 and 8.
Answer (A) is incorrect. Points 2 and 4 and points 6 and 8 will also have equal groundspeed. Answer (C) is incorrect. Point 2 will have a headwind component and 8 a tailwind component. Point 4 will have a headwind component and 6 a tailwind component. These relationships result in unequal groundspeeds.

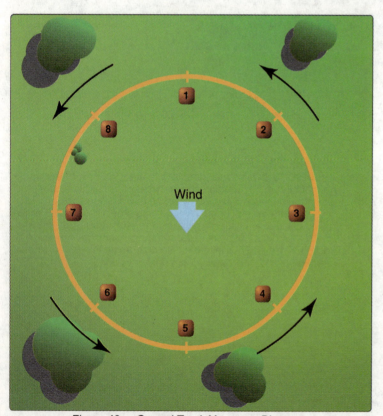

Figure 49. – Ground Track Maneuver Diagram.

SU 9: Flight Maneuvers   347

42. (Refer to Figure 49 on page 346.) The angle of bank will be most nearly equal in which positions?

A. 3 and 7.
B. 1 and 5.
C. 4 and 6.

Answer (B) is correct. *(AFH Chap 6)*
DISCUSSION: In turns around a point, the angle of bank will be most nearly equal when flying crosswind, i.e., points 1 and 5.
Answer (A) is incorrect. The bank is steepest at point 7 and shallowest at point 3. Answer (C) is incorrect. The bank is steeper at point 6 than at point 4.

43. (Refer to Figure 49 on page 346.) Which position will require the steepest bank?

A. 1.
B. 5.
C. 7.

Answer (C) is correct. *(AFH Chap 6)*
DISCUSSION: In turns around a point, the steepest bank is required when the aircraft is headed directly downwind, as at point 7.
Answer (A) is incorrect. At point 1, the aircraft is headed crosswind, not downwind. Answer (B) is incorrect. At point 5, the aircraft is headed crosswind, not downwind.

9.8 S-Turns across a Road

44. (Refer to Figure 51 below.) While practicing S-turns, a consistently smaller half-circle is made on one side of the road than on the other, and this turn is not completed before crossing the road or reference line. This would most likely occur in turn

A. 1-2-3 because the bank is decreased too rapidly during the latter part of the turn.
B. 4-5-6 because the bank is increased too rapidly during the early part of the turn.
C. 4-5-6 because the bank is increased too slowly during the latter part of the turn.

Answer (B) is correct. *(AFH Chap 6)*
DISCUSSION: Note that the wind in Fig. 51 is coming up from the bottom rather than from the top. The consistently smaller half-circle is made when on the upwind side of the road, i.e., 4-5-6. The initial bank is increased too rapidly, resulting in a smaller half-circle. Then an attempt is made to widen the turn out in the latter stages. Thus, the recrossing of the road is done at less than a 90° angle.
Answer (A) is incorrect. Decreasing the bank too rapidly in the latter stages of 1, 2, and 3 on the downwind side of the road increases, not decreases, the size of that half-circle. Answer (C) is incorrect. Increasing the bank too slowly at the latter stages of 4, 5, and 6 would make the half-circle larger, not smaller.

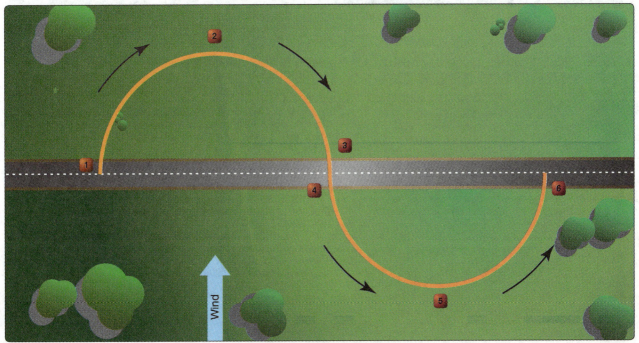

Figure 51. – S-Turn Diagram.

45. (Refer to Figure 50 below.) In which positions will the groundspeeds be equal?

A. 2 and 5.
B. 1 and 6, 2 and 5.
C. 1 and 6, 2 and 5, 3 and 4.

Answer (C) is correct. *(AFH Chap 6)*
DISCUSSION: Groundspeeds are equal when the same components of headwind, crosswind, or tailwind are encountered. The same component of headwind would be encountered at 1 and 6. The same crosswind component would be encountered at 2 and 5. The same tailwind component would be encountered at 3 and 4.
Answer (A) is incorrect. Groundspeeds are also equal at points 1 and 6 and at points 3 and 4. Answer (B) is incorrect. Groundspeeds are also equal at points 3 and 4.

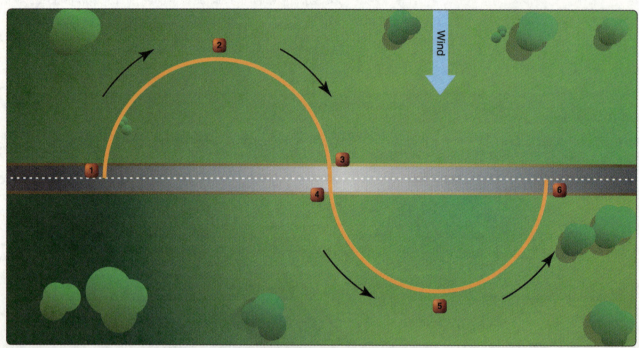

Figure 50. – S-Turn Diagram.

46. (Refer to Figure 50 above.) During S-turn practice, which positions require the steeper angle of bank?

A. 4 and 5.
B. 3 and 4.
C. 2 and 5.

Answer (B) is correct. *(AFH Chap 6)*
DISCUSSION: Steeper angles of bank in ground reference maneuvers are required when one has a tailwind such as at points 3 and 4.
Answer (A) is incorrect. Only at point 5 is a medium bank required due to the direct crosswind. Answer (C) is incorrect. At points 2 and 5, a medium bank is required due to the direct crosswind.

47. (Refer to Figure 50 above.) Proper execution of S-turns across a road requires that the aircraft be crabbed into the wind the greatest amounts at which points?

A. 3 and 4.
B. 2 and 5.
C. 1 and 6.

Answer (B) is correct. *(AFH Chap 6)*
DISCUSSION: The greatest crab in any maneuvering situation is required when encountering a direct crosswind, such as at points 2 and 5.
Answer (A) is incorrect. At points 3 and 4, the steepest angles of bank are required, not the greatest amount of crab. Answer (C) is incorrect. At 1 and 6, the shallowest angles of bank are required and very little crab is needed.

9.9 Eights-on-Pylons

48. The pivotal altitude for eights-on-pylons is dependent primarily upon the

A. groundspeed.
B. true airspeed.
C. distance from the pylon.

Answer (A) is correct. *(AFH Chap 6)*
DISCUSSION: There is a specific altitude at which, when an airplane turns at a given groundspeed, a projection of the reference line will appear to pivot on the pylon. The pivotal altitude does not vary with the angle of bank unless the bank is steep enough to affect the groundspeed.
Answer (B) is incorrect. Groundspeed, not true airspeed, affects the pivotal altitude. Answer (C) is incorrect. The distance from the pylon determines the degree of bank, not pivotal altitude.

49. (Refer to Figure 52 below.) While performing eights-on-pylons, the turn-and-slip indicator appears as shown in "2." The pilot must

A. increase altitude to obtain the correct pivotal altitude, and correct the skidding turn.
B. decrease altitude to obtain the correct pivotal altitude, and correct the slipping turn.
C. decrease the bank to hold the reference point on the pylon without slipping, because the radius of turn is too small.

Answer (A) is correct. *(AFH Chap 6)*
DISCUSSION: In Fig. 52, the turn coordinator indicates a left turn. Illustration 2 shows a skidding turn caused by excessive left rudder, which puts the left wing back. Thus, the reference point was apparently in front of the pylon, which means that the pilot was too low and should increase altitude.
Answer (B) is incorrect. Altitude should be increased, not decreased, and it is a skidding, not a slipping, turn. Answer (C) is incorrect. The amount of bank does not affect whether the reference point is behind or in front of the pylon, the altitude does, and it is a skidding, not a slipping, turn.

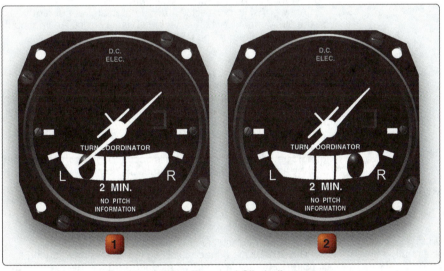

Figure 52. – Turn-and-Slip Indicators.

50. (Refer to Figure 52 above.) Misuse of rudder in attempting to hold the pylon during the performance of eights-on-pylons will result in which turn-and-slip indication?

A. "2" if above or below pivotal altitude.
B. "1" if below pivotal altitude; "2" if above pivotal altitude.
C. "1" if above pivotal altitude; "2" if below pivotal altitude.

Answer (C) is correct. *(AFH Chap 6)*
DISCUSSION: In Fig. 52, the turn coordinator indicates a left turn. Illustration 1 shows a slipping turn caused by excessive right rudder, which moves the left wing forward. Recall that, when one is at too high an altitude, the projected reference line appears to move behind the reference point. Conversely, in 2, left rudder is used in the left turn, which puts the ground reference line further back. Remember that, when one is below altitude, the reference point moves in front of the pylon.
Answer (A) is incorrect. If above the pivotal altitude, the reference point is behind the pylon and left rudder ("2" in Fig. 52) would increase that error. Answer (B) is incorrect. The use of rudder as illustrated corrects for being above pivotal altitude ("1" in Fig. 52) and below pivotal altitude ("2" in Fig. 52).

51. In properly coordinated eights-on-pylons, if the reference point is behind the pylon, it means the

A. angle of bank is too shallow.
B. airplane is above the pivotal altitude.
C. airplane is below the pivotal altitude.

Answer (B) is correct. *(AFH Chap 6)*
DISCUSSION: When the airplane is above the pivotal altitude, the projected reference line of sight on the wing appears to move behind the pylon.
Answer (A) is incorrect. The angle of bank does not affect the proximity point, whether the point is in front of or behind the pylon. Answer (C) is incorrect. If the airplane is below the pivotal altitude, the reference point will move forward in front of the pylon, not behind.

52. If the wing moves behind the pylon during properly coordinated eights-on-pylons, the airplane is

A. flying too fast.
B. below pivotal altitude.
C. above pivotal altitude.

Answer (C) is correct. *(AFH Chap 6)*
DISCUSSION: When the airplane is above the pivotal altitude, the projected reference line of sight on the wing appears to move behind the pylon.
Answer (A) is incorrect. Flying too fast causes the wing to move ahead of the pylon. Answer (B) is incorrect. When one is below pivotal altitude, the wing appears to move forward in front of the pylon.

9.10 Stalls, Spins, and Slow Flight

53. Which stall must be performed during a flight instructor -- airplane practical test?

A. Power-on or power-off.
B. Accelerated.
C. Imminent.

Answer (A) is correct. *(CFI PTS)*
DISCUSSION: At least one proficiency stall (power-on or power-off), at least one demonstration stall (cross-controlled, elevator trim, or secondary), and spins must be performed during a CFI-A practical test. At the discretion of the examiner, a spin sign-off may be accepted in lieu of performing spins.
Answer (B) is incorrect. An accelerated stall is not required on the CFI-A practical test. Answer (C) is incorrect. An imminent stall is not required on the CFI-A practical test.

54. The objective of a cross-control stall demonstration is to

A. emphasize the hazard of an excessive slip during a landing approach.
B. teach the proper recovery technique should this type of stall occur during final approach.
C. show the effect of improper control technique and emphasize the importance of coordinated control when making turns.

Answer (C) is correct. *(AFH Chap 4)*
DISCUSSION: The objective of cross-control stalls is to show the effect of improper control technique and emphasize the importance of using coordinated control pressures when making turns.
Answer (A) is incorrect. Slips are fine as long as adequate airspeed is maintained. Answer (B) is incorrect. The objective is to indicate how cross-control stalls occur so they can be avoided, as they are usually impossible to recover from at low altitudes.

55. If inadequate right rudder is used during a climbing right turn, what may occur if the aircraft stalls?

A. A spin to the left.
B. A tendency to yaw to the right.
C. A tendency to roll to the right.

Answer (A) is correct. *(AFH Chap 4)*
DISCUSSION: If inadequate right rudder is used during a climbing right turn, the ball will move toward the inside of the turn, indicating a slip. If a stall occurs in this situation, the left wing will drop, possibly leading to a spin if the proper corrective technique is not used.
Answer (B) is incorrect. The airplane will tend to yaw to the left, not the right, if inadequate right rudder is used. Answer (C) is incorrect. The airplane will tend to roll to the left, not the right, if inadequate right rudder is used during a stall.

56. Which is a correct spin recovery technique?

A. Apply forward elevator control followed by aileron opposite the spin.
B. Apply full forward elevator control followed by a coordinated rollout.
C. Reduce power to idle, apply opposite rudder and forward elevator control.

Answer (C) is correct. *(AFH Chap 4)*
DISCUSSION: Any time a spin is encountered, regardless of the conditions, the normal spin recovery sequence should be used: (1) reduce power to idle; (2) apply opposite rudder to slow rotation; (3) apply positive forward elevator movement to break the stall; (4) neutralize rudder as spinning stops; and (5) return to level flight.
Answer (A) is incorrect. The power should always be reduced to idle and ailerons should always remain neutral to avoid aggravating the spin characteristics. Answer (B) is incorrect. The power should always be reduced to idle to avoid aggravating the spin characteristics, and opposite rudder should be applied to slow the rotation.

57. Two distinct flight situations should be covered when teaching slow flight. These are the establishment and maintenance of

A. airspeeds appropriate for landing approaches, and flight at reduced airspeeds.
B. an airspeed which gives a stall warning indication, and an airspeed at which complete recovery can be made from stalls.
C. an airspeed at which the airplane is operating on the back side of the power curve, and an airspeed at which the elevator control can be held full-back with no further loss of control.

Answer (A) is correct. *(AFH Chap 4)*
DISCUSSION: Practice in slow flight should cover two distinct flight situations: (1) establishing and maintaining the airspeed appropriate for landing approaches and go-arounds in the airplane used, and (2) turning flight at the slowest airspeed at which the particular airplane is capable of continued controlled flight without stalling.
Answer (B) is incorrect. Minimum controllable airspeed or slow flight means that the airplane does not stall. Answer (C) is incorrect. The back side of the power curve refers to any flight below V_X. The speed at which the elevator control could be held full back with no further loss of control is above slow flight because, at slow flight, it results in a stall.

58. The primary purpose of practicing operations at reduced airspeeds is to enable students to

A. safely fly airport traffic patterns at various airspeeds.
B. develop proficiency at anticipating the onset of power-on stalls.
C. develop proficiency in their sense of feeling and their ability to use the controls properly at various speeds.

Answer (C) is correct. *(AFH Chap 4)*
DISCUSSION: The primary purpose of practicing operations at reduced airspeeds (slow flight) is to enable students to develop proficiency in their sense of feeling and their ability to use the controls properly at various speeds.
Answer (A) is incorrect. Airport traffic patterns should be flown at speeds greater than slow flight. Answer (B) is incorrect. Proficiency in anticipating power-on stalls is learned through the demonstration and practice of power-on stalls, not slow flight.

59. What is the correct procedure to follow if an aircraft is in the region of reverse command during a landing approach?

A. Increase angle of attack and power.
B. Decrease angle of attack and power.
C. Decrease angle of attack and increase power.

Answer (C) is correct. *(AFH Chap 8)*
DISCUSSION: When an aircraft is operating in the region of reverse command, i.e., behind the power curve, only a decrease in angle of attack and a simultaneous increase in power will allow the airplane to accelerate to a normal landing approach speed without an excessive loss of altitude.
Answer (A) is incorrect. An increase in angle of attack would only decrease airspeed further, resulting in a stall. Answer (B) is incorrect. A decrease in power will increase the sink rate, resulting in an excessive loss of altitude.

60. Which can result when operating in the region of reverse command?

A. It is not possible to climb.
B. Increased nose-up pitch does not affect rate of descent.
C. Increased nose-up pitch causes increased rate of descent.

Answer (C) is correct. *(AFH Chap 8)*
DISCUSSION: For a given power setting, an increased nose-up pitch attitude causes an increased rate of descent when flying at an airspeed less than L/D_{MAX}, i.e., region of reverse command. When flying at an airspeed slower than L/D_{MAX}, total drag increases due to induced drag increasing faster (due to higher angle of attack) than parasite drag decreases. Thus, at a given power setting, an increase in angle of attack will increase drag and cause an increased rate of descent.
Answer (A) is incorrect. It is always possible to climb as long as there is sufficient power. Answer (B) is incorrect. Increased nose-up pitch increases the rate of descent due to the increase in induced drag.

61. Common mistakes made by student pilots while first performing intentional stalls are

A. excessive rudder control, excessive airspeed buildup during recovery, and inadvertent secondary stall during recovery.
B. premature recovery, excessive back-elevator pressure, and excessive airspeed building during recovery.
C. fixation on the airspeed indicator, delayed recovery, and inadequate rudder control.

Answer (B) is correct. *(AFH Chap 4)*
DISCUSSION: Common errors in the initial performance of intentional stalls include but are not limited to premature recovery before a full stall is encountered, excessive back-elevator pressure resulting in an exaggerated nose-up attitude during the stall entry, and excessive airspeed building during recovery usually as a result of excessive forward-elevator pressure.
Answer (A) is incorrect. Students commonly use inadequate, not excessive, rudder control during their initial introduction to intentional stalls. Answer (C) is incorrect. Students commonly recover prematurely from their initial intentional stalls.

62. Secondary stalls result from

A. failure to recover from the initial stall.
B. abrupt control movement.
C. exceeding the critical angle of attack during maneuvering flight.

Answer (B) is correct. *(AFH Chap 4)*
DISCUSSION: This stall is called a secondary stall since it may occur after a recovery from a preceding stall. This stall usually occurs when the pilot uses abrupt control input to return to straight-and-level flight after a stall or spin recovery.
Answer (A) is incorrect. Secondary stalls occur after or during the recovery from an initial stall. Answer (C) is incorrect. Exceeding the critical angle of attack during maneuvering flight describes accelerated stalls, not secondary stalls.

9.11 Steep Turns

63. If an accelerated stall occurs in a steep turn, how will the aircraft respond?

A. The inside wing stalls first because it is flying at a higher angle of attack.
B. The outside wing stalls first because it is flying at a higher angle of attack.
C. In a slip, the high wing stalls first; in a skid, the low wing stalls first; in coordinated flight, both wings stall at the same time.

Answer (C) is correct. *(AFH Chap 9)*
DISCUSSION: An airplane will stall during a coordinated steep turn exactly as it does from straight flight except the pitching and rolling actions tend to be more sudden. If the airplane is slipping toward the inside of the turn at the time the stall occurs, it tends to roll rapidly toward the outside of the turn as the nose pitches down because the outside wing stalls before the inside wing. If the airplane is skidding toward the outside of the turn, it will have a tendency to roll to the inside of the turn because the inside wing stalls first.
Answer (A) is incorrect. Which wing stalls first is determined by the interference of airflow over the wing by the fuselage, e.g., in a slip or a skid. Answer (B) is incorrect. Which wing stalls first is determined by interference of airflow over the wing by the fuselage, e.g., in a slip or a skid.

64. If an accelerated stall occurs during a steep turn, in which direction would the aircraft tend to roll?

A. Toward the inside of the turn.
B. Toward the outside of the turn.
C. The direction of roll depends on whether the airplane is slipping, skidding, or in coordinated flight.

Answer (C) is correct. *(AFH Chap 9)*
DISCUSSION: An airplane will stall during a coordinated steep turn exactly as it does from straight flight except the pitching and rolling actions tend to be more sudden. If the airplane is slipping toward the inside of the turn at the time the stall occurs, it tends to roll rapidly toward the outside of the turn as the nose pitches down because the outside wing stalls before the inside wing. If the airplane is skidding toward the outside of the turn, it will have a tendency to roll to the inside of the turn because the inside wing stalls first.
Answer (A) is incorrect. Which wing stalls first is determined by the interference of airflow over the wing by the fuselage, e.g., in a slip or a skid. Answer (B) is incorrect. Which wing stalls first is determined by interference of airflow over the wing by the fuselage, e.g., in a slip or a skid.

65. Students should be taught that throughout a level, 720° steep turn to the right, the rudder is normally used to

A. prevent yawing.
B. control the rate of turn.
C. hold the aircraft in the turn once it is established.

Answer (A) is correct. *(AFH Chap 9)*
DISCUSSION: Throughout straight or turning flight, the rudder is normally used to prevent unwanted yawing. This produces coordinated flight.
Answer (B) is incorrect. The airspeed and the angle of bank control the rate of turn. Answer (C) is incorrect. The airplane holds itself in the turn once it is established.

66. How should a student be taught to correct for a nose-low attitude during a steep turn?

A. Apply back elevator pressure to attain the desired pitch attitude.
B. Reduce the angle of bank, then apply back elevator pressure to attain the desired pitch attitude.
C. Apply back elevator pressure to attain the desired pitch attitude, then reduce the angle of bank.

Answer (B) is correct. *(AFH Chap 9)*
DISCUSSION: To recover from an unintentional nose-low attitude during a steep turn, the pilot should first reduce the angle of bank with coordinated aileron and rudder pressure. Then back elevator pressure should be used to raise the airplane's nose to the desired pitch attitude. Finally, the desired angle of bank can be reestablished.
Answer (A) is incorrect. Attempting to raise the nose by first increasing back elevator pressure or adding power will usually cause a tight descending spiral. Answer (C) is incorrect. One reduces the angle of bank and then applies back elevator pressure rather than the reverse.

9.12 Chandelles

67. What may occur if the initial bank is too shallow when performing a chandelle?

A. Completing the maneuver with excessive airspeed.
B. Stalling the aircraft before reaching the 180° point.
C. Completing the maneuver with too low a pitch attitude.

Answer (B) is correct. *(AFH Chap 9)*
DISCUSSION: If the initial bank in a chandelle is too shallow, the turn to the 90° point may take too long and the aircraft may lose too much airspeed. The result would probably be a stall prior to completing the maneuver.
Answer (A) is incorrect. The maneuver will take excessive time, and excessive airspeed will be lost if the turn rate is too slow. Answer (C) is incorrect. One will not be able to complete the maneuver due to substantive loss of airspeed.

68. Pilots who initiate a chandelle with a bank that is too steep will most likely

A. stall before completing the maneuver.
B. turn more than 180° before completing the rollout.
C. perform a comparatively level steep turn with a nose-high rollout at the 180° point.

Answer (C) is correct. *(AFH Chap 9)*
DISCUSSION: When a chandelle is begun with the bank too steep, the airplane will turn too fast; not enough altitude will be gained and the pilot will increase pitch abruptly to attempt to get to minimum controllable airspeed at 180°.
Answer (A) is incorrect. Although significant back pressure is used, the critical angle of attack is not likely to be reached and therefore a stall could not take place (accelerated stall). Answer (B) is incorrect. Rollout is usually attained at 180° even if airspeed is too high.

69. When performing a chandelle, where should maximum pitch occur?

A. 45° point.
B. 90° point.
C. 180° point.

Answer (B) is correct. *(AFH Chap 9)*
DISCUSSION: At the 90° point, there is maximum pitch. This is when one begins the rollout in the chandelle.
Answer (A) is incorrect. At the 45° point, the pitch is increasing to the maximum pitch at 90°. Answer (C) is incorrect. The pitch is constant from 90° to 180°.

70. Which best describes pitch and bank during the first 90° of a chandelle?

A. Changing pitch and bank.
B. Constant pitch and bank.
C. Constant bank and changing pitch.

Answer (C) is correct. *(AFH Chap 9)*
DISCUSSION: During the first 90° of a chandelle, there is a constant bank and changing pitch. During the second 90° of a chandelle, there is a constant pitch and changing bank.
Answer (A) is incorrect. The bank is constant and the pitch changing during the first 90° of a chandelle. Answer (B) is incorrect. The pitch is changing throughout the first 90° of a chandelle.

71. Which best describes pitch and bank during the second 90° of a chandelle?

A. Changing pitch and bank.
B. Constant pitch and changing bank.
C. Constant bank and changing pitch.

Answer (B) is correct. *(AFH Chap 9)*
DISCUSSION: During the first 90° of a chandelle, there is a constant bank and changing pitch. During the second 90° of a chandelle, there is a constant pitch and changing bank.
Answer (A) is incorrect. The pitch is constant and the bank changing during the second 90° of a chandelle. Answer (C) is incorrect. Constant bank and changing pitch describes pitch and bank during the first 90° of a chandelle.

9.13 Lazy Eights

72. When performing a lazy eight, where should the maximum pitchup attitude occur?

A. 45° point.
B. 90° point.
C. 180° point.

Answer (A) is correct. *(AFH Chap 9)*
DISCUSSION: The maximum pitch-up attitude in a lazy eight is at the 45° point.
Answer (B) is incorrect. At the 90° point, there is a level pitch attitude. Answer (C) is incorrect. At the 180° point, there is a level pitch attitude.

73. When performing a lazy eight, when should the aircraft be at minimum airspeed?

A. 45° point.
B. 90° point.
C. 180° point.

Answer (B) is correct. *(AFH Chap 9)*
DISCUSSION: The minimum airspeed point in a lazy eight is at the 90° point.
Answer (A) is incorrect. At the 45° point, the airspeed is decreasing but not at the minimum. Answer (C) is incorrect. At the 180° point, the airplane is at the maximum airspeed, which is also the entry airspeed.

74. When performing a lazy eight, where should the maximum pitchdown attitude occur?

A. 90° point.
B. 135° point.
C. 180° point.

Answer (B) is correct. *(AFH Chap 9)*
DISCUSSION: In a lazy eight, the maximum pitch-down attitude occurs at the 135° point.
Answer (A) is incorrect. At the 90° point, the airplane is at a level pitch attitude. Answer (C) is incorrect. At the 180° point, the airplane is at a level pitch attitude.

75. When performing a lazy eight, when should the maximum altitude occur?

A. 45° point.
B. 90° point.
C. 180° point.

Answer (B) is correct. *(AFH Chap 9)*
DISCUSSION: The maximum altitude in a lazy eight occurs at the 90° point.
Answer (A) is incorrect. At the 45° point, the maximum pitch, not altitude, occurs. Answer (C) is incorrect. At the 180° point, the airplane is at a minimum altitude, which is also the entry altitude.

76. What should occur at the 90° point of a lazy eight?

A. Airspeed and altitude should be the same as at entry.
B. Maximum pitch attitude, minimum airspeed, and minimum bank.
C. Steepest bank, minimum airspeed, maximum altitude, and level pitch attitude.

Answer (C) is correct. *(AFH Chap 9)*
DISCUSSION: At the 90° point of a lazy eight, one is at the steepest bank, the minimum airspeed, and the maximum altitude with a level pitch attitude.
Answer (A) is incorrect. At the 180° point, not the 90° point, airspeed and altitude should be the same as at entry. Answer (B) is incorrect. The pitch attitude at 90° is level, not maximum, and the bank is maximum, not minimum.

77. Which is the most probable result if a pilot initiates the climbing turn portions of the lazy eight with banks that are too steep?

A. Completing each 180° change of direction with a net gain of altitude.
B. Attaining a pitch attitude that is too steep and stalling at the top of the climbing turn.
C. Turning at a rate too fast for the rate of climb and therefore, completing each 180° change of direction with excessive airspeed.

Answer (C) is correct. *(AFH Chap 9)*
DISCUSSION: At no time is the airplane flown straight or level in the maneuver. If the pilot initiates the climbing turns with too much bank, the turn rate will be too fast for the rate of climb and the turn will be completed with excessive airspeed.
Answer (A) is incorrect. If the turn is too sharp, not enough altitude (rather than too much) will be gained through the first 90° of the maneuver. Answer (B) is incorrect. If the pilot initiates the climbing turn portions of a lazy eight with excessive pitch, not bank, it will result in attaining a pitch attitude that is too steep and stalling at the top of the climbing turn.

78. What would cause the 45° point to be reached before the maximum pitchup attitude during a lazy eight?

A. Beginning with too slow a rate of roll.
B. Beginning with too rapid a rate of roll.
C. Allowing the airspeed to remain too high causing the rate of turn to increase.

Answer (B) is correct. *(AFH Chap 9)*
DISCUSSION: In lazy eights, one would reach the 45° point before the maximum pitch-up attitude if one began with too rapid a rate of roll, i.e., made the turn too fast.
Answer (A) is incorrect. If one made the turn too slowly, one would get to the 45° point too late. Answer (C) is incorrect. If the airspeed is too high, the rate of turn decreases, not increases.

79. At what point in a lazy eight is it most likely necessary to exert opposing aileron and rudder pressures in order to maintain coordinated flight?

A. At the point of slowest speed.
B. At the point of fastest speed.
C. At the point of lowest pitch attitude.

Answer (A) is correct. *(AFH Chap 9)*
DISCUSSION: As the airplane's nose is being lowered toward the 90° reference point in a lazy eight to the right, you should continue to increase the right rudder pressure to compensate for the increased torque. Due to the decreasing airspeed, a slight amount of opposite aileron pressure may be required to prevent the bank from becoming too steep. This is at the point of slowest airspeed.
Answer (B) is incorrect. The point of fastest speed occurs at the 180° point of the maneuver, where the need for right rudder is less. Answer (C) is incorrect. The lowest pitch attitude occurs at the 135° point of the maneuver, where the need for right rudder is less.

SU 9: Flight Maneuvers

80. (Refer to Figure 52 below.) During practice of lazy eights, the most probable cause of the uncoordinated situation at the completion of 90° of turn (indicated by the turn-and-slip indicator shown in "1") is the

A. use of too much right rudder pressure.
B. use of too much left rudder control pressure.
C. use of too little right rudder pressure.

Answer (A) is correct. *(AFH Chap 9)*
DISCUSSION: In Fig. 52, Illustration 1, the turn coordinator indicates a slipping turn to the left. Thus, right rudder pressure must be reduced (or left rudder pressure must be increased) to center the ball and attain coordinated flight.
Answer (B) is incorrect. The ball would be deflected to the right, not left, if insufficient right rudder pressure were used.
Answer (C) is incorrect. The ball would be deflected to the right, not left, if excessive left rudder pressure were used.

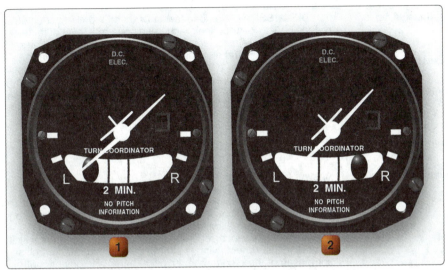

Figure 52. – Turn-and-Slip Indicators.

9.14 Flight by Reference to Instruments

81. Which instrument provides the most pertinent information (primary) for pitch control in straight-and-level flight?

A. Vertical speed indicator.
B. Attitude indicator.
C. Altimeter.

Answer (C) is correct. *(IFH Chap 7)*
DISCUSSION: The altimeter is the primary flight instrument for pitch control in straight-and-level flight.
Answer (A) is incorrect. The vertical speed indicator is a secondary pitch instrument during level flight. Fluctuations in vertical speed indicate changes in pitch. Answer (B) is incorrect. The attitude indicator is a secondary pitch instrument for straight-and-level flight. It aids in maintaining the primary instruments at the desired indication.

82. What instrument(s) is (are) supporting bank instrument(s) when entering a constant airspeed climb from straight-and-level flight?

A. Heading indicator.
B. Turn coordinator and heading indicator.
C. Attitude indicator and turn coordinator.

Answer (C) is correct. *(IFH Chap 7)*
DISCUSSION: The attitude indicator and turn coordinator are supporting instruments for bank during straight flight regardless of pitch attitude.
Answer (A) is incorrect. The heading indicator is the primary, not secondary, bank instrument for straight flight. Answer (B) is incorrect. The heading indicator is the primary, not secondary, bank instrument for straight flight.

83. Which instruments are considered primary and supporting for bank, respectively, when establishing a level standard-rate turn?

A. Turn coordinator and heading indicator.
B. Attitude indicator and turn coordinator.
C. Turn coordinator and attitude indicator.

Answer (B) is correct. *(IFH Chap 7)*
DISCUSSION: When establishing a standard rate turn, the attitude indicator is primary to establish the approximate angle of bank and the turn coordinator is supporting.
Answer (A) is incorrect. The attitude indicator, not turn coordinator, is primary. Answer (C) is incorrect. Only after the standard rate turn has been established do the two instruments change function, and the turn coordinator is now primary and attitude indicator is supporting.

84. If an airplane is in an unusual flight attitude and the attitude indicator has exceeded its limits, which instruments should be relied upon to determine pitch attitude before recovery?

A. Airspeed indicator and altimeter.
B. Turn indicator and vertical speed indicator.
C. Vertical speed indicator and airspeed indicator.

Answer (A) is correct. *(IFH Chap 7)*
DISCUSSION: If the attitude indicator is inoperative, a nose-low or nose-high attitude can be determined by the airspeed and altimeter. In a nose-high attitude, airspeed is decreasing and altimeter is increasing, and vice versa for nose-low attitudes.
Answer (B) is incorrect. The turn indicator indicates nothing about pitch attitude and the vertical speed indicator is much less reliable than the altimeter for immediate altitude sensing.
Answer (C) is incorrect. The vertical speed indicator is much less reliable than the altimeter for altitude sensing.

85. Which is the correct sequence for recovery from a spiraling, nose-low, increasing airspeed, unusual flight attitude?

A. Increase pitch attitude, reduce power, and level wings.
B. Reduce power, correct bank attitude, and raise nose to a level attitude.
C. Reduce power, raise nose to a level attitude, and correct bank attitude.

Answer (B) is correct. *(IFH Chap 7)*
DISCUSSION: If a nose-low unusual attitude is encountered, reduce power, correct bank, and raise nose to a level attitude.
Answer (A) is incorrect. By increasing the pitch first, you will tighten the spiral and also may place an excess load factor on the airplane. Answer (C) is incorrect. By trying to raise the nose before correcting or leveling the wings, you may aggravate the unusual attitude even more by tightening the spiral and also may place an excess load factor on the airplane.

86. What is the first fundamental skill in attitude instrument flying?

A. Aircraft control.
B. Instrument cross-check.
C. Instrument interpretation.

Answer (B) is correct. *(IFH Chap 6)*
DISCUSSION: The first fundamental skill in attitude instrument flying is instrument cross-check. Cross-checking is the continuous and logical observation of instruments for attitude and performance information.
Answer (A) is incorrect. The third, not first, fundamental skill in attitude instrument flying is aircraft control. Aircraft control is composed of three components: pitch, bank, and power control. Answer (C) is incorrect. The second, not first, fundamental skill in attitude instrument flying is instrument interpretation. For each maneuver, you must know the performance to expect and the combination of instruments that you must interpret in order to control airplane attitude during the maneuver.

87. What is the correct sequence in which to use the three skills used in instrument flying?

A. Aircraft control, cross-check, and instrument interpretation.
B. Instrument interpretation, cross-check, and aircraft control.
C. Cross-check, instrument interpretation, and aircraft control.

Answer (C) is correct. *(IFH Chap 6)*
DISCUSSION: The correct sequence in which to use the three fundamental skills of instrument flying is cross-check, instrument interpretation, and aircraft control. Although you learn these skills separately and in deliberate sequence, a measure of your proficiency in precision flying will be your ability to integrate these skills into unified, smooth, positive control responses to maintain any desired flight path.
Answer (A) is incorrect. Aircraft control is the third, not first, skill used in instrument flying. Answer (B) is incorrect. Instrument interpretation is the second, not first, skill and cross-check is the first, not second, skill used in instrument flying.

88. As power is reduced to change airspeed from high to low cruise in level flight, which instruments are primary for pitch, bank, and power, respectively?

A. Attitude indicator, heading indicator, and manifold pressure gauge or tachometer.
B. Altimeter, attitude indicator, and airspeed indicator.
C. Altimeter, heading indicator, and manifold pressure gauge or tachometer.

Answer (C) is correct. *(IFH Chap 6)*
DISCUSSION: In straight-and-level flight, when reducing airspeed from high to low cruise, the primary instrument for pitch is the altimeter; the primary instrument for bank is the heading indicator; and the primary instrument for power is the manifold pressure gauge or tachometer.
Answer (A) is incorrect. The primary pitch instrument is the altimeter, not attitude indicator. Answer (B) is incorrect. The primary bank instrument is the heading indicator, not attitude indicator; and the primary power instrument is the manifold pressure gauge or tachometer, not airspeed indicator.

89. What is the primary bank instrument once a standard-rate turn is established?

A. Attitude indicator.
B. Turn coordinator.
C. Heading indicator.

Answer (B) is correct. *(IFH Chap 6)*
DISCUSSION: After a standard-rate turn is established, the turn coordinator is the primary bank instrument.
Answer (A) is incorrect. The attitude indicator is the primary bank instrument in establishing a standard-rate turn but not for maintaining the turn once established. Answer (C) is incorrect. The heading indicator is the primary bank instrument for straight flight.

90. What is the primary pitch instrument when establishing a constant altitude standard-rate turn?

A. Altimeter.
B. VSI.
C. Airspeed indicator.

Answer (A) is correct. *(IFH Chap 6)*
DISCUSSION: The primary pitch instrument in level flight, either straight or turns, is the altimeter.
Answer (B) is incorrect. The vertical speed indicator is a supporting, not primary, pitch instrument for establishing a level standard-rate turn. Answer (C) is incorrect. The airspeed indicator is the primary power, not pitch, instrument when establishing a constant altitude standard-rate turn.

9.15 Teaching Methods

91. During training flights, an instructor should interject realistic distractions to determine if a student can

A. learn despite stressful conditions.
B. maintain aircraft control while his or her attention is diverted.
C. perform maneuvers using the integrated method of flight instruction.

Answer (B) is correct. *(AIH Chap 8)*
DISCUSSION: The function of distractors, such as pointing out objects on the ground, simulated engine emergencies, reading the outside air temperature gauge, asking questions, removing objects from the glove compartment, etc., is to determine whether student pilots can maintain aircraft control while their attention is diverted.
Answer (A) is incorrect. Stressful conditions discourage learning. Answer (C) is incorrect. The integrated method of flight instruction refers to learning maneuvers by both visual and instrument references, not to the use of distractions.

92. Instructors should include realistic distractions so the student will

A. become confused and disoriented.
B. declare an emergency.
C. develop the skill of coping with the distraction while maintaining positive control of the aircraft.

Answer (C) is correct. *(AIH Chap 9)*
DISCUSSION: The goal of including realistic distractions in training and testing is to ensure that pilot applicants can adjust to the distraction while still maintaining control of the aircraft.
Answer (A) is incorrect. A good instructor never uses methods purposefully designed to discourage learning, but rather always chooses methods to educate the student pilot. Distractions are introduced in flight training to help pilots learn to adapt to real-world situations later in their practical flying experiences. Answer (B) is incorrect. While it is important for a student pilot to know when to declare an emergency, this is not a primary instructional goal of using realistic distractions in flight training.

93. The objective of the Practical Test Standards (PTS) is to ensure the certification of pilots at a high level of performance and proficiency, consistent with

A. the time available.
B. safety.
C. their abilities.

Answer (B) is correct. *(AIH Chap 5)*
DISCUSSION: The objective of the PTS is to ensure the certification of pilots at a high level of performance and proficiency, consistent with safety.
Answer (A) is incorrect. The objective of the PTS is to ensure the certification of pilots at a high level of performance and proficiency, consistent with safety, not the time available. Answer (C) is incorrect. The objective of the PTS is to ensure the certification of pilots at a high level of performance and proficiency, consistent with safety, not their abilities.

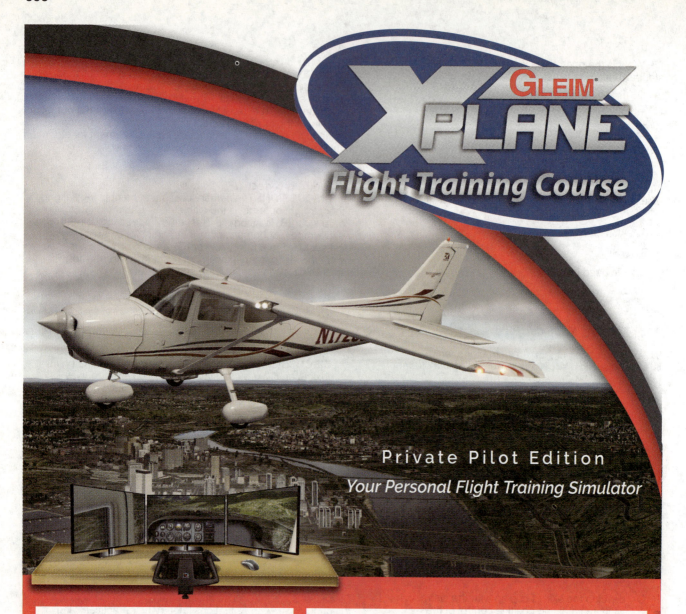

STUDY UNIT TEN
AEROMEDICAL FACTORS AND
AERONAUTICAL DECISION MAKING (ADM)

(5 pages of outline)

10.1	Hypoxia	(9 questions) 359, 363
10.2	Hyperventilation	(3 questions) 360, 365
10.3	Spatial Disorientation and Illusions in Flight	(4 questions) 360, 365
10.4	Night Vision	(2 questions) 360, 366
10.5	Flight after Scuba Diving	(2 questions) 360, 366
10.6	Motion Sickness	(2 questions) 361, 367
10.7	Aeronautical Decision Making (ADM)	(22 questions) 361, 367

This study unit contains outlines of major concepts tested, sample test questions and answers regarding aeromedical factors and aeronautical decision making (ADM), and an explanation of each answer. The table of contents above lists each subunit within this study unit, the number of questions pertaining to that particular subunit, and the pages on which the outlines and questions begin, respectively.

Recall that the **sole purpose** of this book is to expedite your passing of the FAA pilot knowledge test for the CFI, BGI, or AGI certificate. Accordingly, all extraneous material (i.e., topics or regulations not directly tested on the FAA pilot knowledge test) is omitted, even though much more knowledge is necessary to become a proficient flight or ground instructor. This additional material is presented in *Pilot Handbook* and *Flight Instructor Flight Maneuvers and Practical Test Prep*, available from Gleim Publications, Inc. Order online at www.GleimAviation.com.

10.1 HYPOXIA

1. Hypoxia is a lack of sufficient oxygen in the body cells or tissues caused by an inadequate supply of oxygen, inadequate transportation of oxygen, or inability of the body tissues to use oxygen.

    a. As altitude increases (e.g., during a climb to 18,000 ft.), the percentage of oxygen in the atmosphere remains the same, but atmospheric (barometric) pressure drops.

2. When flying in an unpressurized airplane above 15,000 ft. without supplemental oxygen, the most likely physical changes to the occupants are a development of a blue coloration of the lips and fingernails along with tunnel vision.

3. Belligerence or a false sense of security may be symptoms of hypoxia.

    a. The advantage of experiencing hypoxia in an altitude chamber is that it helps pilots learn to recognize their own symptoms in a controlled environment.

    b. Anemic (or hypemic) hypoxia (a reduction in the oxygen-carrying capacity of the blood) has the same symptoms as hypoxic (altitude) hypoxia, but it is most often a result of carbon monoxide poisoning from a leaking exhaust manifold.

4. Alcohol renders a pilot more susceptible to disorientation and hypoxia.

5. Smoking reduces the oxygen-carrying capability of the blood due to the carbon monoxide inhaled.

6. Although not required, supplemental oxygen is recommended for use when flying at night above 5,000 ft. MSL.

10.2 HYPERVENTILATION

1. Hyperventilation occurs when an excessive amount of air is breathed in and out of the lungs, e.g., when one becomes excited and/or undergoes stress, tension, fear, or anxiety.

    a. It is the result of a lack of carbon dioxide in the body.
    b. While a pilot is using supplemental oxygen, hyperventilation can be caused by rapid or extra deep breathing.

2. A pilot should be able to overcome the symptoms of or avoid future occurrences of hyperventilation by slowing the breathing rate to allow the amount of carbon dioxide to increase to the proper level.

10.3 SPATIAL DISORIENTATION AND ILLUSIONS IN FLIGHT

1. Spatial disorientation is a state of temporary spatial confusion resulting from misleading information being sent to the brain by various sensory organs. The condition is sometimes called vertigo.
2. The recommended procedure to prevent or overcome spatial disorientation (in IMC) is to rely entirely on the indications of the flight instruments.
3. An illusion that the aircraft is at a higher altitude than it actually is can be produced by upsloping terrain.
4. A rapid acceleration can create the illusion of being in a nose-up attitude.
5. Atmospheric haze creates the illusion of being at a greater distance from traffic or terrain than you actually are.

10.4 NIGHT VISION

1. One aid in increasing night vision effectiveness is to force the eyes to view off center.
2. Dark adaptation is impaired by exposure to cabin pressure altitudes above 5,000 ft. MSL.

10.5 FLIGHT AFTER SCUBA DIVING

1. A pilot or passenger who intends to fly after scuba diving should allow the body sufficient time to rid itself of excess nitrogen absorbed during the dive.

    a. If the appropriate amount of time is not allowed, decompression sickness due to evolved gas can result, creating a serious in-flight emergency.

2. The recommended waiting times are shown in the table below.

    a. The recommended altitudes are actual flight altitudes above MSL and not pressurized cabin altitudes. This takes into consideration the risk of decompression of the aircraft during flight.

	Dives Not Requiring Controlled Ascent	Dives Requiring Controlled Ascent
Flight at/below altitudes of 8,000 ft. MSL	At least 12 hr.	At least 24 hr.
Flight above altitudes of 8,000 ft. MSL	At least 24 hr.	At least 24 hr.

10.6 MOTION SICKNESS

1. Motion sickness is caused by continued stimulation of the tiny portion of the inner ear that controls the sense of balance.
2. To help their students combat motion sickness, instructors should tell them to avoid unnecessary head movements and keep their eyes on a point outside of the aircraft.

10.7 AERONAUTICAL DECISION MAKING (ADM)

1. The study of human behavior is an attempt to explain how and why humans function the way they do.
    a. The Federal Aviation Administration (FAA) utilizes studies of human behavior in an attempt to reduce human error in aviation.
    b. Three out of four accidents result from human error.
    c. Eliminating human error is an unrealistic goal because errors are a normal part of human behavior.
    d. On the other hand, realizing that many aviation accidents are preventable means designing ways to reduce the consequences of human error. The study of human behavior coupled with pilot training that offsets predictable human error helps achieve that goal.
2. Aeronautical decision making (ADM) can be defined as a systematic approach to the mental process used by pilots to consistently determine the best course of action in response to a given set of circumstances.
3. Risk management is the part of the decision-making process that relies on situational awareness, problem recognition, and good judgment to reduce risks associated with each flight.
    a. The four fundamental risk elements in the ADM process that comprise any given aviation situation are the
        1) Pilot
        2) Aircraft
        3) Environment
        4) Mission (type of operation)
4. One step in the ADM process for good decision making is to identify personal attitudes hazardous to safe flight.
    a. Examples of classical behavioral traps that experienced pilots may fall into are the compulsion to complete a flight as planned, the desire to please passengers, the pressure to meet schedules, and the determination to "get the job done."
    b. At some time, many experienced pilots have fallen prey to dangerous tendencies or behavior problems that must be identified and eliminated, including
        1) Peer pressure
        2) Scud running
        3) Loss of positional or situational awareness
        4) Operating without adequate fuel reserves
    c. In order to gain a realistic perspective on your attitude toward flying, you should take a Self-Assessment Hazardous Attitude Inventory Test.

d. ADM addresses the following five hazardous attitudes:

1) Antiauthority -- "Do not tell me what to do!"

   a) EXAMPLE: During a stall recovery, the CFI allows the student to exceed maneuvering speed. An antiauthority attitude expressed by the CFI would be "The aircraft can handle a lot more than the maneuvering speed."

2) Impulsivity -- "Do something quickly!"
3) Invulnerability -- "It will not happen to me."
4) Macho -- "I can do it."
5) Resignation -- "What is the use?"

5. In the ADM process, the first step in neutralizing a hazardous attitude is recognizing it.

   a. When you recognize a hazardous thought, you should label it as hazardous; then correct the attitude by stating the corresponding antidote.

   b. Hazardous attitudes, which contribute to poor pilot judgment, can be effectively counteracted by the appropriate antidote, as listed below.

   1) Antiauthority -- "Follow the rules. They are usually right."
   2) Impulsivity -- "Not so fast. Think first."
   3) Invulnerability -- "It could happen to me."
   4) Macho -- "Taking chances is foolish."
   5) Resignation -- "I am not helpless. I can make a difference."

6. Success in reducing stress associated with crisis management in the cockpit begins by making a personal assessment of stress in all areas of your life.

   a. To help manage cockpit stress, you should try to relax and think rationally at the first sign of stress.

7. The DECIDE process consists of six elements to help provide a pilot a logical way of approaching ADM. These elements are to

   a. **D**etect
   b. **E**stimate
   c. **C**hoose
   d. **I**dentify
   e. **D**o
   f. **E**valuate

8. A flight instructor should begin teaching ADM when the student has the ability to control the airplane confidently during the most basic maneuvers.

9. Glass cockpits have many benefits, but they also require pilots to recognize the risks associated with them.

   a. All human activity involving technical devices entails some element of risk. Knowledge, experience, and flight requirements tilt the odds in favor of safe and successful flights. The advanced avionics aircraft offers many new capabilities and simplifies the basic flying tasks but only if the pilot is properly trained and all the equipment is working properly.

   b. Most of the aviation community believes automation has made flying safer, but there is a fear that pilots fail to see that automation is a double-edged sword.

   1) Pilots must understand both the advantages and limitations of automation. Experience has shown that automated systems can make some errors more evident while sometimes hiding other errors or making them less obvious.

   2) Humans are characteristically poor monitors of automated systems. When passively monitoring an automated system for faults, abnormalities, or other infrequent events, humans perform poorly. The more reliable the system is, the worse the human performance becomes.

SU 10: Aeromedical Factors and Aeronautical Decision Making (ADM) 363

      3) It is a paradox of automation that technically advanced avionics can both increase and decrease pilot awareness.

  c. Pilots should not be lulled into a false sense of security simply because they have advanced avionics. Judgment and aeronautical decision making serve as the bridge between technology and safety. Any flight you make involves almost infinite combinations of pilot skill, experience, condition, and proficiency; aircraft equipment and performance; environmental conditions; and external influences. Both individually and in combination, these factors can compress the safety buffer provided by your baseline personal minimums.

QUESTIONS AND ANSWER EXPLANATIONS: All of the AGI/CFI knowledge test questions chosen by the FAA for release as well as additional questions selected by Gleim relating to the material in the previous outlines are reproduced on the following pages. These questions have been organized into the same subunits as the outlines. To the immediate right of each question are the correct answer and answer explanation. You should cover these answers and answer explanations while responding to the questions. Refer to the general discussion in the Introduction on how to take the FAA knowledge test.

Remember that the questions from the FAA knowledge test bank have been reordered by topic and organized into a meaningful sequence. Also, the first line of the answer explanation gives the citation of the authoritative source for the answer.

QUESTIONS

10.1 Hypoxia

1. Hypoxia is the result of

A. excessive nitrogen in the bloodstream.
B. reduced barometric pressures at altitude.
C. decreasing amount of oxygen as your altitude increases.

Answer (B) is correct. *(AIM Para 8-1-2)*
DISCUSSION: Hypoxia is a state of oxygen deficiency in the body sufficient to impair functions of the brain and other organs. Hypoxia from exposure to altitude is due only to the reduced barometric pressures encountered at altitude, for the concentration of oxygen remains about 21% from the ground out to space.
Answer (A) is incorrect. Decompression sickness, not hypoxia, is the result of excessive nitrogen in the bloodstream. Answer (C) is incorrect. As altitude increases, the amount of oxygen remains constant at about 21%.

2. During a climb to 18,000 feet, the percentage of oxygen in the atmosphere

A. increases.
B. decreases.
C. remains the same.

Answer (C) is correct. *(AIM Para 8-1-2)*
DISCUSSION: Hypoxia from exposure to altitude is due only to the reduced barometric pressures encountered at altitude. The concentration of oxygen in the atmosphere remains about 21% from the ground out to space.
Answer (A) is incorrect. Although atmospheric pressure changes, the percentage of oxygen in the atmosphere remains the same. Answer (B) is incorrect. Barometric pressure, not the percentage of oxygen, decreases during a climb to 18,000 ft.

3. What physical change would most likely occur to occupants of an unpressurized aircraft flying above 15,000 feet without supplemental oxygen?

A. Gases trapped in the body contract and prevent nitrogen from escaping the bloodstream.
B. The pressure in the middle ear becomes less than the atmospheric pressure in the cabin.
C. A blue coloration of the lips and fingernails develop along with tunnel vision.

Answer (C) is correct. *(AIM Para 8-1-2)*
DISCUSSION: At cabin pressure altitudes above 15,000 ft., without supplemental oxygen, the periphery of the visual field grays out to a point where only central vision remains (tunnel vision). Additionally, a blue coloration (cyanosis) of the fingernails and lips develops.
Answer (A) is incorrect. When climbing in an unpressurized aircraft, gases in your body expand, not contract. Also, nitrogen in the blood will form bubbles to escape from the bloodstream, which causes decompression sickness. Decompression sickness normally does not occur below 25,000 ft., unless you have been scuba diving prior to flying. Answer (B) is incorrect. The ear may actually hold a greater, not lower, pressure temporarily until you equalize with swallowing.

4. Anemic hypoxia has the same symptoms as hypoxic hypoxia, but it is most often a result of

  A. poor blood circulation.
  B. a leaking exhaust manifold.
  C. use of alcohol or drugs before flight.

Answer (B) is correct. *(AC 61-107A)*
DISCUSSION: Anemic hypoxia refers to hypoxia resulting from a reduction in the oxygen-carrying capacity of the blood, rather than from a lack of atmospheric pressure. This can be the result of anemia, of carbon monoxide poisoning from a leaking exhaust manifold, or from smoking.
  Answer (A) is incorrect. Stagnant, not anemic, hypoxia is the result of poor blood circulation. Answer (C) is incorrect. Histotoxic, not anemic, hypoxia is caused by the use of alcohol or drugs before flight.

5. Which statement is true regarding alcohol in the human system?

  A. Alcohol renders a pilot more susceptible to hypoxia.
  B. Small amounts of alcohol will not impair flying skills.
  C. Coffee helps metabolize alcohol and alleviates a hangover.

Answer (A) is correct. *(AIM Para 8-1-2)*
DISCUSSION: Small amounts of alcohol and low doses of certain drugs, such as antihistamines, tranquilizers, sedatives, and analgesics, can, through their depressant action, render the brain much more susceptible to hypoxia.
  Answer (B) is incorrect. Even small amounts of alcohol in the system decrease judgment and decision-making abilities. Answer (C) is incorrect. Neither coffee nor any other substance increases the rate at which the body metabolizes alcohol.

6. Which statement concerning hypoxia is true?

  A. Belligerence or a false sense of security may be symptoms of hypoxia.
  B. Hypoxia is caused by nitrogen bubbles in the joints and bloodstream.
  C. Forcing oneself to concentrate on the flight instruments will help to overcome the effects of hypoxia.

Answer (A) is correct. *(AIM Para 8-1-2)*
DISCUSSION: Symptoms of hypoxia vary, but one of the earliest effects of hypoxia is impairment of judgment. Other symptoms may include belligerence or a sense of well-being, poor coordination, sweating, headache, drowsiness, dizziness, deterioration of vision, etc.
  Answer (B) is incorrect. Decompression sickness, not hypoxia, is caused by nitrogen bubbles in the joints and bloodstream. Answer (C) is incorrect. Forcing oneself to concentrate on the flight instruments will help to overcome the effects of spatial disorientation, not hypoxia.

7. The advantage of experiencing hypoxia in an altitude chamber is

  A. it helps pilots learn to recognize their own symptoms in a controlled environment.
  B. a person will be able to observe many hypoxic symptoms in several people at the same time.
  C. when a person becomes hypoxic, air can quickly be readmitted to the chamber to revive that person.

Answer (A) is correct. *(AIM Para 8-1-2)*
DISCUSSION: The effects of hypoxia are usually quite difficult to recognize, especially when they occur gradually. Because symptoms of hypoxia do not vary in an individual, the ability to recognize hypoxia can be greatly improved by experiencing and witnessing the effects of hypoxia during an altitude chamber "flight."
  Answer (B) is incorrect. The main advantage is pilots can learn to recognize their own symptoms, not those of others. Answer (C) is incorrect. While it is true, the main advantage is pilots can learn to recognize symptoms of hypoxia within themselves.

8. How can smoking affect a pilot?

  A. Can decrease night vision by up to 50 percent.
  B. Reduces the oxygen-carrying capability of the blood.
  C. Creates additional carbon dioxide gases in the body which often leads to hyperventilation.

Answer (B) is correct. *(AIM Para 8-1-2)*
DISCUSSION: Carbon monoxide inhaled in smoking can reduce the oxygen-carrying capacity of the blood to the degree that the amount of oxygen provided to body tissues will already be equivalent to the oxygen provided to the tissues when exposed to a cabin pressure altitude of several thousand feet.
  Answer (A) is incorrect. Smoking can decrease night vision by 20%, not 50%. Answer (C) is incorrect. Smoking creates additional carbon monoxide, not carbon dioxide, in the body which can lead to hypoxia, not hyperventilation.

9. Although not required, supplemental oxygen is recommended for use when flying at night above

  A. 5,000 feet.
  B. 10,000 feet.
  C. 12,500 feet.

Answer (A) is correct. *(AIM Para 8-1-2)*
DISCUSSION: For optimal protection, pilots are encouraged to use supplemental oxygen above 10,000 ft. MSL during the day and above 5,000 ft. MSL at night (when the eyes become more sensitive to oxygen deprivation).
  Answer (B) is incorrect. Oxygen is recommended above 10,000 ft. MSL during the day, not at night. Answer (C) is incorrect. Oxygen is required, not recommended, above 12,500 ft. MSL after 30 min., regardless of day or night.

10.2 Hyperventilation

10. Rapid or extra deep breathing while using oxygen can cause

A. cyanosis.
B. hyperventilation.
C. a build-up of carbon dioxide in the body.

Answer (B) is correct. *(AIM Para 8-1-3)*
DISCUSSION: Hyperventilation is an abnormal increase in the volume of air breathed in and out of the lungs, such as rapid or extra deep breathing while using oxygen. Hyperventilation also causes you to flush from your lungs and blood much of the carbon dioxide your body needs to maintain the proper degree of blood acidity.
Answer (A) is incorrect. Cyanosis (a blue coloration of the fingernails and lips) is a symptom of hypoxia, which is caused by an oxygen deficiency. Rapid or extra deep breathing while using oxygen can cause a deficiency of carbon dioxide, not oxygen. Answer (C) is incorrect. Rapid or extra deep breathing will flush, not build up, much of the carbon dioxide in the body.

11. Hyperventilation results in

A. a lack of carbon dioxide in the body.
B. a need to increase the flow of supplemental oxygen.
C. breathing too rapidly causing a lack of oxygen.

Answer (A) is correct. *(AIM Para 8-1-3)*
DISCUSSION: Hyperventilation, or an abnormal increase in the volume of air breathed in and out of the lungs, can occur subconsciously when a stressful situation is encountered in flight. As hyperventilation decreases the amount of carbon dioxide in the body, a pilot can experience symptoms of lightheadedness, suffocation, drowsiness, tingling in the extremities, and coolness, and react to them with even greater hyperventilation.
Answer (B) is incorrect. Hypoxia, not hyperventilation, results in a need to increase the flow of supplemental oxygen. Answer (C) is incorrect. Breathing too rapidly causes a lack of carbon dioxide, not oxygen.

12. A person should be able to overcome the symptoms of hyperventilation by

A. increasing the breathing rate in order to increase lung ventilation.
B. slowing the breathing rate and increasing the amount of carbon dioxide in the body.
C. refraining from the use of alcohol and over-the-counter drugs such as antihistamines and tranquilizers.

Answer (B) is correct. *(AIM Para 8-1-3)*
DISCUSSION: A person should be able to overcome the symptoms of hyperventilation by consciously slowing his or her breathing rate, allowing the amount of carbon dioxide in the body to increase to the proper level. Carbon dioxide buildup can be hastened by controlled breathing in and out of a paper bag held over the nose and mouth.
Answer (A) is incorrect. Increasing the breathing rate would aggravate the symptoms. Answer (C) is incorrect. Refraining from the use of alcohol and over-the-counter drugs can reduce susceptibility to hypoxia, not hyperventilation.

10.3 Spatial Disorientation and Illusions in Flight

13. An illusion, that the aircraft is at a higher altitude than it actually is, is produced by

A. atmospheric haze.
B. upsloping terrain.
C. downsloping terrain.

Answer (B) is correct. *(AIM Para 8-1-5)*
DISCUSSION: An upsloping runway, upsloping terrain, or both can create the illusion that the aircraft is at a higher altitude than it actually is. The pilot who does not recognize this illusion will fly a lower approach.
Answer (A) is incorrect. Haze can create the illusion of being a greater distance from the runway than you actually are. Answer (C) is incorrect. A downsloping runway can create the illusion that the aircraft is lower, not higher, than it actually is.

14. A rapid acceleration can create the illusion of being in a

A. left turn.
B. noseup attitude.
C. nosedown attitude.

Answer (B) is correct. *(AIM Para 8-1-5)*
DISCUSSION: Rapid acceleration, such as during the takeoff, can lead to somatogravic illusion, which would create the illusion of a nose-up attitude. The disoriented pilot may push the aircraft into a nose-low attitude.
Answer (A) is incorrect. A left turn can be an illusion from the leans, which is caused by an abrupt correction of a banked attitude, or a coriolis illusion, which is caused by an abrupt head movement during a constant rate turn. Answer (C) is incorrect. Rapid deceleration, not acceleration, can create the illusion of a nose-low attitude.

15. Which procedure is recommended to prevent or overcome spatial disorientation?

A. Avoid steep turns and rough control movements.
B. Rely entirely on the indications of the flight instruments.
C. Reduce head and eye movements to the greatest extent possible.

Answer (B) is correct. *(AIM Para 8-1-5)*
DISCUSSION: Various complex motions and forces and certain visual scenes encountered in flight can create illusions of motion and position. Spatial disorientation from these illusions can only be prevented by visual reference to reliable, fixed points on the ground or to flight instruments.
Answer (A) is incorrect. While avoiding steep turns and rough control movements will help prevent spatial disorientation from occurring, only sole reliance on visual references or flight instruments will overcome the effects of spatial disorientation once it occurs. Answer (C) is incorrect. While reducing head and eye movements will help prevent spatial disorientation from occurring, only sole reliance on visual references or flight instruments will overcome the effects of spatial disorientation once it occurs.

16. What effect does haze have on the ability to see traffic or terrain features during flight?

A. Haze causes the eyes to focus at infinity.
B. The eyes tend to overwork in haze and do not detect relative movement easily.
C. All traffic or terrain features appear to be farther away than their actual distance.

Answer (C) is correct. *(AIM Para 8-1-5)*
DISCUSSION: Atmospheric haze can create the illusion of being at a greater distance and height from traffic or terrain than you actually are. The pilot who does not recognize this illusion will fly a lower approach.
Answer (A) is incorrect. In haze the eyes focus at a comfortable distance, which may be only 10 to 30 ft., not infinity, outside the cockpit. Answer (B) is incorrect. In haze the eyes relax, not overwork, and tend to stare outside without really looking.

10.4 Night Vision

17. One aid in increasing night vision effectiveness would be to

A. look directly at objects.
B. force the eyes to view off center.
C. increase intensity of interior lighting.

Answer (B) is correct. *(AFH Chap 10)*
DISCUSSION: In the absence of light, the process of vision is placed almost entirely on the rods. The fact that the rods are distributed in a band around the cones and do not lie directly behind the pupils makes off-center viewing important to night flight.
Answer (A) is incorrect. The cones, which lie in the center portion of the eye, are most effective in the daytime. Answer (C) is incorrect. Increasing the intensity of interior lighting will constrict the pupils, decreasing night vision.

18. Dark adaptation is impaired by exposure to

A. carbon dioxide.
B. vitamin A in the diet.
C. cabin pressure altitudes above 5,000 feet.

Answer (C) is correct. *(AIM Para 8-1-6)*
DISCUSSION: At cabin pressure altitudes above 5,000 ft. MSL, dark adaptation of your vision may be impaired. Also, carbon monoxide from smoking or exhaust fumes, prolonged exposure to bright light, or a deficiency of vitamin A in the diet can impair dark adaptation.
Answer (A) is incorrect. Carbon monoxide, not dioxide, can impair dark adaptation. Answer (B) is incorrect. Vitamin A is beneficial to dark adaptation.

10.5 Flight after Scuba Diving

19. If an individual has gone scuba diving which has not required a controlled ascent and will be flying to cabin pressure altitudes of 8,000 feet or less, the recommended waiting time is at least

A. 4 hours.
B. 12 hours.
C. 24 hours.

Answer (B) is correct. *(AIM Para 8-1-2)*
DISCUSSION: The recommended waiting time before going to flight altitudes of up to 8,000 ft. is at least 12 hr. after diving that has not required controlled ascent (nondecompression stop diving). This allows the body sufficient time to rid itself of excess nitrogen absorbed during diving.
Answer (A) is incorrect. Four hr. is not a recommended waiting period for any type of scuba diving. Answer (C) is incorrect. Twenty-four hr. is the recommended waiting period before flying above, not below, 8,000 ft. after any scuba dive.

20. If an individual has gone scuba diving which has required a controlled ascent and will be flying to cabin pressure altitudes of 8,000 feet or less, the recommended waiting time is at least

A. 8 hours.
B. 12 hours.
C. 24 hours.

Answer (C) is correct. *(AIM Para 8-1-2)*
DISCUSSION: The recommended waiting time before flying at any altitude is at least 24 hr. after diving that has required controlled ascent (decompression stop diving). This allows the body sufficient time to rid itself of excess nitrogen absorbed during diving.
Answer (A) is incorrect. Eight hr. is not a recommended waiting period for any type of scuba diving. Answer (B) is incorrect. Twelve hr. is the recommended waiting period before flying up to 8,000 ft. after a nondecompression stop dive, not after a dive that required a controlled ascent.

10.6 Motion Sickness

21. Motion sickness is caused by

A. continued stimulation of the tiny portion of the inner ear which controls sense of balance.
B. an instability in the brain cells which affects balance and will generally be overcome with experience.
C. the movement of an aircraft causing the stomach to create an acid substance which causes the stomach lining to contract.

Answer (A) is correct. *(PHAK Chap 17)*
DISCUSSION: Motion sickness is caused by continued stimulation of the tiny portion of the inner ear that controls the sense of balance. The desire for food is lost. Then, saliva collects in the mouth and the person begins to perspire. Eventually the person becomes nauseated and disorientated. The head aches and there may be a tendency to vomit.
Answer (B) is incorrect. The problem is caused by the sensory organs in the inner ear sending conflicting signals to the brain, not an instability in the brain cells. Answer (C) is incorrect. There is no chemical cause of motion sickness. Motion sickness results from excessive movement of the inner ear, which controls the sense of balance.

22. What suggestion could you make to students who are experiencing motion sickness?

A. Recommend taking medication to prevent motion sickness.
B. Have the students lower their head, shut their eyes, and take deep breaths.
C. Tell the students to avoid unnecessary head movement and to keep their eyes on a point outside the aircraft.

Answer (C) is correct. *(PHAK Chap 17)*
DISCUSSION: Pilots who are susceptible to airsickness should not take the preventive drugs that are available. Instead, they should open vents, loosen clothing, use supplemental oxygen, keep their eyes on a point outside the airplane, and avoid unnecessary head movements. In the event that you or a passenger become airsick, you should cancel the flight and land as soon as possible.
Answer (A) is incorrect. Pilot performance can be seriously degraded by either prescribed or over-the-counter medications. Answer (B) is incorrect. To overcome motion sickness, you should keep your eyes focused on a point outside the aircraft, not lower your head and shut your eyes.

10.7 Aeronautical Decision Making (ADM)

23. In order to gain a realistic perspective on one's attitude toward flying, a pilot should

A. understand the need to complete the flight.
B. obtain both realistic and thorough flight instruction during training.
C. take a Self-Assessment Hazardous Attitude Inventory Test.

Answer (C) is correct. *(AC 60-22)*
DISCUSSION: In order to gain a realistic perspective on one's attitudes toward flying, a pilot should take a Self-Assessment Hazardous Attitude Inventory Test.
Answer (A) is incorrect. The need to complete a flight is a behavioral trap that must be eliminated, not a way to gain a perspective on one's attitudes toward flying. Answer (B) is incorrect. While realistic and thorough flight instruction during training improves skills, it does not enable a pilot to gain perspective on his or her attitude toward flying.

24. The aeronautical decision making (ADM) process identifies several steps involved in good decision making. One of these steps is

A. making a rational evaluation of the required actions.
B. identifying personal attitudes hazardous to safe flight.
C. developing a "can do" attitude.

Answer (B) is correct. *(AC 60-22)*
DISCUSSION: The ADM process addresses all aspects of decision making in the cockpit and identifies several steps involved in good decision making. One of these steps is to identify personal attitudes hazardous to safe flight.
Answer (A) is incorrect. Making a rational evaluation of the required actions is a step in good judgment, not a step in good decision making. Answer (C) is incorrect. The "can do," or macho, attitude is one of the personal hazardous attitudes to identify in the steps involved in good decision making.

25. Aeronautical decision making (ADM) can be defined as a

A. mental process of analyzing all available information in a particular situation, making a timely decision on what action to take, and when to take the action.

B. decision making process which relies on good judgment to reduce risks associated with each flight.

C. systematic approach to the mental process used by pilots to consistently determine the best course of action in response to a given set of circumstances.

Answer (C) is correct. *(AC 60-22)*
DISCUSSION: ADM is a systematic approach to the mental process used by pilots to consistently determine the best course of action in response to a given set of circumstances.
Answer (A) is incorrect. Judgment, not ADM, can be defined as a mental process of analyzing all available information in a particular situation, making a timely decision on what action to take, and when to take the action. Answer (B) is incorrect. ADM relies not only on good judgment but also on the importance of attitudes in the decision-making process to reduce risks associated with each flight.

26. Human behavior

A. rarely results in accidents unless deliberate actions are performed.

B. causes three out of four accidents.

C. is well understood, so behavioral induced accidents are exceedingly rare occurrences.

Answer (B) is correct. *(RMH Chap 8)*
DISCUSSION: The study of human behavior is an attempt to explain how and why humans function the way they do. The Federal Aviation Administration (FAA) utilizes studies of human behavior in an attempt to reduce human error in aviation. Three out of four accidents result from human error. Eliminating human error is an unrealistic goal since errors are a normal part of human behavior. On the other hand, realizing that many aviation accidents are preventable means designing ways to reduce the consequences of human error. The study of human behavior coupled with pilot training that offsets predictable human error helps achieve that goal.
Answer (A) is incorrect. Many aviation accidents are preventable and are based on human error. In fact, three out of four accidents are a result of human error, which is a normal part of human behavior. Answer (C) is incorrect. Three out of four accidents are a result of human error. Many aviation accidents are preventable, and continued study of human behavior is a necessary step in the goal of reducing the consequences of human error.

27. Risk management, as part of the aeronautical decision making (ADM) process, relies on which features to reduce the risks associated with each flight?

A. Application of stress management and risk element procedures.

B. The mental process of analyzing all information in a particular situation and making a timely decision on what action to take.

C. Situational awareness, problem recognition, and good judgment.

Answer (C) is correct. *(AC 60-22)*
DISCUSSION: Risk management is that part of the ADM process that relies on situational awareness, problem recognition, and good judgment to reduce risks associated with each flight.
Answer (A) is incorrect. Risk management relies on situational awareness, problem recognition, and good judgment, not the application of stress management and risk-element procedures, to reduce the risks associated with each flight. Answer (B) is incorrect. Judgment, not risk management, is the mental process of analyzing all information in a particular situation and making a timely decision on what action to take.

28. What are the four fundamental risk elements in the aeronautical decision making (ADM) process that comprise any given aviation situation?

A. Situational awareness, risk management, judgment, and skill.

B. Pilot, aircraft, environment, and mission.

C. Skill, stress, situational awareness, and aircraft.

Answer (B) is correct. *(AC 60-22)*
DISCUSSION: The four fundamental risk elements in the ADM process that comprise any given aviation situation are the pilot, the aircraft, the environment, and the mission (type of operation).
Answer (A) is incorrect. Risk management, not risk elements, is the part of the decision-making process that relies on situational awareness, problem recognition, and good judgment to reduce the risks associated with each flight. Answer (C) is incorrect. Situational awareness is the accurate perception and understanding of all of the factors and conditions within the four fundamental risk elements (pilot, aircraft, environment, and mission) that affect safety before, during, and after the flight.

29. Examples of classic behavioral traps that experienced pilots may fall into are to

A. promote situational awareness and then necessary changes in behavior.
B. complete a flight as planned, please passengers, meet schedules, and "get the job done."
C. assume additional responsibilities and assert PIC authority.

Answer (B) is correct. *(AC 60-22)*
DISCUSSION: Pilots have been known to fall into a number of classic behavioral traps. Pilots, particularly those with considerable experience, as a rule always try to complete a flight as planned, please passengers, meet schedules, and do what it takes to "get the job done."
Answer (A) is incorrect. To promote situational awareness and then to make necessary changes in behavior are part of learning good decision making, not classical behavioral traps. Answer (C) is incorrect. Assuming additional responsibilities and asserting PIC authority are not examples of classical behavioral traps.

30. All experienced pilots have fallen prey to, or have been tempted by, one or more of these dangerous tendencies or behavior problems at some time in their career. Select the answer that best describes these tendencies.

A. deficiencies in instrument skills and knowledge of aircraft systems or limitations.
B. peer pressure, scud running, loss of situational awareness, and operating with inadequate fuel reserves.
C. performance deficiencies due to stress from human factors such as fatigue, illness, or emotional problems.

Answer (B) is correct. *(AC 60-22)*
DISCUSSION: All experienced pilots have fallen prey to, or have been tempted by, dangerous tendencies or behavior patterns. Some dangerous tendencies or behavior patterns, which must be identified and eliminated, include peer pressure, scud running, loss of situational awareness, and operating with inadequate fuel reserves.
Answer (A) is incorrect. Deficiencies in instrument skills and knowledge of aircraft systems or limitations are factors that increase cockpit stress, not dangerous tendencies and behavior patterns that must be eliminated in experienced pilots. Answer (C) is incorrect. Performance deficiencies due to stress from human factors such as fatigue, illness, or emotional problems are factors that increase stress, not dangerous tendencies or behavior patterns that must be eliminated in experienced pilots.

31. Hazardous attitudes occur to every pilot to some degree at some time. What are some of these hazardous attitudes?

A. Antiauthority, impulsivity, macho, resignation, and invulnerability.
B. Poor situational awareness, snap judgments, and lack of a decision making process.
C. Poor risk management and lack of stress management.

Answer (A) is correct. *(AC 60-22)*
DISCUSSION: The five hazardous attitudes addressed in the ADM process are antiauthority, impulsivity, invulnerability, macho, and resignation.
Answer (B) is incorrect. Poor situational awareness and snap judgments are indications of the lack of a decision-making process, not hazardous attitudes. Answer (C) is incorrect. Poor risk management and lack of stress management lead to poor ADM and are not considered hazardous attitudes.

32. Name some hazardous attitudes that can affect your judgment during the aeronautical decision making (ADM) process.

A. Impulsivity, antiestablishment, and reevaluation.
B. Antiauthority, impulsivity, and resignation.
C. Peer pressure and stress levels.

Answer (B) is correct. *(AC 60-22)*
DISCUSSION: The five hazardous attitudes that can affect your judgment during the ADM process are antiauthority, impulsivity, invulnerability, macho, and resignation.
Answer (A) is incorrect. Reevaluation is not a hazardous attitude in the ADM process. Answer (C) is incorrect. While peer pressure and stress levels may be factors contributing toward hazardous attitudes in the ADM process, they are not attitudes themselves.

33. During a stall recovery, the instructor allows the student to exceed maneuvering speed. Which best illustrates an "antiauthority" reaction by the instructor?

A. The student should know how to recover from a stall by this time.
B. The aircraft can handle a lot more than the maneuvering speed.
C. There hasn't been a problem doing this in the past.

Answer (B) is correct. *(AC 60-22)*
DISCUSSION: When an instructor allows a student to exceed the maneuvering speed during a stall because the instructor thinks the aircraft can handle a lot more than the maneuvering speed, (s)he is exhibiting an antiauthority ("Don't tell me!") attitude. The instructor may regard rules, regulations, and procedures as silly or unnecessary.
Answer (A) is incorrect. The instructor's attitude that the student should know how to recover from a stall by this time illustrates the resignation (leaving the action to the student) attitude. Answer (C) is incorrect. The instructor's attitude that there has not been a problem doing this in the past illustrates the invulnerability ("it will not happen to me") attitude.

34. In the aeronautical decision making (ADM) process, what is the first step in neutralizing a hazardous attitude?

A. Recognizing hazardous thoughts.
B. Recognizing the invulnerability of the situation.
C. Making a rational judgment.

Answer (A) is correct. *(AC 60-22)*
DISCUSSION: Hazardous attitudes, which contribute to poor pilot judgment, can be effectively counteracted by redirecting that hazardous attitude so that appropriate action can be taken. Recognition of hazardous thoughts is the first step in neutralizing them in the ADM process.
Answer (B) is incorrect. Invulnerability is a hazardous attitude. The first step in neutralizing a hazardous attitude is to recognize it. Answer (C) is incorrect. Before a rational judgment can be made, the hazardous attitude must be recognized then redirected so that appropriate action can be taken.

35. What should a pilot do when recognizing a thought as hazardous?

A. Correct this hazardous thought by making a thorough risk assessment.
B. Label the thought as hazardous and then correct that thought by stating the corresponding antidote.
C. Avoid allowing this hazardous thought to develop.

Answer (B) is correct. *(AC 60-22)*
DISCUSSION: When you recognize a hazardous thought, you should label it as hazardous; then correct the attitude by stating the corresponding antidote. Antidotes should be memorized for each of the hazardous attitudes so that they automatically come to mind when needed.
Answer (A) is incorrect. When you recognize a hazardous thought, you should label it as hazardous and then correct the attitude by stating the corresponding antidote, not by making a thorough risk assessment. Answer (C) is incorrect. While you do not want the hazardous thought to develop, the way to avoid this is to recognize and label the thought as hazardous and then correct it by stating the corresponding antidote.

36. Hazardous attitudes which contribute to poor pilot judgment can be effectively counteracted by

A. an appropriate antidote.
B. taking meaningful steps to be more assertive with attitudes.
C. early recognition of these hazardous attitudes.

Answer (A) is correct. *(AC 60-22)*
DISCUSSION: Hazardous attitudes, which contribute to poor pilot judgment, can be effectively counteracted by redirecting them so that appropriate action can be taken. When you recognize a hazardous thought, you should label it as hazardous; then correct the attitude by stating the corresponding antidote.
Answer (B) is incorrect. You should respond to a hazardous attitude with an antidote, not with steps to be more assertive with attitudes. Answer (C) is incorrect. While the first step in neutralizing a hazardous attitude is recognition, to counteract the attitude you must state the appropriate antidote.

37. What is the antidote for a pilot with a "macho" attitude?

A. I'm not helpless. I can make a difference.
B. Follow the rules. They are usually right.
C. Taking chances is foolish.

Answer (C) is correct. *(AC 60-22)*
DISCUSSION: Pilots exhibiting a macho attitude will try to prove themselves by taking risks in order to impress others. When this hazardous attitude is recognized, the pilot should state the antidote "Taking chances is foolish."
Answer (A) is incorrect. The antidote for a resignation, not a macho, attitude is "I'm not helpless. I can make a difference." Answer (B) is incorrect. The antidote for an antiauthority, not a macho, attitude is "Follow the rules. They are usually right."

38. When a pilot believes advanced avionics enable operations closer to personal or environmental limits,

A. greater utilization of the aircraft is achieved.
B. risk is increased.
C. risk is decreased.

Answer (B) is correct. *(RMH Chap 8)*
DISCUSSION: Pilots should not be lulled into a false sense of security simply because they have advanced avionics. Judgment and aeronautical decision making serve as the bridge between technology and safety. Any flight you make involves almost infinite combinations of pilot skill, experience, condition, and proficiency; aircraft equipment and performance; environmental conditions; and external influences. Both individually and in combination, these factors can compress the safety buffer provided by your baseline personal minimums. Consequently, you need a practical way to adjust your baseline personal minimums to accommodate specific conditions.
Answer (A) is incorrect. While one may be able to use an aircraft in more challenging environments, the risks involved with such flights also increase. Therefore, the best answer choice is that risk is increased when a pilot believes advanced avionics enable operations closer to personal or environmental limits. Answer (C) is incorrect. Risk is increased, not decreased, when a pilot believes advanced avionics enable operations closer to personal or environmental limits.

39. Success in reducing stress associated with a crisis in the cockpit begins with

A. eliminating the more serious life and cockpit stress issues.
B. knowing the exact cause of the stress.
C. assessing stress areas in one's personal life.

Answer (C) is correct. *(AC 60-22)*
DISCUSSION: If you hope to succeed in reducing stress associated with crisis management in the cockpit, it is essential to begin by making a personal assessment of stress in all areas of your life.
Answer (A) is incorrect. In order to eliminate the more serious life and cockpit stress issues, you must first make an assessment of stress in all areas of your life to identify those stressors. Answer (B) is incorrect. In order to know the exact cause of the stress, you must first make an assessment of stress in all areas of your life to identify stressors and the causes of them.

40. To help manage cockpit stress, a pilot should

A. think of life stress situations that are similar to those in flying.
B. try to relax and think rationally at the first sign of stress.
C. avoid situations that will degrade the ability to handle cockpit responsibilities.

Answer (B) is correct. *(AC 60-22)*
DISCUSSION: To help manage cockpit stress, you must condition (teach) yourself to relax and think rationally at the first sign of stress.
Answer (A) is incorrect. Many of the stress-coping techniques practiced for life stress management are not practical in flight. Answer (C) is incorrect. Avoiding situations that will degrade a pilot's ability to handle cockpit responsibilities is considered a part of risk management, not cockpit stress management.

41. The DECIDE process consists of six elements to help provide a pilot a logical way of approaching aeronautical decision making. These elements are to

A. estimate, determine, choose, identify, detect, and evaluate.
B. determine, evaluate, choose, identify, do, and eliminate.
C. detect, estimate, choose, identify, do, and evaluate.

Answer (C) is correct. *(AC 60-22)*
DISCUSSION: The DECIDE model, comprised of six elements, is intended to provide a pilot with a logical way of approaching decision making. These six elements, using the acronym DECIDE, are detect, estimate, choose, identify, do, and evaluate.
Answer (A) is incorrect. One of the elements of the DECIDE process is "do," not "determine." Answer (B) is incorrect. Two of the elements of the DECIDE process are "detect," not "determine," and "estimate," not "eliminate."

42. Automation in aircraft has proven

A. to present new hazards in its limitations.
B. that automation is basically flawless.
C. effective in preventing accidents.

Answer (A) is correct. *(RMH Chap 7)*
DISCUSSION: Most of the aviation community believes automation has made flying safer, but there is a fear that pilots fail to see that automation is a double-edged sword. Pilots need to understand the advantages of automation while being aware of its limitations. Experience has shown that automated systems can make some errors more evident while sometimes hiding other errors or making them less obvious. When passively monitoring an automated system for faults, abnormalities, or other infrequent events, humans perform poorly. The more reliable the system is, the worse the human performance becomes. It is a paradox of automation that technically advanced avionics can both increase and decrease pilot awareness.
Answer (B) is incorrect. Automation is not necessarily flawless. Proper use of checklists and systematic training should be used to control common error-prone tasks and notice errors from automation before they become a threat to safety of flight. Answer (C) is incorrect. While automation has prevented accidents, it can also cause accidents from complacency. Therefore, it is not the best answer choice. When passively monitoring an automated system for faults, abnormalities, or other infrequent events, humans perform poorly. The more reliable the system is, the worse the human performance becomes. It is a paradox of automation that technically advanced avionics can both increase and decrease pilot awareness.

43. When should a flight instructor begin teaching aeronautical decision making (ADM) to a student?

A. Beginning with the first lesson.
B. After the student has completed the initial solo flight but before conducting cross country flights.
C. As soon as the student is able to control the aircraft during basic maneuvers.

Answer (C) is correct. *(AC 60-22)*
DISCUSSION: A flight instructor should begin teaching ADM when the student has the ability to control the aircraft confidently during the most basic maneuvers. One suggested starting point is about three flight lessons before the student is expected to solo.
Answer (A) is incorrect. A flight instructor should begin teaching ADM when the student is able to control the aircraft confidently during the most basic maneuvers, not on the first flight lesson. Answer (B) is incorrect. A flight instructor should begin teaching ADM when the student is able to control the aircraft confidently during the most basic maneuvers, which is before, not after, the student is expected to solo.

44. The lighter workloads associated with glass (digital) flight instrumentation

A. are instrumental in decreasing flightcrew fatigue.
B. have proven to increase safety in operations.
C. may lead to complacency by the flightcrew.

Answer (C) is correct. *(RMH Chap 7)*
DISCUSSION: The enhanced situational awareness and automation capabilities offered by a glass flight deck vastly expand its safety and utility, especially for personal transportation use. At the same time, there is some risk that lighter workloads could lead to complacency. Humans are characteristically poor monitors of automated systems. When passively monitoring an automated system for faults, abnormalities, or other infrequent events, humans perform poorly. The more reliable the system is, the worse the human performance becomes. It is a paradox of automation that technically advanced avionics can both increase and decrease pilot awareness.
Answer (A) is incorrect. The introduction of automation is often intended to reduce workload and augment performance; however, this is not always the result. Automation can lead to distraction from the primary task, increased workload, boredom, or complacency. Answer (B) is incorrect. It is helpful to note that all human activity involving technical devices entails some element of risk. Knowledge, experience, and flight requirements tilt the odds in favor of safe and successful flights. The advanced avionics aircraft offers many new capabilities and simplifies the basic flying tasks, but only if the pilot is properly trained and all the equipment is working properly.

APPENDIX A:
ADDITIONAL GROUND INSTRUCTOR QUESTIONS

If you are taking the BGI knowledge test, you should study only questions 1 and 2. If you are taking the AGI knowledge test, you should study questions 2 through 11.

1. The holder of a ground instructor certificate with a basic rating is authorized to provide ground training in the aeronautical knowledge areas required for a recreational or private pilot certificate.

2. The holder of a ground instructor certificate may not exercise the privileges of the certificate unless (s)he has been employed as a ground instructor giving pilot, flight instructor, or ground instructor training in the preceding 12 months.

3. Crewmember means a person assigned to perform duty in an aircraft during flight time.

4. Operational control, with respect to a flight, means the exercise of authority over initiating, conducting, or terminating a flight.

5. Stopway means an area designated for use in decelerating the airplane during an aborted takeoff.

6. V_2 means takeoff safety speed.

7. A second in command of an airplane requiring two pilots may log as instrument flight time all of the time (s)he is controlling the airplane solely by reference to flight instruments.

8. An airline transport pilot may instruct other pilots in air transportation service for a maximum of 36 hr. in any 7-consecutive-day period.

9. The holder of a ground instructor certificate with an advanced rating is authorized to provide ground training in the aeronautical knowledge areas for any pilot certificate or rating except the instrument rating.

10. Under 14 CFR Part 121, if an instrument on a multi-engine airplane becomes inoperative en route, the certificate holder's manual will dictate whether the flight may continue.

11. Under 14 CFR Part 121, all information recorded during normal operation by a required cockpit voice recorder in a passenger-carrying airplane may be erased except for the last 30 min.

QUESTIONS

1. The holder of a Ground Instructor Certificate with a basic rating is authorized to provide ground training required for

- A. a flight instructor refresher course.
- B. any flight review or instrument proficiency check.
- C. all aeronautical knowledge areas for a recreational or private pilot certificate.

Answer (C) is correct. *(14 CFR 61.215)*
   DISCUSSION: A person who holds a basic ground instructor rating is authorized to provide ground training in the aeronautical knowledge areas required for the recreational or private pilot certificate.
   Answer (A) is incorrect. A person who holds an advanced ground instructor rating, not a basic ground instructor rating, is authorized to provide ground training required for a flight instructor refresher course. Answer (B) is incorrect. A person who holds a basic ground instructor rating can provide ground training required for only a recreational or private pilot flight review, not any flight review. To conduct the ground training for an instrument proficiency check, a person must hold an instrument ground instructor rating.

2. The holder of a Ground Instructor Certificate may not exercise the privileges of that certificate unless that person has

- A. successfully completed a refresher course within 3 months prior to expiration.
- B. been employed as a ground instructor giving pilot, flight instructor, or ground instructor training in the preceding 12 months.
- C. passed a practical test within the preceding 12 months.

Answer (B) is correct. *(14 CFR 61.217)*
   DISCUSSION: The holder of a ground instructor certificate may not perform the duties for ground instructor unless that person has been employed as a ground instructor giving pilot, flight instructor, or ground instructor training in the preceding 12 months.
   Answer (A) is incorrect. A ground instructor certificate is issued without an expiration date; thus, there are no refresher course requirements. Answer (C) is incorrect. There is no practical test for the ground instructor certificate.

3. Which is a definition of the term "crewmember"?

- A. Only a pilot, flight engineer, or flight navigator assigned to duty in an aircraft during flight time.
- B. A person assigned to perform duty in an aircraft during flight time.
- C. Any person assigned to duty in an aircraft during flight except a pilot or flight engineer.

Answer (B) is correct. *(14 CFR 1.1)*
   DISCUSSION: A crewmember is a person assigned to perform duty in an aircraft during flight time.
   Answer (A) is incorrect. Only a pilot, flight engineer, or flight navigator assigned to duty in an aircraft during flight time is the definition of the term "flight crewmember," not "crewmember." Answer (C) is incorrect. The term "crewmember" includes the flight (or cockpit) crew as well as cabin crew.

4. Regulations concerning the operational control of a flight refer to

- A. exercising the privileges of pilot in command of an aircraft.
- B. the specific duties of any required crewmember.
- C. exercising authority over initiating, conducting, or terminating a flight.

Answer (C) is correct. *(14 CFR 1.1)*
   DISCUSSION: Operational control refers to the exercise of authority over initiating, conducting, or terminating a flight.
   Answer (A) is incorrect. Regulations concerning the operational control of a flight refer to exercising authority over initiating, conducting, or terminating a flight, not exercising the privileges of pilot in command. Answer (B) is incorrect. Regulations concerning the operational control of a flight refer to exercising authority over initiating, conducting, or terminating a flight, not the specific duties of any required crewmember.

5. A "stopway" can be defined as an area

- A. not as wide as the runway but capable of supporting an airplane during a normal takeoff.
- B. at least the same width as the runway capable of supporting an airplane during a normal takeoff.
- C. designated for use in decelerating the airplane during an aborted takeoff.

Answer (C) is correct. *(14 CFR 1.1)*
   DISCUSSION: A stopway is an area beyond the takeoff runway that is no less wide than the runway and centered upon the extended centerline of the runway. It is able to support the airplane during an aborted takeoff without causing structural damage to the airplane and is designated by airport authorities for use in decelerating the airplane during an aborted takeoff.
   Answer (A) is incorrect. A stopway is the same width or wider, not narrower, than the runway, and is only able to support the weight of the airplane during an aborted takeoff without causing structural damage. It is not capable of supporting an airplane during a normal takeoff. Answer (B) is incorrect. The portion of the runway behind a displaced threshold, not a stopway, is at least the same width as the runway and is capable of supporting an airplane during a normal takeoff.

6. What is V_2 speed?

A. Takeoff decision speed.
B. Takeoff safety speed.
C. Minimum takeoff speed.

Answer (B) is correct. *(14 CFR 1.2)*
DISCUSSION: V_2 is takeoff safety speed. Takeoff safety speed means a referenced airspeed obtained after liftoff at which the required one-engine-inoperative climb performance can be achieved.
Answer (A) is incorrect. V_1, not V_2, means takeoff decision speed. Answer (C) is incorrect. V_{2MIN}, not V_2, is minimum takeoff safety speed.

7. What instrument flight time may be logged by a second in command of an aircraft requiring two pilots?

A. All of the time the second in command is controlling the airplane solely by reference to flight instruments.
B. One-half the time the flight is on an IFR flight plan.
C. One-half the time the airplane is in actual IFR conditions.

Answer (A) is correct. *(14 CFR 61.51)*
DISCUSSION: A pilot may log instrument flight time only for that flight time during which (s)he operates the aircraft solely by reference to flight instruments under actual or simulated instrument flying conditions.
Answer (B) is incorrect. Only when the pilot is flying in actual or simulated instrument flying conditions as sole manipulator of the controls may (s)he log instrument flight time. Answer (C) is incorrect. A pilot may log all flight time in which (s)he is sole manipulator of the controls in IFR conditions as instrument flight time.

8. What restriction is imposed regarding flight instruction of other pilots in air transportation service by an airline transport pilot?

A. 36 hours in any 7-day period.
B. 7 hours in any 1-day period.
C. 30 hours in any 7-day period.

Answer (A) is correct. *(14 CFR 61.167)*
DISCUSSION: The period of time that an airline transport pilot may instruct other pilots in air transportation service, excluding briefings and debriefings, is restricted to 36 hr. in any 7-consecutive-day period.
Answer (B) is incorrect. An airline transport pilot may instruct other pilots in air transportation service for a maximum of 8 hr., not 7 hr., in any 24-consecutive-hour period. Answer (C) is incorrect. An airline transport pilot may instruct other pilots in air transportation service for a maximum of 36 hr., not 30 hr., in any 7-consecutive-day period.

9. The holder of a Ground Instructor Certificate with an advanced rating is authorized to provide

A. ground training in aeronautical knowledge areas for any pilot certificate or rating except the instrument rating.
B. a recommendation for an instrument rating knowledge test.
C. ground training for any flight review or instrument proficiency check.

Answer (A) is correct. *(14 CFR 61.215)*
DISCUSSION: A person who holds an advanced ground instructor rating is authorized to provide ground training in the aeronautical knowledge areas for any pilot certificate or rating except the instrument rating.
Answer (B) is incorrect. A person who holds an instrument, not advanced, ground instructor rating is authorized to provide a recommendation for an instrument rating knowledge test. Answer (C) is incorrect. A person who holds an instrument, not advanced, ground instructor rating is authorized to provide ground training for an instrument proficiency check.

10. If an instrument on a multiengine airplane is inoperative, which document dictates whether the flight may continue en route?

A. Amended flight/dispatch release.
B. Original dispatch release.
C. Certificate holder's manual.

Answer (C) is correct. *(14 CFR 121.135)*
DISCUSSION: A Part 121 certificate holder must prepare and keep current a manual for the use and guidance of flight, ground operations, and management personnel in conducting its operations. One item that must be contained in the certificate holder's manual is en route flight, navigation, and communications procedures, including procedures for the dispatch or release or continuance of a flight if any item of equipment required for the particular type of operation becomes inoperative or unserviceable en route.
Answer (A) is incorrect. An amended flight or dispatch release allows a flight to take off. The certificate holder's manual specifies whether a flight, already in progress, may continue when an instrument becomes inoperative. Answer (B) is incorrect. The original dispatch release allowed the flight to take off. The certificate holder's manual specifies whether a flight, already in progress, may continue when an instrument becomes inoperative.

11. Information recorded during normal operation by a required cockpit voice recorder in a passenger-carrying airplane

A. may all be erased except the last 30 minutes.
B. must be retained for 30 minutes after landing.
C. may be erased only once each flight.

Answer (A) is correct. *(14 CFR 121.359)*

DISCUSSION: All of the information recorded during normal operation of a cockpit voice recorder may be erased or otherwise obliterated except for the last 30 min.

Answer (B) is incorrect. Information recorded by a cockpit voice recorder may all be erased except the last 30 min., not retained for 30 min. after landing. Answer (C) is incorrect. Information recorded by a cockpit voice recorder may all be erased except the last 30 min., not erased only once each flight.

APPENDIX B: SPORT PILOT INSTRUCTOR – AIRPLANE

STEPS TO SPORT PILOT FLIGHT INSTRUCTOR (AIRPLANE)

1. Purchase the Gleim Sport Pilot Flight Instructor Kit, which includes
   - *FAR/AIM*
   - *Pilot Handbook*
   - *Flight/Ground Instructor FAA Knowledge Test Prep*
   - *Fundamentals of Instructing FAA Knowledge Test Prep*
   - Flight/Ground Instructor + FOI FAA Test Prep Online
   - *Sport Pilot Syllabus*
   - *Flight Instructor Flight Maneuvers and Practical Test Prep*
   - Online Ground School for CFI/CGI
   - Online Ground School for FOI
   - Gleim Flight Bag
   - Sport Pilot Instructor–Airplane Study Supplement (which contains the FAA SIA Practical Test Standards)
2. Study for and PASS your Fundamentals of Instructing (FOI) knowledge test.
3. Study for and PASS your Sport Instructor–Airplane (SIA) knowledge test.
4. Study, understand, and practice the tasks and maneuvers included in the *Sport Pilot Syllabus* to prepare for your practical test.
   a. Rely on *Flight Instructor Flight Maneuvers and Practical Test Prep* for the explanations and tolerances required in your practical test.
5. Take and PASS your SIA practical test.
6. Email (aviationquestions@gleim.com) or call (800-874-5346) our aviation training consultants with any questions.

KNOWLEDGE TEST

TEST NAME – Flight Instructor -- Sport Airplane
TEST CODE – SIA
70 questions/2.5 hours/70% minimum passing score

All known questions from the FAA Flight Instructor -- Sport Airplane knowledge test bank are covered in the Gleim *Flight/Ground Instructor Knowledge Test Prep* book, **FAA Test Prep Online**, and the **Online Ground School** (OGS). Gleim has also added additional sample questions that are similar to what you will see on the SIA knowledge test. The study guide on the next page indicates all required sport pilot flight instructor study material for each study unit. Our Sport Pilot Flight Instructor OGS covers ONLY what you need to know to PASS.

The Gleim Sport Pilot Flight Instructor OGS leads you through the study process in an interactive and easy to use environment. When you complete the Sport Pilot Flight Instructor OGS, simply print the required endorsement and pass the SIA FAA Knowledge Test on your first try – guaranteed!

Our **FAA Test Prep Online** and Knowledge Test book provide a step-by-step process to study. The study guide below indicates all required study material for each study unit.

1) Study Unit 1, all subunits
2) Study Unit 2, all subunits except
   5. Multi-Engine Performance
3) Study Unit 3, all subunits except
   7. Manifold Pressure Gauge
   11. Turbocharged Engines
   18. Oxygen Systems
4) Study Unit 4, all subunits
5) Study Unit 5, all subunits except
   4. Weight Change Calculations
6) Study Unit 6, all subunits
7) Study Unit 7, all subtopics except
   61.23 Medical Certificates: Requirement and Duration
   61.31 Type Rating Requirements, Additional Training, and Auth. Requirements
   61.69 Glider Towing: Experience and Training Requirements
   61.101 Recreational Pilot Privileges and Limitations
   61.109 Aeronautical Experience
   61.123 Eligibility Requirements: General
   61.129 Aeronautical Experience
   61.133 Commercial Pilot Privileges and Limitations
   91.109 Flight Instruction; Simulated Instrument Flight and Certain Flight Tests
   91.117 Aircraft Speed
   91.135 Operations in Class A Airspace
   91.157 Special VFR Weather Minimums
   91.211 Supplemental Oxygen
8) Study Unit 8, all subunits except
   6. Distance Measuring Equipment (DME)
   7. VHF Omnidirectional Range (VOR)
9) Study Unit 9, all subunits except
   9. Eights-on-Pylons
   12. Chandelles
   13. Lazy Eights
   18. Flight by Reference to Instruments
10) Study Unit 10, all subunits

Appendix B: Sport Pilot Instructor – Airplane

PRACTICAL TEST

After you complete your knowledge test, focus on your practical test – the sooner the better.

Your SIA (initial) practical test is passed if, in the judgment of the examiner, the applicant demonstrates satisfactory performance with regard to

1. Knowledge of the fundamentals of instructing;
2. Knowledge of the technical subject areas;
3. Knowledge of the flight instructor's responsibilities concerning the pilot certification process;
4. Knowledge of the flight instructor's responsibilities concerning logbook entries and pilot certificate endorsement;
5. Ability to perform the procedures and maneuvers included in the standards at a more precise level than that indicated in the sport pilot tolerances while giving effective instruction;
6. Competence in teaching the procedures and maneuvers selected by the examiner;
7. Competence in describing, recognizing, analyzing, and correcting common errors simulated by the examiner;
8. Knowledge of the development and effective use of a course of training, a syllabus, and a lesson plan.

The SIA Practical Test Standards (PTS) contain three areas of operation for the oral exam portion of your practical test.

I. **FUNDAMENTALS OF INSTRUCTING** – These elements of the SIA PTS are discussed in conjunction with elements of the CFI PTS found in Part II/Study Unit I of the Gleim *Flight Instructor Flight Maneuvers and Practical Test Prep* book.

   Note: In Area I (FOI), the examiner should select TASK F and one other TASK.
   - A. The Learning Process
   - B. Human Behavior and Effective Communication
   - C. The Teaching Process
   - D. Teaching Methods
   - E. Critique and Evaluation
   - F. Flight Instructor Characteristics and Responsibilities
   - G. Planning Instructional Activity

II. **TECHNICAL SUBJECT AREAS** – These elements of the SIA PTS are discussed in conjunction with elements of the CFI PTS found in Part II/Study Unit II of the Gleim *Flight Instructor Flight Maneuvers and Practical Test Prep* book.

   Note: In Area II (technical topics), the examiner should select TASK D and one other TASK.
   - A. Aeromedical Factors
   - B. Visual Scanning and Collision Avoidance
   - C. Federal Aviation Regulations and Publications
   - D. Logbook Entries and Certificate Endorsements

III. **PREFLIGHT LESSON ON A MANEUVER TO BE PERFORMED IN FLIGHT** – These elements of the SIA PTS are discussed in conjunction with elements of the CFI PTS found in Part II/Study Unit IV of the Gleim *Flight Instructor Flight Maneuvers and Practical Test Prep* book.

   Note: Area III is the same as other CFI practical tests.
   - A. Maneuver Lesson

For the flight portion of the practical test, the tasks are taken from the sport pilot airplane PTS; a minimum of 18 of the 40 sport pilot PTS tasks are required as set forth below. Each of these tasks (and maneuvers) are presented in the Sport Pilot Instructor–Airplane Study Supplement. Note that the FAA requires a higher level of proficiency of sport pilot flight instructors than is required of sport pilot applicants. Thus, we recommend you train to CFI standards as set forth in *Flight Instructor Flight Maneuvers and Practical Test Prep*.

CATEGORY/CLASS PRIVILEGES TASK MATRIX FOR INITIAL AIRPLANE

AREA OF OPERATION	TESTING REQUIREMENTS SELECT AT LEAST
I. Preflight Preparation	Two TASKs
II. Preflight Procedures	TASK A and One Other TASK
III. Airport Operations	One TASK
IV. Takeoffs, Landings, and Go-Arounds	One Takeoff TASK, One Landing TASK, and TASKs K and L
V. Performance Maneuvers	Mandatory
VI. Ground Reference Maneuvers	One TASK
VII. Navigation	One TASK
VIII. Slow Flight and Stalls	TASKs A, D, and One Other TASK
IX. Emergency Operations	TASKs A and B
X. Postflight Procedures	TASK A

Note 1: This table is used by the examiner in developing his or her plan of action for a practical test. The examiner may test additional TASKs not listed in the table that (s)he deems necessary to ensure that the pilot can operate the aircraft safely in the National Airspace System.

Note 2: The FAA requires you to perform these tasks (and maneuvers) "at a more precise level than that indicated in the sport pilot tolerances while giving effective instruction." We suggest that you use CFI tolerances as explained in our *Flight Instructor Flight Maneuvers and Practical Test Prep* book, which is included in our Sport Pilot Flight Instructor Kit.

APPENDIX C:
PRACTICE TEST

The following 100 questions have been randomly selected from the airplane questions in our flight/ground instructor test bank. You will be referred to figures (charts, tables, etc.) throughout this book. Be careful not to consult the answers or answer explanations when you look for and at the figures. Topical coverage in this practice test is similar to that of the FAA pilot knowledge test. Use the correct answer listing on page 390 to grade your practice test.

1. (Refer to Figure 28 on page 75.) Determine the approximate total distance required to clear a 50-foot obstacle.

Temperature	35°C
Pressure altitude	3,000 ft
Surface	sod
Weight	5,100 lb
Wind	20 kts headwind

A — 1,969 feet.
B — 2,023 feet.
C — 2,289 feet.

2. GIVEN:

Usable fuel at takeoff	36 gal
Fuel consumption rate	12.4 gal/hr
Constant groundspeed	140 kts
Flight time since takeoff	48 min

According to 14 CFR Part 91, how much farther can an airplane be flown under day VFR?

A — 294 NM.
B — 224 NM.
C — 189 NM.

3. On a cross-country flight, point A is crossed at 1500 hours and the plan is to reach point B at 1530 hours. Use the following information to determine the indicated airspeed required to reach point B on schedule.

Distance between A and B	70 NM
Forecast wind	310° at 15 kts
Pressure altitude	8,000 ft
Ambient temperature	–10°C
True course	270°

The required indicated airspeed would be approximately

A — 126 knots.
B — 137 knots.
C — 152 knots.

4. After 150 miles are flown from the departure point, the aircraft's position is located 8 miles off course. If 160 miles remain to be flown, what approximate total correction should be made to converge on the destination?

A — 6°.
B — 9°.
C — 12°.

5. After 240 miles are flown from the departure point, the aircraft's position is located 25 miles off course. If 100 miles remain to be flown, what approximate total correction should be made to converge on the destination?

A — 15°.
B — 21°.
C — 30°.

6. (Refer to Figure 35 on page 159.) If 50 pounds of weight is located at point X and 100 pounds at point Z, how much weight must be located at point Y to balance the plank?

A — 30 pounds.
B — 50 pounds.
C — 300 pounds.

7. What would increase the density altitude at a given airport?

A — An increase in air temperature.
B — A decrease in relative humidity.
C — An increase in atmospheric pressure.

8. Which statement relates to Bernoulli's principle?

A — For every action there is an equal and opposite reaction.
B — An additional upward force is generated as the lower surface of the wing deflects air downward.
C — Air traveling faster over the curved upper surface of an airfoil causes lower pressure on the top surface.

9. (Refer to Figure 47 on page 139.) What is the normal radius of the outer area (area B)?

A — 10 NM.
B — 20 NM.
C — 25 NM.

10. (Refer to Figure 20 on page 37.) At the airspeed represented by point A, in steady flight, the aircraft will

A — have its maximum lift/drag ratio.
B — have its minimum lift/drag ratio.
C — be developing its maximum coefficient of lift.

11. (Refer to Figure 3 on page 206.) Which station is reporting the wind as calm?

A — KDAL.
B — KFTW.
C — KTYR.

12. (Refer to Figure 3 on page 206.) What is the reported duration of the rain at the time of the observation at KAUS?

A — 25 minutes.
B — 26 minutes.
C — 36 minutes.

13. (Refer to Figure 3 on page 206.) What is the reported duration of the rain at the time of the observation at KBRO?

A — 25 minutes.
B — 6 minutes.
C — 19 minutes.

14. (Refer to Figure 44 on page 297.) The airspace overlying Addison Airport (area 4) is classified as

A — Class D below 3,000 feet.
B — Class B from the surface to 10,000 feet.
C — Class D from the surface up to and including 3,000 feet.

15. (Refer to Figure 44 on page 297.) Select the correct statement concerning the obstruction 7 SM west of McKinney Airport (area 5).

A — The obstruction is unlighted.
B — The obstruction has high-intensity lights.
C — The elevation of the top of the obstruction is 729 feet AGL.

16. (Refer to Figure 44 on page 299.) What altitude should be selected to avoid operating in Class B airspace on a flight from Northwest Airport (area 2) to McKinney Airport (area 5)?

A — 2,500 feet MSL.
B — 3,000 feet MSL.
C — 3,500 feet MSL.

17. (Refer to Figure 45 on page 305.) The airspace beginning at the surface overlying NAS Kingsville (area 2) is

A — an Alert Area.
B — Class D airspace.
C — a military operations area (MOA).

18. (Refer to Figure 46 on page 309.) What is the height of the Class D airspace over Livermore Airport (area 5)?

A — 2,900 feet MSL.
B — 3,000 feet AGL.
C — Base of the overlying Class B airspace.

19. (Refer to Figure 18 on page 40.) What increase in load factor would take place if the angle of bank were increased from 60° to 80°?

A — 2 G's.
B — 3 G's.
C — 4 G's.

20. (Refer to Figure 7 on page 218.) Determine the wind and temperature aloft forecast for DEN at 9,000 feet.

A — 230° true at 53 knots, temperature –47°C.
B — 230° magnetic at 53 knots, temperature 47°C.
C — 230° true at 21 knots, temperature –4°C.

21. (Refer to Figure 42 on page 325.) Which OMNI indication would you receive for aircraft 8?

A — T.
B — V.
C — W.

22. (Refer to Figure 36 on page 161.) Determine the condition of the airplane:

Pilot and copilot	400 lb
Passengers -- aft position	240 lb
Baggage	20 lb
Fuel	75 gal

A — 157 pounds under allowable gross weight; CG is located within limits.
B — 180 pounds under allowable gross weight; CG is located within limits.
C — 180 pounds under allowable gross weight, but CG is located aft of the aft limit.

23. Which statement about longitude and latitude is true?

A — Lines of longitude are parallel to the Equator.
B — Lines of longitude cross the Equator at right angles.
C — The 0° line of latitude passes through Greenwich, England.

24. Choose the true statement pertaining to a slip or skid in an airplane.

A — A skid occurs when the rate of turn is too slow for the amount of bank being used.
B — In a left climbing turn, if insufficient right rudder is applied to compensate for the increased torque effect, a slip will result.
C — In a right descending turn, if excessive left rudder is applied to compensate for the decreased torque effect, a slip will result.

25. During the entry to a right turn, the nose of the aircraft swings slightly to the left before it swings along the horizon to the right. This is a

A — slipping entry, caused by excessive right rudder pressure.
B — skidding entry; more right rudder pressure and less right aileron pressure should have been applied.
C — slipping entry; more right rudder pressure should have been applied for the amount of aileron pressure being used.

26. When approaching taxiway holding lines from the side with the continuous lines, the pilot

A — may continue taxiing.
B — should not cross the lines without ATC clearance.
C — should continue taxiing until all parts of the aircraft have crossed the lines.

27. A slightly low indication on a PAPI glidepath is indicated by

A — four red lights.
B — one red light and three white lights.
C — one white light and three red lights.

28. Within the contiguous United States, the floor of Class A airspace is

A — 14,500 feet MSL.
B — 18,000 feet MSL.
C — 18,000 feet AGL.

29. An airport without a control tower lies within the controlled airspace of an airport with an operating tower. According to regulations, two-way radio communications with ATC are required for landing clearance at

A — both airports, as well as to fly through the area.
B — the tower-controlled airport only, as well as to fly through the area.
C — the tower-controlled airport only, but not required to fly through the area.

30. When operating VFR in Class B airspace, what are the visibility and cloud clearance requirements?

A — 3 SM visibility and clear of clouds.
B — 3 SM visibility, 500 feet below, 1,000 feet above, and 2,000 feet horizontal distance from clouds.
C — 1 SM visibility, 500 feet below, 1,000 feet above, and 2,000 feet horizontal distance from clouds.

31. While in Class G airspace under day VFR conditions, what in-flight visibility is required when flying more than 1,200 feet AGL and less than 10,000 feet MSL?

A — 5 SM.
B — 3 SM.
C — 1 SM.

32. What normally results from excessive airspeed on final approach?

A — Bouncing.
B — Floating.
C — Ballooning.

33. A moist, warm air mass that is being cooled from below is characterized, in part, by

A — smooth air.
B — cumuliform clouds.
C — showers and thunderstorms.

34. Which instruments are considered primary and supporting for bank, respectively, when establishing a level standard-rate turn?

A — Turn coordinator and heading indicator.
B — Attitude indicator and turn coordinator.
C — Turn coordinator and attitude indicator.

35. The first indication of carburetor ice in an aircraft with a fixed-pitch propeller is

A — a decrease in RPM.
B — a decrease in manifold pressure.
C — an increase in manifold pressure.

36. What is an effective way to prevent a collision hazard in the traffic pattern?

A — Enter the pattern in a descent.
B — Maintain the proper traffic pattern altitude and continually scan the area.
C — Rely on radio reports from other aircraft who may be operating in the traffic pattern.

37. When converting from true heading to true course, a pilot should

A — add right wind correction angle.
B — add left deviation correction angle.
C — subtract right wind correction angle.

38. When planning a distance flight, true course measurements on a Sectional Aeronautical Chart should be made at a meridian near the midpoint of the course because the

A — values of isogonic lines change from point to point.
B — angles formed by lines of longitude and the course line vary from point to point.
C — angles formed by isogonic lines and lines of latitude vary from point to point.

39. An aircraft is flying at a constant power setting and constant indicated altitude. If the outside air temperature (OAT) decreases, true airspeed will

A — decrease and true altitude will decrease.
B — increase and true altitude will increase.
C — increase and true altitude will decrease.

40. An electrical system failure (battery and alternator) occurs during flight. In this situation, you would

A — experience avionics equipment failure.
B — probably experience failure of the engine ignition system, fuel gauges, aircraft lighting system, and avionics equipment.
C — probably experience engine failure due to the loss of the engine-driven fuel pump and also experience failure of the radio equipment, lights, and all instruments that require alternating current.

41. When diverting to an alternate airport because of an emergency, pilots should

A — rely upon radio as the primary method of navigation.
B — complete all plotting, measuring, and computations involved before diverting.
C — apply rule-of-thumb computations, estimates, and other appropriate shortcuts to divert to the new course as soon as possible.

42. What may occur if the initial bank is too shallow when performing a chandelle?

A — Completing the maneuver with excessive airspeed.
B — Stalling the aircraft before reaching the 180° point.
C — Completing the maneuver with too low a pitch attitude.

43. What should occur at the 90° point of a lazy eight?

A — Airspeed and altitude should be the same as at entry.
B — Maximum pitch attitude, minimum airspeed, and minimum bank.
C — Steepest bank, minimum airspeed, maximum altitude, and level pitch attitude.

44. On final approach to landing, a faster-than-normal indicated airspeed should be used when

A — turbulent conditions exist.
B — ambient temperatures are above 90°F.
C — landing at airports above 5,000 feet MSL with above standard temperature conditions.

45. Advection fog is formed as a result of

A — moist air moving over a colder surface.
B — the addition of moisture to a mass of cold air as it moves over a body of water.
C — the ground cooling adjacent air to the dewpoint temperature on clear, calm nights.

46. At a constant velocity in airflow, a high aspect ratio wing will have (in comparison with a low aspect ratio wing)

A — increased drag, especially at a low angle of attack.
B — decreased drag, especially at a high angle of attack.
C — increased drag, especially at a high angle of attack.

47. What is characteristic of the indicated airspeed if the CG is at the most forward allowable position and constant power and altitude are maintained?

A — There is no relationship between CG location and indicated airspeed.
B — Indicated airspeed will be less than it would be with the CG in the most rearward allowable position.
C — Indicated airspeed will be greater than it would be with the CG in the most rearward allowable position.

48. Which statement is true concerning the aerodynamic conditions which occur during a spin entry?

A — After a full stall, both wings remain in a stalled condition throughout the rotation.
B — After a partial stall, the wing that drops remains in a stalled condition while the rising wing regains and continues to produce lift, causing the rotation.
C — After a full stall, the wing that drops continues in a stalled condition while the rising wing regains and continues to produce some lift, causing the rotation.

49. (Refer to Figure 48 on page 345.) In flying the rectangular course, which would describe the proper angle of bank?

A — Corner 1 shallow, corner 2 medium, corner 3 steep, and corner 4 shallow.
B — Corner 1 shallow, corner 2 medium to steep, corner 3 steep, and corner 4 medium to shallow.
C — Corner 1 shallow to medium, corner 2 medium to steep, corner 3 steep to medium, and corner 4 medium to shallow.

50. (Refer to Figure 50 on page 348.) During S-turn practice, which positions require the steeper angle of bank?

A — 4 and 5.
B — 3 and 4.
C — 2 and 5.

51. (Refer to Figure 13A on page 215.) After analyzing your flight path through northwestern Illinois and eastern Iowa, you should continue your flight planning by examining

A — AIRMET.
B — SIGMET.
C — PIREP.

52. (Refer to Figure 13 on page 223.) For a flight between San Francisco, CA, and Seattle, WA, you should expect icing to accumulate to 1/4 inch thickness within:

A — 1 hour.
B — between 15 minutes and 1 hour.
C — less than 15 minutes.

53. (Refer to Figure 55 on page 134.) At what time of day does the tower shut down at Dallas Executive?

A — 0330Z.
B — 1400Z.
C — 2100 local.

54. From which of the following can the observed temperature, wind, and temperature/dewpoint spread be determined at specified flight levels?

A — Stability Charts.
B — Winds Aloft Forecasts.
C — Constant Pressure Charts.

55. Which weather chart depicts the conditions forecast to exist at a specific time in the future?

A — Prognostic.
B — Surface Analysis.
C — Weather Depiction.

56. What information is contained in a CONVECTIVE SIGMET in the conterminous United States?

A — Moderate thunderstorms and surface winds greater than 40 knots.
B — Tornadoes, embedded thunderstorms, and hail 3/4 inch or greater in diameter.
C — Severe icing, severe turbulence, or widespread dust storms lowering visibility to less than 3 miles.

57. The angular difference between true north and magnetic north is

A — magnetic deviation.
B — magnetic variation.
C — compass acceleration error.

58. How can smoking affect a pilot?

A — Can decrease night vision by up to 50 percent.
B — Reduces the oxygen-carrying capability of the blood.
C — Creates additional carbon dioxide gases in the body which often leads to hyperventilation.

59. Which procedure is recommended to prevent or overcome spatial disorientation?

A — Avoid steep turns and rough control movements.
B — Rely entirely on the indications of the flight instruments.
C — Reduce head and eye movements to the greatest extent possible.

60. If both the ram-air input and drain hole of the pitot system are blocked, what airspeed indication can be expected?

A — Decrease of indicated airspeed during a climb.
B — Zero indicated airspeed until blockage is removed.
C — No variation of indicated airspeed in level flight even if large power changes are made.

61. If a pitot tube is clogged, which instrument would be affected?

A — Altimeter.
B — Airspeed indicator.
C — Vertical speed indicator.

62. Excessively high engine temperatures, either in the air or on the ground, will

A — increase fuel consumption and may increase power due to the increased heat.
B — result in damage to heat-conducting hoses and warping of cylinder cooling fans.
C — cause loss of power, excessive oil consumption, and possible permanent internal engine damage.

63. On a multiengine airplane with engines which rotate clockwise, the critical engine is the

A — left engine, because the right engine center of thrust is closer to the centerline of the fuselage.
B — right engine, because the left engine center of thrust is closer to the centerline of the fuselage.
C — left engine, because the right engine center of thrust is farther away from the centerline of the fuselage.

64. As the angle of bank is increased, the vertical component of lift

A — increases and the sink rate increases.
B — decreases and the sink rate increases.
C — increases and the sink rate decreases.

65. Propeller slip is the difference between the

A — geometric pitch and blade angle of the propeller.
B — geometric pitch and the effective pitch of the propeller.
C — plane of rotation of the propeller and forward velocity of the aircraft.

66. Who is primarily responsible for maintaining an aircraft in an airworthy condition?

A — Mechanic.
B — Pilot in command.
C — Owner or operator of the aircraft.

67. A warning area is airspace of defined dimensions established

A — for training purposes in the vicinity of military bases.
B — from three nautical miles outward from the coast of the U.S.
C — over either domestic or international waters for the purpose of separating military from civilian aircraft.

68. If a military training route has flights operating at or below 1,500 feet AGL, it will be designated by

A — VR and a three digit number only.
B — IR or VR and a four digit number.
C — IR or VR and a three digit number.

69. When a permanent change of address occurs, pilot or instructor privileges may not be exercised unless the FAA Airmen Certification Branch is notified, in writing, within

A — 30 days.
B — 60 days.
C — 90 days.

70. Flight through a restricted area should not be accomplished unless the pilot has

A — filed a IFR flight plan.
B — received prior authorization from the controlling agency.
C — received prior permission from the commanding officer of the nearest military base.

71. A person whose Flight Instructor Certificate has been suspended may not

A — give flight instruction, but may apply for a rating to be added to that certificate.
B — apply for any rating to be added to that certificate during the period of suspension.
C — apply for any Flight Instructor Certificate for a period of 1 year after the date of the suspension.

72. Which is required equipment for powered aircraft during VFR night flights?

A — Magnetic compass.
B — Sensitive altimeter and landing light.
C — VHF radio communications equipment.

73. Your student has received 3.0 hours of night flight training including five takeoffs and landings. Is your student eligible to take the Private Pilot practical test?

A — Yes, but the pilot certificate would bear the limitation "Night Flying Prohibited."
B — No.
C — Yes, but the pilot certificate would bear the restriction, "Holder does not meet ICAO requirements."

74. What limitation is imposed on a newly certificated commercial airplane pilot if that person does not hold an instrument pilot rating?

A — The carrying of passengers for hire on cross-country flights of more than 50 NM or at night is prohibited.
B — The carrying of passengers for hire on cross-country flights is limited to 50 NM for night flights, but not limited for day flights.
C — The carrying of passengers or property for hire on cross-country flights is limited to 50 NM and the carrying of passengers for hire at night is prohibited.

75. When two or more aircraft are approaching an airport for the purpose of landing, the right-of-way belongs to the aircraft

A — that is the least maneuverable.
B — that is either ahead of or to the other's right regardless of altitude.
C — at the lower altitude, but it shall not take advantage of this rule to cut in front of or to overtake another.

76. NTSB Part 830 requires an immediate notification as a result of which incident?

A — Aircraft collide on the ground.
B — Flight control system malfunction.
C — Damage to property, other than the aircraft, estimated to exceed $10,000.

77. To endorse a student pilot for solo cross-country privileges, an instructor is required, in part, to have

A — determined that the student's preparation, planning, and procedures are adequate for the proposed flight under the existing conditions.
B — assurance from another instructor that the student is prepared to conduct the flight safely under current conditions.
C — given that student the required cross-country flight training and checked the flight planning.

78. A flight instructor recommendation is not required for an ATP applicant except when applying for

A — a retest.
B — a type rating.
C — the addition of a category rating.

79. The minimum distance at which an airplane may be operated over a structure which is located in a sparsely populated area is

A — 500 feet above the ground.
B — 500 feet from the structure.
C — 1,000 feet from the structure.

80. Unless each occupant is provided with supplemental oxygen, no person may operate a civil aircraft of U.S. registry above a cabin pressure altitude of

A — 12,500 feet MSL.
B — 14,000 feet MSL.
C — 15,000 feet MSL.

81. No person may act as pilot in command of a pressurized airplane with a service ceiling or maximum operating altitude, whichever is lower, above 25,000 feet unless that person has

A — completed a physiological training program conducted by the FAA or a military service.
B — received ground and flight training in high altitude operations and a logbook endorsement certifying this training.
C — completed a pilot proficiency check for a pilot or instructor pilot certificate or rating conducted by the FAA after April 15, 1991.

82. When is a recreational pilot required to carry a logbook with the required endorsements?

A — Any flight up to 50 miles from the airport at which instruction was received.
B — When flying during the hours between sunrise and sunset.
C — On all flights when serving as pilot in command.

83. How long will a Flight Service Station hold a VFR flight plan past the proposed departure time?

A — 30 minutes.
B — 1 hour.
C — 2 hours.

84. A student is required to receive a logbook endorsement

A — for each solo flight.
B — to make repeated solo cross-country flights to an airport more than 50 NM from the point of departure.
C — for solo flight each 90 days.

85. To operate an aircraft on a solo flight within Class B airspace, a student must have a logbook endorsement showing that (s)he has

A — received flight instruction from any authorized flight instructor on operating within Class B airspace.
B — received ground instruction on and flight instruction in that specific airspace for which solo flight is authorized.
C — within the preceding 90 days, been found to be competent by any flight instructor having knowledge of the student's experience in that specific airspace.

86. No person may act as a crewmember of a civil aircraft with a minimum blood alcohol level of

A — any detectable amount.
B — 0.04 percent or greater.
C — 0.2 percent or greater.

87. The objective of a cross-control stall demonstration is to

A — emphasize the hazard of an excessive slip during a landing approach.
B — teach the proper recovery technique should this type of stall occur during final approach.
C — show the effect of improper control technique and emphasize the importance of coordinated control when making turns.

88. If the airspeed increases and decreases during longitudinal phugoid oscillations, the aircraft

A — will display poor trimming qualities.
B — is maintaining a nearly constant angle of attack.
C — is constantly changing angle of attack making it difficult for the pilot to reduce the magnitude of the oscillations.

89. When explaining the techniques used for making short- and soft-field takeoffs, it would be correct to state that

A — during soft-field takeoffs, lift-off should be made as soon as possible.
B — during soft-field takeoffs, lift-off should be made only when best angle-of-climb speed is attained.
C — during short-field takeoffs, lift-off should be attempted only after best rate-of-climb speed is attained.

90. Which is the primary driving force of weather on the Earth?

A — The Sun.
B — Coriolis.
C — Rotation of the Earth.

91. Which type of cloud is associated with violent turbulence and a tendency toward the production of funnel clouds?

A — Cumulonimbus mamma.
B — Standing lenticular.
C — Altocumulus castellanus.

92. Which transponder code should the pilot of a civilian aircraft never use?

A — 7500
B — 7600
C — 7777

93. When making routine transponder code changes, pilots should avoid inadvertent selection of which codes?

A — 0700, 1700, 7000.
B — 1200, 1500, 7000.
C — 7500, 7600, 7700.

94. One of the most dangerous features of mountain waves is the turbulent areas in and

A — below rotor clouds.
B — above rotor clouds.
C — below lenticular clouds.

95. Which statement is true regarding wingtip vortices?

A — Helicopter rotors generate downwash turbulence only, not vortices.
B — Vortices generated by helicopters in forward flight are similar to those generated by fixed wing aircraft.
C — Vortices tend to remain level for a period of time before sinking below the generating aircraft's flightpath.

96. Convective circulation patterns associated with sea breezes are caused by

A — land absorbing and radiating heat faster than the water.
B — warm and less dense air moving inland from over the water, causing it to rise.
C — cool and less dense air moving inland from over the water, causing it to rise.

97. Consider the following air mass characteristics:

1. Cumuliform clouds.
2. Stable lapse rate.
3. Unstable lapse rate.
4. Stratiform clouds and fog.
5. Smooth air (above the friction level) and poor visibility.
6. Turbulence up to about 10,000 feet and good visibility except in areas of precipitation.

A moist air mass, which is colder than the surface over which it passes, frequently has which of the above characteristics?

A — 1, 3, and 6.
B — 3, 4, and 5.
C — 2, 4, and 5.

98. Streamers of precipitation trailing beneath clouds but evaporating before reaching the ground are known as

A — virga.
B — sublimation.
C — evaporation.

99. When flying from a high- to a low-pressure area in the Northern Hemisphere, the wind direction and velocity will be from the

A — left and increasing.
B — left and decreasing.
C — right and increasing.

100. Which condition could be expected if a strong temperature inversion exists near the surface?

A — Strong, steady downdrafts and an increase in OAT.
B — A wind shear with the possibility of a sudden loss of airspeed.
C — An OAT increase or decrease with a constant wind condition.

PRACTICE TEST LIST OF ANSWERS

The listing below gives the correct answers for your flight/ground instructor practice knowledge test and the page number in this book on which you will find each question with the complete Gleim answer explanation.

Q. #	Answer	Page	Q. #	Answer	Page	Q. #	Answer	Page	Q. #	Answer	Page
1.	B	74	26.	B	129	51.	C	214	76.	B	281
2.	B	317	27.	C	133	52.	C	223	77.	A	259
3.	B	317	28.	B	137	53.	C	135	78.	A	247
4.	A	321	29.	B	268	54.	C	213	79.	B	267
5.	B	321	30.	A	270	55.	A	216	80.	C	275
6.	C	159	31.	C	271	56.	B	222	81.	B	244
7.	A	65	32.	B	343	57.	B	300	82.	C	255
8.	C	32	33.	A	197	58.	B	364	83.	B	142
9.	B	138	34.	B	355	59.	B	366	84.	C	253
10.	A	37	35.	A	105	60.	C	97	85.	B	255
11.	A	206	36.	B	141	61.	B	98	86.	B	263
12.	B	207	37.	C	306	62.	C	100	87.	C	350
13.	B	207	38.	B	314	63.	C	78	88.	B	49
14.	A	296	39.	A	77	64.	B	46	89.	A	338
15.	B	296	40.	A	114	65.	B	103	90.	A	191
16.	A	298	41.	C	314	66.	C	278	91.	A	202
17.	B	304	42.	B	353	67.	B	136	92.	C	140
18.	A	308	43.	C	354	68.	B	137	93.	C	140
19.	C	41	44.	A	341	69.	A	251	94.	A	200
20.	C	218	45.	A	194	70.	B	136	95.	B	131
21.	C	324	46.	B	42	71.	B	242	96.	A	192
22.	B	160	47.	B	154	72.	A	273	97.	A	197
23.	B	314	48.	C	51	73.	B	256	98.	A	205
24.	C	339	49.	C	344	74.	A	257	99.	A	192
25.	C	339	50.	B	348	75.	C	265	100.	B	201

APPENDIX D:
INTERPOLATION

A. To interpolate means to compute intermediate values between a series of given values.

   1. In many instances when performance is critical, an accurate determination of the performance values is the only acceptable means to enhance safe flight.
   2. Guessing to determine these values should be avoided.

B. Interpolation is simple to perform if the method is understood. The following are examples of how to interpolate, or accurately determine the intermediate values, between a series of given values.

C. The numbers in column A range from 10 to 30, and the numbers in column B range from 50 to 100. Determine the intermediate numerical value in column B that would correspond with an intermediate value of 20 placed in column A.

A	B
10	50
20	X = Unknown
30	100

   1. It can be visualized that 20 is halfway between 10 and 30; therefore, the corresponding value of the unknown number in column B would be halfway between 50 and 100, or 75.

D. Many interpolation problems are more difficult to visualize than the preceding example; therefore, a systematic method must be used to determine the required intermediate value. The following describes one method that can be used.

   1. The numbers in column A range from 10 to 30 with intermediate values of 15, 20, and 25. Determine the intermediate numerical value in column B that would correspond with 15 in column A.

A	B
10	50
15	
20	
25	
30	100

   2. First, in column A, determine the relationship of 15 to the range between 10 and 30 as follows:

$$\frac{15 - 10}{30 - 10} = \frac{5}{20} \text{ or } 1/4$$

      a. It should be noted that 15 is 1/4 of the range between 10 and 30.

3. Now determine 1/4 of the range of column B between 50 and 100 as follows:

$$100 - 50 = 50$$
$$1/4 \text{ of } 50 = 12.5$$

    a. The answer 12.5 represents the number of units, but to arrive at the correct value, 12.5 must be added to the lower number in column B as follows:

$$50 + 12.5 = 62.5$$

4. The interpolation has been completed and 62.5 is the actual value that is 1/4 of the range of column B.

E. Another method of interpolation is shown below:

1. Using the same numbers as in the previous example, a proportion problem based on the relationship of the number can be set up.

```
              A              B
         ┌─10           ┌─50
      5─┤              X─┤
         └─15           └─?
  20─┤     20      50─┤
        25
        └─30           └─100
```

Proportion: $\dfrac{5}{20} = \dfrac{X}{50}$

$$20X = 250$$
$$X = 12.5$$

    a. The answer, 12.5, must be added to 50 to arrive at the actual value of 62.5.

F. The following example illustrates the use of interpolation applied to a problem dealing with one aspect of airplane performance:

Temperature (°F)	Takeoff Distance (ft.)
70	1,173
80	1,356

1. If a distance of 1,173 feet is required for takeoff when the temperature is 70°F and 1,356 feet is required at 80°F, what distance is required when the temperature is 75°F? The solution to the problem can be determined as follows:

```
            ┌─70°             ┌─1,173
        5─┤                 X─┤
   10─┤    └─75° 183─┤          └─?
            └─80°               └─1,356
```

$$\dfrac{5}{10} = \dfrac{X}{183}$$
$$10X = 915$$
$$X = 91.5$$

    a. The answer, 91.5, must be added to 1,173 to arrive at the actual value of 1,264.5 ft.

FAA LISTING OF LEARNING STATEMENT CODES

Reprinted below and on the following pages are all of the FAA's learning statement codes for pilots. These are the codes that will appear on your Airman Computer Test Report. See the example on page 15. Your test report will list the learning statement code of each question answered incorrectly. The statements are designed to represent the knowledge test topic areas in clear verbal terms and encourage applicants to study the entire area of identified weakness instead of merely studying a specific question area. You should discuss your test results with your CFI.

When you receive your Airman Computer Test Report, you can trace the learning statement codes listed on it to these pages to find out which topics you had difficulty with. To determine the knowledge area in which a particular question was incorrectly answered, compare the learning statement code(s) on your Airman Computer Test Report to the listing that follows. The total number of test items missed may differ from the number of learning statement codes shown on your test report because you may have missed more than one question in a certain knowledge area.

Additionally, you should trace the learning statement codes on your Airman Computer Test Report to our cross-reference listing of questions beginning on page 399. Determine which Gleim subunits you need to review.

The FAA will periodically revise the existing learning codes and add new ones. As Gleim learns about any changes, we will update our materials.

PLT001	Calculate a course intercept
PLT002	Calculate aircraft performance - airspeed
PLT003	Calculate aircraft performance - center of gravity
PLT004	Calculate aircraft performance - climb / descent / maneuvering
PLT005	Calculate aircraft performance - density altitude
PLT006	Calculate aircraft performance - glide
PLT007	Calculate aircraft performance - IAS
PLT008	Calculate aircraft performance - landing
PLT009	Calculate aircraft performance - turbine temperatures (MGT, EGT, ITT, T4, etc) / torque / horsepower
PLT010	Calculate aircraft performance - STAB TRIM
PLT011	Calculate aircraft performance - takeoff
PLT012	Calculate aircraft performance - time / speed / distance / course / fuel / wind
PLT013	Calculate crosswind / headwind components
PLT014	Calculate distance / bearing to a station
PLT015	Calculate flight performance / planning - range
PLT016	Calculate fuel - dump time / weight / volume / quantity / consumption
PLT017	Calculate L/D ratio
PLT018	Calculate load factor / stall speed / velocity / angle of attack
PLT019	Calculate pressure altitude
PLT020	Calculate turbulent air penetration
PLT021	Calculate weight and balance
PLT022	Define Aeronautical Decision Making (ADM)
PLT023	Define altitude - absolute / true / indicated / density / pressure
PLT024	Define atmospheric adiabatic process
PLT025	Define Bernoulli's principle
PLT026	Define ceiling
PLT027	Define coning
PLT028	Define crewmember
PLT029	Define critical phase of flight
PLT030	Define false lift
PLT031	Define isobars / associated winds
PLT032	Define MACH speed regimes
PLT033	Define MEA / MOCA / MRA
PLT034	Define stopway / clearway
PLT035	Define Vne / Vno
PLT036	Interpret a MACH meter reading
PLT037	Interpret a Radar Weather Report / National Convective Weather Forecast
PLT038	Interpret aircraft Power Schedule Chart
PLT039	Interpret airport landing indicator
PLT040	Interpret airspace classes - charts / diagrams
PLT041	Interpret altimeter - readings / settings
PLT042	Interpret Constant Pressure charts / Isotachs Chart
PLT043	Interpret Analysis Heights / Temperature Chart
PLT044	Interpret ATC communications / instructions / terminology
PLT045	Interpret Descent Performance Chart
PLT046	Interpret drag ratio from charts
PLT047	Interpret/Program Flight Director/FMS/ Automation - modes / operation / indications / errors
PLT048	Interpret Hovering Ceiling Chart
PLT049	Interpret ILS - charts / RMI / CDI / indications
PLT050	Interpret information on a Brake Energy Limit Chart
PLT051	Interpret information on a Convective Outlook
PLT052	Interpret information on a Departure Procedure Chart
PLT053	Interpret information on a Flight Plan
PLT054	Interpret information on a Glider Performance Graph
PLT055	Interpret information on a High Altitude Chart
PLT056	Interpret information on a Horizontal Situation Indicator (HSI)
PLT057	Interpret information on a Hot Air Balloon Performance Graph
PLT058	Interpret information on a Low Altitude Chart
PLT059	Interpret information on a METAR / SPECI report
PLT060	Interpret information on a Performance Curve Chart
PLT061	Interpret information on a PIREP
PLT062	Interpret information on a Pseudo-Adiabatic Chart / K Index / Lifted Index
PLT063	Deleted
PLT064	Interpret information on a Sectional Chart
PLT065	Interpret information on a Service Ceiling Engine Inoperative Chart

PLT066	Interpret information on a Convective Outlook Chart
PLT067	Interpret information on a SIGMET
PLT068	Interpret information on a Significant Weather Prognostic Chart
PLT069	Interpret information on a Slush/Standing Water Takeoff Chart
PLT070	Interpret information on a Stability Chart
PLT071	Interpret information on a Surface Analysis Chart
PLT072	Interpret information on a Terminal Aerodrome Forecast (TAF)
PLT073	Interpret information on a Tower Enroute Control (TEC)
PLT074	Interpret information on a Velocity/Load Factor Chart
PLT076	Interpret information on a Winds and Temperatures Aloft Forecast (FB)
PLT077	Interpret information on an Airport Diagram
PLT078	Interpret information in a Chart Supplements U.S.
PLT079	Interpret information on an Airways Chart
PLT080	Interpret information on an Arrival Chart
PLT082	Interpret information on an IFR Alternate Airport Minimums Chart
PLT083	Interpret information on an Instrument Approach Procedures (IAP)
PLT084	Interpret information on an Observed Winds Aloft Chart
PLT085	Interpret information on Takeoff Obstacle / Field / Climb Limit Charts
PLT086	Interpret readings on a Turn and Slip Indicator
PLT087	Interpret readings on an Aircraft Course and DME Indicator
PLT088	Interpret speed indicator readings
PLT089	Interpret Takeoff Speeds Chart
PLT090	Interpret VOR - charts / indications / CDI / NAV
PLT091	Interpret VOR / CDI - illustrations / indications / procedures
PLT092	Interpret weight and balance - diagram
PLT093	Recall administration of medical oxygen
PLT094	Recall aerodynamics - airfoil design / pressure distribution / effects of altitude
PLT095	Recall aerodynamics - longitudinal axis / lateral axis
PLT096	Recall aeromedical factors - effects of altitude
PLT097	Recall aeromedical factors - effects of carbon monoxide poisoning
PLT098	Recall aeromedical factors - fitness for flight
PLT099	Recall aeromedical factors - scanning procedures
PLT100	Recall aeronautical charts - IFR En Route Low Altitude
PLT101	Recall aeronautical charts - pilotage
PLT102	Recall aeronautical charts - terminal procedures
PLT103	Recall Aeronautical Decision Making (ADM) - hazardous attitudes
PLT104	Recall Aeronautical Decision Making (ADM) - human factors / CRM
PLT105	Recall airborne radar / thunderstorm detection equipment - use / limitations
PLT106	Recall aircraft air-cycle machine
PLT107	Recall aircraft alternator / generator system
PLT108	Recall aircraft anti-icing / deicing - methods / fluids
PLT109	Recall aircraft batteries - capacity / charging / types / storage / rating / precautions
PLT110	Recall aircraft brake system
PLT111	Recall aircraft circuitry - series / parallel
PLT112	Recall aircraft controls - proper use / techniques
PLT113	Recall aircraft design - categories / limitation factors
PLT114	Recall aircraft design - construction / function
PLT115	Recall aircraft engine - detonation/backfiring/after firing, cause/characteristics
PLT116	Recall aircraft general knowledge / publications / AIM / navigational aids
PLT117	Recall aircraft heated windshields
PLT118	Recall aircraft instruments - gyroscopic
PLT119	Recall aircraft lighting - anti-collision / landing / navigation
PLT120	Recall aircraft limitations - turbulent air penetration
PLT121	Recall aircraft loading - computations
PLT122	Recall aircraft operations - checklist usage
PLT123	Recall aircraft performance - airspeed
PLT124	Recall aircraft performance - atmospheric effects
PLT125	Recall aircraft performance - climb / descent
PLT126	Recall aircraft performance - cold weather operations
PLT127	Recall aircraft performance - density altitude
PLT128	Recall aircraft performance - effects of icing
PLT129	Recall aircraft performance - effects of runway slope / slope landing
PLT130	Recall aircraft performance - fuel
PLT131	Recall aircraft performance - ground effect
PLT132	Recall aircraft performance - instrument markings / airspeed / definitions / indications
PLT133	Recall aircraft performance - normal climb / descent rates
PLT134	Recall aircraft performance - takeoff
PLT135	Recall aircraft pressurization - system / operation
PLT136	Recall aircraft systems - anti-icing / deicing
PLT137	Recall aircraft systems - environmental control
PLT138	Recall aircraft landing gear/tires - types / characteristics
PLT139	Recall aircraft warning systems - stall / fire / retractable gear / terrain awareness
PLT140	Recall airport operations - LAHSO
PLT141	Recall airport operations - markings / signs / lighting
PLT142	Recall airport operations - noise avoidance routes
PLT143	Recall airport operations - rescue / fire fighting vehicles and types of agents
PLT144	Recall airport operations - runway conditions
PLT145	Recall airport operations - runway lighting
PLT146	Recall airport operations - traffic pattern procedures / communication procedures
PLT147	Recall airport operations - visual glidepath indicators
PLT148	Recall airport operations lighting - MALS / ALSF / RCLS / TDZL
PLT149	Recall airport preflight / taxi operations - procedures
PLT150	Recall airport traffic patterns - entry procedures
PLT151	Recall airship - buoyancy
PLT152	Recall airship - flight characteristics / controllability
PLT153	Recall airship - flight operations
PLT154	Recall airship - ground weight-off / static / trim condition
PLT155	Recall airship - maintaining pressure
PLT156	Recall airship - maximum headway / flight at equilibrium
PLT157	Recall airship - pressure height / dampers / position
PLT158	Recall airship - pressure height / manometers
PLT159	Recall airship - pressure height / super heat / valving gas

PLT160	Recall airship - stability / control / positive superheat
PLT161	Recall airspace classes - limits / requirements / restrictions / airspeeds / equipment
PLT162	Recall airspace requirements - operations
PLT163	Recall airspace requirements - visibility / cloud clearance
PLT164	Recall airspeed - effects during a turn
PLT165	Recall altimeter - effect of temperature changes
PLT166	Recall altimeter - settings / setting procedures
PLT167	Recall altimeters - characteristics / accuracy
PLT168	Recall angle of attack - characteristics / forces / principles
PLT169	Recall antitorque system - components / functions
PLT170	Recall approach / landing / taxiing techniques
PLT171	Recall ATC - reporting
PLT172	Recall ATC - system / services
PLT173	Recall atmospheric conditions - measurements / pressure / stability
PLT174	Recall autopilot / yaw damper - components / operating principles / characteristics / failure modes
PLT175	Recall autorotation
PLT176	Recall balance tab - purpose / operation
PLT177	Recall balloon - flight operations
PLT178	Recall balloon - flight operations / gas
PLT179	Recall balloon - ground weigh-off / static equilibrium / load
PLT180	Recall balloon gas/hot air - lift / false lift / characteristics
PLT181	Recall balloon - hot air / physics
PLT182	Recall balloon - inspecting the fabric
PLT183	Recall balloon flight operations - ascent / descent
PLT184	Recall balloon flight operations - launch / landing
PLT185	Recall basic instrument flying - fundamental skills
PLT186	Recall basic instrument flying - pitch instruments
PLT187	Recall basic instrument flying - turn coordinator / turn and slip indicator
PLT188	Recall cabin atmosphere control
PLT189	Recall carburetor - effects of carburetor heat / heat control
PLT190	Recall carburetor ice - factors affecting / causing
PLT191	Recall carburetors - types / components / operating principles / characteristics
PLT192	Recall clouds - types / formation / resulting weather
PLT193	Recall cockpit voice recorder (CVR) - operating principles / characteristics / testing
PLT194	Recall collision avoidance - scanning techniques
PLT195	Recall collision avoidance - TCAS
PLT196	Recall communications - ATIS broadcasts
PLT197	Recall Coriolis effect
PLT198	Recall course / heading - effects of wind
PLT199	Recall cyclic control pressure - characteristics
PLT200	Recall dead reckoning - calculations / charts
PLT201	Recall departure procedures - ODP / SID
PLT202	Recall DME - characteristics / accuracy / indications / Arc
PLT203	Recall earth's atmosphere - layers / characteristics / solar energy
PLT204	Recall effective communication - basic elements
PLT205	Recall effects of alcohol on the body
PLT206	Recall effects of temperature - density altitude / icing
PLT207	Recall electrical system - components / operating principles / characteristics / static bonding and shielding
PLT208	Recall emergency conditions / procedures
PLT209	Deleted
PLT210	Recall engine shutdown - normal / abnormal / emergency / precautions
PLT211	Recall evaluation testing characteristics
PLT212	Recall fire extinguishing systems - components / operating principles / characteristics
PLT213	Recall flight characteristics - longitudinal stability / instability
PLT214	Recall flight characteristics - structural / wing design
PLT215	Recall flight instruments - magnetic compass
PLT216	Recall flight instruments - total energy compensators
PLT217	Recall flight maneuvers - quick stop
PLT218	Recall flight operations - common student errors
PLT219	Recall flight operations - maneuvers
PLT220	Recall flight operations - night and high altitude operations
PLT221	Recall flight operations - takeoff / landing maneuvers
PLT222	Recall flight operations - takeoff procedures
PLT223	Recall flight operations multiengine - engine inoperative procedures
PLT224	Recall flight plan - IFR
PLT225	Recall flight plan - requirements
PLT226	Recall fog - types / formation / resulting weather
PLT227	Recall FOI techniques - integrated flight instruction
PLT228	Recall FOI techniques - lesson plans
PLT229	Recall FOI techniques - professionalism
PLT230	Recall FOI techniques - responsibilities
PLT231	Recall FOI techniques / human behavior - anxiety / fear / stress
PLT232	Recall FOI techniques / human behavior - dangerous tendencies
PLT233	Recall FOI techniques / human behavior - defense mechanisms
PLT234	Recall forces acting on aircraft - 3 axis intersect
PLT235	Recall forces acting on aircraft - aerodynamics
PLT236	Recall forces acting on aircraft - airfoil / center of pressure / mean camber line
PLT237	Recall forces acting on aircraft - airspeed / air density / lift / drag
PLT238	Recall forces acting on aircraft - aspect ratio
PLT239	Recall forces acting on aircraft - buoyancy / drag / gravity / thrust
PLT240	Recall forces acting on aircraft - CG / flight characteristics
PLT241	Recall forces acting on aircraft - drag / gravity / thrust / lift
PLT242	Recall forces acting on aircraft - lift / drag / thrust / weight / stall / limitations
PLT243	Recall forces acting on aircraft - propeller / torque
PLT244	Recall forces acting on aircraft - stability / controllability
PLT245	Recall forces acting on aircraft - stalls / spins
PLT246	Recall forces acting on aircraft - steady state climb / flight
PLT247	Recall forces acting on aircraft - thrust / drag / weight / lift
PLT248	Recall forces acting on aircraft - turns
PLT249	Recall fuel - air mixture
PLT250	Recall fuel - types / characteristics / contamination / fueling / defueling / precautions
PLT251	Recall fuel characteristics / contaminants / additives
PLT252	Recall fuel dump system - components / methods
PLT253	Recall fuel system - components / operating principles / characteristics / leaks
PLT254	Recall fuel tank - components / operating principles / characteristics

PLT255	Recall fueling procedures - safety / grounding / calculating volume
PLT256	Recall glider performance - effect of loading
PLT257	Recall glider performance - speed / distance / ballast / lift / drag
PLT258	Recall ground reference maneuvers - ground track diagram
PLT259	Recall ground resonance - conditions to occur
PLT260	Recall gyroplane - aerodynamics / rotor systems
PLT261	Recall hail - characteristics / hazards
PLT262	Recall helicopter hazards - dynamic rollover / Low G / LTE
PLT263	Recall hazardous weather - fog / icing / turbulence / visibility restriction
PLT264	Recall helicopter approach - settling with power
PLT265	Recall helicopter takeoff / landing - ground resonance action required
PLT266	Recall high lift devices - characteristics / functions
PLT267	Recall hot air balloon - weight-off procedure
PLT268	Recall hovering - aircraft performance / tendencies
PLT269	Recall human behavior - defense mechanism
PLT270	Recall human behavior - social / self-fulfillment / physical
PLT271	Recall human factors (ADM) - judgment
PLT272	Recall human factors - stress management
PLT273	Recall hydraulic systems - components / operating principles / characteristics
PLT274	Recall icing - formation / characteristics
PLT275	Recall ILS - indications / HSI
PLT276	Recall ILS - indications / OBS / CDI
PLT277	Recall ILS - marker beacon / indicator lights / codes
PLT278	Recall indicating systems - airspeed / angle of attack / attitude / heading / manifold pressure / synchro / EGT
PLT279	Recall Inertial/Doppler Navigation System principles / regulations / requirements / limitations
PLT280	Recall inflight illusions - causes / sources
PLT281	Recall information in a Chart Supplements U.S.
PLT282	Recall information in the certificate holder's manual
PLT283	Recall information on a Constant Pressure Analysis Chart
PLT284	Recall information on a Forecast Winds and Temperatures Aloft (FB)
PLT285	Recall information on a Height Velocity Diagram
PLT286	Recall information on a Significant Weather Prognostic Chart
PLT287	Recall information on a Surface Analysis Chart
PLT288	Recall information on a Terminal Aerodrome Forecast (TAF)
PLT289	Recall information on a Weather Depiction Chart
PLT290	Recall information on AIRMETS / SIGMETS
PLT292	Recall information on an Instrument Approach Procedures (IAP)
PLT293	Recall information on an Instrument Departure Procedure Chart
PLT294	Recall information on Inflight Aviation Weather Advisories
PLT295	Recall instructor techniques - obstacles / planning / activities / outcome
PLT296	Recall instrument procedures - holding / circling
PLT297	Recall instrument procedures - unusual attitude / unusual attitude recovery
PLT298	Recall instrument procedures - VFR on top
PLT300	Recall instrument/navigation system checks/ inspections - limits / tuning / identifying / logging
PLT301	Recall inversion layer - characteristics
PLT302	Recall jet stream - types / characteristics
PLT303	Recall L/D ratio
PLT304	Recall launch / aero-tow procedures
PLT305	Recall leading edge devices - types / effect / purpose / operation
PLT306	Recall learning process - levels of learning / transfer of learning / incidental learning
PLT307	Recall learning process - memory / fact / recall
PLT308	Recall learning process - laws of learning elements
PLT309	Recall load factor - angle of bank
PLT310	Recall load factor - characteristics
PLT311	Recall load factor - effect of airspeed
PLT312	Recall load factor - maneuvering / stall speed
PLT313	Recall loading – limitations / terminology
PLT314	Recall longitudinal axis - aerodynamics / center of gravity / direction of motion
PLT315	Recall Machmeter - principles / functions
PLT316	Recall meteorology - severe weather watch (WW)
PLT317	Recall microburst - characteristics / hazards
PLT318	Recall minimum fuel advisory
PLT319	Recall navigation – celestial / navigation chart / characteristics
PLT320	Recall navigation - true north / magnetic north
PLT321	Recall navigation - types of landing systems
PLT322	Recall navigation - VOR / NAV system
PLT323	Recall NOTAMS - classes / information / distribution
PLT324	Recall oil system - types / components / functions / oil specifications
PLT325	Recall operations manual - transportation of prisoner
PLT326	Recall oxygen system - components / operating principles / characteristics
PLT327	Recall oxygen system - install / inspect / repair / service / precautions / leaks
PLT328	Recall performance planning - aircraft loading
PLT329	Recall physiological factors - cabin pressure
PLT330	Recall physiological factors - cause / effects of hypoxia
PLT331	Recall physiological factors - effects of scuba diving / smoking
PLT332	Recall physiological factors - hyperventilation / stress / fatigue
PLT333	Recall physiological factors - night vision
PLT334	Recall physiological factors - spatial disorientation
PLT335	Recall pilotage - calculations
PLT336	Recall pitch control - collective / cyclic
PLT337	Recall pitot-static system - components / operating principles / characteristics
PLT338	Recall pneumatic system - operation
PLT340	Recall positive ex/change of flight controls
PLT341	Recall power settling - characteristics
PLT342	Recall powerplant - controlling engine temperature
PLT343	Recall powerplant - operating principles / operational characteristics / inspecting
PLT344	Recall precipitation - types / characteristics
PLT345	Recall pressure altitude
PLT346	Recall primary / secondary flight controls - types / purpose / functionality / operation
PLT347	Recall principles of flight - critical engine
PLT348	Recall principles of flight - turns
PLT349	Recall procedures for confined areas
PLT350	Recall propeller operations - constant / variable speed
PLT351	Recall propeller system - types / components / operating principles / characteristics
PLT352	Recall purpose / operation of a stabilizer
PLT353	Recall Radar Summary Chart
PLT354	Recall radio - GPS / RNAV / RAIM

PLT355	Recall radio - HSI
PLT356	Recall radio - ILS / compass locator
PLT357	Recall radio - ILS
PLT358	Recall radio - LOC / ILS
PLT359	Deleted
PLT360	Deleted
PLT361	Deleted
PLT362	Deleted
PLT363	Recall radio - VOR / VOT
PLT364	Recall radio system - license requirements / frequencies
PLT365	Recall reciprocating engine - components / operating principles / characteristics
PLT366	Recall regulations - accident / incident reporting and preserving wreckage
PLT367	Recall regulations - additional equipment/ operating requirements large transport aircraft
PLT368	Recall regulations - admission to flight deck
PLT369	Recall regulations - aerobatic flight requirements
PLT370	Recall regulations - Air Traffic Control authorization / clearances
PLT371	Recall regulations - Aircraft Category / Class
PLT372	Recall regulations - aircraft inspection / records / expiration
PLT373	Recall regulations - aircraft operating limitations
PLT374	Recall regulations - aircraft owner / operator responsibilities
PLT375	Recall regulations - aircraft return to service
PLT376	Recall regulations - airspace, other, special use / TFRS
PLT377	Recall regulations - airworthiness certificates / requirements / responsibilities
PLT378	Recall regulations - Airworthiness Directives
PLT379	Recall regulations - alternate airport requirements
PLT380	Recall regulations - alternate airport weather minima
PLT381	Recall regulations - altimeter settings
PLT382	Recall regulations - approach minima
PLT383	Recall regulations - basic flight rules
PLT384	Recall regulations - briefing of passengers
PLT385	Recall regulations - cargo in passenger compartment
PLT386	Recall regulations - certificate issuance / renewal
PLT387	Recall regulations - change of address
PLT388	Recall regulations - cockpit voice / flight data recorder(s)
PLT389	Recall regulations - commercial operation requirements / conditions / OpSpecs
PLT390	Recall regulations - communications en route
PLT391	Recall regulations - communications failure
PLT392	Recall regulations - compliance with local regulations
PLT393	Recall regulations - controlled / restricted airspace - requirements
PLT394	Recall regulations - declaration of an emergency
PLT395	Recall regulations - definitions
PLT396	Recall regulations - departure alternate airport
PLT397	Recall regulations - destination airport visibility
PLT398	Recall regulations - dispatch
PLT399	Recall regulations - display / inspection of licenses and certificates
PLT400	Recall regulations - documents to be carried on aircraft during flight
PLT401	Recall regulations - dropping / aerial application / towing restrictions
PLT402	Recall regulations - ELT requirements
PLT403	Recall regulations - emergency deviation from regulations
PLT404	Recall regulations - emergency equipment
PLT405	Recall regulations - equipment / instrument / certificate requirements
PLT406	Recall regulations - equipment failure
PLT407	Recall regulations - experience / training requirements
PLT408	Recall regulations - fire extinguisher requirements
PLT409	Recall regulations - flight / duty time
PLT410	Recall regulations - flight engineer qualifications / privileges / responsibilities
PLT411	Recall regulations - flight instructor limitations / qualifications
PLT412	Recall regulations - flight release
PLT413	Recall regulations - fuel requirements
PLT414	Recall regulations - general right-of-way rules
PLT415	Recall regulations - IFR flying
PLT416	Recall regulations - immediate notification
PLT417	Recall regulations - individual flotation devices
PLT418	Recall regulations - instructor demonstrations / authorizations
PLT419	Recall regulations - instructor requirements / responsibilities
PLT420	Recall regulations - instrument approach procedures
PLT421	Recall regulations - instrument flight rules
PLT422	Recall regulations - intermediate airport authorizations
PLT423	Recall regulations - knowledge and skill test checks
PLT424	Recall regulations - limits on autopilot usage
PLT425	Recall regulations - maintenance reports / records / entries
PLT426	Recall regulations - maintenance requirements
PLT427	Recall regulations - medical certificate requirements / validity
PLT428	Recall regulations - minimum equipment list
PLT429	Recall regulations - minimum flight / navigation instruments
PLT430	Recall regulations - minimum safe / flight altitude
PLT431	Recall regulations - operating near other aircraft
PLT432	Recall regulations - operational control functions
PLT433	Recall regulations - operational flight plan requirements
PLT434	Recall regulations - operational procedures for a controlled airport
PLT435	Recall regulations - operational procedures for an uncontrolled airport
PLT436	Recall regulations - operations manual
PLT437	Recall regulations - overwater operations
PLT438	Recall regulations - oxygen requirements
PLT439	Recall regulations - persons authorized to perform maintenance
PLT440	Recall regulations - Pilot / Crew duties and responsibilities
PLT441	Recall regulations - pilot briefing
PLT442	Recall regulations - pilot currency requirements
PLT443	Recall regulations - pilot qualifications / privileges / responsibilities / crew complement
PLT444	Recall regulations - pilot-in-command authority / responsibility
PLT445	Recall regulations - preflight requirements
PLT446	Recall regulations - preventative maintenance
PLT447	Recall regulations - privileges / limitations of medical certificates
PLT448	Recall regulations - privileges / limitations of pilot certificates
PLT449	Recall regulations - proficiency check requirements
PLT450	Recall regulations - qualifications / duty time
PLT451	Recall regulations - ratings issued / experience requirements / limitations
PLT452	Recall regulations - re-dispatch
PLT453	Recall regulations - records retention for domestic / flag air carriers
PLT454	Recall regulations - required aircraft / equipment inspections

PLT455	Recall regulations - requirements of a flight plan release
PLT456	Recall regulations - runway requirements
PLT457	Recall regulations - student pilot endorsements / other endorsements
PLT458	Recall regulations - submission / revision of Policy and Procedure Manuals
PLT459	Recall regulations - takeoff procedures / minimums
PLT460	Recall regulations - training programs
PLT461	Recall regulations - use of aircraft lights
PLT462	Recall regulations - use of microphone / megaphone / interphone / public address system
PLT463	Recall regulations alcohol or drugs
PLT464	Recall regulations - use of safety belts / harnesses (crew member)
PLT465	Recall regulations - use of seats / safety belts / harnesses (passenger)
PLT466	Recall regulations - V speeds
PLT467	Recall regulations - visual flight rules and limitations
PLT468	Recall regulations - Visual Meteorological Conditions (VMC)
PLT469	Recall regulations - weather radar
PLT470	Recall rotor system - types / components / operating principles / characteristics
PLT471	Recall rotorcraft transmission - components / operating principles / characteristics
PLT472	Recall rotorcraft vibration - characteristics / sources
PLT473	Recall secondary flight controls - types / purpose / functionality
PLT474	Recall soaring - normal procedures
PLT475	Recall squall lines - formation / characteristics / resulting weather
PLT476	Recall stabilizer - purpose / operation
PLT477	Recall stalls - characteristics / factors / recovery / precautions
PLT478	Recall starter / ignition system - types / components / operating principles / characteristics
PLT479	Recall starter system - starting procedures
PLT480	Recall static/dynamic stability/instability - characteristics
PLT481	Recall student evaluation - learning process
PLT482	Recall student evaluation - written tests / oral quiz / critiques
PLT483	Recall supercharger - characteristics / operation
PLT484	Recall symbols - chart / navigation
PLT485	Recall taxiing / crosswind / techniques
PLT486	Recall taxiing / takeoff - techniques / procedures
PLT487	Recall teaching methods - demonstration / performance
PLT488	Recall teaching methods - group / guided discussion / lecture
PLT489	Recall teaching methods - known to unknown
PLT490	Recall teaching methods - motivation / student feelings of insecurity
PLT491	Recall teaching methods - organizing material / course of training
PLT492	Recall temperature - effects on weather formations
PLT493	Recall the dynamics of frost / ice / snow formation on an aircraft
PLT494	Recall thermals - types / characteristics / formation / locating / maneuvering / corrective actions
PLT495	Recall thunderstorms - types / characteristics / formation / hazards / precipitation static
PLT496	Recall towrope - strength / safety links / positioning
PLT497	Recall transponder - codes / operations / usage
PLT498	Recall Transportation Security Regulations
PLT499	Recall turbine engines - components / operational characteristics / associated instruments
PLT500	Recall turboprop engines - components / operational characteristics
PLT501	Recall turbulence - types / characteristics / reporting / corrective actions
PLT502	Recall universal signals - hand / light / visual
PLT503	Recall use of narcotics / drugs / intoxicating liquor
PLT504	Recall use of training aids - types / function / purpose
PLT505	Recall use of training aids - usefulness / simplicity / compatibility
PLT506	Recall V speeds - maneuvering / flap extended / gear extended / V_1, V_2, r, ne, mo, mc, mg, etc.
PLT507	Recall VOR - indications / VOR / VOT / CDI
PLT508	Recall VOR/altimeter/transponder checks - identification / tuning / identifying / logging
PLT509	Recall wake turbulence - characteristics / avoidance techniques
PLT510	Recall weather - causes / formation
PLT511	Recall weather associated with frontal activity / air masses
PLT512	Recall weather conditions - temperature / moisture / dewpoint
PLT513	Recall weather information - FAA Avcams
PLT514	Recall weather reporting systems - briefings / forecasts / reports / AWOS / ASOS
PLT515	Recall weather services - TIBS / TPC / WFO / HIWAS
PLT516	Recall winds - types / characteristics
PLT517	Recall winds associated with high / low-pressure systems
PLT518	Recall windshear - characteristics / hazards / power management
PLT519	Recall wing spoilers - purpose / operation
PLT520	Calculate density altitude
PLT521	Recall helicopter takeoff / landing – slope operations
PLT522	Recall helicopter – Pinnacle / Ridgeline operations
PLT523	Recall vortex generators – purpose / effects / aerodynamics
PLT524	Interpret / Program information on an avionics display
PLT525	Interpret table – oxygen / fuel / oil / accumulator / fire extinguisher
PLT526	Recall near midair collision report
PLT527	Recall BASIC VFR – weather minimums
PLT528	Recall regulations – small UAS operations / weight limitations
PLT529	Recall physiological factors – prescription and over-the-counter drugs
PLT530	Recall regulations – small UAS aircraft registration / display of registration
PLT531	Recall regulations – operation of multiple sUAs
PLT532	Recall operating limitations – small UAS aircraft visibility / distance from clouds
PLT533	Recall regulations – small UAS operation over humans
PLT534	Recall regulations – small UAS operational control / condition for safe operation / VLOS / frequency interference
PLT535	Recall regulations – hazardous operations
PLT536	Recall physiological factors – dehydration / heat stroke
PLT537	Recall regulations – sUAS waivers

CROSS-REFERENCES TO THE FAA LEARNING STATEMENT CODES

Pages 399 through 406 contain a listing of all of the questions from our flight and ground instructor knowledge test bank. The questions are in FAA learning statement code (LSC) sequence. To the right of each LSC, we present our study unit/question number and our answer. For example, look below and note that PLT004 is cross-referenced to 2-31, which represents our Study Unit 2, question 31; the correct answer is C. Non-airplane questions are excluded.

Pages 393 through 398 contain a complete listing of all the FAA learning statement codes associated with all of the flight and ground instructor questions presented in this book. Use this list to identify the specific topic associated with each learning statement code.

The first line of each of our answer explanations in Study Units 1 through 10 contains

1. The correct answer.
2. A reference for the answer explanation, e.g., *AWS Sect 4*. If this reference is not useful, use the following chart to identify the learning statement code to determine the specific reference appropriate for the question.

FAA Learning Code	Gleim SU/ Q. No.	Gleim Answer	FAA Learning Code	Gleim SU/ Q. No.	Gleim Answer	FAA Learning Code	Gleim SU/ Q. No.	Gleim Answer
PLT004	2–31	C	PLT012	8–49	B	PLT013	2–60	A
PLT004	2–32	A	PLT012	8–50	A	PLT013	2–61	B
PLT004	2–33	C	PLT012	8–51	B	PLT013	2–62	C
PLT005	2–7	C	PLT012	8–52	B	PLT013	2–63	B
PLT005	2–8	C	PLT012	8–53	C	PLT013	2–64	C
PLT006	2–48	A	PLT012	8–55	C	PLT014	8–80	C
PLT006	2–49	C	PLT012	8–56	C	PLT014	8–81	A
PLT006	2–50	C	PLT012	8–57	B	PLT015	8–54	C
PLT008	2–55	B	PLT012	8–58	A	PLT018	1–28	A
PLT008	2–56	A	PLT012	8–59	A	PLT018	1–39	C
PLT008	2–57	C	PLT012	8–60	C	PLT018	1–47	B
PLT011	2–21	C	PLT012	8–61	B	PLT018	1–48	C
PLT011	2–22	B	PLT012	8–62	A	PLT018	1–50	C
PLT011	2–23	B	PLT012	8–63	A	PLT018	1–52	C
PLT011	2–24	C	PLT012	8–64	B	PLT018	1–53	A
PLT011	2–28	A	PLT012	8–65	C	PLT018	2–51	B
PLT011	2–29	B	PLT012	8–66	C	PLT018	2–52	B
PLT011	2–30	C	PLT012	8–67	A	PLT018	2–53	B
PLT012	8–43	B	PLT012	8–68	B	PLT019	2–9	A
PLT012	8–44	C	PLT012	8–69	C	PLT021	5–15	A
PLT012	8–45	B	PLT012	8–70	B	PLT021	5–17	A
PLT012	8–46	A	PLT012	8–71	A	PLT021	5–18	B
PLT012	8–47	A	PLT013	2–58	B	PLT021	5–19	B
PLT012	8–48	A	PLT013	2–59	B	PLT021	5–20	B

FAA Learning Code	Gleim SU/ Q. No.	Gleim Answer	FAA Learning Code	Gleim SU/ Q. No.	Gleim Answer	FAA Learning Code	Gleim SU/ Q. No.	Gleim Answer
PLT021	5–21	B	PLT041	2–4	A	PLT064	8–28	B
PLT021	5–22	B	PLT046	1–34	A	PLT064	8–29	B
PLT021	5–23	C	PLT051	6–127	C	PLT064	8–30	A
PLT021	5–24	A	PLT051	6–129	C	PLT064	8–31	C
PLT021	5–25	C	PLT052	7–120	A	PLT064	8–32	C
PLT021	5–26	C	PLT059	6–80	B	PLT064	8–33	B
PLT021	5–27	A	PLT059	6–81	A	PLT064	8–34	B
PLT021	5–30	A	PLT059	6–82	C	PLT064	8–35	B
PLT021	5–34	C	PLT059	6–83	A	PLT064	8–36	A
PLT021	5–35	C	PLT059	6–84	B	PLT064	8–37	A
PLT021	5–36	A	PLT059	6–85	B	PLT064	8–38	C
PLT021	5–37	C	PLT059	6–86	B	PLT064	8–39	B
PLT021	5–38	B	PLT059	6–89	C	PLT066	6–113	C
PLT021	5–39	A	PLT061	6–87	A	PLT066	6–114	B
PLT021	5–40	C	PLT061	6–90	C	PLT066	6–115	B
PLT021	5–41	A	PLT061	6–91	C	PLT066	6–128	A
PLT021	5–42	C	PLT061	6–92	C	PLT066	6–130	C
PLT021	5–43	B	PLT061	6–93	A	PLT071	6–100	B
PLT021	5–44	C	PLT061	6–94	A	PLT071	6–101	A
PLT022	10–25	C	PLT064	8–1	C	PLT071	6–102	C
PLT022	10–27	C	PLT064	8–2	A	PLT071	6–103	A
PLT022	10–28	B	PLT064	8–3	A	PLT071	6–104	B
PLT022	10–34	A	PLT064	8–4	A	PLT072	6–120	A
PLT023	2–1	C	PLT064	8–5	B	PLT072	6–121	A
PLT023	2–2	A	PLT064	8–6	B	PLT072	6–122	C
PLT023	2–10	B	PLT064	8–7	A	PLT072	6–123	B
PLT023	2–11	B	PLT064	8–8	B	PLT072	6–124	B
PLT023	2–12	A	PLT064	8–9	B	PLT074	1–40	C
PLT023	2–13	B	PLT064	8–11	B	PLT074	1–41	B
PLT023	2–14	B	PLT064	8–13	B	PLT074	1–42	A
PLT024	6–26	A	PLT064	8–14	B	PLT074	1–43	B
PLT025	1–11	C	PLT064	8–15	B	PLT074	1–44	A
PLT034	11–5	C	PLT064	8–16	A	PLT074	1–45	B
PLT037	6–95	B	PLT064	8–17	B	PLT074	1–46	C
PLT037	6–96	C	PLT064	8–18	A	PLT074	1–49	C
PLT039	4–21	C	PLT064	8–19	B	PLT074	1–51	B
PLT040	4–56	C	PLT064	8–20	C	PLT076	6–116	A
PLT040	4–57	B	PLT064	8–21	B	PLT076	6–117	C
PLT040	4–58	B	PLT064	8–22	C	PLT076	6–118	B
PLT040	4–59	A	PLT064	8–25	C	PLT078	4–39	B
PLT040	4–60	C	PLT064	8–26	C	PLT078	4–40	B
PLT040	4–61	C	PLT064	8–27	C	PLT078	4–41	B

Cross-References to the FAA Learning Statement Codes

FAA Learning Code	Gleim SU/ Q. No.	Gleim Answer	FAA Learning Code	Gleim SU/ Q. No.	Gleim Answer	FAA Learning Code	Gleim SU/ Q. No.	Gleim Answer
PLT086	9–9	B	PLT115	3–84	C	PLT141	4–15	C
PLT086	9–49	A	PLT118	3–7	A	PLT141	4–16	B
PLT086	9–50	C	PLT119	4–73	B	PLT141	4–17	B
PLT091	8–83	A	PLT120	1–109	A	PLT141	4–18	B
PLT091	8–84	C	PLT123	2–3	A	PLT141	4–31	C
PLT091	8–85	C	PLT123	2–36	C	PLT141	7–149	A
PLT091	8–86	C	PLT124	2–16	C	PLT145	4–8	A
PLT092	5–28	A	PLT124	2–35	B	PLT146	4–20	C
PLT092	5–29	B	PLT125	1–37	A	PLT146	9–8	A
PLT092	5–31	A	PLT125	1–38	C	PLT147	4–32	C
PLT092	5–32	B	PLT126	3–95	A	PLT147	4–33	C
PLT094	1–13	B	PLT127	2–18	B	PLT147	4–34	C
PLT094	1–16	B	PLT127	2–20	B	PLT147	4–35	A
PLT095	1–72	A	PLT127	2–54	A	PLT147	4–36	C
PLT095	1–73	B	PLT128	6–75	B	PLT149	3–96	A
PLT095	1–99	B	PLT131	1–105	A	PLT149	3–97	C
PLT096	10–2	C	PLT131	1–106	A	PLT149	9–2	C
PLT096	10–3	C	PLT131	1–107	C	PLT149	9–3	B
PLT098	10–19	B	PLT131	1–108	B	PLT149	9–4	B
PLT101	8–40	B	PLT132	2–45	A	PLT150	4–19	B
PLT103	10–23	C	PLT132	3–13	B	PLT161	4–51	C
PLT103	10–24	B	PLT132	3–14	B	PLT161	4–52	B
PLT103	10–31	A	PLT132	3–15	B	PLT161	4–53	C
PLT103	10–32	B	PLT132	3–16	B	PLT161	4–54	B
PLT103	10–33	B	PLT132	3–17	A	PLT161	4–55	A
PLT103	10–35	B	PLT132	11–6	B	PLT161	4–62	B
PLT103	10–36	A	PLT134	2–19	B	PLT161	4–63	C
PLT103	10–37	C	PLT134	2–25	B	PLT161	4–64	B
PLT104	10–26	B	PLT134	2–26	B	PLT161	7–109	C
PLT104	10–38	B	PLT141	4–1	B	PLT161	7–110	B
PLT104	10–42	A	PLT141	4–2	C	PLT161	7–111	C
PLT104	10–44	C	PLT141	4–3	B	PLT161	7–112	B
PLT107	3–89	B	PLT141	4–4	C	PLT161	7–122	B
PLT112	9–1	B	PLT141	4–5	A	PLT161	7–123	C
PLT112	9–10	C	PLT141	4–6	C	PLT161	7–124	C
PLT112	9–12	C	PLT141	4–7	C	PLT161	7–125	C
PLT112	9–33	B	PLT141	4–9	A	PLT161	7–126	A
PLT113	7–2	B	PLT141	4–10	B	PLT161	7–136	A
PLT115	3–77	B	PLT141	4–11	C	PLT161	7–137	B
PLT115	3–78	B	PLT141	4–12	B	PLT161	7–139	B
PLT115	3–81	B	PLT141	4–13	A	PLT161	7–161	B
PLT115	3–82	C	PLT141	4–14	C	PLT162	4–50	C

Cross-References to the FAA Learning Statement Codes

FAA Learning Code	Gleim SU/ Q. No.	Gleim Answer	FAA Learning Code	Gleim SU/ Q. No.	Gleim Answer	FAA Learning Code	Gleim SU/ Q. No.	Gleim Answer
PLT163	7–130	B	PLT190	3–49	C	PLT214	1–64	B
PLT163	7–131	A	PLT190	3–51	C	PLT214	1–66	B
PLT163	7–132	A	PLT190	3–52	C	PLT214	1–67	B
PLT163	7–133	B	PLT190	3–54	C	PLT215	3–1	B
PLT163	7–134	C	PLT190	3–55	C	PLT215	3–2	B
PLT163	7–135	C	PLT190	3–56	C	PLT215	3–3	C
PLT163	7–138	C	PLT191	3–45	C	PLT215	3–4	C
PLT165	3–19	B	PLT191	3–50	B	PLT215	3–5	A
PLT166	9–90	A	PLT191	3–53	C	PLT215	3–6	B
PLT167	3–18	B	PLT192	6–29	C	PLT218	9–11	B
PLT167	3–20	C	PLT192	6–41	C	PLT218	9–18	A
PLT168	1–75	B	PLT192	6–42	C	PLT218	9–61	B
PLT168	1–76	B	PLT192	6–43	B	PLT219	9–5	C
PLT168	1–77	C	PLT192	6–76	B	PLT219	9–14	B
PLT168	1–100	B	PLT192	6–77	A	PLT219	9–48	A
PLT168	1–101	C	PLT192	6–78	A	PLT219	9–51	B
PLT168	1–102	C	PLT194	4–69	C	PLT219	9–52	C
PLT170	9–25	B	PLT194	4–70	B	PLT219	9–57	A
PLT170	9–26	A	PLT194	4–72	B	PLT219	9–58	C
PLT170	9–29	B	PLT195	4–68	B	PLT219	9–65	A
PLT170	9–30	B	PLT196	4–42	C	PLT219	9–66	B
PLT170	9–31	C	PLT196	4–43	C	PLT219	9–67	B
PLT170	9–60	C	PLT197	6–3	C	PLT219	9–68	C
PLT172	7–158	A	PLT198	8–10	B	PLT219	9–69	B
PLT173	6–24	C	PLT200	8–23	A	PLT219	9–70	C
PLT173	6–32	A	PLT200	8–24	C	PLT219	9–71	B
PLT173	6–33	B	PLT200	8–42	B	PLT219	9–72	A
PLT173	6–34	C	PLT202	8–72	B	PLT219	9–73	B
PLT173	6–35	A	PLT202	8–73	B	PLT219	9–74	B
PLT173	6–36	B	PLT202	8–74	C	PLT219	9–75	B
PLT173	6–39	C	PLT202	8–75	B	PLT219	9–76	C
PLT173	6–40	B	PLT203	6–4	B	PLT219	9–77	C
PLT185	9–82	C	PLT203	6–31	A	PLT219	9–78	B
PLT185	9–86	B	PLT205	10–5	A	PLT219	9–79	A
PLT185	9–87	C	PLT206	2–17	C	PLT219	9–80	A
PLT186	9–83	B	PLT206	2–34	A	PLT220	7–104	C
PLT186	9–84	A	PLT207	3–90	A	PLT220	7–152	B
PLT187	1–82	B	PLT208	7–148	A	PLT221	9–21	B
PLT187	1–83	A	PLT208	8–41	C	PLT221	9–23	A
PLT187	9–89	B	PLT208	9–22	B	PLT221	9–27	C
PLT190	3–47	B	PLT214	1–56	B	PLT221	9–28	C
PLT190	3–48	A	PLT214	1–57	C	PLT221	9–59	C

Cross-References to the FAA Learning Statement Codes

FAA Learning Code	Gleim SU/ Q. No.	Gleim Answer	FAA Learning Code	Gleim SU/ Q. No.	Gleim Answer	FAA Learning Code	Gleim SU/ Q. No.	Gleim Answer
PLT376	4–45	B	PLT407	7–51	A	PLT427	7–10	B
PLT376	4–47	A	PLT407	7–65	B	PLT427	7–12	B
PLT376	4–48	B	PLT407	7–66	B	PLT428	7–156	B
PLT376	4–49	B	PLT407	7–67	A	PLT430	7–113	B
PLT376	4–82	C	PLT407	7–70	A	PLT430	7–114	C
PLT384	7–101	B	PLT407	7–71	C	PLT430	7–115	B
PLT386	7–9	A	PLT407	7–72	A	PLT431	7–103	A
PLT386	7–47	C	PLT409	7–34	B	PLT432	11–4	C
PLT386	7–83	B	PLT409	11–7	A	PLT434	7–121	B
PLT386	7–84	A	PLT411	11–8	A	PLT435	4–28	C
PLT386	7–85	C	PLT413	7–127	C	PLT435	4–29	A
PLT386	7–86	B	PLT413	7–128	B	PLT437	7–144	C
PLT386	7–87	A	PLT414	7–105	A	PLT438	3–91	C
PLT386	11–11	A	PLT414	7–106	C	PLT438	3–92	B
PLT387	7–42	A	PLT414	7–107	A	PLT438	7–153	C
PLT387	7–43	A	PLT414	7–108	B	PLT438	7–154	B
PLT393	4–44	B	PLT415	7–102	B	PLT438	10–9	A
PLT393	4–46	B	PLT416	7–176	B	PLT442	7–36	A
PLT395	7–174	A	PLT418	7–29	C	PLT442	7–39	C
PLT395	11–3	B	PLT418	11–9	A	PLT442	7–40	C
PLT399	7–142	C	PLT419	7–33	B	PLT442	7–41	B
PLT400	7–3	A	PLT419	7–48	C	PLT443	7–16	B
PLT400	7–4	A	PLT419	7–73	C	PLT443	7–17	B
PLT400	7–5	C	PLT419	7–76	C	PLT443	7–37	B
PLT402	7–145	B	PLT419	7–78	B	PLT443	7–45	B
PLT402	7–147	B	PLT419	7–79	A	PLT443	7–77	A
PLT403	7–116	C	PLT419	7–80	C	PLT444	7–94	A
PLT404	7–146	A	PLT419	7–81	A	PLT445	7–99	B
PLT404	7–162	C	PLT419	11–1	C	PLT445	7–100	B
PLT405	7–6	B	PLT419	11–2	B	PLT447	7–11	B
PLT405	7–63	B	PLT423	7–19	B	PLT448	7–20	B
PLT405	7–143	A	PLT423	7–21	C	PLT448	7–25	C
PLT405	7–155	B	PLT423	7–26	C	PLT448	7–35	B
PLT405	11–10	C	PLT423	7–27	B	PLT448	7–62	B
PLT406	7–157	C	PLT423	7–28	A	PLT448	7–64	B
PLT407	7–13	B	PLT423	7–30	C	PLT448	7–68	B
PLT407	7–15	C	PLT423	7–31	C	PLT448	7–88	A
PLT407	7–22	A	PLT423	7–32	A	PLT448	7–89	B
PLT407	7–23	B	PLT425	7–165	B	PLT448	7–90	A
PLT407	7–24	C	PLT425	7–166	A	PLT448	7–91	B
PLT407	7–38	A	PLT425	7–172	C	PLT448	7–92	C
PLT407	7–49	B	PLT425	7–173	C	PLT448	7–93	C

FAA Learning Code	Gleim SU/ Q. No.	Gleim Answer
PLT451	7–14	A
PLT451	7–44	C
PLT451	7–60	B
PLT451	7–61	C
PLT451	7–69	B
PLT451	7–75	A
PLT454	7–167	A
PLT454	7–170	B
PLT455	4–75	B
PLT457	7–8	A
PLT457	7–46	B
PLT457	7–50	A
PLT457	7–52	B
PLT457	7–53	C
PLT457	7–54	B
PLT457	7–55	B
PLT457	7–56	B
PLT457	7–57	B
PLT457	7–58	B
PLT457	7–59	B
PLT457	7–74	C
PLT457	7–82	B
PLT461	7–150	A
PLT461	7–151	A
PLT463	7–96	A
PLT463	7–97	B
PLT463	7–98	C
PLT467	7–140	B
PLT467	7–141	C
PLT473	1–1	C
PLT473	1–2	B
PLT473	1–3	A
PLT473	1–4	C
PLT473	1–5	A
PLT473	1–6	B
PLT473	1–7	A
PLT473	1–8	B
PLT473	1–9	C
PLT473	1–10	C
PLT474	6–54	B
PLT475	6–61	B
PLT477	1–19	C
PLT477	9–54	C
PLT477	9–56	C
PLT477	9–62	B
PLT478	3–40	A
PLT478	3–41	C
PLT478	3–43	C
PLT478	3–74	A
PLT479	3–42	A
PLT480	1–88	A
PLT480	1–91	A
PLT480	1–92	A
PLT480	1–93	B
PLT480	1–94	B
PLT480	1–95	A
PLT480	1–96	A
PLT481	9–92	C
PLT481	9–93	B
PLT481	10–43	C
PLT482	7–18	A
PLT484	7–1	A
PLT486	9–6	A
PLT486	9–7	B
PLT487	9–17	B
PLT487	9–53	A
PLT492	6–1	A
PLT492	6–14	B
PLT492	6–25	B
PLT493	6–18	A
PLT493	6–73	A
PLT494	6–11	A
PLT495	6–58	B
PLT495	6–59	B
PLT495	6–60	B
PLT495	6–62	A
PLT495	6–63	C
PLT497	4–66	C
PLT497	4–67	C
PLT497	7–159	C
PLT497	7–160	B
PLT501	6–52	A
PLT501	6–53	B
PLT502	4–65	C
PLT502	7–117	B
PLT502	7–118	A
PLT502	7–119	B
PLT503	7–7	B
PLT507	8–77	C
PLT508	7–171	A
PLT509	4–22	C
PLT509	4–23	B
PLT509	4–24	C
PLT509	4–25	C
PLT509	4–26	A
PLT509	4–27	B
PLT510	6–9	A
PLT510	6–10	A
PLT510	6–12	B
PLT511	6–37	A
PLT511	6–38	A
PLT511	6–47	C
PLT511	6–48	B
PLT511	6–49	C
PLT511	6–50	A
PLT512	6–13	C
PLT512	6–30	C
PLT512	6–45	B
PLT512	6–46	A
PLT512	6–79	A
PLT512	6–105	B
PLT512	6–106	C
PLT512	6–107	A
PLT514	6–88	B
PLT516	6–2	B
PLT517	6–5	B
PLT517	6–6	A
PLT517	6–7	A
PLT517	6–8	C
PLT518	6–55	C
PLT518	6–56	B
PLT518	6–66	A
PLT520	2–5	C
PLT520	2–6	B

ABBREVIATIONS AND ACRONYMS IN
FLIGHT/GROUND INSTRUCTOR FAA KNOWLEDGE TEST PREP

14 CFR	Title 14 of the Code of Federal Regulations		MB	magnetic bearing
AC	Advisory Circular		MC	magnetic course
ACL	Aeronautical Chart Legend		METAR	aviation routine weather report
AD	Airworthiness Directive		MH	magnetic heading
AFH	*Airplane Flying Handbook*		MOA	Military Operations Area
AFSS	Automated Flight Service Station		MSL	mean sea level
AGL	above ground level		MTR	military training route
AIH	*Aviation Instructor Handbook*		MVFR	marginal VFR
AIM	*Aeronautical Information Manual*		NFCT	nonfederal control tower
AIRMET	Airman's Meteorological Information		NM	nautical mile
AME	aviation medical examiner		NOTAM	notice to airmen
ANDS	accelerate north, decelerate south		NTSB	National Transportation Safety Board
AOE	airport of entry		OAT	outside air temperature
ARTS	Automated Radar Terminal System		OBS	omnibearing selector
ASEL	airplane single-engine land		PAPI	precision approach path indicator
ATA	actual time of arrival		PCL	pilot-controlled lighting
ATC	Air Traffic Control		*PHAK*	*Pilot's Handbook of Aeronautical Knowledge*
ATIS	Automatic Terminal Information Service		PIC	pilot in command
AvW	*Aviation Weather*		PIREP	pilot weather report
AWBH	*Aircraft Weight and Balance Handbook*		PTS	practical test standards
AWS	*Aviation Weather Services*		RB	relative bearing
CDI	course deviation indicator		*RFH*	*Rotorcraft Flying Handbook*
CDT	central daylight time		*RMH*	*Risk Management Handbook*
CFI	certificated flight instructor		SFC	surface
CG	center of gravity		SIGMET	Significant Meteorological Information
CH	compass heading		SM	statute mile
CT	control tower		STC	supplemental type certificate
CTAF	Common Traffic Advisory Frequency		SVFR	special VFR
DME	distance measuring equipment		TACAN	Tactical Air Navigation
DT	daylight time		TAF	terminal aerodrome forecast
DUATS	Direct User Access Terminal System		TAS	true airspeed
DVFR	defense VFR		TC	true course
ELT	emergency locator transmitter		TH	true heading
ETA	estimated time of arrival		UHF	ultra high frequency
ETD	estimated time of departure		UTC	Coordinated Universal Time
FAA	Federal Aviation Administration		V_A	maneuvering speed
FAR	Federal Aviation Regulation		VASI	visual approach slope indicator
FBO	fixed-base operator		V_{FE}	maximum flap extended speed
FCC	Federal Communications Commission		VFR	visual flight rules
FD	winds and temperatures aloft forecast		VHF	very high frequency
FL	flight level		VIP	video integrated processor
Fl Comp	flight computer		V_{LE}	maximum landing gear extended speed
FSDO	Flight Standards District Office		V_{NE}	never-exceed speed
FSS	Flight Service Station		V_{NO}	maximum structural cruising speed
FTP	Flight Theory for Pilots – Jeppesen Sanderson, Inc.		VOR	VHF omnidirectional range
			VORTAC	collocated VOR and TACAN
GPH	gallons per hour		VOT	VOR test facility
Hg	mercury		VR	visual route
HP	horsepower		V_{S0}	stalling speed or the minimum steady flight speed in the landing configuration
IAS	indicated airspeed			
ICAO	International Civil Aviation Organization		V_{S1}	stalling speed or the minimum steady flight speed obtained in a specific configuration
IFH	*Instrument Flying Handbook*			
IFR	instrument flight rules		V_X	speed for best angle of climb
IR	instrument route		V_Y	speed for best rate of climb
ISA	International Standard Atmosphere		WCA	wind correction angle
LLWAS	low-level wind-shear alert system		Z	Zulu or UTC time
mb	millibar			

INDEX OF FIGURES

Figure		
2	CONUS Display of CVA Ceiling Analysis..	179, 213
2A	Regional Display of CVA Ceiling Analysis..	179
3	Aviation Routine Weather Reports (METAR)..	206
4	Pilot Weather Report..	208
5	Terminal Aerodrome Forecasts (TAF)..	219
7	Winds and Temperatures Aloft Forecast (FB)..	218
8	Surface Analysis Chart Symbols..	178, 211
9	Surface Analysis Chart Symbols..	178, 211
13	CIP/FIP Icing Severity Plus Supercooled Large Droplets (SLD) – Max Example..	189, 223, 224
13A	GTG Composite Example..	180, 215
15	Day 1 Categorical Convective Outlook..	221
16	Convective Weather Forecast..	188, 217
17	Velocity/Load Factor Chart..	24, 39
18	Stall Speed vs. Load Factor..	25, 40
19	Angle-of-Attack vs. Lift..	22, 35
20	Drag Chart..	23, 37
21	Aspect Ratio..	42
22	Force Vectors..	47
23	Wing Flap Diagrams..	29
24	Density Altitude Chart..	55, 66
25	Airspeed Calibration Stalls/Speeds Chart..	61, 83
26	Takeoff Data Chart..	56, 71, 72
27	Maximum Climb Chart..	58, 76
28	Short-Field Takeoff Distance Chart..	57, 75
29	Glide Distance Chart..	60, 81
30	Wind Component Chart..	64, 87
31	Landing Distance Chart..	63, 85
32	The Law of the Lever..	157
33	Moving the CG of a Board by Shifting the Weights..	157
34	Placement of Weight B to Cause the Board to Balance About Its Center..	158
35	Weight and Balance Diagram..	159
36	Weight and Balance Chart..	148, 161, 163
40	Wind Triangle..	291, 316
42	VOR Indicators..	294, 325
44	Sectional Chart Excerpt. NOTE: Chart is not to scale and should not be used for navigation. Use associated scale..	297, 299, 301
45	Sectional Chart Excerpt. NOTE: Chart is not to scale and should not be used for navigation. Use associated scale..	303, 305, 307
46	Sectional Chart Excerpt. NOTE: Chart is not to scale and should not be used for navigation. Use associated scale..	309, 311, 313
47	Class C Airspace Diagram..	139
48	Rectangular Course..	345
49	Ground Track Maneuver Diagram..	346
50	S-Turn Diagram..	348
51	S-Turn Diagram..	347
52	Turn-and-Slip Indicators..	349, 355
54	Traffic Pattern Indicator..	130
55	Chart Supplements U.S. (formerly Airport/Facility Directory)..	134
56	Leading Edge High Lift Devices..	31

INDEX

14 CFR. 227

Abbreviations
   14 CFR 1. 227
   In book. 407
Acceleration/deceleration error. 89
ADM. 361
ADS-B. 124
Aerodynamics and airplanes. 19
Aeromedical factors. 359
Aeronautical
   Decision making (ADM). 361
   Experience, 14 CFR 61. 231
Aircraft
   Lights, 14 CFR 91. 238
   Speed, 14 CFR 91. 235
Airman Certification Standards (ACS). 337
AIRMET. 185
Airplane
   Categories, 14 CFR 23. 227
   Instruments, engines, and systems. 89
   Performance. 53
   Stability. 27
Airplanes
   And aerodynamics. 19
   Axes of. 26
Airport
   Beacons. 121
   Identifiers. 284
   Traffic patterns. 119
Airports, airspace, and ATC. 117
Airspace
   14 CFR 91 (Class A, B, D, E). 236
   Class
      B. 285
         14 CFR 61. 231
      C. 123, 286
      D. 287
      E. 288
      G. 289
   Controlled. 123
   Special use. 122
Airspeed. 59
   Indicator. 90
Alcohol
   14 CFR 61. 227
   14 CFR 91. 234
Alert areas. 285
Altimeter. 91
Altitude
   Reporting equipment, 14 CFR 91. 238
   Types of. 53
Ambient lapse rate. 171
Angle of
   Attack. 26
   Climb. 23
   Incidence. 25
Aspect ratio of a wing. 26

ATC
   Clearances, 14 CFR 91. 235
   Light signals, 14 CFR 91. 236
   Transponder, 14 CFR 91. 238
      Tests and inspections. 239
ATIS. 122
Atmosphere. 170
Automatic
   Dependent Surveillance-Broadcast. 124
   Terminal Information Service (ATIS). 122
Average lapse rate. 171
Aviation
   Fuel practices. 95
   Routine weather report (METAR). 174
   Weather. 169
Axes of airplanes. 26

Balance and weight. 145
Ballooning. 329
Bernoulli's principle. 21
Best
   Angle-of-climb speed. 59
   Rate-of-climb speed. 59
Blade angle of a propeller. 93

Carburetor. 93
   Icing. 93
Center of
   Gravity (see also CG). 145
   Pressure. 21
Certificates, 14 CFR 61. 227
CG. 145
   Calculations. 146
   Tables. 148
Chandelles. 335
Change of address, 14 CFR 61. 230
Chart Supplements. 121
Cheating, 14 CFR 61. 228
Child restraint systems, 14 CFR 91. 234
Civil aircraft, 14 CFR 91. 237
Class
   A airspace, 14 CFR 91. 236
   B airspace. 285
      14 CFR 61. 231
      14 CFR 91. 236
   C airspace. 123, 286
   D airspace. 287
      14 CFR 91. 236
   E airspace. 288
      14 CFR 91. 236
   G airspace. 289
Clear air turbulence (CAT). 172
Climb calculations. 289
Clouds. 173
Coefficient of
   Drag. 22
   Lift. 22
Cold weather operation. 95
Collision avoidance. 124

Commercial pilot, 14 CFR 61. 232
Common traffic advisory frequency (CTAF). 120
Compass errors. 89
Constant
    Pressure analysis chart. 180
    -Speed propeller. 92
Controllability. 27
Controlled airspace. 123
Convective
    Outlook chart. 185
    SIGMETs. 186
    Weather forecast chart. 182
Coriolis force. 169
Crosswind components. 64
Cumuliform cloud bases. 171

DECIDE process. 362
Demarcation bar. 118
Density altitude. 53
Detonation. 95
Dew point. 170
Displaced threshold. 118
Distance
    Calculations. 290
    Measuring equipment (DME). 292
DME. 292
Downwind landing. 329
Drag. 21
Drugs
    14 CFR 61. 227
    14 CFR 91. 234
Dynamic stability. 27

Echo pattern (LN). 176
Effective pitch. 92
Eights-on-pylons. 333
Electrical system. 95
Elliptical wing. 25
Emergency locator transmitters, 14 CFR 91. 238
Engine
    Cycle. 94
    Ignition system. 93
    Temperature. 91
Estimating wind. 292
Exhaust gas temperature (EGT). 94
Experience, aeronautical, 14 CFR 61. 231

Federal Aviation Regulations. 226
Five hazardous attitudes. 362
Flaps. 19
Flight
    After scuba diving. 360
    By reference to instruments. 336
    Instructor, 14 CFR 61. 232
    Maneuvers. 327
    Plans. 124
    Review, 14 CFR 61. 229
Floating. 329
Fog. 170
Fowler flap. 19
Freezing rain. 173

Fronts. 172
    Types of. 178
Fuel
    /Air mixture. 94
    Calculations. 290
    -Injection system. 93
    Practices. 95
    Requirements, VFR, 14 CFR 91. 236
    Tank vents. 95
Fundamentals of flight. 327

Geometric pitch. 92
Glide distance. 60
Glider towing, 14 CFR 61. 230
GPS. 295
Graphical turbulence guidance (GTG). 180
Green arc. 91
Ground effect. 28
Gyroscopic precession. 28

Hail. 173
Hazardous attitudes. 362
Headwind components. 64
High-pressure air. 170
Hyperventilation. 360
Hypoxia. 359

Ice pellets. 173
Icing. 173
    Potential
        Current (CIP). 188
        Forecast (FIP). 188
Illusions in flight. 360
ILS critical boundary area. 118
Immediate notification, NTSB 830. 240
Induced drag. 21
Inoperative instruments, 14 CFR 91. 238
Inspections, 14 CFR 91. 239
Instructor certificates, 14 CFR 61. 228
Interpolation. 57, 391

Knowledge tests, 14 CFR 61. 228

L/DMAX. 22
Landing
    Direction indicator. 120
    Distance. 62
    Strip indicators. 119
Landings. 329
Lapse rate for pressure, standard. 54
Lazy eights. 336
Leading edges. 20
Learning statement codes. 393
Lift. 21
LN. 176
Load factor. 24
Low-pressure air. 170

Magnetic heading. 291
Maintenance, 14 CFR 91. 239
    Records. 239
Maneuverability. 27
Manifold pressure gauge. 93
Maximum
    Climb. 59
    Lift-drag ratio (L/DMAX). 22
Mean camber line. 25
Medical certificates, 14 CFR 61. 228
METAR. 174
Microbursts. 173
Military
    Operations areas (MOAs). 122
    Training routes (MTRs). 122
Minimum safe altitudes, 14 CFR 91. 235
MOA. 122
Motion sickness. 361
MTR. 122
Multi-engine performance. 59

National Convective Weather Forecast
    (NCWF). 182, 186
Navigation. 283
NCWF. 182, 186
Night
    Flight training, 14 CFR 61. 231
    Vision. 360
NOTAM. 125
Notice to airmen (NOTAM). 125
NTSB Part 830. 240

Obstruction altitude. 284
Off-course corrections. 292
Oxygen systems. 95

PAPI. 121
Parachutes, 14 CFR 91. 239
Parasite drag. 21
Passing grades, 14 CFR 61. 228
Pilot
    -Controlled lighting. 118
    In command, 14 CFR 91. 234
    Logbooks, 14 CFR 61. 229
    Weather report (PIREP). 175
PIREP. 175
Pitot-static system. 90
Plain flap. 19
Practical
    Test Standards (PTS). 337
    Tests, 14 CFR 61. 229
Precision approach path indicator (PAPI). . . 121
Preflight action, 14 CFR 91. 234
Profile drag. 21
Propellers. 92

Radar weather report (SD/ROB). 176
Radio failure. 123
Rate of climb. 23
Ratings, 14 CFR 61. 227
Recent flight experience, 14 CFR 61. 230

Recreational pilots, 14 CFR 61. 231
Rectangular
    Course. 330
    Wing. 25
Relative humidity. 170
Restricted areas. 122
Retesting, 14 CFR 61. 229
Reviewers and contributors. iii
Right-of-way rules, 14 CFR 91. 235
Risk management. 361
Runway
    Exit signs. 118
    Hold position signs. 118
    Marking and lighting. 117

S-turns across a road. 332
Safe altitudes, 14 CFR 91. 235
Safety belts, 14 CFR 91. 234
Scuba diving. 360
SD. 176
Secondary stalls. 333
Sectional charts. 283
Segmented circle. 119
Severe weather outlook chart. 185
Shoulder harness, 14 CFR 91. 234
SIGMET. 185
Significant weather
    Prognostic chart. 181
    Symbols. 182
Simulated instrument flight, 14 CFR 91. 234
Slotted
    Flap. 19
    Fowler flap. 19
Slow flight. 333
Solo cross-country flight, 14 CFR 61. 231
Spatial disorientation. 360
Special
    Use airspace. 122
    VFR weather minimums, Part 91. 237
Speed calculations. 290
Spins. 28, 333
Spiraling slipstream. 28
Split flap. 19
Sport pilot, 14 CFR 61. 233
Stability. 27
    Of air masses. 171
Stall speed. 25, 61
Stalls. 28, 333
Standard
    Lapse rate. 171
        For pressure. 54
    Pressure. 171
Static stability. 27
Steep turns. 334
Student pilots
    Certificates, 14 CFR 61. 227
    Requirements, 14 CFR 61. 230
Sublimation. 170
Supplemental oxygen, 14 CFR 91. 238
Surface analysis chart. 177
Sweptwing. 25

Symbols

- 14 CFR 1. 227
- Significant weather. 182

TAF. 184
Takeoff distance. 55
Takeoffs. 328
Taxiing. 327
Taxiway signs and markings. 118
Teaching methods. 337
Temperature
- Inversion. 171, 172
- Lapse rate. 171

Terminal aerodrome forecast (TAF). 184
Thrust. 21
Thunderstorms. 173
Traffic
- Advisories at uncontrolled airports. 120
- Pattern indicators. 119

Transponder codes. 123
Troposphere. 170
True
- Airspeed. 59
- Heading. 284, 291

Turbocharged engines. 94
Turbulence. 28, 172, 180
Turning error. 90
Turns. 26, 328
- Around a point. 331

Type rating requirements, 14 CFR 61. 228

Uncontrolled airports. 120
Unstable air. 171

VA. 91
Vacuum systems. 90
VASI. 121
Velocity/load factor. 24
VFR
- Flight, 14 CFR 91. . . . . 236, 237
- Weather minimums, 14 CFR 91. 237

VHF omnidirectional range (VOR). 292
- Symbols. 284

Visual approach slope indicator (VASI). 121
VOR. 292
- Symbols. 284

VORTAC. 292

Wake turbulence. 120
Warning area. 122
Weather. 169
- Advisories. 177
- Fronts. 172
- Minimums, 14 CFR 91. 237

Weight
- And balance. 145
- Change calculations. 150

White arc. 91

Wind
- Direction indicator. 120
- Estimation. 292
- Shear. 172
- Triangle. 291

Winds and temperatures aloft forecast (FB). 183
Wings. 25

Yellow arc. 91

AUTHORS' RECOMMENDATIONS

HELPFUL ORGANIZATIONS

Gleim cooperates with and supports all aspects of the flight training industry, particularly organizations that focus on aviation recruitment and flight training. These include the EAA, AOPA, CAP, and WAI.

EXPERIMENTAL AIRCRAFT ASSOCIATION: YOUNG EAGLES PROGRAM

The Experimental Aircraft Association's (EAA) Young Eagles Program set a goal of providing a free introductory flight to 1 million young people ages 8 to 17. They have already exceeded that goal and are still going strong.

The Young Eagles Program is intended to help young people understand the important role aviation plays in our daily lives and, at the same time, provide insight into how an airplane flies, what it takes to become a pilot, and the high standards flying demands in terms of safety and quality.

NOTE: The Gleim "Learn to Fly" booklet (available for free at www.GleimAviation.com/learn-to-fly) is used as "ground school" training for Young Eagles programs. For more information about the Young Eagles Program, visit www.youngeagles.org or call 1-877-806-8902.

AIRCRAFT OWNERS AND PILOTS ASSOCIATION

The Aircraft Owners and Pilots Association (AOPA) hosts an informational web page on getting started in aviation with information for those still dreaming about flying, those who are ready to begin, and those who are already making the journey.

The goal of this program is to encourage people to experience their dreams of flying through an introductory flight. Interested individuals can order a FREE subscription to Flight Training Magazine, which explains how amazing it is to be a pilot. Other resources are available, such as a flight school finder, a guide on what to expect throughout training, an explanation of pilot certification options, a FREE monthly flight training newsletter, and much more. To learn more, visit www.aopa.org and select the Training and Safety link.

CIVIL AIR PATROL: CADET ORIENTATION FLIGHT PROGRAM

The Civil Air Patrol (CAP) Cadet Orientation Flight Program is designed to introduce CAP cadets to flying. The program is voluntary and primarily motivational, and it is designed to stimulate the cadet's interest in and knowledge of aviation.

Each orientation flight is approximately 1 hour, follows a prescribed syllabus, and is usually in the local area of the airport. Except for takeoff, landing, and a few other portions of the flight, cadets are encouraged to handle the controls.

For more information about the CAP cadet program nearest you, visit the CAP website at www.gocivilairpatrol.com.

WOMEN IN AVIATION INTERNATIONAL

Women in Aviation International (WAI) is a nonprofit organization dedicated to the encouragement and advancement of women in all aviation career fields and interests. Its diverse membership includes astronauts, corporate pilots, maintenance technicians, air traffic controllers, business owners, educators, journalists, flight attendants, high school and university students, air show performers, airport managers, and many others.

WAI provides year-round resources to assist women in aviation and to encourage young women to consider aviation as a career. WAI also offers educational outreach programs to educators, aviation industry members, and young people nationally and internationally. An annual Girls in Aviation Day was recently initiated for girls ages 8 to 17.

To learn more about WAI chapters, membership, and outreach programs, visit www.wai.org.

Notes

Notes

Notes

Notes

Notes

Notes

Notes

Notes

Notes